Comments on Flying

Kate Millett:

"'What is this book about?' I wonder out loud, imitating a reviewer. 'Broad goes to Province-town and gets laid.'"

"It's about freedom . . . I say that loving more than one person is a good thing multiplied . . . To get out of monogamy is hard but it's worth it."

The reviewers:

". . . brave, thoughtful . . . being one's honest self."
                                    —*Kirkus Reviews*

"Between consenting adults . . . fine; between author and public, it's better kept private."
                                    —*King Features*

". . . elaborate (romantic and clinical) details of the sexual act itself . . ."
                                    —*Cleveland Plain Dealer*

". . . an unflinching record . . ."
                                    —*New Republic*

". . . the Sexual Revolution party line: no jealousy or possessiveness, each partner free to have lovers without guilt."

Kate's mother:

"It's dirty, filthy, disgusting . . ."

FLYING

by
Kate Millett

BALLANTINE BOOKS • NEW YORK

For Mother
And For Zell Ingram

Library of Congress Catalog Card Number: 73-20766

SBN 345-24393-5-225

This edition published by arrangement with
Alfred A. Knopf, Inc.

First Printing: March, 1975

Printed in the United States of America

BALLANTINE BOOKS
A Division of Random House, Inc.
201 East 50th Street, New York, N.Y. 10022
Simultaneously published by
Ballantine Books, Ltd., Toronto, Canada

As for me—listen well—
my delight is the exquisite;
yes, for me glitter and sunlight and love
are one society.

SAPPHO (Edm II8a)

From *The Love Songs of Sappho*
Translated by Paul Roche
Published by the New American Library, 1966

CONTENTS

PART ONE

VERTIGO

1

FUGUE STATE

A cab to Victoria and then the bus, red and ominous as a city sandwich even though it's for the airport. Riding upstairs I can smoke. There is someone on this bus who threatens me. We go through Chelsea. Lovely English houses, neat as springtime, flowers. Missed it. Missed everything. Here five weeks, never went anywhere. Only the number 19 bus to Cambridge Circus past Soho porn houses, girl's gray breast calling from photo behind glass, fellow in a booth selling tickets. And the bookshops. Accused in a window display, my own enemy in its hideous British cover. And next door in the place that advertises contraception, medical supplies, dusty pamphlets on fertility, ugly women in perverse pose titled *Butch Love*. Written for guys.

Danny La Rue plays the corner at the Palace, wigs and gowns, acceptable British family entertainment. Turn in our door, dread up the stairs, brown carpet hard pinched like England. Betty's face says I don't know how to make movies. Nell is going to turn me into a filmmaker. But I haven't got the footage, never be able to pull it off. Getting up hope while watching the first assembly on Mallory. Technicolor image big enough to fall into, mouth talking relentlessly. Maybe. Lillian next, the second of the three women in my documentary. Can never make a movie out of Lillian. Pacing the office four days over Easter holiday, eighteenth-century slate roofs through the windows, town emptied, stuck here alone with this not-enough. Cutting room dull as its cork walls. The splicer does not move from its shelf. Every object remains in the same place, captured. Mellow gold on buildings, the last light of any Sunday evening's gloom coming at me through the windows and the door to the catwalk. Can't. But you have to. Reshuffle the pieces. Start over.

Nell said freeze it. Screened last night with the freezes in, cut in at the last minute, projectionist on overtime, gray images flicker start stop in the dark of the room. It worked. Slept tired with relief. Robin tough-kid's already cut—an easy film to edit. The movie's done. Going back to America.

Cab driver is pleasant. Gets lost the way I do. We are stranded in space, surreal roadway suspended in the middle of Victoria Station. The cement spiral floats up and disappears. We will never get there. I won't have to go home. No more America. Standing by the car door he looks like a gent, taking out my bags. Says he went to university. Why does he drive a cab? Soft with the kindness of failure. Probably just got lost in life. Maybe what happened to me too. Used to sculpt. Taught English part time at Columbia, thinking I did it for a living. Now what do I do? What am I? Every day the listings for secretaries rebuke me, Alfred Marks's prim little notices barking at me from corners all over London. I read the help wanted ads for dinner, tacky Soho joint, mind off the movie worry. Chicken Kiev every night because it's risky to try anything else. The place full of other losers. We avoid each other's eyes. Management is suspicious of us. There's a depression. No work. Could I get a job?

But I'm rich. Shamefully, pointlessly rich. Figuring

it out behind the newspaper (tonight I'll eat a steak in the Trattoria), I could live three years on my royalties. If I could work I wouldn't need a job. If I had a job I wouldn't have to work. Already turned down Fairbanks. First day back in London from Germany. Three drafts bad typing telling the dean I couldn't come. Did I misspell anything? Wanted to be there next fall. Safe. With the kids. Writing the words, ashamed—I have a book to write, can't come. Can't write a book either. So there'll be nothing. Rest of forever with nothing to do. It can't last long. Sure to go over the ledge before winter's out. How will I live without work?

Light a cigarette. Bus out of London now and into the bleak. Be careful not to pull too hard or the reflex starts. Every day at Nell's gagging when I brush my teeth. Paul saw me do it once. But I never threw up. That's the signal. Started last winter. Waking in the Bowery studio to another morning down empty. Then I remember: today I can escape to Georgia. A plane at noon. Any folly to avoid New York, the Bowery. Home once, now become a cage. Every square foot of loft space recriminates for the old life. Killed dead. Fumio cooks breakfast. Look of a fried egg utterly fatal. Swallow. As the ceremony nears its dull conclusion I stand up. About to say something. Suddenly vomiting all over the rug. One of two Persians from the Connecticut summer days when they sold the first copies of *Sex Pol*. Felt so rich I emptied the bank account. Blew the whole eight hundred dollars in a week of libertine glory, buying an old car and two carpets.

We leaned against the door of the convertible. Just got it that morning. I suggested to Celia that we make love later on the carpet. Tonight in the woods. Oblique, said I fantasized it. In the trees, outdoors, the dark air around us. Could see her body shine white upon the ruby pattern. An odalisque. It was the day we drove to Hollander's to see his two and a half acres. The three of us going to buy it, build a place, live together. Fumio, Celia, and me. Walking through the deep grass planning a long wooden studio for each of us. Then we had a dinner party. Wonderful talk, the doors open into the garden. Mad idea to preserve it in a film. Meet a year hence and do it again. Bring the camera this time, tape it. Keep life. Repeat it even. Illusion.

Fumio watches me clean it up. It has begun to penetrate him. He is finally afraid. While he's off to morning prayers, reading on the toilet, the vomit happens again. Same spot. Like magic. Quiet voice telling myself out loud—here is physical proof of sickness. Never mind you don't believe in shrinks. You're crazy, lady. A speech tonight in Georgia. Already foresee the catastrophe. Opens her mouth and pukes. Splattered pews of Emory University chapel. Pulpit disgorges. Undergraduates' eyes open aghast. Then shut.

Jeannin sat on the floor. I was in a corner. Columbia again. First time since the comeout. The workshop goes on without us. "Lesbianism." I am sick. I do not want to talk to her. She signaled me to leave. She has a message. The floor is cool. I hate her. She is trying to break me. Soothing voice going on about "patterns." She was JayCee's lover. She broke JayCee. Who broke me. Jeannin is talking about her brother. I was in love with my brother, she says. What the hell do I care? Decadent southerners, descendents of a rebel general. Wants me to come to her place and talk, go to her for comfort. "Patterns stick," she says. "I put my pattern on JayCee. She put it on you." Mumbo jumbo. Crap. Magic. "You can get out of them if you try." She says she has succeeded. Finally. Jeannin was JayCee's first. JayCee was my first. Jeannin is a ghost. I want her to die. "We were a chain," she says. She doesn't know. None of them do. It doesn't work with women. For the kids maybe. But never for me. I will go on doing to Vita what Celia did to me. Nothing gets better. "You can break the chain," she says. No, I say. I want to leave. Celia was the new life. Now it's gone.

How crazy am I now in London Airport? Going home
for two more speeches. The last ones. Always the last
ones. Then free: never the public person again. Out of
it, the vulgar insanity. I will be killed up there. Platforms,
airports, newspapers. If I could escape—quit. Time to
buy presents. Brandy for Fumio. Something for Vita.
They're the only two left now. Meeting me at Kennedy.
Counter full of people. Can't get waited on. Everything
too expensive. Forty dollars for a cigarette lighter . . .
Screw you, Dunhill. My fault she's smoking again. Hardly
anything for sale. Pringle sweaters we used to treasure
up in high school. Cashmere. Working in Shunneman's
basement to buy them; thirty hours' standing in the
stocking department worth one Pringle. Give up on it
and get a drink from the bar. No, persevere, buy a scarf
and some material. Vita should learn to like clothes
again. Stop being dumpy Curator's wife, mother of kids.
This present won't make me any less a bastard. I just
can't love her. Friendship is all I want. Can't love anyone. Don't want the hurt. Too risky. Nothing succeeds.
It only works with Fumio. The thing with Celia ended
me. I can't bear Naomi now. Magda didn't want to go
on. Celia. Still no idea what happened. Will never
understand. Look, don't even hope to. Just deal with the
panic. It doesn't work out with women. Should never
have started again. Stick by your principles: Support
Gay Liberation the whole way. But forget the practice.
Nothing in it but the pain. They can say in public that
I'm queer, but that doesn't mean I have to be. Tell the
truth—then outwit it in private.

London Airport. Whole bunch of Americans with
southern accents. All the normal people. Everyone looks
all right. Man takes a picture of his bride. People sit on
the plastic chairs. They do not show that they see. If
they see. But all this year I have seen it, the strangeness.
Looking right through the terror in it. City after city.
As if I saw too much. Discovered the trap in things. I
cannot tell you what it is.

I look at the passengers and I want to yell at them
LIFE IS A PUBLICITY STUNT. A SHILL. YOU'VE BEEN HAD.

But they don't know it so they can still go on. They are not crazy. They don't panic. They do not feel the pain. Madness is merely an agony, a burning in the stomach. I hide my craziness so that I do not shock or give offense, foreseeing that the sight would be obscene, upsetting. I have been crazy for months. Since September, maybe August. And never missed a speech. Only Fumio knows it. If I tell no one else and stay away from doctors, it might get better. It may heal by itself. The shrinks would make me sicker before they would cure me. I may even cure myself. Already the movie has made me better. Now I have finished something. I can be someone else now. Not the one who wrote the goddam book.

Going back to Oxford on a visit. With Fumio, to show him the place I always talked about. Morning lying in bed at Nell's. Afraid to get up and catch the train. I can't tell him. He knows. Horrible to see England again after this. Twelve years and I never went back, always too broke. Said good-bye to the spires next to JayCee on the train, wondering if I'd ever see them again. Must wait for the right time. And now returning this creature of publicity, offensive, dirtied, notorious. Sick. Done for. Despising myself. And the self-pity most loathsome of all.

I had forgotten the way, the streets unfamiliar. Couldn't remember how to find the best spots. Fumio liked it anyway. It was all there still, exquisite in its age and perfection. It will not change. The revolutionary slogans on the wall simply comic relief. Students letting off steam. Felt a sick terror when I saw "Gay Power" painted on the side of St. Giles passageway. It mocks me, an absurdity. Nothing will change. It is some good to know this—it makes security. Try giving up: if you don't bother to hope you will not be disappointed.

Make the tour first and then have lunch. But when we got to the Mitre they'd stopped serving. Walking for miles to find food, a drink out of the question. Ended up eating in an expensive dump near the station, the place becoming a bad trip, all the golden towers falling into

English slum, full thud of depression. When we walked over the bridge he said maybe we'd come back someday: "When I'm famous and have a retrospective at the Tate," he says. My arm nestles under his coat sleeve, his mouth is a slit cut by his own sour joke. We both want to cry. He goes home to America tomorrow. I stay to edit the film. Our fear crosses the bridge. Away from him I will die.

Something remembered from childhood. Waiting for the bus in a snowstorm. Corner of Cleveland and Highland Park Road. Highland Drug behind me in the wind. Warm in there. And they got chocolate malts. But if the bus doesn't see anyone it goes right on. Better wait outside. Ain't got the extra quarter anyway. Can still see the black iron fence of the convent. Slowly disappearing in the snow. We have such a big campus 'cause Derham is the prep school for St. Kate's. I hold all my books in front of me, proud there are so many. This week is the first big tests. French today. Wonder how I did. History tomorrow. The cold is like being sick. The sulfa drugs when I had mastoid. Doctor Flannigan said I was delirious. Wonderful word. Blue car stops for the light. Mercury. Hard to see. Going to be a real blizzard. He's opening the door. Gonna give me a ride. Must be one of Daddy's draftsmen. Why else would he stop? Inside I see his face. But it's not Swanny or one of the other ones. Don't know all of them too well. Their faces come and go, back door to the basement. When I go down to check my math on Daddy's machine they tease me. Look again. Sort of red hair. Nothing familiar. I must convert it to a known face while he is busily fussing over the door. Making sure I don't fall out. So considerate. Locking it. He says stuff about the weather, how cold I must be. Don't know what to say, but I must be polite. Thank him lots of times. Shall we take the river road? The houses of the rich, the trees, the Mississippi. Sure. My favorite way. Of course he knows where I live, friend of the family I am just too dumb to recognize. Mother says I don't pay attention. We turn down toward the river, history test, comfort of warmth, security, convenience. Sense of protection so familiar. I am a girl. People take care of me. The man is talking. Now it seems he needs to remember where I live. Across from St. Thomas College. People think that means Summit Avenue. But it only means Selby. I should remember to say *back* of St. Thomas. There is something funny that he doesn't know where I live. Maybe everything's wrong. Never mind the voice in my stomach saying he's a stranger. Little rise of fear in my gut. He pressed the button on my side. Locked in. Warnings about men in cars. He mustn't know I am thinking this. Guy's being nice. Saw I was a kid waiting for the bus, dark coming on, going to be terrible tonight. Sure, he's being nice. Giving me a ride home. I am wearing my uniform. Doesn't make sense, thinking these things about him. He's asking about my briefcase. I am holding it in front of me, brand new today. Real or imitation? New, my first briefcase. Real, but imitation leather. I admit it. He grabs toward it laughing but touches my front. Breasts, mother says. Sally my big sister says bosoms. So embarrassing. This is a mistake. His laugh is scary—my face is hot. It is not happening. No, the car is not going to stop here with only trees around us. No. There are no houses in this part of the river road. Gray darkness quiet. I refuse this. Deny too that I see his big hands shoving themselves into my blouse. Regulation with a V neck and three cuff buttons. So it can't be. Just not possible the red hands fumbling below my skirt. Trying to enter its Denham Hall accordion pleats. The black serge makes this crazy. Great purple flesh in his lap long huge horrible. Is that what one looks like? This is real now. It's danger. Wild dream awake in the gray evening. Here is the expected terror at last. We are partners. We do things by signals. I am yelling the Virgin Mary, my school, the sin against chastity. But it sounds silly. Every day we say the Blessed Virgin—but we don't scream it. I'm shouting. But there is sometimes no sound because my throat is closed. He will not be able to put the purple thing inside me. That must be what he wants, grabbing to touch me we fight over my underpants his finger hurting me. The purple thing would not fit. He will not be able to do it. He is there and I am here. He must stop the car first 'cause we are still moving. If I could get out. Run away but he's so much bigger. Stronger, hurting me. Now we are wrestling over the door and the button on the door. Is he hitting me? Calling me names. Little bitch. Slut. I run. How can I run if my legs don't work. Run and fall in the snow. Throwing up. Crawl. Hide in the trees. He circles the empty lot in his car. The blue Mercury slowly going around the space where I am, the place without a road where I hide watching it. Time is so long. When he is at the other end I can break and cross. Up the hill. Running with the air blue in the snow. Watching the car disappear is mercy. Then go for the hill. Running the six miles home and halfway there at St. Clair—I discover I have lost it. My turtle. The brace to keep my teeth straight. Spit it out in the snow. I have lost twenty-five dollars. Again. And the last time I promised them. Mother said they could never afford to buy another. Pink plastic in the new white powder almost dark outside the car among the trees. Snow six inches deep. Dark now. I cannot go back and find it. At dinner a fever till they find out it is lost. It is my fault. They must never know how.

Telling on him is telling on me. The pneumonia is weakness, skin hot all the time, dizzy when you sit up. Both lungs. It sounded so important. In the hospital I was special. Got presents. People came to see me. Even Nancy came. The nurse kids me about the shots. "Turn over for another one in your pincushion," she says. But at home now it is just boring. Lunchtime Mrs. Luger comes to make me a sandwich. Campbell's tomato soup. Mother goes out to work. Daddy is gone now. Now I don't have a father. At school I lie and say he's just out of town. In Greenland building an airbase. It's only partly true. Of course he's up there in the ice, he sent us a card, but he's never coming back. Mother found out about him. Told me when I drove her up Cathedral Hill, so icy if I don't pay attention we'll roll backwards the way I do when Sally teaches me and she yells. Thirteen. Can't pass the test for two more years. "Looks like Daddy's car," I said. Black Merc bigger than Mother's little Ford. Harder to drive, you can't see the edges of it. "Yes," she said, "it's your father's car." Now I see there's a lady driving it. Can't be his. She still says it is. "It's time you knew your father has a mistress." Word out of a book. Hearing her and still driving while she says Daddy is going to leave, she can't stand it any more, voice gagging as it has for years at the dinner table, chokes on her food. I drive along Summit past the Walker Houses like castles, my aunt on Daddy's side was married to Chip Walker. Asking, my hands terrified on the wheel, will I still get to see Aunt Christina now. Her house beckoning me like a lover down Virginia Avenue as we pass the corner. Why can't I be her daughter, live with her, no husband now no kids of her own, all that money —I could even give some of it to Mother. Now we won't have any money. How will we live? My mind getting there before she even says it. And we must go home. We don't live up here. No, out in Midway near the river. Back of St. Thomas, and the trees stretch bare gray evening before dinner nights he doesn't come home. Now we won't have to wait dinner for him. Throws his hat in the door first. "You're drunk," her voice messy, then she cries and we hate the way she cries. Like an animal. Now it is just Mother and my little sister Mary. Sally went away to college. Escaped. Mother has a job but she can't make any money. And I'm sick. If I have to drop out of Derham 'cause it costs money I can't ever see Nancy again. She's my best friend.

Lying in bed sick I think about the man. The blue car. I touch myself and my head gets hot. It's a sin. A sin to have gotten in his car. I have been touched by him. Did I lose my virginity? What does it mean really? Not a sin if I escaped. Even if I ran away, was it a sin? But a sin to lose the turtle. Sometimes I want him back. He could put the thing in me. Then I would know what it is. If he put it in me I would stop itching. Look at the

roses in the wallpaper, the yellow spot where Mary threw
up once. Don't sin. Don't think about anything. Think
about the basketball games at St. Thomas. Be one tonight,
it's Friday, but I'm sick. The boys'll be there. Nancy'll
be there too. Ashamed again, thinking that. 'Cause people
act funny about us when we say we're in love. Before
Thanksgiving vacation we told the seniors and they
laughed, kind of scary, like when you've made a mistake.
The nun heard and she got mad. Sally's boyfriend heard
us talking on the phone and said a magic word to Mother.
Lesbian. It takes so long to get well. Already it's eight
weeks. Doctor Flannigan says six more. There's nothing
to do but remember. Over and over. This secret. The
blue Mercury. His face sort of blurry. The terrible purple
thing. Then running. It keeps happening. If I yell no one
hears me, the house is empty. Will he find out where
I live, get me, tell on me? Face hot, sweating, is it the
fever, I wonder. It's a sin and thinking is a sin. How
do I stop it from happening?

In London Airport I have bought Vita a present. That
second trip to Oxford was better than the first—went up
alone to see my tutor. Better already. Feeling good on
the number 19 to Paddington. The advertisements will
not hurt me today. Other mornings riding into Soho
smoking at the top of the bus, one hand dripping the rail
. . . get to the office, don't throw up. But the Gold Leaf
advertisement is no longer a menace. I can see it from
the window. Today it has no power over me. The words
are their words, British. Not mine. It is innocent, it is
a promise; people can get coupons too if they buy
cigarettes. There is nothing of terror in that. Number
19's route is safe today. The land mines are gone. Grey's
Inn isn't death, it's quaint and historic. The Shakespeare
Arms and the brewers' slogan, "Take Courage," hurling
me into panic always. Today I'll tell myself it's a
whimsical advertisement, not an edict, not even a sarcasm.
I may survive. I have succeeded in making a movie of
Mallory. So healthy at Paddington I bought a book to
read on the train. At breakfast Paul teased me: "Will

you bring along a slim volume of Wordsworth?" In the station seeing them all lined up in the booth. I bought one called *The Human Aspects of Sexual Deviation*. Written by a shrink. Read it on the train in front of everyone. Even spread it face down when I went to get a snack. Author a progressive liberal fellow, has a section on homosexuality, maybe there's some comfort in it. Scanning the titles lined up in the booth. Reading the words on the backs. For months the sight of books in airports in bookstores in houses . . .

Sitting down, drinking the watered white coffee, I invented my sentence: "Now that the overpowering sense of absurdity has abated, now that I can look at a porter or a professor or a housewife again without a dizzy feeling of envy followed by nausea, wanting to be them, then realizing they too are caught—now that the illness is past, I can perhaps try to explain it to myself." Bought a notebook to do the explaining with. Got as far as the second sentence. Something about things returning to their normal places again so I could calculate how far they had gotten out of line. Scrappy little exercise book, no room on the page. Cost four new pence. Wouldn't spend two shillings because it wasn't worth it. The first notebook, the one I got in Bryn Mawr, that was a pretty thing. Still has lots of room in it. It sits there now in my bag, its empty pages a waste of shame. When I got to Nell's I put it in the suitcase. Stopped carrying it around with me. If I edit film twelve hours a day I don't have to write. Needn't do both at the same time. The first notebook had a plastic cover, flowers on it for Celia in Connecticut, the days at Brookfield before the fall. Still thought I could write then.

My room in Islington is Nell's library. They gave me the room with books. Probably thought they were doing me a favor. Fear of them haunting me before bed every night. Reading their spines. How big a book one man could write on the Crusades. Another one about a murder. Novels, history, poetry, political stuff, lined up making a wall behind the bed. If I sleep will they fall and crush me? Tried two good ones but couldn't read them. Succeeded with Agatha Christie, chapter a night, just forget what went before and follow the words.

Nell showed me a volume of prison memoirs, thought I'd be pleased. Rare book by early feminist. The object rebuking me from her hand. This woman braved prison. Showing it to me, a claustrophobe, a coward. I have done harm. I have injured the cause. Those brave English women in jail felt siterhood and nothing more suspect than that. They were married, they were certain they were doing the right thing. Nell sits on the bed, the book in her hand is my guilt. I see it. The dead fear in my stomach knows it.

It is all a mistake. The nightmare months of folly. Microphones shoved into my mouth . . . "What is the future of the woman's movement?" How in the hell do I know—I don't run it. Every day in winter more ignorant, weaker. Chicanery of press conferences, interviews, lectures at universities. All arranged. Don't spoil the arrangements. Tired and I don't know any answers. The whole thing is sordid, embarrassing, a fraud. The same questions always. Boring. Reptition of old stuff, no new work. Have I lost faith? If I am bored am I a traitor? They ought to shoot me. Made into a leader. We're not supposed to have leaders. I will be executed in some underground paper, my character assassinated subterraneously.

In the Bowery memorizing the boards on the floor, paper all over the room, all the letters I can't answer. This used to be home. Sculpt all day and then people come by in the late afternoon, drinking around the marble tabletop. Then we'd find some dinner. Last summer there were things like roaring big salads, hunks of chicken, tomatoes red on the lettuce. Strawberries and two kinds of wine. The soft white light of afternoon through the paper shutters.

Then it happened. Friends didn't come any more. A studio without them. Television crews taking up whole mornings and blowing the fuses. Fumio had no place to go. Phone ringing on him all day. Even the months I'm on tour. But then in January I did come home, was there every day. Came home and back to normal. Life would be as if it had never happened. Then was the worst time. Stopped running to discover that what had been my life was empty now. Gone. Over with. Permanently invaded. Sitting alone five o'clock in the evening cold, staring at the cans of film we shot last August. Fumio said it was reckless.

I try to argue back but he's right, and I'm stuck with it. How do you make movies? How does sound get transferred, how can I sync them up? Alien medium. It's too big. What do I do next? Mortified at the waste of money. The stuff is garbage. New York editors look at the rushes, they don't say anything. Finally I abolish the silence to save us all. They have reputations. They are experts, professionals. They don't think it's a movie, just something for discussion groups, educational television. I want to scream—it's three women's whole lives. But I sit there and can't say anything—too scared. I need them so much. They don't want to cut it the way I do. They want a filing system, play one woman against another, first they talk about their fathers, now they talk about their jobs. "That's more dynamic," they said. They are professional. They know. I want to say that I have risked myself upon this footage, love the women in it, their lives a weight I carry everywhere. The editors are busy, they can't work on it. A few give advice, sallow encouragement, the rest disappear.

Run to England into the arms of Mother Machree. Nell herself. She'll know what I meant to say, crazy hat, hands covered with rings, waving in great cirlces of her talk. Dublin and Irish, save me Mother O'Rourke. And she did.

The book in Nell's hand. Scolding me with its finer dedication. How does one get out of the movement? Where is the exit? Nell, I want to tell you I can't do it . . . too afraid even to say the words. I can't be Kate Millett any more. It's an object, a thing. A joke at cocktail parties. It's no one. I'm only the fear in my gut. Just let me watch it from the sidelines. Like other women can. Enjoy the luxury of looking on while someone else does it for us.

After Christmas I stayed on upstate at the farm. After Fumio and the other people went back down to town. Tried to write and I couldn't. It had gone, or never been. After that I didn't risk it often, or only little bursts on a page, scribbling in notebooks on airplanes. Three days snowed in at the farmhouse, at the oak table trying to tell the paper what it was like. Coming out in the media. Publicly queer to the millions in their dentist's office. A Lesbian in ninety-three languages. The shit hitting the *Time* fan for the movement, transforming me into a stick with which to beat other women. And the pain Mother feels. Guilt her retaliation beyond any offense, overkill. My felt pen bleeding red on the white typing paper telling even how it was futile, a service to principle. Celia was gone to me already, lost in New Haven labyrinth of streets, middle of night sitting in front of that big house, no lights in the little apartment off to the side, my hand reaching toward the convertible's big ash tray stubbing out a cigarette, knowing it was over. The farmhouse snowed in. Alone and I read two books; learning from Emma Goldman that I was not a politician, and couldn't write autobiography. Good woman, a religious fanatic all her life. A lifetime given to the anarchist cause without a moment's doubt. Never wavered even in jail. I am all waver, I doubt everything. Becoming really frightened at the size of my unworthiness. So I read Le Duc's *Bastard*. She had already written it: the perfect book. Courageous literary Lesbian. A masterpeice. Told everything. Didn't give a damn. Could do it. Wasn't a political person, no need to be self-conscious. Now, because I am afraid, I can do nothing. My own cowardice begins to sicken me. These two women are art and politics. Reading them I am judged. Better not to try anything.

I know the moment the felt pen stopped, the snow stretching into tedium through the lace curtains, the felt pen coming to a halt. Stopped, trying to speak that

terrible moment at Columbia, Teresa Juarez yelling at
me from the audience, "Are you a Lesbian? Say it. Are
you?" At the start of the panel there, mixed thing of
Gay Lib and Women's Lib, saying it like it was a joke,
my credentials: founding member of Columbia Women's
Liberation and a bisexual. Looking out at my old peers,
professors in the audience, not even thinking they were
finks, just knowing they'd kept the job and I'd lost it.
So I could say things like that. Publicly say I was
AC-DC. Humorous about it. Then into the polemic:
abstractions about homosexual life in our society. My
sex life no more a topic of discussion than anyone
else's.

When I came into Macmillan, Sidney warned there'd
be trouble, the place full of Radical Lesbians wanting
me to clear things up, contradict the press image of nice
married lady. Straight. O.K. Someone from *Time* came
when I talked at DOB in August, candid, one gay to
another. But they didn't pick it up. Chattered Gay Lib
politics with Barbara Love the whole day *Life* interviewed
me. The pregnant lady reporter seemed not to want the
baby. Didn't like me. Said I swore, printed fifteen curse
words in two columns. Misquoted me saying Lesbianism
was "not my bag." Printed a picture of me kissing Fumio.
Saw it one night in a bar when he was gone in Japan.
Drunk and tired, shooting the film. Wept, missing him.
Mother will not have to live with her neighbors reading
the unspeakable. Mother will not thunder at me . . . "Not
my bag."

Time stops: the felt pen recording, the magazine, the
tape recorders, my terrified mind stops remembering it,
while Teresa Juarez's voice loud butches me from the
floor mike center of the room, a bully for all the correct
political reasons. Five hundred people looking at me.
Are you a Lesbian? Everything pauses, faces look up
in terrible silence. I hear them not breathe. That word
in public, the word I waited half a lifetime to hear.
Finally I am accused. "Say it! Say you are a Lesbian."
Yes I said. Yes. Because I know what she means. The
line goes, inflexible as a fascist edict, that bisexuality

is a cop-out. Yes I said yes I am a Lesbian. It was the
last strength I had.

Sitting on a blue chair in London Airport, trying to enjoy
the comforts of international travel, having a drink.
Martini in plastic glass. I have dreamt it again in
England. The dream recurring over and over the years
I was in Oxford. Waiting to die. The terror week after
week until you expect them, grateful, glad they're coming
down the hall to get you. Hope of reprieve so exhausting
it's a relief to give up. Accepting now. Have stopped
trying to prove innocence. Guilty of some crime always
indistinct. Seems to be murder. Something grim, silly
even, something about an illegal operation on a kitchen
table. We were only trying to help a friend. Inside the
gray dream JayCee is my accomplice in most versions,
but it can shift. "Practicing medicine without a license,"
the judge says. He looks down. Robes. Wigs. Asinine
British paraphernalia. "Hanged by the neck until dead."
Sounds crazy. Not only at first, but for weeks I know it's
all a mistake. Got to get it cleared up. Inefficiency. A
little patience until the bureaucracy rectifies itself. The
lawyers still say there's a good chance, merely takes a
while. Then it's a matter of there being a chance at all.
I become uncertain. Maybe the authorities are right. Comfort of agreeing with them. They get their information
mixed up—but in principle they're right. I am guilty, of
something awful. When I am fully reconciled, nobly
composed to die, I will wake up. Wonderful relief. If
I let them kill me in the dream I can wake and live. It's
a trade. A deal.

   And the second time I went up to Oxford I'd bantered
with my tutor about the deal. According to the deal I
give St. Hilda's Library my books and they'd let my
ashes sit in the garden bank unmarked in a blue china
pot underground, beneath the daffodils, the Isis, the swans
going by and the punts. Just a joke. She takes me to
Christchurch meadow, beauty of old towers, mellow green
of trees, outlines soft with age, May day evening. This
morning they sang from Magdalen tower to greet the

spring. Christchurch old stone gold in the evening, grass blue with light of coming dusk. The place tears at me with its beauty. She thinks of leaving it. A senior fellow, leaving it to teach the poor. "I am not a great teacher, only a mediocre scholar, I will go somewhere where I will be of use," she says. I wonder who could leave such a place. It shines in the crisis of my envy, all serenity. I can never reenter it. My mind races, scheming up sham research to take me here. Only a visitor now. Hardly better than a tourist. The doors are shut. I have shut them myself. Contaminated, I will not have shelter in the university. It would have been safety. I have gone beyond the pale, a bit too far out. There is freedom on the outside, but it is dangerous. We had dinner at the Mitre and I missed the train. Seeing myself in the eyes of her distance, remote Oxford don who does not even read the papers. Sitting in her room I am past disputing with her whether girls are as smart as boys or should get into Oxford. Gentle nineteenth-century lady. Always warming her hands against the fire in the grate. She is kind and neither of us can read a train schedule. Her slippers in the bedroom when I used the toilet, the contentment of all those years living in college, surrounded with her colleagues and her students.

A reporter rang the doorbell after Columbia. *Time* lady wants to know if I really said that. They have bugged the university debate. The *Time* people feel a wonderful solicitude that my statement "will hurt the women's movement." Are they protecting themselves from libel—or are they offering me a chance to lie my way out of it? I won't budge. I said it. While she waits in the next room I try to reach Ivy on the phone, get advice, let them know it's going to happen. Not home. Hell with it. It's the truth. That will have to do. I cannot, must not hurt the movement. But the movement cannot sell out on gays, cringe before the dyke-baiting, shuffle into respectability. Calling Sally from Bryn Mawr one night to ask her to help with Mom. Her elder sister's voice tired on the phone out of Nebraska army wife confinement.

"There it goes down the tube for the rest of us. I warned you. It's too hot to confuse with the women's movement."

"I'm not Women's Lib, Sally, just one woman in it who happens also to be a queer."

"I've got every sympathy for homosexuals, but middle America simply can't take this sort of thing."

"Sally, I did what I thought was right." Guilty stomach. "Will you talk to Mother first?"

"They set you up for this, *Time* Magazine, that cover job."

"Yeah, I know now."

But I didn't know. Never knew until it was out. My face on the cover. They asked me whose picture they should use the week of the women's march. I said no one woman but crowds of them, offering some photographs of other demonstrations. Then the shock when the cover was printed, idiots sending it to me for autographs. Just what the movement hates. That time I could explain it was a trick, a portrait painted from a photograph without my knowledge or permission. Will they understand this time?

They're calling the flight. Tighten up. BOAC 821 for John F. Kennedy. In London Ethel asked me—"Will you be all right in New York?" I try to hear Janis doing "Bobby McGee." Paul played it for me one night in London. The upper room, leather sofas, Nell's hot wild wine. Paul's Janis and my terror, every verse a Ferris wheel, the up and rise and spin of fear. "Freedom's just another word for nothing left to lose." Paul shot that last concert before she died. He's playing it to show me courage. The sound blows through my head like madness, something worth checking out for. To have done that first made it all right.

The first day back from Germany Paul was tough with me. Stood in the doorway of the cutting room while I wrote the letter, turned down the last job, finished teaching. I stopped typing and waited for the blow: "Nell can't edit the film with you. We have started to pattern Winnie, it's a long treatment, it will take years. Winnie could be a normal child. You'll have to do the film yourself. No one writes your books for you, either." His voice soft but inflexible under the moustache. So I had to start, doing it alone, Betty cutting for me, sitting at the Steenbeck, her shoulders rigid with disapproval. That night when he gave me Joplin I was grateful.

Passengers for Kennedy . . . they are calling us, they will put me on the plane. I will be stuffed in, sent back to America. Remember Janis in the upper room hitting the Victorian leather, belting out her guts from a silver machine. The kids' faces at Bryn Mawr that day had seen it. *Times* brought me out in Timese: she "acknowledged" and "the disclosure is bound to discredit her as a spokeswoman for her cause." Their young faces had seen it. Scared, shaken. I needed their help. But they were having trouble too. They are eighteen. Just by taking my course they acquire the taint of eccentricity. Now *Time* has told them I discredit the movement. Their faces read the magazines. We are all believers. The media lives in each of us.

On the train going down there I scratch in the flowered notebook, riding the Paoli Local to the last Bryn Mawr lecture, one station as dull and winter-dead as the last. JayCee's stop: Haverford. Finally I am seeing the place she came from, that Main Line first woman, the beginning of it all. Bumble along the track hard hit by attacks and now *Time*'s fool. Coiled in guilt grieving for family and the others hurt by how I live because I defended that life. Obsessed with the loss of Celia. Something like the nadir is reached today. Bitter to remember, last June's fair promise, Brookfield, the new life, clotted over. Canceled.

Hedonist and masochist go at each other inside me, one yearning after art love pleasure joy and summer; the other forever lapsing into shame anguished responsibility despair. And the second has won. Celia. Everything went wrong there. All the threads lead back to that rift, the great torn place, the ache of it literal and organic as a wound. The Paoli Local bumps along all right but I'm derailed. Folly to have given such power over one's life into another's hands. Each moment's peace becomes dependent upon a whim. What collusion of vanity and self-loathing has brought me to the point where I can no longer work or live without the air of her acceptance?

Tomorrow the press conference. We will talk back—for of course we must have a press conference and say the right political things. And I have pulled a coup whereby the women's movement will officially support Gay Liberation. Tomorrow the press conference at the Peace Church. I have not been there since last summer. The night after the concert. Had forgotten to pick up Nell's film after the benefit screening, anxious it might be stolen. Not there. Check the whole building. Alvin must have taken it with him. In the basement I stumble into a Radical Lesbian meeting. It bustles with paranoia in the wake of Lydia's murder.

I stood for a moment on the sidewalk in front of the church. The concert was only last night, just a day ago, twenty-four hours. But what a distance between the two occasions. Last night there was music filling all the floor above, the space between the stone walls alive with Celia's lute. Miriam's voice taking on such greatness it became a force unto itself. I saw Fumio standing in the shadow by the wall, his love beaming out to her from the darkness. Did Miriam see it? Did she know she sang to me as I stood by the door, imagining the sounds were sent to me that I became enamored at last with the power of her art. Too late. She heard only Celia's anger, her order to leave us both. The four of us never really friends again.

Last night the music. But now one hears nothing in the soft August evening. Yesterday's celebration, all that it meant has evaporated like sound. The concert was upstairs: politics is now downstairs in the basement. The music was art and love, even the end of love: the meeting is convened over death. Lydia's murdered. Her body is held at the morgue, captive of the authorities. Friends who loved her may not even gather to mourn or bury their own. We are queer, we are not kin. The police have seized her papers, they are combing over membership lists and diaries. Lydia was in Radical Lesbians. I knew her in the art group too. Was she a painter or a writer? I remember she was tall and thin and nervous. I remember her timidity. The police are picking up her associates There will be questioning and harassment. Murdered, someone says, by an old boyfriend made jealous that she loved women now. The meeting is tense, frenzied, a conventicle of the beleaguered. Leaving, I stood a moment on the pavement before the building, pulled in two directions: upstairs to the past, and what might have been; downstairs to the present. A bitter realization that I live on separate lines parallel into infinity: my friends of yesterday cannot be with me tonight; they are above it, they are not involved. And the other group who fear for their lives, what time do they have for Early Music?

The plane is taking off. That one moment flirting with death. Always the best part of the flight. I am at Bryn Mawr again. I walk from the bookstore across an open field. This place and its beauty of trees. Trees bought with money. I am walking across the field, open ground, remembering the early classes when there were so many students, when I was a curiosity. I have failed as a teacher, not enough time to prepare, too many trips this semester. I have not demanded enough of them either. Last day of classes, there are fewer who come now. Not since the day we grew afraid. The press conference tomorrow. Walking across the field and suddenly I am shot. I see myself hit in the center of empty space, my arms spread in a lavender shirt, my legs fork in the void, two white lines. The figure jumps, poised in space, and crumples. I walk on past it. And when I reach my room I write it down remembering a student's legend that this room once housed a warden who was exposed for a pervert, fired for corrupting her pupils not through seduction but through ideas. Then I lost the notebook.

We are flying over England now, green Sussex below us, hills, the farms cut into bite-sized British patches. Scale is everything: Lilliput or Cinemascope. Coming from Southampton up to Oxford years back sheep looked like toys in their fields. Softer here and always green. It is spring in England as I leave. Starting in the spring last year, just a year ago in New Haven, I slept with a woman for the first time in eight years. Starting in the spring—wrote that on a page and stopped. Naomi suggested I begin the book there starting when it all started again. It started with Carol and it was almost an accident. Woke up one night because I had to tell Fumio, sitting up in bed smoking, terrified, what will he do, will he kill me, will he ever speak to me again, so I made him wake up and I told him. He laughed into his pillow. Why are you laughing? "Well at least you won't get pregnant," . . . giggled, and went back to sleep. I was very disappointed, had expected him to murder me or march out of the house forever. Instead I could lie in bed and look at the ceiling, wondering why it didn't fall. Afterwards Carol regretted it, an experiment she did not choose to repeat. Then Naomi gave me my body. But her masochism and her crazy stage mother were also included. We had to be mister and missus, we had to quarrel, we had to have roles. So I evaded her, failing her as Celia has failed me. I could not solve Naomi's life, I could not write her book for her, I could not fix things. So I defected. And then there was Magda, but all her courage was not enough. At the Congress in May Magda in her beauty and her fierceness talking them all down, being brave enough to think of something else than they had, telling the whole crowd of them to go to hell. Reading her paper: You persecute the few productive women we have, she tells them—"Stars," they yell back, "elitism." Just the glory of it, her great beauty and her nerve, her passionate and careful logic winning the whole audience. Finally only seventeen of the other kind sitting in one corner hissing like snakes in their hatred. She had said what I should have, but was afraid. Then Magda in February having coffee at the Bowery

telling me over the marble tabletop that she didn't have
the courage to go on. "It's really easier to make it with
guys, I haven't got the guts," her voice dull and tight,
"and now I'm pregnant," her own wry smile at the irony
of it. Magda singing in the theater the night of her
abortion, the little ticket from the hospital around her
wrist. Singing with her great Italian courage, still bleeding
inside. Magda remembered in an airplane over the Atlantic. And Celia—now the sense of emptiness again.
Celia who was the new life.

Sitting in the office with Nell. Just a bit more wine before
we're home to Winnie. Her figure against the wall in
her big hat and making Irish comedy out of her crackup.
Gotten drunk with a friend at lunch and they went home
in a cab, but something strange happened and they fell
into each other's arms. "After that I had to go to Spain
for four days and see an analyst." We are having another
glass of wine, feeling guilty about Paul who's waiting
at home for us to do the patterning with Winnie. Nell
playing Paul's daughter to evade her blasting motherhood.
Doctors wanted her to do it again, have another child.
Prove her normality, her breeding power. I met the
friend. She was Magda's twin. How we are afraid to love
each other.

Flying now is flying then, another trip to Podunk, another
speech, scribbling in my notebook then this is an abortion,
a book that didn't get born. Sorrow of a child lost, has
it more satisfaction than this? Something to think about
while riding in a cab. Esteban de Jesus has just received
a summons. He's driving this taxi. Beaten by the pink
native cop who has spent fifteen minutes of our time
illustrating Jesus's crime of turning right from the left
lane. Esteban chooses not to understand. Outraged reason,
the policeman will diagram for us on Esteban's copy
of the *Daily News*. The illustration is done with pencil
lines right over the headline blare of Frazier's victory,
Muhammad's loss. Jesus has done everything he can to
stall, to deny everything, to be a really dumb Puerto

Rican. His hopes and strategies are waves reaching me
in the back seat. Nothing worked and now he's got the
ticket, one more decision against him. He's cornered,
I can feel his rage prickle all over his shoulders. In the
morning, a morning before I came to Europe, in the
morning waking to passion's fantasy. Vita. Had thought
I'd killed desire here, squashed like a coat in a suitcase,
stashed away so thoroughly consciousness didn't even
remember I wanted her. Unconscious sure did. Go down
dream mouth tongue singing on her center tasting knowing
her essence. How difficult it's been made for anyone to
write these words, how much harder for a woman to talk
this way. Then mind's picture sees her head between my
legs, her mouth on my cunt now. And I suck in breath.
The beauty of it, this act. The phone rings. It is Fumio
who jumps out of bed with me. In the dressing room
I suggest it. Back to bed. So it's another act that begins
the day—not that dream I woke to. Good it is, lovely
the fullness of him in me. But need one be torn, forced
to live in one place or another?

Have another airplane daiquiri and arrive at tonight's
Podunk fortified. Never lecture for money. Even if you
give the money away, even if it goes to other people,
even if it goes to the movie. I wanted one thing for myself
so I bought the farm. Fate, let it not become another
stone. Below the wings one more set of snowfields. How
far have we come since the January depression? Since
Montreal?

I hear newsmen in my head, leading questions: will
Women's Lib wear out with the media? This morning
a joke book arrives, cartoon of wife reading me in bed,
husband groans—"Not again tonight." Editor's letter
promises it's all in fun: the sick society has learned to
live with us. Will future historians say that I blew it?
Will they permit my love of Fire Island's summer, the
ferry hitting the waves in the sun, my glory over a long
dress for a party in the Bowery studio in winter. My
passion for spirits like Celia Tyburn or Fumio. Probably
one should never feel such gaiety or such despair. Better

to operate on an even keel like Friedan and Gloria and the others. All far better politicians. But I am not a politician. Not "Kate Millett of Women's Lib" either. Too many years a downtown sculptor. Loving certain human things and having nothing else I knew so well I carved this out of my own self.

Drinking around the marble tabletop at the Bowery one night, all the spaced-out types, Mallory and her troupe, and I said I thought to write about myself. Brother Phillip acidhead said it—"No way. That's going naked, you'd be without any protection." I was surprised, had imagined that's how he lived. But he had called the shot, and judged the danger. Discretion in his dope.

Sitting in an airplane picking my nose among the tourists, this year shooting across the movieola, flights, and speeches: the roar at Boston University, the three standing ovations at Austin. Good moments: Sister Kate is vain and needy enough to treasure them. People are turned on, changed—you can see and feel that—a base for the movement is being built in the university. But the certainty, like a cancer, that there is something desperately wrong with this system, its adulation as depraved as its lonely depersonalized exposure, the seconds of pure terror alone up there on the stage, a mark for attack. The idolatry painful, ridiculous. The whole bloody system is sick: the very notion of leadership, a balloon with a face painted upon it, elected and inflated by media's diabolic need to reduce ideas to personalities.

I cannot write that book. It would have to say that I'm what? And what am I anyway? I hate confessionals. Bless me father for I have sinned. A whining form. And then there's Mother. I hear her on the phone: "What does it mean to be a bisexual, Katie?" "Well, I guess it means to love both men and women, Mother." "How terrible." "What's wrong with it, Mother?" The first time I had ever challenged her, actually said, what's wrong with it? So she told me: it's dirty, filthy, disgusting—and I heard her.

If I try to write, shame will maintain the paper's

purity. Not a fit subject. People will say I don't love Fumio. There is so much people will say that you'd better shut up. Mustn't hurt the movement—they will use you against it. Irony that I had just started writing, really writing, in my own voice, as my thesis went to press. Then slammed with an identity that can no longer say a word; mute with responsibility. Interrupted one afternoon writing that piece on the South that made me drunk with pride and expectation—messenger at the door to deliver the first copy of *Sex Pol*. Holding the book in my lap like a stone, so heavy. Small print, footnotes. New paper but already so old. Finished nine months before. Held it, looked at it, the first fear racing into silent words. Will this object in my hands, offspring already so remote, become a monster? Call the editors, thank them for a handsome job, try to sound delighted, ashamed of my ingratitude as of an infidelity.

That summer's last June days in Brookfield, we three, Celia, Fumio, and me. Then back to town because the book is coming out. That week before it happened, driving the West Side Highway from Miriam's at dawn after we'd talked all night. Along the river and the big ships, windows out of the city cage to Europe. Mind on the *Prostitution Papers,* the rap sessions, another one tonight, each so hurting, a sight of the terrible places women have been that I had only imagined. No sleep for three days. So much to do, the Columbia curriculum, glorious group think tank gathering on the Bowery this afternoon. Drink wine and dream up courses, revolutionize scholarship, illuminate the university in our collective high. Just before the Eighteenth Street exit a long empty stretch, the thousand blank windows of the Raleigh Warehouse sitting huge as fate ahead on the left side of the road. Now I'm choking. Claustrophobia done in a fast car. Cut it out. Open the shirt throat, rub forehead. Talk out loud, you can't fall asleep at the wheel. Watch it. Slowing down with heavy traffic coming hard behind. I see myself park the car, opening the door, legs going over the barrier, the body moving into the other lane, figure crossing the roadway until it explodes into oncoming car. I had almost done it. But how odd. My book is being published. I have written it. There will be a party. Going to my wedding I took a cab, long green coat dress, terribly smart, told the driver my wedding day. Proud to say it. On the way to the hotel where my mother and sisters wanted to dress me in white. We are to have a string quartet playing Mozart. All our friends there, mixture of artists and relatives, oil and water. It is a joke because Immigration is going to deport Fumio. So we got a city hall license. Spouse's petition. Waking together on our wedding morning, rejoicing in the weather. Who could understand my loving him while loving others? Always these eight years and still. But starting in the spring there were women.

I cannot write a book. Tear up the contract, give back the money. The night before Montreal I went to bed writing claustrophobia into my copy of Erikson's book on Gandhi. Telling the flyleaf why I would never write, keep silence. First thing I want to tell you is about the subway. I mean when it stops. That exquisite second when the lights go out. Pristine terror. How does one get that way? Scarcely the question to ask when the central issue is to keep from screaming or breaking a window and bludgeoning the twenty-seven harmless souls who appear to be obstructing my liberty. Heart and lungs doing all they can to respond to suffocation.

And woke with Fumio to begin the day's insanity after the night's. A new edition. At six-thirty we are both pretending to be asleep, pretending even to each other. Things have gotten that bad. By eleven we can't hang out in the womb any more. Get up to find the pipes frozen. No water. Old-time emergencies are almost reassuring by now. Forget about washing your face, deal with the income tax, the bank, the postal onslaught. Choke on an egg and then the scramble of clothes into bag. Today is Montreal. I have some hopes of missing the plane. My taxi "has trouble with the coloreds," is afraid of assault, exhales the city. Woman speeding past on our right has a beautiful hell-for-leather expression. Lady, I wish I felt like you.

Back into the opiate of airport plastic Muzak. Keep running. You can't lose shame. My panic is on again. For six months I've been leaking out, in love lost, in father dead, in work blocked. But January was it, hit bottom. The roller coster of the mind. Every Bowery day one long anxiety attack, cage pacing the studio till I know every knot in its old floor, where the nails shine, where the tin covers void, where the black paint wears down to brown. So scared now, I've ceased to be, prisoner of that monster created in my name. And by this time I'm asking too—what will she ever do now? There seems nothing left, the future so predictably empty it wouldn't be worth sitting through. This is one movie you ought to walk out on.

It keeps going through my head . . . days you lose faith in the movement—and your work, and your self. All one with me now. Moderson's voice reeling at me: "You're traumatized by it all." I looked out the window on Riverside Drive, a mistake to have come up here around Columbia. Those people again. Her voice somehow lecherous in its cruelty: "You'll wear out with it, you can't write now." "They'll eat you alive. You're broken, craven." My guru. When you're depressed, visit a friend.

Up in the sun clouds I meet my double. Lady next to me tries to write pictures of things, a sunset. Another one who worries all the time, a timid one who writes bits and scraps and can't put them together. I do this too, so I ask her how you get over it. Her arm and jaw go rigid with anxiety. When will I learn that no one else can help?

And how can I even remember the bureau drawers of childhood, the ivy wallpaper of closets. Their tedium. Lately so full of self-dislike and crazy enough to have started feeding off the past's sick provender. Want to write and cannot. Hang on as the nausea of failure settles down again. Try to see the house on Selby Avenue, the two windows onto the roof, the closet. I can't do it. Said

I would write about myself. This at a time when I don't even exist. And there's Mother. Fumio. Shut up. That book is fatal, impossible, meaningless, I am a self-exploded humbug, leaving only a dust heap of humiliated consciousness. Yet I'm cornered in it, forcing myself by tearing off shreds of the past, hoping to draw blood and make it flow. Under the rip, only gray livid meat.

Snowfields below are so hateful, so familiar. Where I came from: known and despised. And just to make it a bit duller and more repellent, a country loved still. Since the partition has been installed that separates me now from the someone who felt and existed, I see everything through dirty Plexiglas. The objects recognized are insipid, lifeless; their very sameness contemptible, a reproach. Down there little roads, each farmhouse nakedly lined up right at the edge; trees and privacy are nothing to security. Where I came from and where I'm going. Since already I foresee this summer's farm as jail. Time bleak and endless, look out the window and see the same blank as yesterday and tomorrow. The place a curse even before I get it. Locked in with the heat on the roof, the green of trees full of dead power while I sit empty.

If I were to call any feeling my own it is this terrible unconnected energy consuming itself, like a power drill when the bushings go. Trivial decisions are monumental, dubious, mysteriously impossible. Nothing can be begun since the first step is unknown. In order not to err one does nothing. Competence would require a knowledge and belief far beyond one's power. The illusion of foreknowing every possibility renders action out of the question. Stand still: any step would be hazardous. Or walk around and study the Bowery floorboards, divert everything into the phone, change the mind's subject, drink a cup of coffee. Remember what there is to get from the store. Distract until dinnertime. The life once so various, so beautiful, so new doesn't really end in ignorant armies, the darkling plains are merely the sight of a letter three weeks unanswered. Or some nondescript object standing in just the same spot where it has tortured the gaze for days. A month of this and you'll fly anywhere. Any relief from reality.

Montreal has little solace to offer. Until we reach the mangy student co-op where I stay, the conversation is of repression, martial law, arrests, general despair. A heavier version of our side of the border. There is worse to come. In the usual university ghetto pad, an old house gone hip, I hear about radicals here who are off into madness, suicide, crazy with depression, getting locked up, others breaking their minds with drugs. Everywhere fright and inertia. Like most United States citizens I know less about Quebec than Biafra or the Basque: my education is begun in earnest. The government's martial law regime has delivered a spooky ultimatum—You're the FLQ if you think you are. These people don't know. Are they? Aren't they? Manifestos are fired and terrorism is committed in their name. They are not consulted yet their allegiance is required—by themselves if no one else. The rebels face prison and torture, victims now. As English-speaking residents they belong to the ruling caste, as radicals they have renounced this to identify with French nationalism. Finally they are no one, and the loss of who they are is shattering them.

In bizarre counterpoint to all this is an ongoing emergency over someone's lost dog. One dog is lost, the mongrel with us is a stray; we have to talk about both of them. Seventeen calls are devoted to where we eat dinner. The stray shits on the living room rug at the height of a political exposition. Sentences never end. The conversation veers from police raids to the urgent dog whose odor now permeates the room. Occasionally, like an errant pinball, the talk hits on film. One boy has made a movie. I try to glean information. How do you cut? I have come here sick with my own hysteria. I am obsessed, compulsive: they on the other hand have transcended concentration of any kind. I cannot let them know my confusion. Got to cover the void. Put out little feelers, vague hints to the effect that I'm uncertain what work to do next, fishing for a good project. Blank stares. Panicking trying to find phrases, to elicit direction without confessing I'm in a blind alley, don't know what to do with my life or even whether to bother living it. More of the dog and the phone. Sweat, head buzzes, wanting help so badly. Every time I begin two of the four of them are absent with the phone, the dog, the kitchen.

Finally I give up and await my ordeal in settled dread, the speech before McGill's debating society I've come here to give. There will be no way out. I hate the speech. I hate myself as an impostor, a political apostate going through an act which even in entertainment value is despicable. All I can say are platitudes more tedious with repetition, calling for a revolution vague beyond fantasy, remote beyond hope. For you see, I know we are losing, foresee our defeat. Here in the bosom of the faithful who have the goodness to speed rather than to doubt.

Proceed to a restaurant to break bread with the opposition: liberal student leaders and a journalist. Every detail is seen with the prescience of the condemned: dinner for the prizefighter preordained to lose, for the star poised with the host of those who have made the arrangements and demand the killing farce continue. How much does my futility show? Have enough vibrations escaped to create a sense of impending catastrophe, will some unlikely whim of mercy dissuade them from proceeding with the sacrifice? By no means. I am firmly conducted to do my duty. The hall is bedlam, droves of the curious out for spectacle. And here it is. Reporter wants copy of speech so he won't have to stay. Frantic stuff with mikes for those in the corridors. Crushed by bodies behind stage, one last hope I'll never reach the podium and be let off. Not a chance. Absolutely no alternative, so I go through it, mouth miraculously dry and tongue unmoving through the first four pages. As I fumble along in the timeless vacuum that comes about when one's mouth is open in public, I begin by infinitely slow degrees to mean what I am saying. Believing again. But tired. In the yawn of questions that follow one young fellow argues that my advocacy of Gay Liberation must be a biological contradiction—turns and says to the audience, "She can't be a woman." Here's sensation at

last, a raw wound. Exhaustion but not escape, for it's
right into the next arrangement, the final bathos of a press
conference. Pretension beyond the limits of absurdity—is
she supposed to announce a war? At first it is flattering
when people listen to you and write it down, then it's
silly, then humiliating, then a mocking torture. CBC has
sent a man who knows his wife is fulfilled in serving him.
The rest are either dull questions I have answered already
or good ones I never will be able to. I'm a body past
use now, can be shelved till tomorrow morning's
television.

Back at the pad desultory talk and a little warm
bourbon. The inner circle. Then the predictable needling
about my pacifism. Scatter shot about Vietnam. Nonviolence not their solution; nor South America's. Here
too in Quebec we have a struggle for National Liberation,
they intone, a movie already starting up in their heads.
I have been watching the French-English class thing all
day: English spoken everywhere, then the switch to
French for the servant class of taxi and waitress. Fair
race and dark, never a question who's boss. Every trick
of education and employment to keep the outsiders in
a position of economic disadvantage. Much like Ireland.
A long way from Guatemalan guerrilla war or Vietnam's
battlefields. But the disparity is blurred, is lost in leftist
rhetoric: Montreal French are Third World People, they
inform me.

Then a youngster with a beard, and I will always hear
his voice: "To take up the gun is an act of love." The
sensuality in his voice, the phallic thrill of it. "It shows
how much you care," he goes on caressingly. And the
table is silent with respect. This whole place is a grotesque
play, delirious melodrama of my corruption and their
fantasy. One boy's father is a stockbroker, the fellow
who strokes his arm like a carbine attends classes in
medieval dance. The girls continue to telephone about
dogs: Margaret's has been found at last. Frozen on the
steps of the cathedral. Its coat stuck in the ice when they
picked it up. One whole side torn off. Everything stops
for a moment while we react to this detail. A conversation

then takes place on how to cheat veterinarians of their fee: give a false address and never return. One explicit bit of information, the one moment of intellectual clarity.

Released to fall into the sleeping bag on the floor with full leisure to despise myself all night. So spent with the sense of my imposture, I actually expect to fall asleep. But of course the panic takes over and reasserts itself again. I must be at the end of the well rope by now. Can't believe in anything. I do not want to be part of this chaos, this reverie of arms and warfare. It is not only terrifying, unreal, irresponsible—it's strangling me. All the tight-lipped arsonists in history appear to me, bands of nonentities playing manly games in heavy earnest. You don't make me feel free, I tell them. Then Cleaver playing führer in Algiers, holding Leary under guard. Outside it is eighteen below at midnight. In the front room of a Victorian house, I experience that smothering when the subway stops, the ringing moment when the lights dim.

The one time I killed. Tutoring a spoiled boy from Waseda, got myself invited to his rich daddy's hunting party in the mountains. I'd do the nature walk bit; they could hunt. Feudal pyramid of persons: big daddy, his minions—gun bearers, drivers, business underlings—the complete outfit to laugh at his jokes. I was the double outlander, a foreigner and a woman, Big Daddy treating me with an elaborate respect inexplicably insulting, outrageously waiving his right of precedence to be first into the bath every evening. After they'd thrown me shots for three days, the pressure was on. The Geigin doesn't fire. She was just dumb and arrogant enough to need to prove she could. All day building up tension to shoot. And in the late afternoon managing an overhead shot that astonished and elated me. The mark hit: the bird stopped in air. For a second overjoyed, thoroughly proud. Until it fell at my feet, flapping and bloody, its life for my ego.

I eat meat and am particularly fond of fowl. So what's the point of this? Slaughterhouses are more pernicious than pheasant hunts. But if I think I know what it means to take the life of a bird, what of a man or child? Demonstrate a woman can shoot? What is demonstrated when one stands over the body of one's kill? Will this boy tonight know love then? Will the revolutionary gunman actually know whom to kill? How will he decide? And once begun, will it be necessary, after a while, even to distinguish?

The feeling builds in me, this is not my route. I have only ideas and the anger that lights an advocate. I can and will only argue for change, not coerce it. Something was suggested tonight more by what a girl had said than by the boy. She described a Panther congress in Washington, all parts of the movement brought together, but the thing was total confusion, a disorganized failure. The women were shunted off by themselves to waste a few days together. "And all I remember," she said, "was one moment when the women were in a big room, bewildered, factionalized into little knots, doing nothing. Then the Radical Lesbians came into the room and walked to the center, fifty of them—so together. They sat down and talked in a circle, fondling and caressing each other. The rest of us watched from all parts of the room. I wanted so much to join them. But I couldn't."

Their two statements assaulting me now, the boy's and the girl's, the bare floors cracking with cold, the streetlight shining through the old windows painted red. Suddenly I know what I can do, what I should write, what job could give me belief. It comes together in my mind. A *Sex Pool* of gay and straight, a scholarly objective approach more convincing to the authorities. First lay down a theory about the two cultures, our segregated society. Then find in homosexual literature the emotional truth of the experience as it was lived. Mapping it out in the four hours after midnight. The security of book lists. Work, purpose, relief at last. The farm glows in the summer's distance, not a concentration camp of baffled inactivity, but the refuge of study, purposeful work. There is another way than playing god with life or performing maniac as talking star. I cannot believe in the gun. And as for the leader thing, I am a coward before the crowd, standing before it dizzy with my ignorance. I cannot live with this shame over the dishonesty of repetition, show, applause. What providential release then to see work to be done that transcends this, is real again, new again, uncorrupted. But it was the wrong book. And I knew it already when we landed in Kennedy. Girl next to me at the baggage counter said she wrote her way to liberation. How did you handle first person narrative, I asked her. And said she knew the hole of depression, had been there. But I am out now, I escaped, I told her. "You will fall into it again," she said. Already I was sliding.

But of course Montreal was all the wrong thing. Idiot straw clutching after son, daughter, or whatever of *Sex Pol*, derivative, self-imitation. One night at the farm Vita drank, and I smoked some pot after dinner. Brought out the idea of this book, explaining it had to be a scholarly book, only that would have influence. All the time I'm talking I watch the candles on the oak table, knowing I'm lying, knowing inside that I really want to write another book. But it's too crazy. We got pretty stoned, lying on the living room floor, I said to her—in the old movement there was a nutty lady named Victoria Woodhall who was a free lover, believed in astrology and all sorts of stuff, ran for president on the free love ticket, and married John Jacob Astor. That kind of madwoman made it hard for Susan B. and the regulars. Maybe that's what I am in this movement, an erratic, an eccentric. Getting deeper and deeper into the pot, very heavy stuff, probably hashish. Holding down a screaming desire to mention the other book but don't dare say it because I know she'll encourage me. Vita the enthusiast. And got so stoned I gave in, made it on the living room floor, ugly in my need, giving nothing really, only that terrible desire to be had, brutal stupid sordid. And the next morning I hated myself and had a hangover. Lasted three days, but the wild stuff taught me something that night, showed me what I really wanted to write, and that I didn't dare look it in the face. I

cursed the weed and I threw away the marijuana. Too
dangerous to keep around.

It is gray over the ocean. The captain announces that
Arsenal has won the All-England Cup. Poor Paul backing
Leeds. How I would like to crow at him. After all the
interviews when the BBC man leaned forward asking
a question about commitment. I am afraid. How committed should I be? I said the movement was my life.
But do I have a life? Then I went to meet Doris Lessing
in the hallway at Granada, repairman making a wonderful
noise fixing the door with a stone hammer. She sits quietly
in a corner. But the reporter who arranged the meeting
arrives right away. I don't want him to be there. I'm
sure he's a very nice guy but I hate him. I want to talk
to her, not to him. We're supposed to have a drink but
there is no bar; the bars are not open. We go to a coffee
shop. The coffee is lousy, white, watered, hideous. Her
solicitude for me as I sit there shaking. I ask her about
The Golden Notebook, telling her what it meant to me.
And she said—"But don't you write? You could write
short stories." She imagines I write: poor misguided
woman. She suggests I send a note to Mailer and ask
him to have a drink. That's a funny idea, but it makes
sense. We make a pact to meet again. That man will not
be there, that reporter. We go on to a bar now that the
bars are open. We cross a street with a magic name,
Glasshouse Street. We're going to the Cafe Royal. There
are tarts on the street. "I used to come here often," she
says, "and I knew a lot of tarts." I try to tell her about
the *Prostitution Papers*. I sound stupid—this man is in
our way or I could make her understand. We make conversation at the Cafe Royal bar: She hasn't been there
in years, used to come all the time. I feel the weight of
decades of literati. Is she bored? There is so much I
should ask her and I can't. We try to talk about
prostitutes again. The man does not understand. She explains prostitutes she's known: the sentimental one, and
the unsentimental one, the one who was beautiful, the
one who was smart, the one who was lazy. He asks her

about Clancy. She gives us a scene of Clancy making wonderful pronouncements in honor of his cock and against population control. He is witty, he is impossible. I see Clancy as a man and not the man in the book. Saying good-bye we embrace. I never talked to her and I wanted to so much.

Still over the great gray ocean we will be there soon. New York. Funny I should remember Claire now, and that march to Albany just before I left. Union Square on a gray Sunday morning, bleak, brokenly empty. And like a light shining across the space between the car and the monument, a fag queen sparkles in a silver coat. The first thing I see—what am I doing here? Then the man with the camera over his raincoat. A business suit, topcoat all in order. But the face rouged, youthful. His hair is a strange unreal color. Specter of Aschenbach's specter of us all. Beyond thest two figures I see my friends in the distance: Sidney, Louise, and the rest.

A day of generous contradictions. Woke to find Fumio causing the smell and sizzle of bacon. Odd I should have a husband who sends me off to march for Gay Liberation. I have arrived without a ticket so a spangled queen gives me one free. On the bus I scan a drag mag and find it nauseous. Sitting next to me a blonde kid, fresh and clean as a drugstore beauty. She reads. I scribble. "Claire Bookbinder," she says and returns to her print. "Bookie" the others call her. Inconceivable that anyone on this bus could be reading Brecht's *Galileo*. But she is doing it.

When we stop at Howard Johnson's some innocents from straightsville ask if we are skiers. Sidney and I are very amused. Claire eats her ice cream thoughtfully; her button reads "Don't Pollute—Sail." All along the sad road to Albany I saw the face of my mother. Then Rocky's phallic experience bursting into towers. We volunteer to be marshals, today my first time, excited listening to the instructions. Claire and I stick together, she knows of a ride back to the city. There's a pray-in at the Catholic church. I sit in the pew cynical, resentful, incredulous. Suddenly I understand the church thing because the stained glass becomes the chapel at the convent, then our parish church in St. Paul. Did the church do it to me, my guilt born in this building? But why should I care now, chasing around in the street to find a church and the one Catholic priest they have dug up who says it's all right to be queer? I hate the church, left it when I was seventeen. Why, sitting with this new person Claire, why do I feel this weird little peace?

As we march through the streets the townspeople laugh at us from the sidewalks. An organizer finds me: they want me to make a speech. I have nothing to say. What if I told the truth, the one or two things I know about gay that make it hell? That is bad propaganda. Sidney and the politicals will be furious—but I will say it—shame and fright and suffering have brought us here to make demands of power, and the voices yell out—"Justice, Justice, Justice," the word like a great bell ringing against the windows of the capitol, springing back from every stone wall. I heard the voices shouting and it was beautiful.

We rode back in a Volkswagen, Claire and I tucked away in a little box at the rear of the car. No room to sit up so we crouch wound around each other. Curious way to become friends. We talk about Gandhi and King. When we stop in a place to buy gas and use the toilet there is no toilet paper. For the fun of it we go to the country store and buy ten rolls of it for the whole filling station. I am surprised at the sound of my laughter. First time in months to feel gaiety, believe in summer, imagine the ocean. We talk about Provincetown together. I say I will study this summer, maybe write. She discusses Brecht, some essay he wrote on the artist and politics. She tells me about Solzhenitsyn. Lying on the VW floor looking through the windows I see the trees and think of the sea and the prairie. The afternoon shining red in Claire's face, her odd fluffy ring of yellow hair like some bizarre halo, her green eyes. Am I falling in love with this kid? Locked up in the back of a car, cooped up in this hutch? A few minutes ago while we took a corner my head rested on her feet. She is using my bent knees

as an armrest. I feel comfortable to be touched. There
are trees and the last snow melting in the fields—how far
have I gone now? Crossing the Tappan Zee there is a
mist over the Hudson.

Listening to her crazy talk of dolphins and galaxies,
all her miscellaneous reading, her peculiar ideas, we talk
of love. And how one invents it. "I always thought we
created love," she argues. "Really an invention of our
own, the love of the creature and the creator. Every time
we love we create love all over again." "But then there
are times we can't," I counter. "Loving and not being
loved is suffering." "But you have justice on your side.
To be loved and unable to love is less painful yet
somehow more degrading, because you haven't even got
righteousness then." She laughs at me.

Strange radiant kid—maybe even a little dotty with
all her wild talk about whales and elephants. But how
beautiful her peculiar reverence for life. "The sense the
stars give you of being a created thing," she says. "One
form of life among many. And not all that consequential."
There is something healing in her talk: its religious care
for personhood, its optimism for a humanist revolution,
its love of peace, its never even needing to consider
violence an alternative. She has spent a long time studying
with the Quakers. Coming down the East Side Drive
we fall into one long terrifying look. Everyone in the
car must feel the familiar depression of returning to the
city. But huddled in our box it hurts us less to see the
Lower East Side again, our usual slum. When we look
at each other it is as if some promise were made.

I invite them all up for a drink. So grand to have
people at the studio again, to show the sculptures and
photographs of sculptures, Fumio teasing me that the
Tokyo show was my best since it helped his own
development most. Fumio and Claire like each other.
I must go uptown to a benefit party for the women's
movement tonight. The three of us will stop by for a
moment and then will go off to see Chikamatsu's
Monagatori, a film Fumio has been keeping as a surprise
for me.

Showplace apartment on Riverside Drive. Never used to have to go to this sort of thing, but now they use my name on the agitprop, it becomes an obligation. We arrive too late to be introduced. My intention had been only to keep faith with the promise to show my face one minute before it was over. But my hope had been to see Betty Friedan and talk. There have been so many months we should have. Columbia Liberation tried to engineer a meeting but I did not want it. I see her talking energetically to a bunch, a bald man who is a bore and several vultures. She seems mellow and there aren't too many people left. She could still cut me down to a nod and that would be it. But she wants to talk, wants to explain the article in *Social Policy*. I look at her face, haggard, beautiful, and ugly. In the center that great nose they all hate, so grandly Jewish. And a bit mick now with the drinks. Tonight I'll be able to tell her my respect, that I have changed beyond the kid righteously denouncing her as a conservative and revisionist, have seen enough now of the sophisms or whatever young ambition uses to clothe its naked will to power. Betty jeered in print and pilloried in Carl's idiotic slander. Where else in politics would they stoop to the rancor of an ex-spouse?

I must explain the purpose of the press conference on the gay issue, sputtering volubility. She keeps interrupting—the fourth time I'm demanding: "Betty, you've got to hear me out." She eyes me, dubious but unpredictable. I say Gay Liberation is valid for the same reasons as feminism, but acknowledge it's also my own personal commitment. She allows it to be my right, is almost supportive. People crowd around like they want to eat us, voyeurs seeing us together, wanting to soak up our conversation. We try another room and a plush sofa. Enormous pressure of time, there is so much to say now we are finally talking. In the rush I am barbarous enough to stub out a cigarette in a marble cigarette box. Someone comes to fuss with it. By now we're bargaining. It seems Betty would like me to shut up about Gay Lib for a while and I won't. Issues shift and it seems to be how to cool gay-straight warring in the women's movement. She wants to meet us. I suggest Barbara and Sidney. Unlikely they could agree on anything and I wouldn't be there to mediate—going to England so soon. Then I say that I want to write on the gay issue. "Write whatever you like," she says. Seems too good to be true. Has Betty become my mother, is she now a permissive parent? A white butterfly perches on the table and we ask her to leave us alone. Then we find our common ground, our mutual fear that it could all come to nothing, that the movement might dissipate before it can make concrete gains. We are both depressed. "We have only two years and we used to think we had twenty," she says. "If we get women to hope and then we can't come through and produce, then what will happen?" I ask. She suggests a meeting in June with Sheila Tobias at the Hamptons. A summit. We embrace good-bye.

Claire has waited in the car because she can't stand this kind of party. Then we are all off to see Mesaguchi's film of a boat captured in stillness, emblem of all the pity and hopelessness of romantic love. I want to make films again. Mesaguchi has proven they are art, not technology, not entertainment, not business. We go to a Chinese restaurant. Claire tells a story of a Zen master in chess. It is about concentration and compassion. It is about editing, about Vita, and about Mallory. She is teaching me what I should know when I edit the film. I see the affection of Fumio and Claire, enjoying it. Over the ocean now and I remember the look on the highway. Like a promise made that someday we'd be lovers. But of course that's silly; don't get involved again. Stay away from it. If you can't succeed at relationships you really shouldn't start them.

A London evening walked along the Embankment after Bob Morris's playground opening at the Tate. Makes films too. When I met him at a party the week before he was confident about the show. Cynthia Braverman's, the flat full of people, talking, smoking grass, I sat by myself and read an article that explained Virginia Woolf, how she went crazy. Being Virginia Woolf wasn't enough: still she was afraid. Morris came in and sat next to me. I was surprised by his kindness. He is not afraid, works big, so many pieces. All the Americans in London at the Tate drinking wine, playing with the sculptures, being "free," showing off. A likeable girl pours us champagne, says she is trying to make it as curator, is very involved in art. She is glad I was doing all these things for women, since she hasn't the time. I walk away from the museum still angry through Whitehall toward Trafalgar where the demonstrations are, past the Houses of Parliament, the government buildings, saying to myself, They are artists, you're supposed to do politics. Everything is lit up like the tourist London I knew when I was a student coming down to town on weekends to see plays. The buildings are huge blocs illuminated from below. Everything is history, names you whisper all your life, reading. I am an artist, too, damn it. The buildings are enormous sci-fi insects that can crush me. Across from Parliament's dramatic sepia lighting, there's a church. Sign says they'll be playing Early Music there on Sunday: some other name is listed to play the lute. Celia. So far from home in London and certain it's all past now. Not to hear her play again. Dante reminds me the worst is remembering the best in a bad moment. I pause and think to go in but cannot move, pawn in a field of force, its terminals each grabbing me: politics, art, love. Dinner alone in a red plush place, steak joint for Americans, looking over Trafalgar's fountains. Fresh evening water playing, this great square, its centuries of politics, our own Black Friday enacted just over there before the doors of the National Gallery. I am overwhelmed by England. The waiter snickers. I overtip and have to go home without cigarettes, just enough change for the number 19 bus. Looking at the fountains moving calm majestic, still arguing with them that I too am an artist, lost.

Over the ocean soon be back there New York, I remember the night before England. Fumio, Vita, Louise sitting about the marble tabletop. Vita's bronzed foods.

Her strange art a poetical humor. Listening to the
Grateful Dead driving a great train full of cocaine, Jack
Daniel's with the ice in the middle of the table. The last
night in America. I'm gonna cook chicken for the whole
bunch if I can find a pot. Vita quotes the Paramitra Sutra.
Fumio gets out the text, translating as he goes along:
"Nothing stays in the same place, form is emptiness,
emptiness is form. There is no limit to the senses. The
eternal world is the same. Men do not understand the
anguish of life and why it happens, nor do they note it
all passes. Those who know the anguish of life and its
reasons know it will pass. And for these there is no old
age." Vita wants to know the date. Fumio guesses it's
three hundred years before Christ. While they talk I see
the water towers again as I did yesterday driving across
town. Watching me from the tops of buildings, guardians
of all the Bowery years. Sentinels of downtown, protecting my trips to the Grand Union on dreary winter evenings. I could survive those years with their help. Now
I leave New York seeing them and hearing the poetry
shared with my friends. In this moment held, captured,
the ceremony of communication. Fumio plays Oiwaki,
Shinjiku crossroads. Parting. The total loneliness of the
flute. The music of exile. Then the swing passage, but
Christ it's tearing sad. All the partings of this year—my
father dead and now only a serene figure in the past.
Celia. Tonight my country and these friends, leaving
them now. We play Shakespeare, my favorite song from
As You Like It. "It was a lover and his lass," taunted
by all it meant in Brookfield's summer. The three of us
singing it always, driving about the countryside: Fumio,
Celia, and me.

That night's dream. A trial by the movement. Figures
of women ranged about a room question and cut at my
life, the place unrecognizable but familiar in its location,
just beyond the reach of recall. Curious sensation that
the room is associated with some current friend but which
one? Tenor of the questions is critical. That probing
wounding judgmental quality one so fears in friends. Odd

impression they are helpful as well, instructive. They
badger me about roles. Questioners seem to be of the
straight faction, those who have the most to accuse me
of.

I awake in midtrial and hear Fumio sigh. How sym-
biotic we are. Tomorrow we leave what used to be our
home, a heavy inexplicable sense of banishment in both
of us predicated on the possibility of my editing the film
over there, which could separate us for several months.
Three weeks separation last summer tried us beyond
measure, convincing him Japan was for him now uninhabitable and that I had to be his America or he was
homeless. He has returned to his new world. But what
finally do I have to give him besides this pain and my
own insanity? I am not much good to him however much
I love him.

Gray ocean gray like my father dead since the bottom
of January. The night my father died I yelled at him
on paper. Words for the occasion:
So it's happened. My father dead. I say the words
as I walk upstairs, hear them as I go to tell Fumio. Only
when they are out in the air, knocking up against the
dirty plasterboard in front of my eyes as I climb to the
landing. Only then do they have breath outside of me.
The words go ahead of me, still hanging and echoing
as I turn to face Fumio above the second flight of stairs.
Sitting on a low stool, with the skeleton of a kite at his
knees, tying threads. His apron on. The sawdust all over
his socks. His steady look.
Jim Millett dead. Elder calling at 9:30: "Dad died
three hours ago. Shelagh has just let us know." What
was I doing, three hours ago, at 6:30? The moment my
father stopped. Was I buying bourbon, and potatoes,
and some parsley? Or had we already sat down to have
a drink. Are you dead, then, Dad? What will it mean
for me? Who were you? I remember the picture of you,
pale and handsome young man, a little frightened-looking,
ghostly, even, because your photographer overexposed
you. You have died so many times for me. You have

been dead so long. Twenty-one years. Then resurrected last May. To pay a visit in New York. Reconciled.

You died again last month, when Elder called to say you would die, had to die. Too ill now and weak to live. I yelled and wept for you half the night. Kept Fumio up. Fending off the end of a life that hadn't had or done much, made mistakes and never fixed them, then fathered three more lives too young to lose you. I cried for you, man, for your manhood, even—that strange thing you had to live by, which I never understood, only loved and suffered from.

You're dead already, and we never talked. I saw you last spring: old man unrecognizable in an airport, identifiable only by the chuckle in your voice when you spoke.

You arrived while Mallory and I had coffee, nurturing our various hangovers. Mallory who was Mary once, before she changed her name. The flight was early and we missed you. Even fathers get to be strangers in twenty-one years. I was terrified I'd have to approach every middle-aged man in Newark Airport with the absurd and monumental question, "Are you my father?" But Mallory knew you, had seen you only a year before. She could spot you in a group of nondescripts, lined up in plastic chairs.

Awkward greetings. You talked to Mallory, but not to me. I went to get the car, sure it was all a hoax and you an impersonator. Random middle-aged male looking improbably respectable. Until I heard the laugh. While we drove into town, you still talked only to her. The two of you flirting across my jealousy. I sensed you were dodging me, too. I was the one who loved you—so I was expendable. And you loved Sally more. You loved Sally best. I could be your slave. When you caroused and broke your foot, you could sit in the big, overstuffed chair sacred to your use and complain that only Kate paid attention to your needs. As if that one insignificant name were proof of your neglect. So you came to see us. Mallory and me, two women who were once your daughters. After an apologetic letter that almost begged

permission. And we had four days of plays and dinners.
But we never talked then, either. Even a family feast
on the Bowery, with music and booze. But you're not
drinking now. Teetotaling with heart trouble. Mallory
and I whispering—shall we turn him on to pot, then
retreating from the idea. For twenty years I dreamed
of getting drunk with you and telling you everything.
And when we did meet, at last, you could no longer
swallow the stuff. So we never talked. People never do.
Probably they can only meet under the agreement that
they won't. But in the awkward pauses, the polite little
silences, you knew. You heard me curse and love you.
And I saw your apology in your eyes, under your
admirable poise, impressive in an elderly man with little
education who has come to see a child he abandoned
twenty years before. Asking me not to hurt you. I
couldn't. You were already dead. The bully, whose
beatings I can never forget or forgive, was gone—destroyed. Replaced by this kindly, carefully inoffensive
old man. Jowly. Two men about the same height, but
bearing no relationship to each other.

Now, really dead. Literally and finally. I've mourned
you so many years, I wonder, now, what it will be like
to start again. To walk over and tell Mallory. To hesitate
at flying west for the funeral, the ordeal of the funeral
parlor and the grave. The sight of your new wife and
children—your real family. And the Milletts. The grand
and terrible aunts with their accusing eyes, their power
to annihiliate. Still with an indifference superb beyond
condemnation. I can see their gray-eyed superior stare
arched over an open grave, measuring me and refusing
my application: "No, you are not a Millett."

Tonight will be bad for Mother. Divorced but still
married. Fifty years your wife. For three decades, a priest
admonished her each Friday afternoon at five o'clock
to bear her cross. Heavy door of the parish house, its
servile housekeeper ushers her in in a whisper until his
eminence comes grave and final. At the end of every week
she brought him her dilemma and he would solve it for
her. Surer than any psychiatrist. And cheaper. She

obeyed. Until one Sunday morning twenty years ago when the worm turned and she kicked you out. One of her kin calling on a tip she couldn't ignore, forcing her to confront the apartment on Cathedral Hill.

We'd known it, somehow, already. Known it a long time. Through the clothes chute Elder and I listened to him booking rooms for Mr. and Mrs. Millett at the Palmer House in Chicago, and knew he wasn't taking her. Heard the fight then, when she came into the kitchen, sensing his deception with the infallible antennae of an abject. We'd known it, in a way, but without quite letting ourselves know we did. The point was that she knew now too, or rather, that she'd finally admit it. That she'd say, at last, she did know.

And that Easter, when you left, was our resurrection and beginning. Out of the dead trees toward the river, and across the playing field of St. Thomas, ragged against the gray middle-western sky, we could go on, free of you. Our family died, and we four women formed another. We wanted it. But she didn't. Mother only wanted you. So Mallory and I walked her back from the Marshall Avenue Bridge sometimes. Where I had spotted a suicide one day from the saddle of my bike, a woman floating in the Mississippi, her red dress awash like an oil drum in the dirty water.

After you sold the Canadian farms and blew it flying Shelagh in airplanes, I know there were times you lay in a motel bed somewhere like Florida, drank whiskey, and remembered us. And felt like hell. It's O.K. You had no other choices.

I felt rotten about those letters. Nights I was made to sit down and write you at that crummy gray desk I'd found and refinished myself. And made a botch of it. Under the ugly fluorescent lamp, compelled by Mother's desperation, her wonderful shamelessness, to beg you for money. "He's making eighteen hundred a month in Greenland working for the government. We need some of it."

You seldom answered. After a while I could stop

writing. So Mother took care of us. Using her phrase, "we managed somehow" through years of stew, her visceral anxiety, our bullying, the sound of her frightened tight little voice on the phone, pleading with people she didn't know, names from a mailing list, strangers imposed upon with the machine's insistent ring, asking them to buy the insurance she sold.

And she carried your name still. Carried it through the town like a stone. She carries mine, now. And it may be worse. You at least were her Jim, the only man she ever had. All this time passed. Still faithful to her humiliation. A woman abandoned.

And so I went over to Mallory's to tell her the news. Fumio and I brought whiskey. When we got there Philip said, "Isn't that an indulgence—to drink whiskey?" Could have strangled the little bastard right then and there. Stoned on pot and acid all day long, he calls it indulgence if we drink a little whiskey the night the old man dies. Arrogant young puppy. And then a faggot comes in totally theatrical and silly and I must sit there and listen while I want to say, Little sister, our dad is dead tonight, can't we talk about that? Finally she takes me off to the tent. They have built a tent in the house. Conglomeration of Turkish bedspreads, pillows, candles, and whatever. We'll leave the men to themselves. Crouch there shoulder to shoulder, two sisters the night their father died. But we do not talk. Mallory is bragging about how wonderful it is to live with Philip. "Perfect relationship." I try to talk about Dad, about writing to him too late, but she is not listening. But one thing she said to me inside the tent scared me for a long time. She said, "Look, Dad's dead, but you can't write any more until Mother dies. Whatever you wanna say now would kill her." And I look at her and wonder, is this Mallory who replaced me as the family rebel? Her voice insisting I shouldn't write any more because of Mother. Sits there in the tent then curled up in her own preoccupations. She's so oppressed, she's so poor, and the loft is being inspected by the Buildings Department. She can't really pay attention that her father's dead. But she is sure that I should stop writing. Frightening me with my mother's death.

Mother in the gray light of ocean becoming America as we touch its borders. And the storm begins. Surely now we will be killed. Suddenly you look down there and it's America. Even from this height it is unmistakable, whole scale and color values so known, dull and gross by comparison to the English countryside. And like all things that belong to oneself, somehow unspectacular. Discouragingly familiar, bringing with it the melancholy realization of what one is stuck with. What one is trapped in being. And under this self-dissatisfaction an older assurance that one loves it fiercely. Mother, you are finally the problem: If I write do I kill you? You are home. You are the final criterion, the last judge. You are the beginning.

Ethel's voice penetrating my drunk that night amidst my ravings over the last year's pain and failure and madness, asking "Will you be all right there in New York—will you be able to cope," her voice going up the way theirs do. I'll know soon. In my own studio in my own city without fright. It is supposed to be a homecoming. Is there a special dread we live in now—Not Mailer's prizefight but something so generic we cannot escape it? Landing like on a foreign planet. *Time* Magazine is ridiculing all the liberation movements on my lap. Equating the Mafia's Italian-American civil rights with Gay Liberation with Women's Liberation with the Blacks, niggers all the niggers it can afford to shit on. We are coming into America in a terrible storm. The plane will have to break. It is a nightmare. Is this home? The gray sky black now with lightning the plane trembling in all its pieces. There will be a way out because we will have to fall and die. It is disappointing to come home this way but it is a solution. We cannot possibly land. The whole thing vibrating wild, dangerous beyond any weather I've ever known. Surely we'll be spared the

making it. Yet somehow we get down. Somehow they
have to do this. And as we hit the ground I saw a broken
plane outside the Lockheed hangar. Huge monstrous
thing like a bug severed in the middle. Is it an omen
finally?

2

It is the same. No better. Worse because it is the same.
There is some happiness in seeing Fumio. Then Vita
spoils everything by losing the car in a parking lot. We
are two hours immobile in the rain till Fumio finds it.
Walking up the stairway at the Bowery I wonder how
anyone could live here ten years. There is still Fumio.
The movie is done. But on the way to our ceremonial
dinner at the Finale I crack into pieces again in the
nightmare search for a parking place. He reads me the
lesson of New York: acquire patience or go berserk. The
back yard has all its good gay ambiance, scene of so
many feasts of love. And one really bad trip here with
Celia. At dinner we wonder over her latest enigma, the
first tentative communication, a postcard with no return
address.

Next morning I explode at the Bowery cockroach
kitchen. Just twice. The rest is cool. I am cured. There
is still Fumio. And at the farm a superhigh, a tree splurge,
buying in the rain, planting in the late afternoon. Fumio's
figure over me against the sky. We lay back in the mud,
looking up and around at what we owned now. The place
green, changed wonderfully from its winter bleak.
Beautiful even in the rain. Bourbon, steak, and animal
exhaustion. At night Mother's Day guilt. Can't get

through on long distance. Too beat to stay up. There
is still Mother.

And there are still the speeches. The best is already
savored by the time we're back in town. Heaps of mail,
the usual confusion, demands, tension. And there is still
Vita. At the Bowery today, rescuing. Staving off the
pervasive stench of failure, the heaps of screaming unanswered mail, each piece a sentence against any future
time or space. She has been opening my mail while I was
in England. Fumio tried to answer letters but his English
is too original. Someone, Vita or Mallory, had to check
it. Now Vita has offered to help with the mail. Out of
friendship. It is so kind—but it makes me nervous . . .
Surely she must have better things to do than this pile
of tedious paper.

That winter night home from Salt Lake. Fumio was in
Philadelphia. Called Magda, Naomi. No one home. Going
through the address book . . . I used to know so many
people in New York. Do they avoid me now? Try Lila
and Renos. Miriam. Not home. No one else suits. I cannot show them my condition, frighten them with my
weakness. Walking the floors of the Bowery, cold, in
panic, I stop at the red table where I wrote a book, so
long ago—writing for professors. Writing when I did not
even want to be a writer, just burning with an idea that
could make me do a book, call it a thesis, rip off a Ph.D.
Now I am sick with wanting to write. There is nothing
to say; you cannot make a book from air. I have lost
myself. Gone with Celia. The phone rings. Actually rings.
Someone calling me. It will be some idiot intrusion, the
media wanting entertainment, the movement wanting a
speech. Not a friend. But it's Vita. Vita and Fred Nielson,
art world couple we've known for ten years. He's a
curator and critic, the best the Modern has now. Vita's
a poet, does pieces where tar melts over automobile tires
and words are written in neon colors. Haven't seen her
since the Flag Show.

Vita said she could not get arrested because she was
a mother, still shook up from Stuttgart where the Plexus

Group were harassed by the police. Her face is afraid. Fumio and I are taking down my piece, talking over the power drill, removing the screws. The District Attorney has indicted my sculpture, a toilet in a cage, the American flag washing out of it like an overflow. "Offensive to the citizens of New York State: people's evidence number one." John and Toche and Faith Ringgold have been arrested. After a week of ignoring us the cops came last night when no one expected them. They should have got me too, all of us on the Committee. I do not want to be arrested right now because the plane for North Carolina leaves in two hours: another speech. I look at Vita over a two-by-four, the screws are in my hand. The way she announces the mother thing sounds a bit righteous, but I respect her fear. I have had fear since that first night. Another fear. It started with Jill.

The Flag Show just opening at Judson. Walking in is like coming home. Toche and Jon Hendricks behind the table, chuckling at our conspiracy, winking whenever they imagine they see a plainclothesman. We will defy the law, attack their icon. See if they'll bust us. A big hug from Vita, just back from Stuttgart. Then I see Jill. Standing in the shadow, Levi's and shades. The other world again. Vita introduces us, a redundancy: we met years ago before at a party. Jill never noticed me, does not remember. Marjory Strider and Michael Kirby's studio, Noguchi, Schecter, a lot of art world guns in attendance. The whole dinner was chili con carne and crackers. I made the wrong remark about some dancer, tripped making an effort to enter the conversation. Jill took care of me in no time: a look, an intake of breath, one phrase. Vita says Jill would like to ask me a favor, then she starts up the stairs with Fumio. Jill stands in the corner, tall, comic-strip scary. Would I go on Channel 13, be gay on television? I groan at the prospect of further immersion in media. But something in her manner is sinister, hazardous. I mumble obediently that it's a good thing media is dealing with the issue and say I am doing a gay panel at Columbia soon. Yes, I'll do the television. Then in a rush I'm telling Jill how sick I am of media altogether. And for months I have been hearing my Elder sister's voice that night after dinner, angry almost despairing in a place like Nebraska. Exasperated tone—she has every sympathy for what homosexuals are put through but don't blow it for the rest of us, confuse the two things in the minds of the great unwashed. Women are just beginning to get confidence, how will their fragile claims stand up when their husbands hear this stuff? Most women aren't queer, they have enough troubles of their own. I hear the voice of expediency in it. PR thinking. But my own sister's grief and outrage too. And the familiar granite prejudices of middle America, St. Paul. Travel beyond the charmed circle of the art world and the echo of the movement—it's a long way from Omaha to Judson. Elder's right and I know it. She's wrong too. And I know that with the colorless certainty which accompanies moral decisions.

Stumbling out my worries to Jill. Suddenly she's furious. Spitting out the names of poet and composer, art world paragons, all the celebrities who've turned her down already. Wouldn't go on record. I'm not feeling like any damn celebrity, wishing that weren't why I am being asked. I'm simply confused and trying to express it. I haven't turned her down, never intended to. Merely wanted a hearing for my dilemma. Why is she so mad? Calling me a fink. I snap out of the growing belligerence of our talk to realize we are shouting. Fumio and Vita have stopped halfway up the stairs. Jon and Tosh watch us from the table. A crowd observes us. Everything is going wrong. I don't want to quarrel with Jill. I like her. All these years reading her column. It's good what she's trying to do. I want to help, we should talk it out, but I can't right now.

Already forty minutes late for the symposium upstairs. I'm a sponsor, I should be there, I have to speak—explaining this to Jill. She could care less. Her miraculous indifference to me as a human being both terrifying and curiously admirable. There is only one cause in the world. Hers. She is going to St. Adrian's now. I can meet her there later. Hating the honcho feel of the place, air of young stud painter heavier than the Old Cedar or Max's, I search desperately for the name of another bar and can't find one. We have moved to the top of the stairs. Jill lounges in her long denim legs while I run to check the time. How many moments' grace before I have to go on? My hope of sitting through the other speakers, picking up energy and making notes so that I might make sense when my turn came—no chance of that now. Scurrying back and forth between the Mephistophelian figure of Jill and the guy who clocks the speakers, I am transformed into the totally fearsome little woman. Jill's butch disdain looks on, more bullying than any male performance I can remember.

Called on to talk five minutes ahead of time, I speak with too much unpremeditated feeling, then sit down to regret it. The place is crawling with police agents. Paranoid, I suspect the young man interviewing me for the New York University student paper of collusion with the CIA. The symposium grinds along, Abbie Hoffman doing his thing for the cameras. Good Jewish comedian, understands show business, knows his media, as persuasive as Attorney Lefcourt rehearsing case by case the arbitrary enforcement, the philosophic absurdity of flag laws. Listening, I begin to understand we are here about something even more serious than artistic freedom. The thought of being arrested has been with me all day, a special jittery dread of the cage, of it being all up with me, of being in their hands and helpless. But just as strong my hunch that we will be able to get by with this, art and artists just inconsequential enough to escape the system's attention. Finally I'm sure it won't happen tonight. Free to leave, find Jill, work it out.

At St. Adrain's things only get worse. She's with some guy who wrote a book on the new movies. Would like to talk to him, tell him I used it for my class. But not now. He is between us, making Jill distant. He treats me like an intruder, my hands shake, why did I come? Jill and I square off, defensive moves, snide remarks. We have hurt each other too much to continue. The conversation goes underground and dies. I leave, furious with myself for my rudeness in refusing to let them pay for my drink, a graceless gesture. Still aggravated on the street, can't remember where I parked the car, detained even later from the long night drive ahead. All along the Taconic I curse her out, the personal arrogance with which she treats me, the art world snobbishness (Judson art is out now, old hat, etc.). The way she chick-hassled the waitress, her outbursts of butch rhetoric ("Sometimes I'd just like to fuck broads like guys do—I have nothing to say to them anyway—damn women anyhow, they need some liberation"). Then the other outburst, her astonishing fit of tears. Was it self-pity, manipulation, real unhappiness? I do not understand her. Yet all the time I know she's right. Where she stands I am a fink ever to have paused or considered. I know as well as she does that if women are vulnerable to the dyke-baiting we are vulnerable to everything, a paper movement, helpless even before words. If I demur before televised true confessions, knowing that the media is delighted to exploit one's sexuality in this quite as in any other manner, and terrified of the upshot with my family as well as the movement, she can counter with The Closet. We will never be free unless we relinquish the comfort of our disguises. The argument that even closet gays pass out of a legitimate need for protection cannot move her. Like Sherman—and now I understand Jill's power over me—she wears her gay like a cross, like Sherman does. But it made Sherman kind. It has not made Jill kind. Why should it? So she is right, however wrong to me, right in her abstract pitiless justice to dismiss all my reservations, if not right in punishing them. But even this, her scorn and anger for the timid—this too has its cause in all the lukewarm and the discreet who have finally denied their own, passing on to safety in respectable silence. Yes, she's right. You've got to say you're queer even on telly.

The whole night quarreling with Jill in her absence. When I get to the bungalow it is after midnight. In the terrible country dark struggling for minutes to find the keyhole. Somewhere out of sight the lock refuses, the

key twists and breaks. I am locked out. I cannot think.
Stupid to drive back to the city. Find somewhere near
to spend the night. No one in Millbrook I know well
enough to break in on. There are friends in New Haven.
And there is Celia. But of course the friends, Carol,
Betsy, are only a pretext to bring me to Celia's town.
To Celia's house in the dead of night that I might ask
for shelter, throw myself on her mercy, confront her as
I have nearly done some hundred times these months.
Each time the sanity of self-defense has saved me. Work,
travel, the bungalow have saved me. Tonight I have the
perfect excuse. The bungalow has betrayed me,
evaded me. Now my delirium intones, I must go to Celia.
Some part of my understanding knows this is hokum, but
I go. Floundering down to New Haven, lost on the little roads, lying to myself that I can still go to Carol's
instead. Rehearsing the scene of reconciliation. Celia is
up. The light is on. She is reading. She smiles. Her beautiful eyes. The shoulders rise, the arms spread out to
take me. It's over. The long estrangement passed. Our
light glows in her bedroom. Alternate version: Celia's
house dark, she wakes outraged at my imposition, no
smile, no embrace, only annoyance, then contempt. She
dismisses me, snarls the final words. It's over.

I stop in an empty Connecticut village for directions.
The only light is the police station. I go in. Three
policemen each wearing the American flag on a sleeve.
Over the muscle. My mind plays little games. Was the
Flag Show broadcast up here tonight? We had television
there. Or will they simply arrest me out of some intuition
of the blood? I am afraid of them. I fall back on
femininity, stupidity, my most-inoffensive-person routine.
They find it unreasonable I should want to go to New
Haven when it is not convenient to get there from here.
The sergeant is loud and knowledgeable but soon runs
out of information and turns away in disgust. A rookie
stays on, trying to help me with all the rights and lefts
and highway numbers I must absorb to reach the road,
the one I cannot miss. Then one last humiliating request—
the toilet. Where is the toilet? He gestures upstairs with

his flag arm. I who put his flag in a toilet follow with an animal's gratitude. Jill climbs back into the car with me. A mad voice insisting, will not go away, hammering again at my cowardice. My self fights back, defending, explaining, pleading. But she has smelt my fear and will never relent. She is my better less corruptible half. I am become another, all the others who would prevaricate, who would not make the thing an issue, who would fink. She has sensed complicity in my diplomacy, individualism in my insistence on privacy or at least the freedom to choose my own times and places. She has hit upon my final vulnerability, that I lose at love, that the experience I am to defend has become only a gray mud waste. If I am brave for it I am now merely an automaton speaking only from principle, from a commitment purely moral. Cerebral not sensual: abstract, de-eroticized. There is none of the joy it began with, this great flower of my infatuation, Celia, last summer's grand new way to live. The great gay fight is gay as death, a campaign from despair.

The landmarks are familiar and treacherous all at once, a reservoir, a bridge, a hill, a turn. I have seen them all before but do not know if they signify that I am going toward or away from my destination. Like hearing directions in a foreign language you only partially understand: are they saying the thing is this way or that?— recognizing a word but failing to catch the context. The headlights see black trees, fences, roads that escape off into corners and disappear. Once into New Haven I am lost again along the tracks of my former errors. Again I forget if it is Church Street or Temple where you turn right, just as I have forgotten countless times before. Or is it Chapel Street? Trapped in the labyrinth of past confusions, my confidence evaporating before I have found the calm to begin again. Finally the correct street, up the hill, the proper turn. I have made no effort to go to Carol's, lying silently to myself that I'll just check Celia's first. Her house at last, huge, frightening. Almost relieved to see there is no light on. But if her car is there . . . Parking my own blue convertible, bought in order to please her, suitably large and even vulgar, the lower-middle-class edition. Back and forth, deceived in the dark by a convertible which is actually green, then by another, spurious castoff of the wrong manufacturer, too large, too new. Then by a third the right size and color but on closer inspection not a convertible at all—damn hardtops.

Sitting in the dark before her deserted house I relive the last visit. Drove up from New York in a rainstorm. Local television. And I was late. Numb with embarrassment at having forced them to go on the air without their advertised "guest." Warding off the hostility of Connecticut housewives trapped in their split-level ranch styles with chores and children, and a fiery distaste for Women's Lib. A shrieking horde, they telephone the station to denounce me. A few begin calling in support, then more. A battle of suburbanites. The gentleman interviewer, type of genial humorist who presides over all women's programs everywhere, aglow at the "response." Hot topic. Good show. Leaving the station I know already I will be taken there to stand in front of that big house in the rain. Her car not there that day either. Fatuous enough to ring the bell and wait in terror. Then lingering on hour after hour on the chance she might be out shopping. No one came. Tonight in the darkness no one will come either. I wait on in a depression rather like relief. Spared the final exile. Saved too from a lower order of bondage. I do not want Celia back on these terms, loathe slaves as much as she, am as arrogant.

We did not begin this way: started off peers, brave and witty, equally independent; perfectly matched. But subject to moments of need, insecurity—did Celia have hers when she joined us at Brookfield? Fumio glad to see her too, welcomed her, the three of us living for ten days in a bliss of summer green, feasts, flowers, and music. Yet she never forgave us that she needed to be with us, that she came to us, and that we saw it. The blow to her pride. Later when Fumio went home to Japan and I was shooting the movie, falling apart from pressure, from media, I needed her. Unforgiving to herself, just as heartless to me, she withdrew. Seeing my love recede in the distance I pursued, desperate to recover my happiness. She grew adamant, cold, a bully. I begged. She despised.

Sitting in the dark before her house. Three-thirty in the morning. Possibility is crushed out in a cigarette butt. It is time to start back. The caretaker can be found, the bungalow opened, some work done, the weekend partly saved. Celia is lost. Jill has won. I will do what I must, though it be for nothing.

Halfway back to Millbrook I pull up exhausted at a diner. Dawn morning on a lonely road. Two women cleaning up, preparing for the onslaught of truckers, alone before the men arrive. I order hotcakes then can't eat them because my head in danger of falling into my breakfast requires my full attention. The younger woman mops with overpowering chemicals. Ammonia, once a lady's smelling salts. It sickens me. Awake now. Too nauseated to eat. The weak coffee heals. They go on mopping, I watch. I who am supposed to help women. But I cannot help these two marooned in their tawdry diner at five in the morning. Instead, they help me. They are kind, concealing even their surprise at my strange appearance.

Vita's voice is tired, bored. Fred is not home. Would I come over for a drink? I do not want to go. She sounds as far down as I am. I want a lover. Vita's a married lady. But there is nowhere else and I cannot bear the idea of staying in the Bowery this whole evening alone. My own company will drive me crazy. Once I went to Japan in order to learn how to be alone; now I have forgotten again. I am afraid of Vita. At her place last fall with Fumio after Cissie's party, enduring the people all night, acquaintances mostly, but people I'd known from before the book, guys mostly, telling me I was "famous," partly in envy, partly in contempt, watching me like a freak. I wore a long dress and tried to look serene. Back at her place I smoked pot. I sat in a wicker swing in the living room. She waited till I'd talk. The

drug easing me away, my protection failing me till I
admitted I was miserable. I think I did not say Celia.
But the other things, the loneliness, being a thing for
people, a joke, a puppet given orders in a place alien
to my old life. Fumio watched. He was, I think,
surprised, frightened. Perched across from me she seemed
a witch, expecting, making it happen that I became so
vulnerable. It is a comfort to tell someone. It is also
worse. I'm terrified I have given her power over me. She
knows my weakness now. My panic. For it was beginning,
perhaps that was the first time I felt it, and the drug,
lightening my head, making it feel empty, with a wind
in it.

I remember that night when I get to her house.
Drinking bourbon, sitting there warm in my red sweater.
Mallory bought it from a mountain woman in Mexico
ten years ago, kept me alive those Bowery winters, I wore
it even to bed. It is no comfort now. Again Vita is asking
questions, digging into my secret, my shakiness. She is
staring at me. Oddly. Dressing to go out tonight I had
a second's fantasy she might make some gesture toward
me. But of course that is impossible, married woman
with kids. Fred's wife. He is out tonight. He has a lover.
She speaks with such feeling—it has put her through hell
she says. A year of it. Does she have lovers? Fumio and
I have decided we will love other people too, not that
it works out very well. Does she have wifely guilt? No—
not at all—why should she? I have, plenty, feeling foolish
admitting it. There was a guy she says, some expert on
war or something, a Frenchman, met him at Christmas,
a Harvard College reunion. How she despises Fred and
his friends. I like them. But the man rejected her, has
a wife. All a secret. Whole thing sounds like a bad idea
but I pity her pain, thinking she is like me, rushes in,
type who gets pushed in the face.

Seeing her again that time at Judson when I did a
happening in the downstairs gallery. Put the whole
audience into a cage, walking them into the basement
in the dark. Nailed in before they knew it. Pentagon day.
Regular little America complete with sound effects: toilets

flushing, footsteps, Protestant hymns, the kind of movie music you eat popcorn to before the curtain goes up, a bugle playing taps. Just at the end Lil Piccard bent the bars, the first one to get out. Big hurry because she had to go on television that night. But Vita, when it was all over and the lights on and everyone had made their escape—no one had lynched me or trashed my lumber— Vita climbed right over the top. Looked fat, awkward, overeager. Acting like a child but looking like a fool because she's a grown woman and too heavy, too large to squeeze through between the top of the cage and the ceiling. Thought she'd get jammed there. Sticky moment. Stubborn—she made it. But the whole act wrong somehow. Unsightly, overenthusiastic. Now she's staring at me and I begin thinking I must protect this in her that gets hurt.

Now she wants me to go with her to her writing room. Smoke some pot. I'm reluctant. The way she stares embarrasses me. It cannot mean what it says. I will be entrapped in some ridiculous pass and denounced. I was in that room once before, one night Fumio and I were there for dinner. Middle of a conversation about Yoko Ono, Vita starts calling her names, insisting Yoko abandoned her child. I'm defending Yoko because she's an old friend, arguing with Vita that half the painters we know in New York abandon their kids; do it all the time, no one puts them down, they're artists. "You are only shocked when a woman does it." Vita is getting mad but I don't realize it till she's saying—"Repeat that and I'll leave the room." I can't believe she's serious. This is a dinner party at her house. I start explaining to her why she is so angry but she has already left the table. I'll be damned if I'm going to feel criminal over this childish behavior. But I do anyway, struggling through dinner with the two men. The three of us absurdly pretending it hasn't happened. Vita controls us from down the hall as she pounds around in her room. Fred putters along explaining she has been unhappy. He is her father. She is five years old. Poor bastard lives with this. Why don't I get up and try to

bring her back? It is like the fights I had with my sisters
when we were children. I know just how she feels. I know
just how I feel. She wants me to plead with her. I do.
But she wants too much pleading. I won't. Then the
quarreling stops and I look at the beautiful avocado tree
she has grown. She shows me her poems and her new
paintings. We are adults now. I leave and she comes down
in her own time. But I have always resented that evening.
That she made me feel like a bully because when I said
what I thought, she refused to remain at the level of
argument, escalated, resorted to the violence of leaving
her table.

So I do not relish this room when we get there. It is
different now. The avocado is gone. Dead. There is a
mattress in the room. It is her whole house now. She says
she sleeps here, away from Fred. They are going to
divorce. Her hands rolling pot into paper sticks. It is
very strong. I'm stoned in no time. Now her eyes staring
at me hypnotize when she takes my hand. This is an innocent gesture, she is an old friend who is unhappy in
her marriage. Telling me she loves me: I must have heard
her wrong. She says it again. An eerie sense of being
tempted. I cannot even see her eyes boring into mine,
my glasses off and the pot has made me dizzy. What
is this stuff? It has other things in it, Fred got it from
one of the curators, it worries him to keep it here. Same
stuff I smoked last time. She is pressing my hand. I want
to be loved, wonderful if some woman loved me. They
are all gone now. Magda avoids me. There is no hope
with Celia. I do not want to see Naomi. The last time
it was grotesque, got turned on dancing at Paolo's then
we had nowhere to go—she had gotten herself another
roommate. There was nothing left but the role playing,
the terrible scenes of childwife and boor she invents for
me like an iron band, making me a man. I would be an
idiot to begin with another woman. Nothing works.
Should know that by now. If I cannot succeed in
relationships I am wrong to enjoy the lovemaking. That
I have despaired inspires Vita, she will give me assurance.
I am too stoned to be making this decision, instinct

revolting at it, weakness craving, needing, willing to tell myself Vita is like me, a loser. Like me, only more so, more vulnerable, she has been hurt even worse. If a woman can love me I am not finished. There is something left. She is telling me I am beautiful. I feel I am. I would like to tell her she is beautiful but I don't think she is. She looks weird, her eyes like big draining holes pulling me . . . Need. But I have need too. Forgive and take solace. I tell her she is good, believing in her goodness. She is pulling on my arm, wanting me to kiss her. Does she know what she is doing? Ask her. She says yes. I cannot seduce women. Only men, and men are scarcely a problem to seduce. Last desperate hope that she will not expect some odd butch behavior from me—or even butch courage. But it's Vita who's making love to me now in the blur. Dizzy feeling the painful ease of being touched by a woman. But no orgasm. She may not know but I do. Appalled, getting sober too late, knowing then I do not want her body. Do not want to see it, caress it, go down on it. Now I am trapped. I have sinned against love, taking but not giving. Fall asleep but a few hours later awakened to make love dishonestly. Of course she demands it. Silently, her outrage smoldering if I flinch. I feel like a criminal. My God this is the first time she has made love with a woman and it should be this barren ordeal. All the time she is rejoicing, saying it's beautiful, crying out yes yes yes. I want to shout no at her—no, it is false. But she is a woman in love today hanging upon me. I cannot so insult her with truth. I am even hoping I will grow infatuated as soon as I recover from the shock of being here at all. If not I will have to tell her the truth. The one thing so hard to say to anyone we invent a thousand reasons and excuses. Never could say it to a man's face that I did not want him. Almost inhumanly offensive. Surely this is worse what I am doing.

Next day on the phone she has married me. I am Fred now. Already Vita's an appendage, leaning on me, a whole building's heft of dependency. I told her no, I don't want to be lovers, just can't handle it, all my fault,

I am not worth what you offer. She says I am ridiculous. I am. Also scared. Wonderful how she backs off, just didn't realize what she'd done. Now she does. Has no intention of leaning any more. We are after all old friends—I cling to that idea like sanity. Says she would like the relationship to be physical but if I don't want that, she only wants to be my friend, she cares for me . . . I listen feeling like a rat, small relief I'm off the hook, guilty this way too. So much I can hardly ever rest, the accusation always in my gut, the endless reproach in her letters to me in England.

There is still Vita and the mail. The whole litter a judgment on my total inability to be the creature they've created. White crap all over the big red table, blotting out the space in which I was supposed to write something actual. Paper all over like fungi infesting the Bowery so I can never come here except to find more underwear before I catch an airplane. We have struggled for hours, my panic rising with each cup of coffee and still we're nowhere.

Then it finally happened. Celia Tyburn is on the phone. To Fumio. Vita goes upstairs to get him. I can sit there, ears ringing to the silence of that black thing lying on the desk in the next room. Run, pick up the tube to her voice. I don't move. They both descend. He walks through the room. Both of them can see my face. Fumio's voice is on the phone. Vita back in her chair across the table. And we actually proceed with the mail. Incredible, but I literally read six letters of insistence that I be at some conference before I get up and stand beside him at the phone, writing on the back of an envelope so he can see it—tell her I'm back from England, I'm here, will she talk to me?

Her voice is warm to snuggly. The perfect humor of it gay and gallant. Lady, what a super front you have. Or are you really incapable of pain? Can anyone be this happy in life? For my part, I'm phony, genial. But I sound good.

She lives in New York now. Has already divulged

an address and a phone number. I see it in Fumio's writing while I hear an ambivalent description of her recent semimonogamy. "Not really my sort of thing," the Don Juan chuckle. Musique Ancienne's in a depression funk. No work. The Renaissance a luxury folks are doing without. Did she call because she's bored, idle? Do I have Sidney's phone number? She is thinking of joining the gay politicals. Elegant Lesbian not into marching, evasive and amused when I asked her to come out in last June's streets. Was it only for a phone number she called? "Will you go to Brookfield this summer?" And her voice sounds like she remembers it. "No, but we'll be neighbors up there, now. We got an old farm near Poughkeepsie." Pride of my life to show it to her. Did I buy that damn farm to give it to her? After the scheme for the three of us to buy land together faded with her disappearance. Did I hunt all over upstate New York still loyal to the collective illusion she and Fumio had long since wised up to? Telling Nell one drunken night in London, just a week ago, that to live with Celia Tyburn and Fumio was all I wanted in the world—just that.

And now her voice sounding glad about the farm, "Love to see it. We must get together." "I'm going up there tomorrow and then back to London to pick up the movie print as soon as it's ready. Call me next week, won't you?" Probably she won't. Then just before hanging up, says she is going back into the hospital in July. "It will be the last time." Did she call because she thinks she'll die?

Vita has been trying to leave all through this but I ask her with a gesture to wait. Ashamed she has to see it, watch the radiance I cannot hide, hear me crow when I hang up. How asinine it all is: A loves B loves C loves D who has a vibrator. Not a sign of reciprocity anywhere. Gay, yes, hilarious, Masie and Sadie all over town. Is Vita my slave because I'm Celia's? Knowledge is only further disappointment. There is no cure. Bending down at the top of the stairs, I see Vita in her goodness accept my apology. My eyes fill up with shame when they reach hers.

Fumio gives me a glass of Jack Daniel's, with a sermon on how adolescent I am. Of course. I hate hearing his judgment. Too close to the shrink's for comfort. Standing in the kitchen, noticing how dirty the stove is, but for once not giving a damn, I tell him I won. I won because I wrote her last September that it was up to her now, that my pursuit hadn't worked, it was her move and she finally made it. Once in New Haven, sitting on the sofa in the sunlight of the six lovely windows, I said we were both gamblers. "Let's call a truce. We grew up on the win and lose game. Let's not play it." She grinned and agreed. Did she already know she was a better player? Then the balance fell off and the teeter-totter put her at the top. Winning is so silly—till you lose.

"No, I won," he says, "I mailed her necklace back to her. First she sent that postcard, and then she called. It's because I moved," he insists. I look at him astonished. Just before England I had taken that necklace out of my suitcase after carrying it around for eight months, the companion of all my travels. Silly French glass birds and flowers—would you believe how the thing suited her? Five times I drove to New Haven, bringing it along as an excuse. Four gray afternoons and one dawn when I would have crawled about the yard and barked. Fortunately she was never there. One trip I resorted to magic before trying the doorbell: smoked a joint getting courage.

I look at the whiskey now, knowing I've finished the movie. Maybe I'm not over, can still make things, go on, live. A sense of triumph spreads with the booze. Fumio walks around, beautiful in his pale blue work shirt, telling of Yoshiko. How perfect it was. Twelve years. How blasting when she died. His tortured Samurai eyes redden only a little. "Sex is so difficult. To make love's the easy part. To make a friendship so hard." Then angrily: "Your theories are crazy." I know it. The biggest down of the spiral was to bear my growing understanding that all my freedom talk was hot air. Not for the others perhaps, but for me. Miles from what I future-preached, a relic of every hangup knocking me down till I believed in sin again at the bottom of the ride. I know that every time he attacks this way he's saying he won't say he's jealous. And there is nothing left for him either, and that's my fault too. Living with me hasn't made him appear the single woman's notion of an eligible. So they take him on, and then drop him, just as they do me. Why should the two of us want more than we have, when it's more than they have? Mere marks, we get philandered and ripped off, kicked back into the cold comforts of a monogamy we didn't want. Licking our wounds together, drinking whiskey those bad winter nights across the stone tabletop in the Bowery. Tonight it's not quite that same conversation we've had for months, the stalemate of his pain and my desire. Fumio growing sullen and belligerent as he drinks, while I am shredded against my dilemma: I dare not hurt this man yet I cannot stop wanting women. Nor can I succeed with them, repeating with each the old illnesses of gay. It's better tonight. Yet something of the old depression lingers on in our talk of the failing lives of the people we love. Naomi's not writing. Elder will never go to law school. Haus Merberich has blown up, killing Milly's family of dogs and cats.

Tonight the mellow feeling will get us fairly high and cook a good meal. "Let's go to Times Square," Fumio says, happy enough to give his favorite challenge, his delighted child's idea of what to do whenever the work is going well. All these eight years we've ended our really perfect evenings gazing at cowboys, eating popcorn among smelly vagrants, snoring drunks. And one evening, after the lights of Frankenstein went up, we discovered a whole balcony of faggots necking: we were the straight minority. The phone rings as we finish eating. Unimportant mechanical interruption, we'll be leaving in a minute. I'm bringing in the coffee when I see the look on his face. Going to be something bad. It's Washburn. She says Zell is dead. Crackpot phrase, don't believe it. Dead three days in a room in Harlem. Tabloid stuff. It must happen all the time, but to other people. People without friends. She's up there with Billy and the three-day body.

Zell a body. But I remember such a handsome man. Mustachios of a señor. Brass-buttoned blazer, senatorial bearing, beaming with one hand in the pocket of a really good raincoat. I always wanted you, Zell, but we never got around to it. Years going by and we were never free the same moment. So we forgot about it: ten years' friendship was better anyway. Our great fondness, flirting with each oher at parties. Zell, I don't want to see your great brown body a swollen shape on a bed.

Washburn and Billy up there this morning, found him. They haven't eaten all day. I get on the phone and tell Wash to clear out of there, go somewhere and eat. We'll be down to Centre Street later, with a bottle. To wake Zell drinking. Time for a flick while they eat and come downtown. Fumio goes to the corner for the *Village Voice* movie listings. While he's gone I begin to catch on. If I don't want to see Zell's face tonight, how must they feel up there with his paintings, his kitchen, his view, and that thing in the bedroom. Obscene to go to a movie when we ought to drive up and rescue them. Line's busy. So we start anyway. Catch them before they leave. Traffic lights shine on black slick of Houston Street, the East Side Drive lordly and immediate tonight. Like the West Side Highway, it can convert the flaccid moments of city life into something alive. Tonight the city has significance because of his death, the skyline ringing with it past the U.N. towers and the bridges into Queens. Exit at 137th Street, the car careening through Harlem's edge to Lenox Heights. Zell ended in this nigger heaven looking down over Manhattan's lights. He gave up painting. All those years doing social work, his goodness spent upon other people's children, counseling messed-over ghetto kids. Then, suddenly, at fifty-five, quitting a good job and going to college. Finding Plato in his age. Already a finished man, the mellow glow of the classics a last patina to his perfection. A final elegance. And painting again. But he died the night of his first show. Full, mellow, ripe, master of the art of friendship, untainted by the artist's win evils, poverty and envy. Dead the night of his first show.

Doorman says they've left. Mr. Ingram's dead—we don't want to see him, deciding for us. By now I really do. Then renounce the urge as something perverse. Follow Bill and Janey Washburn downtown. And we do drink for him, friends made close after a drift. Zell hugging us together like a homecoming. After the winter's madness to be with old friends again. Yet we seem inattentive. We don't really concentrate on Zell, the talk going in all directions. Probably best, 'cause Billy's reeling. The great friend of his life gone.

When Zell didn't come to the opening Bill Rivers started up to Harlem on the subway. At two A.M. and the damned thing stopped. Has to give up and go back downtown. Try again in the morning. Finds him dead, gone since Monday. Each of Zell's two girl friends fancies she's a widow. Grotesque error, the straight world cannot even honor friendship's love. Bill's the widow, his life's buddy lost.

It is my idea to get the "communist party" together for Zell. It will be his funeral. Billy says yes, right thing to do. Our CP's a rough collection of old friends, painters mostly, who make a feast each Thanksgiving, chipping in on money and the cleaning up. True communism: a party. Tonight feels like home, the whole winter's monotonous series of airport arrivals never happened—the town each time distant, stinking, gray through a cab window. Drinking gin and orange juice tonight, like last summer, before things went crazy. The glass stands solid and golden on the table. Objects are real again. Being their friend, I become someone I recognize. Standing up to leave, Billy's arm on my shoulder, favoring me with a long impossible Carolina ghost story. His gift.

I wake that night to Fumio's agony. Full-scale migraine. Water turning my hands soft, burning. One washrag after another. Carrying them steaming to his forehead on the pillow. His frail body bursting out of bed to vomit in the john, shivering back under the quilt again, so small. Start over with the compresses. Hours in the middle of the night. Dawn before he sleeps. He has seen his own death in Zell's. Next morning driving to the farm, he lies in the back seat still trembling under the sun.

We got to take off the old wallpaper, my idea, can't stand how the farmhouse looks. Same wallpaper lace-curtain look as January when I tried to write and couldn't. Fumio hates this job, wasting his sculpture time on the house, convinced he'll grow old taking off wallpaper, doesn't care how it looks where he lives. I do. Always the quarrel between us that I mind the space around me, my environment I tell him. And the Bowery studio was a refuge made habitable after ten years struggle, sanctuary from street, city, even life—our high white light place where people came and went away drunk on Fumio's Mickey Finn bartending, enchanted for having been in a different world with strange objects his kites hanging in air, all the wooden bicycles on the top floor floating in the cathedral ceiling.

If the farm is to be any use it's got to change into our place from Horner's despairing finally abandoned homestead. Fumio grudgingly with the steamer, me with lesser tools, scraping wallpaper. The awful tedium of this job. But it's real, when the paper is off you know it. Not like art—always slipping from the grasp of confidence falling dead in midair vacuum nowhere gone. Sweating over bilious green living room I am writing in my head, only place I dare. Crazy idea anyway, but it keeps coming at me that day at Jenny Spitz's. Sun in the kitchen of her brownstone. Surprised when I saw where she lived, so bourgeois for a radical tiger. Knew I had to go there. Carol bludgeoning it at me in the car night before. "We want to know why you signed your book." Like that. Why sign it? Why not? Hardly even defending myself yet that I did it from custom; signed my thesis, signed a contract long before with the publisher, delighted that someday I'd be in my college library, Oxford. Real book people could read, not just a microfilm thesis at Columbia. Carol who I wanted to love next to me on the car seat terrorizing me: she and Jenny have decided I shouldn't sign my name. Why didn't they tell me in time? Why did they decide for me? I'm scared, my stomach quivering, hands out of control on the wheel, parked thank God under the Bowery windows in the dark of First Street. Carol keeps talking, I wonder if they will kill me somehow. Jenny told her, Jenny's idea. "Did you question it, why do you only talk to her not me?" She is crying now, saying she did talk to me, is doing it now. "But you already decided for me. Why?" " 'Cause it should be anonymous, should be an anonymous woman, Jenny said." But I remember the unsigned thing at Artworkers Coalition, paper passed around one night supposed to be a statement of the whole group but one guy wrote it, wouldn't admit his name, everybody furious, what if this went to the *Times* as a statement for the organization, and no one but him making it, the text kept saying "we"? Carol repeats Jenny: they want *Sex Pol* to be anonymous so it can be the whole movement talking. "But I wrote it and it's not the movement speaking, it's me. It's my mistakes in there, my hobby horses, my literary criticism, half of it not even politics but just what I wanted to say about certain writers I grew up with." At New Haven in Carol's kitchen, she had just read the galleys, pointing out where I'd forgotten a footnote, ought to put in another clause about Engels, is there still time? I had wanted to make a long footnote on the theory Roberta worked out, that the origins of patriarchy were dependent upon the discovery of paternity, which opened the way to a population explosion whereby the male could, because the means were now at hand—through knowledge, this great biological discovery—could enslave women and children, the latter deliberately produced for serf labor. And now workers and property could come into being, the developing class system breaking the communal life of neolithic village roundhouse and in time the numbers would grow to those required for building the early cities, those hordes of nonpersons, sealing the division of labor in the second agricultural revolution, reclaiming the Indus

Valley's unpromising soil, a whole population slid into peonage toiling for an elite priest and prince god at the top, pyramid building finally. I had guessed the discovery of paternity was the door of sceintific knowledge, Roberta had added the final piece in the puzzle: a population explosion, man empowered to use woman and child as objects in the manner already discovered through stock breeding. It made sense. Jenny was coming to the same conclusions in New York. Go see her and work out the theory, complete your own speculations and round out what little can be guessed at so far on the origins of human social relations.

I walk up the brownstone stairs thinking how to finish that paragraph in the Engels chapter, must be a clear and thorough discussion, acknowledging my friend's work and completing the thesis on this point. But already I am sick with fear at what Carol has said, realizing we should have gotten together while I was working this out the first time—Jenny never answered her phone—I needed the help of an anthropologist. Jenny's the real thing, though fired now from Brooklyn for being radical about grades and letting students run classes, WBAI reporting on her fight long before I met her, the first Miss America Pageant riding back in the dark with a student of mine from Barnard, beautiful girl I kept trying not to fall in love with. Jenny in the dark of the bus, her hair shining under the light of a street lamp, all of us so afraid of the goons. Atlantic City home of the Ku Klux Klan, the gangs maybe waiting for us in the parking lot. Being walked back along the boardwalk, a cop on either side of me suddenly welcome in spite of Columbia's other night. I want to take their arms. Will the people lined up rush us gang rape behind the police barricades? Cop to cop their body line protecting our mere hundred while we shout the things that sting their minds to violence, laugh at their beauty contests, kick their war. Jenny and the five who were chosen to go inside the hall are busted now, their banner shouting Women's Lib at the cameras— producers said point your lens there and you're fired—so we never got on telly. And the stink bomb they got

arrested for, horrible sulfur smell still all over the bus
when we have sprung our friends and can go back the
five long bumpy hours shaken to New York. On the
boardwalk calling lawyers from a phone booth, trying
to act like I knew what you do in a bust. Then with Flo
Kennedy in the police station, tough black lady, Rap
Brown's lawyer once, never misses even one political
number 'cause it's all "polka dots" she says, every
pressure point helps bring down the building. Then
presenting the bail collected bit by bit in the buses till
we had enough. Now Jenny back with us safe, talking,
her lovely yellow hair against the black window, her
Oklahoma cracker accent. Outside the Panthers in the
parking lot, invisible blacks in the night protecting us
from white men. At lunch they were remote superior
figures in costume. Beret, black jacket. You wonder if
they carry guns, afraid of their condemnation and the
mandate of their danger. Now they are warmth out there
in the summer night, the only reassuring shapes in the
unknown—they are giving us safety. They are kindness
and friends. The sulfur stench hangs in the bus waiting,
engines running, Jenny spills out the whole year's hurt
of her struggle to bring democracy to the classroom. My
student sitting next to me and we listen both admiring,
shy with each other. Surprised when I spotted her making
signs at Union Square before we left the city—for the first
time on a demo with one of my kids. Embarrassed sitting
next to her during a break in the marching, noticing the
hair on my legs, should I have shaved them? In line and
singing, my usual tuneless way, she must have heard it.
Ashamed for her having such a teacher. Later she quit
school broke, Mom and the relatives holding out on the
money her father left her. In my office trying to help but
she's had it with college, wants to hop around the country
with some guitar boy. Only hope he's good to her. And
in my movie class, the best student, she saw *Jason,* said
it was interesting, she hadn't known anything about
homosexuality before: "Funny how you still never see
anything about Lesbians." Electrocuted in my swivel
chair wearing a stupid pink schoolteacher dress, I stiffen

and despair. Walking into the student lounge to get coffee before class, her eyes on my back will know I harbor perverse symptoms for her. Condemned by her rigid logic, her virtue. Daydreaming about her on lazy mornings only to become further convinced one should never covet students. Unfair somehow, even when they are overwilling, always the elder has a certain manipulative advantage; they think you are the power of all the poets you merely teach them, helpless before their own admiration, a prey to use. And this very beautiful kid must find me disgusting, having figured out, I'll bet, what I never wanted her to know. The main thing is to help her but I can't because she's leaving school anyway. I can call the dean, the housing folks, the scholarship office, whatever, but no use. Maybe better she does what she likes, but will she ever come back and finish, too fine a mind to waste. Believing then in the degree like it was magic. Now the torture of sitting next to her the long night way back to New York. Everyoné is sprawled out sleeping, their heads on each other's shoulders. We cannot do that, sitting bolt upright her white sweater so beautiful in the dark, long straight black hair, a face of such perfect line, such exquisite intelligence. Finally she moved to another seat. So I am contaminating, but at least permitted to rest until the bus drops me at my Bowery door. She saw where I lived, could always find me. But of course she never came. A hundred times playing the scenario of her arrival late at night a runaway and I could sit her down give her coffee & advice till she confessed why she really showed up. Ending every sequence in disgust at the very notion. I was married loved my husband taught at college did not sleep with women any more. Could limit the worst self to a few daydreams, the realm of never happen. Idle morning fantasies over students, kids, last thing I'd ever do. Mornings on my days off, mornings I should have been sculpting—but staying on in bed to daydream. Part of me even then suspecting this stoked-down thing was no good: wasted time, sapped strength, took energy better used on sculpture.

And once out on Long Island staying with Emerson when the first draft of the thesis was finished, reading it on a rock near the ocean, hating it for being so bad, have to rewrite that second chapter, three and four also lousy—at dinner that night Marchesi asked me, didn't I ever miss women. So I told her how much I loved Fumio, how his penis felt the first time we made love, how it felt against my stomach shrunk to a soft thing the moment he collapsed on me, his Yoshiko dead now. That night we got loaded in Shinji-ku, a cab bringing us home in the Tokyo morning took a corner bringing us together, fell into each other's arms and started to kiss. Our astonishment that, good friends, we were wanting each other as lovers. And I a friend of dead Yoshiko's too, his consolation long nights after the funeral drinking in the Kotatsu, he told me all his life with her, wanting to die now too. But I am trying to make him live, not kill himself. As I guessed he might, watching the toast burn in the kitchen while he's sobbing into the phone saying he's just seen the cancer, his cousin the surgeon had him watch the operation, whole of her insides white with it, she'll have to die. Thinking, you will then too, you're twins. How the two of them looked going off one morning from the next house, like children—brother and sister—while Toshiko stood with me at the window. "How lovely they are," she said. Toshiko with me because she'd got drunk, threw up all over everything, middle of the party, had to wash it up furious over the straw mat ruined. Later had to give her a bath in the wooden tub in the back yard and she's kissing me asking me to make love to her. Next morning after we did the dishes she said it was an "interesting experience," the very words negating the fact that it had ever happened. For months sick with need of her, my own terrible loneliness there. When I'd call she was always busy, her voice resenting even that I wanted to have dinner with her. Then the last night in Tokyo she got herself drunk again and kissed me in front of people at Nishi Ogikubo pub. Went back with me to the studio. And I didn't want to because now I belonged to Fumio. My lover, climbing

into the window of my house from his house when his
mother would leave for elder brother's place every evening
at nine. But she kissed me long and terrible taking away
my soul, a witch in the night, her life's cold celibacy,
her mad drawings, the lonely beautiful wooden room
of books where she lived. W. H. Auden admired her
poetry and Takiguchi encouraged her to show. But she
teaches the first grade, stuck with translating for all the
visiting artists because she was born in England and
speaks the language more beautifully than my American.
Toshiko, torn between two cultures. Hating the marauding
Caucasians, a hostess during the Occupation enduring
GI talk about Jap cunt, forced to return to Japan during
the war, her father reluctant to forgo the antiquities of
the British Museum merely because of a war. And when
they got home her brother more valuable, a boy, worth
saving from foreign devils, was accepted in Japanese
schools, she wasn't. Toshiko shunted off to an upper-class
Protestant school, speaking no Japanese, illiterate in her
own land, a traitor to the emperor god. Her loved and
envied brother, younger than she, now a big successful
literary critic with two sons. Toshiko still unmarried,
her mother grieved for her. Finally they had to shorten
her kimono sleeves for grand occasions, the *omiai* never
worked out, the matchmakers' photos were sent back.
Here she is past thirty unmarried, probably some guy's
mistress, wouldn't be surprised if he works at her school.
Then fired from this job, living on in the house by the
gardenia bushes, a pallet bed just big enough for a nun,
an artist unsure and never doing enough work, her only
solace a few other women artists who are often gone
abroad. "Everyone comes and goes but I stay," she says.
Visits her mother and the brother's family every Saturday.
I asked her to be Mori-San's friend when I left, giving
my best friends to each other, hoping they could give
each other strength.

I made a whole circle of friends, Yo-chan the
glamorous and Kon the struggling architect, Fumio and
these two women. Fumio's in America again waiting for
me. The circle will fall apart. They will not stay together

when I leave—though they love our parties at Toshiko's or the wild nights in Ginza, Shinji-ku, Shibuya, Ropongi, dancing eating long dinners in bars. Mori-San laughed in the car going to Yokohama to put me on the boat. I am the tiresome foreigner, the *gei-gin,* always-in-a-hurry American. "You are freer than we are," she says. Mori-San a virgin at forty, face of a child, still supporting her mother, father, uncle, and the brother who went blind during the Occupation when there was no medicine. But one brother is a high court judge, has independence and a family. After the neighborhood bar Mori-San has to climb in a window of the house she owns and supports lest uncle find out how late it is. The maid is her accomplice. Mori-San a sculptor doing commercial art on the side to support this menage where everybody's her boss. She came late one night to the brown folk-art studio I rented from Izumi. Soon he'll evict me to plant his first son's arranged marriage there, bride off an IBM card, a backgound in art, the proper qualifications to be a wife to a folk-art shop even though number-one son wanted to be a car salesman. His children hated the store and its lovely pots. So I became Izumi's daughter, traveled all over the island with him to the pottery villages, their straw roofs, bamboo water clocks making gentle noises as we walked through cedar forests to discover the potter at his wheel.

The second year I lived in Fumio's big house while he went to America. Yoshiko was to follow as soon as he could find them a place. But when he left she got strange, wouldn't go out, didn't want to play with us. And never saw the promised land they saved ten years to see, Fumio thinking she would be freer there. So we threw her ashes from the Coney Island ferry. Every year in March the two of us together bringing daffodils to the boat, throwing them from the deck in memory, afraid people would think the package contained an aborted child and arrest us.

Mori-San in a cab late one night came to that first studio, wanting to be held. So I held her kissed her, but she could no more and wanted to go home. Feeling that floor again, the two of us leaning against the pillar on the clean boards, the place I did my first good work, sculpture worth saving, a Don Quixote from a log, some pipes and the wooden grille from the ladies' room of the boat I came on. Starting from nothing, broke, couldn't speak the language so couldn't buy materials, no money anyway, just the five hundred yen a day for screws, hammer, chisels. I built wooden cars, chugs—because the McMann boys broke mine when I was twelve? New in Japan, just making things, not having to be a sculptor, nobody watching. I found things, walking late at night, picking up junk to use. And once I heard music, standing outside a bamboo fence. Beyond in the darkness in the house I cannot see, Japanese are playing Beethoven's Violin Concerto. The terrible hurt of childhood over music, the beloved aunt who gave me those records. Now I am disowned by all the Milletts.

So far away from home when Mother's letter came saying she'd sell the house on Selby Avenue—all I had left, the only root in the world. I sat on a straw mat in my own *kotatsu* stunned. She cannot sell it, my childhood, the place she made our fortress when Dad left. Funny-shaped roof, geraniums in window box, neat, small-town. Every time I went back it looked smaller, the rooms shrinking. Stopped there on my way to Japan for Mallory's wedding. She was still Mary then, my younger sister. Now I am the only one left unmarried, target for Mother's relatives to discuss at Thanksgiving and Christmas the way they did Cousin Carol, Cousin Lenore. Long dull overfed afternoons of my childhood. Hardship cases. Outstanding failures. That visit Mother's bathroom redecorated, the place getting a *House and Gardens* look so different from when I lived there. The tub doesn't have feet any more, lavender rug and towels so elegant, bath powder smelling ladylike. Mother has a bedroom of her own now—not theirs—the place where they held out on Saturday afternoons doing we always figured what. Now gauze curtains, and only her clothes in the closet, feminine light blue. And her office things, a success at life insurance, all the clippings of the time she was Man of the Year for her company. Her prizes, her gold certificates. The wall full of daughters and grandchildren. She has their photos tinted. I am there in my sorority girl picture, a Theta in my Lanz dress cropped hair college coed. Also oxford black and white with bunny fur hood. Baby picture with dirty shoes sitting on a piano stool, mother forgot to whiten them till the man had already poked his head under the black curtain—the shame of her life, those shoes will be dirty forever. The bathroom is so clean, after my two years on the Bowery, a gray ring around my neck like a bas-relief from sleeping with the dog for warmth, the sheets too black ever to ungray. I lived with a girl. Zooey. And Mother knew. Her face makes a face when she comes near the topic but we stay afar, mutual consent. No more Zooey now anyway, gone, left.

I brought the dog, it was our dog—I'm stuck with the baby, going to take it to Japan. But it got fucked by Roger the sage neighborhood mutt the very day of the wedding. Terrible scandal, this example upon the lawn. University of Minnesota vet washed it out. Blamed dog too frigid to breed when we tried, or the stud too effete, helping their organs in a Bronx living room having answered an ad in the paper. Zooey wanted puppies. But then Customs says no dog. Sent it back to Zooey; her baby till it died. Hard to leave this tidy bourgeois bathroom for my adventure, going without money to Japan. Nine hundred dollars and no ticket back. Asked Elder to buy a drawing: she says her money belongs to Edward and her sons. Mallory can't buy a drawing because it's her wedding so she must have it for a present. I did a series in Mother's basement, huge black strokes, final product of a year's daily discipline, two hours every afternoon. No one bought them. Carried them on the boat, wandering on my way, seventeen days on a freighter. Frightened when the pilot went down at the Golden Gate, watching his body leave me a girl in a white dress in the night, alone with all the Japanese sailors, lights shining on the magnificent bridge as it recedes. Now I am stuck going to Japan.

Cold eggs for breakfast—that's Western food. Cribbage at night learning to gamble in Japanese numbers with the officers. When they crossed the line they gave me champagne and again when a wire came from Zoe for my birthday. Till I saw Yokohama harbor one gray morning—it was so ugly I wanted to turn around. Hauling all the suitcases through the subway afraid to ask in English for a train to Tokyo, noisy tiled underground world. And between Yokohama and Tokyo one long dull gray industrial blight, billboards through the window awful. Where was the tale of Genji, the world of art and court and beauty I devoured in print and expected, though I had warned myself not to?

After it became clear New York was making everybody sick crazy or alcoholic, all my friends in their twenties cracking their hearts against the city. "Everybody sleeps around." The art world's a tough place—"You got to be a survivor to make it." Watching them, afraid I'd turn game player, get hard. But I have no inner strength, cannot stay home nights I feel evening coil around the Bowery's bricks beckoning me to adventure, rebuffed always, gay bar or straight. Coming home empty, more empty when laid than otherwise. So I took a Harlem kindergarten job, stopped living on Mother's kindly dole of forty a month. Started saving to escape, get the money to leave, though I still didn't know where to go. Till I heard Nina Simone at Town Hall. Sitting in the middle of the concert, Japan came to me. Just happened and now I'm going.

Jack Thomas urged me on, big warm black man lover, soldier over there on furloughs, thought the Japanese free of racism. A delusion, but he needed it. Crooning to me Japanese words, "Ladies who run bars are called *mama-sans*." We laughed. Teasing me why don't I marry him. Couldn't mean it, every time I call he's got some woman there. Stop by and there's another one in the bed. Bathtub in the kitchen; when he takes a bath he looks like Neptune, huge beautiful body. Kind, singing to me the world's a bad place, one night I just gave up and cried. He comforted me like a mother.

"What would your mama say if you came home with this black man?" he yelled while I stood at the bureau drawers, my back to him. He only wants to test me, has no intention of getting himself tied up. And when I was in Japan Zooey wrote me that he'd raped her. My best friend. Wanted both of us and she wouldn't, so he forced her, huge body of a football player pinning her to the bed, bruising, beating her. Afterwards she crept out and walked the streets with the dog. When I read this letter I cursed him even in racist terms, called him a black bastard not just a bastard. Helpless in Tokyo watching the light bleed through the trees outside my studio, falling on the concrete driveway where I did my drawings because I couldn't dirty Izumi's floor. Wrote Janey—don't let him come to the Bowery for dinner any more. She was better than me. She let him. Janey said he only did it because he couldn't write, was having a nervous breakdown instead. While I lived in Japan Zoe went crazy from this wound and from life in the place she moved to on Tenth Street. No windows, the whole apartment just one room. And not one window. Paid rent for that. When I came home to New York he rang the bell shouting, "Hey baby you're back." I went down and then I did a cold bold thing. Told him I never wanted to see him again. He lived a block away on Second Street. Every time I went to the store I could see him through the plate-glass of the Cooper Union store front, bustling about, becoming a figure in New York politics. Not running his maid service any more. Not writing either. Bumping into him on the street once coming home from the polls after the CORE campaign. A down moment anyway, we had to vote for LBJ. So hard not to say hello, stay loyal to Zoe, forgetting his tenderness and the good times: the night we went to Coney Island, people staring at us on the train, nigger and white chick. Staring right back. Laughed all day and bought popcorn, cotton candy, shooting range, swimming, merry-go-round catching rings even, laughing more. Wanted to make it on the beach but he was afraid. When we got back to his place, thinking as he entered me there goes the sound barrier—

hoping I had not said it out loud "you're black"—a whole piece of America breaking in me, free.

I'm telling Marchesi that I love Fumio, knew when I felt him lying there in his gentleness that I would always love him. "That's not what I asked you," she said—"I didn't ask you if you loved Fumio, I asked you if you missed women. No I said, and I lied in my confusion, imagining that loving Fumio was incompatible with missing women, with loving anyone else at all.

That was at dinner. Drinking before dinner we had a quarrel over racism. I said we all had it. Marchesi said she didn't. Emerson either. But we have to have it, I insisted—think of how we're taught, going back to that first time I touched a black hand; parties at Minnesota, JayCee and a few other graduate students, and the old-line leftists who had quit academe to become waiters. And Nova the queen bee presiding. Lots of black men there, Pullman porters, one named Jimmy danced on sand, wonderful to watch. We sat around and listened to Dylan Thomas records. Blacks very rare people in Minneapolis, peers not available, Pullman porters did for Nova while she and Hank got drunk on rum and Coke. I was an undergraduate startled. But when I touched Jimmy's hand I knew how well I'd been taught because of the fright in my gut. I told them this. They said I was full of crap. Asked then had they ever slept with someone black. No, but that didn't matter. We did not have a very good time bluffing each other. Went back to Emerson's disgruntled. Up to the second story where she put me to be out of reach. Hugged her good night before I went up. But she gave no signal. Protesting my marriage.

Getting rid of the wallpaper, haunted by Jenny Spitz. She would not want me to write a book. Warned me then. In dread of her, climbing the stairs of her brownstone, knowing beforehand I am about to be assassinated for the crime of individualism. But she has a neighbor there, we sit in the sunny kitchen talking about Catholic girlhoods because the other woman had one too, boisterous jokes about the confessional. Maybe it won't happen. Maybe she'll stay and Jenny won't start on me.

But my ally leaves, and I know I'm done for when Jenny moves me to the dark living room for grilling. Endless attack and defense. Why doesn't she write her own book, I'll help her—She still hasn't written her thesis and now she's got excellent stuff for a real anthropological book. If she'd drop the project on semantics she started with and do another thesis. "My prof seduced me then stole my ideas and got famous," she says. "No one ever helped me. I have been used." Her voice shakes. "You can do articles anyway," I venture, already choking with fear. "Ha—" she spits on books, it is bourgeois to write. Her collaborator's gone out to California with her husband. "Do it yourself then." My eyes fall on the child. Last year, the second Atlantic City demonstration, Jenny looking like hell, pregnant, clothes dirty, hair uncombed. Here is the child. She says she understands woman's oppression better now. I wince considering the price, this child an unwanted atonement for a baby she had long ago when unmarried and gave away. Has done this to herself now. She is righteousness mouthing the line about anonymity, the collective Maoist this and that. She was not there to write my thesis collectively so I signed it myself. Now it's too late. I go into the bathroom in the middle of our fight trembling behind the door, almost too afraid of her to come out, malingering there, safe. She screams at me through the afternoon, wounding tearing hurting. She says the book will be important, terribly important. She exaggerates, publishers be lucky if they recover their advance, will they want their four thousand back if they never sell any copies? "You will regret you ever signed it," she warns, sibyl more than she knew. Words I hear again through slabs of wallpaper. Then she decides to nurse the baby, her great beautiful breasts showing her miracle of milk. "Try it," she dares me. "Let him take your nipple." "But I have nothing," I say, "he will not suckle." Then she urges me and I'm modest but game, curious. He rejects me. I am judged. Condemned by the child. Dave comes in on his way to a meeting then off again in a rush. They will leave the city and wander. He will give up engineering to roam around in a trailer. She will never write anything now. Her life has closed down. He leaves and I know she is locked in this place, can't even go to the movies, baby too small to take along. I can leave through the door but she cannot. I worry for the child; it would have to be a boy. I put my hand on her shoulder but she pulls away, nearly striking me. What is she afraid of? It was affection, I tell her, "We are sisters." "Sisterhood is bullshit," she says. "You are not my sister"—shrieking now, our friendship crashing into pieces on the rug. "Forget the movement, Jenny, we're friends. Dave and Fumio like each other too. Remember the great times we've had nights you came over for dinner?" But she is the movement. She makes my decisions. "Look, we must be human first," pleading with her, "If we can't hold on to that the political thing can become insanity." Now she is shouting she will call everyone in her address book and denounce me. She glares at me like I am the kind she will shoot when she has power. "I will love you even when you hate me," I say, afraid of the promise as I make it. "Get out of here, you disgust me"—I leave, limp down the stairs, raped by her hatred.

That May at the Congress Jenny and a bunch from New Haven sounding like everyone's Weatherman boyfriend, making each resolution a bellowing match, using trash tactics, preventing free speech. I tried to mediate, caught in the middle, bitten by friends on both sides, Carol and the bunch from New Haven calling me a pig, the NOW women calling me to come away from those freaks. Nothing is hated worse than a peacemaker. Finally there were resolutions saying movement women could only write by lot, no inspiration till it's your turn, turn off. All money from publication to go to a central committee, you may apply to them for groceries and carfare but the neediest women in the city will be funded first and radical charity will find plenty of needies, so forget it.

Three days raining fire on the "stars" till Magda silenced their hisses. Magda battered into trauma by a consciousness-raising group who acted like playground bullies, cornering her until she wept, other theater people giving her hell for her hard work in the feminist theater, a whole year destroying her ability to work. I declined an insulting invitation to be a star panelist and gave my airtime to the Radical Lesbians, whose takeover that first night was the only lovely moment in the whole bloodbath. Actually got up courage to come out over the microphone near the end of the first session—everyone putting on their coats, too bored and sleepy to hear my great confession.

How can I write a book now, sign it when Jenny would forbid it, and the right wing would use it as grist for their mill? If I signed the last one, wanting credit for my work, would signing this one be an act of courage? Large piece of wallpaper fallen. But how dare I still? One thing to say you're queer, another thing to prove it—detail the truth in print? Don't write, just go on degenerating.

After the wallpaper the evening closes down. When dinner is over we have coffee and a fight. Fumio says it was a mistake to buy the farm. "I am yanked out of my studio in New York to peel wallpaper. I have lost my system to come up here." His face a rage, yelling at me. "Fine time to say so. It *cannot* be a mistake, we have done it." I am holding a paring knife. If he does not stop I will put it through the palm of my hand. I bring it down on the table instead. "The wallpaper is only three days more. They are building your studio, you have the technology money for tools. It would be the best shop we ever had. Then you can start. You haven't worked for a year. You should make new things, not just the same kites. It will be an empty room. Fill it, you have another show in January." But I know he is afraid. So am I. Of course it is a mistake. He will sit there alone in a new studio and nothing will come. I have dared to affect his life, trying to help. But if he stayed on at the Bowery alone, like last winter? A whole day to tie one knot because the phone keeps ringing, because my life is devouring his time. No, the farm has got to work, begging him to take it back, unsay it—say it was not a mistake. My eyes on the knife, my mind trying to beat it into my hand, trying also not to do that, not hurt my hand. "I have no money," he shouts finally, "I cannot have a new studio, contractors, band saws." "Why in hell not? Who cares?" I shout back. He does, his samurai pride cares. The only times we ever fight are when he is broke and won't mention it till he explodes. Still keeping a record of what he owes me. But when he came to America, eight hundred dollars, all he had in a foreign country—three months while I hunted for a job, any job— he loaned me finally to the last dollar of it. Calling agencies, women's voices, "Don't come in if you don't type." At the end I passed a test, got to be a file clerk, Olsten's Temporary. An Oxford M.A., I knew the alphabet, so I could eat. Took two years to pay him back. But he cannot pay me back. It is probably six months since he sold anything. Vita was to mail the letter with the price list. Drove us to the airport when we went to England, Fumio still writing it down in the car, asked her to mail the letter for him. That winter he had two exhibitions but nothing was sold. No price list. He got home to discover the Nebraska Museum had turned away customers. Then the Chicago dealer went bankrupt and disappeared with all the sculptures. How can he sell art in a depression? Now we have a joint bank account, why didn't I think of that before? We will never know then how much he owes me. We are still fighting over whether it was a mistake, the farm. He will not unsay it, he is stubborn, tired, afraid. We go to bed like enemies in a cease-fire.

Driving to New York for Zell's funeral. Fumio sulks in his corner. "What are you thinking about?" "My own things"—darkly—"my work, my life." I will shut him out and think to myself, talking in my head, not writing because I have nothing important to say. Merely thinking about the car. Fumio hates it, not safe to have in the country, always breaking down. All winter cheated by mechanics trying to get it right—"Man if you could just get this car in shape for me." They say sure, keep it for twelve weeks, charge twice what we agreed on and the whole time they never even manage to fix the gas gauge. I squirm, adding up the money thrown into it, a big bargain for three hundred and fifty dollars, now it's cost fourteen hundred altogether and still won't work. So damn cheap that now you're paying one hundred dollars per thousand miles for the fourteen thousand put on it since last summer. Figure out what Hertz charges, you could have rented one at this rate. Aristocrat and peasant thrashing away inside me, a quarrel of Millett and Feely, male and female, father and mother. This car is a proletairan version of the Cadillac or Buick elegance of my Millett aunts, those beautiful women. I wept my fourteenth summer away mooning over pictures of them, the tragedy that they were not their own twenties any more, a youth so superior to mine. Very Scott Fitzgerald, they drove open cars in the winter in those days—people from my town—wearing bearskin coats, drinking booze. And Claire Brick their cousin died on her twenty-first birthday. Didn't see the new traffic island installed on University Avenue. A crash of yellow hair.

My father might have understood this car. What a struggle to contain both these forces in one body, Millett and Feely, money and fear. Dad and his sisters, 'cause he was their Jamie, squaring off against Mother's reproach, her justice. I am on her side—quit being a Millett years ago when they kicked me out. Then Celia remembered me I was a Millett too, those New Haven first days of our love, laughing at the joke of her family and the Irish. Old American money, they imported Irish labor for their Connecticut Shipworks. The Tyburn men carried on in business, the women carried on in guilt. Little charities to ease their conscience. I am Irish but I know the Irish sniveled, whined, had runny noses, were thoroughly unpleasant in their poverty, ill health, their complaints marshaled with slave's cunning. A Protestant, Celia was sent to the workers' Catholic schools, and they kept the rosary a secret from her in revenge. She cried telling it. I was amused anyone would want to know that stuff—"They shoved it down our throats." We both laughed, sun in the six big windows, those early June days, thinking we had solved the class problem with our love, with time, with humor. The Shipworks are gone, we are another generation, sisters, lovers. Wasn't I Irish gentry after all, a Millett, with their looks, their arrogance? Then trips to New Haven with the door locked on me, I turned out to be not a Millett, but Mother—the one who gets hurt. Hearing Mother's voice— "You are always for the underdog"—almost as if it were a reproach. But it was what she made me, her lesson.

Mother's peasant finds this car a crime. The aristocratic Millett in me argues beguilingly for the glamour of its ride, easy big old boat, almost floats on the highway. Mother's peasant is disgusted by the waste. The effusion of a showy car that won't even run properly, has already cost a scandalous amount of money. I burn over the transparent folly of my insistence on this aging Ford convertible, Galaxie 500, lines like sculpture, solid trunk, big enough for the whole movie, all those machines. Shooting last summer we always kept the top down driving through the city, you see all the buildings, even the upper floors where there are gargoyles and carvings downtown. This is the car I wanted when I was fifteen and couldn't have because of course we could not afford it. Pointless to mention you might want something like that. And now I have it, my teenage fantasy fulfilled. This greaser's dream, fuel pump to the energy of cracker America, everything it finds beautiful and exciting. It needs a spinner on the wheel, baby boots dangling from the rearview mirror, leopard-skin seat covers. Dances, corsages, tooling around town picking up girls. I defy nature in owning it. No car for a dame unless she borrows her boyfriend's and wears a tight purple sweater driving it all tits. The car helps me understand men sometimes when I think I'm losing them, off in my world of women. Men make up their minds right away, either they like me for having such a car, or they smell intrusion, honk on the highway, yell dirty words. Would laugh to see her crack up against the guard rail, demented redneck hostility that can always shit on cunt and niggers. But most men love a car like this. They look at it and see their own youth. Mine too. Discovering in one horrified moment that I cling to it because it's Celia, no, not Celia, but the hope of her return. Because it means last summer when Brookfield was the life beyond the revolution. The three of us in love with friendship, living in an old house, a commune with a bunch of college kids, youngsters who were Fumio's apprentices. The great dinners and the music afterwards, wild flowers on the table. We slept like three children in a row. Celia in her bed beside us. Never made love the whole time and never missed it. Somehow it would have been excess. And we could not hurt Fumio. The kids' feet at night softly visiting each other, but we were chaste. Talking was our dissipation.

One night we went for a walk in the woods and I tried to kiss Celia with some obscure Lawrentian passion. We would make love here. But it was so dark and frightening, the notion seemed ridiculous. So we sat on the steps of an old railroad station, our arms around each other while she told me her brother betrayed her in school and her father frightened her so that she forgot how to talk. And I asked her not to be Fumio's lover because I was afraid. Hardest thing to ask, ashamed doing it. One morning I read manuscript in bed, the thing on Smith and Vassar, my first piece trying to write a new way. Celia favored regular sentences. She came into our bed giggling with Fumio, kissing him. And I should have picked up my papers, gone downstairs and concentrated. Maybe I did leave. But I had already gotten her word, prevented them. Only the car remains in the waste of hope. Last summer gone while another comes out in green on the Taconic going by. There will not be much in it.

Taking up time on the way to death, anyone's time, talking about a car. You cannot write this stuff, it is not important. Politics are important. Of course Montaigne could do it, just write about his personality—as if that were significant—and it was. He invented the self. But I had better not write anything down, my self trivial as this car.

Driving the warm streets over to the Finale. Vita and me. A nice evening in New York, almost seems like this could be a fun place to live, looking at the West Village streets, shady and quiet, but with the city's throb of bars, music. Things going on all over town this early summer night.

The awnings roll back when we sit down, tree branches and brick walls, pale sky giving way in time to the candles, drinks, warmth, and chatter. We go over the crazy year again, its pain so remote for a moment. One long error set right now being home. That too an illusion probably. In no time the mania will come back, readjust itself for another go. The familiar will disappear again, a waiter or a newspaper will reassert themselves as portents, an ad enunciate despair, the commonplace revealing its true sinister character. But for now Vita can hand me Jill's Marmalade book for a present, we can talk about our friends' shows, bringing the downtown people to bear, building with names and faces something like a community. I am still living, not lost. And the old ethic of doing what you like no matter. Since the middle class doesn't exist, their morality is unknown, their lumber room of prejudices too negligible to furnish anything but humor. She tells me that a friend did a happening last week at Judson: shaved from the neck down. Whole body. Took all day. "Remarkable look, you should have seen the naked backs of his hands." "Aleatoric art," she says. "It got late so he threw an I Ching to see if he should go on up and do the beard and scalp." "Jesus, the I Ching!" It takes a full moment to realize this is funny. And with each laugh more of the evening sky and the branches stretching out to summer fall into my mind, bringing delivery from the ridiculous solemnity of politics. Hysterical scramble to take sides—but for Christsakes which is the right side?

Next morning erranding around to the bank to find I'm poorer than I thought. They have lost four hundred dollars in the machine. All the records go to New Jersey on IBM cards. It is irremediable. And how will I pay the income tax? Then to the supermarket for chicken. Soul food for the "communist party" tonight. With the sun out downtown it feels like my town again. The old neighborhood Bleecker Street artists looking fine and scruffy in their big hair and boots. How exciting New York is, my provincial conviction whispering that this is where it all happens. In New York we take chances. After a winter lecturing middle America I'd forgotten that. That we are the ones who do it—downtown. Then the Lexington Avenue Subway and the *Village Voice* to snack off while riding uptown. I will get that tourist agent to refund my ticket. There will be no London for a while since the print isn't ready yet. England can wait. I'm home.

There is sun all over the buildings uptown and I love Park Avenue, street of doormen. Some leer and some whistle. Some laugh. The funny people in business suits walk around. I have arranged it so they look cheerful today. Everything is so splendid, each face open. All winter I made them look like cops or the damned. But how long will the new truce last? Worrying the question as I did last night lying in Vita's snug study—why did I go crazy? What was it about? Has anyone ever gone mad from media before?

"You believed in it partly, partly you must have believed in the whole charade," Vita said last night. Not even an accusation. Just a fact. Plastic bags strangle children. I am not a child, only childish. A fool in that total environment. After it stopped being funny. And started to swell.

Pop back into the subway. Get that chicken cooked. At last I can be unrecognizable again after *Time* sold my image to strangers on airplanes. How satisfactory to be no one, a short rather plump subway rider, neutral, inoffensive. The perfect getup to cancel a self. A subversive's mind tucked under the camouflage, plotting art or ideas. Then the guy next to me on the bench betrays me and leans over to ask if I'm Kate Millett. Crash into Astor Place goes the morning.

He looks sheepish. I ought to ask him why he asked me. But I know. It's just to congratulate himself on the feat of recognition. Once I saw Taylor Mead on the

Lexington line. Picking his nose and reading a comic book. I didn't ask him. It wasn't necessary. My guy gets out at Bleecker Street. It's my stop so I follow. He's nervous. Does he think I'm pursuing him? I want to. I want to scare him. I want to become a nuisance to him. I want to go up and interview him. But he looks like a poor nudge and it is a nasty thing to do.

Memorial for a black artist. Bill and Washburn have made this for Zell. Days of telephoning to friends, coping with the strangeness of coroners, cremators, lawyers, all the square machinery of death, functionaries we were too isolated to have happened upon. We never had a funeral before. We always had parties. Exhibitions. Maybe even a wedding. Though few of us bothered to get married. Zell loved weddings. Talked about ours for years in parental pride. I realized one night that I had asked him to be a witness because he looked like my own uncle who looked like a senator giving the bride away at my sister's wedding. Lover, I wanted you for a father figure too.

Park the car in front of the Peace Church. Leave Fumio's fried chicken in the back, it's for later, tonight's communist party. Washburn at the door when we come up the steps. Frock on even. Greeting people. I've got my poem rehearsed. There's actually a program: Romy Bearden, John Bell, me. I'm too white to read Zell's friend Langston out loud to black people. Wonder why they asked me. Proud too that they did. But the others have better justification. Romy's the dean of black painters. Bell's a philosopher from New York University, Zell's teacher. Nervousness like before a speech.

Standing at the door, I spot a kid off the street calling to me, Bryn Mawr student, arriving out of nowhere, looking for an art school in New York. Already got herself the right kind of clothes and a boyfriend. "Try the School of the Visual Arts." Looking at her, this new one starting out. Inside, it's Zell's finish line. Then a man saying hello to me. He's an apparition. On one of the ten high Brookfield days last summer he took my picture for *Time. Sexual Politics* hadn't come out yet, was only a thing about to happen. And *Time* might be reviewing it. A nice guy, knew a lot of painters, the two of us laughing as he posed me against a tree. It was fun. When *Time* stamped me on its cover they gave that photograph to Alice Neal to base her portrait on. How sinister that picture grew. Surprising that he knows this—and apologizes for what was done to his work.

Sitting next to Washburn, looking up at the dimness, other moments come full circle. A black woman sings. I hear Miriam's soprano and Celia's lute still lingering in the air here from last summer, and the meeting the next night after Lydia was shot. And then the press conference on the Gay issue. Such discordant things. For an agnostic. I spend a lot of important moments in churches, bumping around through people and places.

Memorial for a black artist. The church full of New York's black painters. The young ones, like Jackie Witten, dandy legs, endearing optimism, grinning at his conquests. Overstreet's rancorous bandit handlebar, his rage against the white world bitter as a rapist's lust. Vanna striding in militancy. It was different, even harder, for their elders: Zell, Romy, Bill. The white world left Zell dead. And let Romy make it. It made Bill fight despair and liquor thirty years. Almost too late when his luck changed. The music's getting to me. Green Kleenex in Washburn's hand. Her whisper: "Hang on, Millett." We were at college together eighteen years ago. Still calling each other by our last names like prep school kids. We cut classes to go skiing, big children inventing nicknames: Washbag, Milletface. Piled her old man's rickety Cadillac into snowbanks and just laughed. Self-consciously learning to drink, waiting for nausea, listening to Leadbelly and Dixieland.

Romy's talking now, eloquent on friendship, bringing Zell back so hard it hurts. Then Zell's teacher, John Bell. Sunday afternoons Zell came by the Bowery. His black face under the white hair glowing with Faulkner, with Marlowe, with Agamemnon dead. He'd dig me out from under a pile of freshman themes written badly and reluctantly by middle-class kids who merely endured their education, to remind me what a student really is. I used to think he interrupted me, wasted the afternoon. Teaching me again now as I sit here and grin at my vanity for wondering if I could get up this big a crowd if it were my funeral. Half of them would be the same people. Zell now making me understand there's just so much time before it's over. Friends, other artists, come, and they add you up. It is all a matter of what you get done before this happens. Remind me, Zell, to come home; to get going.

At the party the air is serene around the gray rafters. Early summer evening, the loft full of people. Some paint brushes shoved back on a table to make room for the bar, beans warming on a hot plate. The beauty of his life. Coming home, kissing each one. In conversation noticing the warmth of one friend's skin, the black of another's eye patch, still another's grizzled hair. If I said to them, "I have come through alive, through to the other side of a tunnel," they might understand. Walter tells the story of Rothko's overcoat. How the old man grew too paranoid to exhibit. Ten years working on his murals. Still insecure, begging for praise and assurance when people dropped by. Rothko cold in the winter, but wouldn't call Bloomingdale's and just order something warm. Had to wait to settle on the proper thing from the British American store, where a collector would trade for a drawing. Haggling took time. So the master died with five million dollars but no overcoat. Stupid misery of fame and money. Always we were safe from it, mistaking our obscurity for a curse when it was a treasure. Free to make what we liked, to be ourselves, even do nothing at all. No one watching. We could be real. Their sanity cures me as the party ripens. Slipping into myself. Just be. Go on living. Work again.

Then I met Bill Hutson. A black painter seven years in Rome. "I was watching you from over there, and wondered how you felt," he said. I told him I felt scared. He nodded. "Things going way out of control. Each day knowing less and less. Depleted. More tired all the time.

You think crazy things like even you might get shot. Now I feel better." He's looking at me hard, like he knows. It is gratifying, but somehow puzzling. Said he'd come by for a drink and never did. I am left wondering was it just a come-on.

Juan explodes on arrival. All Puerto Rican militancy, movie maker, and super queer. "I'm a faggot," he bellows, hugging me. "I'm a dyke." And we dance around. No one's shook. It wasn't always this way. In the old days I struggled to pass, so they wouldn't have to know, have to face it. And they all knew. Struggling not to admit they knew, so I wouldn't have to face it. Everybody uncomfortable, a waste of energy. I suppose even good Zell knew. One can hardly faze a black man with twenty years in social work. My fault if we never talked of it, never mentioned it.

Everybody eating now, Fumio's chicken a huge success. All the talk of summer conjuring places like the Hamptons, Provincetown, Joe and Nancy are going to the Island, Jackie and Maria are off to Greece. Summer, and the urgency of life. Flavor and sweetness in the water and the sand. Why not admit to pleasure? Live these times, too. We have wonderful inebriated conversations on politics: amateur, pointless, good-willed, with only a few gestures. That world keeps at bay tonight.

Tonight seems to distill the goodness of every night in New York. Surpassing every meeting of the communist party to date. Chuck's studio is archetypal: he got it finished just in time for it to be condemned by the city.

Part of me is still waiting for Zell to show up. But I'm feeling too how much closer all of us are become. Hovering toward the consciousness we are a group. Made whole through a defection. At the end we stand and toast him. Fullness. Then past the big round oak tables, down the long loft staircases, into the streets. Home.

He's driving. We are back at the farm. He is practicing for his test. I am making phrases, apologizing to an imaginary reader. Underbelly book. The backside of writing. People who know what they're doing never tell

you this. The dirty fingernails of art and politics. And
close to the bone. Making chicken Kiev for a bunch of
people once I watched my hands tear the pink meat off
the ribs with a sharp knife. I am afraid of everyone. I
am even afraid of him. Fumio—after all these years. While
he puts the car in the garage I play with the new machine.
Whispering into this Sony tape recorder that I can go
on. I have just bought two notebooks: one with flowers,
one with flag stars. It seems possible to keep on going.
Drunken excitement in my hands and stomach. He comes
in. I start off in the notebook. He sits down at the table,
eating potato salad. The paper rattles. I'm caught. But
he is my Fumio. I want to ask his permission, but I am
afraid.

So I show it to him. Give him this paragraph to read,
the one I've just written down. "Do you want some
coffee?" Bribe the reader, serve him. While he settles
down to it I search frantically for the pot. Nowhere.
Don't interrupt while he's reading. Keep looking for the
blasted dripper that never works anyway. What will he
say? He sits there in a dark blue shirt, a great bowl of
quince blossoms before him on the table. I look at him
through the flowers, their strange Chinese color, neither
pink nor red, the navy denim of his shirt. His golden
face, black hair, a head the shape of a boy's. I am adoring
his beauty.

Yesterday Vita read the first notebook and said I
should go on. We sat on the kitchen floor here at the
farm, her back against the refrigerator, mine against the
sink. "I stayed up all night reading it," she says. My
heart races listening. "Of course it may only be gossip
and nothing serious," she says, my blood freezes and
waits—I should risk my life on gossip? "Hard to say yet
what it would be like, it's just fragments," she says
judiciously. My throat is up in the air. Instinct tells me
she is playing with me, manipulating my fear. It is our
bond. She knows, has discovered long ago, I am afraid.
The deal had seemed to be that in return for her knowledge I should give her love. She has helped me. The
trouble is I could never quite love her—moments, but

I cannot hold on to it. Instead I am only grateful. And Vita has helped me so much, bailed me out when the movie ran aground. She helped me then, more than I could repay. So I told myself the work itself must be her reward; she has nothing in her life she values worth doing and no work of her own. She will go to pieces without work. The art gallery never came through, the bookstore didn't work out, she cannot even get a job. She is a poet who is a housewife trying to break free. The movie is a purpose. It can start her out. If she learns to be a film editor she will have a profession.

And I needed help. That was my weakness, that I let myself be helped. Sitting in the Bowery one night after failing with another editor, Fumio Vita and me. And I was on the floor, done for. The two of them listening to me rave. "I'll type the transcript," Vita said, "It's an offer." "It's drudgery," I warned her, but already I was letting myself be saved. I said to her, "You must do this for the film itself, for what it is saying, because you think it's worth finishing." "Yes of course," she said. But how can I ever be sure? When we had dubbed the tapes and the transcripts were done, I took it all to England, edited it myself. She saw it leave her hands.

And now this book. She has decided it's a tract for Gay Liberation, wanting that. It is not what I want. She is a convert now, nouveau gay, burning for instant propaganda, narrow and without ambivalence. But who else is encouraging me to go on with it? She is the only one who's seen the notebooks. She's a writer. I hardly know any writers. She says I shouldn't show things to Fumio, "It might not be a good idea. For a while." "But he's my best friend," I said. "We've always worked side by side. I can't do things he doesn't know about." Realizing that his felt disapproval has held me back for months. What if he had said go on, do it, or said what he always says when I show him a drawing of a sculpture, my awkward lines on a page and some words, after redrawing it himself with his great skill—"Just Go Head." His face turned toward me waiting, pushing me. Vita likes secrets. I hate them. I will not keep secrets from

him. She cannot be so mad as to try to pry us apart.
Surely no one is that crazy. But no, she says, it's just
that he "wouldn't understand." While Vita and I talk
he fixes the front door. I feel his disapprobation through
the wall.

Later he brought me flowers, pear blossoms and the
quince. Was he afraid? All these dry months telling him
I will not leave him and does he still not believe me?
Now he stops and laughs at the line about permission. I
discover the coffee pot on the table. He had even poured
me a cup. He puts on a straw hat: "Let's go to work."
"Look," I say to him, "I showed that to you for a
reason." "Well tell you the truth I can't read your writing
about eighty percent." He grins. So I read it out loud
to him. Now he must hear me. His face is beautiful under
the straw hat. "O.K. Just Go Head."

I start in the notebook. Vita said I could make it
anywhere, could play games with time. That means I
can make it Bond Street last summer. When I sat in the
car with Celia. I showed her the big loft building. "I
could buy that maybe and we could all live there, you
and Miriam and me and Fumio. We could be a group
marriage"—using some word out of an old book. She
makes a face. It was the wrong thing to say.

Or I can make it England. Roll on cookie, spin mac-
aroon, how does mind cheat time and make it that last
night in London when we drank our wine out in the garden. Flagstones and the shining yellow of the daffodils.
"Burgeoning," we'd say each spring morning as we willed
them into bloom. This curious family I am part of now,
Nell Paul and Winnie—leaving them tomorrow. Wild dago
red in big round goblets, ruby in the English evening
gray around the rooftops. We talk of a friend in politics
who wants to write plays. "What if she wrote down all
she knew about politics," I suggest, pretending merely
to sketch out a notion. Feeling like a tub of hypocrisy
because of course I'd thought of doing that myself and
then collapsed into silence. Because it was too hard.
"They'll kill you," the Editor screamed—the Editor in
my head—negating me day after day until I quivered and

came to a halt. Just stopped. Chicken, and the dread
inside too much to go on with. And when I'd stopped
the disgust took over. Now, like a one-armed carpenter
I begin insinuating that Ethel should write such a book,
launching forth into rationalizations: surely it would be
useful for others to hear how one really feels, what one
actually thinks, what is experienced by the persons
thrashing about hoping to bring change into being. Nell
interrupts with a magnificent gesture. "It cannot be.
Under no circumstances," she thunders. The reason why
is impressive. "It would stop politics. The entire
mythology would be endangered and politics depend
on everyone believing in magic, images, media, lies,
versions—all made up and ready to be religion. The notion
of change might excuse telling the truth. But politics
never"—her very sarcasm a challenge.

First I must write a preface. On the picnic table in
the farmyard, under the sun, fighting out each sentence.
Writing to find out who I am. Looking up for a second
to find Zell a part of it too. I called it a necessary pre-
amble, a bridge between the voice talking in my head
and prose as I'd known it. It was to explain myself to
myself—ponderous, self-conscious. It went like this:

No apology justifies what I have done. A coward
pushed into risk, the next moment squirming in it. I will
always clutch after extenuation. With all the bravado
of the truly intimidated, I will admit that excuses are
in themselves both servile and presumptuous. But let this
be brought forward by way of explanation: *it had occurred to me to treat my own existence as documentary.*

There are many reasons why I shouldn't have. Among
them some credit is due to common sense. I did realize
my scheme was in bad taste, a divulgence superfluous
even before one considers its impropriety. I have a
powerful respect for the pleasing, reasonable dishonesty
of civilized discretion. One reason I thought it worth
doing is because I'm fairly sure that had someone once
tried to tell me all this I would have been interested.

Especially if I had heard it while there was still time. One's impressions during such an experience, the bits of what an observer sees and thinks then—recording them, even if they were my own, might, I hoped, just conceivably have some marginal value. I'm still not sure.

As a sculptor I was happy with our minimal need for introspection. I was not a secretive person, so my ordinary reticence was more than adequate in a life about which, understandably, no one but a few friends had any curiosity. As a visual artist I had done something unusual by maintaining a link with scholarship, even completing a doctoral degree in comparative literature. With the publication of my thesis (an unlikely event in itself) my decent anonymity was blasted into a ruin of interviews, articles, attacks, a banal paper war of thunderous volume if minute proportion. At first I responded to the novelty of this attention with naive excitement. For a week or two it was fun to be "fámous"—I was thirty-five and had never yet had a proper art exhibition. Here were people so interested in what I might say they were prepared to write it down or broadcast it. So I chattered for reporters with an ingenuous candor I now find it particularly grating to recall. Flattering at first, amusing too since it was so transparently silly, the American hype of ads and photos, the paraprose of journalism. Like the gallantries of a drunk, it was all so overstated as to be comic before it became perplexing. Yet when it persists, one becomes nervous and embarrassed. Soon it grew tedious, an indignity. One was made passive, led obediently, trotted out to perform, to be cooperative so as not to disappoint promoters, all the nice people who had gone to so much trouble. For a good while I imagined I was using a diseased system to attack exploitation itself in advocating radical ideas. A tricky proposition.

As the subject of controversy I suddenly acquired significance for others just as I ceased to hold any for myself. Filed and catalogued as a phenomenon, whatever purpose I might hold for myself now evaded me. As it was no longer mine, my life grew loathsome, repeating itself like a failing mimeograph, more and more swiftly proliferating the malign tide of unreason. Steps had to be taken.

It had never before occurred to me to regard myself as subject matter. Though I like to imagine this is my first book, I seemed, at thirty-six, to be past the age of the obligatory autobiographical novel. Sensible friends recommended research topics: pollution, erudition, etc. The confessional should wait upon one's ripe old age. But it was apparent to me that I might have no ripe old age, was sure not to have one, if I did not take some steps towards recovering my being.

The timid are devious: a number of hallucinations occurred to me, each more meretricious than the last. First fantasy: merely an editor, I shall sign some preface with my name and claim that someone else wrote the rest of the thing. Fantasty two and of greater relish: sign another name to the preface, my own to the book, and announce the author's death straightaway. Forgo the humor of promising a personal appearance on publication date, and leave it at that—she's dead. Then the delightful prospect of living into a serene old age, varied with gardening and an occasional sculpture show under a pseudonym. Too easy. If a feeling of misplaced pride in work led me to sign a book before, owning up to this one—despite any masochistic overtones—is also the mandatory acknowledgment of fact, even if it be error.

You may well ask how I expect to assert my privacy by resorting to the outrageous publicity of being one's actual self on paper. There's a possibility of it working if one chooses the terms, to wit: outshouting image-gimmick America through a quietly desperate search for self. And being honest enough. Of course it is impossible to tell the truth. For example, how does one know it? I will not belabor the difficulty by telling you how hard I have tried. And if compulsion forces me to tell the truth, it may also lead me into error, or invention.

Vita comes downstairs. She has just typed the preface and the part on Zell. We are at the farm. Her feet pound down the stairs and into the dining room. She is my editor, coming down to give me a conference. It is arranged. I wait for her afraid. What will she say? Last week she told me on the phone that she wants a salary for being my editor. She is above being a secretary now—she is my boss. At first she suggested she would be my collaborator. Her voice sounded like my mother's. "No." I refused, struggling to find the nerve. "How can I have a collaborator when I'm writing this out of my own gut? It's my life I'm doing, Vita." Then she said she had to have a salary. It was fair. I was relieved. If she has a salary I am not exploiting her. "It would be less exploitative," she corrected me. I cannot afford to pay a salary, keep a dependent, I do not want to hire people, be a capitalist, exploit women. Since last winter she has wanted to be my secretary. "But I don't even approve of the idea of secretaries," I argued. Now I am so behind it seems necessary. Mail piles up. Vita volunteered to help and I accepted it. But she makes so many letters out of sometihng simple. People keep writing. The mail accumulates. She seems to like making it complicated. Calling long distance every day, ten phone calls over what I wear to make a speech. Now she demands a salary. I said I could not pay much, the salary would be contemptible. I have spent all my money fixing the barn over into a studio, making the movie. "It's the principle of the thing," she told me, her voice an accusation. I tell her I dislike there being money between friends. Maybe that's just snobbery. She says it is. Then I wonder if it is a bad idea since we were now lovers; money could be poison there. She says this is conventional thinking. We are above it. And I ought to pay her, she has already done work, and after all, she says, she is poor.

At times Vita is a woman with a penthouse and a husband. Fred is a curator on full time. I was offered half his salary for two-thirds time. Vita thought it was too much. "He has worked for that museum for years," she said. "I have worked everywhere for years and never made more than three or four thousand dollars," I countered. Or does she resent it that I can earn a living? Once she offered to invest in my movie, said she had private resources. Other times she is a pauper with no money of her own. "It all goes for the children's clothing." Probably all of this is true but somehow it's still mysterious. Has she got stock somewhere? Now she needs some spending money for her independence. She is an oppressed woman; I am covered with guilt. The salary will ease my conscience. I hate myself. Vita is my crime now. When she does nothing for ten days it is still a crime: I am a slave driver, a cheap bastard wanting my money's worth. One night we worked it out in her room, I sat there terrified she'd name a salary I couldn't pay. I want to pay her for what she does, so much per manuscript page as I always do. But she wants a regular retaining fee. Then it will be a real job. She is nobody's typist, she says. She will be my editor and farm out the typing to a girl. I plead with her to do it herself. Because of the punctuation. "You are a writer, you understand how to do it right. I don't know punctuation; some writers claim it's like choreography."

Now she is coming into the room. I am trapped in a corner. She sits down at the table. I expect my fate. She says it's good. "What I've read so far . . ." Now I can breathe. I stand up walking around the room feeling confident. "But the preface," she says. Quickly I tell her I'll rewrite it, just an early version. "It's servile," she says. Now I am Celia's Katey, the cringing one she threw away. I will hang on, argue, like I did with Marcus, knowing I'd have to give in anyway. "How is it servile?" "Just take a look at the diction, the vocabulary as you scan the first paragraph: apology, justifies, coward, squirming, clutched, extenuation, intimidated, presumptuous." She reads my words. They accuse me, I am hopelessly servile. I should be a brave homosexual, a militant. A brassy writer, full of myself. And I'm not. It's all waste paper. Then she turns to the part on Zell, or rather Celia, 'cause it's Celia she doesn't like. I asked her wouldn't it bother her—the stuff on other people: Celia, Claire. "No of course not I'm an editor I've done this work before," she said. It seems miraculous to me, her objectivity. How can I say my freedom preaching was "only gas," she demands. People will misunderstand, think I was a hypocrite. "No, it only means I could not live the way I advocated, recommended to other people. That I was not free myself. We're all finding this out. A lot of my friends say the same thing, we recognize the gap between what we say and how we really live. It depresses us . . . We have discovered ambivalence," I say dramatically, hoping she'll laugh. No such thing—she is a tyrant, without humor, commanding me from the dining room table. "Anyway all this is just subjective stuff, a reader would have to realize that. It's a personal book, merely what I think, you are aware of the fact that I am not Women's Lib? Personified? In the flesh?" Wheedling. "If I am to be your editor you will listen to me!" Now she is pounding the table yelling at me she is the absolute judge, an editor doesn't take back chat. I have an editor already at my publishers. But I wanted to finish the whole manuscript before they saw it. To be sure that it will be my own book. So now I have Vita shouting at me. This is ridiculous, I tell myself. But I need her help. I am so unsure. She says she understands what I'm doing, she will help me go on. We subside, I walk to another corner.

With my back turned I hear her pronounce that "Academic writing is dead." There goes *Sex Pol* shot in midair, four hundred pages of rubbish. I'll agree. I'll agree to anything. Vita has never even read it, is bogged down in Chapter Two. I say skip it if it's dull, boring, go on to the last four, they're more entertaining. Hoping still she will find something to admire and to comment on in these pages I venture that I liked the ending of the part on Zell. Vita had not noticed. She says the last sentence of the preface doesn't sound like a last sentence. I rush to fix it. Her feet thud back upstairs.

3

Verde's Garden. I'm here, Celia isn't. We were supposed to meet here. After all the months of not meeting. But of course it's a fuck-up, and now it looks like she won't show. Half suspect I do these things to myself on purpose, deliberately set traps to fall into. Last week we arranged to meet at four thirty "in that Italian place with a garden on Sixth Avenue near the Waverly Theatre." There was something vague about calling again on Friday morning before I drove to town. Was it to cancel or affirm, I can't remember now. I left the farm early and since this morning I've been out of reach by phone. Yet I could have called her and confirmed at any time all during the day. My final arrogance—testing perhaps, sticking her to the original plan. Naturally I'm the one who gets stuck.

Verde's is some tough bar, the garden a little nugget behind it. I have known so many good afternoons here under the trees, the beer yellow and white in its steins, the warm look of French bread and butter. It would have been a pleasant way to meet again. And won't be now. I shuffle back and forth to the phone, a woman alone, the barflies heckle me, I am conspicuous, I even look stood up. The waitress is anxious over me. Check the other places on Sixth Avenue, the next place has a garden too. But no Celia. Back at Verde's to find my garden infested with a drunk and his lady friend, types from the bar strayed out of their territory.

"Whatcha had to eat all day, Louie?"

"This ain't bread, this is calsamite an' water. Take this tomato shit off the shrimps. I paid money for this."

"He's right. It's junk. We eat junk in this country."

"Ninety cents for this? It's garbage."

"You're right, Louie. Eat the lettuce."

"I'm not a rabbit."

"What else you wanna eat?"

"You."

"Stop being so fresh or I'll smack you with the bread. Take me to the movies tonight, they gotta double feature Dracula at midnight. We can hold hands and kiss."

"Nah, you stink of garlic."

"You've been drinking whiskey since eleven o'clock this morning."

"You're too fat."

"Do you make me fat? Do you feed me? I'm not your mistress. You can't talk to me like that."

"Shut up."

The afternoon collapses in the movements of their jaws, the sight of spinach between her choppers, the noise of his voice, his big hand smashing the bread, demonstrating its triviality, a whole basket destroyed in one fist.

Phone Celia again. She's been here and gone. Is not interested in coming back. "I know it's disappointing for you," the patronization like a silk lining to her voice. She's busy preparing some food for a picnic and doesn't wish to be disturbed. I petition her. Noblesse oblige she consents to return. It will happen, I will see her, I am not abandoned to the waitress's comforts and the stares of the men along the bar.

Sit down and consider the rich reluctance in her voice. Should have said, "Skip it." Maintained some cool. Now you're the victim of her charity. Remember that girl in college, who was also Irish and called Katie, also her lover. And Celia's superb dismissal: "She was servile." Last summer you ran like a hare so the ax wouldn't catch you, bought clothes, talked incessantly in an effort to dazzle. But only fatigued. And with each sinking inch of dependency she retreated another city block.

I change tables to escape the roar of my neighbors. Of course choosing the wrong table, one that's too big. They'll be needing it soon, the place is filling up. It is in the center, obvious, in bad taste. The right one is over there in the corner. I cannot bear the publicity of moving again. The footsteps of new arrivals crunch upon the gravel. Time hovers and dodges the waitress's frantic haste. And still she does not come. Chilly now, the afternoon gone.

Two young men at a table against the wall, lovers tête-à-tête these three hours; they had a nice time today. Now a couple seat themselves at the table I covet, then another pair at the next one. There it goes: I must wait here chained to the wrong table where everyone can hear our conversation as if to ensure that we never have one. And next I must worry, since the thought has just occurred to me, how will we greet each other? Do I dare embrace her? It will not be the friendly unself-conscious hug I had counted on. Not now. Her voice over the phone like a tired husband, dragged down here again, doing me a favor.

Then it happens, I look up to find her barreling down on me. Little half round of a tomboy's grin, a cloth bag thrown over her shoulder bouncing against her hip. I struggle to rise in the hurried confusion of her embrace. Always beyond calculation, Celia does not sit down across from me at the table where hope had placed her these two hours past. Instead she plunks down next to me on the bench. Do we look strange? Will the people stare at us?

Once in her face, I forget them all to remember her eyes' light penetrating green, the iris freckled with scattershot brown. And relentless, whether it chose to enthrall or to repel. It was always her eyes for me. And the grin. Restored to me together with what I had blasphemously forgotten, those small creases at the corners of her smile, the cheek nearly child soft. She looks older; it is almost a year.

We laugh perhaps a bit less than we used to when things were continuously funny. And as we talk an odd notion comes to me that the time in between has somehow run parallel for us, confessing to her how I grew to hate the things I was doing.

"I thought you would."

"It was repetition, Celia. Spinning your wheels in the same place, not making anything new. I got scared." I avoid her eyes, saying this. "How was Musique Ancienne?"

Her hand wipes the table: "When you tour, you find easy ways to get through stuff. You never practice because there's no time. And you lose yourself traveling, being in a group. I found this winter very oppressive."

The word, spoken in her voice, sounds peculiar, powerful. "The summer feels like it will be so short. I'm afraid it will begin all over again next winter." She has named my own terror.

"Look, we can't live by the weather," I argue. But without a trace of conviction.

"We played for some people last night. They all drank too much and wanted to talk about the traffic instead of the music. When the chairman of the board handed me our check, a lady, beautiful old woman, leaned over and vomited in her lap. Fat man next to her, finishing a story, didn't pause or stop, just talked louder."

I try to explain the months I traveled around the country, a little crazy, seeing things. People going about their business, comfortably unaware they were sealed in. Trapped. "What was spooky was to discover their predicament, that it's the same as mine, but unconscious. What I envied in each of them was their appearance of being undisturbed because they hadn't discovered it. I was going crazy with what I saw."

"You were a little crazy last summer." This is how she puts it.

"I've been crazier since." Her eyes watching me, while I say that I think perhaps I had actually fought off madness, and won.

"Fine thing to do," she says. Is she putting me on?

We order another beer. And then, together, eat the steak I ordered, cutting it for her after she decides she's hungry, passing the pieces of meat across the table. "We did a lot of things wrong. We blew it." She nods. What a relief to say it finally and agree on it. That it was going to be so special, and we blew it.

Several times she admits she's glad she came, wants to meet again and see the farm. She knows how to hang wallpaper, can teach us. A demonstration of this, with all the paraphernalia of her humor, the charm of it as good as new. A certain unkillable hope starts up its engines again. But there is no hurry. Because I see her, Celia becomes human again. The hydraulic force of illusion dissipates, then rises again, what if she came back? No, fool, think beyond that.

I display the symptoms of my composure: I remember the time, I call for the check, I gather my things and stand up, ready to leave. When she emerges from the toilet I am checking an address at the phone booth. She sidles up next to me, poring over the directory.

"How do you spell it?"

"It's just a meeting, Celia."

"Let me have your number again, Ann threw it in the waste basket by mistake."

Outside on the street we are friendly but noncommittal, each telling the other to call. Suddenly we are holding each other in the middle of Sixth Avenue. Is it just a friend's bearhug good-bye, my hand feeling the flesh of her back under the shirt? Or an embrace, my mouth kissing the soft of her neck? Or only another instance of her splendid disregard for public opinion, having chosen the very center of the sidewalk? Then for a moment fallen through grace, all the good things it was come hurtling back and hang spinning there on the pavement in the summer evening, crowded into one point and fixed. The city's avenues line up at our sides, stretching away into time, turning on an axis.

When we broke, I'm sure she didn't look back either. But I blessed the top of a parking meter with my hand, feeling the air cool around my head as I walked down Bleecker Street.

Sidney said I was welcome: "The meeting is over at

Fosta's place but it doesn't start till eight. Come by first and have a drink; it's been a long time."

How to describe CR, consciousness raising, arcane sacrament of the women's movement, when the very term smacks of an evangelism faintly embarrassing to a lapsed Catholic and an art snob? I can tell you the emotions it engenders: fear and joy. Fear mostly, the fear of being judged by other women. And really, they ought to kick my tail, Funnyville electing me a leader; how much of it my own complicity? Perhaps my only safeguard against such defection is my personal terror of that consuming responsibility, my knowledge it could kill the artist in me. I have stayed away from this part of the movement too long, isolated from the democratic guts of things. And I know I am going now out of loneliness. Yesterday I came home to my friends in art, tonight I return to the movement. What will they say to me?

Sitting in the car with Sidney before we go up, discussing our strange lives, parked in front of a church. Sidney's model monogamy, gay version, is threatened now, Barbara spending part of herself on someone else. Claire.

"It has all hurt so much," Sidney extracts the words slowly, painfully. "You don't own people, so it wasn't that. It was as if the focus were lost. I no longer held all of Barbara's attention, I knew part of it was elsewhere. And that was hell. Nowadays it seems we've ceased to have private lives separate from politics, so the group all know. And they help; there's a great relief in other people. For someone alone, like Fumio, it must be harder."

I feel closer to Sidney than I've been in months, freed of the reproach of her once implacable optimism. We agree there are no rules to go by in this new life we live, making up our ethic as we go along. "But Sidney, I've still got a guilty skepticism that can't quit, won't quit. Are we trying to invent a new existence, whizzing through decades of social evolution in an afternoon? Or only joyriding? Do we mistake the emotions of pop music for a higher theory? Think of the puritan revolutionaries who disapprove of fun in bed. Or remember square definitions: my mother would call me an adultress. In the suburbs, they would call it 'swinging.'

"And if the only morality lies in not hurting others, then we still fail. Others are hurt. What freedom of ours can justify their suffering? It always comes to this, and I know that no freedom of mine justifies someone else's pain. When I offended straight sensibilities, even my own mother, by supporting Gay Liberation, I had the excuse that gay folk were in what I knew to be a greater misery. But in being gay myself don't I blow it, hurting Fumio, who says 'Do what you like,' but can never quite mean it."

Sidney nods, letting me go on:

"Yesterday, up at the farm, I went out to where the carpenters were fixing the roof with the radio blaring. A magic lady bounced right out of the box at me. The Poughkeepsie station congratulates itself on granting time to public opinion on social issues. Here she is, the little person, for the first time ever, asked her opinion. She's gonna tell you. With the same deluded vocalism of all those telephone talk-show callers I remember wrestling with in medialand. People so repressed they can neither make sense nor know when to shut up. In their whole neglected lives, this is their first chance to be listened to. And what they've got to say you don't wanna hear. Revolutionaries have to reckon with the fact that these are the people too. She's announcing over the air waves in this shaky emotion laden voice that Women's Liberation is ruining woman's precious femininity. She's still there, and baby, she's most people."

"Yeah, I suppose she is." Sidney shifts in her seat. Now I must tell her the real problem: "Look, if you can molest children, fuck monkeys or Coke bottles and get by with it, provided you keep your secret, you can also tell *Time* Magazine you're bixexual, be AC-DC in the international edition, and then go celibate. I did it for a while. Hung for a sheep and a lamb both in the same instant. But it may be unforgivable not to keep silence on the details. The problem is, I write, I even hope writing has some usefulness. What final purpose does evasion serve? Plenty of immediate ones of course, if the movement is a civil rights number about jobs and not a revoltuion in the entire way we live. All right, but then come on strong with ultraradical purism, and I really come off badly. 'Cause in every relationship I form I watch the familiar straight political games cropping up, like dockweed in the grass of friendship. So why do things badly? Why not quit? Go straight. Go dead."

Sidney looks puzzled, helpless. I must beg her for a sign:

"On the way over to your place tonight I passed a VW bus on Houston Street, a woman's voice yelling my name. I turned but didn't recognize the face: 'When'd you get back from London, Kate?' Eerie, people knowing me and I don't know them. Another stranger's head pokes out from the back door, laughing: 'Sisterhood is powerful, even lethal. It can kill—sisters mostly.' Ti-Grace's bitter old slogan. We grin at each other in the solidarity of disappointment. 'Take care of yourself,' she calls out. And they vanish around a corner. An apparition. Ominous maybe, but I feel a strange little elation: paranoia may not be the answer."

Sidney smiles and squeezes my arm: "We've been waiting for you a long time; we've missed you." I am reassured. Then afraid all over again when I enter the room. Will the rest of them chew me up in little phrases, recite the Line mercilessly, call me to book? This is a gay group: looking at them I condemn my imperfect faith, my apprehension they would look hunky dyke, grotesque with the queerness that has been my own bad breath for a lifetime. Though I know it is the others who have made us ugly, the knowledge has never furnished me relief. I have taken their squint of disapproval into my own eyes, fearful of mirrors since adolescence. Here are my doubles, so many pier glasses ranged around the room. And I like the look of them, am overcome by their welcome. It is not a trap. Paranoia speaks forth from the gut: wait till they know you better.

There is the usual earnest tedium about the purpose

of the group, soul searching by the younger ones, graduate students keeping us on course. Viki O'Flynn outlines the problem: How, without drowning in the swamps of group therapy, can this unit be of some help in our own lives, and since so many of us are activists, how can it furnish energy for the work we do in the movement? Ruth starts, describing the ordeal of holding DOB together, punished by every faction, letting her own book slide in overwork, exhausted by abuse, tired, discouraged. My hunted animal relaxes. Of course they understand. How stupid not to have gone to them before.

I unload my winter on them: Sister Kate in stardom, the whole number. "I read Gandhi all winter and fantasized some Mrs. Christ nonsense, thinking I'd go through it for the movement. Not waking till I felt the nails break skin. Then it was get out of here or go crazy. And to hell with responsibility. But you can't begin life in a convent and maintain that attitude. So it's a double bind; can't quit and can't stay in there either. All the while the movement is sending double signals: you absolutely must preach at our panel, star at our conference—implying, fink if you don't . . . and at the same time laying down a wonderfully uptight line about elitism. Why can't we stick by what we knew was right to start with—no bloody leaders?" Of course the whole world is convinced this is impracticable. They may even be right. But I agree with anti-elitism. Despite the countless sermons against elitism I've observed to come from dogmatic adolescents or envious females, each spinning in her own righteous circle, tripping on ambition, making herself famous in her own little pond for her superior insights.

Because I still remember the dark of those speechifying days, arriving in airports, met by some little knot of greeters selected by committee like the prize at a lottery. If it's the larval Rotarians of student government, then they just insult you in simple candor, asking how it feels to be an overnight sensation, a celebrity. Have you been doing the lecture circuit long? One hears the translation: "We've paid for your appearance here as a freak, we think it would be fun to know how long you've been growing stale in the carnival, and what it's really like to be a whore." I would like to slap their smug little faces and tell them I'm vomiting with terror. The prospect of being their evening's entertainment brings on a delirious need for booze throughout the day. But if I ask for a drink before dinner, they're sure I'm an alcoholic. It seems they often lose lecturers in bars, particularly authors. I escape their anxious attention (bought object: don't let it escape) for the ladies' room and a quick fantasy of jumping through the window to freedom.

If the radicals are chosen for the airport reception, methods differ: there's lots of sympathy, inside poop, followed by insidious putdown inferences, punitive examination questions. Either bunch greedy to suck you so dry before you talk that your voice may not quite be able to. For eight to sixteen hours they treat you to all the indignities of a performer, meeting after class after meal, all carefully arranged, ruthlessly scheduled so that you must talk, and are never permitted to listen or learn from them. Continuously registering how you're going over with them, what they find interesting, comprehensible, repetitious, looking their boredom when you are forced to answer the identical question seven consecutive times.

Then you come home to find everybody in New York invents scandalous legends while you're gone, and three purists have just put forth an edict on your treason. There is no one to talk to, since New Yorkers are so busy even friends require an appointment. And they find it unreasonable I should have a problem when their own books are really the issue, or the rent money, or tomorrow's rehearsal. What the hell do you mean calling up on this short notice? Of course it's unheard of to tell someone over the phone: "Look, I'm lonely, I have an idiot craving to be held." One never says it, knowing ahead of time the price will be five hours of scrutiny: How's she holding up? Or recriminations: "You're not going to treat me like a sex object. Why aren't you here when I want you?" "Because I was in Nebraska." "Well, I'm busy through Thursday."

Thursday I'll be in Indiana, talking on an empty stomach after some hideous little communal meal, a hot dish or a Kentucky Colonel devoured on someone's floor at the party got up especially in my honor, though no one speaks to me during the entire meal since I'm not a friend, just the visiting weirdie. All the time thinking, my God, we're doing this to each other, remembering other long-ago trips only last semester when I'd visit places as a sister, an organizer, a peer, staying up all night to laugh. Above the click of plastic spoons a voice still screaming within me: I was a teacher and you were my students; I am a woman in the movement and you were my sisters. Why have you made me a curiosity, a photograph, the letters of a name?

A lady at Wesleyan, over a picnic table and rum punch, informs me in a satisfied voice: "The media need a scapegoat right now, it's all so amusing, so useful for the movement." She fiddles with the diamond on her finger till it catches the sun. "And you're it," her laughter like a blow along the wind. Even beyond my fury I feel a humbler emotion, a desire to beg her to go on, imagine for a moment it might be an actual person she were addressing. But it's pointless: I am not even real to her.

I stop remembering and look around at the women in Fosta's room. The group has decided to give me special time at my first meeting. I go on to the worst part. "It was feeling a traitor to the movement, party to a shady deal, assenting while we cooperate with the System to create this fool of a leader we exploit full voltage while condemning the idea full volume. One is used and used up. Terrified to think it could happen that one might get hooked on the applause, the diversions of travel, the attention, and the snare of distraction—the worst drug of all. Airplanes are a great excuse not to work. All right, it's not work, it's a job. You do it for the movement, knowing it's wrong, but hoping that it builds the thing on campus now that the Grownups have been polarized into For and Against, media static having transformed most hope for change into garbled nonsense, faddish advertisements, television jokes.

"But month after month is buried under crosses on the calendar, the very future seems walled away. And always the sinking fear that it is time utterly wasted, the right wing scoring ahead in the apathy on young faces. While I grow shoddier in my own eyes, pacing the floor between trips, despising myself for not rewriting speeches out of laziness and the more depressing conviction that there's no point in it anyway: What is old, gray, dreary to me, is new to them, what they have to hear. While I go on, loathing the pompous lecture language, its cold abstraction the very antithesis of that vital hurt coming now, living it."

So I kvetch this out to the group, expecting accusations to fly, hell to break loose. Instead, they give me the joy of being understood, that wonderful euphoria of first meetings when a woman finds all her crazy irritations shared by others, her private grievances revealed as part of the social fabric. Ruth has had to give ninety-six speeches to my thirty. Most of us have worked in the movement a long time. We are a hopelessly elitist group, mostly writers, architects, students, artists on welfare.

We've grown very secular on the wine and are now a little drunk. By the time the others have finished their testimony we have developed a special *gemütlichkeit*, standing hugging, arms around each other, or sitting holding each other's hands, then dancing, yelling back and forth through the rooms, singing nonsense, the meeting passing beyond into another kind of communication.

Are we all enjoying it too much, making it too easy for ourselves? Their gratitude assuring me I did not hurt the movement by holding out for gay. "The boondocks are surviving the shock nicely. As to the leaderspeak follies, of course it's oppressive to everyone. Relax, Kate, the job's over. Welcome home."

Claire is here. Kissed her when I came in, seeing her for the first time since the ride back from Albany when our happy proximity ended in the promise of one long look at nightfall as the city shut down over us through the East Side's slum. She's here and I find myself wanting her. Which is not very political. How do you file Eros in the revolution?

Claire glows at me, magical, alive. But it is not radical to like blondes. Is there a taint in my desire? Is it her youth and beauty that attract me? Fosta's stout middle age has no such effect, finding myself embarrassed I cannot return her urge toward me. Should I? Fosta is thanking me for what I said at Albany, her heavy shoulder leaning on me is warmth itself. My absurd ritual prostitution fantasy recurs: Prove purity of motive by making it with young, old, ugly, gorgeous, indiscriminate. The pecking order is built upon looks, sight judgment, like a meat display in the supermarket. All wrong. Yet how to account for desire? It is no solution to take refuge in aesthetics and blather about art. Have I won the prettiest girl and the approval of the majority by coming over here and playing the martyred heroine? For I felt Claire's arm along the back of the couch encouraging me when I talked, the kindest event in the evening.

Later when I put the question, "How do you live with yourself when our theories don't work in practice?" she made a nice political observation by pointing out, "one egotist to another," that it was pride after all to tailspin this way over difficulties. Everyone laughed. "It's all right for the other people to fall short, but you've got to be perfect," O'Flynn smiled, grave and scholastic. " 'Cause you're so special." Exactly. Of course it's pride. But let me fall short the regulation number of times and when I'm judged will I get the usual handicap? Still childishly asking life to be fair.

Claire is offering to buy me a drink.

Going over the mail when I came home from London I found a cryptic note advising me she had a pair of socks I lost somehow at Albany, together with a beer in the fridge if I'd care to come by for either. The charm of such an invitation. But I did not answer it till this afternoon when I telephoned and no one answered. The next instant regretting I had done it at all in my purse-mouthed determination to stay out of any more beds, covered with shame each time my need relents with Vita, giving her nothing, finally, but my own jerked-off guilt. But after tonight's warm affirmation among peers, tolerant and fallible, gay too, why not come back to life, climb down off that perch, just admit I'd be delighted to accept?

Together outside on the street we become self-conscious. She looks shy, awkward. Her awkwardness is lovely. It is right somehow, honest. "Where shall we go?" I notice a bar restaurant sign down the way, pointing toward it. "There's a place right over there." She smiles. "That's the Inferno." Not until we are closer do I realize it's Paolo's. Odd how I always forget the location, often driving around for hours, searching through the labyrinth of repression.

Place of shame. One goes there to remember. In case the new life lets you forget. It takes but a second to locate each figure arrested in the same gesture as ten years before, the entire tableau frozen just as I dreaded it. Feeling safe, I fancy I look good hitting the door, with someone, swimming fast through the mob at the bar. But still nervous at being sized up, still not many inches away from all the wallflower nights in years-ago bars clinging in desperation to a fifty-cent beer.

All the last romantics crowded into one room. And do we look awful. The whole charm of the place lies in the fact that it shouldn't exist. Every thrill the forbidden has to offer. And I love them all. This shame is ours, our rebate, our ghetto of the heart. How logical of gay politics to put a priority on finding new places of assembly, weaning us from this tinseled fleur de mal. But something in me never wants to relinquish what took so many years hunting down. This emptiness I discovered: all I would ever receive in exchange.

Homosexuality was invented by a straight world dealing with its own bisexuality. But finding this difficult, and preferring not to admit it, it invented a pariah state, a leper colony for the incorrigible whose very existence, when tolerated openly, was admonition to all. We queers keep everyone straight as whores keep matrons virtuous. I have borne this label so long it is a victory to embrace it, a way of life accepted. For the kids and the converts this nostalgia over a sick subculture is merely gratuitous. Yet there are times I am angry they do not know the past, are free to forget what should never be forgotten. The few youngsters here seem like misfits, deficient in self-hatred; still beautiful, still women. But so are we. And herein lies my treason: I never wished to look the part. Once, passing was an effort to overcome ignorance or my own unconscious self-accusation. After eight years in the straight world, some clothes, a dash of self-respect, I'm damned if I'll ever again disfigure myself to fulfill some twisted notion of how a "pervert" should look.

Of them but not of them, I love and hate such places. For the bad whiskey, the police treatment, the supervision—we are put on line like children to go to the toilet. Protest, and the bouncers are there to throw you into the street; behind them stand the Mafia. For this you get to sit and drink, neck a little, even dance together like ordinary people do at decent prices all over town. To be together in public and imagine you belong to society, some kind of society, however covert. The solace of knowing you are no longer the only freak in the world.

The last time I was here with Naomi. In November, the day before *Time* "exposed" me. Already it seemed like a last fling. Dancing, we got carried away, and were very nearly thrown out. I insisted we leave in a huff, delighted to have cheated them of the cover charge. It all seemed so funny, a good story to tell my friends. Way back then, before the reckoning.

Claire agrees that the best thing about the place is the popcorn. We order some, eating it in a delirium all of our own, the place turning us on because we understand it, and because we are falling in love. I am learning her. Each new bit of information precious, giving me who she is. Carefully, I gather up the habits of her mind: her obsession with astronomy, her method of couching her references in jokes, calling it a nice day on planet earth or apologizing for an insatiable curiosity over Andromeda.

"I have a very satisfactory job, all I do is play with children. It's a preschool program. I have the afternoons to read. On lucky days I work on my book. But at the rate I'm going it will take me fifteen years. When I get all done, I'll call it *The Human Spirit* by C. Bookbinder." She is hilarious at her own absurdity. "No, better yet, I'll call it *The Human Spirit* by A. Young Woman."

There is something fine and remote in her love for children and other creatures, her insistence that dolphins have brains—"We ought to let them into the United Nations." An idealism so intense it has tactfully disguised itself as humor. I watch her, astonished to discover she is good as well as beautiful. Best of all she's funny. We have another drink, heady with the place. No longer garish, it is transformed with the loveliness of our desire. I feel her tongue in the palm of my hand, I kiss her neck, tasting the flesh soft and delicious in my mouth. This mean and ugly bar undergoes a metamorphosis, our desire reaches out its tendrils and spreads through it like a superimposition, colors bursting into its black and white. The jukebox dissolves into pale peonies in an ivory bowl.

My god, she has picked me. Forget the endless speculation into every motive, only be thankful to be picked. How much I would like to go with her now. But I promised Vita, am late already." Saying good-bye to Claire at Fifth Street: "You have to go home now," she says, meaning Fumio. "No, it was someone else I promised to see." Driving off choking for a moment at the idiocy of going to Vita when it was the dawn on Fifth Street I wanted. Yet somehow it doesn't matter now. The ease of letting go tonight makes it possible to be with Vita, finally. Nothing could be better.

I walk into the dark room hearing her speak to me from the bed: Did the meeting just break up? Now fancying a reproach in the question, I should have answered it, but I'm in her arms already now, my mind's mouth going down on her even before we kiss. What I have so long wanted to give, possible at last. And the acceptance pouring in. Self, woman, flesh.

Later I recall that the car is asmoke in the middle of the street, crippled by the usual radiator problems. We are both famished. So there is reason to venture out at five in the morning toward the 22¢ Chicken on the corner. Closed. We must go up to Seventieth Street, crawling with junkie and hustler, night peoole like us finding refuge in a hamburger stand. On the left are two blacks cock-sizing about their age and agility; behind us a cracker kid dressed midnight cowboy-like, all alone. Across the counter, the all-American white boy making big eyes for me. Jesus, not a reader, or a media freak! No, lots better, he's a letch. Stepping up to us on the pavement when we leave, standing his ground, shitproof: How would we like to go home with him and his buddy? We wouldn't. "Just tryin' to get laid," he says. The words wail down Eighth Avenue's canyon. Easiest thing in the world, yet utterly impossible. And by now he's had to forget any other form of contact that might have gone along with it, the first priority grown big as a building, doing a fine job of blocking off human beings altogether. Three guys hunting in the street sweep by us. One gooses Vita into a new perception of urban life's little indignities. We return from the battlefield, back to bed.

But her eyes are so tired in the dawn, I lose hope again. And wake in the usual anxiety I am probably still crazy and it is madness to write such a book.

Coming down. Out of the window a moon in the warm breathing sky. I lie in bed and watch it. Drove back. Didn't stay with Vita. Fumio seeing us off, waving from the Bowery window, his black head among avocado leaves, the white curtains blowing. So when we got to her place my gratitude to him made duty turn round and come home.

Coming back into the studio, seeing him asleep in the bed, the familiar tan paperback unread beside him on the blue of the quilt, the strange Japanese print. Endearing habit, always falling asleep when he reads. The sight of it brings an ache of tenderness. Do I wrong him whom I love so well? Hurting one in loving many. An agony to watch his head asleep in the pillow's crazy flowers, the terrible black sheen of his hair against their red, yellow, green. I touch the soft of his ear and his legs rub mine happily. But he's not waking.

I am. Waking under the moon and the night, each so alive. It had seemed too late to stop by Fifth Street to hear Claire's voice and see the crisp of her yellow hair. Now it is even later. Just lying in bed I can walk the warm streets a few blocks toward the east, climb the stinking staircase to her door. Or just as easily meet her for a drink downstairs at Hilly's. She has invited me for a sail off Staten Island. Lying here, I feel the wind, the sun cracking off the water.

The moon is still there. Straight up through the window, a haze lighting a cloud across its full corner. Pleasure occurs in and out of the mind, blowing through the city, running the grid of streets to the sea. Coming down from a flying day.

I see back into the afternoon. The light falling in splashes through the white oaks today at Wellesley. The sound of chairs folding after Commencement. Ceremony laid waste and heaped back into the red and white Avis trucks. Somehow this sight can squeeze six years at Columbia into one twilight on the last day of school, waiting in apprehension as the dome of Earl Hall expands to fill my office window with panic. I stand lost by a file cabinet crammed with useless stencils, leftover learning in the blurred sheaves of mimeographed verse undergraduates would never be troubled over again. My full envy hearing their voices below in the grass. Now in the gray light beyond the dome summer stretches in a crisis of emptiness: time without the kids. My shameful teacher's love each year deserted afresh by the youth it feeds upon, a fixed point in their flux, aging hungrier with each semester. A yearning for Columbia surprises me here at Wellesley, the College Walk suddenly superimposed on this other landscape. A quick glimpse of its gates, now shut to me, seen from a bus window weeks ago. Lose Columbia and gain what? Fired twice from Barnard, I am still reluctant to follow fickleness and take a job somewhere else.

Wellesley is beautiful in the afternoon, light falling in many greens through the trees. A valley of rhododendrons a hundred years old. This was JayCee's school. How peculiar that I should have been invited to speak at its graduation. The anomaly of my life now: one year's crashing change ago I stood in line for Columbia's diploma, that portentous thesis my graduation from the Bowery years' better obscurity.

JayCee, her presence all day reprimanding me as an interloper. There were her grounds, her classmates singing under lanterns, ringed round by torches set on stakes at last evening's upper-middle class ritual. Now walking past the tennis courts I suddenly recall, in some other player's golden skin and white cottons, the first man's body that I loved. Rick didn't get invitations to play on courts like these. South St. Paul he was, his old man a supervisor at Armour's packing plant. Even for us it was slumming when I took to practicing my signature as Mrs. Richard Grinell all over school notebooks. My aunt's money sending me to Oxford was to save me from being the mother of what by now must be his five children. Until the Milletts discovered JayCee, and a fate still worse.

Rick playing championship tennis, like a young god in his whites. A sensitive student with a bad complexion. He courted me with early Hemingway stories, Greek tragedies, cool jazz, impressionist prints. Giving me his treasures: we were two provincial kids groping their way toward Culture. One of his brothers was already working in the stockyard, but Jerry, the one who was a doctor, taught us opera.

At the university Rick got lonesome, missed the support of being a poet for the gang from South St. Paul High School, slobs who were what he loved most in the world, loved with the manly friendship of beer and auto engines. None of your queer stuff. All husbands now.

The other guys had trouble finding dates, so they hung around us, conferring on me the dubious privilege of being the only girl running in the pack, my ears curling to their talk of Getting Her To First Base, Making Her Go All The Way, Getting Your End In. How they needed it, despising the need, and the Dumb Broads who put out. Rick swearing that our own pawings about in the back seat parked on the river road in peril of a cop's flashlight were events never reported to the gang.

Lost at the university, Rick did the only thing he knew; he let them make a Marine out of him, Korean War bayonet lust bringing him home unrecognizable. A killer now, scared of everybody. Unable to breathe without his buddies. Returned to the university, closed to new friends, shut off even from learning. Mad at the women teachers. There were so few—how did he get two of them? My own great Marjorie Kauffman giving him a B. Rick wanted to strangle her, together with the lady math professor who failed to be impressed by his scientific ability.

Less joy than ever in our sex, ground out in cars. And one stolen time in bed while his folks were out of town. We were not friends: we did not talk to each other. And he refused to meet my friends, now that his own gang bored me. Just before Christmas he watched me getting drunk with JayCee, sitting on the floor of her apartment one night after the symphony. And guessed. Next day he came by and delivered his present, Handel's *Messiah*, one ski mitt extending the precious boxed album, hesitant in the front hall of Mother's house, his face pinched tight, his glasses steaming in the cold.

I broke the news that I had another date for New Year's Eve. His face registered the betrayal: "That settles it, it's over." But of course it wasn't that at all. Of course it was JayCee. He had felt it, smelled it out. When I hardly knew it yet myself. The other date was Thom. Who never learned until he came one soldier's furlough from Germany over to Oxford at the next Christmas, loaded with hams and brandy. We ended up drunk, reading John Donne's naughty poems, screwing on the sofa. JayCee slamming out of the house into the night. Thom left after the next morning's bleak interview: he would have to give me up since I was "like that."

These two boys discovering the monstrous, afraid even to give it a name. I saw Rick only one time again, passing each other in Follwell Hall between classes, his eyes open, blank, empty along the corridor. When I spoke he didn't answer. Even before the end of the semester he had left the university for the packing plant. For Thom it was the second cheat. There had been Becky Bradley, my big sister in Theta. And I had loved her too. Bringing myself to speak the words up in Megan Bridgewright's room at the Theta House, one evening after Washburn and I got particularly tight on a concoction we called "tennis shoes," and I smashed my hand in the door of her dad's old Cadillac. Sober now and prone in the heroic pain of seven stitches I confessed to an extraordinary emotion. Becky sitting on the bed across the room, prim in her Lanz dress, said, "Yes, but it is not a good idea." I had to agree. Such things couldn't be. We were sorority sisters; her folks lived in St. Paul.

She solved it by getting religion. Coming home to Minnesota after a year away at Mills, reciting the Lord's Prayer in a loud Seventh Day Adventist voice across from me in the Stadium Cafe. Her round face horribly transformed, madness revealing itself in a friend right there in the middle of a campus beer hall. The awful words of the prayer stunning the room's usual havoc to silence. Obscene here. Thunderous. I had never seen anyone I knew go crazy before. Remembering the despair I knew then, I despair again to recall the embarrassment I felt as well. Becky had found the wrong formula: this was more grievous socially than queers and fairies. Then, for a year or two keeping her in sight, a pinball joggled between gospel nuts and psychiatrists till she fell down the trap and disappeared.

Late sun-filled afternoon at Wellesley. I am now in JayCee's place. JayCee who initiated me in my senior year of college. Washington's Birthday, gray evening outside the crummy rooming house where she moved after leaving Leonard, the psychologist she married to go straight, rebelling against a Wasp family by marrying a Jew. Washington's Birthday. Landmark for a decade: day of my creation and my fall.

We had sat across the room from each other all afternoon, talking about Life while I imbibed the wisdom of her six years' seniority, wanting her, and frightened. I'd come over in the morning, driven Mother's car. JayCee hadn't got up yet, was wearing those ghastly yellow pajamas like Dr. Dentons which made me so profoundly uneasy. I had seen her nakedness changing into them, a week before, when that graudate student was there and stayed over. The two of them sending me home. Were they lovers? JayCee stood partly hidden by the closet door. I could still see her if I looked. I didn't want to look. I wanted to see her body as a sacrament the day she'd give it to me. So I could not profane her by looking when she was merely a woman changing clothes. She looked overweight, ordinary: it was not prayer.

There had been mystic times already. Confessing love to *Così fan tutte* before Christmas, and she nearly did it to me on the couch, bodies pressed together till I was all fever. She was married, and her husband came home at the end of the afternoon. Did he read my crime? Driving back to Mother's, the Mozart soared nearly choking me, ecstasy replayed a thousand times, fed upon through the dry weeks when I saw her only on Saturdays.

Once she let me kiss her, parked behind the library. I said it was awful. She said it was not awful at all, it had been a woman who had first taught her to love. A week later she called it off in a cafe lunch hour, saying the word: "I don't want a homosexual affair with you." My face went hot in shame. I haunted her, a lifetime's starvation in my beggar's need. JayCee was my obsession: notes, visits, the phone, borrowing Mother's car to go over to the university at odd hours. Mother's car; her Gordian knot. Mother's voice shouting harsh from downstairs as I reach the landing: "What on earth is

the matter with you—are you in love with this woman?"
I looked up and saw myself in the mirror, discovered.
The accusation convicted me already of madness, obscenity, the unspeakable. The word said aloud, the word
I used to whisper to my mirrored self when I was drunk
in college, getting drunk so I could do it. Standing in
the toilet in beer joints, mesmerized, asking the image
softly in dazed and fascinated horror, "Are you queer?"—
repeating my own name—"Are you queer?" Leaving the
secret there when I went back to the table, shaky lest
everyone see; all my friends who were normal.

Washington's Birthday, a hopeless dun-colored
afternoon, and at dusk she spoke to me, "Come here."
Telling me to do it. She sat there on the bed and said
it twice. The first time I couldn't believe it. Then I knew
I heard it, and I got up and walked there, passing the
neat little piles of flash cards prepared for Anglo-Saxon
class, the letters perfectly formed in her immaculate hand.
Went to her, and her arms opened, taking me trembling,
crying. Then laughing. I'd never come before in my life.
And couldn't yet understand why I was making for her
now whole puddles in the sheets. Crossed into the
unknown, the pure thrill of fear, the rhapsody of evil.
Daring, in my panic, to do the incredible, the risk of
it demanding all the courage of my life. And the mystery
finally revealed, as it never had been in those hot ugly
moments hurting from Rick.

Once she asked me had I ever made it with a guy,
the crude terms of the question making me wince though
I was proud I could say yes. I had some qualifications,
wasn't a virgin at least. But she called me a virgin in
her bed, seemed pleased that this should be my first time
with a woman. Will it show, that I don't even know how
it's done? Then in my ardor touching her. Playing a lover
to another human being the first glorious time. Finding
it didn't matter that I didn't know how: I could invent
it. When she went down on me I lay there appalled to
receive such honor. Shameful place, unworthy of her,
dirty. Trying to do it myself, later, in a frenzy of embarrassment, my face blushing as I forced my head along

her body in this unheard-of gesture. Awful it was, this
joy and terror, tenderness beating in my chest like a bird's
wings until I shook.

Hours later, still athirst. I would never have enough
of her for my insatiable need. At one in the morning we
went out so I could phone Mother from a hamburger
stand, lie to her, and say that I was staying at the Theta
House with Hilda, a respectable friend. And when I was
discovered, Mother's detective soul relentless, checking
out the story—I grew fierce, lying still to save my life,
knowing beforehand I was damned. It was not possible
to imagine any challenge to Mother's sense of sin. I knew
my depravity to be just that horror she suspected. Mother
made reality. Her definitions codified life itself. One could
not live outside them except as an outlaw. Henceforward
everyone will know, though deception's most scrupulous
care might be given to hide the monster.

But next day we met in poetry calss. Our eyes finding
each other's reaffirmed the miracle: it had happened. The
room, the other students, dull things with overshoes and
briefcases, vanish in the collusion of that look; we are
isolated as deities while Allen Tate's sonorous voice,
priestly, if a trifle affected, one full hour intones the *Rape
of the Lock*. Only we two hear the music of its lambent
eroticism, cognoscenti more subtle than our master, the
only persons in the world who comprehend.

Now there are two utterly different existences: the
real world, which is like Mother, the profs, my classmates—they will catch me—and the forbidden sensuality
I learn in JayCee's room making love, listening to Mozart, eating steak and artichokes. We cannot go out because we will be discovered. If one of us walks by herself on campus or in Dinkeytown among the bookstores
and the soda shops, she becomes invisible, merely an ordinary coed. But together we become something else,
recognizable by all, our bodies, clothes, walk, transformed
now, giving us away, stamped with the certainty of our
guilt, shouting our criminality. They will all see us; they
will all know.

The afternoon light falls through the trees at Wellesley

over JayCee's school and her people. Once she condescended to say I was fairly well brought up for someone Catholic Irish from St. Paul. It was the first time I'd heard the news: it had never occurred to us. JayCee came from the East to tell me we were not the chosen people. Saturday afternoon in her teaching assistant's office, I'd sit in the chair reserved for undergraduates. Scared, insulted, admiring (she had been to an Ivy League college and had already lived in her own apartment in Greenwich Village in New York City), sat there knowing that this was arrogant crap, what she said, yet still burning inside— if the Milletts had sent me away to school like they sent Elder to Mills, I could be as good as you are. Imagining once that all you did was pay admission. Until catalogs from the women's colleges, names famous and revered since childhood, warned me quietly from out of their brown wrappers that I didn't have the credentials, might not pass the College Aptitude Tests they never coached us for in convent prep. Turning the pages, conjuring on the magic syllables of Holyoke, I thirsted over the booklet's gushing prose and the photos of the elect in their cloisters. Once Elder showed me a pile of photographs from her magic college life. That afternoon I spread them all on the living room carpet, studied them for hours absorbing every nuance of those shining lives, their brief four years of flower past now. And wept for them because they were all dead, each spirit already flown, those beautiful young women who had passed me forever in their aura. By the end of summer it was finally obvious even to me that no one intended to send me away to college. There would be no world of my own peers perfectly sealed from banality; instead I would be stuck with Mother, and the "U," and the gray thereness of always.

Watching the tennis players dance as the sun filters through Wellesley's trees onto the big lawns, I try to sort out spite's deprivation and separate my provincial snobbery from the beauty of the place. The Wasp aesthetic: how difficult to concede they have one, since this is to concede their humanity, a fact which radical presumption

is allowed, perhaps even obliged, to ignore. Eastern
seaboard summers, boating sneakers, Nantucket Island,
and the very taste of blond and privileged pleasure, sharp
as when you lick the salt from your arm after spending
an hour under the first sun of June. Racquets and
sailboats and clubs, always the sun children blond and
easy, their voices casual and empty, since content is not
a fixed requirement; manner carries all in merely replacing
it. So hate them then, become ensnared in a fervor of
denouncing them; are you not guilty still of the yen to
belong, to be a member, not merely a visitor condescended to with reverence? Envy may always be vin-
dicated in that inevitable moment when their glow turns
cold and shallow, their best intentions fade, and they
simply remind you you're not quite right, not really their
kind. Celia.

The night before, arriving at Wellesley, we found no
one there. I was furious they would not meet us, feed
us, bother with a greeting. During our sweaty walk into
the village to buy whiskey my class hatred cursed their
cake-eater hospitality, monotonously referring to them
under the rubric of "these people," grinding Vita's nose
in her own Wasphood. But she fails to crack under this.
And it seems gratuitous, merely further revenge on Celia
Tyburn, nothing but pointless bullying, since Vita doesn't
even look Anglo-Saxon. Perhaps a mick or some other
minority loser, tall and redheaded and in exile.

An attendant finally taking notice of us blandly
recommends we forage in the grass: there's a picnic in
progress somewhere. The grounds are huge, we trek along
dead tired, lost on circuitous paths, unable to find the
tent. Vita is patience silently reminding me I am a noisy
ill-tempered bitch. When at last we stumble into the
alumnae dinner we are fixed by the gimlet eyes of elderly
ladies sitting correctly before the remains of turkey and
gravy on paper plates. The feast is already over. We are
too late. I want a drink. They stare: the cocktails were
earlier, and it is doubtful even if there are any more
dinners left. We are causing a stir of unwelcome attention.
If there were just the prospect of a decent meal they could

cheerfully ignore us. But now they are fussing. I am ashamed at my petulance. Mrs. McKnight is going to take us to a restaurant. She attends to the less important visitors. I am a more important visitor she says, so I am not actually her department really but Mrs. White's. I have fallen to her through default. She is a comfortable middle-aged Scotswoman with a sense of humor.

Over dinner she describes how she once contemplated the murder of her husband; dead drunk after a Harvard reunion he insisted on walking home alone since he was in no mood to tolerate her driving. He strides along ahead of the car so she cannot even drive off and leave him in the lurch. "Should I run him down or not?" telling the story with exquisite ladylike charm. Then she turns to Vita and together they dissect their class's snobbery. Vita attended the right dancing class, the one that still excludes the Irish. I dare to ask why. "Because you cannot be too careful." Vita becomes a deeper mystery. Really then she is Brahmin, hiding the fact under those dreadful clothes, and the penthouse no one ever repairs, that beautiful old place masquerading as a slum.

When we return to where we are billeted, a soulless modern error indistinguishable from a motel, I am avoiding her again. I want to sleep. It is so false being here, letting Vita come with me. All day she has been introducing herself as my secretary. I don't want to have a secretary, keep trying to introduce her as my friend. Why did I let all this happen? Vita all week on the phone from New York giving trivia dimension, "What size mortarboard do you wear?" her voice patient as with a fractious child if I refer to the cost of long distance or the fact that I'm trying to write. I did not want her to come with me, but she has received her own invitation from the treasurer, an old friend. She desires it so fervently, has labored so over the arrangements that they are a maze of complexity. I will need her help; she has promised to give me the confidence I need since I do not like my speech, hated composing it, forced back into the old abstract language—don't want to write that way any more—staring at the beautiful last afternoon light

through the farmhouse doors, its refuge wasted because
I am not doing what I want to, the dread of public places
flooding back again, the academic world accusing me
for my defection. If I have to go to these places, women's
colleges, and particularly this kind, the sacred groves
of the seven elite sisters, I am vulnerable enough among
them so that I should go alone.

Actually, they are being rather decent to let me come
back for a day, a public Lesbian, and they must know
it. It is a sin against their hospitality to arrive with Vita
parading as my secretary. It is phony. Her obsequious
perfect helper routine—look I can get that spot off your
dress—only compounds my crime. How do I get out of
this mess? I will never live through that speech tomorrow.
Vita faithfully swearing I will, keeping me up later and
later to apologize for the deficiencies of my desire, the
two of us insanely pursuing the source of my frigidity.
Since of course it's my fault, we must discover what
neurosis turns me off. I must confess the corruption of
my inclination. Suspicion points toward Claire. Shouldn't
I love all women, regardless of what they look like, aged,
fat, whatever? And you look wonderful sometimes, Vita,
so happy when unobserved, laughing with someone. This
conversation is a nightmare, but I must know why I find
Claire, for example, so attractive; is it only for her
beauty, perceiving that I am hopelessly shallow. Then
Vita says it is vivacity, joy, energy—revealing it to me
through the words. It is such relief that I go to her,
listening while she explains this has been killed in her,
how she had it once before all the married years, fifteen
of them, but this marriage crushed something in her. "You
must recover yourself, when you were still you, not theirs.
How far back can you remember?" I ask. "When I was
sixteen." "Then go back to then, and begin again."

Vita asleep in my arms while I contemplate her
prospects. Fred takes the kids all the time now. She is
getting free. Her face will not look so tired. She will grow
up, escape from the willful child in her. In England I
asked Nell where Vita could learn film, and she recommended Joe Kaplan. I relayed the message to Vita and

already she has started. The work she did on my film was a beginning. Joe cannot pay her anything but she has the little salary I give her. When she has finished her apprenticeship with Joe she will have a way of earning a living, become independent, find jobs. Then she will have herself. It will work out for her.

Once more seeing the light pour through the trees of this place, remembering this afternoon with an uneasy satisfaction. The speech went well: Vita must have helped me. In the morning reassuring me while I fiddle, running through the thing beforehand, waiting for the terrible moment, Vita glowing at me, her heroine. Of course it is foolish, but I am faint when the procession starts, the local high school band attempting to sound baroque and stately. And the occasion, the robes, the horns. What could they possibly mean, having me here? I should be suspicious of acceptance, yet am grateful for the faculty's tolerance of my unremarkable text, the kids' charming affection, rows of them beaming at me, having made me some curious symbol in their heads. Hard, so hard not to love them; our future. The bright faces above their black gowns brush by me two by two: change will sweep them to a further point than we will ever reach. Or will they end up dead and brittle like the alumna lady prattling about her "offspring," as she calls them, who attend the fancy horse-jumping academies pictured in the ads of the *New York Times* educational supplement, one of those dead women I met the night before, women mortared into their husbands' positions, nubile young women suddenly ossified and chipped into place by this type of college, so often nothing but a quarry for the graying edifice of class.

I succeeded far too well today and am frightened they approved of me, distressed that the trustees didn't dislike me enough. Over lunch arguing with one about American medicine, a distinguished physician who must be finding me tiresome while I describe emergency cases screaming at St. Vincent's, blacks and Puerto Ricans with stab wounds. And not enough doctors, so they must wait for hours. Or watching a man die on the Bowery because the ambulance is held up in traffic, actually watching the light go out of his eyes as he bleeds propped up against the wall before my house. How strange to be landed here today, amidst these lawns' somnolent privilege, liking them and then appalled at the idea, ashamed I had a good time, lionized, the women so kind to me.

Captive in the limousine behind the college chauffeur, I asked him to stop the car so I could jump a fence and examine a cheap convertible with a For Sale sign on its window, squatting in the dirt bargaining with the seller even though I am on the way to an airport and cannot possibly buy a car, am only shopping. Then cooped up in the hearse again riding through the landscape of wealth, its slow shady roads, its systematic gardening, its expensive quiet privacy. I experience the same fantasy I had once on my way to Bryn Mawr, the fantasy that the rich are merely uneducated: if you just told these people how things really are, they'd change. If they could be made suddenly to understand that most people, who after all are not living in upper suburbia, and are therefore unaware of the tight-assed limitations of its aesthetic, have in fact been hankering for years after these very yards and their domestic architecture. Imagining they would instantly come to, explain they simply hadn't been informed, had never guessed that the blacks felt this way or that the poor are pinched and envious. Ridiculous. Of course they know. That is why they invite radicals to speak at Commencement, to lend a veneer of good faith to their grasp on power, the world of privilege it would never seriously occur to them to relinquish.

Now the moon shines and I think of Vita. As each mile freed us of the place my desire put forth its leaves, wilted by the presence of the old world servant driver, then thwarted again by an argument on the plane about why I keep feeling married to Vita when she insists it's all my imagination. I explain my fears of being married, inquiring if somehow unconsciously she might be playing wife. No, she is sure she isn't. After all, she sleeps with Claudia too, another lover she acquired while I was in England. Vita accuses Claudia of constantly "disappearing" on her. So neither of us is equal to the task of her need. Vita had composed a poem in which she feels she is caught in a whirlpool. Claudia and I, charged with the responsibility of keeping her aloft, are found derelict in our duty. Vita becomes my mother, a woman scorned, disappointed, leveling reproaches.

Then we both stop quarreling and share a rare good moment over a martini. It would be better if I told her everything. Which means I must confess to wanting Claire in order to receive absolution. Vita says that's just fine; she is not interested in monogamy, has ceased to be a wife months ago. She reads her magazine. I continue to wonder why she can't stop seeming like a wife. Surely I am wrong not to love her, constantly irritated by the way she makes herself look; does anyone actually require the calculated tackiness of bright red anklets? And the way she moves, so wrong in each limb. Hating her so at times, then telling myself she is like me; when I despise her it is only myself I condemn. I must accept her completely. Soon I will like her enough. I will improve, stop being so demanding, snobbish, perverse. Or she will change, relax, learn to dance, stop moving in that elephantine whirl, loudly announcing her joy, ignoring the music.

We sit back and relish our martinis. Vita looks down on her birthplace, Newport, green below us. She points out some hill, jumping up and down in her seat, an ominous child. There is something monstrous in a grown woman still acting like an eight-year-old. I look at the hill trying to enter into her rapture, seeing Newport. With a twinge of guilt I remember Claire's Boston too, noticing that Vita has no trace of an accent, murdered it long ago, whereas Claire's is still comically broad, a delight to her.

The moon in focus through the casements, spreading its kind light on the old New York bricks. Life is just young and good enough tonight to make it nearly a matter of indifference if one goes out or stays. Free of greed at last I can relive a hundred nights' strain after adventure, like a party missed in childhood, scrabbling need and never enough love. But all the perquisite questions hang still in the air: am I not a great romantic never-grow-up fool who, because more than one soul's body is willing to sleep with it, imagines Casanova? Deprived so long, how not to fall into every puddle? And how does one construct a decent present using the warped lumber of past experience? Do we bring neurosis to friendship and save pathology for sex?

But the moon inspires one to hope. I will go to Vita, my desire uncovered at last, great as I had wished it to be. And lady you deserve no less, though desert has ever the effect of saltpeter. Assuring myself this is not obligatory—I really want to go there. Putting on sandals, standing in the dressing room, feeling free, unmarried, with adulthood's privileges of coming and going when one likes. Yes, I'll go. Outside there are no police to stop me, the car swimming crosstown. One is finally prevented only by those forces one permits to crowd the mind.

I say her name, opening the door, afraid. I left her only an hour ago. Will she be with Fred? Will Claudia be there? In the dark I know there is someone. Embarrassed, amused, perhaps a trifle impressed. It is Lily, staying with them since she became a runaway wife. Vita announced importantly to Fred that Lily would be seeking "sanctuary" over the weekend. Does she imagine her home is a church? Lily is sick tonight; Vita is ministering. Curious healing, they are both naked. Lily rustles past me in the dark. I feel silly but rather flattered to be given precedence. One moment's wonderful mortification, then it is merely funny, a trifle awkward.

That Vita lets me into her arms is miracle. So fierce for her, proud even to have arrived at last, her lover. Self-consciousness and anxiety are swept away with the brush of her flesh, my hand on her shoulder, the fingertips finally appreciative, able to concentrate. I will succeed. But the ghost I see in orgasm is only myself in the great white dress of fear I wore today, getting through a speech because she helped me. My Aztec princess getup, an apotheosis of colors, swirling in a kind of glory in the sun, transformed through the intensity of her admiration and my own vanity. I lie back washed up in nausea against my damned and ubiquitous self. Like an iceberg, the chunks of its need melting ought to make possible some estimate of its outrageous size. And now it has bedeviled me in a vision. I recall one of O'Flynn's cynical remarks that the lover as revolutionary gives generously out of an excess of self-love. Preserve the lowest possible estimate of things, it's simpler. I will be cynical and cancel my words to her in the dark: "I love you," meaning it. Cancel too her voice coming back: "Sure, I know you do."

It's just been graphically proven to me that I cannot love Vita. Yet. Will it ever get better? Progress slow enough to justify any cheap despair. Smoking afterwards in the dark we exchange childhoods: the special ennui of the schools she went to, the boy in the class ahead of her who committed suicide, the cult of sailing from which she was excluded, relegated to tend the roses that were thoughtfully included in the curriculum to impart a communion with nature. I realize with fascinated horror how little Vita has ever told me about herself. Nor have I ever talked to her, trying now to give myself to her, taking her back to where I came from, the convent prep where, unconscious it was against the rules, I had at thirteen fallen histrionically in love with a classmate named Nancy Kelly. We announced our miracle to the seniors. They laughed at us. We became ridiculous. Hearing one of our telephone raptures, Elder's boyfriend warned Mother I was diseased. Finding it more difficult to take this seriously than to simply ignore it, Mother was willing to dismiss it as adolescent crush. Midyear my aunt took me out of school for a trip South to cool off. And the next summer I was sent to camp with Cousin Colleen. Devices no one probably ever recognized.

Meanwhile the convent's ripe eroticism: the thrills of apostasy and reconversion, nuns taking communion with veils lowered, the privilege of the Scola, the early masses singing plainsong infatuated with the Virgin and the saints or the sound of the novices singing the requiem for a nun. Endlessly in love with a teacher, or a senior, or all the seniors at once, remote superior beings in white gowns with peroxided hair. And through four rapturous adolescent years somehow faithful to Nancy Kelly, the entire thing erupting again on a new plane of danger in senior year. And a few days after graduation Mother left me in charge of the house. Poised at the pinnacle of freedom to give parties and drive her car, Nancy staying with me, lying in the parental bed open to the balcony's perfect June air, the outline of geraniums at the window box in the dark. We might have made love that night. But when she touched me, I felt horror. Mumbled some rigid thing about impurity. Sin.

All through senior year kissing in furtive ecstasy, embracing behind the wheel of a car on the darkest side streets. I can still see the stripe of her blouse, feel its ironed freshness along her arms. I will always have this. Even touched her breasts, not knowing if it was reality or the gentle rubber with which she improved her figure. Nancy was the most popular girl in our class. Each morning during Religion she whispered the names of the boys who had phoned the night before. I listened in a daze of uncertainty as to whether I were merely another conquest or an event of a higher order. Lesser members of the clique snitched our notes, gave them to the homeroom nun and demanded justice before the whole class. We became a scandal. Earnest to model ourselves after books and enjoy the immunity of art, we read up on Achilles and Patroclus, Jonathan and David.

We had both parked with boys in cars. For me it was tedium varied with crude excitement, a friction never satisfied: fear and the convent's interdiction fell between. Sin was a live thing in the stomach. Protestant kids had petting and French kisses, we had mortal sins: Going All The Way meant hell, loss of virginity an irretrievable fall, original and terminal sin. More experimental, Nancy might have actually arrived at this crisis with her steady. As best friend, my role required that I pander to their love, contriving that they meet by stealth in Mother's garage or back yard, safe from her folks and his military school.

Now, in Mother's bed, her hand finding me, tentative upon the dark triangle of my legs' fork. Desire so fresh it is sharp as needles, hurting even. It is all so new, forbidden almost beyond the shade of thought, yet familiar as one's basest acts. Surely this is the very essence of evil. And I cannot do it. After four years of wanting this, wanting it even when I did not know what it was. But I cannot do it. Everything stops during the moment of my treason. My hand taking her hand away. In one movement betraying her past any forgiveness.

That summer we had jobs together filing insurance records in metal cabinets, slaves to an infinity of dull yellow folders. At work the next morning, hoping she would contradict me, argue for it, persuade me, I mimicked the voices of our spiritual masters in a tight and smutty whisper, saying I had never guessed she was capable of "something vile like that." She only looked at me. Probably the last time she ever looked at me. If I live to be old, I shall never forgive myself for that statement. Next year I hung about her nursing school, lovesick as ever, and wiser. But she was already beyond my reach.

In the morning Fred is feeding the kids, their bodies naked, happy, eating griddle cakes. He dishes some out for us, the three of us breakfasting together way at the top of the penthuse in its scaggle of a garden, our table a weathered timber spool ripped off Con Edison. I sit across from them, observing the two together, Vita and the man she lives with, once her husband, now her friend, feeling contentment in their gentleness with each other. How peculiar we are, transitional people generous toward each other with a special understanding. Fred is patriarchal in his big beard, his shirt off, while we tease him about the pallor of his slender arms. We sit lazily watching the three kids play on the fire escape, inventing a drama of their own. Vita tells the story of my arrival in the middle of the night to find Lily with her. We laugh over the moral: Never make use of a key without telephoning first. The kids are uproarious two stories below us—Fred fills my cup. It is melancholy to think of leaving this airy sun-filled eagle's nest, the early morning laze of coffee drinking, stretching in the comfort of it, like a summer spread out in the ease of slow talk where there is so much to say that we do it without words—in smiles, or by passing the sugar. I ought to go home and pack, but the day is too perfect for anything but speculation.

At the Bowery Fumio is gathering up the tools for his new studio. I fiddle with a lampshade that should have been repapered months ago. We are both in a distracted mood. I begin to write downstairs at the maple table, reembering last night's moon on paper. Fumio walks by, wondering what to do with the afternoon, surely too inviting for work. Sensing each other's truancy, we consider the possibilities: today is Sunday, Celia plays a concert this afternoon at the Cloisters. Why not go and hear it, live rather than write?

Not writing it until three in the afternoon the next Sunday at the farm, beginning just at the stroke of three, choosing the same moment in competition, wanting, forever wanting to make music as others can, a monotone burning to sing, going silent in envy's self-belittlement. That time and this time. Then it was their music; and now in another place, I set to the task of making the sound strong, building it in words during the time's single and unique hour from three to four on a Sunday afternoon. While deception fiddles with its watch, resetting by ten minutes, cheating in my chicken coop, sitting down to croak over a battered table. Looking out upon green golden trees, a pond, and the one bird always on a reed, steady, standing there.

With words turning time back, making this Sunday the one before, today's own concert beginning miles away now unheard, transformed into its predecessor as Fumio telephones to confirm the time, warned by that catastrophe a year ago when a museum official misled us on the telephone, told us it began at four, when of course it was three. And when we got there it was over. My hand striking the stone wall in rage before the guard's malign satisfaction at having thwarted pleasure, prevented adoration, his face looking on astonished at its success. A year ago, when the whole world was lost in one hour's music.

It will be different today. Up the West Side Highway along the Hudson to where the Cloisters' tower peaks above the trees. Playing music there each Sunday last June, Celia had in her arbitrary fancy renamed the place, calling the small red-tiled lip that tops the furry branches a clitoris. "It's not cloistered any more, we've liberated the joint," she chuckled. The cap of tiles and the old masonry emerge softly above the foliage as the road turns. It is the road you take upstate to the farm; I see the landmark now and remember her boast as I have remembered it a hundred times, wincing at how mood, like moment, perishes. But today there is hardly a trace of pain for the year intervening. Yet I am still impatient going up the drive, fuming while we wait for some unhurried moron to relinquish a parking place. We are already a few moments late. I brush a white cotton leg against a greasy fender, losing the elegance I had preened in hope, ruined in a dirty knee. Then almost philosophic when we find the chapel full, the music already begun.

Miriam is there. We had not expected her. They are singing the very songs we missed that day a year ago. But there are also numbers from the next concert, the one we did get to on time the following Sunday, recording it with a small machine from where we sat upon the floor. A tape I fed upon the summer through, my portable joy, playing it once for friends up at Columbia when I brought roses for them from Connecticut. Another time hearing it stoned at sunrise with some of the movie company. Portable joy to carry anywhere until it sickened strangely with autumn and the love gone bad, a cassette broken upon a shelf somewhere.

These two singers had been a paradise to us, my own folly beckoning Fumio on. Then lost, the cancer beginning in August, spoiling on through the fall and the winter's madness. This Sunday then is also that other, a year ago, floating again within that sound, the glory their voices made with lute and viol as we leaned against the chapel's cool reverberating stone, made one with the elect by friendship with such magical persons. Aware even how the harmony of their music, their distinctive art, is the child of their own long love. I watch from my corner by the door, incredulous to find them playing there upon the altar once more. Returned to me now behind the busy heads of onlookers. Time, turning cycle, grasped and held again, it is not lost. That day, and this one too.

Writing it, still another Sunday, at the farm seven days later in my chicken coop looking out over the pond. They are playing again now in the stone chapel. Just three o'clock and the music is beginning, swelling to fill the stone walls again. Then this Sunday becomes last Sunday. I see Miriam and am surprised again and afraid for Fumio, who loved her. And then once more, it is that day last year of Celia's triumph—she had just made Musique Ancienne, her friends filling the place with bravos. But today only a routine museum mob, indifferent, noisy. They block the entrance and we must stand outside the door, unable to hear. Then a few of them leave, making an opening. I crawl through to sit on the stone floor near the altar. Fumio must be behind me. They see us. Smiles and nods, greetings lip-read. We are special listeners whose straining and perfect attention will focus the rustle of shoe-grinding commoners, still their coughs, silence their chair scrapings. I look on amused while a hippie kid sprawls, touseled head upon his lady's lap, a page boy in the court of today. But he is spotted by the pension-holding guard, fringe-benefit Irish, coming in great boots to arrest the concert midnote and reprimand. Wonderful, Celia's consummate patience while she waits upon this fool's interruption. My own error was never so forgiven. But a year has passed her too since that quarrel.

I turn to find Fumio gone. Missed beyond the heads in the doorway, I cannot see him. I must listen alone this time. And will they play for me? Seeing their two heads again cut fine as cameo against the old yellow stone, the chapel wall before me pirated block by block from France. Celia's profile bending in grace against its mellow color, tracing the line of her face above the lute, a Madonna intent upon her curious wooden treasure. I hang upon the fall of her gown, its brown velvet draped over a foot so exquisite in its sandal yet so firm upon the block where it rests to help her cradle the lute.

I look across the pond now as my mind's eye drinks that moment in color—and matches it against the black and white a Pentax saw, saw and held last summer at Brookfield as the sun fell in scatters through sycamore leaves. Celia, her hair uncombed after breakfast, played the lute for us in the open air. Now only these portraits remain: my mind's version in motion and sound, and the still shot upon paper. Celia bending then upon her lute, playing it in sunlight one fine morning our summer of delight, her straight hair merely braided, not dressed as now in five choirs upon her head for concert. A figure outlined against a white New England wall, wearing the yellow jersey that with the true cheekiness of an aristocrat she never seemed to change, and a pair of faded jeans I bought her on the Bowery. Celia a profile leaning over the great pear-shaped lute. Strange instrument, only its face showing in the photo, its back hidden against her body, the wonderfully carved facets of polished wood fileted together in perfect laminations, the very shape of craft and song. Examining again her tomboy succulence that Connecticut June day, the extravagant delicacy of her face, something even of her eyes' fine beauty captured one forever time ago to pierce me now as they did that muddled September night I scrawled on yellow paper, cursing her good-bye. Eyes like a light through the tunnel of loss. And now the music rises, sound in air expanding as the lyrics come crisp and Elizabethan—"Every bush new springing." The lute speaks, then their two different soprano voices in low and lovely measure, threading each other in air, superior art of song defeating mere prose in its finer medium. Time, and again in time recurring.

Sound once lost in space, now miraculously reassembled here within the same stones' echoes as it echoes in the mind while I sit here before a table bending time to will, the music heard into being again, this moment erasing the bird's chatter about the pond a hundred miles upriver from where the sound now echoes to their miracle performed. Really performed, as I merely conjure the distance of time and place at my own far remove from where the music now draws to its close unheard. Because, Celia, today I did not go to hear you but stayed behind to scrape in simultaneous emulation. And here late afternoon light falls upon the pond and the one bird silent upon its reed. While there, inside the stone room you stand and bow. The audience rises, I rise with them. Applause breaks for your lighter, purer, more amorous form, echoing still. Lost, then found again; watching in an ecstasy as you pass near me.

Fumio appears, kissing Miriam. I look on, happy to see the grace in his slender figure, his face sundark above the stripes of his shirt, his feet in sandals. Is she a stone she cannot see his beauty? Refusing him always though he loves her. Then the music people flock around and we are excluded, outsiders who are not of their world. Driving home down Broadway past black kids opening hydrants. In this contained version of class warfare they are particularly delighted to fire upon a convertible. Within the instant when the water hits I see again that arm preternaturally beautiful as it swept the lute. The same hand strummed me once. And I can feel, even now when it is lost, some solace in the knowledge that this happened once within the time of my life.

Fumio remembers we have no food at home. Shall we eat out? Shall we dig up a friend? I suggest we pick up Vita. Or Claire Bookbinder. Realizing after I've said it that both are lovers as well as friends. How about Lila and Renos instead? "Out of town," Fumio objects. "Who then?" "Whoever you'd like," he says. I'd like to see Claire. She lives right near here, perched between Puerto Ricans and the Hell's Angels in a tenement crammed with peaceniks who have painted the word LOVE across their brickfront, a beacon in the middle of chaos. I wonder if I should call first. But there are no phones and we are here already.

I ring and she answers. Then up the urine-soaked stairs of last week. We made love then, for the first time. Scared, shy, both of us so frightened I can remember nothing of it, have ceased to believe it ever happened. She cooked a steak for me, both of us forgetting it until it resembled old tree bark. Will the door open again upon that classical Lower East Side pad? Is she still there behind the crazy mottoes she has pinned on the door, Tiny Tim blessing us one and all in Camp right next to the police lock? And on the walls, in photograph, all her saints: Gandhi, Casals, a complete and progressive self-portrait of Van Gogh. Fifteen in the series; with and without the ear. The place crammed with books. All her bibles: Tolstoi, Piaget, Unamuno. And her magic astral paraphernalia of moon journeys, telescopes, the stars ubiquitous in Ektachrome. Even in the toilet. Floor to ceiling she has transformed the walls, papered them with her philosophers, her galaxies, her ideals. She smiles while I apologize for being "spontaneous," neglecting to call first. "We drove past and wanted to have dinner with you." "I approve of spontaneity, one of the few tolerable things in a dull and all too frequently vicious existence," she answers in that defensive abstraction which is her specialty. Again I wonder who she is; hearing the outrageous Boston accent I cling to the hope she might be Boston Irish after all, and forget the Saxon look. My eyes survey her place again, two rooms with ivy on the windows, the bathtub in the kitchen. She lives here writing some crazy book intended to connect the universe with two drunks loafing on the steps of Trinity Church, while the other lone survivor of the planet is the junkie squatting in the building across Fifth Street. Bookie. I marvel at how the two cramped little rooms have become the picture of her soul, its clean simplicity of table, chair, bed, and five hangers. She has had supper already but will go with us while we eat. Only to be with her again is a delight, to follow the chops of golden hair flying about her head, to feel the elated vitality of her humor. We go down the stairs to join Fumio, the three of us sitting in the front with the top down. She takes one look and defines my folly: "Some sort of teen-ager's car. Except that no self-respecting kid would be caught dead in it unless the radio worked. Get it fixed." How delighted I am with her put-down.

We can drink before dinner for free if we stop off at the Bowery, sitting in the day's last light from transom and casement, the talk beginning in the trivia of what kind of car I ought to buy. Both of them tease me for persevering with my exhausted treasure. And then they hit upon their own subject, the pair of them exclaiming over whales, Fumio elaborating on his love for Moby Dick. "First time I slept with Kate I felt like a sardine," he chirps, "so I called her my whale. But she didn't understand my compliment." Claire dazzles us with erudite accounts of whale language and brain size. Fumio responds with something he has read about the scope of their genitals. We remind him that the reader defines himself by what he remembers.

Mellowing high, Fumio grows delightfully incoherent, jumping topics like a Zen acrobat. The two of them like each other. We are all happy with the power this studio has to hold off the world in its insulated euphoria, Fumio's sculpture hanging airy and contemplative against the ceiling a mere thirty feet from the horrors of the Bowery. We discuss time in writing. Claire rolls out her hobbyhorses, wishing to fix our attention upon the galaxies, announcing that time is either distance or intimacy. I protest I do not have the comfort of the stars, merely a few details and a camera eye. So it worries me when she denigrates photographers like Updike. "There's panning, and then there's cinematography," I quibble, defending my turf. "But Proust's cookie made him remember, whereas I appear to be stuck at the level of mere reminiscence." "Everything's cyclical," she assures me, "*again* is not such a bad word."

Several drinks into things. I launch into my favorite nonsense: the room you see when you read a book. Henry

James's fireplaces, for example. I have unearthed them after the lengthy investigation it surprises me that no one else bothers to undertake. Felt the excitement of being on the other side of the blueprint discovering I used a certain old house in St. Paul as the site of Osmond's fatal interview with Isabelle in *Portrait of a Lady*. Then found I had chosen a physical setup actually inaccurate (the fireplace was to the right in Maudie St. John's house, to the left in James—or vice versa, I can't remember now). But what I was pursuing in his pages—and tracked down only when I compared his description against the visual memory I supplied—was in fact an early trauma that matched the emotional atmosphere of his scene, a visit to this great house one night with my aunt after the symphony: I was given champagne and spilled it on the floor.

Similarly, I taught Kafka's bug nine times until I realized Gregor's bedroom was my own rose-wallpapered child hell. Then I had to quit. Since Gregor's hideous nuclear family occupied an apartment, his floor plan was all on one level; the dining room and the forbidden yet edible apple were actually next door to him. It had taken me years to realize that since our dining room was down on the first floor, my parallel setting here was not a dining room at all but the parental bedroom. Intolerable inaccuracy, correct beyond endurance. And I am mystified that no critic pursues the topic, no reader ever checks out his rooms. "Don't people see pictures when they read? How could they fail to compare their own spatial reference against the book's, notice the discrepancies, and then follow the clue to the room they have supplied in place of the author's, and pursuing the motives of their choice, discover themselves?"

While I wonder on in this manner, the two of them have enthusiastically reembraced the whale, Fumio creating a Japanese fishing village inhabited only by women pearl divers: "All the men off in Antarctica, chasing whales," he declaims. I see a parade of them running in the snow. As I listen, relishing their enjoyment of each other, this morning's conversation with Fred plays in counterpart, our Sunday morning leisure of coffee outside the penthouse, Fred grave and gentle with the children while we deliberate the new life. Fred describing his Vita Nuova; after spending a year in a commune, coming out, discovering he loved men. His kindness serving up hot cakes and bacon while he listens to my interminable doubts and fears, quietly preventing his children from stepping either upon the garden or the conversation.

Claire and Fumio beam at each other and shift gears—from whales to food and back to aesthetics. And then to love, and how people abuse it. Claire doing a nice parody of the romantic grabber who insists that he or she love continuously, without a moment's hesitation or ambivalence. On the way to the bathroom she shouts out an imitation of the determined lunatic. The three of us laugh together at the familiar. There are moments in friendship, Fred had said, when the thing spreads beyond the ordinary margins, when something is said that carries you beyond the little guidemarks of restraint or indifference, like watercolors merging on a page, a moment when you survey a relationship from some transcendent point and see it's beauty, the beauty of persons, of friendship itself. It's these few moments that make the difference. I watch the two of them before me in this light, aware each of us knows that communion now.

There is a slow increase in the frequency of our references to rolling out for something to eat. Just before we leave we listen to Deller sing Shakespeare's songs, Claire having chosen the record out of some uncanny rapport for the concert we'd just come from. In my hubris I try to explain how an exquisite verse of rococo cipher—likening breasts to flowers, nipples to mountain crowns—first bewitched me when Celia sang it in New Haven. Fumio cannot follow the conceit; neither of them can catch the lyrics. I admit, provisionally, how difficult it is to share one's own ineffables.

On the street I discover they're both drunk and I'm not. Stumbling along, three abreast, infinitely pleased with

ourselves, a menace to passersby, I feel her fingernails
express themselves in the palm of my hand. There is no
need to go across town to the Village; Claire knows of
a restaurant right in our neighborhood. It turns out to
be the Paradox. Macrobiotic pseudofood, Fumio grumbles, outraged anyone would voluntarily eat the brown
rice he gagged on during the Yankee Occupation. Grown
purist, he disapproves of what they have the nerve here
to call tempura. I agree the salad is green grabage, but
I like the garden. Fumio reminds us it's covered with
a parachute. The Occupation continues as East meets
West. Claire's not hungry.

Two black guys arrive, one with an underfed dog. It
seems they know us, are friends of Janey and Bill. The
man with the dog is Josh Tarkington. Now I remember
backing him up in a debate with an uptown dealer one
night at St. Adrian's. Lily-white gallery man's usual line:
He'd be glad to have black artists, but no "qualified"
black painters ever seem to apply. Tarkington and the
other fellow pause at our table. We talk of Zell. Josh
and his buddy furnish versions of how they missed the
funeral. They sit down with us next to Claire, Josh running through a script of maliciously flattering clichés:
she has the complexion of a baby, looks like a Christmas
angel. They snicker and continue to bait her, this white
"chick," like boys torturing an insect. It is a familiar
militant arrogance, a knee in the crotch revenging itself
on women for having kissed the white man's ass all those
years. Forced to listen, I find myself further irritated
by the realization that I've been seeing a Florentine angel
in her golden hair the whole week past, idly watching
Kevin in his youth and his long curls working on the roof
of the barn up at the farm, a blond boy standing high
in the sun with a goodness lovely as hers and beautiful
as a girl. Hardly as cruel as his role requires, Josh stops
short of outright insult. Since Fumio cannot follow, he
cannot play the protective role convention would assign
him. And how unfair the custom that demands I sit by
while her beauty is humiliated, not even permitted to
praise it before others. But Claire is holding her own.

I change the subject to politics and try to impress them with what I saw in Europe, showing off, beginning to enjoy myself.

All of a sudden she's leaving. And will give no explanation. I follow her into the scullery passage to hear her say bitterly that the evening's a dead end. Her pride insisting that she's tired, she might as well go home. I am afraid now; I have bungled as always. Clutching for an opportunity to apologize: "If I come by in a while will you give me a cup of coffee?"

Desultory conversation back at the table: Josh's outrage at that Uncle Tom show in Texas, his fury at Larry Rivers for playing the great white father, edging out the black artists. All of us, except Josh's buddy, who's having an exhibition at this moment, agree the art world's been a vacuous bore for the last five years. "Since Pop Art," Fumio insists. Josh's buddy insists that what's going on in New York now is *his* show. His truth. Why not? First show I had I would have paid people cab fare to get them there.

Our visitors leave us to our own devices. Fumio asks what shall we do now? I say I'll drop off that article on physics which Claire forgot on my way home. "To Bookie's? Wonderful, let's go," he says happily, ready to leave. "I'm going alone." His face shows the hurt surprise. A second later I realize there are kinder, more intelligent ways to do it. Discovering that till now he hadn't known. But I was following his wishes. For six years my father practiced deception badly. Hating it still, I'd rather not try to at all. But last month Fumio asked me to stop bothering him with the truth. It is difficult not to. The noncommittal easily becomes a lie or an awkward moment like this when the door of friendship closes in his face. He's right to be angry. The exclusion is unjust. How would I feel if men were getting it together, falling in love with each other in the process, locking *me* out? And it's no good, my being the person at the center. How would I survive a weekend with Fumio and some friend of his, Frieda, for example? I wish he'd try me out. Without the fairness of parity, without a balance on each side, we have only invented a new way to mistreat each other.

His face darkens with the hit to his pride, and something more than pride, telling me how, one night when Barbara was away, he and Sidney talked: "I told her that the trouble was not possessiveness, or the jealousy, it's knowing she's with someone and you're alone. And she understood what I meant." Guilt is creeping all over me. "I know it. But I can't fix it." He answers with a disgusted look. "I can't fix your loneliness. You'll have to do it by finding other people." "They are all disappointments," he argues. And I know he's serious. "Then decide what you want. Or if you want only to sculpt." He admits he cannot decide. And then he turns on me: "You can't fix it, but you cause it." "Shall I stop and become your wife?" "No, do what you like. But your theories are just crap. You invent them only to explain your pleasure." Usually I accept this. Tonight it feels good not to, even suspecting he rather likes me for refusing that judgment. Paying the bill and walking down toward Fifth Street we're friends again. When I turn down to Claire's, he gives me a comradely grin, naughty and tender: "Crazy way to live."

I am exhilarated caution, keeping clear of the Hell's Angels until I am safe in the stench of Claire's staircase. But for a long time after arriving I cannot tell her, rhetoric around the room instead: "The problem is I'm trying to live a life that isn't possible to anyone yet. Top of that, it's against the rules and so naturally no one approves of it." She waits patiently till I'm coherent. I am ashamed to my stomach for blowing it: naïve please-myself fool, delighted at being with both of them, finally an entanglement to each. Then she's apologizing for having left abruptly, then denying she ever called the evening a bust. I am riddled with Fumio's pain, and intruding it on her, knowing that's not fair.

"There's your life too, and the both of you won't be dying on the same day," she tells me steadily. "Only don't be cruel, not even unkind. And tell me, what is in this contract? What have you got, you two?" "We got past Immigration. Anything good you might say for marriage we had already, two years before the license. We have been each other's everything for eight years now. It is the first good relationship I ever had in my life. But now I want other people too. Women. And I can't hurt him." Then she surprises me by asking the question I ask myself so often. "What are you really doing anyway?"

"I'll answer you, in your own vein. You know that habit of upper-case abstraction you've invented so you can say what you like without being put down, since your wry method of delivery and the Donald Duck intonation guarantee everyone it's only a joke?" She nods, amused at my appreciation of her tactics. "Well, I'll use that then, all your three-syllable diction, suspect from overuse, bearable only when exaggerated, pronounced with a glint in the eye. What I want is outrageous: all the possible pleasures of freedom. I want to go beyond the old system of possession, the notion of person as thing owned. Like so many of us now, I'm experimenting with life, trying to get it right, to do it better, aware how often we're merely rationalizing—but still trying to create a new kind of social existence." "So, if that's it, you'll have to take responsibility for what you do." She says it firmly and in good will.

My guilt slides off like an old coat in her arms. "And what is it that you get from women?" Asking me what I never asked myself. "I don't know. Is it energy, support, tenderness? The wonder of rapport, a life experience close enough so you know the same jokes. Did your mother always warn you to wear clean underwear, just in case you had an accident?"

By the third cup of coffee we are enjoying ourselves enough to exchange horror stories on demagoguery in the movement. I do a few sequences of Rita Mae Brown explaining the necessity of killing when the time comes: "I'll behead men in the streets if necessary . . ." The two of us giggling over the sort of logic Rita Mae might scrape together to explain the political utility of a beheading. Claire goes back to the night she fed her friend

French Rothman a pork chop, only to find French, at the first hint of diagreement, pointing a knife—"My knife!" Claire explodes, laughing. "And there's French shouting: 'It's your kind that has to be killed.' This, after eating my pork chop, with my knife—and there's French lining me up against the wall to shoot me."

We condole with each other over those times when the Right is nothing to the madness of the Left, one's own kind and yet so heartbreaking. But it's all merely funny tonight. We are getting high on coffee. Then we begin a long debate, a chess game between Claire's sense of the apocryphal and my own sense of the ironic, two points of view making love through definitions. "Irony is how one copes with disappointment," I move. "Apocrypha is the superior perspective of the cosmos," she counters. I demonstrate her theory contradicted in the way Chaucer causes Troilus's soul to laugh down at his former wretched existence from a star. Trying to incorporate irony into the solar system and thereby subvert Bookie's argument from the galaxy, I offer a compromise: "There is synthesis in romantic irony. Can I sleep in your bed?" "Whenever you like. It's a pleasant variation on the joys of solitude." I watch her across the table, the lamp glowing upon her wonderful hair as she talks. "I've lived here for five years as a hermit. Never went out except to see the librarian or the shrink." She winks and purses her mouth. "Recently I've abandoned asceticism and returned to the flesh." I'm relieved to know I'll be spared those little exercises where sex is a power pawn, the dishonest games we play on men, not very inventively and with less justification turned upon each other.

In bed, in her arms, in her softness, and she asks me how irony deals with this situation. "It searches out a witty phrase to explain the Tampax you are destined to find anyway." "I have prescience and knew it was there already," she replies serenely. Smiling at me: "We are now incorporated, the flesh of one actually assimilated into the other," her eyes so fine and green they hurt. A good day on planet earth.

Loving, even seven undisturbed and insatiable hours of it, all runs together. Only a few things wash up on memory: last time the wet of her coming all over my hand, the feel of it startling me at odd moments during the week. Tonight we enrich our familiarity with the classics, rendering the Ninth Symphony as a crisis, and when Handel's soprano who knows that her redeemer liveth gets her needle stuck in the middle of things we lie there laughing, coming to liveth-liveth-liveth, shaking the bed with our mirth and the ease of intimacy and tenderness. My prima noces superstition that one never matches or surpasses the first time is conquered now, gone with its thrill of taboo and fear, all those rules which give us a morbid rebate for the expense to our spirit, the waste of our shame. Tonight I beat that rap without ever renouncing that incomparable moment when I saw Celia's eyes as we found each other's center, and stayed there. Energy. Emotion. Stillness. Friction. Spirit. Flesh. Building till sight went blind.

And tonight blots out all the voices of my life, their squalid words hitting like stones: sin, perversity, infidelity, scandal. Now I outcry them, certain, not only through the joys of sense which in themselves become an ethic, but through a new perception that virtue, ultimately, is only another human being. Rejoicing in our bodies' woman's beauty, I can refute them, knowing that when I die I will have lived in these moments: comes to it, you have the world in your time, or you didn't. Mine now is looking down on the gold of her head between my thighs while the white sky brings its first light through the ivy's green in the windows.

We wake to a gasman's pounding doors on floor after floor, announcing to no one that Con Edison is the fate that waits them. No one answers. "And why should anyone surrender their few precious moments of sleep or intimacy to a monopoly?" Claire inquires, not moving. "You should be here when the exterminator comes. Imagine waking to that." She bursts out laughing, causing the narrow bed to tremble dangerously at the thought of that word coming into sleep's little death. Snuggled safely, the two of us savor a Lower East Side morning, its casual endurance of the lesser indignities of squalor.

Using her ragged toothbrush I remember how little two hundred dollars a month really is. She has given me her vulnerability: that she has never known a man, is afraid of them, was abandoned by her father when she was four. Should I build her a decent bed, big enough for two, one of my special wood and foam rubber creations—but that implies a future. As I leave I notice a wan inscription pinned over the police lock: "Is it possible there might be even one pure motive?" The one near the bed reads more urgently: "How shall I deal with the terror of history?" Outside in the fine morning I meet my favorite graffiti on the wall of the music store at the corner: "Reporter—Mr. Gandhi, what do you think of Western Civilization? Gandhi—I think it would be a good idea."

Fumio smiles at me, a friend again with a sense of humor, teasing me over how much sleep I got, laughing at the madwoman with whom he cohabits. And when we get to the farm, the barn building all month, his studio, is finally finished and magnificent, its white walls, its old beams beautiful even beyond our hopes and ready for him. No more wallpaper to peel. His work crisis past, he wants to sculpt again. We rock out on the front porch like country grotesques, drunk on the flowering juniper, Fumio alight with all the pieces he will make: a wooden typewriter, so many bicycles, a coronet—"an artichoke too," he boasts, rising to express his perfect delight and thorough sense of ease in the place by pissing against the old maple on the lawn. The full moon breathes down upon the cutout of his shape at the base of the huge tree. The pride of his stance. The sound of his content.

PART TWO

THE NEW
LIFE

4

Sitting in the sculpture garden at the Modern. Why are gardens so important to me? Came here to read Milly's letter, the German postmark hoarded like foreign money all morning. Such a long while since I have been uptown—which means publishers, the media, the fright. But today on Fiftieth Street in the morning, the day fresh early summer, why not go to the museum do something carefree like the old days? Sit in the sun and listen to Milly's voice far away black exile in Deutschland. Never come home again she swears. This letter will tell two things, flipping it in my lap, knowing beforehand what it will say, only waiting to hear how she says it in her own wild language. Milly talking of Zell dead now, will have heard it from us, from Janey and Bill. Loved him too, always turning him down, wouldn't be his little wife. Not Milly tough mother. But the hurt of him gone now forever jumping off her typewriter speeding along as she ignores punctuation and sentence structure. Flood of her American talking. Grief speaking out in a foreign place unheard until I read it. Two years ago she stopped by

at the Bowery, back in the States because her mother
died, I looked and saw Milly standing again on my studio
floor, spot where her dog shit punctually each morning
that whole year she sublet while I was away in Japan.
Zell hovered over, courting her, not giving up though
she was having none of him. Tried to tie her down. Then
she was off again. I used to think she had a beau over
there, some racist Kraut probably wouldn't marry her.
But when we went to visit, flying over after Paris, we
met Gerda, the German girl she lives with, her life. And
saw Haus Merberich, the magic studio they'd had two
years and losing it now. Milly spending plenty brought
us home in style, a cab all the way from the airport, so
different from her surly black girl number when she lived
on Second Avenue and would meet me on the street
summer mornings. If I wouldn't come to her place she
wouldn't come to mine. Stood right in front of the door
at the Bowery refusing to come up for coffee. And once
Fumio and I ran over to the storefront on Third Street
wanting to invite her for a big Sunday dinner—"We'll
have roast beef." "Uh uh. Not eating with no more white
folks ever again." Just like that. No explanation, though
we knew she'd quarreled with Nickelman the Sunday
before, ready to walk out on his party only Zell wouldn't
let her. Fumio wanted to cry, he wasn't white anyway.

Haus Merberich. We inspect the great Deco mansion
now decaying. Just leave it as it is in the middle of the
German countryside, the paint falling off the walls, would
lose its savor if you fixed it, chase out the ghosts of so
many artists who have lived here: Kandinsky, Klee, the
rest. Built by a baroness amateur fond of art, Milly tells
us as we stroll along a country road, some strange trees
on either side, plane trees, going to see her friend who
keeps the museum of local art and speaks no English,
the warm handshake of a potter. Inside the pure white
walls, old pastor's house, the artifacts carefully saved.
Local pottery, carvings, weaving. I stare at them,
homesick and tired in Germany. Seized with depression
at the futility of all human effort finally put under glass

saved preserved guarded to stifle in a case in silence. Why do we bother finally? Our things sitting alone in rooms too clean and perfect for people to come to.

Today the Modern doesn't seem this way. It's full of people chattering in its garden. Even a bird. And always the fountains. Coming in I spied a New York painter sitting in glorious idleness under a tree, the whole day before him and nothing to do but enjoy it. Privilege of the unemployed all over him makes me taste again those first days in the Bowery, skipping down the street in the morning while truckers sweated delivering beer to the bars and I had no job to go to. Free. He calls out hello. Know each other from Cedar Bar days and the Flag Show. Lost our case against patriotic fascism, had to pay a fine. Feel like winners anyway the whole thing's funny. How peculiar we would seem to our former selves, greedy little bar spongers, eye on the main chance ragging up our egos at the Cedar. Or trying to, though a girl is less convincing here. Then we never gave a damn for politics, too high-mindedly selfish. Aesthetics was all, let people go to hell, we felt our insignificance pretty keenly downtown. Now we sit in the morning sun with our coffee, actually citizens as if this town were Florence once was like this. Can it be that things are changing? Becoming involved, connected, we could turn the basilisk around and run it; Kaprow once said find the levers and the buttons cease to be a victim, let the artist become a man of the world. A nice bubble, watching my iced tea filling in the cafeteria, find a spot under a tree and muse. Lady in line to daughter-in-law, speaking impossible language of old people rather than new, her voice grabbing at the youngster, "Baby's very cute now eating regularly not spitting up, soon I'll be getting to hold it." Hearing her I wish she wouldn't. And the youngster loathing it, coerced through life, each day a uniform, dragooned this morning into white-gloves museum tour. Yes she says yes to everything.

Beyond the glass windows the sculpture stands sunning itself in the open. In this corner I once saw Calder, old master in a blue shirt and an amazing red tie. Nighttime preview, had wangled a ticket and crept up, touched him on his coat or was it his sleeve, all reverence. He turned his beautiful old man's face white hair over ruddy flesh, pure light-blue eyes. Uncanny fool I felt pretending to be peering at a piece or out the window, coughing, rearranging whatever costume I'd gotten together for the occasion. Had touched greatness anyway, my face aflame.

Settled now in sunshine, treat myself to Milly. After Zell she'll thank us for the bread we sent when Haus Merberich blew up in a freak explosion of cats and dogs, wandering now the pair of them bereft through Europe. The great beautiful studio gone now, bitter way for it to end, that mellow refuge. We came there shaken from our terrible media year, the two of us hunted through Europe. Fumio's first sight of it finally after eight years postponement in America while I rotted through graduate school. Milly sat us down in the dining room to a spread of cheese beer brown bread and a great row of windows overlooking a pond. Solace of countryside and the big garden in back where I played out my Gethsemane, Vita on long distance from America, Fairbanks was demanding an answer would I teach next fall? So we asked Milly to forgive us and went to the garden for a little crisis, lying under some apple trees plucking at the grass, crazy with the pressure. Wailing my panic to him, look I must write this book. But give up for the last time safety, academic or establishment, the hardest risk of all still ahead of me? Trying to tell him how I had to do the thing for gay, still planning an academic son daughter bastard of *Sex Pol,* prove the psychologists were wrong solve the dilemma of a fragmented society we're all bisexual anyway. And so forth. Saying that but the still more dangerous secret lurking inside me, to write my own book, dump polemics, come out as myself. So sick of the wars, so wanting myself again. Haus Merberich did it. Milly too, her distanced compassion listening to my wreck of nerves. "Baby I just hang out here livin' simple," the example of her life removed from the ugly monotonous twist of making it. Milly at rest.

That last afternoon in the garden, the three of us on an old stone wall among roses overgrown to chaos. There are naked thorns. Later there will be flowers. Summer ahead of me now, a warm day in early March the German mist rising a little to let in some light. Already I cannot bear to think of fool August coming to wreck me again, then, no not another winter like the last one. Celia. Why go on when you have had by now so much more than you can take? Why not just get out of things, vanish. If only you could die. Milly and Fumio are in the sunlight remembering old parties, dinners at Janey's red tablecloth everyone tanked on wine and yelling about Pop Art or racism or whether Martha Jackson kept a stable. They are happy together in the light, the two of them knowing who they are. I have separated myself into darkness and see only the dead roses. I do not really want to go on. Tomorrow back to England to cut the film. Fumio forgoing a trip on his own to Italy, Florence, the Uffizi. "I am not art student," he grins, "and we both know about arrivals at midnight in Rome without the money they got there, not a word of Italian, no hotel room. And the toilets, just I get accustomed to one and it's time to move. We will go to Florence some other time, together," his face making a smile as if we'd last that long. But he will stay on with Milly to play a few days before the cold samurai rigor of life alone in the Bowery.

I will be steel, go to England right away, not linger even a day. Told Betty we'd start cutting Monday, I'll be there. All the exits are closed, now is the time to gamble everything finish the movie and write. Sick with dread just hearing the sentence in my mind. Milly sent me off in the boom of her voice, "You let me see it soon's you're done. I'll project it on the damn living room wall if I have to." How could I tell her it was junk, might never be finished?

A young girl recognizes me and says hello, she liked my book. For the first time I am not afraid. Perhaps I can be Kate Millett after all though it's still ponderous and a little silly. This morning Vita and I had breakfast in a bistro, blowing the cashier's mind with an open forum on our lives. It happens to be our breakfast, so we talk freely even as he peers into our plates, sniffing after sex. References to men were simply the cherry at the top of the ice cream sundae we presented him, a banquet of workingman's scandal, set him up for the day. Rarely gets customers so giving.

Brood here over iced tea watching the sun ripen the stones of St. Thomas Church while over to the right townhouses and clubs are created in the reflections spread across the windows of the Modern's new wing. I hear the fountains echo Trafalgar's splash accusing me of trivia, expecting today's little high to end in the usual betrayal or a bigger fall. When will the failure of nerve come again? This morning Vita diagnosed my condition: "You are either superwoman or broken wing. And they are both ridiculous." And our friend Cissie is the same. And Mallory. And the list went on, so many women I know now standing up new and huge with beginnings then falling over the next moment. Want to go so far, then relapse back into the little woman, the past jiggles underfoot and we capsize continuously.

On the subway Vita showed me her poems. Nice recriminatory verses, yet how good that she is writing again. Some bitchy songs and one better than the others, though all Stein, goes this way: "Woman sees woman as no one. Yet sees herself as everyone. Nobody everybody somebody anybody. Who could she be if she were some one." Commentary of a sort. Then we took the escalator watching a couple kissing out of the corners of our eyes. We grinned thinking they were girls in long hair. Chastened when we saw one's a guy in curls to his shoulders. Things are not changing all that damn fast. Coming up into the air I stopped dead to tell myself like a policeman: if you are so fragile blown by notoriety or media, what if prison comes?

I am expansive in the sun, claustrophobe and artist, fond of gardens and comforted by the Maillol bending to the water washing her full womanlimbs while another falls all abandoned into a pool. Moore, my early hero with his perpetual family. A real bird innocent upon the concrete, trees, Rodin's *Balzac* poised melodramatically on his pedestal overlooking two easy young lovers. I walk among them, they are old friends, saluting a favorite here or there, like Elie Nadelman's *Man in the Open Air* so urbanely naked under his bronze hat. Similarity of pose remembers me my joy coming upon Donatello's stuff in the Bargello gardens. There must have been a young man with a hat in that bunch too. Traveling alone to Florence after the Oxford examinations, years ago when I fell out of scholarship into art. And when will I ever sculpt again? It has been so long I have not made a piece I dare not even add up the months. Am I still a sculptor looking at the works of better sculptors? Time to leave them. One last walk around to see the new technical exhibit up there on the top level. Deciding there are two principles in life, reality and pleasure. Here are scientists, making soulless structures, perfect example of reality principle. Here am I just taking notes on the back of an envelope because it is not important enough to write out. Next to me a girl scribbles in her notebook. Probably keeps a journal. Centuries of our sensibility huddled into diaries, the kind of writing you don't publish, just a little safety valve of self. But she has a tougher self and hangs on to her table, whereas I have relinquished mine to some imposing European tourists, three German pushers have grabbed my writing surface. Take it.

Claire waves *The New York Times*. Her oracle. A scientist predicts in fine print, very interior page, that the cultural isolation of Planet Earth is drawing to an end. "We will become part of galactic civilization. Probably its most retarded member." Nevertheless she is sanguine. "With a history so catastrophic it is unlikely we will have anything to contribute. But on the other hand, the extraterrestrial types may have overlooked certain things, Bach for example, or the sailboat. Think of it, the solar age, a whole new stair of evolution." I remind her how past hopes like the Industrial Revolution began with the conversion of human beings into draft animals dragging coal through the mines of Victorian England. And ended in the debris of her Fifth Street tenement.

It is hours before the meeting. We can drink beer while the green light sifts through her ivy windows, our friendship chattering on will lose all track of time. I notice a message pinned to the broken iron gates over one window. Originally it was addressed "To the Thief." Then French delivered one of her political lectures, said it should read "Dear Brother." So it does. Timidly advising him not to bust her again, she has not replaced the typewriter. On the desk the long sheets of manuscript, ruled yellow paper conquered by her relentless felt pen. Her maybe crazy maybe beautiful manuscript. But today she went sailing. And today I worked because she was out, deciding to stay home self-sufficient since there were no distractions to be found. It seemed a step. Angela Davis in handcuffs pinned before us on the wall. Angela never out of mind, face I saw in airplanes all year, knowing she takes the rap locked in a solitary cage while we sit here and discuss civilization.

Claire is optimism arguing for a new age in the photographs pinned against the grating where the light blazes through her latest space shots. I am a skeptic: "Is there a store somewhere that specializes in this stuff, a clientele of fanatics sufficient to keep them in business?" "Shut up, we will learn to be gentle, there is no alternative. Anyway we know too much now not to be wise, too much psychological insight is available by now to continue in our old patterns." Since we converse in books and pictures I quote the Mass Psychology of Fascism, offering snapshots of Dachau. "You see that figure there pinned to a fence, only bones left of him now. A whole society can go crazy." And yet I live upon her hope, my sustenance, just as I am her "reward" she calls it, on Fridays. "All week I can bear it, that hour when evening falls gray on the desk, so sick of reading and writing I think of death that time of day alone." Red coming into the green of her eyes. So I do not wish to break her optimism, only make it real, the mad things

she says while Casals' photo conducts in the next room,
a whole wall of him concentrating in the kitchen, and
over the tub right next to the sink, frowning down in
double-chinned ecstasy while she slams the ice-box door
and opens another beer, yelling at me like a good-natured
bully, "Stop your whining and write whatever the hell
you please. You can impose your will on reality." "Crap,
Bookie. Nonsense." "So fuck yourself and go on doing
nothing." I am leery of will and imposition, having
realized at last that everybody's literary myth is a hoax,
just their own milieu and I had believed them all. Should
I dare to listen while she urges me on? "Take hold of
time while you live it, you are placed so as to have opportunity, that's responsibility too; anyway, try as hard
as you can to make things happen, change. Use your
damn head, then go beyond it." "No," I say, "delusions
of grandeur, I am only trying to cope. If you flatter me
I cannot be your friend." "Altogether your own problem.
This is my kitchen. My kitchen where I will express my
mind. Modesty doesn't trouble me."

She is twenty-five, unpublished, living in a cold-water
walk-up, and has just announced she'll be the first writer
to convert science fiction to literature. Our friendship
is talking, so much talking that we always burn the food
if we cook too. Infatuation of the mind. I can rarely
remember what we say, it is a mood. We are writers.
We encourage each other in our delusions. She is sure
of mine. I am never sure of hers, often suspect she has
gone wacky in her hermitage. How can she be so com-
pelling in her conviction that everything is possible?
Testing her again: "The junkie I saw crossing Thirteenth
Street this morning was even white, yet so full of self-hate
he needed to poison his own brain." "Of course. It's a
running sore. My own neighborhood festers so that I
would like to become a Band-Aid, a sticking plaster for
all the chancres I have to look at. My intention is to
become utterly harmless." "Bookie, really . . ." "Sounds
easy, doesn't it? Well it's not. We are always hurting
somebody, stepping on something while we're not looking."

Back at her desk over yesterday's roast beef, which she calls an antipasto, she muses on, forgetting to eat it while I hold out for a good meal after the meeting. She tells me about her preschool kids. The long struggle beating racism; her own, theirs. I see her there, the only white. And so very white that black children are fascinated by her blond head and black teachers sullen over the lunch table. "The process of being accepted never ends, I succeed only so-so. It's exhausting. When you are near children you realize everything has been settled too far back. If we had a shred of intelligence we would rearrange our priorities, put every available resource into protecting the psychic life of the child. Anything else is superficial." She is dogmatic too. We drink another beer swapping kindergarten experiences. Hers from the Lower East Side, mine from a Harlem winter years ago. I had forty kids, free but out of control, nearly went mad from the noise, was never patient enough, learned the monster in myself and hated what I saw. The professional kindergarteners in the room across the hall, old ladies in calm authority, their kids forever in line or making Christmas trees, little hands neatly laid on the desk, ran a quiet totaliarian state while I was anarchy next door. I did not know enough.

My other missionary trip, the loony bin, Claire did that too, college kids on summer jobs determined to create sanity. Discovering we have the same past, the excitement of becoming friends finding we have journeyed through identical country: civil rights, kids, crazies. Was Claire less absurd than we were, three freshmen with a year of Abnormal Psych setting out for the snake pit? We would stick together, subvert the bureaucracy in unison. They were too smart for us, let us pass the test, "Can you tell people are crazy by their eyes?" Vote liberal, say no. But then they farmed Hilda out to Hastings, Bakula to the feebleminds in Faribeault, and me to St. Simon. Every night quarreling in beer joints with the guys who were aides on the Men's Side, their bigger voices insisting, "You gotta beat these bastards, that's all they understand." Lonely among the bumpkins till

I found Maggie, a nun who had leapt over the wall, now a crack nurse on the Women's Side, privy to all my grand schemes of music therapy, playing my old 78 rpms in the library—most patients just nod. Or tennis. Hardly anyone notices the ball.

Maggie and I drank beer and went out with the New York Giants training that summer in the sticks. Big football pro trying to fuck me in his car, mind resisting hysterically—my God he's married. And really I loved Maggie. But I let Rick climb through the window of the nurse's annex so I could lose my virginity, bored uncomfortable, sweating, it hurts, does he know what he's doing? How will it ever fit? For the first time the key to a room of my own, here is opportunity, he said we had to do it finally. Stood by a dreary oak bureau grimly resolved to go through with it. So we did. Next morning looked in the mirror over the bureau to see if I was different. Supposed to be a woman now. Nothing had happened so I read forty books on psychology in as many days, ransacking the library so I would understand how to make people well. Long afternoons sitting next to vegetable women in smocks. Wanted to touch them, kiss their faces, anything, any response. But they stay in their place, shut away. No one has cigarettes. They are wards of the state, their people have gladly forgotten them, not even an allowance, they cannot earn and taxpayers will not buy ice cream except through my salary. So I bought ice cream, a cigarette roller, and a bag of Bull Durham and rolled our own. We all smoke when nurse says we may. I hand out matches living among women who scream in agony at night. Wrap the womanboy in cloth, change the bloody sheets again, ordered to tie her to the bed so she will not tear off her skin and bleed to death during the night shift. Daytime count silverware after meals, dizzy with the stench of slops. We will have the same chicken downstairs later. First two weeks I lost fifteen pounds.

And why do it? Taking the bus to the first interview with Big Nurse, a smart college kid who asked to see the wards, got a guided tour of horror, yells, figures jumping out at me. Will I be killed here or go crazy, long files of things who used to be women now mere ghosts perched in bird rows on the benches that line the halls, gray, dead, in unthinkable haircuts and shapeless dresses that are really flour sacks. Who could stay sane here? Scared riding back to St. Paul on the Greyhound with Don Quixote for Humanities class. Undergraduate sense of humor delighted with the ironic perfection of the assignment. I was afraid but I went anyway. Dared by it, stubborn, fatuously expecting miracles of healing, whole wards marching into the sunlight to the tune of my pipe dreams. That summer learned me reality. The job itself solid as the bars, hard as the keys I wore on my belt. "Keep them in your pocket," they warned me, an unwilling jailer, always losing them or fighting the pull to open every door and let people out of hell. But where would they go? All I had was my good will. It wasn't enough. It was ignorance.

The only psychiatrist in the whole place was an administrator for eight thousand people. Two part-time psychologists interviewed a few promising patients a week. Get to see a doctor if you break a leg, discredited physicians from the city. One invites me over for Schubert and starts to come on. Rumors they abuse the female patients, fucking hopelessly crazy bodies. Mind all gone do they feel the indignity of use? I read Menninger and decided the aides are the key, only personnel close to the patient. Retrain them and the nursing staff. In Big Nurse's office of an evening outlining my schemes. I would stay on without salary, had already earned the six hundred permitted me as my mother's dependent, so I would become a free-lance therapist with my own program. Maggie would change the whole tenor of the staff, classes, reorientation, New Attitudes. Big Nurse looks down six feet at me. Not even for free.

Then Mallory was going to die. I walk up the front steps, Mother's house transformed by the quarantine signs. Huge letters across the front door of Selby Avenue, fatal contagion of poliomyelitis. Bulbar, worst kind, give you maybe three days to make it or not. Afterwards no crutches or iron braces. I cannot go inside, must sleep at the neighbor's while the kid sister I love is murdered tonight in Anchor Public Hospital darkness of children screaming and even parents cannot watch them die. There was an epidemic every summer. Jimmy Spencer had died. Jimmy Spencer who I beat up in first grade when I was a gang leader. His mother called. My mother clucked and said it was a terrible thing, she's a girl. Then he disappeared in August. Only the week before he had shot me in the fanny with his BB gun when I rode my bike past his house. Waiting up through the nights with Mother till Mallory lived, dearer but strangely nervous, the carefree blond child had died and this new sister was temperamental, bullying, something in her spine malicious, holding its own.

So I would write exposés of St. Simon for the local papers, or drag my fellow citizens through its hell on guided tours, force them to watch the brutality of the place and the persons they had put in charge of their aged or disgraceful relations. The big Polack aide swinging her plunger ready to strike if patients cannot shit on the dot of schedule, ramming their naked bodies blue against the stone walls of the weekly showers. But Mother and her family said I was a fanatic. And I backed off, afraid the system was bigger than me at eighteen.

Claire, her yellow hair lit like an aureole in the day's last sunlight, was there too. At McLean's in Boston. Telling it, she makes the usual comedy of her trauma. I listen, loving, yes, both her goodness and her humor, marveling before her beauty as she describes how she was socked into understanding. "By a woman, mind you, my favorite patient, real progress, special rapport, the whole ego trip of healing. Then she punches me right in the nose. So I look down and notice the whole front of my uniform is covered with blood. Then I figured it out. There'd been an accident at the gas station while I was going to work. I drive in and tell the guy to fill the tank, enjoying myself, a big shot. Smack, a car whizzes past me and piles into a tree ten feet away. The crowd thinks I'm a nurse. Could have been a waitress, same uniform. Of course I'm just an aide and don't know a damned thing. The woman at the wheel of the car has her head smashed and is bleeding all over everything. Half of the crowd is yelling I've got to be a nurse, do something. I keep trying to explain I don't know anything. Only thing I can think of at this moment is to suggest she remove her wristwatch, the blood is spoiling the works. Swear to god this moronic suggestion is all that occurs to me for a full thirty seconds. Everybody's yelling. But the other half of the crowd has a totally different point of view, they're shouting don't touch her you'll get sued. Isn't it wonderful, this single-minded obsession in the face of human suffering had to be nothing but an impulse toward the lowest form of self-protection? The filling station man says my tank is full, I'm incompetent, the ambulance has already been called. So I leave. Then I march in on my patient, scare hell out of her with my bloodstains, and she cracks me in the mouth. Enough reality for a full-scale nervous breakdown. Madness is everywhere, it's endemic." She dissolves into her own peculiar laughter, thoroughly infectious, yet with just a tinge of hysteria in it always. "Never forget that day. Faulkner died too. Same day."

We open another sixpack to console the futility of our younger selves. Her friend Muriel drops in and diverts our attention to Dorothy Day, one of the saints on the wall near the door but too real for either of them. Muriel and Claire are both under her spell. Muriel who is much younger than we are—no, seeing her with Muriel, Claire suddenly seems much younger than I am—Muriel a volunteer at the *Catholic Worker* around the corner. Muriel is critical, making the usual radical denunciations of charity, a drop in the bucket, no bottom to it, doesn't help, we need a revolution instead. I tend to agree, but am taken by the lady's gallantry. "Imagine all those years fighting the Church. I grew up hearing her denounced from the pulpit as a dirty commie while still chained by Mother to my pew, cheering her on, another rebel. Anyway, she's not that apolitical either, she's endorsing some pretty violent means lately, that ought to please you," I tell Muriel. "She's an authoritarian, doesn't see the people around her." Muriel means herself. "Maybe she's busy with her purpose and the . . . young people who help her come and go," watching Muriel whistle at the word "kid," I had almost said it but didn't quite, seeing the mistake too late. I am saddened by the acid of righteous youthful criticism spilt all over an aged saint like Day who would wither into ashes if she knew how casually she can be dismissed by someone twenty-three. Gingerly, I try to explain to Muriel that maturity might be the trick of recognizing accomplishment without mercilessly discarding it as you become disillusioned by the sight of its limitations. Muriel glares, so does Claire. Then they laugh at me. I feel like a member of the faculty, which is to say frankly ridiculous.

Then the three of us embark on a fantastic conspiracy to improve the business of sainthood. Renovoate, reconstruct, throw out asceticism, give an infusion of humor, hedonism, flexibility. We grow boisterous, eloquent, brilliant. Saints and religion are not my sort of thing, they are however one of Claire's obsessions. Our favorite argument is how to bring about nonviolence without hocus-pocus. "You must have spiritual leadership, an ultimate purpose beyond humanity. How else could Gandhi cool out the masculine preoccupation with violence in a whole nation?" "No, I prefer that men free *themselves* of their gun-prick thing. And look, it's already happening, lots of young guys are becoming gentle, human, beautiful in their long hair, their very gesture softer. This generation has resisted the draft. Men can change." "But there's no direction, no purpose still, the Left might revert to violence any time . . ." She protests, launching off into the cosmos and its creator, hunting around for God in a new getup, calling him the star-maker. If the culture's to be overhauled and renovated, a pie-in-the-sky social order made up while the three of us drink beer, Claire's for saints if they're sufficiently novel, imaginative. Crowing that she wants to be one herself. Crazy ambition I think, watching her, uneasy at how friends call her our saint only half teasing, her reputation going ahead of her a little way in our circles, always worrying me that her curious goodness, real in its peculiar way, and loved, recognized, will turn her head, make her fanatical or proud. Does her humor give enough perspective to her isolation, her youth's gigantic desire to excel, still unapplauded, unrecognized, unpublished? "You had better finish that book. We're out of beer and it's time for meeting."

That night she fell off the bar stool at Chumley's. Meeting went on too long in O'Flynn's cramped little slum room where the topic was money. All of us honest enough to admit we're ambivalent. Want it, have wanted it, but think it's filth too, a weight, an illness in the system. We are still dishonest enough to be matching middle-class origins against the fortunate who hold the credentials of a proletarian childhood. It is hot. Marta just steals things, which we admire and don't admire. She is not open enough to discuss it and my mind woolgathers on the radical rip-off. Is it only a half-pint criminal thing, ultimately antisocial rather than revolutionary, simply inconsiderate of those who have to pay, the squares? Is it perhaps even petty and self-serving? Half the people I know feed on welfare. Do we bring down the system or are we just selfish? Or am I only a puritan from St. Paul? Welfare gives you time to write, call it state assistance to the arts. If Claudia quit architecture she'd be free to make movies full time. But on welfare wouldn't have the money. Money, how much one wants it never having it, then have it as Ruth did in a good job and give it up to become an activist, free now to write but still doesn't because there is always just enough trivia to distract and serving others an excuse not to serve oneself. I do this, too, it's our bond. But Ruth's broke and I have enough money to buy a farm, still guilty about it. Shut up and use it, they say. I will but I'm never sure. Debbie hates her orthodox Jewish parents, immigrant slaves in the garment district through a shriveled lifetime stitching gloves. "They're penury and joyless deprivation, I want a sports car. And I love all the sleazy blouses I get at discount from my cousins who got rich quick and go around in silk ties and striped suits. They're not the same capitalist pigs as the old moneyed WASPs," she says. I know what she means but I quiz her, will she someday forgive her parents for what they had to be because they remain that until you know and accept them, becoming yourself. I ask because I am trying to love my mother and where I come from. But Ruth says stop lecturing, it happens in time. O'Flynn who quit Columbia Graduate School of Archaeology has also stopped going with the guy who held on with his money, she is now Debbie's lover and needs ten dollars to print a pamphlet. People are even tired of money now and want to go home. I write out a check frantic to escape and have dinner with Claire, less a group member than a lover tonight. Meetings can be too long.

And here is Claire falling off the stool at Chumley's, midsentence of one of her tirades on peace. When we got to the restaurant she didn't want dinner, just split a bottle of wine, she wasn't hungry. "Berrigan's in solitary. Jackson and Angela are awaiting trial. What the system does is to kill the future each time it appears . . ." Bartender picking her up, huge black man infinitely kind finding it all very funny. Claire's unshaken dignity finishes the sentence sobered. So am I. Tonight's meeting taught me nothing at all. Here she is drunk because she hasn't eaten. Because she had no money and wouldn't admit it or be taken out to dinner and imperil her integrity. Never occurred to me. We decide to regulate our tastes to the level of her necessity. I am to be permitted my creature comforts but not at an expense beyond her means. Which from now on she'll have to learn to divulge.

In the morning she left for work and returned. Mumbled she had forgotten something and then climbed back into bed. It is the Bowery bed that Fumio built, and I have broken its marital taboo a first time. He has more sense and has slept here with several people. For me it was the first time with another. We have had no sleep because we are so fervid we are ridiculous. And dangerous. No one calls in sick without contrition. It comes in the midst of coming she turns off. Then sits up in bed to announce: "I have decided you're the mother Fumio's the father I'm the baby." I'm horrified. "Freudian claptrap, really the most absurd thing I've ever listened to." "Look, I didn't spend my grandfather's legacy for nothing. Seven thosand dollars, all the money I'd ever got in my life. Brought the whole mess of it to a clinic and said cure me of everything. Remarkable really, it took exactly that amount to do it." She's angry. "This is my particular neurosis for the morning and I will attend to it immediately myself."

But first I cook breakfast, making scrambled eggs with cream sermonizing on the glories of good food: painters and sculptors know how to eat. "It is fortunate you are already married or I would marry you for your eggs," she says. I am uneasy before the specter of roles. "Who'd be what?" I ask. "Never mind, I have located my problem, now I go home to fix it." But it is still in her eyes when she tears off a good-bye and bolts down the staircase, afire to recover her independence, both of us afraid we are too in love for safety. Why do people always mess it up? It is my fault, I am older, have no job to get up for. We are not doing well. Is it our fate to mess up even more than most people?

When I get to Mallory's it all comes back at the table. Mallory's kitchen where we made the movie. Word has come from England that a piece of film has been lost at the lab, that bit on the beach I used for our titles. They cannot proceed with the print until it is duplicated. Today we must reshoot it. I await my fate at the table. The movie company; nine women who are like lovers, like enemies, like fear itself. Mallory found her kitchen table in the street, a classic Lower East Side model with an enamel top. Mother had the same kind when we were kids. This is the table Rhoda banged during our biggest fight when she threw it on the floor, meaning to throw it at me. Going to kill me that moment because she wanted to be director. And because she was younger.

I am the oldest of the company. I had just written some crazy book they had never heard of. And I had the bread. So I said we'll share it, make movies together, be a company. Then I wanted to go further, become a collective. No very clear idea of what that meant, but it was the new line against individualism. The book might make me individualistic. And the media, just starting their tour of me that fatal August. I would guard against ego tripping, multiply my accidental good fortune, share it, make something for all women. The movie company was my dream and it became a nightmare. We made a hell for ourselves right there in Mallory's loft. Their resentment. My insecurity. Their rancor and my fantasies living among us as real as Celia.

Each day there were meetings, people announce their problems, get help. Delora's baby-sitter? Fixable, we'll rip it off the company I said, trying to alienate the money from myself, first money I ever saw in my life, calling the publishers and begging for more, would have rolled on the floor to get it and go on. But what if it were wasted, movies can be done cheaply or expensively. We wouldn't bother with rentals, the capitalists who rip it off you and leave you nothing but the bill. Since the lens is bad, they forgot to give you the battery and you do not know enough to check. So Rhoda hustled free equipment through two weeks of wheedling on the phone. We got it together, we outsmarted the system. But when the chips fell, and one of the borrowed cameras was stolen because those who were supposed to guard it left it in the doorway open to the street and a junkie walked off with a two-thousand-dollar box borrowed from a hell of a nice guy who had it from his college, his job, his ass in a sling—no, then we were not a collective—it was just me who was out all that bread. Sick facing them that hot damn night near the end of the shooting. No one said a word. They stare at me, the fool. No one offered me five dollars. My heart broke while I looked at them. So I bought the guy another camera and he said he was surprised because people say they will but they don't.

Rhoda's problem is that she owes somebody fifteen hundred dollars, has got to split to pull a deal on the Mexican border. Putting the make on me or she'll leave. I learn to say go. And she stayed. Then Robin's endless distrust, each day another child fascist examination to discover if I am real enough. She comes by my studio and repeats every movement rumor: they're saying you're this or that. Could invent them if she didn't hear them. But I must last through it, prove myself, give her everything: affection, my house to live in while I'm gone, every mark of trust imaginable. If I trust her utterly then she will trust me a little. Enough for the movie. Radical Lesbians have voted that no member can be in our film. They are paranoid, they are afraid. They are also a group deciding arbitrarily what people can do or not do. And that girl Bobbie plainly wanted to do it, even if she's a bit frightened, who wouldn't be? And when no one would trust me and I wanted so much to have one of the three women in the film to be a gay one, Robin offered. Tough, gallant, scared but wouldn't say so. She gave me herself for the film so I could give it to others. She has courage.

At the meeting where we tell our needs I said I had a plan to go to Provincetown with Celia the week after the shooting is over. We must finish it on time. This is what I want most in the world, I'm in love with her. Please let me, so they say yes. But Shirley keeps asking questions about who is fucking who while I shiver at the word until Fumio and Miriam and Celia are all spread out on the table. Under her gaze we look crazy. Shirley's very cool, says she may have started out in convent school but she's made it with chicks too, has even sold it. Woman of the world. I am accepted. Everyone's problem can be solved if we are totally honest and cooperate in good will. We will even waive the rule about having men on the set and permit husbands to come when we shoot Lillian at Long Beach. Celia can come too they say, or Fumio. Then it turned out neither of them wanted to go finally. They resent the intrusion the company represents. And the company resents them as it resents

Mallory's Philip, everybody's husband and kids. The company is compulsive marriage.

We will be completely open with each other, give each other everything. Then we won't again, battling savagely. One week before shooting is to end they quit. Only Mallory and June stay on to spend whole days on the phone coaxing the others back. We could keep the cameras an extra week and still finish it. If I did not go to Provincetown. Called Celia, said it killed me not to go, she said "Go right ahead, make your movie. It doesn't matter at all." Was it the crime past forgiving or was it really unimportant to her? To me it was watching life itself recede. Hysterical with her one night parked in front of my house, the movie is making me crazy, the media, the pressure. Celia is trying to help by holding my hand and kissing me with the top down when along walks my paperback editor. In tears trying to be civil. Then we picked up Fumio and the three of us went to the Finale for a ghastly supper. I lay down on the bench and couldn't eat. Celia had had it. Fumio got off at the Bowery and we went uptown to Miriam's empty apartment. Hoping for love during one of Celia's rare visits to New York. Sleep together. Just what we did. Playing director, Rhoda had ordered a seven A.M. call. I was on time. After two hours sleep, no love only its death in Celia's exasperation: I was crazy, I wasn't fun any more, I was a drag. Rhoda did not bother to show up till eleven-thirty. That time I was angry. The others said cool it. I did. But they had lost me Celia, which was what they wanted, knowing it or not. Sympathetic on the surface but at bottom her enemy because they suspected I wanted her more than the company. And finally I didn't. I chose the movie, her rival, my work. The choice she would have made herself.

The movie company, torture and psychodrama, no one of us wise enough to comprehend or call a halt. We were a capsule scenario of every oppressed unit on earth, a Chinese village on Great Jones Street around Mallory's kitchen table. Every role in history: male and female, capitalist and proletariat, backward people and tech-

nocrat, fascist junta and the one who is chosen for
execution. On the box of film which cost six hundred
dollars cash the guys at Kodak had scribbled *Womens
Lib Stay in the Kitchen* in place of an address. We consult with male authority over the phone about light read-
ings and film stock. Shirley's husband wanders in the
open door of the Wooster Street location, begins giving
advice with the best of intentions and we lose three hours
of shooting time. Otherwise there are no men on the set
but me. 'Cause it is my money I am the resident male
chauvinist pig. Also the capitalist cigar. I am a man
because I am Mallory's Philip who happens to be out
of town, or her ex-husband who happens to be still on
her mind and because in those days she could still make
a husband out of anyone who was bigger or together or
had enough money to buy dinner, a wife so long she was
a con artist as wives are, trapped in the habit of its convenience. My sister leading the daily revolts. The others
deciding if Kate's own sister says she's a pig she's gotta
be. A nest of oppressed women screaming at me like
machine guns. How difficult to resist the role, not become
a man and yell back when they start on me making me
someone else, my very self slipping away in panic. My
terror seeing they could do this to me—. But I will be
a woman too, crying when they beat on me, humble,
groveling, sniveling, begging for mercy. I am my mother.
It does not occur to me to demand they stop. And I must
be evil because their voices insist I am. They are oppressed women, queer am I a woman too? Guilty I might
be butch somewhere, not as female as they, especially
Mallory my pretty sister, the tantrum star. How do you
match that? Furious then learning not to shout back at
her, be humorous instead. "Come on Mallory, we must
transcend our origins." Refusing to quarrel, then falling
back into it again, the blood game like when we were
kids and I tried to be her bully like Sal was mine. But
she accused me, fought back, said I was fat, could always
get me that way. I had had no weapons against Sally,
waiting till it hurt too much my arm behind my back
twisted till my stomach went water and I said yes

anything. I tried that on Mallory, wanting to have my moment too a victor, but she wouldn't let it happen. And by then I had conscience. Sometimes, not always. But when I forgot justice she could always call me fat. So in one way we had triumphed already, broken the circle.

Each day of the shooting I made more strenuous efforts to be gentle, inoffensive, never assert anything, becoming so vague they screamed harder, needing orders. They had always had them before and they missed them. Beyond my reticence and haziness was my intuition that they would take no initiative unless they had to. And it was my dream to be peers, artists together. Despite what it cost it worked, the whole bunch of them giving Mallory energy at the kitchen table while she rapped for the camera. Or interviewing Lillian without me the night I had to speak at DOB, taping the passages that saved the film. Mallory did it and Sybil. Robin and June, Lillian's own daughter, hammering away at her myth till Lillian gave clues that the Adjusted Woman wasn't all of it, and grew honest. Beautiful and moving, this middle-aged woman who trusted us while we took her life and shook it for meaning.

I sit tense at Mallory's kitchen table waiting for the company. "Relax, they'll show," Mallory chuckles, stirring her coffee. Days when everybody quit Mallory never quit. And now it's nearly finished. Nell said stop complaining go ahead and reshoot that bit. "It will change your mind about movies." "Having to reshoot is a nuisance and I hate being dependent on them, their slave again," I whined back. "Just do it," says Machree long distance from London. And it feels good to be back, as if something nice will happen. The old dream flying in my head again how we would be the muses times three, all the energy of our nine genius, the Movie Company.

They drop in one at a time, the red arrow on the elevator lighting up another arrival. No one is punctual, we are nine individualists. Will they hate the movie now that it's cut? Will they assassinate me at the screening? Already the din has begun, everyone talking at once exchanging the year in between. There are jokes and laughter, Mallory's wit knocking about the room. It is last year again as the chairs fill around the table. But it is this year too. Delora did not have that next baby, looks wonderful, has been shooting a lot. June has graduated and started the job hunt. Rhoda has made a movie with Donna about a baby being born. Sybil has got a job at City. Shirley's car got stolen. Mallory is getting parts downtown. Rhoda and Robin, always the most problematic, are the last to arrive. We are a short crew. Sybil, Shirley, and Donna are not coming. I describe the finished movie, hoping for their approval and wishing I had it with me on the spot to show. I am less afraid now because they are different. They will not hurt me, we are all one year older now. Our first film is nearly done. Only a few hundred feet of film stand between us and the finish line, the pittance of one color roll lost.

Odd how it should be that bit on the beach where I first saw film, what it could do, composing the shots, timing them to the second. The rest of the movie was a happening, but this one short piece was a dance directed, the three women poised in a blue light before the ocean, three female figures in configuration and behind them infinity. We did it carefully, making diagrams in the sand. I held the watch and called the shots, looking through the lens before each one like a real director. I was sculpting life.

Smoking pot one night at someone's studio in Westbeth and playing with a set of masks a sculptor had done for a group of dancers, I realized that film was the golden mask. I had watched them as they improvised a mime. Then they stopped to rest. Pick a mask to wear they said. I looked over the strange metal objects laid out on the table, intriguing, sometimes ominous. And picked the gray one most like a cage, my usual figure, sculpt it myself, have lived in it always. "Pick another," they said, so I picked the gold one, rich, foreign as Cleopatra behind it, green dangerous luxury. "Put it on and tell us what you see." They smiled strangely while my mask spoke of all that film could be, medium that contains all the others like Chinese boxes: words, movement, colors, space, most plastic of all forms, can make any miracle occur. Glowing in the golden mask to remember that glimpse on the beach, film as it might be, the vehicle of greatest possibilities, purer than music, light its very substance. How did Nell know I should repeat this experience again, but differently, more workmanlike this time? Reaching for the impossible to make something happen twice the same color, to achieve frames identical with that strange blue light we got the first time, so unearthly and accidental.

Driving to Long Beach in the dark, top down on the movie car, six of us stuffed in, laughing, becoming friends again or perhaps for the first time since we have already learned each other to the very bottom better or more brutally than friends or family during those three terrible weeks. We have been so far away so long it is communion, this hilarious ride lost on back roads. "Maybe we will get there sometime before we run out of gas," Robin is caustic and Rhoda shows off emptying the pumps of a forlorn place on the unlighted highway. Next we must forage for food. "A company must be fed," Mallory commands, finding a Dunkin Donuts where everyone treats everyone else, the waitress treating us all. Mallory remarks loudly that no one ever eats coconut to a man eating coconut, the morsel poised at the rim of his mouth. And suddenly he laughs. We are our own fantasy selves doing the most romantic thing in the world, making movies. Today brings back the euphoria of that first day when we picked up the equipment and rode in an open car down Seventh Avenue, all the precious machinery piled high, Rhoda in her Superman shirt perched arm in arm with Robin up on the top of the back seat, all of us bellowing the Hallelujah Chorus. We were real. We could talk a cop out of a ticket by just conveying our excitement at doing the greatest thing imaginable. And he understood. Because everyone in America wants to make movies.

Celebrating this again when we come upon a filling station a whole car full of uproar pulling in out of the dark, Robin stretched from the back seat to the front, necking with Rhoda to scandalize the proprietor, all of us delighted to watch his response. Remarkable man disappoints us, wiping the windows as if we don't exist behind it in our lawlessness off in our own world, too many of us to challenge. "Kerouac and his buddies lived like this and it was important," Rhoda says. Can we achieve such validity ourselves, could I give my friends life on paper? Not unless I can listen harder, remember exactly what people say. So far I'm trapped in self, trying to find me. Rhoda encourages me to write in the first person, a friend of hers left husband and child for the solitude of a cabin where her whole life poured out suddenly upon paper. "This is our time. We will see our fantasies take shape before our eyes, we have magic now."

We forgive each other for last year. Delora giggles plump and helpless in the back seat, recalling how I announced I'd put six hundred dollars in the bank, "My God, she expected to do a film with that." We shout together exhuming pieces of my innocence, our collective insanity, the pathology of our role playing, the wars between the "technical people" who dealt in the mysteries versus the "people people" who merely dealt in the personalities of the women in the film, or the agony of the changing bag in the August heat of Mallory's elevator where we searched for perfect darkness. Amid our present uproar I return to that strange brown evening when all nine of us, sick of each other and needing peace, danced for hours stationed at intervals across the huge floor of Mallory's loft, each alone in her space, women's bodies moving in the somber light against an immaculate white wall.

For us the movie will always be the shooting, never that thing on the screen which I made, editing it alone. It will be what we endured together making it, our orgies of recrimination and re-creation. For me it will be the feel of their hands on my body holding me high in air

that first day of shoooting when Robin led the trust game
and I was "it" in darkness, blindfolded, having to depend
on them. They did not fail me. Then she made us hold
hands and look into each other's eyes. I held Mallory's,
asking her to give herself when we shot, hold nothing
back. And always the movie will be one sequence we
never even used, Mallory in the skylight loft one morning
dancing alone, my sister life itself to the Beatles' "Here
Comes the Sun," Mallory moving in her perfect rhythm,
motion connected to force, a figure sensual, yellow, the
first thing of day, hope even before coffee.

I read the paper while the others check cameras and
meters, rituals of technology. Here's an interview with
Erich Segal, once a good professor of classics at Yale
who wrote a silly book that undergraduates labeled
reactionary, driving him from his university. "Success
kills," he says. Wanted to go back to the time before
it happened. So did I. Now maybe I will stop wanting
that and go on, getting up to shoot in the bright ocean
morning, timing again, directing, the bunch of us a team
at last cooperating. "It's the little egos that cause the
trouble," Robin prounounces like a sage sitting crosslegged on the beach, around us the mystery of ocean, the
light, the color of their violet clothes against the sand. The
moment comes, they are composed before us far away
through our lens. There the three of them sit motionless
before us upon the sand. And here stand the three of
us—Rhoda, Delora, and I—light, sight and idea in league
behind the camera. They are still there while the seconds
spin on the dial, I hold time in my hand while life
becomes its record in the spin of a machine. Powerful
as God. Even while we do it I realize we have failed.
Of course Mallory was right, her belligerent voice maintaining there is no such thing as an identical retake, "We
will do something better, meaning different." But I
wanted the same thing, did not change the sequences.
She carries on like union labor when we ask for extra
takes. Robin's hair is too long for continuity. Rhoda used
the wrong f stop on our only roll of 7255. We did not

get it. There are clear images on the 7252, good enough to use but not the same. Never the same, that peculiar blue of the first time, its eerie mood lost forever from the film, a crucial ambiance no one will ever miss but me, mourning it permanently. This very dissatisfaction will ensure that I go on, make more movies, pursuing the ineluctable forever. Of course Nell was right.

So we didn't get it. What we got was something else, better than film. We got together. Healing the wound made in each of us last summer. Driving back in the afternoon's mellow light we are better people and we feel it, smoking pot in the open car, serene and happy. Rhoda holds forth, our lecturer on the sexual revolution, "We must accept everything human, even the roles, play each one of them, crazy as they are, go through them in sequence. And we must develop a new sensuality, more general, less specific, genital sex is too confining, too unimaginative, too limited and ungenerous." "Did you ever make love with two people at once?" I ask her. "Yes, and I want to tell you it was a catastrophe. Jealousy surprised us. The lines of affection snapped like that. We are still lost to each other."

I hear and try to understand that dawn when Celia gave me Miriam. An afternoon of hard crying, Miriam's red nose an indignity of snuffles. And Celia cruel I felt, mediating between the one's dependence and the other's fear of being tied. Celia a fishwife astonished me. My compassion for Miriam's need is because her fate is always before me till it was mine. After the ease of tears Miriam slept, leaving us to dine in a Mafia restaurant, me to gape at murderers, Celia to congratulate herself for knowing such hangouts. Then Celia brought me back to Miriam. Afraid, a bit modest, some stoic bravado covering my diffidence before so new and maybe dangerous an experience, undressing in the bathroom and coming out to see that we were three nudes, three white bodies in the white dawn reflected from the ceiling and filling the room, a silverpoint of shadows, still at times, then moving chiaroscuro. It was very beautiful.

Then it failed. Because I wanted Celia and did not know Miriam. Celia had taken from us our first time, we had not yet had each other alone, just Miriam and me to concentrate only upon the other. We were only friends who made jokes together, hilarious simply by pronouncing together words like Bemidji, Oshkosh, Duluth, twins of a middlewestern childhood where there was enough to eat but people were too poor to have music. Miriam has crushed all the gray melancholy of our October evenings after the grain is cut and winter coming and put that sorrow into her music. I have already loved her in her voice, but never in those other senses of the flesh.

Now Celia is directing life, she will solve jealousy by hurrying us, be sure the slow drift we have already made toward being lovers is completed. Miriam is making love to Celia who is making love to me. And then I stopped it. Told Celia she could not bring me there, was not even competent. And so I cannot bring Miriam, my hand on her failing, unable to know her so suddenly. This is not right for a first time. Theoretical Celia playing God to the rest of us. But how much of it was my fault, the greed of my preference for Celia?

So I take issue with Rhoda, telling her three is not wrong in itself, merely a matter of how well you do it. "I have been with two women I loved. And it was beautiful. But it became terrible too. Why should it be?" "We don't understand jealousy yet," she answers. And we riddle it together. Is it possession? No, we have ceased to believe we own. Insecurity then? If so, what kind? Deprivation and loss? Of what then? The focus of attention, time together, the power of choosing time and occasion to meet, a convenience now shared with another? Or a deeper craving never satisfied because there was never enough love in our lives, we have been forever hungry since childhood, our unfed appetite still whammering? So one satisfiies it with the love of many, loving more than one, and hits the wall of the unknown, the experiment releasing what kind of forces never understood? While we talk I wonder if what I remember is what happened. And what does Celia remember? What does Miriam? But we never talked, did not discover, comprehend. In silence we may die, not knowing. Of course we may be insane or profligate to some who have no faith in love, no interest in the mystery of the mind, the senses, the self, the past, the most crucial forms of understanding. But such things are a fascination to us, friends driving home in the long golden afternoon of trees until the hellish landscape of man begins near the city, the industrial blight that starts around Elizabeth. Driving along, each of us practices seeing this stretch, how to shoot it, obsessed with the outer eye as much as the inner. In the city, parked in front of Delora's apartment house on Sixth Avenue, we linger an hour talking movies, machines, our plans and ambitions. Delora says I should shoot now myself, she will teach me camera, generous to me in her way as Rhoda.

Claire does not come. We are all here now, the whole group except Claire. Barbara and I are both her lover and we are both worried. Pretense of interest in the meeting, what topic shall we choose? The talk is easy rather than earnest. Witty, exuberant, relaxing. I wander between it and the telephone where Barbara has reached Claire and is holding her in the black plastic against her ear. She will not come, is sick, is busy, is something. I ask to talk. Claire says she has a cold. I was afraid of this, knew it was coming in that nonsense about her neurosis. She will disappear from me now. I cannot hold her, she will go faster. Yes, take care of that cold.

We decide to forget the meeting and hold an informal discussion on the body. "The flesh," Barbara and I tease them. "No, the body and its image," O'Flynn corrects us. "By now there is the new gay and the old," Ruth begins, "the new Lesbian radicals who are the vanguard. Young, good-looking, a type of elite. And the old bar dykes like derricks in their duck-ass haircuts, their mannish leather belts. Our ghetto people. How do we feel about them?" I feel so many things, fascinated repelled contemptuous compassionate loyal dishonest. My ideal always an image of two beautiful women in ecstasy. And they have defiled it with their ugliness, their cheap imitation man and woman. Femme is mere tinsel. And butch is the shadow that has fallen across all our lives, the false self that lives in wait to capture you, to seize your shoulders and make them self-conscious, wrong, to give you away as you cross a room, your body betraying you like a stranger before accusing eyes.

Another spot in my mind is wondering why I do not want Fosta. Who is no bull dyke, only a large matronly woman but so fat that she needs a special chair, always a problem at meetings. I want to know why Fosta is fat. I have been fat but not this fat, surely she inflicts it on herself. And why can't I desire every woman, sister, Lesbian? Not practical. Not enough time. Life is not an orgy. Only "relationships" justify sexual pleasure. Friendship is what it's about finally. And there are great obligations in friendship. But if you love your friends, why is it you do not want to sleep with all of them? What is sensuality, where does it stop between the gratification of touch and the hot genital current between the legs?

In New Haven Carol's group had a party, the women upstairs and their men downstairs talking and smoking grass. Upstairs we sat on the big bed. Tonight this segregation by floors is some sort of experiment, later we'd join the men. We are drinking wine and singing, the door to the hallway is partly shut, it is a little dark in the room. Higher on the wine we talk softly, sprawling on the bed we touch each other and do not say excuse me. Someone touches my hair I am not sure who, smoothing it gently. My hand is kind on someone's face. When women touch your face their hands so sensitive it makes you feel special, important, recognized. Now we are kissing. I am frightened, eight years I have not done this, and then never when it was many. I am straight now, married. Their hands on my face, a woman's cheek soft brushing mine, the lips kissing. Don't even know whose it is. Where is my friend Carol, the others I hardly know, Carol is from Minnesota too, I am staying at her place up here. She is kissing someone else and it is beautiful to see. Their heads are against the light from

the door. My side is dark. I do not have to worry about
who is pretty, the tyranny of my own eyes, the continual
tyranny of looks. Mine. Theirs. My hand is gentle to
a shoulder, or is it a leg? A woman's cheek touches my
cheek softly. It is lovely. It is different from sex but it
is sex. Where will it stop? Doesn't matter feels so good
feels wonderful. But we cannot do this. The movement
cannot be queer, dykes the papers call us. No, straight
we rush to assure them, showing wedding rings and
children, pushing the prettiest ones forward to go on
television. How can we have this pleasure, it must be
wrong, must not be. Afraid, my body alive with it and
how curious that it doesn't matter that I cannot recognize faces, a woman, just a woman is touching me,
touching woman itself. Tender, and you don't even know
who it is. Is this an orgy, never been to one—an oil man
from Texas bought paintings and gave orgies, lots of
painters went. Years ago.

He came to dinner upstairs at Janey's and I went up
for a drink. Zoe wouldn't go. She was shy. "He's a
bastard anyway," she said. I was sitting on a high stool
over by the window and he said which are you the butch
or the femme? I stared. No one had ever called me a
dyke to my face. Except one guy I met in the Cedar Bar
who said he knew Durrell and the people in the *Alexan-
dria Quartet,* so cultured, fascinating, handsome gray-
haired man. My friends now do not read many books,
they are painters, I have stopped telling people I went
to Oxford. He pays me court, I am flattered. We went
over to Tommy McNutt's loft afterwards, whole bunch
of us drunk and and happy. But now he is standing on
a tabletop and announcing to the others there is a Lesbian
here. Pointing at me. I will go mad listening to him the
unthinkable word, people can hear him. Jesus, McNutt,
make him get down, save me, I'm your friend, it's your
house. McNutt doesn't do a thing. The monster still
talking, now they are all looking at me in my red sweater
unmasked, naked, people's eyes staring. Zooey sits in
the corner dazed, her eyes lost. There are no words in
my head, it is empty. Only waves buzzing. Will I faint?

Can I die? Disappear? Later he asked why are your fingernails short? My mouth is preparing to say because of the plaster I work in plaster I told you I was a sculptor, always so proud to say it waiting my chance to say I am an artist when I meet people. "But of course they are short because you are a Lesbian." His voice is clipped with assurance. It is like being hit. He is saying we do it with our hands. Hands are ridiculous, you cannot make love with your hands, it looks funny in a book.

This bastard from Texas with his terms I've never heard of. My face burns before his brash curiosity. He is not embarrassed, I am. So I am a fool kid, a hick among sophisticated people and he is smart and grown up. I have no words. The others watch me while I am humiliated. No one speaks. Janey and Bill look on silent.

Then I am downstairs again in my own loft banging things yelling fuck wondering if they can hear me upstairs, throwing the books on the floor, the precious leather sets from Oxford. Zooey's face is beaten. Washburn comes downstairs, my own Janey from college, how can she let such people in her house—he's a pervert! Proud, puritan, furious. Janey "knows" but the three of us are polite and overlook it, never mention that it is hard. Once she walked into the bedroom when we were in bed and just grinned, "Don't get up, Milletface." We pretend there is nothing, Zoe and I are roommates. Now she is soothing me, how her divine tolerance irritates me. Then one day after Zoe left, Billy said that my new girlfriend was pretty. I rejoiced at the pretty, resented the girlfriend, ignored the remark. No one could reach me behind my defense. Nickelman stopped by one day and mentioned that the new girl who was subletting his apartment never gave them any trouble: "After all, she's a Lesbian." He might as well have said nigger, I was outraged. Why did I pretend the word was not there when it is me? No word more terrifying, in my mother's mouth it is a snake hissing, Lesbian, intake of breath the unspeakable word.

Are we being Lesbian on the bed in New Haven or

is this some sisterly business, an experiment in sensual understanding, the new line on touch gratification? Is it contaminated or not? What if it were not wrong to touch people, gently enjoying it? Is this sex or does it stop somewhere short? What is love, this friendly feeling carried further, or something different? Do all these things coexist: sex, love, sensuality? Or are there rules where you shake hands or fuck with nothing in between? I lie here their hands upon me knowing only that this is. A discovery so moving, so strange. Then it stopped. Someone came into the room or left it. There was a noise. Did something frighten us? I cannot remember how it came to an end.

After a while downstairs with the men, a little guilty trying very hard to enjoy ourselves. I liked them. Some people had guitars, the rest of us made music on pots and pans. I delighted myself with a kettle. We danced around in circles. Tense again saying good-byes at the door. Each man claiming his woman. We had frightened them. Telling ourselves they didn't know, but of course they must have felt it. So possessive and the women passive now, obedient, contrite.

When Carol and I got home we fell together in the bed. One year ago February in New Haven. It was the first time in eight years I had been with a woman. Cried remembering it again in her arms. But the whole thing so barren and awkward. She was closed to me, dry, I could not teach her since really she did not want it, not me or anyone. All those years being fucked by some black militant. Had never had an orgasm. The next month she learned to masturbate with a vibrator, the machine her final companion.

Fosta is getting pretty sick of the discussion we're having on weight. She has guessed that my little generalizations about self-attitude are directed at her, has seen through my deviously apologetic openers, "Like I've got this magical notion people look how they feel." I drift off again thinking how sometimes I look like hell, sometimes I'm beautiful depending on how I like myself or if I'm busy I try to look crummy when I work so as not to distract myself. Other times I'm the most fatuous narcissist because I have been beautiful for only a little while and am not used to it yet. Since New Haven. Women gave me beauty. Fumio does not find it interesting, suspects it. Says I'm tiresome when I preen for him. His favorite photograph is one he took where I look like an Irish washerwoman. I prefer one Louise Mark did where I look beautiful. Someone else saw it and said my eyes were frightened.

Fumio is very beautiful but his aunt once said he was ugly. He was four years old when she made up a song about his looking like a monkey. Forty years later he still believes it. For a decade I have admired his beauty to no avail whatever. Elegant figure dark and lithe, twenty-six-inch waist. Love the feel of him in my hands, the slender chest and hips, no seat at all, his skin so smooth and hairless, and his magical penis wonderful change when you touch it stands up grows strong hard lovely feeling when it enters holding it inside melting me till it melts. I can squeeze it till he gasps coming and I worry about his heart. His father died fucking. He is always evading me because he will not believe he is beautiful or that I love him. Then he revenges himself with glumness, the shadowy feudal samurai world dead now still living on in him. And the war has broken his hope. A whole generation of them have it in their eyes, his classmates, the artists I met over there. Fumio's eyes at eighteen saw Hiroshima, a boy sailor posted in a boat offshore sent in to bring out the dead and dying, their withered figures walking toward him along the railroad tracks, naked, bald, all hair and clothes burned off, only the rubber elastic band from their underwear still left about their waists. The skin hanging off their arms like long kimono sleeves. So when I believe in a new life he is dubious always, critical. He awaits me, a nest of disapproval, distrusting me for a mere enthusiast. And when I stalk him he escapes me. I will pursue him all my life and never have him.

Fosta is angry now, defending herself. Admirable in her immensity saying she has a beautiful life, is loved.

Ruth loves fat women not skinny ones, she insists. I am wrong. Wrong for loving beauty. Also wrong for not just accepting that I do. And confused. Calder was beautiful. It is character Fumio always says. It is health and intelligence I always argue. Fosta has all these and is not attractive to me. Should I really want everyone, what is impartial love? What if I love just one—sufficiently? No, now I want to love many people.

We give up on the discussion and Claudia shows her movies. I see a whole world of women, they are all Lesbians and they are beautiful. Women photographed in nature in the country or at parties. An architect making these remarkable home movies. Edited with extraordinary care right in the camera. I decide home movies are where it's at, their intimacy a thousand times more real and interesting than screenplay fiction. Those boring story lines. I know some of the people and some I don't, but they all look wonderful in Claudia's eyes, lovely, serene. Lesbians are the only people who inhabit the screen, we are beautiful. Always I have been ashamed of us that we were ugly. Now we are transformed into a whole world that is us. I want all of them. Watching in love with women in love.

Ruth is inviting me to the houseboat tomorrow. I was to go sailing with Claire but she has invited Claudia as well. I do not want to go when there is someone else along. Maybe I should leave Claire to herself and go to the houseboat. It is the world of Claudia's movie. I can drive Ruth and Vita. Ruth is one of Vita's lovers now, but we do not feel jealousy, have overcome it by loving many, our jargon calls it "multiple relationships." I am a great advocate of it at this moment, sure we are conquering jealousy, leaving it behind, all of us friends and immune to who is paired with whom. Vita would love an outing, never gets a holiday. I will leave Claire alone for a while.

As we are leaving, Sidney points out contemptuously that we are merely a network: "Everybody knows everybody else and they are all sleeping together." "No," I protest, "it's cynical to talk like that. We are a new way to live." But I do not even know what I mean, am only a greedy child running hungrily down the staircase. Going to Claire to see what is wrong. There is a dance at DOB. I drive the others over and wait while they get out. They all know where I'm going. Behind the wheel, self-conscious and annoyed as they close the car doors, teasing me or saying nothing. Barbara has gone inside. Sidney stays in the car. "You may be doing something very dangerous." "Why?" "You may lose her." "I am her friend, if she is really sick or even if she's just mixed up, it's my job to help her, isn't that what it means?" Knowing I am also in love and will lose of course because I can never stay back. But I will try. "Get out and let me alone."

When I arrive she opens the door. Always she lets me in when I come to her door and yet each time I am afraid she will not. She is gay till she tells me her news. She has decided to become an ascetic again: "Life in the flesh does not agree with me finally. It was wrong to resume it. It hinders me in my pursuits. All the mystics advise against it. I have been reading them by the sackful. I hope very much you can still love me."

I answer yes. Wasn't Vita this generous with me? Yes it's fine, but my stomach isn't, my stomach is scared. Celia did this to me in a little note on yellow foolscap last summer, a little note to tell me we had better go platonic: "You know what that means. No SEX." The vulgarity of it astounded me. She had drawn a line between everything else and love, making it *sex*, something suddenly crude, obscene, singled out, it became my carnality, the thirsting beast Carol made me feel. Catholic guilt of the flesh ravening now for being forbidden. With Celia it was hardly as simple as sex, it was different, a strange communion of spirit looking in her eyes those endless seconds while we touched each other's center, perfectly, just the fingertip upon the clitoris moving more and more slowly, our eyes steady on each other and the delicate pressure fine and more fine until all motion stopped in one still point remembered always, a vision. And then I did not know her pleasure from mine, my body from hers. We fell into and became each other. Then we slipped over the edge, entered and made love.

Yes I will still love you of course I say, panicking for a way to change this ending. So I set out to amuse, give a parody of the meeting, a replay of Claudia's movies, enthuse about home movies, how Claudia has captured our reality on film. "It is necessary we believe in it. And we must go to the dance." I cannot remain here with this catastrophe. A miracle occurs and she agrees to go. Our arrival is debonair, both of us playing it cool, joking with the kids who sell the beer, young girls who have taken off their shirts. Rachel Goodwin says it's freedom, men do it. The kids say it's hot. I say it's beautiful, their young breasts lovely and small, how delightful to see them. "Take yours off," they dare me. But I am afraid, I am not twenty, my breasts are larger, all my life ashamed of their size. When I got fired from Columbia I could quit wearing a bra and dresses. Then I gave up the schoolmarm bun and wore my hair down. Mother drew in her breath and said I looked like a hippie. She waits like a martyred saint for my luggage, "Of course you'll have dresses in there Katie it makes a bad impression to wear pants on airplanes." "No, I didn't bring any dresses, Mother, just more pants." Like a novena Mother keeps on whispering, "Katie you can't have done this to me," as if repetition will fill the suitcases coming down the ramp with clothes appropriate to dinner with her friends. After the *Time* cover Mother raised the ante, now I looked like an old Indian crone. Cousin Rosalyn who used to be a nurse said I'd get breast cancer for sure without a bra. Now I could feel my nipples against the cloth, tripping on the sensuality of it for days after discovering them. But I cannot take off my shirt. Neither can most of my friends. But the youngsters can, dancing in the center of the room all in a tribe of bodies and breasts weaving in the pale dark of the turning lamps. Magnificent how free they are, the bodies of women in the strange light spinning many colors on their flesh, their breasts moving, their arms thrown out. Claire seems to offer me her body again in the dance. I remark on her inconsistency and she laughs, we are both laughing; nearly all we ever do, everything is funny to us. It will be all right.

She will buy me a drink at Paolo's. Ill at ease again in this nether world that is not our world, so much less so than the dance. This dark place bristling with the unconscious, the famished self rampant all through the room. Two women stand near us, figures staring out like lost children, looking always looking out their futile eyes searching good God for love. They will not find it in the stud bracelet of the blond at the next table, the expensive trousers of the bartenders, the tough butch supervising the humiliating queue into the toilet. Here and there the new ones, kids in big hats with bookbags on their shoulders.

Against this background Claire casts the shadow of Barabbas: "A he-man like Hemingway, type of guy who'd call Jesus a skinny creep who looks like Fred Astaire." Then she shifts gears and begins telling it seriously, adapting Kazantzakis to conversation. "Barabbas is out to save his neck though no one could imagine why. And when he's done it and is back on the streets again he's still plagued by those Jesus freaks, this cult of fanatics he is forever running into or being mistaken for and confused with by other people. The whole business irritates him unspeakably. After it's over, all the hullabaloo and the crucifixion, he meets this poisonous female, a hairlip, whiny and unbelievable ugly, dragging herself along the road coming home from Golgotha. Barabbas raped her once and you really don't need to see people you have this sort of relationship with. She snivels, he loathes the sight of her. But she's a Jesus creep and he's exasperated with it at last, so he asks her what, just what was so great about that guy? 'He told us to love one another' she says, and it hits him like a stone. After all," Claire concludes, "miracles are simply the effect of circumstances or even personalities that are capable of radically altering human behavior."

I counter with Marius the Epicurean, since I must always take issue: "On the side of Aurelius, not the angels perhaps, but civilized. One of the last civilized persons in Rome's degraded welfare state of free bread and carnage. Must have been appalling to be a late Roman noble and observe the Christian hordes take over, a religion of underdogs and drudges winning out. You might even wonder why it was this particular bunch that won out over the hundreds of others, some probably still crazier, the late Empire a welter of them, a Dionysian madness of sects springing up into the void now that the Republic's rotted into Empire. Falling apart, you might say, overextended like America, and bankrupt through expensive and badly managed foreign wars." Our heads nearly touch each other during these peculiar ruminations, our delirium of talk, quaintly academic in these surroundings, our eyes in love again when we are silent for a moment. The management has already extended more butter for our popcorn. I look up to see Paolo's transformed into Roman decadence through the kind cooperation of the Mafia, and suggest a comparison between the DOB and the early Christians, the women dancing there tonight pure in their grotto, a loft hidden in Soho's abandoned night streets, their naked breasts a ritual of chastity compared to the careful butch costumes we see here. All revolution is religion changed, but not that much.

It can also be a new and terrible orthodoxy with purge and heretic, its Inquisition ending in a firing squad right next to the stake. How to maintain that gentle communion of new persons whom Marius could admire but never join. And I know that hesitancy of his, though he was fair enough to acknowledge this new spirit as a finer thing than laws and bridges, the achievements of Roman efficiency and technology. So very American they were, a culture of management and administration. Our new people now on communes, or in CR groups, our liberation movements like cults springing up everywhere, succeeding each other, their new spirit infusing our Rome's tottering Empire, rigid still against real change. Shall we pass on to political revolution like Russia, Cuba, China, Algiers, which are, yes, better than the starvation that preceded them, but dull police states too in some ways. Change on the surface, the political and economic structure, leaving the spirit oppressed still in many ways. Shall we put the queers in concentration camps, jail the dissenters, purge, execute, forever abandoning change itself in the obsessive drive for power? Or shall we find a new way, finally change everything, not just the usual categories of politics or economy, but society itself, the dynamic of roles and identity, all the basic structures, the family, sexual identity, the self itself? And do it for freedom's sake without coercion, violence, killing? A problem too difficult to solve at Paolo's.

Back at Fifth Street, under a host of photographic icons I am awarded the bed while Claire pursues holiness in a sleeping bag on the floor next to me, holding hands in a sweet absurdity I shall always treasure. Chekhov smiles down at me from tintype. Claire reports that he wanted champagne when he knew he was dying: "After all he hadn't had any for a long time, consumption you know. He drank a toast and was quiet. His wife slept then and woke. He was dead already. There was sunlight on the corpse. A morning without Chekhov. The funeral was a terrible mess. Only a few friends showed up 'cause they held it out in the country. And the mourners got lost and followed the wrong coffin, turned out to be a general. Retracing their steps they tried to catch up with a wagon that looked like it might be the hearse and had some writing on it. So they hurried and hurried, managed to overtake it and read the lettering. On the tailgate it said 'OYSTERS.' "

5

First thing Vita says as she wakes up: "I was once as fine as Celia." Odd, can she be this embroiled, actively jealous? Has she fallen into my cult? Yet I can guess what she is saying on another level, that she is Celia's kind and has lost it, herself, who she was, or used to be before the fifteen year of wife. Yesterday walking up the beach I recognized the Brahmin in her. Underneath, they always knew what to wear. And for the trip to the houseboat Vita had slipped and permitted herself a simple jersey with a fine white boating sweater tied around the neck. Exactly the right thing, it had been there all along hiding under an assumed ugliness. She was young again, lovely. I congratulated her. "You've found something you threw away. Rummage among your beginnings and pick out what works, you needn't keep their arrogance and that sort of thing. Discriminate, make new combinations." Later, shopping in the Village, I even detected a Waspish snobbery in the wrinkle of her nose at a loud Mexican border, letting me know it was unthinkable I should be so gross as to consider it. Made me nervous, bit overmuch of the Saxon manner. Snottiness, we used to call it in parochial school.

Vita yawns comfortably. She is finally ready to discuss the manuscript. Yesterday she refused categorically, a punitive mother withholding the simplest comment, manipulating me crazy. Impossible that the stuff involves her too much. Denied me any word until she snapped, "You've got to stop saying I kissed the soft of her neck twice in ten pages." Then closed up again like a turtle. Today her remarks are pointedly editorial: "Why did

200

you want to change tables waiting for Celia at Verde's, how could you be so craven?" her voice full of scorn recognizing that Katie who got the ax. "It was snobbery." "Exactly," and she loathes me a bit more openly. "No, a different snobbery, an outsider's, it's a kind of collusion with people who despise you, like the Jew falls into while lusting after the fancy Christians in *Goodbye, Columbus*. I saw it in myself and couldn't deny it."

Vita still doesn't see the point. I change the subject, mention that I wrote the passage right there while I waited, but of course you can tell that. No, she hadn't noticed. Suddenly Vita claims to be thunderstruck by this detail of composition as if it were some miracle. Now I am getting scared, this sort of praise is more dangerous than blame or coldness. But it has made me start building things in air, over the bed, out the casements to the Bowery, a roof spanning the city, a shimmering hope this book might make our lives live, our Downtown real. Only a clique of friends, but what did Dante have to make the *Vita Nuova* but a club of fellow poets and their odd little cult of love, calling it a new life. And because he did it happened. For ages after people were living it, in one corner of their souls he had invaded them. Vita grows restless. Hearing Dante she suspects Beatrice. Gives me a look like I was in graduate school too long.

Instead she unwraps her bright new ideology, it should all be political, it should wave a flag. I try to argue that propaganda is a bore, has no magic. "You're an instant Lesbian, you're not really gay. It's something you learn through years of eating shit." "But I've found at last my own community, the gay world has given me a home." "That's nice." Looking for cigarettes I have time to regret my sarcasm.

Already feeling lost when I walk into the dressing room. Fumio's clothes are there, the suits we never bothered to hide from Mother, only the shoes and the shaving cream buried out of sight in the living room—kitchen during two years of visits when she arrived openly wanting to know did he love her daughter, when was he going to marry her? How many different directions converge here? Every time I enter this room I lose my book. It happened all winter. I stand dazed among laundry baskets, perplexed by definitions. Facing me is the small oil Kawashima gave at the wedding. Not really abstract at all, a frankly sexual pattern, bright red on white. Loaded when I saw it first, I made some asinine speech about how he uses Japanese crests in his work. The wedding guests laughed, I was as embarrassed as a virgin bride. On the opposite wall a drawing by Black Jackie Witten, another friend of our existence as a couple. How dare I be queer and live with this guy?

What am I then, some pulp Sappho? The library of cheap paperback Lesbian affairs full of sentiment I hoarded once because they were the only books where one woman kissed another, touched her, transported to read finally in a book what had been the dearest part of my experience recognized at last in print. Kept them hidden in a drawer so visitors would never spy me out. Afraid the sublet might find them, I burned them before I set out for Japan. Really I was ashamed of them as writing, the treacle of their fantasy, the cliché of their predicament, heartbroken butch murders her dog, etc. The only blooms in a desert, they were also books about grotesques. No, the problem is impossible, Vita's comment about too much soft of neck convicts me, I will never get beyond the tawdry.

I go back to the bed where Vita has ensconced herself for the day. Then I see him. The voyeur. Staring at us from across the way. Framed in the window of an abandoned loft building on First Street, probably a squatter. Looking right at us across one hundred yards of clean summer morning air. I jump back, my hands longing for a gun would gladly shoot him. Spying on us, the bastard, how dare he? Vita never moves. She has no twenty years of hiding to run from. She only smiles. The morning is preternaturally clear. The building and the man are cut as clean as de Chirico, the geometry of infinitide. And suddenly he's funny—and what does it really matter? He can't hurt us. I look at him, he is not even "a man," "a voyeur," he is a person with a beard and warm eyes and a smile. Vita has taught me something. Now he is playing a guitar to us while we sit smoking, naked, we actually wave at each other. I would not do this with Claire, nor would she sit through such a thing, so shy, so tenuous after her long history with the shrinks. I would want to protect her from this man. Because Claire is gay. Vita isn't gay, she is beyond it. Where I want to be, moving there now, watching the figure across the clean morning light. His girlfriend has joined him, both waving to us now, their arms about each other. They are naked too but the window blocks the view below their shoulders. Greater access to privacy than my casements afford, but never mind. It is a moment of amnesty. I shudder at the violence I felt a moment past. Ready to shoot, and calls herself a pacifist. The four of us, naked and with music, the four of us are peace. There is a buzz and things stop, frozen after a little dizziness like the private signal I used to get when first seeing a sculpture that would be important to me, the Miroku Bosatsu or a late Donatello, moments when the significant is not only present but announces itself. I look across at the couple in the window, then back at us. This, Vita, is what we mean, the new life, here in a moment on a Sunday morning, prefigured, as symbols are consummation long before the fact, but in their name we follow after dreams.

So Vita is dear to me this rare fragment of time out of time, momentary cessation in our long hostilities, the war of attrition she has declared on me because I will not love her as she demands, never forgiving me for that. And why should she? It is the thing one cannot forgive. At the same time she prevents me from loving by always finding just the perfect irritant, the finally unbearable accusation. Because it will prevail, that angry screaming red-faced child in her, still hating the world and perhaps her father in particular for not having loved her sufficiently once. So that it will be damned if it will now or ever relent, obdurate that it will not be loved where it wishes to be. And where it is loved, will despise the lover for loving . . . shit. Which is what she thinks she is. This is Vita. It is me too. It is even Celia. All in our different ways. But Vita is the most stubbornly determined to stay that way. Celia the most stubbornly deceptive, claiming this is not the case; she is a blithe spirit and above this rot. And I the most stubbornly desperate to escape this trap into the new life where we are absolved, free at last because we grant each other mercy, transcending aversions till aversions cease and we fly above their causes which are only those terrible moments long ago when we were young and damaged, before we had defenses. Vita is to be loved as we all are to be loved, and I have loved her, this moment.

We renew our pact of gratitude. She has seen me through the movie blues and dug me out of a writing rut. I have brought her out and urged her past her long childwifehood into self, job, independence. Both drowning, we clung to each other, yes, using each other—it had to be that way. And somehow Vita will get through. And somehow I will be her instrument though she burn me nearly mad using me in passage.

And because I felt so close I said it—"Come be my accomplice, there is a concert today. You will see it all at three o'clock. Just let me work for an hour, then we'll go." Vita is off to find food, still the expert at rendering services. When will I learn that Vita's free-for-nothing favors cost more than a fleet of secretaries, chefs, caterers? The price is two tainted pork chops from the sunny window of a Puerto Rican bodega. Everything else is closed, it's Sunday. The chicken yes, it moves fast. Otherwise you don't buy meat from slum grocers, you wait until Monday or open a can. I try to explain this to Vita, who is a wife and mother and has cooked this poisonous food for me which I am not eating just pushing around my plate, trying to beguile her with talk so she will not notice. But of course she does, furious. "You are spoiled, a gourmet. And I hate cooking, have done it three times a day for other people for fifteen years." "Right. So why offer to cook bad food and force me to eat it?" Back to square one.

But of course I am just as fanatic driving up the West

Side Highway, full of intrigue. I will have no collaborator but Vita can be my confederate. She will see the raw material, sift the ingredients, know the secret, visit the inner sanctum. Fussing over a parking place, already a moment late, march right through the crowd at the door, drop safe into my place on the stone floor. Glowing for them, recognized. Vita glowers next to me. My idea has not been a success. I jump into the music and escape. It is like flying as the sound darts about in air skipping across the chapel vault, disporting itself, showing off, then swells and enfolds me with it till I am wrapped in it like a coat. Just before I disappear I notice from the corner of my eye Vita resolutely planted on the ground, refusing to move. So be it.

Afterwards I introduce Vita to Celia. The two stand measuring each other, Celia appearing kind and cordial, not threatened. Vita does her most ingratiating kid's grin, the nose wrinkles, and she praises the music profusely. Celia's eyes question me: arch, amused, inquiring. I smile back, a magus satisfied with my traceries, aware that it is all too complex to explain.

Driving home Vita astonishes me by staging a tantrum: she had no idea where we were going, didn't figure it out till we got there, saw it was music, it must be Celia, etc. I wonder if her hearing is erratic, surely I explained, she has *read* about these concerts. Never mind, her nerves are undergoing a deadly attack which only whiskey can relieve. She absolutely must have a drink . . . after what I've done to her . . . the last sentence suitably in italics as befits her style. But Vita is incapable of jealousy, has told me so on any number of occasions.

So ruthlessly I pursue my notion of our complicity, lovingly analyzing the figures of my myth. Celia, Fumio, Miriam. Explaining how Fumio loved Miriam for her music, Miriam whom Celia had loved so long that it made music. How at times Celia would go to Miriam only in duty, her desire watered down to a New England conscience. "Imagine going to someone like Miriam from mere duty." Vita imagines very well indeed, has already become Miriam, taken her side, cannot think of enough

ways to say that Celia is a spoiled child, indulged, rotten
with adulation. What is it in Celia she so admires that
she detests her? Or is it only the paragon, the loveliest
girl in the country day school where Vita was a washout
among her tribe? Her Celia, not mine. Not mine even
the grand lady with lute performing and admired before
people. A Celia I love to observe only because it makes
dearer that other Celia, private and mine, the mischievous
tomboy who seduced me, the secret troubadour who
courted me in a slouch hat and big flowered pants playing the lute as I lay helpless on Carol's seedy New
Haven carpet already too weak to get up.

Vita's will to control rages so that she can't wait
till we get downtown. "Stop the car at the nearest bar."
We are passing the West End. Columbia's West End,
all those years after a faculty meeting getting drunk in
a sudden hour with Kate Morgan or Bobby or Mary or
some other fellow teacher. In a rush becoming human
with each other, breaking from the competitive rabbit
life of junior faculty on those rare and furtive occasions
where we permitted ourselves to be friends, five or ten
times in six years. The reason people get pie-eyed at office
parties. Yes, we will stop at the West End. Sitting in
a booth with them now, not Vita. And those precious
moments relieved of the strain of our false selves, with
two drinks so precipitously united. Then I am torn again
because Fumio is waiting alone on the Bowery. On the
happiest occasions we would all pile into a cab, chattering
frenetically all the way downtown, arriving to delight
him, still sober but grateful we have come to share
whatever half a chicken we will now spread over four
people. Or going to Chinatown still more blotto. Finally
talking to each other like friends, pouring out hopes fears
hatreds ambitions, affections building. Then so cut off
again next morning in the office.

All of us had been to school in England. Bobby was
our mascot, we patronized him. But Morgan was my
peer, my paragon, my rival. Morgan and I who shared
the same office, even the same first name, twins in the
idolatrous eyes of our students. In those days we figured

we were the two smartest dames who ever taught college, elbowing each other to be superteach. I was the more adventurous, lugging the avant-garde to Barnard, teaching happenings, dada and Genet, underground movies, Ginsberg probably the first to do so at his own university—of course the place he was most despised. Then it went from art to politics, and again I was adventurous. A better campus politician, Morgan is still here, she kept the job. How can I ever forgive that she has kept the job? And how can she ever forgive that in losing it I became so many things she must have wanted too, one part of her, the part that lives downtown and writes novels in the vacations. Does the other still want to be dean of Bryn Mawr? And I who went such a different way, just as befuddled being myself, sitting here in the old bar out of term yammering about a lost love to Vita, an angry woman who imagines herself dedication scorned, possession deprived of its prize. But I am a free spirit now, an artist banished without the walls. The gates of Columbia are closed. But one part cries out still that they open again upon that vanishing segment of myself which would still rather have that job, the job Morgan has—remembering Bentley's quip on Nietzsche, who would rather have been professor at Basel than God. Lost the job so he had to be Nietzsche.

At the West End Bar I desert Vita. To rejoin Eric Bentley the night they called the cops at Columbia. "I'll resign," the great professor said to our room full of youngsters, impressive to us that he would even be here among the powerless who could not vote in the councils of the ad hoc faculty convened below in Philosophy Lounge, their endless hours of Roman oratory still refusing the demand for student amnesty. "If the police are called I'll resign," Bentley said. And he did. The rest of us got fired.

Because we never believed the cops would come that night to attack our students, their heads broken all over the College Walk. And one boy's eye impaled upon a snow fence. Police like an army invasion, twelve hundred of them, soldiers really, armed against our nonviolence.

I imagined my silly arm band, red for strike, green for amnesty, but white for faculty would so terrify them with a scholar's petty authority they would stop and curtsy with respect. "Over our bodies," we declared, like parents protecting children. Our kids, kissing the last good-bye, taking the subway home. I had been guarding Low twenty-two hours a day while my own sculpture show went down the drain, Fumio saving it for me in continuous phone calls to get fresh instructions on how far apart the holes should be drilled. But when I got to the Bowery, Columbia's radio station is urgent, the bust will come tonight, is starting. Probably another fool's errand but it was against this moment we endured all that waiting, the absence from each other day after day. Fumio sitting up in bed, "It's your job to get there. There's three dollars on the dresser. Take a cab."

Through the gates just in time. A long hassle at the barricades counting on faculty privilege. Almost too low on the totem even to deserve it. I only teach at Barnard, the girls' school. And my other persona, a mere graduate student, you would never get in on the ID tonight. All brass, I make it through the gates an inch ahead of the bullies, mob of plainclothesmen impenetrably disguised in their idea of Joe College, got up in sweatshirts. A few even carried books, little toys in the arms of giants. Get to Low before the dark ranks of the police, the black lines coming over the hill. Then hand in hand with a few other faculty, disappointed there are so few who stay to see it happen, our hands sweating in each other's palms, a gentle frail old Russian scholar, a staunch young man in humanities. I do not see any other women. They let so few of us teach on this side of the street. And no Barnard women faculty except Sue Larson, brave enough to camp out on the stone steps against the violence of either side. Our whole cause here is to see that no one is hurt.

And now I stand here in the dark, holding hands with strangers, mad enough to stand against a stone wall and sing, yes for God's sake we are singing it, "We Shall Overcome," a love song, like the old times in civil rights.

In greater danger now than I have ever been in my life,
gigantic physical coward who was beaten in childhood.
Got myself into this and now I have to stick, tears in
my eyes, loving the words as we sing them. Even
Columbia, I loved you that night. For the first time,
forgetting for once to hate your daily insult, your
bureaucracy, the registration forms where you check
Second Sex if you are female, forms where I lie by signing
my own name and putting Mother down as next of kin
(if I admit to Fumio they will make me use his name
and married women have even less chance at scholarships). For a few glorious days the strike has given
the university to its students. So forget even the weekly
humiliation of graduate seminar where Professor Langbaum encourages the young men to sophomoric humor
over the quality of female intelligence while the four
women among us sit in silence. Professor Langbaum's
favorite young man repeats his point that Morris's
"Guinevere" is a mess of a poem because of course it
seeks to recapitulate the confusions of female thinking.
"Which we all know is a mess." Automatic laughter.
The professor smiles. Forget it, the cops are coming,
twelve hundred black shapes against the sky, darker than
its night, the jocks cheering them on from the walls, "Kill
them." Till they got clobbered too, betrayed by what
they had fancied to be fellow spirits but were really my
Irish cousins who hate the guts of these blond frat boys
rich enough to fool around at college uptown. Waiting
for days, the nightstick drumming nervously in hand to
beat shit out of these brats, unable even to distinguish
them from the other brats, the intellectuals and the radicals endlessly provoking them not only in WASP but in
Jew-who's-made-it arrogance, calling them "pigs."

Here in the East you're brave to say you're Irish, since
it means reactionary, if not the fascists who live in Queens
and work for the city. Morgan laughed a superior laugh
at Mike Quill the barbarian union boss with a brogue
daring to deprive her of the subway a whole month in
winter. So they are coming now, these Irish cops. And
I know them, have enough of their wild mad rage in me

at times to tremble for myself, another killer. But lined up now against a wall for nonviolence, pitted against my own people's hot joy, a blow the only expression finally that we can rely on when pushed to our edge. They are coming at me in the dark, male as my father's brutality in childhood.

But then they surprised us, raped Low sideways, came in through the tunnels. I hear the students bellowing in pain behind my back and the windows breaking. The building is already lost and all my never-budged heroism only comedy. We are finished, the tactical police, helmet and boot already lined solid before Mathematics where it will go hardest. No chance now to break in and bleed on its steps. And try to remember that the job is to be sure no one is hurt rather than to confront policemen armed with gun and club, yourself only a body to offer for breaking. Try to realize that right now the TPF are stampeding people down those dangerous steps below Uris Hall, concrete and iron, narrow, winding, if someone falls they'll be trampled. That horrible passage in Tolstoi. Already running terrorized in the sea of moving bodies, shouting, "Move slowly," till I do it myself, then, "Careful, don't run," becoming the marshal I'm supposed to be, getting people down these stairs and out. But I have not thrown in so much, a whole exhibition, maybe my job, and all this time and fear, just to get on that subway and give up.

So I found another way to get back inside the gates and line up with the others still not evicted from our sacred way, the College Walk. Watching in dull amazement as the dark police outlines lead their prisoners to the caged wagons parked smack upon the Walk. Once only the president of the university could park here. Now all of these kids in handcuffs beautiful, but most of all my own, the girls unsung at Barnard who will never be mentioned in the papers, my own, these beautiful young women dragged along by armed men. What horrors have been performed on them by groping cops righteous at last in kicking a girl in the face, the groin, the breast? My students down these stairs beaten, but no not beaten because they persist in the ritual savage sacrifice, the whole thing barbarous as war brought into our groves. No, not beaten, they were something else I'll tell you, because they yelled it—UP AGAINST THE WALL MOTHER-FUCKER—a chant as grotesque as their captors, but in their mouths glorious. I nearly died from love and pride. My kids were heroines. For a whole moment silence on all sides. Then all hell cops breaking ranks crazed, you could hear their captains calling out so ineffectual it sounded silly, "Hold your lines," while they went berserk to hear a four-letter word in a girlmouth, utterly maddened their sacred values mother virgin whore torn asunder frantic beating every head in sight. We were stampeded down South Field where a boy fell in front of me, the crack of his head on the stone forever ringing in mine. And the shape of the cop clubbing him, posed like a sodomist, finishing the job, his notion of manliness his nightstick.

Now I have again the impossible duty to prevent hurt. Foreseeing how they will be driven up against the fences, captured on iron spikes till beaten to shred pulp blood flesh soft over iron gratings. I must get to Johnson Hall ahead of the pack, hysterically ordering janitors to open the basement doors into the streets so people can escape back to the world again rather than be trapped in dormitory rooms where who would ever know how it happened? I pull rank outrageously, even under these circumstances ashamed to play professor to the broom men, university "personnel," a type of drudge, some gamma out of Huxley's *Brave New World* consistently, pointedly treated as if subhuman. But I am just enough the madwoman to overwhelm their bureaucratic rules that these doors are never opened except on express orders of Buildings and Grounds. I have saved life. Or tried to. Unnecessary finally because the police stopped short at the end of South Field and turned their clubs on stragglers. Watching powerless through the night as the lounge of Philosophy filled with casualties. The scene of uneasy graduate coffee hours transformed into a hospital, bloody sheets all over the Oriental rugs heretofore innocent of everything but the worn nervous shoes of scholarship students.

And the next day I piped up in Barnard's solemn council. As one of the two faculty members who had actually seen the bust we are now discussing so calmly I waived my usual superior artistic boredom with faculty meeting and spoke out. The blood still before my eyes, trying to make them see it. The president, a good woman and better than most, is trying to maneuver this conservative faculty into directing a mild censure at Columbia's administration. Nothing very rude of course, we are Columbia's little sister, an inferior institution knows its place. She orders me to sit down. "This is not show and tell." I am a grade school pupil annihilated by teacher. The faculty roars in delight. I can forgive anything but cheap jokes on smaller people. And they are so easy. I have taught for years and know all the gimmicks, if someone gets out of line you ridicule them; using the handle of authority you appeal to the slave in the others, who will betray themselves by jeering on your side against the one who spoke out for them. But I do not speak for anyone here because last night they were in bed or watching TV or grading papers. Girls' schools do not get into stuff like police riots, radical politics. No, our duty lies in gently leading docile females on to become the docile wives of the doctors or lawyers making it across Broadway behind Columbia's gates. It was not our girls' fight. But they broke and ran to it anyway.

This bar reminds me of too much. So many afternoons with students. Movie class met down here during the strike. Even my Victorians moved out of Barnard Hall to keep on meeting in St. Paul's basement. Of course we were on strike but we still wanted to talk about the books and with each other. So it reminds me of being loved. And of being despised. That night of our little cabal in Nick Olafson's apartment, the five "radical" faculty members trying to figure out how we could alert the students against the new strike rules coming from Albany and beyond that from Washington. "How can we warn them that their acceptance endangers every academic freedom all across the board, not only students but faculty and staff too, our jobs, not just a student's registration card—they can take their money somewhere else—faculty and staff cannot." I offered to write a piece for the campus paper explaining the implications of the rules, advising the students to vote against them. There was a long hesitation. "No, not you," someone said. "Don't write anything, you'd ruin it." The others nodded. And before I knew it I was in tears to realize I was evicted now from the last trust I had, pariah even with them.

One month later came the Cambodian War. But by then I was a red witch heard by no one the few times I was permitted to speak, urging on them the actuality that people are being slaughtered, people real to me as Fumio are being slaughtered, cornered now in schoolhouses and shot against concrete walls amid screams and the piles of corpses loaded on trucks shift after shift through the night. While our faculty debates Incompletes and Absences, resolutely avoiding the issue of whether it would join a peace strike across the country on behalf of persons killed far away, across the world, not just across Broadway. They had stopped listening. I was merely an irritant, irrelevant as some unwashed nut trying to put them on with prophecy. It was over for me.

The six years at Columbia all ended here in this bar, closest I ever come to the university now. Used to boast that when they fired me I'd hold my classes here, eternal unpaid teacher. But my students are gone now. And that last spring as an organizer along the East Coast I discovered students are everywhere. At Smith I sat and listened to them, an anonymous outside agitator during Cambodia while the great assembly hall rang out to their shouts STRIKE STRIKE STRIKE. Knowing I had helped that moment come. And that I was already beyond the university, having entered something wilder like life. And there were other places besides Barnard. Even besides Columbia.

The whiskey glints on its ice, the glass stands solid on the old wood table. I am beyond the university another way now. Wanting to write, sitting before my judge, Vita. Tell me, are my people, the ones in the book, Celia, Fumio, Miriam, are they subject fit for writing? Tell me, is it possible? But she will not. Cannot. So we drink up and go home.

Lying across the bed I hear her banging around the Bowery. She is taking my files away from me. When I ask where, she says her place, to put them in order. I should be glad. All the weight of the impossible responsibility, the women from all over whom I can't help enough. That letter from a black woman in Chicago still not answered. I cannot solve her life, am ashamed she asked me: "This is the first time I've ever written to a famous person." My God, a famous person. Then her whole trap laid out, that she has no money of her own, a husband who won't let her work, two kids, and wants to know what books to read. Should I send book lists? Books? When what she needs is another life. Her letter a nice down-home description of black macho, her old man, what it's like to be his nigger. And I cannot solve these lives, can hardly hold on to my own. And now Vita is taking the pieces from my hands. The six years' record I have struggled to keep, forever inadequate, yet there is still enough paper here to choke me. I cannot run the movement from my own studio, why do all these people write? Cases, lives, researchers, women scholars, Gay Lib, peace, women's studies. My stomach listens while she takes all this away, the final obstacle. I should be relieved. Yet I am terrified. What a mess could be made of these folders, not very tidy to start with. I am weeks behind. Will she buy new folders, rearrange in elegantly labeled manila? Methodical Vita, her faultless office, her labels. Will she steal them, reduce them to chaos?

Back to the bed. Keep on writing revising reading into the tape while she slams about packing. Going off with most of me. Keep scribbling. She is out the door. I go on insanely trying to finish the part about Wellesley. Already unsure, sensing there are things left out because she'll see it. Faked so Vita will appear the inspirer, the shining star, the warm mother helping me, always helping me. Saving me from madness. While instinct whispers from the gut, "She's sabotaging you. Escape her or there's going to be no book." "All nonsense," her stolid figure bustles back at me, "you imagine it, you project." And when I say, as if casually, humorously, just an observation, etc., "Could it be possible you're blocking me? Unconsciously I mean, you know how weird I am, people get that way trying to write books. Of course this is merely my way of seeing it, the whole thing is subjective as we both know." She snorts at the very idea. Yet this afternoon when I teased her that she had seduced me, Vita stood there furious, her big lanky body stiff as it is now. Dire threats upon me if I ever said that word again. Vita banging down the stairs and out. I breathe freer, running against time. Vita is a shape sitting on my chest.

In the old farm kitchen, painting chests. Mrs. Horner told me her daughter once had this kitchen for a Home Ec project. The problem: how do you convert to modern use? Has seven doors which always seem like eight and no place for counter space. A railroad station. The daughter fought and was defeated and took her D. Someone recommended we take out the floor above and make it a cathedral ceiling, a "radical solution" he called it. Then I would lose my secret room at the top of the old unheated wing. It is romantic. Also silly. Hopeless to fix, its ceiling falling down. How can I ever conquer this place? Material things are so hard, solid, resistant. They will not move when you will them, the problem of sculpture without its significance.

Like the Bowery all those years with Zoe. We made no effect on the place whatsoever. Zoe wasn't even interested: "Just leave it, we're paying rent." So it was filthy and unreclaimed. Raved about it when I was in Japan, remembered it as glorious space, a thousand plans

to make it civilized, even beautiful. Fumio resisted the
Bowery at first, took one quick look and said the place
was uninhabitable.

His four rooms on Seventh Avenue where we made
love all day. So glad to be together again. He had painted
the floor green for my arrival. Waiting for me to come
to him from Japan. We walked down Seventh Avenue
arm in arm under the tall buildings. We owned New York
and sang in the street. We kissed in front of shop windows. We made love seven times in one day, and when
we got to Janey's for the big party to welcome me home,
Fumio had migraine. In the midst of the roast beef, just
the moment we are sitting down, Bill's knife poised to
carve. Fumio suddenly must go back to Seventh Avenue
to bed. I should go with him. But I am the guest of honor
with my old friends. I must stay, save face for both of
us. I am also having a great time. Moments later contrite
at the thought of how sick he is and leave. Waiting up
all night while he sobs in a pain I have never seen before,
frightened.

When his vacation is over Fumio goes back to the
sweatshop, painting the Santa Clauses made ready for
Christmas in the August heat at one dollar seventy-five
cents an hour. Foreign labor, not a white man. I fix the
Bowery alone, Janey's cat shit, Milly's dog shit. Sweating
away on a ladder doing the ceiling, the paint stinging
my eyes. Even doing the impossible and fixing the electricity. In the evening he is leaning out the window on
Seventh Avenue over Duchin's Hardware Store, his head
and shoulders waiting for me. My chest hurts seeing him,
tears in my eyes, finally someone loves me in my life.
We take baths in his kitchen and drink vodka. He has
been drinking out of loneliness in this new country. Every
night a pint. It worries me.

In the living room his kites sit by the fireplace. He
has been a painter all his life, now he sculpts, the first
bamboo and paper kites sitting before us next to the
fireplace that doesn't work. There is a girl next door who
cannot sleep. She is a Japanese painter, middle aged,
desperate. They console one another talking in Japanese

against the city. She got Fumio this place through Matsumi. Matsumi is a gossip and has told Fumio I'm a Lesbian. I had told him too, but differently. When he went to America I said meet Zoe, she is someone I have loved. And so they had dinner in Chinatown and he liked her, was kind to her sadness. Met Janey too, went to a party where someone cooked lobsters on a hot plate. Took seven hours for the water to boil. Everyone got drunk. Some people got impatient and left. Some people necked on a bed. "They took turns," Fumio reported, shocked. Then Janey leaned over and threw up in his lap. Fumio held her head, nursing her. Naturally he thinks the Americans are crazy. But he has discovered Joseph Cornell at the Whitney, his whole face shining when he tells people he has found the best American artist. The New York school bore him, my heroes Kline and de Kooning. They are a mess, sloppy, he claims, puffing Calder. "Calder made the invention, made sculpture fly, didn't care if people said it was a toy." His kites sit by the fireplace, growing.

When the Bowery was finished he would sleep but not work there, rented a studio on Forsythe Street with two other guys. Each time I visit him they make me feel unwelcome. Important men, big canvases. Fighting with one of them, Dick, in a Chinese restaurant about *Flaming Creatures,* I say the film is ambiguous, maybe evil. Feeling red in the face, losing, I am being moralistic. Dick says that the sadism is irrelevant and homosexuality is just an interesting theme for art. And it doesn't matter what things mean. Kind of guy who would have enjoyed beating up faggots on Eighth Street in the old Cedar Bar days. But now like everyone else he respects Warhol's success. It's chic to be queer now, provided you're a guy.

The big pop artists at parties wearing dark glasses. No one talks to anyone any more. Once all you needed was to overhear an address in the Cedar Bar, now you need to be invited. We were invited to the big bash for Marjory Strider's opening in her loft, Pace Gallery hired two bands. People pass by. Even if they know you they don't say hello. People wear outrageous clothes but they have the faces of insurance salesmen. There is money now, everyone is doing business. No conversation any more. Only the dancing is real, this frantic exhibition of energy under deafening sound. I am not very good but Fumio is braver since he knows even less. In the center of a circle dancing with two girls. He is inventing it as he goes along, slender and alive, flirting with his ass. Everyone loves it. They cheer. I am excited seeing him, proud.

Duchamps liked his kites. Invited us to tea. And it was tea, though his wife Teenie had said tea or sherry. I could use the sherry but there isn't any and I dare not ask, intimidated by the great old man, harsh beside his chessboard. He is all mind. He can see I am dull, sifting me with a look. Fumio chatters happily. Duchamps is just a name to him. In Japan I was this free with Takiguchi, old saint of young artists, our poet, gray-haired dean of all-night parties, his health broken by prison. Wrote a book on Miro that made reference to the artist's pacifism. Military government thought it was subversive. Jailed for art criticism. Locked in a cell with bedbugs he aged twenty years in the two of his confinement. Fumio could find him intimidating at first but I never found him anything but a lovable papa who took gallant satisfaction in escorting wild young women like me and Yoko to the dives of Shinjiku. Duchamps however was intimidating.

At Cissie's dinner party the important people are to have their plates pasted down afterwards, people like Duchamps, their leavings embedded in polyester by a Greek assemblagist. We do not have our food pasted down because we are young artists and very lucky to be here anyway. We don't talk because it is all in French. Fumio cannot understand. I can follow but will not speak and risk my accent. At my elbow Copley needles me, "Talk French, you are not educated if you don't, Jefferson did, and Franklin." I glare at him and keep silent. Duchamps thought we were interesting because we never said a word. A week later Teenie arrived at the Bowery in Mrs. Staempfli's limousine with a driver, the big black Jaguar parked in the middle of the bums. The ladies inspect my things on the second floor. Then we go to Forsyth Street to see Fumio's kites.

Duchamps' place on Tenth Street, somber ground floor fronted with balustrades, plaque outside says that Mark Twain lived here. Inside the walls are rich to madness, real Impressionists, Monets, Renoirs, Cézannes crowded next to each other. They are not paper reproductions like everyone else has. It is unreal to see them here in a house rather than a museum. The only American is Cornell. Duchamps is taking two of Fumio's kites. They will hang with Cornell and the other masters. Here, over the door, the old man says. They discuss the price. Fumio is courageous, he is asking seventy-five dollars apiece. Later Duchamps said it was too much. Fumio is fierce and samurai. He will take no money, they are a gift. I am in awe of his dignity, his rage burning inside him makes him shine. His face golden and set under his black hair. His small body is big with its pride. When Duchamps walks us to the door I try to speak up, say something to him. Ask because I can't think of anything else to say, did he know Henry Miller in Paris? Want to tell him that I had written an appreciation of Miller in Japan for Waseda, and would like to have the courage to send it to him. Duchamps does not even look at me. His face looks ahead. I do not interest him. "Yes." All he says, quickly. We are out the door.

Teenie wears split-pea earrings. She is easy to talk to, she is not so serious. Her kindness recommends us to PVI, a new gallery, all the good young people in it. Lady dealer says I'm ready to have a show. Then she changes her mind, she will have an all-male show for a hundred men. I have been back in New York for three years now and hardly shown at all. The dealers never even look at the photographs while you stand there a beggar. I must try harder, bring a piece up in Cissie's car to show Mrs. Fischbach. But it's a Volks, don't understand the shift. Have forgotten how to drive. Heart attacks at the traffic, hours finding a place to park. Mrs.

Fischbach is impatient while I assemble the piece. When I am finished, taking infinite care not to scratch the paint, the blue and white squares along the bottom like the pattern on the walls of Katsura Palace, design which I spent the entire month of February painting—when I am finished, she says it is "cute." My throat closes so that it will not scream at her. So that it will not say anything at all, carefully rewrapping each part and carrying it back to the car. One last hope, stop by and show the piece to PVI. When I run up the stairs she is walking around, giving orders. PVI is closing, bankrupt. Group shows have ruined her, didn't have the faith to pick her artists and back them. I beg her to look at the piece anyway. She refuses. I am pleading, if she would only look. Only say it was good even. She turns her back.

When the man from the Modern comes to see Fumio's work he must walk through my studio first. Janey and Bill have gone to Spain and Fumio has the third floor. The curator must see my things on his way up the stairs. I watch him walking fast. His head does not turn at all. When they come down, he has chosen something, a tall blackbird to show at the Penthouse. Fumio sees him down to the street and I am crying because the guy wouldn't even look, went right through. Fumio is happy, he will be in the Modern. I do not want to cry. If Fumio makes it, has success, some money, I do not want to take it from him, his gladness. Only that the man would look at my stuff too, only look. Infuriating how they pay more atention to Fumio because he is a man. A foreigner, and Japanese are popular now. But they are appreciating him for the wrong reasons, they imagine his broken English is some Zen wisdom. I must stick around to help with the language or there are fatal misunderstandings. Yet I must stay back because I'm only a girl friend and I do not want to be a pushy woman. Everyone writes articles and makes remarks about the bitchy American females these days.

Fumio always tries to make them look, "These are Kate's things," pointing them out as they go through my room. The uptown people stare, the lady breaks a high heel on the floorboard, Fumio sometimes gets afraid and says my wife, though we are not married. No one ever looks at a wife's work. With the other artists some like his work best, some like mine. Even here I do not want them to choose or have favorites. It is so hard to be two artists living together. People expect one. If there are two they still expect one. But I want them to notice both of us. No one will do this, but we insist. It is our pact. Fumio tried it before with Yoshiko. In Japan all the neighbors laughed when he went shopping with his basket. Friends said he was tied to her apron. In the basement of the Wah Kee in Chinatown I lose the argument with Dick from Forsyth Street. He is now explaining homosexuality to me. Next moment I am quarreling with Zooey across from me. She says that if two people are artists, it's the man's work that should matter, come first. I stare at her. This is Zooey I used to live with. Who was the man then? But we never had to worry about those things. Dick is fucking Zooey, it is what people do to her now.

At Inokuma's house I am introduced as Mrs. Yoshimura, the old painter being good to me, making an honest woman out of me as I sit next to Isamu Noguchi, trying to get him to talk to me about sculpture. He will not. I am a wife. How do I tell him that I'm not, that my name is Kate Millett and that I had a show in Tokyo a Minami Gallery, he even knows my work. The man across from us is writing a book about Japan. He lived there eighteen months, doesn't speak the language at all. I would like to say in Japanese to Isamu that this guy is a fool posing as an authority though he didn't even bother to learn the language in all that time. But I am supposed to be polite. Inokuma and Noguchi are sacred persons, men who can help Fumio, his elders. We reverence them. No one speaks to me except Noguchi, bantering now about women, outlining the submissiveness he finds attractive. I am expected to listen; should I obey the instructions or are they given only to underline the futility of my aspiration? Noguchi is so strong, so sensual. Looking across at his shaven head on my right, a man of such magnificent vitality at fifty. If I were not so angry I could like him. Inokuma's wife is called Fumiko, a name like Fumio's. I like her because her name reminds me of his. They are a love match too, they ran away together. She has breast cancer, we are all afraid she will die. I think this during dessert, keeping my temper with the old painter at my left, patting my hand, lisping, calling me Okusan—wife.

Now the farm again, painting chests. For the dressing room. Still have no furniture but now at least a place to put our clothes. The workmen have left. It is lonely without them, the crowd of men busy on the roof, radio going full blast like a block party on the Lower East Side while I write in my chicken coop. They are a gang, they can tackle big projects like beams and roofs. Now they are gone. Fumio stands in the huge new studio, dwarfed in space, shaking his head: "It is so big and I am so small, it is too much." He must fix the floor alone because we have run out of money, to encourage himself he disparages the carpenters, becomes didactic about the superiority of the apprentice system. "The Americans are wood wreckers. In Japan they are two years just to learn the plane. They still have the craftsmanship. Even the pickpockets . . ." Venting his sarcasm on the shoddy barn doors that Vince threw together at the end, anxious to be done with our job while he still had hopes of a profit.

Mother Millett taught me how to hound a workman, the example of her man Danny ever before me and the nervous penury of women living alone compelled to hire a man to bully them for their ignorance. Danny was generally drunk, accosted me strangely once in the bathroom, had a habit of showing up just before one of Mother's polite dinner parties stoned, demanding the money to finish a binge. But our Vince is sober, chirpy like the reddleman in *The Return of the Native,* some neatlegged forester out of Lawrence bounding around doing the whole job in a month's time. I worry if he is making any money, By his own account the situation is tragic. I clutch after the possibility of overstatement, calculating his glibness. Fumio hangs back and will not assert himself to these big white men. He will not interrupt Vince in the long nervous speeches that come before he tells us it's going to be three hundred dollars to build these crummy doors, talking English so fast and so long I too surrender by the time he gets to the point.

The workmen now address themselves only to me. Up here a man is boss. But a woman can be boss if she has money. At first all questions were routinely referred to Fumio. I was a wife, maybe a schoolteacher, something solid. Then someone tipped off the carpenter that the money was my money. From that day forward they ignored Fumio. They have decided us. I am humiliated and defeated by this; I want it to stop. I do not want to have to be the wife, but neither do I wish this on Fumio. Treated like a nonentity up here because the neighbors think that I'm rich or notorious or a freak. I am insulted with his insults. I must find a way to stop it. How does a woman insist that a man be respected? It was easier to fight for myself. And how dare they punish his poverty? If Fumio is not a man to them, what is he? A paramour? A child? A curiosity? Vince talks to him in endless ingratiating speeches about his sculpture as if it were some miracle of frivolity more delicate than watchmaking but totally pointless. With customary irony Fumio insists that it is. "I only make the useless things," he smiles.

The paint brush goes on, slowly, methodically. The drawers of the chests are piled up primed and white, ready for the colors. In the barn Fumio is patiently rebuilding his floor. Board by board, using the old lumber he has scavenged around the place. There is no money left for new planking, the lumber up here poor and overpriced. No decent hardware stores or tool shops. The countryside is more bankrupt than the city. Everything is packaged, is shopping center, supermarket. Artificial, the new America. And no plumber. One evening a man drove up and handed me his card. My savior, a plumber looking for work! Takes one look at the problem, figures the pipes are buried in a wall, can't figure out which one, and never comes back. Probably couldn't afford him anyway. So we will have to do without plumbing, or with partial plumbing. I love the colors I have concocted: cobalt blue, lavender, French blue. And the pink, which is not turning out right. How can I write that sort of book up here? I have neighbors who think I'm a wife. Like Baker down the road who is a used-car salesman and has found Fumio a good secondhand station wagon.

After a week combing the countryside, following back roads, squatting in the dirt making deals or being hustled by showy big-lot salesmen who read the papers and keep calling me Kate, all familiarity. Then at Buchanan's we found a beautiful old Lincoln. It is ridiculous I should buy a Lincoln, I am a radical. But just have a look. Engine purrs like a well-kept madam, it will last forever. Belonged to a rich lady over in Millbrook, all the buttons work, luxury machinery fascinating me against my will. And Buchanan, the tired old man who runs this gas station, is selling the car on commission, its svelte body blooming in the weeds behind the parched dirt driveways and cracked cement of his garage. Like children who have discovered a wreck in an empty lot Fumio and I take turns sitting behind the wheel. It has distinction and it's vintage, I suggest. It's cheap and probably solid he decides. For two hours a fever of possessing, arranging the insurance, bring the checkbook with the money from my Commencement speech.

And then this weird bumpkin, the proprietor, changed his mind. Won't sell, his wife wants the car for her son. A fat evil woman staring us down from a corner. She gives off the scent of the tyrant, forbidding him to keep his honor when he has already made a deal. He looks a fool now. And we are trifled with, our time is wasted. When we drive off in a huff I turn to see them grinning at us and feel a terrible urge to machine-gun the whole wizened and moronic family circle. Then Baker saved us. Our neighbor the miraculously honest car salesman. He drove over with five gallons of water the first time the pump broke. Baker took charge and discovered it was the fuses in the barn. Since then he's been our mainstay.

I should be writing Chapter One today. Just beginning to take shape, how to do it. Going back to when I was crazy and unable to start. Frightens me to go back there, afraid I'll go crazy again putting myself in that pit as I have to just to write it. I made a beginning last evening. Then I went down to the creek and swam and wrote that bit about the long moment at Columbia. Hardest part, always get stuck there. Baker says I can use his pool any time, but the creek seems better, neutral somehow. A gang of boys were playing on the bridge, daring each other to jump. They yell faggot at the timid one. He hangs around me, asking if I'm a doctor. Do I have any odd jobs for him? I can't tell if he's moonstruck or just wants pocket money. His pals torture him for speaking to me. Terrible how they make each other suffer. I remember my nephew Steven who stayed a few days last week on his way to Germany. He brought good news. His mother is starting law school this fall. Elder, my sister Sally, will be a lawyer, fulfill my own ambitions. Steven volunteered to put the farm in order for us, paint the barn doors, mow the lawn—a thousand projects. But he is still a child, gets tired, must comb his hair with a boy's vanity. Stop everything when he gets a cut.

Steven is fascinating to watch and I like him. When I was fourteen I could not even see boys, so great a gulf between us then. Only by instinct could you guess if they were jealous, envious, hurt, arrogant. Watching this boy Steven now carrying a desk from the barn into the house, a big oak farmer's desk for me to write on, he and Fumio struggling with it. It will not fit in the back door. It falls on his beautiful young foot. I wonder what he will do. He is a miracle of courage, the ugly beast of furniture wedged between two doors, furious with the pain but not seriously hurt. When I drive him to the airport it is Steven who finds the signs for the obscure North Terminal where the charters are. Inside there are thousands of people who all look alike, army or army dependents. Same cookie cutter, same shirts from the

PX. Boy children in grotesque ties you pity them for. I have an attack of tribal pride wanting to protect this lovely youngster from his fate as army brat, God forfend he should be processed into mediocrity like the rest.

It is Steven's idea to treat me to dinner so we go off to the Luxury of Pan Am. In the bar he waits bored while I drink, reading his Michener on Hawaii. Yesterday Claire and I took him sailing. In the morning we were thirty minutes late picking him up at Mallory's loft. An attack of passion at the breakfast table just as we were about to leave. Claire standing in front of me as I sat on a chair, both of us embarrassed and afraid by it. We go back to bed made guilty. If I had been with Fumio would I feel this way? Steven complained when we couldn't get out of the harbor, teasing Claire's inefficiency enjoying himself. The men at the marina laugh at her too, the blonde with the little Sunfish. Taught herself to sail by capsizing in storms and spent the whole first day learning to put up the mast, every sailor on the pier giving her advice. But they respect her now for sticking with it, for the part-time job that paid for the boat, her one exit from the slum. After sailing we ate fried chicken in a small place beautiful for its vulgarity, the old songs on the jukebox, and I tell Claire, because Steven is not paying attention, how much my father loved joints like this. To make the whole world always a roadhouse at five o'clock on a fine afternoon. He drank so it would happen. Buying drinks for his men. Ripe afternoons twenty years ago. Freezing time in its perfection. How I have loved him for this terrible deal. How completely I am his daughter still, sitting on a barstool watching him, knowing we have to go home to Mother, knowing how happy he is. Sad already for the split beginning even then. And I still have it. Realizing suddenly with ferocious pain how I loved you Jim Millett, my Jamie too. And we never talked. Life that made you lie than made you silent.

Steven still reading his book in the Pan Am Bar. I tell him to stop reading that damn book, this nephew whom I like but who is irritating me so. We talk family.

He reports there is to be another cousins' party next month—the eighty-six descendants of our peasant grandfather Patrick Henry Feely. "I'll have to miss it, there's a demonstration then." "Some Women's Lib stuff?" he asks, a gruff boy. "No," I tell him, fear rising in me, "It's Gay Liberation." "What's that?" "It's homosexuals." "Huh." "Mother is very down on me for supporting Gay Liberation," I tell him, being diplomatic. "Grandmother is pretty old-fashioned." He shrugs. I'm impressed. "What's wrong with being homosexual? If that's what people want they should have their rights," he announces, all urbanity. He is fourteen, I think. Inconceivable, he lives in Nebraska. The old glitter of hope the family might accept me.

By the time we are eating I have decided he's great. He orders dinner grandly calling for extra French fries, a kid spending his first money. Whatever Steven eats is under ketchup. He is going to Germany, his German will be good for school. He wants to be a doctor, is earnest, ambitious. In a surge of love I want to buy him *Buddenbrooks* in the bookstore so he can read it on the plane, no better way to meet the Germans. He tells me he is going alone with a friend of his to Paris. The adventure of two fourteen-year-old boys in that city. It is beautiful. Now we must go, the hostess beaming at us down the stairs. Does she think we are lovers? Will she think he is my son? Proud that she might. Steven has forgotten his knapsack. I am touched he is so vulnerable, loses things. Giving him a hug as we run down the stairs laughing.

When I come back from the creek Fumio says Baker has invited us over for dinner. We have no neighbors, only Baker. Our only neighbor. And didn't we have a fine time over there two days ago when we closed the deal on the station wagon, sitting by the pool drinking and talking cars? Could Baker get me an old Buick convertible like my aunt used to have? No, but maybe he can find another Ford Galaxie like mine but with a good engine, an engine that some son of a bitch hasn't raped and murdered just before joining the army. Baker loves cars, the two of us rhapsodize together on the older engines, the better bodies of once upon a time.

And now Baker is inviting us for dinner. I should stay home and work because I go to England soon and won't have time to finish Chapter One. But we have only one neighbor. Fumio wants to go. He adores Baker for having rescued him from my convertible, hates it, his notion of a car pure transportation. "Let's go, it's fun to have neighbors."

When we get there it isn't dinner it's drinks and country music. Baker and the missus and their best friends Bert and Alison. And Alison sings, a great lusty Wife of Bath woman, huge behind her guitar. Breasts as big as a man's head. I love it. Fumio is enraptured. Alison has a red face and yellow hair, her head thrown back laughing. We talk about yodeling and hollering, Fumio uses the word diaphragm, meaning the voice, Alison begins five minutes of dirty jokes meaning—but he can't follow so I explain off to the side. She overwhelms him and he appreciates her like some great natural force. Alison laughs and bangs hell out of her guitar.

I go into the kitchen and talk to the men standing by the ice box. Baker and his friend Bert say the farm was a bargain. "George Horner's not the businessman he thinks he is. He donated his other farmhouse to the LaGrange Fire Department. Burned it down for practice. Solid 1835 farmhouse." I love this story, it makes me feel astute, it feeds my favorite hallucination, the financial genius. But when Mrs. Horner stopped by the farm a few days ago she told me how they had always wanted to fix up the house themselves. Looking at the fireplaces we built she said if George could see this he would cry. Suddenly I felt so sorry he had not built it himself. They are talking about flying. Bert was a pilot in the first war. Enormous man with yellow hair on his arms, something comforting that he has all this force but is gentle and funny telling how the folks around here warned him when he came home from France that he ought to give up flying 'cause it was impractical and had no future. Suddenly I remember my father who flew me upside down strapped in a one-engine when I was a child, the memory of it like dementia. The notion creeps into my head that it would be fun to learn. One of my students did, a Classics major, had me writing letters of recommendation for her to the government swearing she was not subversive, dutifully certifying her patriotism in triplicate to the Aeronautics Board so my kid could fly. If she could, why couldn't I? Everything is possible, I am tipsy.

I will have a little sober-up in the pool, racing myself to see if I can still do it. Then Baker is at the side of the pool. By the diving board saying he wants to be neighbors. I am really afraid. "I don't know who you two are but I'd sure like to be neighbors. My nephew said you made a talk at his college and wrote some book. Are you in some kinda politics with this Women's Lib business?" He wants to know who I am, his confusion is genuine. So is mine. I close my eyes feeling the smart of the chlorine. Baker if you knew who I really am—I see myself drowning. No, be sensible. I laugh: "Well, I'm one of those radical nuts." He chuckles. "I expect you gotta lotta ideas I wouldn't agree with." I laugh again. "Afraid so." "Well it don't matter. Gives us something to argue about." I'm enjoying the prospect of Baker's conversion to utopian socialism when I am pulled up short to hear him saying what a nice guy Fumio is. "You two sure are a nice couple." Baker thinks I'm Fumio's wife. Naturally. How could I tell him what I am? His first conclusion would be that I "don't love my husband." My mother's voice on the phone moaning, "Katie what is this bisexual stuff, what does that mean?" I am something Baker cannot understand, can only be hurt by. As I tread water, polluting the man's swimming pool, he wants to shake hands and be neighbors.

That was last night. And this morning the asters opened blue in the meadow and in the long grass before the barn, so fresh I wanted to brush my hair and start right to work. But after breakfast I am pulled apart by who I'm supposed to be because my neighbors think I am. Today is only good for painting chests. Here is good Roger Baker at the side of his swimming pool and I would like to be his neighbor. Next week is Gay Pride week. Even playing it safe and painting a chest, my life is so inexplicably bizarre that it is hard to choose what color to begin with. Blue is safe. How can I write a book when I have neighbors? Still worse, my mother has neighbors. I have just one neighbor and could lose him. Will I have to lose the farm? This is decal country, the flag on every bumper. Will ruffians burn the cross on my lawn? Am I living two lives even though I deceive no one? Have always been honest with Fumio and the media obligingly does the rest for me. But I chickened out with Baker.

There is plenty of paint left over. I will paint my big ugly desk. This will be a positive gesture, like some sort of magic it will help me start again. The drawers are easy, they can be two shades of blue. I will make the top lavender out of some self-ironical gay patriotism. I do one design and am not satisfied. But it has given me an hour while the paint dries to figure out how to put things together, what to remember, going over the old notebooks again. Even looking at them brings back the panic. I am pretty much well now, I don't want to be sick again. Is it even authentic to write the first chapter second? The thing just pieces so far, unrelated. A mess. Never add up to a damn thing. Fumio comes in and I worry to him. He will repaint the lavender top for me. We are both laughing at what it means, but I am also hysterical, repeating like an incantation that this color must work or I can't do it. It will be a sign. He works patiently, like a painter making a painting of the top, balancing the white and the lavender, changing it again and again. I am a house painter. He is an artist. He will help me write whatever I write. My gratitude watching him, his head bent concentrating, crooning his vague little hum.

Last night when we came home from Baker's we stayed up eating cold chicken and talking about Mann. How grand he is, a master, can do anything. Fumio is reading *The Magic Mountain* and praised it till I despaired. I cannot think about writing. No, not in that way, not at all. Just to get it down, remembering, keeping a record.

In ten days I must go to England: I have nothing done and I do not know who I am.

I see it from across the street. Finally it has happened. I lug the two big shopping bags from Bloomingdale's, one in each hand. Saleslady had never seen anyone buy this many sheets. But it was the only thing Nell wanted . . . "You Americans have these incredibly smart sheets." I select them in an orgy of purchase, scads of them in every color, coveting them all myself, a monster of mouth-watering acquisition. They are my present, the only thing I'm permitted to give in return for all the help she gave me with the film, Movie Nell who saw me through it and for whom payment is out of the question. Only that one clue about sheets to relieve the weight of my obligation, now twenty pounds heft in each hand as I gaze down Bleecker Street seeing the unbelievable.

My house. The door a gaping black hole in the brick wall. My house open to the world. I am robbed. Ripped off. Just two hours ago I stopped by here to pick up the mail. So it's not because I was absent in the country, neglecting the place. Just two hours ago I was here, removing the telltale pile of mail visible through the glass door that lets them know you are out of town so they can bust you. And by God they have, the door yawning open to rape by any stranger. In an afternoon the whole place could be stripped. If I had already left for England they would have taken the paint off the walls by the time I got back. Now as I watch, ten years' sculpture and all my manuscripts lie prone waiting for them, every enemy.

When you are robbed the whole world betrays you in that moment. I came up the stairs that first time seeing all the drawers open, knew immediately. And the dog rushed me, that silly little cocker who would have welcomed any thief, bitchlike wagging her tail, turning over to show her belly. But somehow she had given him a scare and he beat her. Big white Russian with crazy blue eyes, told me once how he'd busted an artist on Second Avenue but the jerk had nothing to steal so he razored all the canvases not to have wasted a trip. Used to meet him on the Bowery: "Gimme a cigarette, I'm your robber." Insisting on our special relationship while he looked down at the dog, telling me what he'd done to her.

That time it was my clothes, all the ski sweaters from the lush Oxford days. Even took the peanut butter, the tuna fish. My typewriter, the silver cigarette box JayCee gave me when I got a First. I would have whored to get it back. All these treasures gone for a dollar or two in the thieves' market on Rivington Street. After the second bust I spotted the Russian in one of my sweaters in the Palace Bar, cornered him and got a cop. Take off that sweater. But it's second rate and so are the three others underneath. All the good ones were gone already.

The cop wants me to have him arrested. I go upstairs to get a coat. Strange noises come up from the hallway, the cop is actually beating the guy up. My robber. For a second I relish the sound. Bastard took all I had, winter coming and no warm clothes even. I listen to the slow steady thud. Then I can't stand it. Screaming at him to stop it. "Not in my place buddy. And forget the arrest. What good does it do me if he rots in jail?" Everything gone already, I can never get the silver box back again, my whole past wiped out in the few things I owned. If there's an arraignment it will be three days' pay as a substitute teacher. I just started this job, I need the money. If I send him to jail he'll kill me when he gets out. Justice is too expensive. The next time I was robbed the police stood around and grinned: "Girl like you has no business living down here anyway." After that I no longer bothered to notify them.

And now the open door stares at me again. I stand across the street by Fat Harry's hardware store, my art supply house, offering unlimited credit for the last ten years. When I was broke Fat Harry would always let me charge it: "Sure kiddo, go on working, pay when you can, I trust you." Fat Harry to whom I own my career in the arts. I look across the street at the black hole, which looks back at me. Then I cross and start shaking up the stairs, should I go down and get Tony the pawnbroker from the first floor to help me? If they're still there they might kill me in their fear if cornered. Tony behind me more frightened than I am. So I go up first, saving his face as a man, asking him to look here and there and then doing it for him. It's safe, they are gone. So is the TV. That's fine, we never use it any more. Fumio and I gave it to each other one Christmas. Greedy as children, we broke down and collected it as early as Thanksgiving, watched it like addicts. Three months even eating dinner in front of it. I began to think our whole relationship had died in boredom the way it had been with Zoe. Then that February I slept with a woman again in New Haven. Things got better, we were not through. Enough problems now to keep us interested forever.

Damn. They got the music. Left the turntable. Bitter feeling when I see the amplifier and the speakers gone. And the bicycle. Left my old typewriter, too heavy. Nothing else to take unless they go berserk and wreck Fumio's sculpture. Go to the third floor and check it. Mine is okay too. That final vulnerability, our work. And my possibly scandalous life, letters, tapes, manuscript. I must be prepared to lose everything. Or prepared to keep nothing here again I cannot afford to lose or could be hurt by. Thinking while I walk through the rooms still trembling, If I finish my book I will have no secrets to be afraid for, corrupted over, tied to, as I have been all my life, hiding.

Fat Harry will sell me a padlock, but there is no way to secure this place unless I make it a prison and sleep behind bars. The casements no longer open to the murderer I wait for every night, the pimps and Mafia I have lived with, my own horror movie replayed every night I sleep here alone since the *Prostitution Papers*. How do people live in New York? How do people live? And how can I live here still? Knowing already how crucial it will be to sleep here tonight. In my own place where I'm paying rent, where I have always lived, this studio my very life for a long ten years. No, I will not give it up, scared shitless.

"Of course you are coming, Bici's divorce is tonight." She is not interested in my robbery. Vita is interested in the divorce, ordering me to be there. "John and Yoko are coming." Her voice makes that important. I am a rat, I had forgotten her divorce, had wanted to be with Claire. And now I am at Bici's divorce, which is being conducted as a happening. When you enter the brownstone the door is divided, you have to choose "his" or "hers." I must choose hers not Goeff's. They are stringing barbed wire across the living room door, separating it from the kitchen where I could get a drink if I were on Geoff's side. The barbed wire hurts my eyes, it is new and shiny but it is still barbed wire. Fred's adolescent lover rolls the wire off a spool. George Maciunias is here too, giving instructions, he is master of ceremonies. I can't stand this place I'm hungry. Since they are late starting I ask if there's time enough to run out and get a bite to eat. Fred and Vita are both annoyed by the question. It is a relief to be out of there and into the normality of the 22¢ chicken, flirting happily with the Puerto Rican chicken men who give me extra pieces because they have made a mistake and we all think it's funny. Just in front of Bici's I see the Beatle car. A limousine for Godsake. Maybe it's not theirs after all; don't peer in the windows you'll look like an autograph hunter. But then Yoko's face appears out of our old neighborhood bar in Nishi Ogikubo. She gives me a hug, her voice rushing to tell me I have been doing all these good things that she's been trying to do for years but she always gets in trouble. I am embarrassed because she is praising me when I want to praise her. How the young men artists hated her when she did those great happenings in Tokyo, brilliant pieces night after night. Then Tony who made her have the baby, no way out, too many abortions already. And still with him, still doing concerts with him in New York the last time I saw her. The two of them off to England with a lot of wild talk about astrology. Fumio and I listened nervously. Next time I read she was a Beatle. Yoko up there so high and lonely when she called from California on my birthday.

Found me at Alvin's cottage where I was hiding out. "You're famous now, I read about you everywhere." "It's insane, horrible, I'm going crazy." She is going crazy too but has found the perfect remedy in California. "John and I are getting primal scream therapy." "What?" "It's very simple, don't you see what we all want is our mother's breast." It is incomprehensible to me—I want Celia. "Yoko, you mustn't believe what you read about me in the papers, I don't carry an ax like they say." "Well, they say I broke up the Beatles." "Of course I don't believe them." "There is always some truth in the media." I was shocked by the idea.

In the elevator Yoko seems so distant, so far away in these four years. John and Yoko like some myth alive in our time. Royalty, legend has entered the room and taken a seat on the davenport. All eyes inspect them. I sit next to John Lennon dying to whisper wow I'm glad to meet you I think your music is great it's wonderful how you care about peace. Instead I offer him some chicken trying to be cool and nonchalant, to defend him from the eyes that devour them. In my smaller way I know how it feels. He doesn't want chicken. Neither does she. We are pinned to the couch under a roomful of eyes. It is impossible to talk to each other, so I make pathetic little jokes in Japanese. Yoko explains them to John, her voice shaky like a child reciting a lesson. "Kate says Yoko is *sugoi onna,* that means I'm like some hell of a dame, maybe a witch, a tornado. Kate talks this awful tough Japanese she picked up in bars, it's like men's Japanese 'cause it was men taught her. It's terribly unladylike, that's why it's so funny." Of course John can't find it funny, so the three of us sit in a morose little file on the sofa. We don't say a word. Everyone keeps on staring.

Now we must go upstairs for the "division of property." It is hot in the bedroom where Geoff and Bici are tearing the sheets in half, pretending to be greedy. But looking like they are. It was supposed to be a joke, a farce carried out in the wooden-faced manner of happening theater. But it has become real. It is terrible to watch. I look away at my friends. Louise Mark is here taking pictures. There are Sidney and Barbara Love. Then I see Claire. She is with Barbara. Bici tugs mightily at her end of the sheet. People cheer. It is so hot I am going to be sick crowded here in a corner. Claudia runs the faucet in an alcove and hands me a glass of water. Yoko is holding John's hand like a child, terrified to be out of his sight. She looks infantilized, hangs, depends, cringes. She leads him away. I stay to watch, stoic, horrified.

They are going to saw the bed in half. The bed they made together, their bed for eight years, the bed they built and made love in and slept in. Now the power saw is ripping it in half. First he runs it then she does it, showing how she can do it, run the big tool herself, like a petulant child, pushing too hard. We are cheering her because this is supposed to be about Women's Liberation and they are brave to do this. But the scene is very powerful, a true happening, one of the best I've ever seen, for once not effete and abstract but right to the bone of life. The power saw buzzes, then they use a handsaw. I am sick watching the wood cut and bleed. I do not want to do this with Fumio. We have taken off our rings. Maybe we should do more. Not the legal silliness of divorce, but not this either. Maybe if we had a party, like the living-in-sin parties we used to have on the anniversary of the day I came to him from Japan . . . Next the foam rubber, cutting it like flesh with mat knives. No I will not cut our foam rubber like that. One more moment of this and I'll throw up. It is barbarous, primitive, the people yelling obscenely at this execution of a past. Vita's last Event consisted of burning all her paintings. She hung and photographed each one before shredding and throwing it in the fire. A set of murals she had worked on for eight years. Why this desperate compulsion to destroy? Of course she had the slides afterwards. But after this there is no more, only the snapshots everyone filming it. The heated air is split with flashbulbs.

I go down and stand in the hallway. Jill leans against

the wall by the toilet. There are police barricades
everywhere that you must step over. We stand and talk
by the toilet. Jill says Germaine says I blew it. What
does that mean? Jill seems to have quarreled with
Germaine Greer on her last trip to New York. All I get
is a confused picture of Germaine drinking champagne
in a hotel room and preferring young men to Jill. I refuse
to go for the bait, she goes on. "Germaine says you blew
it with the media by coming out." This from Jill. "Ruined
your media image." I have never met Germaine Greer
but I know she didn't say this. Suddenly I am furious
at the triviality of Jill's phrase, remembering the idiotic
"discussion" shows where I struggled to give dignity to
my argument while the "panel" snickered that women
are ridiculous, our humanity reduced to Susskind jokes
about who does the dishes. The way I had to beg Cavett
to hold back the commerical so I might have three unin-
terrupted moments to describe Hiroshima as Fumio saw
it. Lying in bed the night before in tears of concentration,
how to find words eloquent enough to make such an event
real for his gray nothing-under-glass which reached
millions of people. The media is an opportunity that
is finally merely a fraud, no opportunity at all, only a
method of neutralizing every idea into nothingness, plastic
thought, a dangerous totalitarian force which you think
you can control when you start off and discover too late
that you cannot. I turn to Jill. "The media is a mind
fuck." I wonder if they will madden Germaine as they
did me. But she is stronger, better at it, constantly witty,
an actress. Still I worry for her. Jill humphs.

We go outside to the rooftop and discuss our nervous
breakdowns. Jill's preface to her book said it happened
to her twice. I describe my craziness and ask after hers.
But hers is incomprehensible to me, I cannot imagine
what it was like. She said she was flying. Was it drugs?
"No just flying happy with someone, then I fell." Landed
in a hospital. I think mine was different, essentially it
was the panic. And airplanes were my hospital, the
Bowery, the hell I carried with me everywhere. Jill understands my craziness no better than I understand hers.

We try to add up the experience. I am hoping to come out ahead. Did the storm of pain and distorted vision give my anything usable? Is it a breakthrough of some kind that leaves you changed somehow? An asset? So would you then pursue it like some terrible jolt to the imagination? No, that is false as well as dangerous. Mostly I am terrified it will come again. Winter. Jill is kind, comforting.

There is a party going on inside. They are dancing in the apartment in Geoff's studio, the msuic pounds away above the quiet of the rooftops. Vita comes out. She sees us talking, two notables together. She approves and goes back inside. The evening is soft and gray, the garden merely a rubble but it is a summer night in New York, our world. Squatting in the dirt we talk about writing. Like a kid holding a frog in its hands, I mention my book, hoping for help. For once Jill seems gentle. Her book is out now. Already it has helped me to dare to talk about myself as she has done, using the ordinary things that happen to us. Claire comes out, I introduce them. Jill looks through her. Claire is a writer too I say, trying to defend her from Jill's indifference. But Jill has never heard of Claire, so she doesn't exist. I know Claire has admired Jill for her courage and is disappointed. She is proud as well as shy and she leaves us. Charlotte Moorman flies into our garden full of cries and embraces. Jill has heard of Charlotte. They teeter together in a theatrical embrace while Jill brags of having inveigled John and Yoko and the media to come and drink champagne on the new *Queen Elizabeth*. Jill calls it *QE II*. Charlotte is admiring this. Jill is very pleased at how she is making things happen, creating art in life. I decide we are all remarkable and leave.

Inside men are dancing with women. But men are also dancing with men. And women are dancing with women. Claire finds me to dance. She seems to want me again in front of all the people, not only the women in our group, but even some straight people looking on while she kisses me, leaning toward me giving herself. I am embarrassed but I also don't care. Let them see, even

if I am frightened letting them, so happy she has changed
her mind. Probably we shouldn't be doing this, probably
it is against the spirit of the group, probably we should
be dancing circle dances with them, but my body is so
excited in my jeans and my breasts in my shirt it is
delicious to kiss her. Even if she is boyish courting me,
finding me again to dance with, following me. I feel
conspicuous but I love it, wanting it so that she wants
me again.

When there are no more people in the room she is
shy. We sit by the fireplace. We hold hands feeling
ridiculous. Someone wanders in, so we leave and go
outside to the roof. There are two young men there. We
walk to the other side and just sit there together while
she hands me the stars in one of her astronomical raps
across the city roofs into space, her eccentric probably
half-mad obsession with the future carefully reduced to
a joke about how it's her modest ambition to participate
in galactic culture within her lifetime. "Try to imagine
my chagrin at having to leave before the news came."
I don't much care if she is crazy, intoxicated looking
up into her face, it is youth and goodness the sweetness
of her golden head laughing by the light of a streetlamp
from below. What does it matter? She is the promise
of summer.

When we finally go back inside people are already
leaving. John and Yoko look bored in the living room.
I pour a drink in the kitchen, thinking how in a little
while it will be time to have our talk, me and Yoko,
relishing the prospect. When a few more people clear
out, I sit near the front door with Ruth and Vita. Jill
sees Claire finally, sees her as a pretty blonde. Feeling
the hunter in Jill I wish she weren't so irredeemably
butch, an old-time dyke with a man's head, so brave
up front, while behind it all there is a frightened woman
hard to reach. She has just heard that Fred and Vita
have come out. "It's wonderful, everyone's doing it," Jill
whizzes on like an advertisement for gay transformation,
eager to write it all up in the *Voice*.

Suddenly John and Yoko are leaving, walking through

us out the door. It is too late now to call out "Stop we have not had our talk come back." They are already in the glass jar of the limousine. Yoko is living inside a bubble, I am cut off from my friend. It is unjust, surreal. Is it my fault for not going to her earlier? Was it a mistake dancing with Claire? Would Yoko understand that? And now she is disappearing from me behind glass, leaving me to become the prisoner of a limousine, separated from me behind the panes of a sealed car. Aloft in the Beatle world beyond reach. Must be hell there, my own was bad enough. Now I am free, living an ordinary life, sitting in the dust of the penthouse stairs I have friends again, down to earth in my own town. I was able to escape back to myself, if not the self before, then the one after. Catching sight of Claire out of the corner of my eye for no reason.

Vita brings out some pictures taken at the houseboat. There is one where she is laughing. In profile, she looks entirely free, beautiful. I want it, it is the Vita I want and never see, caught for a moment, unconscious as she never is, relaxed which she never is, admired by women, which she is coming to be. But only once, here in this photograph, have I seen that Vita realized. In this picture is what she can become.

A moment later she becomes again what she has been, the maternal inquisitor. Because Claire has asked me for a ride home. O'Flynn needs one too. I said yes. Vita looks her accusation. I surprise myself and look back at her that I will do what I want, sleep in my own place. With Claire who has broken the code: gay honor like straight goes home with the one it comes with, and Barbara is nowhere in sight, must have left. That damage is already done. I am sorry, even condemn Claire's callousness but how can I judge, wanting her so that I see it detected in Vita's eyes. They reproach me now. Of course she expected me to stay with her—tonight of all nights—I read the phrase she would have chosen. But I want out of this thing, it gives me the creeps. And Vita has Ruth, who sits beside her on the steps perhaps accusing me too, knowing Vita has reduced her to second best and made me top dog, a cur. I would not have chosen Ruth, was surprised when Vita did. But Vita did choose her and now ostentatiously seems to value her less than me. Ruth bears it in agony, a ghetto Jew with a bad complexion, it wrenches the heart to see her swallow such insult. But what defense has Ruth, in love and imagining Vita a beautiful woman. The very thing I wish her to become and she hasn't yet, pouting in self-pity, stewing in hatred, her bottomless eyes menacing me from the top step.

Spring up the stairs at Bank Street, past the little foyer with its Japanese prints, negotiate the screen that keeps the cats inside, and get a great big hug from Lila. Sign of health that I am able now to jump into a marathon talk session on Bank Street, Lila and I a mile a minute as we have for years. Lila curls in her chair, body languorous as one of her cats while the mind is a coiled spring of talk, this lady of conversation and salon life, settling herself in the cushions as she must have done every afternoon in London those eleven years she lived in Nell's town and was her friend even before she was mine. Today Lila is very princess, has been to the hairdresser and got herself a Jewish afro.

"I'm nigger-Jew baby," she giggles toddling toward the kitchen, her soft shape wobbling about under one of her usual zaftig bags. Today as helpless as ever in a red and blue number while I make my own drink. Place still has no decent ice cubes. Someday I must remember to buy her a real tray. "Been afraid to see you writing mama 'cause I was crazy and couldn't write." "The crazy part is hard, the not writing part's a bit harder," she says, both of us knowing she hasn't written much in a long three years. Not since that novel cost her the family, the ghosts of her parental characterizations still living in the mythical apartment out in Forest Hills. And big brother a shrink in Brooklyn who will never speak to her again. Mommy and Daddy revenge themselves in illnesses. But Daddy pays visits, bringing along a good sherry just as he brought to all his mistresses, five decades of them. Daddy's girl, Lila adores his visits and treasures the gifts. Mother burns away at home, a bitter no-life woman cancerous with rage to see her daughter live at all, ready to turn up any guilt to prevent that. "We're our mothers' fantasies come true, and worse. I write for Mother Millett who wanted to and does now, in me. It's just that she wants to be the resident censor as well. Takes over like a shopkeeper's steel door sliding down between me and the paper." Lila settles in her sofa. "Mothers are the core of the problem. Sometimes it seems incredible that broads like us ever do anything at all, given all the prevention. Your young man writer pushes pen and screws. Each erection adds to his stature. Whole different number for us baby. Harlot, pervert, whatever. But if you can't talk plain you haven't got much to say."

"I've decided I'm queer, Lila," camping for her, "I'm resolved to accept my condition at last. Funny thing is, I'm feeling better already. It was driving me bananas, with my sainted mother at the wheel. She has set it up so that either I go bananas or she does, one. I've decided I'm not going." "Lots of luck baby," tucking her feet up and sipping her fuzzy concoction, both of us aware this chirpy talk is only a smokescreen against the fires of our guilt. Of course we care, stranded in the drought which Lila accepts with a grace I cannot.

"You know the funny thing is, when you're crazy people don't help, don't even want to know about it. Afterwards they say—but you should have told me. Maybe even believing that they might have wanted to know." "Of course they don't want to know. Why should they? They can't cope with their own inferno. I went to see Momma yesterday. She's had a stroke. O God, I'm getting out of town. Away from those eyes on that pillow. There's this place in Switzerland where Renos can teach acting and I can do some courses on woman writers. Switzerland will give me a little peace. And I can write about my mother's mind in that bed. I know her completely, every inch of her life, every thought in the head lying on that pillow. I can get it all on paper. But I can not look at it any more."

"And so you're into it with women?" Looking across at me. "Every time I see you high, like last summer, it seems to be about that. What's it do for you?" "I'm not sure I know myself. It's something like energy. I seem to operate best on that kind of support. And I seem to fall apart without it. Of course there are other things, the beauty of women's bodies, a special kind of tenderness." Lila smiles benignly while I spread out my theories about loving more than one person, how there is variety and less dependency, how there can be obligation, commitment and permanence without the exclusiveness of *I own you, so you can't.* "It makes sense but I can't do it," she says. "I'm not there so I stay where I am. But I want to hear about it. What's your theory got to say about men?" "There you got me, I'm inconsistent. Maybe I don't get involved with men out of some last fidelity to Fumio. I'm not there anyway, it's with women I want to be now. I've been thinking that it's possible we're in some transitional state where we'll be closer to each other for a while than we can be to men. Till things change. Till men change. But some men are doing that already, becoming beautiful human beings, especially the young ones."

"Well, what's it like with women?" I look across at Lila. It is hard to explain to her. Afraid to admit failure. Afraid of her sense of satire. But she seems genuinely curious. "You know, it often doesn't work out with women." She looks at me steadily. "You know it didn't work at all with Celia, I'll never know why, because there are so many reasons, and because she never talks. Mostly it doesn't work because the old games happen, all the dried-up roles we had for breakfast lunch and dinner all our lives, the same old tired crusts, just the sex changed. No, nothing like what you can see, not the butch and femme barreling about looking grotesque in the Village. No, more subtle, nice, fine, deadly."

"Tell me about now." So I tell her about Claire and Vita, holding Claire back a little, protecting her perhaps because she is gay. And Vita's habits are a story. "And this Vita's playing your secretary?" Bang, I can see it in her eyes, a terrible instant revelation of how much this isn't a good idea. Scrambling to explain that Vita's also an old friend who volunteered and later needed some money. Lila squints and tilts her head skeptically. "Actually, Vita's a great help, I could start writing again, she keeps the world at bay."

Lila nods, like a fortune-teller. "Tell me your book." "It's myself. It's a record as I go along doing my thing. Like a documentary. Since I did those three other women in my film, it seemed only fair to subject myself to the same process. It demands I remember everything and be honest." But already I am sitting in a nest of red ants. Lila has just made me see something awful. Vita should not be my secretary. My head is full of critics' ridiculing and the endless refrain of what will people say. "Baby, they'll say anything and everything. Relax and await your misconstruction." "Will they say I'm screwing my secretary? My God, and me in Women's Lib . . ." We both find this very funny till I find it more than I can bear. "Fuck the orthodoxy. Put it in," Lila chuckles. "Put everything in and they'll murder you again, even and especially the movement ladies who murder each other until I am exhausted with the spectacle. How pleasant Switzerland appears already, innocent of our odious and sordid little factions. But do it anyway. If you want to write you got to and if you don't tell it, it kills you."

Renos arrives from a day of cab driving and auditions, a heroic Greek in a flowered shirt who needs a shower. Standing in the doorway like a big bear. It's delightful to see him again. We go to find dinner, strolling along Bleeker Street, the three of us, how good to be together again, headed for a new garden restaurant they've discovered. Lila disapproves of my title: "*Living It* . . . nope, too much like Podhoretz's *Making It*." "What's that about, I never read it." "Well, don't bother to."

Lila feels the food here has fallen off in quality, gets into her Jewish-American princess act and raises hell with the waitress. All through dinner the three of us invent titles out of pop songs, clichés, literally monuments and bric-a-brac. I cannot remember them because as usual I have sought advice in order to ignore it. Nor would our humor sit well on paper, it is the perfume of a mood, each candidate title more ridiculous than the last until we are choking, Lila wheedling like a used clothing merchant after each new horror—"But it worked for him." How about *Prisoner of Sex?* and the three of us shout with laughter another time. "Look kid ya gotta remember it worked for him," Lila snorts in dialect, all Jewish Mafia coming to steer this little goy along the road toward comercial understanding. The three of us blissfully silly in the summer air of an evening in our town, New York a fine and Cosmopolitan place to lose such nights in gardens under an ailanthus, the only rat-like tree that can grow in our soil, tougher than concrete.

Renos bores us with a description of how boring Sartre's *Condemned of Altona* really is and we listen meekly because any man who can tolerate the prolonged company of libbies is a saint. Renos is also a fine talker. But Lila and I always want to talk only to each other and Fumio is not here tonight to divert Renos's great conversational energy. Renos says I never listen to him and he's right, I don't. But I love the air around the fine curly hair of his head, the warmth of his company and hers. So many nights they have patiently endured my drinking Irish-American revolutionary tirades, holding forth on their squeaky leather chairs or sprawled on the big white rug the cat shit on the very day they bought it. Fumio cleaned it up while Lila raved. Fumio who adores every spoiled inch of Lila, giggling and calling her his movie queen, his sex symbol every since the first nibble came from Hollywood for her novel. Loving the sensual Eastern shine of her as I do watching her now in a garden. And the grandeur of Renos, the integrity of his spirit in that colossal frame, this Francophile Greek who can never go home again because of the junta. Renos living now with his father's death since last winter as I live with mine. Renos kicked about in foreign America, a great actor forever denied parts because of the accent, Renos presently reciting Sartre's long deadly speeches in order to demonstrate their logical errors. Watching the two of them, one in each hand, man and woman in their world, knowing that in an hour I enter a cavern of Lesbians in a loft on an obscure downtown street. Watching them with loving eyes and feeling all the tension of two worlds, two cultures sealed away from each other, two entire societies separated so often it seems permanently, the crevases between tearing me apart like a mulatto who passes. When do things come together?

6

It starts in the car. The thing with Vita. That spot on the highway. Which spot? How strange that I have never discovered it again, the very road a peril, but the place itself disappeared. Lost as I was lost, dizzy the moment it began. Innocently enough as we drive upstate to the farm, Vita and I are going to make a home movie of the place as a present for Nell. My friend Louise is coming up to do some photographs of me and Fumio, plump and pacific amidst her cameras. Next to her in the back seat her friend Peg, lean as a knife, expectant. It is a beautiful day for an outing, we have just come from a workshop on gay consciousness and the arts. All this week there have been panels and discussions, parties and dances. They have made a spiderweb of hope, inside it I have hung tentative, waiting for the culmination of Christopher Day, the march through the city.

My left arm lolls on the steering wheel, my right arm is stretched against the sun's warm cheek along the back of the seat toward Vita. Expansive, I say that I have great hopes for the march tomorrow, losing America the next day by flying to England. Can I count on the euphoria of our week to sustain me there, food in an alien place? It is asking for a boost, the support we give each other nowadays. Troubled again by the habitual quarrel with Vita last night, Vita again denying me my book. Like a bad conscience it obtrudes once more to becloud my mood. If I refer to it out loud, turn the depression into a joke and then a problem, we can analyze it and understand. Peg and Louise will help us solve it, together we will whittle out what is wrong. "We had a little tiff last night which seems to be bringing me down . . ."

Suddenly Vita is screaming, hitting me with words—"damn well ought to feel like shit about last night, you really deserve to feel bad—I'm telling you for your own good, it's the honesty of a friend"—her mouth open yelling into my face until I can no longer hear but must hang on to the wheel so that we are not crashed into the gray concrete and steel barricades coming up fast into my very skull like her words. Peg and Louise are frozen shut in the back seat as Vita enacts the scene of injured wife insistent upon preserving the privacy of the married state while taking sweet revenge on husband in company. Right on, Vita, so you must have waged your woman's war for years. But I am not your husband. Yet already the felt hat grows upon my head, my father's gray fedora now a crown of thorns. What is happening to me? Vita's thunder is transforming me, I have lost myself, disappeared into her version of me, surely the truth, any feeble croaking in my defense only renders me more guilty, comical, ripe for the firing squad. Vita the indomitable proletarian woman, utterly righteous, her heavy inexorable steps approaching without mercy, a fanatic armed with exact orthodoxy, one hundred percent pure. Her Truth carried before her in a sealed bottle, clear, vacuous, sacred.

I want to get out of this car. Stop it. Evaporate into the woods intact before her rant incriminates me further. Peg and Louise are shocked into silence, paralyzed as I am by her bellow. She is now jumping up and down in her seat, full fit. I have ceased to hear her words, irrelevant clichés from soap opera and magazine, what matters is the force of her hatred's injury. Words are superfluous to the energy bouncing off her body, every vibration accusing. With the accusation I cannot outlive. Surely she will have finished me off by nightfall. Lila was right. Vita should not be my secretary. Inevitably I have oppressed, exploited her. Whether in reality or imagination, what difference does it make? It is a terrible error which has closed around us now like a trap. The question now is how do we escape? But there is no exit, Vita will see to it that we are locked into these positions forever, are they not to her moral advantage? Yet some instinct perceives that while Vita is on the boil I must feed her stove, bring it to a head. Like the hand of a pickpocket the notion slides into mind, what if I brought it to an issue, broke free? It would mean doing without Vita, cutting loose, going it alone. Is it worth it? Listen to the alternative in her trumpet of outrage . . .

There is no solution in teasing her out of some futile hope that sanity might be just another mile up the pike: Look Vita, we are being ridiculous, my tits are bigger than yours, do you realize what we are doing? We will be caught in these roles, they will become a track we can't switch out of. Top of that I simply refuse to be your oppressor, don't want the job. I resign. Undaunted, she fires off another volley of indictments whose sheer force of embittered femininity is unanswerable. In our world women are always right. By now she must have done it, alerted Peg and Louise to my crimes, allied them against me. Now I am exposed, the total pig, the enemy of women, the male chauvinist. Judas within the ranks. My self-ideal, that shoddy altogether fortuitous mixture of egotism and sham reduced by her fierce searching to its true elements. I am unmasked. My head is brought in on the cover of *Playboy*. Knew it all along.

We drove along the river at Redwing, Mother and I. And she said was I a Lesbian with that Zoe, living out in New York. I was driving. Mother would always let me drive, her foot frantically pedaling the floor but finding nothing since the brake is on my side, not hers. Strangling just before the head-on collision, the little

gurgling noises in her throat every time she spots a car.
I was my father, her tormenter, always untrue. A de-
ceiver.

And now Vita. Peg and Louise will see it. Everyone
will see it. I cannot hide any more, she will proclaim
me to the world, because of course—my innards complete
one full revolution—I'll have to put this catastrophe into
my book. Now Vita has stopped the book, who I want
to be, has exterminated that self with her all-seeing eyes,
convicted it of the irredeemable sin, worse than the one
against the Holy Ghost. I am a running dog Vita has
brought to judgment before the people, exposed on the
wrong side of the party line and beyond the pale. All
hearts burst applauding her, the little woman. Will the
movement accept my resignation? Vita has meta-
morphosed me into the bullying male, my father's hat
sprouting like horns, the brim firm over my eyes while
I drive on. From a great distance I observe our profiles
as we settle, each in our fixed position in silence, Mr.
and Mrs. Hideous Alliance.

But we are not an unmixed catastrophe, one thing at
least is settled, we have severed our nefarious relationship, Vita will not be my secretary any more.

The farm is ashes in my mouth. Pride in ownership had
drooled to show it off: the barn fixed, the chimneys in,
the lamp hung over the table so it makes a great blue
tulip of light at evening. The door framing it a glow of
home as it beckons poised over the wild flowers Fumio
has picked. His love walking abroad through the fields
in search of them, then an afternoon's concentration to
the exact form of a bouquet. As the car stops I hear his
windbells overhead. Broken pop bottles, bell jars, old
nails, assorted hardware, the tongues of the clappers sway
on junk ribbons cut from some scrap of plastic. The bells
are in memory of Yoshiko, living still he says in the wind.
How can I drink their peace and permanence in this fog
of rage? Vita springs headlong out of the car, maniacal
with her Super-8 shooting everything in sight, a monster
enthusiast devouring Fumio and his barn. Fumio, the

sight of him so gentle under his straw hat. Living up here
he has become a farmer or a hermit, looking up like a
Mexican waking to an invasion. Dazed, tearing himself
away from the wooden typewriter, his slow steady all-
summer project. Vita's rabid lens consumes beams, man,
flowers, trees, the whole place fuel to her gulf of
acquisition. The rest of us seem dwarfed and lethargic,
our greeting poor and inadequate. This is no homecoming.

We sit around the dining room table. I see Fumio
through the flowers and across the vale of misery Vita
seems to make for me, ashamed before my guests. The
four of us hardly able to make conversation while she
whizzes about, in and out of doors, shooting her movie
right there on the spot. I have no heart to shoot. Maybe
tomorrow, knowing already I won't do it then. Vita has
taken it from me, appropriated even the farm, gobbled
it up in her powerful urge while the rest of us sit in embarrassment examining the pieces and pretending to have
a drink.

Then Celia is on the phone to invite me to a party
Sunday. But Sunday is the march. No, her concert is
the same time as the march, the party is afterwards,
around five. "I can't march, so do it for me. I'll play
the lute, you yell the slogans." "Nice, that way we get
the revolution to music and flowers." "That's getting
it together," she chuckles and then tangents off to some
article on masie-sadie lib she read months ago in the
Voice. "What has this got to do with anything?" I ask,
already afraid. "Well, that's getting it together too," she
comes back. Taking flight then in the usual evasion of
fey jokes.

When I sit down again with the others her insult has
already taken form. How dare she say this to my face,
say that I'm her masochist, a label, a trifle, her thing
to torture. Louise takes a few more pictures of my
ravaged condition. Under the big straw brim Fumio's
face is radiant as the shutter clicks. There is some relief
in this evidence that one of us is still whole and sane,
chattering away in his gladness to see people. Friendship

is his life, his love always generous, vulnerable, so ready for anyone who is willing to take the trouble, understand his English. Vita rockets in and out behind her Super-B, the great directrice. Got her hat on today. The one she wears when she's a big shot. I glower not making my movie.

The remarkable day peters out into twilight, our whole group variously miserable. All except Vita who is having the time of her life. Louise and Peg sulk by the picnic table, determined to quit America, Louise bitter and drinking, the taste of the Peace Corps and then the peace movement two failures rancid in her mouth. And their recent hassles with Peg's folks, liberals trying to work it through and accept the idea of these two together. Things go along smoothly and then erupt again on the nights they all try to go out to dinner as a group. Their latest quarrel with Peg's parents is now another one between the two of them as they sit in the sad gray light, squaring off, Peg on the bench, Louise facing the yard desperate remembering another farm where she kept goats with some other lover through long-ago winters, the animals dying one by one till they went broke. I hover about in a feeble attempt to play hostess. Inside Vita has switched over to instant editor, busily cutting her last home movie. She thunders about the lighted rooms. We have surrendered the house to her, Fumio and I venture in only when obeying the instructions bellowed out about scotch tape, scissors, a command to fetch more paper clips. Louise and Peg may not want us here but there is nowhere else to go. I fix more drinks and start on one myself. It is one of those occasions when even the soda crackers are soggy.

An hour later I am bent over the potatoes, deriving comfort from the spud when the next problem arises, a surprise visit from Elizabeth and Jacob. Here they are, two friends of our marriage, witnesses at the wedding. And here are Peg and Louise in T-shirts which proclaim Gay Revolution in large print. It will have a clarity. Lovely time for my two worlds to come crashing together. Louise is drunk and Vita is too manic to be presentable.

Jacob met Vita up here on some other visit when she was probably calling herself my secretary. Jacob stayed overnight and the incorrigible satyr tried to put the make on her.

Jacob is a charming Slavic soul with an insatiable taste for women and a tattoo on his arm from Auschwitz. The first time I saw it, his shirt sleeve rolled up in summer, I had no idea what it meant and teased him it must be a phone number. The camps, he said, a term which meant Girl Guides and Boy Scouts to me, till he said "Auschwitz," the word like a blow to my ignorance. Wept at my stupidity and still cringe at the numbers in his flesh and the capital A. An adolescence spent in hell. After another year as a refugee stowing away in trucks to find his village gone, Jacob came to America and waited on kosher tables working his way through school. The only place to study was Coney Island. Then scholarships and the miracle of his intelligence made him a physicist. When I met him he was a nihilist who drove an old car and mourned a schizophrenic wife, his indefatigable hope goading him to read each new publication on the subject. Jacob was the first person rash enough to buy my sculpture so I could go to Japan and find Fumio. And Jacob could stay here and find Elizabeth who deserves him better than I did. Jacob calling to me from the bottom of the Bowery staircase "I love you." Night I sent him home, copped out by saying I was gay. When really I loved him too much to be a lover while not loving him enough. After Japan Jacob became the patron of our poverty, buying Fumio's stuff when mine got too far out for his tastes. Loaning us his car and the cottage in Millbrook, my hide-and-run place till we got the farm. Scene of tonight's disaster. I concentrate on the potatoes, intent on the special recipe Nell and I worked out in London, a tuber ecstasy of butter fry. The separate societies will just have to sort everything out themselves, I am cooking.

Vita is bouncing about in the living room, threatening the floorboards, endangering the foundations, dancing her inner frenzy. Louise is drunk and egging her on, the

two of them contorting in some wild fashion. Jacob, who
can't dance either, is bewitched by the spectacle and joins
in, the three of them hopping about to Joplin while I
stay with my stove, furious, the slave in the kitchen. Vita
winding through offers to help, but I will have no help,
perversely angry that they have all gone off and no one
but me has given a thought to dinner. Elizabeth comes
to stand by the sink and keep me company, sporting and
enlightened liberal about some gay militants who trashed
this year's book conference in Denver. I hang grimly on
to the stove. Miracles of integration go on all around
me while I, the relentless integrationist, am sick to death
of the whole damn bunch of them. To think that I must
produce a full-blast dinner for seven people when the
table is not even set yet. How to keep patience and not
break the dishes or throw the mess of food on the floor,
spuds running over the rug in an unsightly breach of
hospitality. And blaspheme the only mass I know any
more, a dinner party?

Finally we are seated. All right, damnit it, pass the
meat, I will preside over this farce, try to make them
happy. There is white wine in the glasses and toasts to
get us going. But it is very little work after all, they find
each other fascinating. If I could block out Vita and
smile, amuse, find the big mouth for a bit of whiskey
Irish blather. The tulip glows over us and the wild flowers
in the center, a lace of buttercups, alfalfa, daisies, even
baby's breath. In Japan they call it "spring mist." I see
Jacob's Pan-like beard jutting to my left, then Peg, her
face its own sadness, Louise's cherubic adipose, Fumio's
dark face shining for his friends, talking that zany poetic
English of his, a language fresh minted every time he
speaks. And Vita, yes, you are there. I must finally love
the sight of you having a fine time. My eyes resting on
each face around the table, know its comfort and delight.
And down through the flowers Elizabeth's fine woman's
face smiling at me through their filigree, the sight of it
so touching, strong. The circle complete now in the
miracle of friendship. It is peace.

I wake knowing it is Christopher Day. And turn to Fumio still sleepy when I touch him wanting him, rousing his slumber soft in my hand till it wakes while I repeat to myself, idiotically excited by the word, his member. What an odd word. An enchanting thing stirring in my caress while he grins in his boy's face. Probably it intrigues him too, that grace of reliability which only lets him down when he's drunk. Giving his little growl do you feel horny? the term so absurd in his English, then whispering in Japanese, "Skaebi," his dear body small in my arms so frail and strong. Lushness then entering me while I see the barns out past the windows gray ships of familiar morning the trees green heavy the fresh asters open as I am open the sun blessing this day. Let me be all things his moving within me the trees and barns as well as the city cries moving in the march as we did last year shouting we would be in the open free as the feel of him now just him as the other things fade, his face over me nearly fierce his strokes riding high so gentle but here coming strong moving the feel of him coming bigger growing at the tip that second or two so short yet long as the years we've had, when I know a few more thrusts and his bursting as I hold him tighter as he gathers each part of me happening when he does, slower together in the all going soft I hear his cry, my name as if his heart would burst to our tenderness in that great shaking kiss I would give him my soul while he swoons nearly, his man's body so tender in my arms.

Breakfast is a disaster. Peg has a hangover and a mood. Louise is afraid for her book cover. They have paid her for the picture but there's no guarantee they'll print it. Vita watches me load the 16 mm, hexing my fingers on the sprockets. With a few bits of motherly advice she delivers a death blow to the idea of me and machinery. Within three minutes I have run afoul of technology loading a camera I have loaded hundreds of times. But today I cannot. Vita comments that I behave like a child. Any ten-year-old kid in a temper, of my own rage. She's right, I am being silly. But Vita is cool and competent boxing her shots. I go outside and begin to shoot. But there is not enough time to study, to brood and see. I rip off a few feet of the barn, doing it badly. The camera jams. Go back to the house and check it. Just as inexplicably it unjams. Begin again, sitting in the long grass beginning to care, to do it properly. It jams again. I cannot understand this machine, begin to hate the buttons and knobs like a savage. Lose my temper and give up.

We are late already. The movie company is going to film the march and will be waiting at Sutter's. If I'm late they'll be furious. Peg and Louise are ready to go. Suddenly Vita is at it once again. We look on astonished, she becomes incoherent force, inexplicable venom throwing boxes of film around the dining room. This time she is oppressed as "an unpaid movie director." For doing the farm on Super-8. The knowledge comes to me like an inspiration, I am being bullied. For once I can see the end of the tunnel, this time she is wrong I'm right. For once sure even in my own relentless judgment, since I am Vita as well, always on her side against me—why not, I seem to have more than she does and I know it, aware that by helping another one inevitably patronizes. Vita is a woman breaking out of three kids and half a lifetime as a childwife. This does not prevent my disgust at the way she asks for something out of the trunk of the car, the tone not that of a sensible statement, not even a friendly order, but the despairing petition of a prisoner who holds every key to guilt and plays them like an expert.

Saying good-bye to Fumio, will not see him again before going to England tomorrow. I kiss him and can hardly let go of his shoulder. Like a child losing her father lover brother friend mother, everything. Center of my life. Terrified as last time when we walked over the bridge at Oxford, knowing we'd be apart for weeks while I stayed on to edit. "Bring that movie home this time," he teases, nervous, afraid probably too. It is losing an arm to start the car while he stands there a small figure in a striped shirt and straw hat isolated on a farm, his own loneliness ahead of him.

When we reach the highway I ask Peg to drive. There
is one bag of hateful mail and some of it may be urgent.
Vita is not going to be my secretary any more, we
decided that yesterday. But she wants to do this last
bunch of letters just to wind up the job properly. It's
perfectly all right, she swears she is not oppressed. I
should write a note on each piece sketching out how to
answer it. Tearing the letters open I know already what
a bad idea it is, foreseeing her repercussions as well as
further more impersonal ones if I leave the country
without attending to the mail. Peg is driving like a hack,
which she is, the holder of a taxi license, rocketing the
old convertible way above the manageable speed. I worry
about the steering and remember the brakes are soft. Do
I dare ask her to slow down? I read the mail in a crisis
of fear, the car will crash, the march will fail me, the
movie company are waiting in a murderous mood, the
letters are screaming for answers, each one a hidden trap
if ignored, Fumio is gone behind me, England is only
tomorrow. Vita erupts in yet another animal fury next
to me in the back seat of our closed car. Demanding
everyone's full attention weeping and screaming mysteriously, her pain grander than all others. Sobbing with
strange mad sounds—I have never heard such weeping. When Yoshiko died Fumio sobbed a terrible sound,
it was probably the first time he had ever cried. So
that is what it's like when a man does it, I thought.
Mother said Dad cried when Ryan the dog was run over
by a car, Elder walking home with the body in her arms,
her ferocious tears. And when Poland fell he cried for
the Jews. Always talked like an anti-Semite, then he cried
for the Jews. Somehow I wish I'd heard him, it would
have made me love him better.

I am trying to love Vita in her sobs, shaking the car
and engulfing all of us like a spell, laying claim to our
sympathy. I put the letters out of sight. Just have to give
up tidiness. Peg's driving more disturbed, we careen on
and off the shoulders of the road by now. First I must
get her to slow down, careful not to give offense. Then
attend to Vita. An arm around her, what is it she wants,

a lover friend mother husband wife? What, I wonder, trying each of them while she resists them all, thrashing away in her seat. When will she have punished me enough? Come dear . . . I try tenderness, humor. Nothing works. She is too angry at everything and I am handy. I am also the capitalist cigar and she the poor working girl exploited beyond al revolutionary revenge, I should be stomped to death by mobs. I comfort her with an embrace not entirely sincere, it's hard to caress this regressive force. "You won't even let me cry!" Her final ultimate reproach. I nearly laugh out loud. It is all so asinine, wanting to shout it to the two in front so we can all break up into hilarious sanity together, put the top down and sing, the four of us bound for a festival in the bright morning air. That might make sense. But of course it's not to be that way. Vita will not have it and Vita is in charge. And I am too harried for singing, my execution so imminent.

If only the other two in front would help the two of us in back. Surely they could interject some reason. At least say something . . . But they are intimidated. Vita, though fond of scenes, loathes communication, a believer in private life made scandalous through noisy demonstration while the matter remains inscrutable. Perhaps if I simply wait, holding her, she will talk. And she does, the whole problem is not me, it is never me, it is always something else, just as she denies my theories on roles and games for more obscure explanations personal to herself. The problem is her new job. How odd that she never mentioned it before. Joe Kaplan is "shoving her out of the nest," she divulges significantly. Monday she is going to start cutting for a real movie. Of course there will be no pay now but may be later if the guy sells it. She wails that it might be the first legitimate paying job of her life. I listen, finding it hard to believe Vita is thirty-five has never made a living wage. Even before you were married? No. And married, she still had her stocks. "Why do you think we have a penthouse?" She hurls the question like an accusation. "Money holds you back," Vita sobs, crying now for her money. Vita has announced her grievance, now we can all unite to cheer her up and give her confidence. I can take over the wheel and prevent Peggy's mayhem. But we are still wonderfully late, calling Sutter's from a phone booth and getting three wrong numbers till a thoroughly uncordial man finally grumbles he'll give the message if he can find them. "Looka fella, how many women do you have in there carrying movie cameras . . ."

The air is bright and alive with expectation. When we get to Sheridan Square it's the balloons everywhere like small clusters of sun, free as the day they float in, balloons gleaming yellow in the bright of intersections, darker lights in the narrow streets where the marchers are assembling. Gay, even giddy. I see the Lesbians at the front of the parade under a big lavender banner. Gulp at the sight of my own kind, ranging all the way from beautiful young women to super butch muscle. And someone who has nearly managed to grow a beard. There is so much I cannot understand. A creature in an impenetrable costume and a sign that says he, she, it is from Philadelphia, a face hidden by a grotesque mask and a body in a strange gray sack of a getup that is designed to imitate an enema bag. There is Enema Lib too? So it seems. And all the queens in a frolic of silver spangles sling heels like the fifties, a parody of women. And the male creatures inside have become today what females were to start with. But no, on second thought, never were. Either. No matter, it is some young man's dream come true. The rest of us have another, the handsome young Gay Liberation men who are manly as any man and a bit better-looking than most. Their beards and muscles reach the full gamut to leather and tattoo. It takes all kinds. We got them.

My own eyes focus as if they were Delora's lens, now nearly out of sight in the distance. No problem, she knows her thing. And I am doing mine, all my friends and fellow politicals swimming into view. Even the ones who denounce me most days of the years have kisses today. Christopher Street Day. Three years ago on this day the "fags" fought the police in the streets when the Stonewall Bar was raided. One young man, an alien in the United States illegally, jumped from a window to escape discovery and arrest. He landed on a spiked fence and lingered ten days in St. Vincent's Hospital. That night the cops gave way before our rage and in this act of resistance our movement was born. Everywhere there are cameras and tape recorders. We are making it happen, history is media is now. Here's a fellow from the *Voice* with a mike. Nothing to be leery of, just the neighborhood paper. It's Arthur Bell, and I'm happy to tell his machine we are become a Community and this our holiday, the heady sensation of community suddenly overwhelming. Feeling that we are proud and do live in our own city. They have given us the streets.

There's Jill. Do I want some coffee? Sure. But Delora needs a recheck of our film stock. We didn't buy much, not really sure what to do with this footage, just know that it happens only once, so catch it. Rhoda has already overshot. Make peace somehow about who gets the extra magazine. Where is Vita? Here are my friends from the group. Why don't we all get together with the other women at the top of the march near the banner. There are so few of us and so many men that the women are outnumbered. Mustn't come on heavy, merely suggest. People agree with the idea but there is so much going on right here where we are, a hug for someone, the attention for another's joke, looking up the name of someone to get in touch with in Boston or where to get your article printed, some college needs speakers, yes, the movie will be out soon, they're doing a Women's Lib course in Rochester, here's Jill with the coffee.

Crowds drive her nuts. Jill whispers over the din that there's a party for John and Yoko at Pan Am around ten tomorrow night. I could catch it on my way to England. My life is a trip, I think, forgetting the winter dark in the sea of bright balloons, the many friends. And today's a day you live a year for, Christopher Day, the day we come out into the public sun and make our beginning, summer people that we are. There is Claire shy by the curb, confused expression, bright circle of yellow curls. Wearing her "Don't Pollute—Sail" button. Ethereal apolitical creature behind her years of pacifist study, the Quakers and all those people who have nonviolent conferences out in the countryside. Turned now toward the stars or inward toward mysticism after seven years of reading psychology. Laughing and protesting, "Can't imagine why I'm here," her eyes demonstrating the collective insanity of the occasion. We embrace midstreet. You can do things like that today. So happy to see her that I experience one entire moment free of guilt that my place should be with Vita. We promised to march together and now she isn't here. Claire disappears into the crowd. I lose her.

Then a great shout and the march has started. Did Delora get them from the front, that splendid second of triumph the marchers moving but arrested forever in time held upon the paper suspended in the stills I have seen of marches past? In our different magic the figures will move and go on moving. Or cut, just as one chooses. Where is Vita? Look around as we swing easy under the quiet trees of the Village toward the big Avenue of Americas reserved for us today. We are straggling a bit. Where are my friends? One should be courageous, but I am uneasy without them. There is Claudia looking for Vita. Ruth too. We are three mothers, not one of us adequate. Then she pops up in our midst perfectly contented behind her Super-8. Had gone to get more film.

Sixth Avenue full-throated Village main street past the Waverly Theater and O. Henry's where I used to have dinner with Terrence Dwyer on dates with an uptown doctor in a Brooks Brothers suit. An old friend denounced me once in the street in front of Dylan's Tavern, dark and her voice yelling through the lamppost canyon of her anger at seeing me with him, with six feet of man and not with Zoe who had left me. That same year the friend left her women lover to marry a moustache who abandoned her with a child on Christmas Eve. The year before I went to Japan where there was Fumio. How it all goes back and forth. And here years later I am in daylight come out a second time in the streets to let the world see, not shaking yet, because still downtown.

Ruth is a marshal, running along the line calling out the chants. I do not want to bellow that gay is twice as good as straight, knowing it is nonsense, but knowing why they say it, defensive, niggarized, starving for rhetoric's overkill. How tediously every cause imitates the Panthers, like the women's movement's giant step backwards into neosegregation, crablike yet maybe inevitable while getting our own thing together. The circles it goes in, politics. That somehow you must emphasize race to be rid of its emphasis. And with sex too, the same unavoidable squaring off, the factions, the fads, the slogans. Because people learn so slowly. And one's own inner self slowest of all, poisoned with a past that poisons the future.

But the New Haven Lesbians marching ahead of us have music and a rollicking beat that is fun to sing to. The best moment in feminism I ever saw was a bit of footage from the English women's march, a group street dancing a mocking cancan to an impossibly corny old ditty—"Look young and beautiful if you want to be loved," the song coming out of an antique gramophone wheeled along in a baby carriage as their long beautiful velvet trousered legs kicked high, arms on each other's shoulders, a chorus line winding slowly down a London street covered with silent and surprising snow. A moment of absolute Camp. Like a breath of air these new women, their long wonderful legs, their faces grinning at their own perfection of rhythm, up and out, the joy of the act itself. The song the very thing they laughed at having brought them together in this pride and affection. They were freedom and style and a sense of humor. Today we have a man who has climbed a telephone pole to reveal the rose sewn over his asshole. And a man dressed as a fairy queen six feet high tripping along with wings outstretched. May not help us much to make a strong case for equal employment practices, but the real revolution is in accepting. Which means everything and everybody, the overweight uglies, the truck dykes slickass haircut, the swish of queens, all the faces of alcohol. Yes, but what of that curious enema figure persistently wandering in and out of vision? Surreal, somehow terrifying. Is it the unknown or is it madness?

Crowds lining the street. Looking up at loft windows in the twenties I remember last year and the exhilaration of the march. We had risked ourselves in the streets even before the blinding eye of network television where your mother can learn about you on the evening news. More seasoned travelers, we can joke about it today. The placard I'm carrying reads, "Hi mom come on out. Gay is good." The marchers around me take particular delight in the message, joking about it. Yet one side of me knows with each block going by that Mother is the heart of the matter, Utopia shining in the sign's ungentle pride. What if she could ever let me be? What even if she'd just climb out of my gut, some triumph of my own delivering myself of her?

I look around again for Vita, playing happily with her camera. Claudia is filming it too. These will be the best movies, the ones of friends, the intimate side of the event, our own march. And the movie company's footage another more general record, a larger validation. I spot Rhoda and Robin shooting film from a rooftop. How on earth did they manage to talk their way through a bar and a staircase and a hatch to arrive at the top like heroines getting it all bird's eye? Vita is everywhere at once. She is not marching with me, she is not marching with anyone, she is working. Is the parade a happening for Vita the busy technician? All around me people are cameras. And I another, my eyes and mind the lens and film, but will they be able to give it back, put it on paper later? Never mind, for once just live it, be, and the whole thing enters the self. I will do it then, live my life, my own now maybe. I will be who I am. I must get that first, learn not through words but through feeling what that means. Then later I can go on, act, live for other people. If I have felt it enough. Lived it myself.

It is not a happening for me, it is my life, all these

years hiding, and then not hiding. Last year for the first time. My arm around Claire's shoulder can feel her trembling, nobody's political Lesbian but gay too, like me. Vita cannot know that. Cannot know what we feel moving together watching ourselves watched. We see that we are two women together radiant with the happiness of love. But what do they see, the crowds lining the streets? Their faces are closed shut. You do not know what they think. At Forty-second Street it grows tense, scary. Here is the brute in New York gathered, belly button asshole of the world, junkie figures cruising in the nights cops Puerto Rican painted whore. Groping dark of movie house manhood fantasy, balcony toilets where the casual queer hunter shows prick to stranger. Butch America. Porky pig faces jeer us by in shouts. Claire is shaking, I can feel her fright through her determined little speeches how you should never say "pig" to anyone, "Overwhelm them with gentleness instead." She waves her hand as if it were magic, laughing at herself, her parody miracle. And it takes place in the sun of her hair, the perfect goodness of her face. For a moment there is no evil.

But there is still the enigma of uptown job faces packed into the Time-Life Plaza. Masked. Blank. You want to know what they think but they only stare at you. Is their hooded look less frightening than the construction workers in the next block who spit down insults and give us the finger? Gay men macho them back, perpetuating the dilemma, or taunt them in queen voices—"Try it once the other way sweety." The murderous offers of fuck you taken in vain. I am relieved they are seventy feet in air, hoping that we haven't unsettled them on their perch. Hard work, being a man. Or a waiter at the Hilton, all of them lined up in a pink-jacketed row, mocked men mocking others who are mocked. Or are they in sympathy? Who knows. And the tourist ladies in the little hats with veils over their sparkle glasses, my mother's hats from my own Middle West. And the suited salesmen from anywhere. For a moment embarrassed at having assaulted their reality, its values neatly arranged like Mother's. In order. Is it not some species of cruelty even to exist when your existence so affronts others? Was it out of this consideration that we have hidden for centuries? We who are your children.

At Fifty-fourth Street the CBS Building, next to where you turn down to go to Magda's. But I never go there any more, I frightened her and she is never home. CBS its big chunky block letters before a brown glass basilisk of television, lies for a whole America to believe, having nothing else. But now we have forestalled them with the fact itself, media who reports it all for the millions is surpassed by actuality as we pass the bluff unbelieving faces lined along the curbs watching us in stunned horror from the safe distance of the pavements.

At Fifty-seventh Street, street of galleries and dealers, another tension. Up there in old clothes on Tuesday nights, opening nights with Janey and Zoe timid after an afternoon's dressing on the Bowery, having found at last enough pieces to put together, old decencies our folks had bought us in college. Some young women wore big hats and bravura costumes. We were too small-town for that. And must bathe first in a tin tub with water heated off the hot plate, trying to appear respectable over the velvet collar of my Peck & Peck, its original color turned every shade of drab like a dead rat withered on poison. Or trembling, the manila evelope dampening in my hand as I offer the dealer my photographs. Waits in the outer office while an editor decided whether to be "in" or not . . . And at Fifty-seventh Street I kiss Claire amidst the galleries and the publishers, those ultimate powers who can tell you you're bad where it hurts most, your ambition. And your art. Kissed her squeezing her shoulder, wow this is a political act, do you feel brave? "Invincible, Katsie, I'm supermouse." Using that idiotic name she has invented for me, the way I call Fumio Bird and he calls me Pumpkin, the sort of thing you would die rather than let people know, would think you're a moron. Kiss Claire at Fifty-seventh Street, beginning to realize how much I'm in love, experience so high and adventurous, so opposite to the banality of the phrase itself: in love—that power over the world so convincing at the time, such folly and emptiness later. But today as substantial as the cement in the street.

And then we hit the park. Ahead of us a solid shout of new people, the young and hip giving us peace signs. Now there is green around us, we are safe. And the heat of afternoon has a chance at our attention. Vita appears with a sixpack of cold beer. I bless her receiving a can. One for me but none for Claire. Scolding that she needs the rest for her own friends, Ruth, Claudia, etc. I take a swig and pass it to Claire, answering Vita's eye of reproach with one of my own, she need not have refused Claire to her face. Too hot to march any further, the crowd now a leisurely dispersal toward the Meadow. There will be no speeches. I hear the news with a mixture of relief and disappointment, surprised by the latter. I had actually gotten up wind for a sentence or two. There's no hurry, have a hot dog. The movie company appears for a conference. Claire evaporates into a book sitting on a bench in the near distance, eating print at the usual rate, having a little read in peace, the world far too much with her here. Heavy day for this spiritual dirigible. Rhoda wants more film. I have no money. She insists. What the hell then, take this traveler's check and get a cab. But she doesn't want to bother going herself and can't find a runner to go downtown to the one place near Wall Street that's open all the time, even Sundays. We hustle around trying to find someone who is willing to be such a lackey, do what neither of us wants to. Naturally there's no one. Pleasant the way things occasionally solve themselves.

As we wander over to the Sheep Meadow for the be-in phase, a lady reporter from some impossible place, Turkey, Greece, Tunisia, wants to know what I'm doing here . . . Didn't know Women's Lib was up to this sort of thing, etc., her voice ominously confident, not only that I'm Women's Lib in some abstract essence, but that I'm also at the wrong parade. I am trapped in the heat having to explain dutifully how I am merely one person

in the women's movement, there because I'm a woman.
But also gay and therefore in Gay Liberation. She stares.
My friends go on ahead, but I am pinned here having
to recite formulæ on how much the two movements have
in common. Hot, tired, truding out the analytical stuff
about sex roles, identity. She's never heard of it, start
over again from zero. How I would like to be out of this
nonsense and into the shade. Claire was bored and went
on. But there is always the job to do, my friends grin
back implying it is the earnest guilt of a Catholic girlhood. I would prefer to hope it might be merely responsibility. Never very sure myself. And by now the
reporter has become a woman, a person asking a question that cannot be ignored. Claire wanders out of
sight.

I look for Vita in the grass. Fred sprawls next to her
naked to the waist frolicking with the three children,
the fierce little daughter and their son Sandro, a waif in
a sailor suit, his mouth red with candy, and the elder
son, Jerome. Vita is with Ruth. Fred's lover is a boy. It is
an interesting family. I flop down among them and do not
realize for a moment that Claire is sitting softly behind
me. I turn and try to include her in the conversation.
Shy, removed, she is not to be included. All around us
gay men are taking their clothes off. Delightful spectacle,
I think, a woman never sees enough naked men. The exhibition is scarcely done in my honor, but freedom is
for all so I gander penises. Bodies are so much simpler,
too simple when naked . . . Where does the personhood
fly in a crowd of nudes who are strangers to the on-
looker? Into the beard and the face possibly?

The women move off into the shade, a quiet spot under
the trees, a glade of our own. We lie in the grass, heads
upon laps, at peace, contentedly reviewing the afternoon.
How pleasant to be here, spread out with the cool grass
under my back, admiring Claire until it's time to leave
for Celia's party. Rhoda delivers the camera which it
is now my duty to carry, protect, return safely to the
rental agency. Do we have all its parts, this beautiful
big Ari, so precious, so complex? Vita has agreed to

let me store it in her strongroom until tomorrow when
the offices are open. Rhoda rechecks the boxes, loading
the equipment on my back, I am ready. Claire is on her
way home, she will help me carry it out of the park as
far as the subway. Vita bridles at the sight of us leaving
together. "But you aren't going home yet and Claire is."
Vita's bottomless eyes attempt the double whammy.
"Private property is dead" . . . I have said it, told her,
the way I would love to tell people off but never manage,
kindness and cowardice putting me on their side, inventing my best lines the day after. Vita vibrates
supernatural energy from every pore but I am unscathed
for once. I'll have my independence. And Celia calls.
I'm in a hurry.

Two worshippers carrying an idol, Claire and I exit
grandly with the camera. At the first opportunity I must
invest her with its powers so that she too can taste the
wondrous drug of the machine, play director. How she
will enjoy that, Claire with her obsession after the heroic.
People stare, a man asks if it's ours. The temptation is
overpowering. The park is enchanted as we pass through
it. Marching along shoulder to shoulder we imitate and
then exceed great personages all the way to the Plaza
Hotel. Our dalliance has taken half an hour and I am
now too late to take the subway. But it doesn't matter,
nothing matters, everything is remediable—here is a taxi.
Now it transpires that Claire needs thirty-five cents to
get downtown, as always she ignores money until it
presents itself, refusing to borrow a whole dollar when
she only needs change. Nothing ruffles us, everything is
amusing. And it is how we say good-bye, pragmatic,
undemonstrative, practical. As quickly as she puts me
into the cab and slams the door. "I'll see you after England."

"Did you shoot that thing today?" The weight of office
has made me feel significant enough to admit my own
unimportance. "No, I'm the gofer returning it to the
store." Wrinkling her nose to laugh, Celia's eyes regard

me as definitely less impressive. We are both delighted and she is surprisingly kind, solicitous that I am tired, fetching me a drink.

I am installed in a chair with Celia at my feet. This is a change. Or a restoration, I the lady now and she my page. But it was thus at New Haven when she could love me. When I was still to be courted. Nervous glass in my hand still shaking from the weight of the camera and my hurry. Will Celia be ashamed of me before the Musique Ancienne? Or will she lionize me instead? Dreading either possibility. Only to love her. Her lover again someday? Seeing the rare delicacy of her face before me. I might have survived winters on the sight of that misty hair under the straw hat she wore once, a great floppy thing she called her Provincetown hat; yes, that or something more exquisite, the fineness of feature, the absolute beauty of her eyes, their total intelligence, humor, spirit. Her mysterious postcard to the two of us said that she would like to be friends again. So today I am just her friend, settle for that. And be introduced to the Musique Ancienne. Even to her Ann at last, a sharp young face and not very friendly, on the other side of the room. The Musique Ancienne regard me, I hold my breath. Someone asks about the camera. I explain, telling them where I have been, shooting the Gay Liberation march and the gathering in Central Park. "It was very beautiful and very important to me." There is no catastrophe. A few even say they wish they might have gone, but went instead to hear Celia at the Cloisters. I am surprised by their tolerance, then by the realization that for several of them it is their march too. Is the group a stronger force than politics, I wonder, music people so strangely close and closed always to outsiders. "It's still going on over in the Park," I say, testing them. Two young men volunteer to go over later. Celia is curious to see it too. We'll go out together in a little while.

Today is one of those rare days I feel good enough to be as good as I would wish, brave enough to announce myself to these fastidious strangers and now brave enough to cross the room to sit next to Ann. We talk about

George Eliot, her awkwardness in mustering the passionate, the way Dorothea's sexual frenzy ends in being ridiculous, the heroine panting about the room and then onto the bed for a swoon. We laugh about it, our pretended superiority covering our fear of each other, our enthusiasm for Eliot the excuse for our rapport. I am surprised to find I like her.

The rest of them are debating the notion of costume. A woman, dark and gypsy beautiful, says that long dresses make concerts feel special, festive. One of the young men going with us to the Park argues that costumes keep away the proletariat. "Why should the poor not enjoy Early Music too?" "There are six thousand reasons why they stay away from your concerts, but clothes are surely near the bottom of the list," I tease him. "And your shirt is a costume as well," someone else adds on my right. He looks down at it, an embroidered Third World thing that becomes him. We all laugh. The dark woman goes on, "If special clothes, and they needn't be Period, mark off the attention of an event, celebrate it, why not?" He's losing the argument, but undaunted talks louder. One must admire his masculine certitude. Afterwards, standing near him eating shrimp, I apologize for what he might have felt was a put-down, knowing how it feels and usually on his side, a political against the aesthetes. He grumbles and prolongs the tedious argument, aping the Left's prejudice against art, its infallible habit of losing the point and the fun of things.

At the door there is confusion and farewell. One of the musicians is planning to quit the group and the rest are distressed, this party has been in his honor. He seems unable to decide, the others wheedle and persuade. It is still unsettled as we leave for the Park, Celia, Ann, and the two young men whom I have privately named Butch and Softer, together with the lute and the camera. Coming out of the elevator, Softer makes a cruel joke about the breasts of the dark woman who had argued for costume against him. Watching her pain I feel less like a kind aunt toward him. She leaves us to go home to her children.

The two young men walk ahead of us, their conversation making it appear artistic and rather fashionable to be homosexual nowadays. They are joining a co-op upstate, naming the names of the grand who will be participating. "John Cage" they say in a proprietary tone. Celia and Ann defer to them. How adept they are at appropriation, these young men, the events in the Park have become their property, a monopoly. I feel I am being tolerated as a novice and must remind myself I was here before them. Just as I can remember Cage from ten years ago when he was despised among this sort of musician, a lonely man during the intermission of his own concert at the New School, looking like a big California farmer, the face all lined even then.

In the Park there is hardly anyone left. It is over. We have arrived too late for the spectacle. Only a few demonstrators linger about on the lawns. Butch and Softer are petulant, they stare about contemptuously as if to tell the stragglers that only the real drags are still around. And the poor and the black, some interesting young black women playing with frisbees. But the young men with us do not perceive them as "anyone."

Leaving the Park we pass the Tavern on the Green, its music moving toward us across the grass like an invitation. I wonder idly when the day will come that a group like ours might just drop in at such a place and dance together. There is the hopeless feeling of evening. Celia beside me, our paces matched over the gray cement blocks underfoot. Worrying about Ann, will she be angry, jealous? Warmed by the sound of Celia's voice softly teasing me the old way, flirting, making me laugh at her or at myself, her voice like a caress, like a tongue in my ear.

We will go downtown to the parties. But first we must stop at Celia's place to feed the cats. I will see where they live. It's Ann's idea and very kind, leading me up flights of stairs in the West Nineties to two little rooms and two cats. Their personalities are outlined for me while I admire and transcend the smell, loathing cat shit. Only death or imprisonment exceed it in odium. There is a small inescapable pain on seeing where they live, the fireplace that really works, the exciting painting over the bed, the less interesting one in the hall . . . wondering if these are aesthetic judgments or reaction to circumstance. But they too prefer the one in the bedroom, the one in the hall is duller, that's why they put it there. Already it is time to leave. Down the stairs, noticing the filigreed tin ceiling as I go, my eyes resting on an irrelevant and disregarded niche in the wall of a landing. It once held a statue or a flower, is now empty. Then another flight of stairs, their sanctum receding as my prospects do. Ann has made things clear to me. I will respect that. No advocate of monogamy, but up there she revealed her youth and innocence in a phrase—"All this is very new to me." Her eyes frank, but not imploring. Listening I realize that Celia brought her out and has a responsibility now to that trust.

We drive down to the West Side Highway, the road calling after other days, the day we drove it after a concert, Fumio and I leading the way in my car, Celia and Miriam in the other. Miriam did not want to come downtown with us for dinner because Celia, in a moment of arbitrary flirtation, had whispered it would be nice to be alone. We stopped under the bridge. Celia got out of the car and said she had doubts. But they came on anyway, though Miriam was sick by the time we got downtown. Fumio served her with soup and hot packs and his gentleness. Miriam's eyes needed Celia like a dog's, one had to feel compassion. And they sang duets for us, Bach's love songs, their voices so perfect together it hurt us to listen. Celia was in a victorious mood and made me a present of her most appropriate hat, which I sinned by losing one night in a bar. I feel Celia's arm around me now. Platonism or flirtation? Or my imagination? "Get it while you can," Joplin's husky voice advises from the grave. But there is Ann. Butch inquires from the front seat how he can transport Celia's sailboat from Maryland to the farm where the four of them will spend the summer. Celia gives instructions about the Chesapeake Bay ferry, the details ordinary to her, even boring. Butch's tone implies that the very act of going to Maryland is moneyed and glamorous. Snobbery, I wonder, checking it against my own, deciding for once I'm off the hook. We must stop first at Vita's, asking them to wait in the car while I store the camera.

No one seems to be home, so I will just pop the thing into the strongroom. Fred appears in the hallway. I explain about the camera, suddenly catching sight of Celia and her pals. Wandered right into the house. Vita springs out of the living room. Even Ruth. Fred's boyfriend. There is a whole crowd in the hallway. I have managed to bring oil and water together again, dwindling through the introductions and wondering how they will receive each other. But they get along swimmingly, the mutual admiration of artists.

Celia has ensconced herself in the swing. She will flirt with us all, a queen, the reigning coquette of the room, exerting that curious power she has to delight people, to make them happy. I watch her singing madrigals with Vita, careless and triumphant in the bamboo swing, Vita dark and graceful sitting next to her at the end of the couch, her eyes following Celia's encouragement. They have discovered a bond, because of course Vita went to the kind of school where you learned madrigals. Once told me she'd been sitting in a cafe in Berlin with the four other avant-gardists in her set and it turned out that they'd all gone to the same prep school in Virginia. It surprised them so, she said. It surprises me less. Yet how delightful to hear Vita singing in a good voice that only needs affirmation, confident for once, sparkling with self-expression.

I sit off to the side, an observer as Celia becomes the Celia I know, swinging her legs in their flowered pants and singing bawdy, a parody on courtly effusion where the lover begins humbly enough, but the lady is too coy and he tires of the game, his refrain ending, "So kiss my ass." We shout in laughter protesting its authenticity, but Celia swears it's seventeenth century. "Just that they would have said ars rather than ass," beaming down at us in that bravado Fumio always refers to as

her "mischief." On the shelf next to me Fred's slides
neatly stacked and labeled from his catalogues. Just out
of eyesight Butch sits nervously, making me nervous
since no one is talking to him. Finally Fred comes over
and shows him a book. They discuss it importantly together. Ruth teaches the rest of us a round about an Irish
boardinghouse raucous enough even for me to sing,
unnoticed, enjoying myself, daring to let Celia see my
mouth move, confident she cannot hear me. The old fear
of singing, my voice disappearing in school when we had
to stand one by one to have our voices tested. Everyone
watches me while I stand paralyzed, unable to make a
sound. The nun waits forever before she slaps me. If I
could make a noise, any noise, she would let me sing
The Messiah with the others. But I stand there and no
sound comes out, the clean starched shirtsleeves on my
arms, the accordion pleats of my black serge uniform
tremble, sweat runs down my nylons into the regulation
saddle shoes . . . I look back at Celia, singing with her.

Time for television. The coverage of the march. We
crowd around the set eager to see ourselves. But in fact
we do not. No women demonstrators are interviewed.
Gay Liberation appears to be a masculine province. One
station shows only the queens and assesses the event by
its eccentricities, the other is ultraconservative, skeptical
even of our civil rights demands. The whole of our day
is dismissed in one fleeting moment. We appear to have
made no impression on the American media. My expec-
tations dim like the tube switched off, a gray surface
blank and cheerless. The job seems bigger than ever.
Even here where one might expect the enthusiasm of the
committed, we are downcast, fractious. Butch and Softer
are fidgety to get downtown; Fred warns that the parties
are already over. Vita won't come, she must type. I try
to persuade her to let it go. No no, all martyred wife.
Hanging back next to Ruth, who will see to it that she
doesn't type tonight.

First the Firehouse, where a lone watcher is turning
off the lights. It's over. Then to Mattachine. Everything's

closed here too. "Since we have tried your places, let us try ours." The men object, they are not allowed at DOB. It's unfair, they argue, blaming me. We must beg them even to let us check if DOB is open. "If it's closed you can all go uptown together, if it's open I'll drive Celia and Ann home." They walk behind us, their resentment propelling me into fright. Now I can't find the place in the dark Soho streets, each one looking alike. Celia is walking beside me. We complain quietly of the men, what bullies they are, complaining loudly behind us. I am more and more frightened. Lost now. And then I find it just in time. Celia and I climb the stairs. The door is locked. Somehow it is worth it just to see her here on this staircase, here in the netherworld of our shame, healing the breach between staircases I felt last August on the pavement before the Peach Church the night after her concert. Last year.

We walk back to the Volkswagen, Celia and I lingering to say good-bye, nailed by the beam of its headlights. I balance Ann's needs against my own and the urgency of time, England is tomorrow. "When is the operation?" "July sixteenth." The young men wait impatiently in the car, Ann with them, the headlights glare a shabby and penurious farewell. Wanting to tell Celia, to say it, "I love you." But she would despise me for saying it. The headlights on us provide as much privacy as the media. All that I can risk, my love so desperate, futile anyway, another moment and I might cry or show the passion she does not want. Just a phrase. "Be O.K., Celia . . ." "Sure." We hug good-bye. A second feeling her in my arms. Damn your headlights. And she's gone.

The street empty, a bit like an old picture, New York in the Nineties. For a moment I feel like a drunk rolling home to some Irish slum, a cat crossing my path appropriately under the streetlamp. Celia is owned. Vita is with Ruth. Fumio is at the farm. Claire? Said good-bye to her already, if I show up at this hour she might be offended. Would be so easy to lose her, always a bit remote. Feeling sorry for myself, going home alone. But no, not really. Examining the mood again, it's rather

nice. Unexpected little peace with myself. I can be someone independent, self-sufficient, walking Soho at night
and driving off rather daring alone, big easy car coast-
ing home to my own studio. My life is improbably adventurous, I make movies and go to England. In the
morning wake up and work on my first chapter, get it
finished before I fly. My existence is astonishing, dramatic. Turning at Houston Street and seeing the lights
reflected on the pavement. I thank Zell, remembering.
Then the usual terror up the stairs at being alone in that
place at night. But too tired to tremble in bed. Out.

The phone keeps ringing. I cannot take it off the hook.
The old number is disconnected but only temporarily.
Still hoping to turn it back on and be in the phonebook
as always. So that when someone needs me they can
find me. Should be accessible to any woman in the
movement. Something repellent and elitist about an unlisted number. But the old one rang over a hundred
times a day. Had to shut it off. And by now everyone
knows the unlisted number.

Rings and keeps on ringing. In a few hours, tonight
in fact, I must fly to England, how can I finish the first
chapter when I am interrupted continuously by this diabolic machine? People call for favors, give us a little
blurb, make us a speech, write us a free article so we
can decide if we want it or not. Or they ring up over
trivia, have you read the latest insult? Or to gossip, somebody said at a party—is that true?

I will never get any work done today. Yet I still can't
find the nerve to take it off the hook. It rebukes me and
talks back. Used to be a beep, now it's a real voice talking far away, "Put your phone back on the hook." She's
a record. They have put her into a can, like the implacable one who says the number when you have contacted is
not a working number while you sweat in a phone booth
knowing there are no more dimes anywhere in the
world. And my curiosity is my undoing, you never know
who you're missing. Maybe a friend, might even be
Celia. Pick it up.

Vita again. Calling from work. Still in Joe's nest. To-day she is bustling me off to England. Then Mallory. "Mallory, if I could get someone to take this camera back and pick up my ticket I might have time to get my chapter drafted before the plane." But Mallory has plenty of problems herself, this also happens to be a very busy day for her. Her own exciting situation requires all her attention. She has been trying to write herself but never finds the time. "I certainly can't do errands for you, Kate, it would never even occur to me to ask such a thing, it's totally oppressive." "June's over there, could she do it?" "June can't drive well enough." All right, I'll take the camera back myself. But when can I write? "Just write it on the plane," she says. "You'll have a lit-tle free time then."

I hang up ready to wring her neck, eager in fact. Paul had said that no one writes your books for you. Clearly no one is going to help me find the time to write this one. The most irritating part of it is that Mallory's right, you must do your own shit work. And it is easier, ulti-mately, to do things yourself, cheaper in the long run than favors and free rides. But I am still furious at the prospect of midtown traffic, the hours it will take to get that thing up Eighth Avenue. Am I going to lose this book to the marginalia of movie making?

As I lock the Bowery door I see her blue workshirt across the street, waving at me, her face radiant. She has changed her mind. Dear Mallory, she has relented, wouldn't let me down. We are sisters, she has come to help. Mallory negotiates the traffic like a heroine and walks toward me all smiles. But she has come to get the fan. As a favor I drove it back from Long Beach for her last week. "Be so nice to have it in the summer heat. Just run up and bring it down for me." Mallory follows this order with a little speech on female oppression. Her own in particular. She talks like *Sexual Politics*. "Yes of course you're right, Mallory, no one should do an-other person's work. Right, Mallory, I agree entirely. Look, Mallory, why don't you do some writing, find the time, remember how much that editor liked your wild-sound tapes for the film, the story about the rubber tree? That stuff should be typed up and worked over. Why don't you sit down and transcribe them? Write like you talk Mickey Mouth, you can woman-rap even better than Roslyn Drexler." Burying my rage in praise and a big hug good-bye—"I'll bring you back your movie, superstar." Her fan in one hand she hugs me good-bye, my adored and infuriating kid sister. Turning the key in the ignition I realize she won't return that camera 'cause she didn't shoot with us yesterday, though I tried three times to phone and include her. She is probably mad as hell at me for writing. My only salvation is to get her to write too. Off my back.

As I drive along I argue with the movie company, with Vita, with Mallory. With my mother. Then with Vita again. Why do women go on thwarting each other, preventing each other from working when it would be so much more sensible and productive to help? Why not escape to England? Write the book over there. Never come home again. Once before you escaped to England with JayCee. But when you got there you were her prisoner. Of course, her writing was better than my scholarship, nobler. Writers are the real people, the ones who make the stuff scholars merely sniff over with our little vigil lamps to Keats. I would support her for life so she could write. With the job in California I could support JayCee's old friend Pauline too when she decided to come to live with us. JayCee would write, Pauline would paint. I would teach to support them and someday I would open an art gallery. Meanwhile I would encourage creativity on my salary, doing Freshman English all day while Pauline and JayCee . . . did they make love while I was gone? Low of me even to suspect such a thing but JayCee was so removed now, no longer seemed to want me. Braving dynamite asked her one night going to bed. She didn't say anything for a long moment. Then she said yes they did. Everything broke inside me, the world and everything in it that was reasoned, ordered, comprehensible, broke, fell into pieces. I went downstairs to sit by the fireplace, planning how

I should kill them, commit the deed of blood, Greek tragedy, the action called for. Sweating to discover things weren't like that. I could do nothing. And so I became an animal, the family dog. They permitted me to use the living room, the study, the kitchen, the single bedroom now assigned me. They lived in the front bedroom, their room, sanctum I was never permitted to enter. Reckless I suggested we might all be lovers, had had a momentary urge toward Pauline but had stamped it out as an infidelity. They rejected the notion and went on living behind the door of their room, once our room. I went on paying the bills and going crazy sickened with jealousy. When they would threaten to leave I'd get frightened. What if JayCee changed again someday, loved me again someday as suddenly as she stopped loving me for Pauline? I might miss that moment if she went away. Wept and pleaded with them to stay. One day they threatened again. In a rage of courage I said go. But why remember this now?

Park in front of Amy Perkins's. Next door to Vita's. Amy's a professional, I'll tell her how we're fighting over the credits, put it up to her. "The credits are always a headache. And the fights are routine. People go a little crazy making movies. The hardest part is near the end, after the high of shooting wears off and till it's safely edited. They'll like it when they see it, don't be afraid of them. "You could have done your credits straight, just said filmmakers and listed the names alphabetically. But if people want work they need specific designations, camera, lights, whatever." "But what should I be called?" "Well, what did you do for the film?" "I thought it up. I found the people to do it. I got it shot. I paid for it. Then I edited it." "Then you're the director. If other people want to call themselves director and you let them, you're being silly. To sign yourself as 'filmmaker' is not so grandoise as 'director,' but you certainly deserve it."

She puts the lid on her garbage can and disappears. I go up Vita's stairs and inside to get the camera. Wrangling with the lock on the strongroom dissatisfied with

Amy's verdict. The very verdict I had hoped for, mature, sensible, just. But I feel guilty and selfish calling myself the filmmaker. What is the ethic here? We should have been a collective—and weren't. A collective would have arrived at the concept together, so we were off base from the very start since the concept was mine. Even wanting to make a film at all was my idea, pushing cajoling the others, finding them through hearsay, meeting them by accident. Met Rhoda at the Carmine Street pool. She'd just left a play, was free, said it would be fun, Rhoda a stranger in a swimming suit, somebody Robin knew. And I'd met Robin only once at a meeting. Then too, a collective would have operated from a general fund, rather than on one individual's own money.

How do they edit a collective film? Who does it? Do they vote on each cut? In the editing it was my mind that made every decision, so that the seven hours of rushes became seventy minutes of film, so that Mallory would say this and never say that, so that she would say this first and that second, so that you would learn one piece of information only after you had learned a first one, building her personality in little incremental bits into the only one the audience would ever know. It was not all that Mallory said, only what I chose she would say. Choosing it carefully so it would say the most fastest. And the three times I got into trouble, Nell gave me clues . . . her "brilliant exits."

But we were not a collective. Maybe we got as far as a cooperative . . . So it was a failure, admit it when you've failed. Grow up. And the movie got to be yours through default when you were the only one left. But then you wanted to be "director" and Sybil took it from you. She and Robin and Rhoda were the directors, Sybil yelling me down on long distance. I rolled on the carpet in Nell's office and cried. Had wanted that director's credit so badly. Then you had to give up wanting that. All right, so it was pompous to want to be "director." But I must have some title, an artist wants credit for work, some recognition. I don't want to be in a collective. It annihilates the person. I am an individualist after all.

An egotist? No, you don't want to be that either. Should I get no credit at all? Take my name off the film? Then I disappear. And they can't sell it, counting on my name to interest distributors. It is insoluble, and I can't make the lock work either. Call Vita on the phone. Her voice patiently repeats the combination. "Try it." "It works! You're right of course, I must be nervous, thanks."

Driving uptown still grabbing at the hope of writing in England. Arguing, defending myself against Vita. I could do the movie there, away from the movie company. If I write there I won't have an editor. No more Vita. I will be free. Escape her like I did the movie company just to get the job done. Everyone I know talks—beautifully, brilliantly, incessantly. So few of them get things done. But I have to, that's my thing, my special curse, that I finish things. Two black truckers pull up next to me at a stoplight. "That your baby?" Their eyes point to the camera next to me on the seat. I drive with one hand cradling it like an infant. Now I must confess it's only rented. We all three giggle at the idea. They like it, this chick with a black super-prick thing like that in an open car. We grin at each other, my mind kissing each of them. Moment of amnesty.

At Columbus Circle I see the banners of the Italian-American Civil Rights Day parade. Always held the day after the gay march. Happy coincidence, since the Mafia runs both the Italians and the queers, bleeding us in our bars. The pennants strung across the road are a signal of our collusion, our secret sympathy. The Mafia and the homo, we are both outlaws, our world right next-door neighbor to pimp prostitute pusher. Claire and I at Paolo's billing and cooing over pacifism, necking through history and civilization are really part of a gangster movie. The banners flap money. Must spend a mint decorating for this thing. Yesterday the queers didn't have a dime. And how do they feel in their march, the Italians, is it the release we knew, the roller coaster high on identity before a whole town puts them down? Wops. Zoe was a wop.

Just beyond Columbus Circle the road divides. Take

the fork that goes to Columbia. The adventure continues feverish, but what to call the thing? Prescient, drugged, mystical with excitement, call if the *New Life Talky*. That way it's pop, not serious. If it's a joke people will excuse, are more likely to forgive. Call it talky so it's Camp, contemporary, not Dante's new life then but our own now. Call it talky 'cause it's a movie, a sound track. Put a notice at the front explaining that what I'm trying to do is to supply the voiceover for the pictures I make. With this caveat people might understand or at least put up with it. Closer to Columbia, disturbing visions of disgusted reader throwing the book on the floor. How do I dare take up his time? I see his annoyance with a brilliant clarity. A he rather than a she. Can I refund his money? Should I tell him to fuck off and learn to steal books the way I used to and he won't lose his investment? Who will ever want to read this book, this collection of the clutter in my mind? Vita jumps back into my head accusing me. Then I have a revelation on Columbus Avenue.

A revelation that Vita is my mother. I've been telling her all along that she makes me her husband. She's been telling me all along that it's not about that at all, it's about mothers. And maybe it is. I am not Vita's mother, have never even met the woman. But Vita is somehow my mother, which must be why she makes me feel so lousy. Mother operates loudest, convinces me I am the worst . . . her Lesbian daughter. Vita has revealed it to me, now I realize I was my mother's man, opening car doors, driving for her, taking her arm across the ice. When Dad left she said we replaced him. And we did. She arranged it, needing that. Mother weeping and hysterical when we were bad, two insubordinate daughters with no man to keep them in line. Elder was already away at school. Mallory who was Mary then and the two of us could now yell back. Mother was little, threatening to spank us and we'd laugh. And Mother a woman drowning while holding on to two children. I was to be her pillar. Fourteen and going down too, my own adolescent emergencies merely bubbles on the lake of our greater trauma.

A schoolgirl with a crush on Nancy Kelly gushing our usual way through a phone call while Elder's "beau" sits in the living room, paying a visit. The beau who taught me how to draw horses, serene on the rocker calmly chatting with my mother. Then his voice crisp and clinical, "You should realize your daughter's a Lesbian." I heard it. The word. His voice pronouncing a word I have never heard but understand immediately, comprehending his voice. His voice makes it a disease. Mother says nothing. But I am warned now to hide. People mustn't hear me. Stay in my room most of the time and read. When I use the phone it must be from the downstairs extension at night when she is upstairs. Pause when she picks up the phone. "You kids have been blabbing forever, get off, I have a client." Fill in with a sentence or two on the Regimental Ball at St. Thomas Military Academy across the street, "Who are you gonna go with?" Things I am supposed to talk about, learning deception from the same woman who taught me to tell the truth.

Learning through accusation. Did you go to mass? Yes, Mother. Having spent the mass hour sitting in her car parked on one of the dull little streets near the parish church reading a novel, checking the missal before turning home to be ready for cross-examination. What was the sermon about? I invent one from the Ordinary, some clue from today's Gospel or Espistle. Then veer off into the priests' habits of delivery, comparing Father Corrigan's tedium to Father Gilligan's. "You are sarcastic," she says. "Your laugh is cruel. You make fun of people." If I have to go with her to her own favorite mass, the ten o'clock, I use the occasion to practice my Latin. Smug that she knows no Latin. "Shall I teach you, it's more fun if you follow." Mother stung, humiliated. "No, don't teach me."

And then I told her once, doing the washing in the basement. The big old lead tubs. The stationary tubs, she call them. I stood by the washing machine and watched the funny-shaped thing in the middle whirl, the agitator, and said it—I don't go to mass any more. "I have lost my faith." The agitator whirls between us, and the tubs stand rigid, the tubs where I am in charge of the washing now, doing it alone every week to help her. My job in the stocking department of Schunneman's basement pays the utilities bill. Even the phone bill now with my baby-sitting business, a real ad in the Highland Village paper, nice families, new part of town. They are Jewish. They pick me up and bring me home. I wash the dishes and clean the house for thirty-five cents an hour. The kids like me. I am an excellent babysitter. I look through their drawers and discover contraceptives. Protestants have them too. There is a breast pump I have to try. The boys have penises. Once I touched it and it stood up. Tried it with a cousin. Didn't work. Too little. Too soft. Knew it was wrong, a mortal sin. Wrong even beyond that because I am doing it to him, he is not doing it with me, does not even understand, is just a baby. But I had to know how it would feel. My face is hot. What is it like? Men and women do it. His little thing doesn't do anything. When you do it you're a woman. Grown up. The mystery they never talk about but it's everywhere. Explains everything they do. Get married. Have babies. Families. I have file cards for my families. When a black voice from Rondo Avenue calls, Mother says it is too dangerous I can't go. In the icebox at one place there are suppositories. Try it, melts up your ass. What's it supposed to do? It must be a sin. Also snoopy. But so fascinating.

Frankie Luger showed us his penis. How boys pee. We stood in the toilet in the Lugers' basement. He was five, I was eight. Frankie peed for us. We watched. It looks easier. You don't have to sit down or take your pants off. He could shoot it. Funny looking. Cute. Next let's have a look at the new bar in the rec room that Mr. Luger built himself. But just then Frankie's sisters caught us. They made it important. Frankie is just a little kid, what he does is not important. But his sisters are older and they said we were bad, dirty. When we ate Campbell's Tomato Soup in Mother's kitchen Tim McMann asked me did Sally make blood like the soup, same color? I knew he was dirty 'cause of the Luger girls. And Sally would be furious if she could hear. Tim is so good but he said that. His brother Donald is dirty and he peed in their garage wanting to show us but by now I know it's bad so I won't look. Then Mrs. McMann called Mother and said I should stop playing with boys. Getting too old for that she said. Frankie and Tim and the other Tim. All my gang. No more Purple Feather Club with Grandma McMann going to sew costumes for us out of that beautiful rayon you get up on Marshall Avenue in the dry-goods store that has everything, I could stay there all day. And now I have to play with girls. So I bought a chug from the McMann boys for twenty-five cents but they came that night and broke it. Mrs. McMann has had me kicked out of the gang. No more snow forts or dugouts in the vacant lot near Murphy's. You could crawl into the packing crates and live there. And in the spring when they trim the poplars across the street at St. Thomas you can build wigwams with them. Sit there all day and smoke cigarettes like we do when we go exploring down by the river, Indian file, watching out for enemies and bums. There's a grotto down by the seminary that has outdoor stations of the cross. Pious in the woods we do the stations, feeling sorry for Jesus. The cross hurt so, his face shows it. Don't look at the other thing around his waist. "Up down up down, stations of the cross," Daddy laughs at them. But Good Friday and the wonderful darkness. The Tenebrae is in Latin and takes forever but it's exciting. Only the boys get to sing it 'cause they can go up on the altar and we can't. The candles get put out one by one and the chant is so rising and falling I will cry I love it so and our church does it three times during Holy Week. Then Easter.

"You must go to confession," she says from her side of the tub. At Derham my homeroom teacher Sister Agatha Marie is very young and beautiful, everyone says so. I love to watch her walk tall, the long skirts swing then her beads click. She catches us in the toilet down the hall from homeroom. We go there to talk. The lounge is for the seniors and the toilet is the only place for freshman to talk. It's where you go to smoke everyone knows about it but you can get expelled for smoking. Sometimes Nancy and I go there and talk about how much we love each other. It is the most interesting subject. I can feel my heart getting excited. When I see her walking ahead of me down the stairs to chapel or through the cloisters with the white gauze veil on I want to faint maybe, she is so beautiful. My heart gets exicted walking along. I will love God a lot. The Blessed Virgin. We only sing her mass at my school. We study her all day. Nancy gave me a beautiful holy card. "Today is the last chance if you're going to do your Easter duty," Mother keeps saying. She doesn't understand that I can't. Last time I told about Nancy Kelly. The priest said I should go to the priest house afterwards and see him. If he sees me he'll know who I am and tell Mother. Now I can't ever go to confession any more, counting up the sins against charity, the lies, or the hard ones, the sins against purity. That's when you touch yourself or even think about it. I think about it a lot. So just find a good number for the times you tried it with a pencil or whatever you can find around to experiment.

But by Easter I can't go to confession any more because last time I told him I kissed Nancy Kelly. You have to tell kisses. I don't know if it's mortal or venial. So I said I kissed a girl. That's probably venial. He said what? So I had to say it again. Then he said why? His voice was scary. I didn't know what to say so I just said 'cause I love her. When I said it I was counting on it not being so bad as with a boy. But it was worse. After the way Agatha Marie and the seniors acted I should know this by now, but you are supposed to tell the truth. Now I have to tell Mother why I can't go to confession. I can't say why really because then she'll know too. So I say I have lost my faith. It's dramatic. Like big words, like fate. Losing your faith, the worst thing for Catholics it's like death. I feel important when I say it. More important than I had meant to feel. She says I am a smart

aleck reading those Protestant books. Last summer I read
H. G. Wells's *The Outline of History* in four volumes.
And Van Loon who said the Catholics did awful things
in the Inquisition. She calls me a smart aleck but really
she's scared, crying now. What has she done to raise such
a child? Daddy is gone. We are all scared. I didn't mean
to scare her so much I'm scared too. Last time the priest
refused me absolution if I didn't go to the priest house.
So he could see who I was and call my mother. I ran
out of the church and straight home. If I go to confession
again God will know it and make the absolution not work
'cause I'm getting it on a lie. If I die now I'm done for
'cause it's a mortal sin. The rest of my life will have to
be fake.

She says I have to go up there it's Holy Saturday today
and confessions only go on till seven. I have just until
tonight or it's another mortal sin, failing to make your
Easter duty. The people stand patiently in line, the nice
darkness and the smell. Light of the candles up on the
altar. I kneel down, knowing I have to make it up now.
It is not just cheating on the number, everyone does that,
how can you ever remember just how many uncharitable
thoughts? The main thing is to say what you did, confess.
But this time I'll be lying. Receiving a sacrament in bad
conscience, like we say in religion class. Bad conscience
is when you know beforehand. But she won't let me back
in the house if I can't swear to her that I've been to
confession. And she'll watch me tomorrow at communion
time. Is it better to go to confession the wrong way and
walk all black up to the rail and get God in the flat white
bread, my tongue caressing it against the roof of my
mouth all these times since the first? If I confess then
at least some sin might get erased, if not Nancy, then the
usual stuff about touching myself or telling lies or just
not honoring my parents. I have only one parent, my
mother . . .

Watch out for that car. And remember where you're
going—Daedalus to get that airplane ticket. Crazy name

for an airline. Of course Vita is Mother and I have slept
with Vita in bad faith, which is a sacrilege. So of course
that makes her my mother, the one who can accuse me.
Moreover she has a nervous tic of swallowing all the time,
just as Mother used to. My mother, the first wronged
woman. And Vita is a woman wronged, she has never
stopped telling me that. I am supposed to champion
women as I did my mother, her mainstay while she cried
and carried on during dinner dishes.

Time plunging back to the time of recriminations.
Mother wrings her hands, weeping her terrible powerless
tears. "We have no money. We will starve. Everyone
in St. Paul knows about his drinking. You can be darn
sure they talk about how he's left us. And the two of
you are Jim Millett for sure. Took up right where he
left off." Mother crying and yelling at us till we are crying
and yelling too, Mary completely hysterical in no time.
I hold on till my stomach is going to throw up in the
sink over the dishwater and the rectangular tin of garbage, the mashed potatoes left over still yellow from the
butter. The green of the peas. And still now we are poor. I
cannot make her rich. And she says I am as bad as him.
The man I should hate, my father, that bully. Underneath
I'm even worse, still, hanging on to my infatuation with
him and all the Milletts. Does that mean I am one of
them? If I'm like my father am I still a girl? But Mother
is right and he is wrong, bad, he left us. But he laughed.
He could dance. Sing. Tell stories. He is handsome. And
so friendly when he took us out to dinner that one time
we saw him after he left. And I adore my Aunt Christina,
wish to God I could be her child. When we go to her
house at Christmas there is a fire and all the Milletts make
it feel like a party. The grownups drink and all the aunts
and uncles laugh. Afterwards they sing funny songs like
"When Hastings Was but a Pasture" that they made up
themselves. They dance crazy dances and Uncle Rog
comes down from the attic dressed up like a lady with
a lampshade on his head. He draws pictures 'cause his
father was an artist and he was born in France. And
Maude and Uncle Dennis argue about Governor Stassen.

It's a quarrel but not a fight. Everything's so beautiful.
The glasses, and the table is mahogany. You hear music
when you eat. And there are so many presents wrapped
in gold and silver foil with special wide colored ribbons.
Once the butler floated down a great big whale from
the balcony. It was my present. Wouldn't it be wonderful
if I could get adopted. But I'm Mother's kid and I must
stick here and see that we survive, be strong for her. There
are just the three of us now. This is where I live. But
I'm rotten from the Milletts and I can not earn enough
money.

Around Easter that first year he was gone we brought
her from the river one on each side of her. I was afraid
she might commit suicide from the Marshall Avenue
Bridge. Floss McCarthy and I already saw a woman
drown there. We stopped our bikes and looked. The fire
department was there. Her dress was pink like an old
tin can rusted, an oil drum. Pink dress like a woman's
body just floating. We watched. I am already a junior
lifesaver. I am learning in the gym class at Derham. We
have a pool at Derham 'cause we're the high school to
a college and we get to use their pool two days a week.
If you don't want to swim you say it's your period.
Nancy tells them that 'cause she doesn't want to get her
hair wet. We have curtains to hang in front of our stalls
when we change into our suits. The nuns don't come here.
Some kids go along and jerk your curtain off the hooks
and laugh. If they do it to me the other kids might see
me. What if Nancy saw? She has nothing on her front.
Mine are big already so I must hide them.

In lifesaving class I want to save Nancy, who is supposed to float on her back waiting to be saved. There
is the head carry but the cross chest is nicer, like hugging
or kissing. We practice. People pretend they are
drowning. They fight and try to drown you. But you've
got to pick them up from the bottom under the water
along their body up the sides. Otherwise you'll both
drown. The agitator goes on, the clothes flop back and
forth. Mother looks down into the washing machine. She
is an abandoned woman now.

Here I am at Daedalus. They actually call it Daedalus, fine name for a fly-by-night charter. What's all this nonsense about swimming and flying? Sly old Joyce with his exile silence and cunning. Daedalus is a nondescript old brownstone in a deserted block in the eighties. From the looks of the place it will probably go down without even taking the trouble to melt. The cop on the corner is going to let me park illegally. Daedalus is risky but it's the risk of air over water. Vita is drowning in New York. I would help her but she is drowning me too, speaking my evil in her silences. She will drive me crazy. Don't you write finally for Vita and Mother? But they are drowning me. So I'm skipping town. The cop has no idea I'm working for Mother. And Vita. Forging the consciousness of our race, etc. I tell him an innocuous story about buying an airplane ticket. Does he suspect I am escaping Vita and Mother, saving my own neck by taking off on them?

A black man in the foyer points to his left without a word. He understands. He is magical. A guide. Daedalus turns out to be either Peter or Stephanie. Vita has called them, made the reservation. Do they have my ticket? Yes. Here's the money. Peter wishes me luck and assures me it is an honor to be fired from Columbia. He recognizes me and seems to approve of me. Vita should have undeceived him. Can I write on the plane? Stephanie says she even types on airplanes. "Screw the sleepers." She is bold, a real writer, a journalism major at Columbia. She is printed. I will never be printed again because the last time made me crazy. Now I have started up again but I can't finish even the first part in time. Before England, where it will be too late. The cop outside is still letting me park. Daedalus will save me over water. From Vita.

At the corner a Sabrett cart. A black man in a business suit is buying a hot dog. The Sabrett man squirts him with a water gun. The Sabrett is a white man, looks Italian. A little boy jumps up and down laughing. The black man turns and says did you do that? The Sabrett man blames it on the kid. It is an absurd, impossible transaction. I watch it from my car window knowing who shot who and tasting the black man's humiliation, which tastes the same as the old outrage felt for elderly white men mugged on the Bowery by young black toughs, Social Security checks torn out of their hands by the gang who hung out under my windows a few summers ago. If I try to stop them they'll get me, break the glass door, come up and cut my throat. Each one carries a razor. Whole afternoons torn again and again by the squeals of little old men totally humiliated while one young guy holds his arms and another sees through his pockets for change. A nickel all he had. Doing it for fun. The real money is in pimping. Or in dope. This is just a game to hurt, done for amusement, cheap racial revenge.

Now the black man by the hot-dog stand can do nothing but swallow his insult from this idiotic little white bastard squirting a water gun. The black man is understandably furious, the white man is palpably crazy with the madness of his kind. The incident is as emblematic as it is ridiculous. The whole city seethes with violence today. Some days you can reach out and feel it. As I wait here for the stoplight it explodes in the air and coats the metal of the car like paint. Violence is swallowing us. There is no gentleness left. New York, America, is blowing up, choking on its spleen. Everybody hates. Will the black attack the Sabrett? I wait. No. He is leaving. I want to comfort him but he walks off with his briefcase. I should have spoken out because I saw what happened. When you know you are responsible.

On Ninth Avenue I cannot say really that I know. But I sense something powerful in the Fifties. Cops everywhere. Something's happened. The streets are full of Maf. You can actually tell them by their cars, only Mafia have cars like that. And the faces behind the glass of the windows, impossible faces. Going through the intersection I catch sight of a gold-lettered sign—Roosevelt Hospital. Someone's been killed. A big one. Swarms of police. Has a diplomat been shot? Now the shit hits the fan. The sensation of murder is pervasive, choking like a sense of doom.

Now the city is to be torn apart, you can feel it going mad. Get out of here and get downtown. Cops and Mafia seem at times to be the same people in different costumes. But the Left wears its jeans and stompers and is dying to kill you too, it's so revolutionary. America is a prick on the rampage, a diseased bull in fury. New York America is a gangster movie going on right now this afternoon. Hurry home and work, it's the only sanity. And scuttle that crap about *New Life Talky,* too American. Like our movies and the city, lovable, hateful, finally unbearable. I want to escape violence, my own no less than the rest. Daedalus will save me, safe in my pocket. Frenzied on downtown, all the feelers out, my own heart beating in the collective ecstasy of kill.

Park the car staving off my demons. And sit down at the dining room table to become crazier still trying to get it done before England, save the book that is me, bits from the old notebook when I was mad in the winter, scraps I wrote then lying all over the table. There are more of them in the shopping bag where I keep the book itself, a ragpicker's specialty. Like an old crone frantic that I will lose some piece of it, the scraps floating at the bottom, must put them together to make sense. Blend to a unity the scribble of my madness, a collage of the evil winter, splinters of the explosion written furtively on airplanes. I must save myself and then escape Vita. But England looms ahead like pressure, swollen bag of water we must cross tonight. The plane takes off at eleven. Hurry. Don't lose the book again.

A panic of haste against the phone's interruptions. Vita again. When should she come over? Faithful Vita driving me to the airport, my endless favor-doer seeing me off. I am giving her my car. Dubious present that might make her freer if it doesn't break down. "Please don't come over yet." Fighting her in my mind. It's not her book. It's mine. I've got to smuggle it out of the country. Away from her eyes. Get rid of this Editor. Censor. Scrambling back to my chair. Then the doorbell.

Mallory is here to pick up my keys. On her way to the
grocery store, decides since she is going there anyway
it would not be too difficult to pick up a can of something
for me. Assures me it would be no imposition whatsoever.
I have not eaten since yesterday's hot dog in the park.
I go upstairs for the money. Mallory mounts behind me,
her tread like fate. I must tell her now even if she kills
me. Make a clean breast for her to stab at. My back to
her, "Mallory I have something to tell you." I do not
see her face. Would never have found the nerve to say
it with her eyes on me. "It's about the credits. My
credit." We are up the stairs and walking toward my
work table. Now she's interrogating full force. "Yes, I've
been meaning to ask you," her voice shrill and sarcastic.
"Just what *is* your credit, Kate?" My very name like
a stab of guilt. Everyone else has their credit. Invented
them themselves. Mallory has given herself three. We
stand on either side of my writing table, the precious
papers strewn about. I gather a desperate strength from
their presence. "I said in the last frame that I was the
filmmaker." Her voice takes off like a siren. "Oh yesss.
You couldn't be just *one* of the directors like Sybil and
Robin and Rhoda you had to be *special. Elitist,*" she
spits at me. Quaking, I try to explain—"I thought about
it for a long time. I think what I did is fair, represents
what I did for the film." "You are a fascist pig you are
the president of General Motors you are a capitalist shit."
Mallory always knows what to say, where to hit. I turn
away and walk on shaky legs through my sculptures,
wooden people on magic chairs sitting all through the
room, calm presences who have kept me company for
years. Sculpture is silent. Then suddenly Mallory subsides,
just quits, changes the subject. "What do you want at
the store?" I have been preparing to die, have waited
for this moment in buses, in beds, in airplanes, driving.
For weeks I have dreaded her denunciation, tantamount
to an execution, judgment on all I am or hope to be.
And she lacks even the concentration to carry through.
She has lost interest after two sentences. I am reprieved.
And strangely annoyed: she has the mind of a butterfly,

the attention span of a kindergartner. I have gone through torture, was preparing my soul for death. And she wants to know what I want from the store. "Campbell's Baked Beans." My hand still shaking giving her the money. She'll pick up the keys on her way back.

Giving me ten minutes grace to struggle with the fragments, more unruly each time I try to organize them. Mallory doorbells my concentration again. This time with a hippie boy in tow. Another Philip? We were all so relieved to be rid of him, Philip crazy on his acid. By the end Mallory claims he was trying to kill her, she had to change the locks. Where did she find another one of these creeps in ten minutes? On the street yet, a perfect stranger. I'll give her the keys and the minute she's asleep he'll be back here to clean me out. I try to give her the eye, for Christsakes hide these when you get home. His cheerful little face grins past me up the stairs, casing the joint. If I say one word she'll blow up at me. And he'll be warned. One word of caution and Mallory will have a tantrum, I don't treat her like an adult, etc. It will go on for hours. I must surrender everything to some stray she has found on the street. On the other hand when I called her from England and asked her to guard the place while Fumio saw Italy, she said—just leave it to me. And came through beautifully. So trust her now. You must trust people. Not all people but the calculated risk. Hard as it is. That is how we did the movie. All on trust. It is magic and it works, it you totally surrender doubt, people rarely fail you. Gamble on it. Here are the keys.

Back again with the scramble of papers, the outline now finally coming together. Pieces falling into place under a felt pen on a tablet of typing paper. An elaborate key to the confusion of notebooks, labeling and coding the passages, the glimpses of self snatched on planes. Moments escaped from the Bowery. Fumio's disapproval. Then his okay. Suddenly it hits me, insane as the book itself. I will dedicate this book to Mother. To Zell of course for starting me. But to Mother too. It will heal. The perfect pipe dream, ultimate pie in the sky. She will read me and know who I am and accept. Always she says, "Write a book I can show to my friends." This will hardly satisfy that requirement. Mother living in St. Paul with my queer notoriety, her first pride in my success turned to gall. And now how much worse this time? But what if she accepted my dedication? I'll try it. But wait a minute, is it cheating to finish Chapter One on the plane tonight, cheating because it's backwards? The real Chapter One takes place going toward America and tonight's plane goes the other direction toward England. Well, try to remember the feel of it in the gray over ocean, in it again.

One more thing, where are the words from the flyleaf of Erikson's *Gandhi*, the worst part, bottom of winter, night of the ultimate despair when I knew for sure I couldn't write? Maybe they won't fit but I'll try to squeeze them in. Finding the book on the floor by the bed where it's been for months. Excited. Still there on the last page where I wrote them when I couldn't sleep. Thinking about a razor. Finish it off. Intimidated by Beckett, master of all masters, the manner in which he distills. A poem on my cages. The panic traced to claustrophobia, then to being a woman and queer. Copy it out so you won't have to lug the whole book to England. There, the skeleton plan is completed. The last piece is in place. Happy, I walk the Bowery floorboards. I can be a writer. Quick, back to the table. There is no time to gloat, it may have already cost you something, some piece lost at the bottom of the shopping bag.

Almost finished when I hear her key in the lock, the climb up the stairs and across the floor of the living room. Vita is framed in the door of my studio. I turn to see. Her eyes are a spaniel's waiting for a blow, inviting me to be my father's heavy hand. I am already tried and indicted by these eyes. No. I have spent my life trying not to be my father. Damned if I'll hang for this. Cheerful instead, telling her I've got it all, crowing at her. The worst thing I could say, but it's my salvation. I'm not going to drown in those awful dark pits of her eyes.

Vita disappears into the other room. I should go on writing, there is still an hour, I could finish. But I may have hurt her. She is a guest, give her a drink. I don't feel like it. She sits down and I get out the ice. It is a relief to wait on Vita in any capacity. She's explaining how Joe knows everything, can understand her completely, can tell when she has made the right shot or the wrong one. He's infallible. I listen full of objections, may be her movie teacher but he's not God. Who is this guy that she's so slavish about him? Sounds like a newly-wed. Annoyed at the way she works for him for nothing. Me, I pay her, she hasn't even finished the two pieces she insisted on typing. Had two weeks to do them. Now she's saying she'll send them to me. Her voice is pitiful. Her face is ground like the poor.

Standing behind the kitchen table I go for a showdown. "Look, Vita, we're through with the secretary business. We're out of it." No, be gentle. "Why don't you just give me the tapes? I'll have them typed in England." I stand in front of her with a drink. She really does look sad. Very gently I ask to have the manuscript back, it would be easier for her. I can find someone in England. Afire now to pay in money rather than blood. I see myself copying it in longhand on Nell's dining room table. No, she says, she wants to finish the job. The peasant in me argues that I have already paid her. Her eyes plead. Now I am a bully even to suggest it. Instinct would have them back at any cost, is willing to beg her to surrender the stuff. Or to tear it out of her hands. No, settle for Chapter One and the few bits already typed that I can bring with me, the preface, Zell's funeral. Remember all she'd done, that huge transcript for the movie, her loyalty, her efficiency each time I'd call from England for a piece of track, the long day she spent with Fumio hauling boxes of the precious original negatives to the shipping company. I could never have started the book without her. I am grateful. "Let's forgive each other, Vita, maybe we're just cutting loose to take our own first steps." She is tragic about our future. I insist again that I do not quit on people. Gradually we slip into being friends sitting on the rug and having a drink, talking about movies.

I lie back on the floor by the file cabinet. I want to make love to her. All day I have wanted to make love to Vita once, with my whole heart. Before I leave tonight. She tells me she has finally heard the tapes. "I wouldn't love you so much if you were not such an electric writer." It sounds nice. Then it sounds overdone. "Will I have to repeat this remark and look like a fool regurgitating compliments?" "What's the most embarrassing thing in it so far?" "The weekend I was screwing my secretary." "That's just a delusion of your own. It was never that sort of relationship at all." "Yes it was. For two days you made it that." Vita refuses to admit it even happened. She is stubborn. And I am turned off. How can I get turned on again? I want to be her lover before I go. We have another drink and check the luggage. "Would you like to cut out footage from the gay march?" The idea pleases her. I begin to dread what might happen working with Vita again.

We lie down on the bed and have another drink. There is still time. We have discussed all our friends, she has praised Joe, and I have done an imitation of Nell. The mood is right. We are both "corked" today, as Fumio would put it, our simultaneous periods a kind of twinhood. Vita is laughing. I like her again. Her body so lovely. Like a girl's. Her skin on my skin the length of our bodies naked. Making love to her with all my attention. I feel tenderness and the power to give her joy. When she comes she says "that's what it's about," did I feel it? "I don't know your experience it was different from mine," I evade. "Oh well, maybe next time . . ." Vita is nonchalant. Yes I answer my face turned way on the pillow ashamed to say it or that it was not quite what I wanted. I wanted what she had, not what she gave.

Of course it's all good. I decide philosophically in the shower. Shame is silly. Perhaps that is what she was saying. Odd how the world condemns. The asshole, for example, even with a man sometimes, but nothing you can do very often, raises hell with the bowels. How do faggots manage? I grin into the water, remembering

Marcus and that passage in Mailer where I thought
Rojack was fucking his wife in the ass. Marcus shut the
door of his office and said no, it's analingus. What's that?
I was ashamed I didn't know. Marcus tough as a city
editor explaining it's the tongue in the asshole. We had
wonderful conferences. And wonderful quarrels. Whole
scholarly sessions that were nothing but an amazing exchange of four-letter words. But Marcus betrayed me
and told Mailer, who ridiculed my ignorance in a
magazine. In the shower it all seems rather funny. I was
a ninny before Mailer's expertise. Scholarship yelps for
clarification. Should I revise, amend, write another footnote practicing learned witticisms, acknowledging Mailer's
kindness in "rectifying error," look up the exact reference,
get all those damn numbers, volumes, thingamajigs, page,
date, etc.?

Leaving the house warm with each other, the exchange
of the flesh still with us, chattering about class, hers, mine,
Celia's, feeling a kindred in our insights and subtleties.
Dissecting our movie teachers or Ireland or the film Vita
is planning to make about the place where she spent her
summers as a child, a private beach that her family
owned, their own beach the way Celia's people had. Vita
will shoot a poem to its memory. As we enter the Queens
tunnel we are talking about mirrors and how we feel in
them. For Vita they are only something to use in poems.
"Become an editor and make movies, Vita, but don't
forget you are a poet." "Mirrors are endless reflections,
lovely like water and light. In another woman you see
yourself." "The shrinks call it narcissism." But for me
my mirrored self has always been a stigma, accusing me.
"Someone ought to do a job on the mirror as a symbol
in homosexual writing. Starting with Dorian's portrait.
Capote uses them too, and other writers seem to resort
to them when identity is questioned. Or feared." We
discuss the notion, Vita is tempted, but finally disagrees.
    We are already out of the city and bowling along
Grand Central Parkway. Vita begins to claim that I do
not listen to her. I defend myself by claiming she never

talks to me, has told me very little of herself or her past.
"It's because you talk too much." "I'd be delighted to
shut down if you'd open up. I feel just as deprived of
you as you feel surfeited." "My father silenced me in
childhood and I have never talked since." What is it
about WASP fathers? Celia said the same thing. And
Celia wants to write. "All my life I've written only in
order to say the things I couldn't say out loud," Vita says
quietly. We feel close again, sharing between us all the
things that prevent women from talking aloud. All the
things we mustn't say. Haven't we shared them tonight?

Vita is annoyed and disgusted with Fred about his
work. And about his Keith. "Keith is not his peer." Self-
righteously, we agree that we will never understand
homosexual men. They are as different a breed as straight
men. Growing up as men they do the same things to each
other they would do to women if they had the chance.
And with each other they lack even the defenses women
have against men, the trick of frigidity, for example.
Among themselves it must be no holds barred. How
they must hurt each other. What agony that world must
be for a sensitive man. What a trap of promiscuity and
exploitation. We congratulate ourselves on being out of
it, ignoring our own pernicious, if more subtle, sadism.
We are women censuring men.

At Pan Am there is no party. Not even a bar. John and
Yoko are nowhere in sight. It is too late for everything.
Only a cheese sandwich, pure wax it looks. I won't buy
it. Vita makes a face that I am spoiled. In her commune
they eat hot dishes. Her communards pay rent or exchange rooms in return for baby-sitting. Comtemplating
the sandwich, I wonder vaguely if it's a commune or
a boarding house. When I refuse the sandwich Vita
regards me adoringly as some tempestuous exquisite like
my aunt. Facing the gray tedium of the sandwich counter
she describes a happening where everyone sent in food.
"Don't you find these things effete sometimes?" I object.
"No, I sent in something that I ate when I was nursing
my daughter." Somehow that makes it more serious. Vita
is a mother and I have never nursed a child. We sit next

to each other on plastic chairs while two men give us the eye. For Lesbians? For broads? For what? We out-face them, discussing the problems of letter writing. I am full of good intentions having just decided it's the letters to my father in childhood that started my block on correspondence. I am exuberant with new resolve. I will write hundreds of letters in England, each like a plenary indulgence, a gold star pasted on the forehead in grade school when you brought money for the pagan baby or coathangers for the scrap metal drive. We giggle and stare back at the two businessmen, probably innocents too.

It'll be seven hours to England. I will starve. Already getting grumpy. We hear there is food at the International Arrivals Building. Hurrying, our clothes running along the pavements. Tearing up the escalator. A food stand open at the end of a corridor. Thank God for a ham-burger and a shake. Vita cannot understand why this is different from the dead sandwich. I explain I can eat good food or Yankee crap, nothing in between. And that I love the American kid food I never had in childhood because Mother wouldn't buy it. We had different childhoods I think, watching the bastard who cooks hamburgers here and gets high on ignoring customers. I bark at them. He barks back. We're both Irish. My rage turns to laughter with him.

We run back to the parking lot. Vita has lost the car again. I pray for her. Suddenly she is whooping and jumping up and down, arms flailing. Playing movie chase we careen back to the cattle pen for my charter, the waste of airport roads like the second canto of the inferno. Vita's labyrinth is Kennedy as mine is New Haven. Are we too late? No, just in time. But I have no cigarettes. I contemplate the seven hours ahead trying to write without a weed. Vita takes a dollar and begs change while I hang on to my place in line. It is the act of a saint. Vita is utterly charming cadging quarters off middle-aged Americans. The rest of the passengers are kids. The Sarah Lawrence choir is going to England with me. Everyone is smiling, we are all excited taking a trip. Vita is selfless friendship buying cigarettes at a machine. When she shoves them into my hand we are at peace with each other at last. Her generosity is pure, it asks no reward. When we kiss good-bye I am infatuated with her. Finally in love.

And now I will be who I am becoming. Alone in the bus I am pleased with myself. I will put on my blue glasses, the glamorous ones, the ones where people can recognize me. it is incomprehensible how sometimes people can recognize me, sometimes they can't. Does it depend on the energy one gives off? I will go ahead then and be Kate Millett. Putting on the blue glasses. Showing off. Then guilty again in a moment. I should want always to be anonymous. It is less individualistic, etc. But it is more fun just now to play Kate Millett. And because I feel so happy I will dare it, step into that scary mannequin, fill its clothes, make it reality. Where before it was pasteboard. Someone else's invention. Not me. Or anyone. I will make her alive, animate the corpse, convert it to an actual person. Go get that movie. In my blue glasses. Vanity of a public person, folly and delight. Tonight it's all kids and I don't care if they see me. They might even be kind. And if they are cruel it will not hurt. They're my kids and I a wandering scholar in the media age flying around in airplanes.

No place to sit. I am last on the plane, a poor survivor in the scramble. Never was good at the subway either. I am embarrassed standing here without a seat. Conspicuous. Feel like an old woman, fat, ugly. One moment past I was young, beautiful. Famous and enjoyed it for a moment, ego tripping. No one recognizes me, no one has the faintest idea who I am. After an awkward eternity the hostess finds me a seat next to a pair of newlyweds. We take off. I spill my drink on my shirt. Up the aisle are two beautiful girls. Their faces talking. Their lovely hair. One comes down the aisle toward me in a green shirt. Yellow hair. Youth. I feel tired. Maybe I can't do it. No Chapter One after all.

The dark is lifting and the light is coming toward us

across the heavens as we run to meet it. I start working,
putting the pieces together, making a beginning. Outside
the sun becoming morning becoming light. Go on working. Light billowing in the airplane windows like the
clear air around the boat going to Japan. Light, medium
of images, of vision, of beginning. Say that you finish
this book, what would you do next? Study politics maybe? Die? Could I bear to live with this book public?
You should be grateful just to write it. Ask nothing
else. Aftermath. Scandal. Reviews. Kill me in print. Further rounds of shame. Poisonous movement denunciations. Why not live on with your friends? Not die. But
will they be strong enough? Will I lose them again, like
Celia?

All night the plane flies against time toward the east,
America's blackness becoming light, the day moving
back and now the dawn. The old world is ahead like
the sunrise. Ruminate on tradition, Italy and England.
Rome was realer to me than Dublin till the Milletts
stuffed me full of Celtic twilight. Both of them more real
than America. My Uncle Dennis, family historian who
died before I could tap him, an enthusiast for Sinn Fein
operating in lovely amateur fashion by drinking with
the drinking priests, probably collecting money. Talking like God, a raconteur all his life. My hero, my
model, our only poet. Why should he pass the bar and
bother to be a lawyer when he could live off a rich sister and tell such lovely stories? Celia gave me the Milletts again, myself recovered.

The plane stretching in the light of England flat ahead
of us. And Ireland over there. Daedalus floats in the
morning light triumphant as creation. The kids around
me. Young men so gentle, beautiful, good, you want to
reach out a tongue and lick their arm, kiss a forehead or
an ear. Another shipload of new world to the old. They
all carry knapsacks, the student alpine group on board
as well as the musicians. Daedalus is flying full of sky
climbers, mountaineers with the whole summer in their
packs, traveling light with ten-dollar traveler's checks.
Light pouring from the skies over England. The plane

going down to the land, kissing clouds as it enters them. I'm Dante tripping. Celia those three days in New Haven laughing in the light of the six windows that paradise morning, basking since the night before in the glory of being her lover, and in the morning seeing in her face every nation, the Florentine primitives, Spain, every true princess, so many Renaissance paintings, even the Irish poor. Confessing how once I had hated such hair as hers, "The girls in convent school with funny hair like yours, we hated them for the shanty look." How we laughed at the idea, how we laughed at everything. Celia demonstrating how the truck drivers would talk to her when she went slumming with her college buddies to Northhampton neighborhood bars. Big resentful man jerking a thumb, calling her a switch hitter. Celia hearing him in the dread of discovery. Laughed even at this. Sisters. Lovers. Never guessing then I could lose her, laughing in the light of the cupola's six windows and marble floor, the roses blowing outside down away into the back garden. One time ago. In the evening I picked both red and white. Asked her to choose. Enlightened generosity, I picked some for another love of hers who stopped by, young lady actually named Isolde. There was no need for jealousy. So long as there is Celia for me. Celia enough to fill my times, why should I care if another enjoys when I am gone?

The light fills the skies over England and the ocean as we dive to touch it. And the new life is found as Celia is found, is present. Outside us the sky where we float, strangely now as if entering heaven. The sun rises, no, not rises, bursts into wonder, an explosion of light. And in the miracle performed beyond our windows is Celia's smooth hair, her heavy braids bending upon a lute. Some improbable how she has found her way into the English sky like a diamond, the sharpest light of all as we move slowly through hallways of clouds drenched in the soak of light like orange juice over whipped cream.

Celia is the new life here beside me. More tangible as spirit and light than when she stood before the head-

lights in the Soho street saying good-bye a day ago in
New York. And now England and its sea in light the
sky around our cabin brilliant with day. One might expect
to catch sight of a seraph out the window in the greater
miracle of light. Light pure as the future or as promises,
all possibility flooding with its increase. We fly into the
very sun and do not fall. Any glory is justified here where
belief in light keeps one aloft. And all my handwringing
but a way of finding faith to be a troubadour of the
troubadour in floppy pants. Celia. England, eyes green
as Ireland, Ireland beneath us now. Then a little while,
then England. Rising fast to meet our wheels. Celia
a year since that night your eyes so fine, beautiful under
a cheap pink lamp. Just a year ago. Since then all hell
to pass beyond. Now friends again. Not lovers. Yet.

Hit Britain with a thump. English voices greet us and
we drown in Muzak. Does a boy's voice say plane
wreck? I look below to see the shade merely of that
Lockheed at Kennedy. Checking the curious orange
boats on the green field beneath us. We are safe, it is
only an echo. Planes here are the color of the sun. Chapter One is finished. Trust paradise. Daedalus never
melted.

PART THREE

BLICK.
THE ENGLISH
NOTEBOOK

7

Miles of tunnel. Labryrinth through which the Yankee is spewed into Britain. But the sewer backs up at Customs. The line of suitcases kicked inch by inch up a corridor. Flower children crowd, intent on their baggage hurry. The grab for places. So tired I would like to ask someone for help. But they are a bunch of Americans out for themselves. Already I feel separated from them. Neat British customs man begins the whole rigmarole of who I am. Wonder myself. Which should I tell him: sculptor, writer, teacher, filmmaker? Movies, I'm here for the movies. Looks me over suspiciously, can't be a movie director she's a dame. Next it's a dirty movie, what other kind? And your production costs? Low budget, do I strike you as an American heiress type? He is getting annoyed. I am getting to like him. Flirting, I answer back in his own marble English. The thing he will not endure. Reminds me I do not hold a British passport as if it were the ticket to heaven. Get in line sister or they won't let you in their country. I retreat to inoffensive person and get through. The first encounter not much to my credit. I'm not doing so well in England I figure, floating up the escalator. Even the escalator is different.

We line up for baggage. The American kids all knapsacks and flowing locks. We are new, I think, watching them. We are flooding this old place. It will have to change. Summer children, an invading army. How can Europe resist it? Conquest by culture shock. A Fabian, I'll just have a little rest and wait for the results. Why hustle baggage? The junk shows up when it will. I sit on the floor amidst my kingdom of belongings content to wait.

Next some vast and horrible railroad station. Even uglier than America, British ghastliness grafted onto the Coca-Cola sign. Gatwick. We are out in the sticks. In the money line the lady teller converts my dollars to pounds. Transubstantiation. I am myself when I came as a student and thought I was Isabel Archer, reading myself in Modern Library James on a cross-country train. And here I am a strange grown-up version of the same person who has come to England to collect a movie. How could I have made a movie? Everything in this place is so much bigger than I am and I have too much baggage. Dragging six boxes around and asking for cabs. "Too dear," they say. The peasant takes over, decides on the train, arms and legs yelling for cab comfort. Lie back on the leather and have a cigarette.

But it's all right, I have friends. Call Nell. The old mistake about the A and B button. A strange voice at the house in Islington. Says she's Ursula. So Berda has left them and there's a new one. Ursula sounds nice. Expecting me. Should I go to the house or to the office? Would be nice to get rid of this junk. But it's still early. Could get to work right away. Show the new footage to Betty this afternoon. Go to Victoria. You can make up your mind when you get there, in London at least.

At the barrier I jolly the ticket man. He gets me a porter. I let him have most of my property but hang on to the film cans, the shopping bag. A brown paper bag, huge lettering on the front tells you everyone's shopping at International Food Stores now. Crammed full of wrinkled paper. It's my book. Then I see it behind the conductor's head, British railroad poster speaking to me from the wall: "Weekend Engineering Works May Affect Your Journey." Impossible to stick around in a place where they talk like that. I'd lose my book. The porter reappears like a miracle on the platform. He is honest, I am still intact. Ask what I should tip him. He suggests one-fourth of what I had in mind. I give him half. We laugh about it as he tucks me into the smoking section. Lovely cockney way he talks. Bumping along to Victoria the poster returns to jinx me. It's their English, not mine. Get out of this place, you can't write here. Hysterical reminding myself I have friends here. A house in Islington. An English bed. They expect me. American tourists converse in Pure Long Island across the aisle. I would be the superior anti-American self I used to affect in my student days over here. It was not a success, they always spotted me by my Peck & Peck raincoat, knew me for American even if a matriculated student sworn-in-Latin member of the University. After two sentences they'd ask what state are you from? My tutor had never heard of Minnesota. Mustn't trouble her, mumble vaguely that it's in the middle at the top, near Canada. Today I need you, silk-suited Americans who give off the feeling that you're just taking the D train to Coney Island. Show no excitement at all. Whereas I am mad to see this landscape again, England kept in mind twelve years. Used to break my soul against the plaster walls of Mizz Prichert's duplex in Greensboro when JayCee left me, gone a thousand miles into the room at the top of the stairs in the sound of their lovemaking. JayCee off with another while I listened dry-mouthed, remembering England back in America. Weak to see again those toy sheep, the little trees of the journey up from Southampton, replaying the pictures in my mind while the red-leather Spenser stares at me open on the desk. You have a lecture to write. Fielding smiles from the bookcase in matched volumes reminding me it would go in her going. Trying not to cry while teaching Eng Lit to cracker kids because each line was Oxford, which was JayCee, two years wiped out as if it had never happened. Because it had never happened to me but to us. JayCee my England. Had none of my own. The parasite though she lived off me. Hearing them upstairs. The gray Carolina winter jumps into place outside the train window. The train trestle, but I could not do it. Came home cold in my peacoat. JayCee sees me cry. It doesn't matter. Her face says it doesn't matter at all. Outside it is again the English countryside. Why is it that winter now?

Quick light a cigarette, careful don't gag. Look out through the window at the fields. The little trees they have here. It's England. Now I have it again through the window, my own England. Twice seen in one summer, outrageous luxury after twelve years' exile. Given England again. But I will lose the book, the whole American point of it misdirected in this extravagant journey. Should have sent for the film. Stayed home. Worked. My book is in America with my friends. This is the wrong place. But I have friends in England, Nell, Paul, and Winnie.

Victoria Station. Walking along the platform gray to the gate and the queue outside, whispering the English word to myself, smug that I know it. How funny they look, the English forever lining up, will wait for anything, even the licensing hours. Now it is my turn, the cab parked a bit out from the curb. I have all my things. They are crowded around me on the ground. A voice is saying my name. I turn. My hand is shaking a hand. Face I know but can't remember here. Sally David from my first teaching job in North Carolina. The terrible year. Still there, but now she's here in London. It is so hard to understand: a figure out of then, years ago, that year, into the bursting now. Hasn't seen me since I got so important, etc. Feel silly. Ridiculed. Wish people wouldn't say these things. Big warm woman embarrassing me with this talk. She is effusive, proud of me. Does she reproach me in her hyperbole? I left Carolina. Have I betrayed that time by living through it, going on? She will share my cab so we can have a visit.

I will go to the office. See Nell right away. Can't wait now. In triumph tell the driver Soho Old Compton Street just off Cambridge Circus, giving directions like a native, all my bundles safe in the cab.

The buildings flash by white and handsome in the sun of London, Sally says she is here for the summer doing some work on Herrick. A good time of year for Herrick. She names a poem. I can only remember Corinna's Going a Maying. We grow urbane playing scholar on summer vacation. This town is crawling with American teachers of English. I wonder distractedly if I could remember Eng Lit exam answers. Have I lost being a scholar now that I'm out of the university? But it doesn't matter, I am high on movies today, thinking how glad I am not to be a professor. I'm writing a book. It's all in my shopping bag up front. All so wonderfully outrageous, I think, cocky as we pass the monument of Victoria, an old woman frowning in a chair high up on a pedestal. The big squares going by, the wonderful names, the perfect regency façades, St. James, the green of a park vivid. Everything is scrubbed painted glistening in the light. Sally says the chairman didn't promote another woman teacher who had to leave, go to another college, Kansas someplace. We grumble at discrimination. "What is this book of yours?" "Myself, and may get me in trouble." Her bulk next to me, closeted for years, kindly, possibly afraid. I am afraid. Then I am not. Her generation is caught, but we are getting out, young and can do it. It was harder for them always, stuck in little towns, confining jobs, doing pedantry and calling it scholarship. Even their good stubborn teaching never honored. How unfair that we should be luckier. And the kids in colleges now are hardly damaged at all. Those undergraduates at Fairbanks coming out without a qualm, they claimed. Sitting on the grass with them last spring I asked have you ever been to a gay bar? They said of course not. No reason why they should. Surrounded by the easy climate of their own generation, little reason why they should be troubled. But older people have had to be alone. Cautiously, proceeding side-

ways, I introduce the ominous, telling her we have just
shot the big Gay Liberation parade in New York. "It
was beautiful, people felt free. Everything is changing."

Maybe now she'll have gotten the message, this
middle-aged schoolteacher relaxing on the leather seat,
heavy, good-willed. Going back to Carolina at the end of
the summer. I must encourage Sally in her age and her
dress and her weight. Going back alone to Greensboro,
the terrible heat of summer, the thunder of August
there, the boredom I remember going to drive-in movies
with my dog.

Shaftesbury Avenue now, the sex flicks menacing with
*Scandinavian Love, Her Hottest Moment, Babbette's
Profession.* The sort of thing the English seem to need
now. And some play that has been running for twenty
years. *The Mousetrap.* Pictures of old-fashioned actors,
stomachs full of gas, pronouncing their British lines in
revivals. Even this street shines when Sally comes up with
an idea as good as a gift, telling me it is lovely to eat
on the river, I should go to an inn along the Thames,
take a barge, dine on the water. Such a fine day, and
just arriving in London one can imagine doing this in
the evening. I will take Nell and Paul tonight.

Now we are there. She insists on paying for the cab.
She will get out here. Will I have time while in London
to have dinner? I am vague. My attention is on my
friends, we are right in front of the office. I have come
from America just to go up these stairs. Victorious as
a warrior, looking up at the windows, wanting to shout
up to the attic where they are, "I have come back! I have
brought everything!" Nell's sheets, my film cans, work
print and originals, suitcase. Then I see that I cannot
see it. The shopping bag is not there. My book is gone.
It's all in the shopping bag. But there is no shopping
bag. Incredible, it's not in the front with the driver.
Should have carried it with me in the back. My God
where did I lose it? It was in my hand waiting for the
cab. Now my heart is running, Compton Street spins,
people passing, man in a green knit shirt. The windows
are far away. The driver waits, looks. Did I have it when

I got in? We must go back. I apologize to Sally. Tell
him take us back to Victoria. She will go with me. I am
so glad of her now, a warm presence while I go right
into the vertigo, my hands wringing each other frantically,
one so upset it squeezes my arm in terror. It is ridiculous,
but I have lost my book in Victoria Station. First we
must make it past the statue, which is miles from the
station. We approach her sour look, the marble's white
dead now, stiff as despair, frozen still. The old queen's
eye a basilisk destroying me as we go by, racing. We
have lost. And next to me on the seat this woman I used
to be a teacher with, knew only casually for one year
over ten years ago. She looks at Victoria, chuckles—"I
expect she wouldn't approve." I laugh, still grabbing
my forearm tanned from the farm hurting as I hold it
tightly the flesh on the bone. "Victoria said such things
didn't exist. Could believe it of Wilde but for women
the notion was impossible." We laugh like conspirators.
Now we are both leaning forward, pushing the cab faster
with our energy to save. Sally is not even behaving as
a parent might, or anyone for that matter, chiding me
with the obvious; I know I am a fool. How could I lose
my book the first minute I am in England enjoying
myself? The cab running slowly now along the lineup.
I see it! It is there on the pavement. An object.
Miraculous how it stands there jutting up from the flat
of the sidewalk. People near it. Cars pulling away. My
God they *are* honest, jumping out, saving it, saved. "You
must have put it down when you met me," she says as
I bounce up and down on the seat, exultant, protected
by magic. But why did I lose it? What frightened me
seeing an old teacher from my first job, my first thought
only a snobbish reaction that here was an American intrusion at a time when I did not wish to be interrupted,
here at the end of my journey, excited at the prospect
of seeing my English friends? I am ashamed even to be
writing this. What if she read it and were hurt, Sally,
the kindest being imaginable, riding next to me back to
Soho. Sally, who has seen me quail and be an idiot. I
was so cocky. I was so rich, such a profligate in life and

art, making movies, writing books. Then fell on my face. Sally watched it all. And never recriminated, comforted me, stayed on even after such an obvious stupidity—to lose the whole new book. I peer down into the mess, had a hundred-dollar tape recorder near the bottom. Would never have lasted beyond the turn of your back in New York. We pass Victoria again and I grin up at her, winning this time. She still runs England but I am not her subject. I have my shopping bag again.

In front of Nell's. No bravado this time, smaller and shaken hauling the heavy packages into the hallway, waving good-bye to Sally, ringing the bell. No answer, have to drag all this stuff up four flights, can't leave anything unwatched. In Soho they do steal. Betty and I caught two guys going through our purses the first day we cut together. Landing by landing, run back to get the other packages can't carry all six at once. So tired now, flying all night, the trip took twenty hours and have been writing almost nonstop for two days. Here is our door, wood and brass, the big handle in the middle, the kind they have here, a very English door. I call up for a hand. Here at last. They will all run down to help. A voice answers but no one shows. The last stretch past cork walls and the brown carpet. "I'm back." No one notices. There's someone new on the phone. She says it was Joe Colombo who was shot in New York while I drove down Ninth Avenue past Roosevelt Hospital. Yesterday in New York. Now there will be a gang war. The Mafia, composing the news to myself—"and when I got to London they said it was Joe Colombo on Ninth Avenue when I drove by and felt the Maf." Now, in New York, where violence was an electricity in the streets yesterday. That city's terrible vitality. But here in London it merely sounds bizarre. New York only a foreign madness from this distance. But in New York you feel the city. If you're living close to it, it pulses inside you. London is outside. Behind glass. Looking at the handsome buildings shining white in the afternoon from a cab window.

Nell is in "conference." Some producer, little man

in a goatee, ordering a commercial. I must wait outside.
Then she strides out in her hat, arms outstretched, embracing me like movie people. Wearing hot pants, black
nylon stockings running up her long legs. And one of
those nutty satin T-shirts she likes. Bought her another
in Poughkeepsie one day with Fumio, head shop up there
in the woods. Has a big satin star in it. This one has
Mickey Mouse on it for Godsake. Lots of people in
London think O'Rourke's a crackpot. Trendy. I know
her for a sibyl. "Superstar!" she says hugging me
theatrically, all rings and bracelets. "Mother Machree,
I'm back again." One moment's attention. Then the
phone rings. She's off again. I sit down to wait in the
waiting room. Read a magazine. Talk to the new girl.
Nell comes back. "You'll have Angus," she says. "Betty's
on vacation. Ellen's gone back to Canada. Angus's the
only one around. He'll be your editor." Nell waves a
ring. It's settled. My private voice rebels. It was supposed
to be women all the way through the movie, only women
working on it. I shut out the voice and surrender. Feel
like a bigot even bringing it up. Angus doesn't know the
film, talks so slowly, mumbles, I can't understand his
accent. So soft in his long orange hair, an impression
of total ineffectuality. My eyes running sadly along the
file cabinet in Nell's office, the statue of the old Cowboy,
the hi-fi and the liquor cabinet, the phone—I would not
have come back if I'd known Betty was gone. No one
seems to know if the freezes are finished. Angus says he
will call the lab tomorrow morning. Now he is busy getting some prints ordered for Nell. I cannot understand
him when he gives explanations. Where is my film? What
will happen to it when the neg cutter is finished? Of
course it will all fall apart. It will go out of sync, things
will be lost. I must sit down again and wait. Angus is
on the phone. I am impatient. The people here are so
slow, and a little vague. Why did Nell say I should
reshoot? In New York they insisted there was no need.
You have a work print, just strike a print off that, they
said. Joe Kaplan claimed that even if the original were
lost we had only to renew the work print in some solution

to remove the scratches and then print again. Marvin
at Cinelab said the same thing. "Fluid gate," they called
it. Could it be that Betty simply didn't want to bother
picking out the bits and sending them off to the lab?
When I'm not watching everyone neglects the movie.
They don't care. How can anyone care enough about
somebody else's movie? On the long distance Nell kept
shouting that I had to reshoot. Then a long incoherent
explanation about flashes at the beginning and the end
of the work print that made it unusable. Did Nell want
me to come back because of Winnie? I had asked her
if it would help, if I came back as soon as I could. "No,
you've been a wonderful help and it's good to have a
third person in the house with us. It relieves the tension.
And we'll manage about Winnie." But I know she can
never ask. Give but never ask. So I pushed her. Finally
she said yes it would help if I came back right away.
And I didn't. While the film was getting lost and not
found I started my book. Everything is a mistake. Now
I may lose the book, interrupting it with this England.

When I woke up the Japanese flowers already looked
sick. Nell gave me a pot of them, putting me to bed. I
think we were both drunk. So tired I fell asleep in the
chair, my arm and shoulder doing funny things. Strange
numb sensation. "You never should have left," Nell said,
"You missed the greatest thing on TV." Big hat runs
through the movie, playing everybody. It's a western
with a gunslinging dyke opposite our heroine the town
schoolteacher. They shoot it out in the main street. Nell
lines up the saloons and the whores. She's the dyke
marching through town in her boots and shorts. Paul
and I are her audience, gleeful over what Hollywood
distributes so innocently. Then Nell is our heroine
shooting the dyke to protect her man, cavalry colonel,
the two of them off arm in arm into happiness sunset
ever after. Is Paul the colonel, am I the dyke? We sit
on the floor in Winnie's room surrounded by the new
sheets, their colors leaping out of their plastic bags and
covering the carpet, brown like the one at the office, but

charged now with frantic spots of color, bright vivid brought from America.

Winnie's room in the basement. There against the wall is the crawl box. They have lined it with Morris wallpaper from Liberty's. He hates it anyway. When I went down he didn't know me, pitiful little figure prone on the floor crucified in his brace. Then he knew me, crawled into my lap. I was so grateful. As if he forgave me for leaving him. He looked better. Nell comes down with a drink. Says Winnie's stuck. On a plateau. Has made no progress for weeks. Is fighting back now. He bites. He plays on the rug while we talk. "We will make a film," Nell is full of surreal schemes. A friend of ours who does happenings is to ride in a baby carriage, I'm to be severe, have a square face and push her. What else am I supposed to do? "Think things up," Nell says. I am nervous. It is just talk again. She will never make this movie. Then Paul comes down and she does the western for us. I'm more nervous. Sounds like a parody of the three of us—or a premonition. Paul says we cannot eat on the river. There is no one to stay with Winnie. The new girl is out. Her night off. "Then let's go tomorrow." "It's for tourists, you wouldn't like it." "Let's go and pretend we are tourists. It would be fun." "No." "Paul, we're only tourists if we think we are." "No." I feel I am wheedling my father. We eat dinner and Paul goes upstairs. Nell and I sit in the kitchen and drink. We jabber like maniacs. Everything she says so funny or so wise. I hear her but I cannot listen hard enough to remember it all. I will never be able to reproduce it. Goes right to my gut, healing everything. Till I fall asleep.

But in the morning everything is different. I wake hearing a voice—that book is all about your sex life. You just can't say those things. I look at the pot of flowers on the trunk next to my bed. They are wilting already. The room is the same, and the sameness is a defeat. The books behind my bed are less formidable. Paul's military prints stare me down from the wall. More of them than last time. And the mod sign from the nineties that says id soap. Still no clothes-hangers. No desk. Could I use the trunk top? How could I ever write here, in a room without a desk? Maybe the dining room table . . . No one ever uses it. But I hate the tablecloth. Victorian velvet antique. There are hundreds of blue and white plates, Paul's collection. This is really such a beautiful house, pure Georgian, restored magnificiently. Decorated. Full of stuff. But it depresses me unspeakably. Small. Claustrophobic. When I first saw it I knew I'd never last. "Imagine living in a place that has one hundred and seventeen antique clocks and only one of them tells time." I looked at Fumio with the eyes of a madwoman. He grinned. I go into the sitting room. There is Paul's big color television. And Nell's women, turn-of-the-century plaster heroines out of myth. Boadicea. Federica. Looking like lionesses. They used to terrify me. Today they are less imposing. Rather funny even. Why should that deco lady hanging in a long dress against her lamppost always strike me with such despair? It is not as bad as last time but the plumbing still doesn't work. You flush the toilet and hope. Then you try again. Hold your breath and count. If you are very patient it works. The garden is my salvation. Burgeoning like a volcano. So much color. There are roses. But I am late for work and mustn't linger. Breakfast is cornflakes. The vulgar American box jumps from the darkness of a fifteenth-century Spanish armoire.

On the street I realize I cannot write the book. The people rebuke me with their faces, the tobacco shop, the butcher, brick walls like North Oxford, the slums, dull clothes. Working-class England. The advertisements frown. What would my tutor say, serene and maternal lady? I miss the number 19 bus and have to take a cab to the office, wondering if what Nell really wants is for me to make that movie with her, or force her somehow to do it herself. As usual it is probably only talk. Everything is hard to do here. The climate of the place seems to thwart every hope.

In the cutting room Angus's tennis shoes keep running back and forth answering the phone. I shouldn't have come to England. Should have waited or else finished the film before going home last time. It's messy. It ruins the shape of the book, running back and forth to England, doing things twice. Forever needing to repeat things. I can't write here. Everything's different. Even the words. And the people here are their clothes, just their clothes, the trendy gear worn by a handful of promising people. The rest of the population looks and feels exactly like twelve years ago. Things don't make sense. The ideas we have in New York seem idiotic over here. On the way to the office the intersection mocked me—what do you celebrate, a bunch of Lesbians in New York City—blabbling away as if their lives were glorious, had significance? I look at the people in the street, agreeing with their triumphant commonsense, but full of anxiety to know just what it is that they live for.

In the cutting room I look at the movie again. So unfamiliar. Yet I know every word on the track. I can't pay attention to Mallory. The reels are inside out and I don't know how to rewind them. Lillian's movie has become incomprehensible. I need to see it on a screen the right size. I watch the old beach footage in the window of the Steembeck. We didn't match it with the new takes. The film running back and forth through the spools and the little window of the machine. It's the bay behind Lillian's house. I was just there last week. It was better.

Turn off the machine. Go out and buy a notebook. Just go down the stairs and do it. Be brave. Go in the bookstore and ask if they have them, if not, they might know the nearest place. They won't remember you. But he does. Wants to know if *Sex Pol* is selling in France. I never ask, I say, not asking how it's doing here in England. It stared at me through the window when I went in. After two months here last time they still had some of the fifty signed copies left. Never entered the store because I was embarrassed. I am ashamed that it doesn't sell. In America it sold too much. And here not at all. He rubs his hands, a gay, one of us, but nance. Distracted. Doesn't look me in the eye. "Stationer's right down the street." There it is, a green sign behind the fat legs of a lady in square plastic high heels. British shoes. I buy a green notebook, plain cover, none of your flowered nonsense over here if you please. Blick's Student Notebook, it announces on the front. I am supposed to be looking at my movie today. But instead here I am scratching away like a truant in a new notebook. Look back to the cover, check the apostrophe "s" in Blick's. Even their notebooks discourage, imagine naming anything Blick.

But of course they're right and I'm wrong. England is static, a whole society resistant to change. When you look at people in the street you know they haven't moved. But the people in the street are going to work, doing the right thing, living sane, wholesome lives. Had felt so great to start a new life, but it was clearly off the wall. After a day here you realize you are out of step. Yesterday I told Nell I'd gone gay. Just said it. Two of us riding in a cab to the house. Paul had gone on ahead to pattern Winnie. We ride along excited, talking ferociously, so much to say. The packages heaped on the floor of the cab, her lavender boots perched on top of them. She said, "But you look wonderful." Even Paul said it. "You've lost weight. You look tremendous." His eyes appreciative. I leaned against the wall by the coat closet, so tired, so disappointed, a little crazy, my mind full of trivia. Twenty hours to England I never slept. Wrote on the plane. Finishing Chapter One and doing some new stuff last few hours about light and Celia scribbled in a miniature notebook, probably incoherent. Nonsense anyway. Probably lost it. I smile at Paul. He demands stoicism. Has so much himself. The dignity of a lord. I told him I'd gotten happy, happy at his compliment. Paul never used to notice that I'm a woman. But now he notices. Now that I'm queer. But I do not tell him, I tell Nell. "Maybe I've finally solved it Nell, stopped fighting it. Already I feel so much better." Brave enough to make an anouncement, looked at her lavender boots and knew I had to tell her. Her long legs arrange themselves on the packages. The sheets. "How's Celia?" "Going to have all her plumbing removed in The Mercy

Hospital July sixteenth." "Mean operation, that one. You better get back in time."

Yesterday I had so much strength but today I look ugly in the mirror. In the toilet next to the cutting room. Third trip of the morning. Diarrhea. It is not panic yet. Angus is a guy. There are two and then three guys in the next cutting room. I cannot even find the masking tape to hold the film on the spool. Will they notice that I have no idea what I'm doing? Find some adhesive tape then and get to work. This movie will take a lot more time to finish than you thought. Got to keep on top of it.

Paul is ordering me to stop writing this minute and come to lunch. Even teasing and bullying he gives off such tiredness, he has not written or made a film for a long time. We go to the old place, American hamburgers, a firehouse staircase. Paul sits at the round table: "I have this morning written a letter to Sir Steven Runciman, requesting the rights for his book on the Crusades. I should love to shoot it. A *Forsyte Saga* with cavalry." "Let's have some wine over here before I expire"—this from Nell. Their voices are crossed knives today. Hard not to compete in the movies.

I tell Nell how Lila will be hanging out for five hours in the London airport on her way to Geneva. "Let's dash out and see her. We could have a lovely visit in the bar." She is less enthusiastic than I thought. Odd, they've been friends for years, Lila introduced me to Nell. Nell asks where Paul can buy some foam rubber, Winnie's cracking his head on the crawl box. It's got to be lined. Then answers herself. "Ask Angus. He's an expert on foam rubber. Stuffed his whole bloody house full of it." Winnie's plateau comes back like dread, the fighting back. It's not going forward. I order fish and chips since this is England. Paul has a malt to quiet his ulcer. Nell and I start on the first bottle of pink. I ask Paul what a scampi is—it's on the menu.

"It's a cross between a lobster and a shrimp. More of the lobster species, very hard carapace." He says it, he says "carapace." Nell and I try not to smile. Paul under his big droopy moustache. Body of a football hero, soul of an art historian. Nell tells us that Ethel, whom they both call Mother, is in a "working crisis." Ready to give up the cross of holding Antiapartheid together. Been too many years alone, the public's apathy, and the flak they give her inside the organization. The guys below her in the hierarchy bitch her for her little salary and then go out for long expensive lunches. "Ethel's killing herself doing benefits to provide their calories. She's also beginning to realize that she can't work within the system, gets one nowhere, Ethel's beginning to realize finally that they have to have a revolution in South Africa." I remember Ethel, her sensual lips, her dark Jewish face, the stout force of her body. It was Ethel whom I wanted to write that book, what it was like to be in politics. Living in politics.

I am scribbling on the back of the menu. Paul asks what I'm writing. A new book. I protect myself with the affectation Claire uses, telling him it's a documentary of my existence. "Oh, the crucible of life," his voice ridiculing the words. I consider Paul, the put-down artist, the gentle bully, capable of thrusts that take one's breath away. Paul is a cynic now, telling of his days in the Party. "Used to be magazine called *Masses and Mainstream*. Every week they had an article in there whose second paragraph ended with the phrase 'in the crucible of life.' The line would arrive in England via Romania. Printed up in something called *Lasting Peace*. Every week a new truth. Translated from German. The most lugubrious English conceivable. We sat about and exchanged significant phrases. Then they fingered me for trying to take over what they called the mass cultural organization. Everybody in it—and it was hardly massive—happened to be a member of the Party. Except Steinberg. Who was a front. It just occurred to me now, Nell, that it was the ugly head of sex that lured me into the Party. That dark one, do you remember?"

Nell ignores the question and declares flatly that men should be required to learn typing. "Wonderful idea, they do it in the army," I remind her. Paul says he types very well. "Then why did you ask me to type that manuscript for you?" "But you see I'm not accustomed to electric machines." "You do it gently," Nell reproves him, setting down a knife. Under her big lavender hat she passes on to myth. "Who is that lady who ran for president in eighteen something on the platform of orgasm for all?" "Victoria Woodhull, my double. She was a bit too far out for the practical feminists, free love was considered too great a risk." "I think she was super," Nell crows. "She was also a bit crazy," I say, "she believed in astrology and married John Jacob Astor. At least I haven't gone that far over the dock," words I hold out against judgment. "No, Woodhull's more like Germaine," Nell decides.

"The one I like is Florence Foster Jenkins." Nell does it. Giving us the little old lady who couldn't sing a note and hired Carnegie Hall to do it in. "Of course everyone came to see. So she quavers out *Die Fledermaus*." Nell fills the restaurant, full quaver. "People sent up roses, dozens, thousands. Cruelest thing anyone ever did, of course. Florence Foster Jenkins keeps singing the same fancy passage, throwing the roses back to the audience. Dee dum. Dee dum. One by one. Then she asks they be collected so she can do it again." I shudder, hearing myself described. Nell too maybe. But how I would love to see her do this on film. How I would love to make a movie of her.

"There is this book called *The Wilder Shores of Love*," Nell starts up again. I see it in my bedroom with the other books. Nell goes into gear. "All about exotic heroines of love. There is Jane Digby El Mezrac. Lived in a cave with a brigand chief. Things not going well, Jane at the end of her rope. Married all the crowned heads of Europe one by one. Captured them. Head after head. But, as her biographer says, the black tents of Islam beckoned. So now she's in one or a reasonable facsimile with brigand chief and it's a bust. Crying her heart out for civilization."

Nell goes on with her litany of heroines, each story enacted with extravagant and gallant humor. I watch, torn between adoring the performance and being murdered by its futility. "What I like are those old lady explorers like Isabel Eberhardt, big long awful dress. Rode all through Asia and the desert on a mule. Right there in the middle of the nineteenth century. She got to a town and told people she'd come through the desert alone. They said really? She said she met a tiger, a real one. Isabel knew how to deal with it. Lifted her umbrella and said shoo. And the damn thing did. Slowly, of course."

"When I shot the Suffragette Centennial I got this crazy lady off the David Frost show. He was having some political panel. Everybody up there doing the thing with the clenched fist. Heavy Black Liberation. Maoists. Whole number. Then this dame pipes up from the audience. 'I too was a revolutionary.' Oh what did you do? They think she's funny. 'I bombed buildings. Mrs. Pankhurst called a meeting, said the situation was intolerable. I decided upon a course. We were careful to destroy only abandoned and unoccupied properties.' Well, how many did you bomb? 'I am not free to tell you the precise number, but it was around sixty.' Dried up fragile little thing, Lady Lynton. 'Mrs. Pankhurst said do what you must, but do not harm human life.'"

She has talked herself into a high. But soon all the grand ladies who just went out and did things begin to bring her down. "We've got to get that foam rubber. Winnie is all bruises. He's biting all the time, it's horrible. I can't take it. I'm trapped. I've got to have some room." Now she is arranging, maneuvering Paul toward a vacation in Yugoslavia. She can handle Winnie alone, she says. And she wants me to stay and make a film with her. She'll have room if Paul is away. Paul should take a trip. Paul says he's trapped too. He could manage Winnie on his own. "But we can't do it together any more. It isn't the patterning, after all that's just a few hours a day, it's what we do to each other with it." Now they are talking to me like friends, honestly rather than like married people with secrets to hide. I am candid with Nell: "I think it's what you do by turning Paul into your old man and then dredging up all that rich Catholic guilt about sin, so you make him your monster and then resist by going frigid or getting drunk in Soho and not showing up to pattern." I tell her straight and she takes it straight. "The whole thing is too big to solve," Paul says, forlorn in his big body. Nell takes off for a screening, leaving us together to talk. Paul seems to want to. It is the first time.

I look at Paul. "It simply won't work any more," he says, "I want to get out." I am afraid for her, hearing him. Usually it is Nell raising hell and Paul holding on. Now he has had enough. "Winnie bites. He fights me like an animal. Times I want to kill him." I look at Paul's huge arms. Endlessly patient. Endlessly gentle. Devoted to this thing who might become his son. But still a vegetable. Hidden in the basement for years while they hoped he'd die. Then Paul heard of the patterning. Flew to Philadelphia. Surgery. Instructions. But the new program of therapy takes everything you have for years. Everything in time, money, and energy. It is a mission, a way of life. It is inhuman. Already it has cost them too much in four months. Paul looks so miserable. Surely he should escape if he has to. Then Nell could do what she wants too. But what of the noble experiment? I am afraid for it as well. "But there is Winnie, how does he get his chance?" I ask. "We could board him. There are people on the coast who know the program. Or one of us could take him. But we can't do it together any more." "What would you do?" I ask him. "I could go somewhere and write." "But you can write anywhere, Paul, I've been doing it on airplanes." "Then I'll stay home and write. I don't even know what I want to do but I know I've got to get out." I tell him what happened to me, the gay thing and accepting it finally. How much easier it is now. "Last time I was here I was more than a little crazy. Had something like a nervous breakdown. Finishing the film saved my life. Both of you saved my life. When I went back to New York I started to write again. I have energy. From letting myself be." Paul agrees that may be a good thing, but what he feels is entirely different, trapped. "But how sad to break up what you have. You've been together a long time. Why throw all that away?" "It's gone already," he says. "It's been dissipating for years. Our sensual relationship has completely degenerated. It can no longer be said to exist." Paul's term. Sensual relationship. Incredible phrase. How I love him for it. This huge man capable of such delicate phrases, such delicacy of feeling. Paul a Canadian who played American pro football, surely they said fuck.

"Paul, I'm in the peculiar position of being a woman yet knowing how you feel being a man rejected by a woman. I was in love with a woman who turned away from me. It hurt. I felt like shit. It made me feel like a monster, carnal, awful. Unbearable guilt. I hated myself. Women can make you feel like hell. If we are Lesbian we do it to each other the same way we do it to men. Then I decided I wasn't that bad really. Neither are you. You're a beautiful man. What have you done that makes you want to punish yourself so much?" He fiddles with his spoon. I think he doesn't hear me.

"Paul, I've watched how movement women treat the men around them. Like dirt. It infuriates me the way they treat Fumio. If he were white he could say boo and bully them. If he were black they'd be all reverence. But he's quiet, doesn't assert himself. Is delighted they are his guests while they go on yakking to each other one thousand miles a minute. Never even notice he exists. All the time he's fixing them another drink. They treat him like a Jap houseboy. Ignore him while they drink his liquor. If they could they'd make him ashamed even to be alive. We always do that to the nearest sympathetic soul. I've seen black guys do it to the white women who live with them. Nearest honky they can trash, only one in fact."

"We used to have such good times in the beginning." His eyes look like they are bleeding. "For years. But it's gone flat. It's pointless to continue. I want only to see her happy. I wouldn't mind even if she preferred that chap in New York." I suppose he means Alvin. "Look, I met the guy. He was crackers about her and I felt very sorry for him. But then I met you and I thought she had made the right decision. You're a hundred times the man he is." I feel silly saying something like this, idiotic old chauvinist phrase, but it happens to be what I think. I dismiss Alvin ruthlessly, Alvin with his flattery and his favors, Alvin getting film processed for me free at his big ad agency once or twice then disappearing. Then Alvin showing up again all need, a crybaby, a nudge who'd hang about when he needed to play broken hearts, his over Nell, mine over Celia. Each of us in splendid isolation from the other. And finally Alvin off with his new girl friend. I take a last look at Alvin and push him off the table like a cockroach. Paul is far better, loving him for how much he loves my friend O'Rourke.

Paul sags. I wish I could hug him. "Nothing matters but that she suits herself. Maybe what she needs is a lady." Hearing him, my God. "No, I don't think so, Paul. She's got a worse case of Catholic guilt than I do. And I went crazy. I'm sure Nell could never handle that sort of thing. She told me she had a brush of it with a friend of hers. Had to go to Spain and then to the shrink. They did awful things to Nell when she was a child. I think she is still terrified. And this is lots harder than getting it together with a guy." Knowing it is in one way, not in another. But sure I'm right in her case. Paul wants her to go to the shrink again. I want to find out what can be done to help. What is concrete? Real? Do-able so I can do it? We go around in circles. I feel helpless.

Paul picks up the check. No, he will not let me pay my part. Becoming the masterful male again like the day he took me to lunch to solve the problem of the credits. Paul with a pad of yellow paper blocking out the end titles while making faces at how corny my backgrounds were till I was ashamed of my film. Paul insisting I be called the director. While I felt like a traitor for even listening to him. Advice from a male chauvinist, etc. "You are the director," he shouted. "Paul, they will murder me if I print that." Afraid to tell him that by now I had come to agree with them. Nonsense, he said. "Politics can kill an artist. I did not work for two years after I left the Party. *Crise de travail*—you could call it a nervous breakdown if you prefer that. The symptoms are the same." Then we all settled for "filmmaker." Nell said if I didn't take that she'd never speak to me again. "Mention it one more time and I'll scream."

On the way back we stop for cigars. Paul's Dunhill is being repaired. He is witty and talks tough with the men behind the counter. "Your incompetence is remarkable. I am taking my business elsewhere." When we leave I look up, questioning him. "It's our little joke. They've been friends of mine for years." I tag along feeling like his little sister. I will never understand Paul. Then I remember my notes scribbled on the menu. "I have to go back, Paul. I forgot something." He interrogates me like a priest. Grinning down at me under his moustache. I am ridiculous in his eyes. A devious child. A neurotic woman. He stops dead on the pavement and snorts at me. Though he slay me with contempt I will go back for them. Running till I find the green paper. "King Bomba" it announces grandly, under a drawing of the sun. My orange felt pen writing on the back. The notes run down the side: wine, Lila, carapace, foam rubber, Ethel, crucible of life, Party and sex, Victoria Woodhull, typing, Florence Foster Jenkins, Jane Digby El Mezrac, Isabel Eberhardt, shoo to a tiger, Lynton the arsonist.

I say good-bye to Angus at the corner outside the office. The two of us working together for hours have accomplished nothing. He is patient. I am frantic. Technology is defeating me again, my elaborate ignorance of film process. Should I have an internegative cut here? Or is it better to do it at home? Why the devil did I come over? The sight of Old Compton Street hits me like a truck. A row of crummy restaurants and strip joints. The Gents Coiffure to the right, its hideous wigs on display like painted straw over two improbable plastic heads daubed in bronze. Like cannibal trophies. And tits through the window in the next block, gray negative breasts of pornography. Old men gazing at pictures of Lesbians in the bookstore. Futile England's attempt to recover from puritanism with prurience. I feel such despair. England stays the same. Compton Street has not moved. Beyond the pinball houses at the Movie Palace *The Sound of Music* continues its gigantic queue, thousands of people want to see it. They will not want to see my movie. Or the movies I would want them to see. They want this instead. They need it. The cute little drug pictures stuck on the wall outside the cinema. Inside is fairyland. Cartoon figures jump through flowers. Not real flowers. Cutouts. Paper roses. English women above their big feet squeezed into plastic shoes, the spreading highheel weight of bodies imprisoned in elastic corsets stretched tight. Ugly and improbable cloth dresses. Men in sad English suits. No depression like this depression, all of it looking so damned cheerful.

I am among straight people. Normal people. Who remain the same. Surrounded by them and feeling crazy because I am different. Should I go to the sandwich shop on the corner? Cheery proprietor, recently opened. And doing a landslide business. If I go in it is like before. It is before. Therefore I am crazy again because I was crazy before. Always two chicken sandwiches with watercress on white bread because I am not that adventurous and still from St. Paul. Six new-penny bottle of milk. Then back to the editing room. Just as before. Nothing has changed places. No, I will go to the old place for chicken Kiev.

The brown dress of the whore constant on our corner. Waiting for me to see her again. She is all orange. Hair, fabric, shoes. Shoes in very bad repair. Unprofessional really. A mess. She haunts me. Still there in her one dress and those terrible eyes. What age, is she ageless? Where does she wash? It is clear that she does not change. Same clothes. The use of the plural here is impolite as well as inaccurate. And still smoking too much. Odd I should worry about that but I do. Her suffering so overwhelms that one can only approach its edges. Last time and now this time. Still I do not speak to her. So present in my mind. It is difficult to approach the great. Their pain so fierce it is a net about them. One feels so foolish. One's unworthiness a kind of idiocy that must be hidden. It is shame.

Take the bums on the Bowery. I would give more often if I were not so embarrassed being asked. Fumio and I quarrel. It is alms, he argues, bourgeois charity. Can the bum wait for capitalism to fall when it's now that he needs this drink? But different with hippies. When they hustle me in the East Village I can sometimes feel annoyed. Just a few minutes blue-jean nice-day stroll from my home turf where need is real. Theirs must be too, or why should they ask? Surely to ask for help is difficult. Behold Nell the never-asker.

Tonight in London I will settle for the chicken Kiev. My glass of white wine ascending from the bar in the basement. Two tabloids for dinner. But I do not open them. My mind on giving. Giving and taking. How Nell and I are always trading favors. I was in her movie. Then I tried to help distribute it. No luck, they lost the print somewhere in Texas. Should I have tried harder to find it? Next she helped me with my movie. The perfect teacher, knew just when to give, how much. And when not to—the hardest part. In trouble herself and had the size to help someone else. Vita did too for that matter. But Nell never asks to be paid. O'Rourke who has done so much for me. So I tried to find something to do for her and found Winnie. First seeing it as Winnie for her. Then only later for himself, for what he could be, become, a child. The great experiment. And now it's falling apart. Nell and Paul, what could I do for these two people that I love? How hard even to consider it, both of them proud as nobles. How does one even aspire to help them? Reserved, superior people. So special it seems ambitious even to imagine being of assistance. First a hard look at what they need. Nell needs her work. Paul too. But there's Winnie. So instead of the films they should be making there are the commercials. And lately not enough of them. Paul told me this afternoon that they are going into bankruptcy. Winnie's the war in Vietnam, so urgent it has to be fixed before all else. And how can I fix Winnie? I could stay and pattern, print the film over here and pattern Winnie full time. In abandoning him to my book these weeks, have I let everyone down? But how do you baby-sit transatlantic, commute the ocean for a kid? Why not? Luxury of expense, unreal. I cannot sacrifice everything for this may-be child. Yet they have to. The parents. If kids belong to eveyone as I am always yapping, then Winnie is my job. How does one be a friend? How much does it take? There are so many obligations in life. One has them even to oneself. And this book like a baby that I haul bleeding through the world, abandoning it in railroad stations. My self. No, it's a mistake to be here. It's not good for the book. Long dull afternoons in London doing exercises with a brain-defective child, what kind of material is that? No one would care. These things do not interest readers. But there are no readers anyway. The book will never be written. Fuck the book. People have got to come first. Winnie just could be a person. On the long shot. And there are Nell and Paul, two tortured people in a trap. You make a cult of friendship, better live up to it.

The telly glows in the dark at the top of the stairs. Paul sits on the couch drugging himself with the box. Nell is sick. The helpers didn't show up to pattern. So it was just the two of them without the necessary third to hold Winnie's head. They got through one set of exercises alone. Then she collapsed in a fever. I suggest putting in a call to Lila. If Nell is up to it tomorrow she should keep that date out at Gatwick. She could use a shot of old friend right now. Paul sighs, "Of course she'd go in a minute." Obvious that he disapproves, a teetotaler who hates her drinking. "Paul, it's not the booze it's the cheer." And how marvelous the way you can call America direct, a communication victory, pinpointing Renos through a busy signal. I can still hear him in the din of ocean, other people's conversations, a tiny voice saying

they go straight to Geneva. Won't stop over after all.
There will be no shot in the arm for O'Rourke.

I go up to see her. The light on. A sacrosanct terror.
Their bedroom. The lair of Paul's Nell, not mine. She's
a wife here, not my friend. I feel a violator. Her delicate
face asleep on the pillow. "God Bless Our Home," a
sampler cries over the bed. A Camp joke that now seems
only cruel. Does she know he will leave her? Nell in a
room full of old pocket watches. She should get out from
under these antiques. But instead she protests by getting
sick. Her face on the pillow asleep, I do not wake her.

Downstairs three Russian astronauts are perishing on
television. In comfort we watch them die. It has no
reality. Yet strange how real the Bengal famine looked.
You wanted to grab the starving off the screen and feed
them. Not the astronauts. Death by weightlessness, the
announcer says. Intriguing term. Experts debate the
question. One argues that reentry after a long period of
weightlessness is fatal. Gravity will have its revenge.
Could that be my problem in England? The astronauts
were up there three weeks. But it would take a lot longer
than that to reach the other planets. Bodes ill for Earth's
isolation. Hard news for Claire.

Paul solves it all by suggesting artificial gravity. Expert
backs him up from the screen one second later. I look
over at Paul. Here is a man who can solve the problems
of space killing his mind with the boredom of evening
television. Then I notice the toffee. My God, we are back
to eating candy and watching telly. Paul generously
remarks he's already eaten my favorite kind. We are stuck
now, glued to our despair, adrift for the evening in a
blue china boat full of colored wrappers. Tedium and
call it health, boredom and call it everyday living. We
three could have been on the river tonight. If we worked
hard at patterning and played afterwards it would not
be so wretched. There is no need to live this way.

The doorbell. An old pal of Nell's, a musician in
London this week to do a gig. He'll be drinking in the
bar across the street if she feels like recovering. Paul
doesn't tell her. Instead he has called the doctor. A grave

man, all black clothes, bag, etc. He says it's bronchitis. More serious than I thought. Thank God we have Paul. Huge. Responsible. Just the sight of his bulk reduces one to comfortable dependence. Telly mumbles on into a bad old movie. Paul like a prince in slippers reclining on the exquisite leather sofa. In Nell's spot. I am on the other sofa, to the right side of the technicolor altar, Paul's spot. Usually I sit in the rocker, my back to the set. When telly overpowers all hope of conversation I watch it from the floor.

I go up again to the invalid's room. Drop of tea and a giggle. "Look, Machree, what can be done? Tell me what I can do." We rehearse the dilemma again. She flounces her pillow—"If there were enough people to pattern, a whole phalanx like they have in America, cast of hundreds, regular setup, so when one gets sick another fills in, etc., all those club ladies you've got over there, nothing or little to do. But England is short on do-gooders. They don't volunteer like you do in the States. And I can't ask the movement. They are fixated on their own problems—nannies, *au pairs,* constant crises over that sort of thing. They're not about to take on other people's children. Particularly if they're semi-idiots. England is full of child vegetables tucked away in back rooms or calmly sunning themselves in front windows. One of ten births is defective. Everyone's ashamed, of course. Don't even admit it exists. Child usually languishes into death between eight and eleven. Even sooner if you're lucky. Winnie on the other hand could make it, but the two of us can't do it alone. I don't see him as property any more, my child how dare you and all that. He's a creature to be saved, but it will take a lot of people. We've tried everything, all your church groups, ladies' auxiliaries, but no luck. If there were a steady team of volunteers, a big mob who'd hang in. But it won't work with friends. They do it once or twice for a favor. Then they're bored, call in sick, have to go on holiday this weekend."

Can she be telling me I should put all this together? That I should organize the pattern? But how could I ever organize the English, I'm a foreigner, don't even know anyone in England. How could I possibly? Getting the point but resisting.

Paul comes in and takes off his jacket. For a mad moment I fantasize us all settled into bed together. Amused and horrified at the picture. Sexual liberation has carried me out of my orbit. Forget it and get back to business, the problem at hand. Paul stands by the bureau. He'll drive down to Cheltenham on Friday, a number of people there know the pattern. He'll ask around, see if there's someone he can trust to board Winnie with. They have to give up doing the program themselves. But it will still take a while before all this is settled. I feel such despair as he says it. He'll leave her. Winnie the noble experiment is a washout. A sinking feeling watching the towel thrown in. It had seemed so fine a thing to do. Such a brilliant gamble. So gallant. So like them. Proud even to be a little part of this, an adjunct. And I worry at the notion of anyone doing it for money, those people he would be boarding with, would they put enough into it? Winnie could make it only through the fanatic dedication of people who put the full and terrible energy of love into the program. You don't often get that with hirelings.

I sit on the end of the bed and talk to both of them. "Look, I'll stay. I'll print the film here. That's two weeks. I can pattern every day. Twice if need be. That frees one of you entirely. Or you can take turns. It isn't much but I'll put all my time at your disposal while I'm here. Just give me orders. Now I'm off to bed. But promise me one thing." Paul looks up. "Try, dammit, to enjoy yourselves a little, promise me you'll go out." He grins his slow elegant grin under the moustache, his exquisitely modulated voice chuckles. And won't promise a thing. O'Rourke laughs in her new sheets. I go downstairs.

Falling asleep in my yellow bed. Think Celia's name. And see a doorway. The refectory at the convent, large dark place and cool. Along the corridor to Sister Saint Sebastian's piano room. The upright rigid against the wall. I cannot tell my right hand from my left. Right

is the treble. It is like north. North is when you stand
at Mother's house and look toward the back yard. I have
not practiced. She slaps me. Once she gave me a slip
of the begonia on the window sill. I lost it on the way
home. Desolated by my betrayal. The day I fly home
from England Celia will have her privates no say the
word cunt torn apart by doctors. I never kissed it good-
bye. Never kept a plant till the avocados on the Bowery.
Fumio's avocados. Mr. Amendula pinched my cheek
when I went for lessons. Smelled of garlic, Mr. Amendula
who coached the professionals of the Minneapolis Symphony wasting his time on me. Must have needed the
money. Aunt Christina paid. Paid all the music teachers.
Several actually turned me down. Needed the money
and still said I wasn't worth teaching. Mother said
practice, your aunt has bought you a piano. But I hated
it. Dull black spots on the page, even Mozart so tedious
the business of doing things over and over. So I talked
Amendula into teaching me theory. It would be less like
cheating since I could never learn music. Theory is like
algebra, little puzzles. The higher algebra in junior year.
It's so much fun doing it on the steetcar going back and
forth to my job at Schunneman's. Then I fell behind,
couldn't understand Sister Agatha Marie. We were
enemies now. I could no longer follow her, the marks
she made on the blackboard. Dropped the course. They
told Mother it was all right, it was an extra course, the
load was too heavy. The ushers line up in their long black
skirts and white blouses along the gangways at Northrup
Hall. I am in the university now. We rustle in our
uniforms waiting for concert time. We talk music like
experts. Now I can go to the symphony every Friday
night free for nothing. At intermission I kiss my Aunt
Christina. But I am here on my own. I do not have to
wait for an invitation to sit in the other seat second row
first balcony. Friday nights in high school having to decide
between that seat in the first balcony or one next to
Nancy and the gang at the basketball games. There is
Uncle Frederick now anyway. He sits there now in the
seat that was my seat, the extra seat. He wears pumps.

And a tuxedo. He is the most elegant man in the world. But cruel. Made a joke during intermission the night Janey's Uncle Archie committed suicide. Frederick plays the piano at Christmas. Studied in Vienna. When they found out about JayCee that summer before Oxford the Milletts flew in from all parts, regular tribal conference. And Frederick said, "After all it's her own life." When I heard it I thought it the strangest statement in the world. No one has their own life: we are a family. And I was its outlaw. Christina took me to lunch at her club. Said she'd once saved Aunt Celia from a similar fate. Or was it Celia who saved Christina? I can hardly hear her. We do not talk in words but in silences. She will not use the word. I would deny it anyway. I would lie. "That woman dominates you," she tells me. It was a mistake ever to bring JayCee out there, the big house by the lake where she moved with Frederick after Virginia Avenue. But I wanted to show them off to each other, asking JayCee to read aloud from *Tristram Shady* after lunch. Of course my aunt will admire too, fine voice, her own favorite book, has a first edition of it. But she called JayCee a divorcée. Mother said it too. "But so are you," I said. So is my mother. My aunt calls her "that Stein woman" using her husband's name, emphasizing its strangeness, the fact that it is Jewish. "Her name is Markham," I said. She went to Wellesley. I listen to my aunt, trembling behind the chicken salad. You get such nice helpings here. Even Mother would think it was worth every cent of the eight dollars. This club has a special entrance for women. The doorman told me I couldn't go in the front door.

Celia will be cut by knives, steel instruments in a man's hand. Didn't walk in the garden tonight, just too tired. And I will never be her lover. Months the tissue healing. But even then. Yes, maybe someday. I should have said it then that night. Standing in front of the headlights. I should have said that I love her. Sidewalk so far away now. But she would have made a face. And if she hadn't? If we started over? No, I would only become her victim again.

I say, ashamed for being critical. "Wit replaces energy. Last night Nell looked up from her pillow and told me she has no energy, none whatsoever." "Yes," he says dreamily. His body gives off no energy at all. Then his tennis shoes run meekly to the phone.

In the afternoon we deliver the negative to the cutters. "Hello chicken," the big guy named Pat says to Angus. I stand by unnoticed, the girl who came along to carry the cans. Angus introduces me as the director of the film to be cut. Pat shakes my hand like it is a fly to brush away. The men get to business. I am permitted to listen. I want to shout—this is my movie damn it, kindly condescend to explain slowly and carefully what you are saying. Nell reclined on her sofa balancing a wine glass, telling me it's all routine. "You pay union wages to some bloke on a shoot and he can't even find the clappers. Stands there with his arms hanging down, daring me to be director of this bloody thing when everyone can see I'm a cunt."

An hour later I am in the midst of an anxiety attack on the phone with the neg cutter. They have just lost three rolls of film. That bit at the end of Lillian's film where it all goes black. The movie fails without it. No mister, I can't "just delete that material." And all the credit photos are on the same reel. "Look . . . ," I say, exhaling smoke while trying to retain some shred of patience, wanting to just fucking cry and go home to America, big mistake to do it here, bloody English costs are two times as high as ours someone told me yesterday, hearing again Paul's old veteran's remark—"Labs of course can ruin your film, once it's cut there's no guarantee you'll ever see it" . . . tears on the edge of my voice as the lab man reacts to the accent, "Look, you will simply have to look. No, never mind, I'll look *for* you. Be right over." Dragging Angus along, primed with filmmaker paranoia through Soho streets and up rickety elevator. Rummaging wildly through every tin in sight 'cause by now I don't give a damn if it's manners or protocol, that movie's my baby. And the company waiting at home! Searching till we find part of it, this big Pat guy convinced by now that of course the broad must be crazy. Then back to our place to sweat through all the trims, two maniacs going through each roll however tiny till we know with certainty that it isn't there. Then the cutter on the phone again, "Yes, they have just now located it." Reacting stiffly to his insufferable British correctness while I swear inside, full repertory of my American street talk reaching all the way back to my first four-letter words acquired in the convent but perfected on the Bowery. Again to the lab to watch them cut it in. Told to wait in a waiting room while men accomplish. I wander out to find big Pat asking Angus to make a major decision on the color of another segment. No one bothered to consult me. Put them straight. Then Angus comes up with a brave idea to go all the way to black for one eighth of a second as a way to stretch those last eleven feet that are ruined now. Back in a dead run to cut it in. Then out of breath up the old elevator one last time, the thing sure to stop, one hundred years if it's a day—I will be left here in an iron cage forever, a claustrophobe. Till it lands at the cutter's door and we explode with the footage, handed over a minute before closing time. Now it's in the oven.

Wanda and I watch the fountains. Trafalgar. Same restaurant where I watched one bleak night last time. How different this afternoon. Walking through Soho and the Square, the sun flashing a London summer day I could measure the distance. Here with a friend and well. I chirp with movie talk, confidence, the glory of it being nearly finished now. Expanding for Wanda, who has seen me through it, watched it on the Steembeck in its scotch tape days. Sat through three versions of Mallory. And so many drinks in pubs at evening time while we talked America, Wanda yearning to do Mallory's thing, walk out slam her husband's door and into the arms of her Philip, a boy lover same as Mallory's but different. To make the break. Not be Henry's wife, a newspaperman's hostess any more. Between bouts of her thing and my thing we discuss Paul and Nell and the problem of Winnie. And what it does to the two of them. I complain that it is making Paul a bully. Wanda, Paul's own sister, says, "Yes, Paul can be a hell of a bully," and flicks her cigarette, her face ambiguous, helpless. "But really he's a victim, his first marriage was a disaster too." From the vantage point of London Paul's sister watching him caged all these months. She feels there is no solution. But I have hopes of the movement here in England. If Nell is afraid to ask them I'm not. A Yankee going to town. Making plans. How to organize. "You help them by being there," Wanda says, always a stroker. "But then I leave and it's no lasting help, one extra person to pattern is nothing."

The waiters give us the eye. Glamorous Wanda, seeing her that first time in the office back in March when Fumio was here, a mod lady all purple velvet, one would never guess she was fifty and broke. She was also a tyro sculptor, nervously showing Fumio her pictures. He encourages her. Then I remember seeing her stuff at the Star Turtle Gallery across from my studio on the Bowery. And liking it. Pieces she'd made in Provincetown the summer before. Living with Philip till Henry whistled her home, pulled the strings of money and her age. She stayed the winter, trying to go back to the old life till she couldn't work any more. Then it was just hanging on, a frightened woman, her trapped eyes fixed upon an airplane ticket. Paul and Nell worry how she'll live if she bolts, praying for some settlement from Henry. It is very hard on him too. I saw promise in her works, her terrible need to do it, in any case good bad or otherwise, a life in art might justify itself if a necessity. Telling her now as I do every time if you throw away security, London, the place here and the husband—do it for what you're going to make, make it a run to New York or Provincetown in order to sculpt. Terrified to think her old and poor and having done it for some kid who might not even be there for her tomorrow. The work would always be there if she gambles on it and not on love. Philip has a tantrum every time she changes the date, always postponing the time when she will fly to him, this middle-aged and beautiful woman who has never quite had a life of her own. Has

had four husbands instead, plus a whole deck of
semicareers. Wanda ready finally now to fly to a boy
waiting for her in a crummy loft on Chrystie Street in
Manhattan.

Today, as the sun plays fountains shine splash down
bright light of hope, Wanda has finally booked her ticket.
I tease her, "How many dates have you set already?"
"No this time it's final." And for once I believe her. It
is some satisfaction to see one of them sprung. After the
thousand conferences in the office or at the house in
Islington or the assortment of cheery evening pubs where
Wanda and I exchanged worries and egged each other
on. To do what we wanted to do anyway. But were
frightened.

And now the last drink together watching Trafalgar's
late afternoon golden glow before she goes to tell Henry.
Who knows she is leaving but does not yet know the date.
Wanda toys with the notion of simply disappearing on
him. "No, dammit, don't just leave him a note, be
decent," I argue. "But I'm scared of him." "You needn't
be cowed, but remember his pain." She fidgets, so long
a girl taken care of by men, so many of them, always
a beauty. And the pathos of her age. Even a slipped disk,
Paul sounded dubious when he told me. Henry calls her
an old woman unwell and regards her ambition to sculpt
as madness.

I am eating dinner, Wanda is holding off in order to
play hostess for Henry's *conversazione*. As a last fling
he has invited a slew of editors, getting the entire list
of people he owes dinners out of the way. Before she
leaves him. Strange details of bourgeois existence. But
the life in Wanda's eyes now as she describes how she
will live again when she arrives in America. Together
we extol its energy, shaking our heads over the depressing
atmosphere of England. One more martini and we'll
leave, old friends mellow in our conspiracy as Trafalgar
turns pink in the twilight. We are the politics of mere
existence. Proclaiming one can go on, live, do it yourself.
arrive there with a fellow spirit. Love, friendship, work—
are a life still despite the system. Trafalgar rebukes us

for romanticism, privatism, an ignorance of institutions. The fountains relenting then as we pay the check and go out into the Square's soft evening air. Other times in London flooding back into view as I look across it, my first Oxford visits on theater nights, St. Martin's Lane, dinners in French restaurants with JayCee, afternoons in the National Gallery. The sidewalk artists still at it in the beaming evening when I have put Wanda in a cab. Henry and the cordial ahead of her while I walk the old streets back to Soho for the number 19. Eating out I have saved them the trouble at home. How nice to have London to myself with money enough for the bus and cigarettes. Everything improves upon the past.

Hedda has come by tonight to have dinner. She and Nell still linger in the garden over their wine. Paul scouts female company in favor of television. He has given up eating dinner altogether. The ulcer roars in its cage. Out of loyalty to my sex and hatred of the tube I join the ladies. Last week Hedda tried acid. "Utterly delightful," she says. This week she is "into" astrology. I listen in a semblance of good manners. Nell is fascinated. Everything captures her interest. All the fads in London find a welcome before her lovely indiscriminate curiosity. Next they discuss the season's new book, Castaneda's *Don Juan*. Nell wants to film it. "Everything would fly," she says, creating a thousand gray phantoms in the twilight. Her hands wave in the darkness making films. Hedda's gossip by now is literary. Cooper's *Death of the Family* is still causing a sensation. "They are roasting Cooper for being an alcoholic." She giggles maliciously. "They would have to accuse him of something," I offer. "He is rattling their cage. When that poor bugger what's-his-name put out a sex education film they burned him alive in your papers. The Archbishop of Canterbury says premarital sex isn't Christian behavior. He should know, has a monopoly on it and the thousands benighted enough to believe him."

They ignore me. They are best friends playing "keep away." I am the "pickle" in the middle, they will not give me the ball. Hedda's saying all works of art are revolutionary. "Bullshit," I say. Every painter in New York wants to be in Rocky's collection. I used to spend whole mornings fantasizing his great studio visit myself. And when SDS came one night to the Artworkers' Coalition and documented the collusion between the trustees of the Modern Art and the System, the artists couldn't afford to care. They still wanted to be in the Museum. Rockefeller owns a large part of Venezuela. People starve there. "You are a political bigot," Hedda says. As they continue to exclude me I have time to think it over and decide she's right. Yes, all works of art are revolutionary. My sense of irritation revives as we lock horns over prostitution. Hedda says it's merely earning a living. I object that it is a special hell. Remembering last summer listening to prostitutes rap for hours. "It's not so bright and easy as you claim, the sufferings those women described were blasting to hear." Hedda counters with tales of career women who exploit young boys the same way. "Never heard of it," I say. "Well, you just haven't been around much," she sniggers. It is a cordial evening spent wondering why in hell I don't go upstairs and keep Paul company. Hedda is driving me batty. In six more minutes I may hit her on the head. But I am fascinated by her superiority, tantalized by her indifferent hostility, the nerves in my stomach vibrating to her dislike of me.

Finally I do leave. Paul has the telly on but he turns it off to talk. He lectures me on politics, an old master with a store of knowledge who has memorized the history of the Communist Party, American radicalism since the Founding Fathers, and every wrinkle of the New Left. Paul teaching me. His affection. Also his sternness. Every fact he produces intimidates me further, elaborate evidence of my absolute incapacity to be what I'm supposed to. Or what Paul has in mind. One assassination follows another in his recital, the full panorama of historical bad faith. I protest against the inevitable pattern. "You are too soft," he says, dismissing me. Now I am a cream puff. I sag. "An artist has no business in politics anyway," he resumes, summoning up O'Casey, Gorky,

García Lorca. He has done this to me before. I feel bullied. I also feel absurd. In paying me the compliment of taking me seriously, he takes me too seriously. Paul has got it in his head I am some kind of politico or another. "Look, Paul, I just care about change. I'd like to dedicate myself to that somehow. I'm not quite sure what it is or what I can do. But I know it's not about power. And what I have in mind is somehow more basic to experience than a 'politics' that is 'out there,' which is about money and office. I'm interested in something entirely different and trying to figure it out with myself first—how I could get it together, change myself." His moustache rumbles. "Of course I am terribly vague, Paul. But as you have just demonstrated, politics brings little change at best, at worst none or terrible new crimes. And ordinarily it sells out all it advertises." He agrees but says he worries about me: I am so "unfit for things." "Well, I am getting better and I feel less alone now." "But the mere media could annihilate you. You couldn't stand the beating you took last winter." "I'm human, Paul, and you can't say the mere media. It's the millions who believe in it who give it reality. When *Times* tells my mother that Ginsberg is a dirty-mouthed faggot who recites illiterate obscenities in Town Hall, she believes it entirely. When I land in Minnesota a week after the reading to tell her it was moving and beautiful and that Ginsberg has written an elegy on his own mother's death that is hideously painful to read as well as beautiful, *Time* has already arrived before me. She simply can't believe me. And how many people, people like my mother, have even the hope of an alternate version? The media control all the avenues of information available to the general public. We can't just play artist and dismiss the media as hot air. Its power is a very real force. One plays with it at hazard." "And you got burned," he reminds me. "Yes, but what is the alternative? There is no change if it's a handful of bright people having discussions. I may be sore as hell at the personal expense, but it seems unavoidable."

The door slams Hedda into a cab. Nell appears with

the usual. Valpolicella. Two glasses on a tray. Paul is going to bed. We enact the scene we have enacted already
a thousand times. He stands by the door admonishing
her to come up soon. She waves him out. I do not know
which way to jump. Since I adore her conversation
I inevitably fall into temptation and stay up with her. She
is outwaiting him. He is outwaiting her. I am merely satisfying my craving to listen to O'Rourke, sibyl, friend,
teacher. And yet tonight for once I wish she would sleep.
But she insists, she wants company. Nell draped upon
her couch. So ill. So wrecked.

As before, I think of suggesting I stay somewhere
else, timidly offering even the last time when I was editing and needed her odd moments to discuss the film and
nauseam. Paul continually intervening to forbid it. "I
could stay with Liz Moore over in Swiss Cottage, or rent
a bed and breakfast somewhere." Nell will not hear of
it. "No it's good you are here. Paul thinks so too. We
need a neutral force, a buffer." "Nell, I couldn't bear to
have prolonged houseguests in my studio." "How odd.
We have them all the time. But you are the first one
who ever contributed one damn thing." I am flattered,
but still uneasy. Yet by now how could I leave? By now
there is the patterning. I am part of the team, have to stay
to keep my promise, a bonafide member of the house-
hold. Which is in trouble. "We are locked in our roles,"
Nell says. "When I feed Badger the cat on one dish,
Paul would have it done on the other. If I cook sausages
for Winnie they are cooked inaccurately. All I can do
not to throw them at his head." Paul reappears in his
red bathrobe to haul her to bed. He is grumpy. She is
sulking. Paul is a tyrannical father, tender of her welfare. Nell is a whipped child defiantly resisting every inch
of the way. I look from his massive and wonderful legs
to her broken little girl's face. They are ridiculous and
tragic figures. I love them but I cannot help. It is so
dismal to watch. The first day we could discuss it, even
parody it, the two of them playing at Bluebeard and fair
maiden till we all laughed out loud. The whole thing a
huge joke, Paul wonderfully witty, even playful at last.

Now we only discuss it while acting it out. Soon we will merely perform it without speaking. This pace is quicksand. We all know what we are doing and go right on doing it.

I walk in the garden. Their masterpiece. The light is on in the kitchen. One sees such a beautiful house, magic as those on quiet streets in the West Village when you walk along and imagine who lives there, concocting whole short stories in the sight of a lamp or a bookcase. I look back at this house in London, a fine solid place. Look at this house from its garden and you are sure the people here are outrageously happy. Such exquisite taste. All bought with O'Rourke's commercials: prize-winning chocolate bars, fantastic superimpositions, every inch of film technically outstanding. But not what she wants to do. Or so she says, part of her wavering always as Paul does between the most rigorous demands of art, unflinching integrity, perfect honor. And the buck. Of course people can get hung on bourgeois comfort, I have met a thousand drunks at parties uptown who wanted to be artists but made money instead. But these two are not like that. More real. Both have done good films already. No, they are not ordinary middle-class types. But what choice have they? Winnie requires it. The tyrant in the basement demands the comforts of a whole house with a room for Ursula, and another for Letty, the American girl who is living in the little room next to Winnie this summer. Patterning this morning with Letty and Ursula I thought how easy it is for outsiders to do this work. How cheerful and amusing Winnie is. We were three women playing with a child who was not our child. Playing with a child between coffee breaks and gossip. Patterning was not the heavy stressful business it is with Nell and Paul, the long *Angst* of frustration, hope, anger—Winnie and the pattening making a cage of their lives. They are killing their work by supporting this invalid child. Winnie demands huge sums for the American surgery, the cost of the program. And the helpers Ursula and Letty. So they can run an office that pays for it all. So the office makes commercials and requires twenty thousand a year just to stay afloat. And the office is going broke.

The structure rises and falls as I watch the Georgian bricks build and diminish in air. It is insoluble. Here two days and already defeated. None of my bloody business anyway. Imposing on people's lives. If I could think of a solution it would be different. Perhaps excusable. I have no motive but my affection. They are my friends that I love. But check this out carefully. Sort it through and seek for any impurity. No, I don't have designs on either. I am a neuter. The queer in the house. Unctious homosexual eager to prove its human worth to these archetypal straights, save itself by saving the child, save the marriage. So I am properly repressed, disinterested, whatever. And say I were not, how would that invalidate my desire to help with their dilemma? My most probable culpability is the anxiety produced by my sense of obligation. They have done so much more for me than I have done for them, saving my life and my sanity by getting me through that movie. *Giri no ong,* they call it in Japan, the oppressive weight of obligation beyond what one repays. Or can repay. And what do I offer? A few hours patterning and the habit of staying up to get blasted with Nell in the evenings. She may enjoy it but Paul scarcely does. Nell insists it is her right to enjoy herself with her friends. Paul has none. He will let himself have none, though he knows so many people in London and is said to grow wonderfully sociable when Nell's out of town. It is hard to be Paul's friend, he resists such an intrusion. And though I adore him he refuses to like me. I once got Paul to the point of saying he'd let me take them out to dinner. Katagiri met with his approval. In a fatal error I shall always regret I made a face over the imitation Japanese food invariably overpriced. Paul is relentless, it was the last time he consented.

Well, dammit, I am as stubborn as he is. Take leave of the roses, enter the hallway, and face the one functioning clock in the house. Like our predicament it is enormous. All right then, it is insoluble, but I'll stay and gamble.

8

Winnie's room is full of odd sounds. Abuzz with static.
Part of the treatment. He cannot have music, only these
irritating noises on tape. Lovingly, scrupulously composed by Paul. Neither music nor bright colors. "They
stimulate the subcortex, the baser, more primitive section of the brain," Paul informs me, casually making
inferences I resent more every time I hear them explained. "Medical philistinism," I say. "Science," Paul
assures me. Winnie. His strange big head crawls over
to hug me. So much more a child now. The vacancy
nearly gone. Next he gives me a shove. The new violence
is a good sign. He resists while we coerce, willing him,
even pushing him into mind. It is the energy of our
willpower finally that might do the trick. Far more than
the exercises, it will be the dogged persistence of our
wanting him. The knowledge of our hands insisting. His
enemy the crawl box looks sinister under its gay Liberty
lining. There are ropes stretched across it to keep him
from jumping out. We pattern him again on the table
his head rolling between my hands as always. I am back
here now, a derelict returned to post, feeling the exercise
tiring my back again, where I sprained it once, stranded
on the Bowery floor, a sanding machine still buzzing
away ominously across the room while I lay flat, pure
Gregor Samsa, buglike and immobile.

Winnie's head turning his little body on the table between us while we count, my back nagging as time
pauses, hangs till the endless count to two hundred. What
is it like to be Winnie? What does it feel like? Off in his
place. Is it pleasant? Is it nothingness, vacuous as his

347

face when he drools, holding the miniature red London
bus in his hand? *Toooo—Tooooo—Toooo,* the pointless little whistle he makes. It is animal, disgusting, idiot,
yet terrifying seductive. I have dreadful premonitions
that if I surrendered to it, I could sit by him and dream
forever, recovering again the empty company of infants
on baby-sitting afternoons in teen-age. No future and
the present a bondage. His odd little whistle, this little
sound of his own. Does he sing to himself? Is it comfort?
Does it encourage his self? The head lolls again. But
rarer now. Winnie, his arms and legs moving in rhythm
to three adults bored beyond endurance, sweating, waiting for the cigarette break and the next cup of coffee but
intent in rhythm together, planting the pattern of the
child's crawl that he never learned within a four-year-
old body whose mind is over three years behind it. The
movements we engrave remorselessly on the lateral
nerves, hoping to force the living cells to take over the
work of the dead. Paul says he has already gained four
months of childhood through the program. Neurologi-
cally eight months to start with, he is now up to twelve.

Winnie's head turning in our force. My reverie
drowning in Winnie's spell, the power of motion, rhythm,
repelling the hypnotic pull of his lassitude, the peace
of his sensual buzz. We struggle against his strength. I
feel him luring us toward him. I feel it more than they
do, surely more than Paul, who would sniff at such a
notion. Or would he? If he admitted it at all would he
recognize it for the enemy? So we founder on, reversing
Winnie's force. We will make him like us. And cancel
his magic.

I saw him first last winter among company upstairs,
an idiot carried into the room like an error, doddering
in arms. The drool on his mouth. Eyes empty of
everything. It was a moment of terrible embarrassment.
The thing was obscene. One averted the eyes. Yet closer,
he tempted me. The staring eyes, mouth softly whistling
to itself. What place is his? What is it like there? What
echoes did I know of that region? And how valuable
the objective world that has since deafened me to this

sea of passivity? Beckoning to me again, reminding me of something I had known. I would watch him for hours, head hanging over a flashlight or the inevitable red bus. Then we began it, this gamble. Going to make Winnie a child. Seeing it work, the eyes beginning to focus, the mind beginning to form. He no longer croons, he looks, actually looks at things and sees them. He is coming alive inside, angry even. I glance again at the crawl box, a wooden slide with ropes across the chute. He is inserted into it twenty-four times a day by main force. Yes, force. Ashamed of ourselves we force him down it, torturing him in his rage. He hates it.

I thought the whole project American quackery in the beginning. Something they'd fallen for in their despair. But it worked. Exercises, diagrams, wooden structures that Paul and Angus built, charts, tables, timing regulations, rules about food, color, music. A whole bureaucracy. But the results were real. Winnie, at another structure, one he has mastered and can even like now, he stands on his toes walking below the overhead bars, his hands gripping, even the bad hand, the right one. He is smiling, showing me what he has learned while I was gone. Then he falls into my arms.

Last spring I did not want to do it. Don't get involved in some baby-saving program. Forget it and just work on the film. Hoping is a trip, and it's hopeless anyway. Leave him in his idiocy. Limpid, serene. But the risk was too beautiful. And then it started to work. The results threatened to become addiction. My hands turning his head on the table, the three of us one country together over his small body. After a while, carried away sometimes, wondering if this wouldn't be a purpose to live for, there being so few. Then I left them, didn't come back right away, stayed to be in America in my own place with friends, Fumio, fixing the farm. I started the book. Have I let them down? Push comes to shove, they are the parents. It's not fair. Winnie is everyone's problem. When will there be enough people to help? Winnie pulls against our work, our books and films. But he is art too, we are creating him. Can we do all of it or must we choose? They are choosing now.

Watching Winnie I become a zealot again. Why have I listened to them, believing that their work mattered and nothing else, only that they live and make things? Believed them when they said they were caught, couldn't go on. Winnine is what matters. They must save him. Keep the office. Make money. Pattern Winnie. Pay the American doctors, hire more people to help. Nell's commercials got a silver lion at Cannes.

Drinking last night upstairs, Nell dropping on her sofa, green eyes a blur of tears, said, "I'm not winning. Barely even surviving. Why should I buy Paul a wall full of military prints? I hate commercials. I'm not making any money, scarcely paying the bills. We're still behind ten thousand dollars on the last operation. I've been supporting Paul for a year and a half now and I find I resent it. Where is my life going anyway?" We go on counting, Winnie's head turns in my hands. It is insoluble.

In the mercury of her mood she had poured another drink and launched into plans. She is going to New York, get Tommy Hutchens to give her a whole bunch of money to film Carlos Castaneda's book. Shoot in New Mexico. Be her own person again. No Winnie, no Paul, no movie company, no house in London, no Badger the cat. Then kicks out her skirt telling me again what she wants to do in films, the images no one has even seen yet, the reality beneath life's surface. I follow her poetry until I cannot see it, switch to the new film of Alain-Fournier's *Wanderer* which I have been urging her to see, the vague pale colors, the mystery, the way it narrates entirely in visuals. "That would be a great kind of film to make. But why film somebody else's book, O'Rourke? Write the stuff yourself and shoot it now." But she draws back. Shooting a commercial next week.

While they are at the office Ursula and I eat strawberries in the garden. Ripe enough. So we pick them and eat. Nell and Paul never eat them. The idea that we do at first seems outrageous. It is breaking a pattern. We laugh at rigidity. "Dry as a bone," she says, her brown finger scrabbling on the brown ground. I look for the hose, meaning to water them. Ursula tells me about South Africa where her husband, a writer, was a political prisoner. Ursula is here twelve hours a day. Not an employee, since for her Winnie is a cause. I hesitate before turning on the hose. Would Paul resent my doing this? Is it correct? Go on, continue to be reckless. But use the water can, filling it in the kitchen sink where I used to try not to vomit while brushing my teeth. Paul might see me. Last spring. Today over the noise of the faucet I suddenly hear Claire's voice, teasing me. "Well, sweetheart," it drawls, the word "heart" sounding like "hot" in her broad Boston vulgar. Does Claire exist? I stand at the sink, confounded by the idea that such a person might be real rather than a figure of my imagination.

Yesterday I drew a line through the white band of my Blick's English notebook. A magical gesture made in orange ink. Blick itself is an olive drab and bears only a pale resemblance to the emerald green of King Bomba's menu. In the restaurant the orange pencil looked fresh upon the green and white. By these small moves I resist England. As if I were Ireland. For a moment I thought the pencil lost. I keep losing and finding it like my notebooks or my shopping bag. England, the place stops me. Riding along past signs glimpsed from the bus window I see that the *Daily Express* features Cardinal Something's Sunday special, "The Making of a Bishop," and the *Daily Mail* advertises "Christian Heroism" in huge black letters from the shoddy stationers' fronts on Upper Street. Prime Minister Heath flashes on the set to address a banquet. His face is jolly like an overfed athlete's, assuring us things are going splendidly here in Britain. All radical ideas are denounced each morning at breakfast by the London *Times*. Everyone looks so poor, so depressed, the shops, the people on the streets. Things seem so unnecessarily tacky. I watch the faces behind the glass windows of another bus. Remote as ants on flypaper.

When I came home Nell was working in the garden. Writing for her movie. Orange hair bent over her pencil. How cunning she is to have gotten sick so she can write. I observe her through the kitchen window, very pleased with events. Things are looking up. Such a fine evening, I will walk out in London. Give myself the city I missed last time. On the street I run into Letty, our flower child, a blond kid looking American summer in the dull English street. She has spent the day in the Regent's Park rose garden writing letters. I see Claire's hair in hers, each reflecting the sun. I notice that the house on the corner has a new orange door. They have painted it. They are making it new again. Or better than new because it is a fine old Georgian house restored. But they are the middle class. People like Nell and Paul. Pass on to the other houses in the block, the working class. Here it is dull brick slum-council house. Restoration wouldn't help them. And no one feels up to restoring; the very curtains seem discouraged. Like North Oxford where I lived in the not quite slums of the mind, the England I knew before twelve years ago. Lawns and swans for the privileged, hopeless brick dreary for the rest. Bare comfort without humor or style. The orange door appears to be a portent. Should I paint the farm doors this same orange? Red I thought at first, like New England. Common, Vita said, make them yellow. When I have painted the doors I have changed the place.

Walking North London streets past the bike shop and the tobacconists and ads for patent medicine. Everything going into brick dullness again. It blots me out. House agents, secretarial bureaus, beauty parlors. The old culture. I conjure up snapshots of my friends and project them on the screen behind my eyes for reassurance and walk on toward the Angel. Here is a cheerful pub. And I have found a rose garden across the way where I can muse until it opens. The Angel and Crown, admirable name. I sit on the grass, breaking rules. A little old man comes by, says, "Are you writing to that lady over there? She's writing to you." Look up and see a woman on a bench. True, she's writing. What can he mean? Curious flirtation. Everything is a little odd over here, or is it the day?

At the pub they watch me while I order my beer. Catching my accent. "Girl all by herself," they tease. "Yes, love, lager's the coldest," men rough and cheery as Lawrentian woodsmen. "Cold enough for you now, dearie?" Fresh cool frost on the glass. I let them badger me, grinning back at them, relishing the sound of the words in their mouths. It feels very summer, sitting alone under an umbrella at the front of the pub. Mr. and Mrs. at the next table. Invariable pink beefy face flat cap. Her impossible clothes talking about the nephews. We smile at each other. Lovely evening. I am in England writing in my notebook. In love with them. In love with everything.

Today Stephanie is here to help us pattern, crisp and likable in her starched summer dress, silk gloves beside her on the table. After the ardors in the basement we take our wine out in the garden. Stephanie discusses psychology with Nell. I detach myself from the conversation to dream the afternoon among roses and the clear fine evening. London and America too, my friends, transporting them in a trice, arranging them on chairs around me. Fumio chuckles to see Nell the mad Irish lady. Claire has never seen England at all. She nods her big golden head with interest: "Though I've never ventured beyond the Ohio River, I travel in my mind," she quibbles. Vita glows as Nell praises her: "Real heroine of that movie, soldiered through finding all those bits of track you were always needing on the long distance." Celia risks coming back, England where she cracked up once, right here in Islington, rooming house with a gentle boy who took care of her while she recovered from having fallen in love with a schoolgirl on her first job out of college. A teen-ager alternately leading her on and lapsing into obscure French convent innocence. This *jeune*

fille, half dodge, half real. Celia took her and her classmates skiing and on picnics, felt made a fool of and
quit. Might have been fired if she hadn't come from the
right family. Took a ship for England, never coming back.
Until of course she did. Back all the way to the family
place in Connecticut to lock herself in with a lute.
Learning it from scratch the six years until she was ready.
Then they disappear, fade out of my proprietary fantasy;
they have seen what I so wanted them to see, an English
garden on the evening of a fine day.

Psychology reasserts itself in conversation to my left.
Nell goes off to seek another bottle of red. I look at
Stephanie and just tell her, scarcely remembering how
I found the key, perhaps some sarcasm at the absurdity
of the experts, having no idea whatsoever, yet they pretend to tell us who we are, insisting they know, professionals. "Take a case like mine, a real freak, a bisexual, a thing quite unheard of in their theories. Of
course Freud said we are all bisexual, but he had no intention we should practice it. To him it seemed to mean
that we all had elements of the other utterly foreign sexual
personality, rather like oil and water, but you are
admonished to stultify your opposite sex when it intrudes,
all too often, like a trick knee betraying you. Of course
that is not what I mean by being bisexual." Stephanie
looks away. Flicks her cigarette. "How did you get that
way?" as if it were leprosy. "Queer, you mean?" "Well,
if you like. Did you get that way in college?" I do not
answer the question because I do not know the answer.
Instead I answer the question's inference by saying I think
we are all bisexual. "And I'm a scandalous person with
a mass of outrageous notions, such as that we're neither
hetero- nor homosexual. Training and experience seem
to lock us into one or the other." Stephanie is clearly uncomfortable. I have just suggested she could be as weird
as I am, a Lesbian, a pervert and so forth. This is far
more unsettling even than my previous gaffe. She pushes
it away. "Then none of us knows clearly who we are
and my life is already too difficult." "Some people go
on to be straight as programmed, and some for various

reasons don't. But to start with, we're just sexual. Though that's tricky too. There's no proof people would have intercourse without instruction of some kind. Maybe the only thing we can count on is the pleasure principle. Which might get one as far as masturbation without benefit of schooling, but the rest's rather unclear." "But what of the sensual gratification of nursing, fondling, affection, and so forth," Stephanie objects, interested now in the discussion. "Yes, that goes rather a long way, but it's all complicated by tribal habits, methods of child rearing. And we're talking about complex social feelings now and not just organs."

We are both relieved by O'Rourke's return and another glass of dago red while I thank the sky for not falling. I have laid it on someone, not for a friend but a stranger. A little announcement she scarcely needed, and received in the usual liberal attitude of—I wish so much you would not impose these things upon me, I would be so pleased to overlook it. The talk strides on as O'Rourke brags about the Lesbians and prostitutes who used to live in her boardinghouse, great friends they were in the days when she worked in the market. Took her off to their bars and all that, used to see wonderful brawls and hair-pulling fights. Grand it was. Still knows where they are. Over in Nottinghill Gate. She offers to take me. I accept, knowing she won't. Nor will I wish for the nerve to remind her, piqued at this shower of the bizarre. "People think I'm a Lesbian," she says, presenting us with the impossible. "Sure, why not? Here I am, professional lady, pretty tough one at that, so they think—what else could she be? Ask me to my face, guys in the business, while I'm sitting next to some frail type, some old friend of mine in television who really is gay, but how can I protect her? I used to go crackers keeping her secret from these pushy blokes, all eyes and inferences—broad like you making all that money has got to be chuckling some little sweety of her own on the side, now doesn't she?"

The world amazes me. I have another drink. Stephanie is taking her leave. Paul is refusing dinner again. Nell and I will cook up some potatoes, the usual Irish experiment combined with a few more bottles of the un-varying red. I listen to O'Rourke perform her talk want-ing to make it a movie. A tape. Anything so it is not lost, this talent for words, for life. Preserve it somehow so it is not lost forever on the airways, dead in the morning kitchen, its dazzle diminished to hang-over. Her vast potential never heard by a soul but me getting drunk at her kitchen table. This prodigious Irish-talking lady scattering emeralds into the sink and garbage can, waving her gold rings into desolate age unheard, the green eyes already dying. A face so much older than her years, younger than I am but so much aged in trouble that I feel she is an aunt, a mother, a hag, a witch, a saint, a fairy six feet tall—the old kind we had in Ireland before the English cut us down to size. For once the stranger people rode on white horses, blew horns, would call you to the hunt and you would never come back, disappear into death like Machree now dying in her pain, a thirty-four-year-old professional woman movie director in London and mother of a defective child cooking potatoes in butter while she talks a blue streak. Theme and variation on the absurdity of making movies nowadays when they already bring you war on television. "Look see the people die. Now for the football scores. A little sermon by mealy-mouth on Christian charity and they bring on 'God Save the Queen.'" So much a performance one cannot reproduce it on paper, which has neither tone of voice nor gesture. If I could only tape everything, but it would ruin the occasion, make us self-conscious. The devouring present historian in me is a monster. If I could bug my own head, go direct from brainwaves to paper, skip even the interference of voice, not to mention the labors of composition . . . my favorite fantasy racing on as I dish up the spuds on the blue and white at Nell's kitchen table where once in London Lila wrote her book.

I bewail my own now to my guru. "How can I write in England? The pedestrians accuse me of full-blown insanity. On Shaftesbury Avenue their faces expressed the most outraged surprise at an American dyke intent upon creating myth out of a handful of Lesbians in New York City and a few other friends while the real world, the employed and responsible, have a routine and reality to accomplish. I rode in a cab and their faces conveyed it all through the window." "Naturally," she says. "English cabs are like hearses. Look, you're better off here. You were flying when you arrived. Now you're down to earth. You had power. I didn't like you. Kindly stop calling yourself a queer. It's a cruel word, sharp at the edges. You're cutting yourself on it." "No, I'm coming to find it proud." She smiles at me. "I've watched you testing people this visit, announcing yourself, probing them. There's something touching about it. You're becoming gay within yourself, getting identity, rounding it out. But it's not all you are. There is Fumio too." "Yes, but there's been Fumio such a long time. And I've been gay again only a year or so. I must get right the balance. Besides, the whole world's confident it's no crime to love a man." "Just where you're wrong. Places there will be. Bigotry lives on all sides and gay chauvinism, which will come because it's inevitable, will make it very hard for you futuristic bisexual types before you win out."

"But the outrage, Nell, is outrageous. People are so threatened." "Ultimately it's simple, a matter of fear. Or no fear and the remembrance of fear. They're all of them or bloody nearly all of them scared right I mean Right out of their minds. Nothing so unsettles us, men women and children I mean the lot, as our own precarious sexual identity. And there you are blowing the lid by calling it all into question. Of course they will want your head for dinner. Hang it up on the wall after your brain is picked."

"I should be stoic?" "Stoicism is beside the point. If the shoe pinches you, you can say it hurts. Why not? That's the truth. Your job's only to tell the truth. To hell with that image business, most destructive nonsense of all. Are you a prizefighter, for Godsake?" Puts her fork down, does prizefighter till I laugh. Bantams about the kitchen, scraggly red hair abounce under the edges of the big hat she wears all the time to protect her hair from her dislike of it. Dances, boxing on her toes about the kitchen very Norman the Mailer, then sits down and performs the routine of "soldiering through," a habit England has forced upon the skinny shoulders in her dungaree jacket spare with the weight of the world and Winnie. "O'Rourke I love you." She twinkles back in imitation of Doris Day. "Pale not O'Rourke this is disinterested appreciation, a nearly aesthetic detachment before the world's greatest free movie." Yes, and sad great lady scorned by each and every circumstance. How do I bail you out who bailed me out each time, patient, loyal, or flighty? Even when playing temperamental queen of hangovers, generous beyond any woman I have ever known.

Sarah drops in from her flat around the corner. Graduate student and mainstay of Winnie's program. And of Ethel's antiapartheid. A gentle solitary vulnerable person giving so much to other people. People who are older and fond of her. And Sarah taking what she gets back fills the void of her loneliness. But it is easy to mistake her for empty. I did when I first met her, a bit of arrogance on my part, thinking thank God I've escaped graduate school, those horrendous dull projects like dissertions on obscuranta that inevitably make one as dull as they are. Especially over here where the illness lingers for years; Sarah has been writing this thesis for half a decade and of course it bores her to distraction. That was before I knew her. How much easier to spy out the cages in foreign parts, so much more predictable and obvious in another landscape. How easily one misses sight of the people inside.

All things conspire to educate me. Today I am emerging into the world. Out of Winnie's basement to an antiapartheid conference. Sarah goes on ahead to buoy up Ethel the organizer. I will follow in a cab when the pattern's done. May miss the first speeches, but the thing goes on all day. I will not miss Caroline Hunter. Up the stairs through hawking Leftist bustle of pamphlets, hit for two pounds of mimeo lit before I get to the door. Then redecorated with Angela buttons. Angela in her grandeur reduced to a smudge. Angela real as prison and the world flaunting her courage, riding on that wind of heroism while an actual women is in handcuffs behind real bars somewhere taking the rap for our emotional effusions. And possibly for the expediency of the left as well. Those of the right go without mention, their predictable inhumanity. And now I remember I still have not composed my letter to Devlin, roasted on the box and in newsprint this week. Having a baby on her own. Lady interviewer turns the knife, "Won't that mean your career?" Mick Bernadette, her face only human and beautiful, parries thrust while I groan for her, stuck in a soft spot of scandal once myself.

Ethel is at the door all mother in girth and bosom coordinating the political with the merely human, even the sociable, introducing me to Caroline Hunter. Nell said that when Baldwin couldn't come they thought of me for a moment. "But your pacifism was an obstacle." Took the wind out of me. "Not the only obstacle, O'Rourke, I am an ignoramus on South Africa. Two full days of briefing and every pamphlet in London still leaves me nothing to say." Paul grumbles about the double-edged exploitation of writers poking their noses into politics, "Consider poor Baldwin." I remind him Baldwin's speech last time was magnificent. Not a speech about economy statistics political ideology—but about suffering. Which is what South Africa is. "Writers," Paul says, murdering the word with contempt. "Watch Caroline Hunter today and you'll see a pro."

Caroline is a remarkable woman. At eighteen she organized the Polaroid strike in Cambridge, Massachusetts, then traveled to South Africa for an on-the-spot survey of how a genuine fascist state controls its citizens with identity cards, photo, fingerprints, superbureaus filing its victims, a model for global controls until other governments catch up. We begin cheerfully with black humor on the totalitarian computer future, Kafka's nightmare wide awake. I admire her enormously, the competence, the fire. Even the wit. Try her out on my own political

bends, rapping on the suicide trip of white boys in the
American Left persuaded that change is an old movie
bang prick bang till they kill us dead the show is over
and the lid comes down. She nods, agreeing. We get on
to women but a white man invades us, wanting to hear
the proceedings, then insisting that I'm unrealistic, delivering a lecture on how power invested will never resign on its own volition. Next her black African soul
brother joins us. He's been two years in prison for just
handing out leaflets. Caroline passes over into paranoia
out of solidarity, claiming she'd get busted by London
bobbies if she even put her foot out of the door, racism
here is as bad as South Africa. . . . Distinctions blur,
the volume goes up. The men take over. Caroline becomes their echo. Everyone begins yelling. My own argument for the possibility, even the preferability, of
nonviolent change had referred to America. I cannot
speak about Africa, would incline to be convinced that
wars of liberation are inevitable there. But wars of national liberation are not necessarily revolutions. And the
situation as well as the changes we wish to see brought
about in America are entirely different. But now all
three are bellowing that violence is the only way, armed
revolution in the streets, Chicago, let the street people go
guerrilla, Caroline is reciting, "Kill the Pigs." Nixon's
army?

In two minutes my contemptible honky nonviolence
is up against the wall, the white English male intellectual
most strident of all, the black brother heavy insistence,
Caroline all follower. I would like to point out the superior military force of the opposition, argue expediency, at least they might take that into account. But in
such a conflagration of murdering voices it seems futile
to mention that my own real criterion is morality.

Caroline has been taken from me. We are no longer
discussing anything. We are several people merely
shouting. I have become the target for everyone's irrational violence toward nonviolence. So I go off mumbling to myself the things they would never permit me
to say, a bit more convinced than ever. Humiliated but

not really angry, only a trifle depressed. This encounter
is a cliché in my life. A monotony of being outshouted.
At times one makes one's point better by refusing com-
bat. But it does hurt that Caroline and I cannot be
friends. In the dark auditorium the predictable audience
of white women and black men. Since it is a special
occasion there are also even some white men. Prominent
on stage. Things like this are run on a daily basis by
white women acting out of a spirit of service, the unglam-
orous reality of operation, leaflet, the lifelines of help
and accomplishment such as they are, conducted vicari-
ously and at great distances from the scene of the crimes.
Black men emerge at important moments as heroes and
the authentic people. White men condescend to grace
high holidays like this with their expertise. Black women
are no place any time, always the most ignored and
abused, though a few sprinkle the audience today. And
Caroline for figurehead. Room for one heroine.

I have come to learn so I get to it, frantically scribbling in my notebook, an undergraduate again at a lecture. War is going on in some places already. Angola.
Mozambique. Tenuous guerrilla operations gaining and
holding ground in one place, losing it in another. British
intellectuals are airing the situation. Economy. Geography. Facts of South African and Rhodesian financial
strength, efficiency of operation, expanding gross national
product, support by world trade. Banners on stage behind
the panel reads "South African Freedom Day." The
phrase nearly seems a mockery. London is so far away.
Yet of course it is better than someone try to do something, inform themselves, try to tell others that certain
atrocities take place daily somewhere else. One speaker
finally putting it on the line: "Rattle the investment system in hell holes like South Africa and Rhodesia and
you make a fundamental challenge to the capitalist system, which in America and Europe is expanding in a
period of false growth, its huge new profits derived from
forced labor elsewhere, the peonage in South America
and parts of Asia, or actual slave labor as in these parts

of Africa. Rattle that system and you end up attacking the very society in which you yourself are living."

The British Industrial Relations Act and the new Immigration Bill are both versions of this new colonial money empire. Currency is a far cheaper and more efficient conqueror than arms, behold the dollar these two decades ruling the world. And other methods now suggest themselves for use on us here at home, a new subgovernment through citizen control, the computer records already spreading through the American system where government has by its own admission catalogued one in eight of its subjects in secret files. Many of those currently neglected are still children or too old or poor for notice as yet. And so one arrives at South Africa, a good model for potential worldwide systems. It threatens all of us. The issue is greater even than racism. It is slavery and freedom. It is a matter of a new slave economy in one place and a totalitarian bureaucracy in another. Western, especially British, financial stability depends on African apartheid. But by the extension of the methods and controls perfected by government in South Africa, Westerners may in time experience the apartheid system at home. Rigged, of course, by class, in addition to or in place of race.

Remedies seem so pitiful. England, France, and America are all fighting to sell arms to apartheid, which is getting so smart it's beginning to learn to build them itself. Africa states are taking graft, selling out their people or looking the other way in order to survive. Indeed, the only hope does seem to lie in insurrection. Yet I wonder still why no one remembers Gandhi's tricks for dealing with imperialism. He started out in South Africa. And this is a British-educated audience who should remember India. Has everyone forgotten? But how could it work anyway? Admitted himself he had only the British to deal with. How would it be if he had to go against Hitler? Yet remember that the Norwegians didn't do that bad a job of it. But South Africa today? Or the Portuguese, such brutal imperialists there in Angola. The mandatory solution seems to be violent revolution there. Well, so you agree then. So why quarrel with Caroline? Because we began by talking about America and America is a different place: different social conditions, economy, a different stage of industrial development than African states or South America. Even its victims have different experiences than the slavery of South Africa, the peonage of South America. It is sloppy to say that Harlem is Vietnam or Bed-Stuy the same as Capetown. Even the point of rhetoric is lost when mere analogy is preached blabber Leftist rhetoric right smack into absolute sameness. It is a kind of violence to language, even to common sense. One ceases to be able to think. It is different to be high on skag in a urine hallway 125th Street than to be napalmed, skin burning and village gone. Housewife and faggot may be shit on, but they are not starving to death tonight in Bangladesh. Not even the Mississippi black or cracker baby with rickets is quite as bad off on food stamps as the little bodies already dead. There are differences and differences are facts. Does even suffering have objective gradations?

All right, say one acknowledges that, could we change America by changing ourselves? And then take it over? And how, for Godsake? I don't know, I am incapable of a program, intent first upon my own transformation. Or is there even time, since America runs everybody else's disaster too? How does change, which is, by logical definition, the end of violence of all kinds, take power without violence? Better yet, how does change eliminate power, convert it to order, the ideal politics, that rational ordering of human affairs based on justice and good will? How does the question of social transformation grapple with the hard fact of politics as it is now, control based upon force, ultimately violent, ultimately monetary, ultimately military? Monetary (the bloodstream) military (the sinew). All of it ultimately masculine. Ultimately bureaucratic, institutional, and impersonal, a machine greater, more deadly because entrenched in offices, officers, and the fate of millions trained from infancy in religious and unthinking obedience to folly, an ideology ultimately greater and more potent ever than their tyrants. Nixon is paper, replaceable as a washroom napkin. There would always be another.

My attention returns to the Englishman making his speech: political, coherent, masculine. I take notes and concentrate, trying to master the charts of products and companies, figures and dates. Then off to the left of my vision something astounding takes place. A crazy enters the hall in bare feet, flowers, bundles of mimeo paper in his arms. Yells nonsense at the speakers, sits, claps, shouts. The speaker resumes his statistics. The crazy spreads flowers on the apron of the stage. Playing mother, Ethel tries to quiet the crazy. "There is at this moment a war going on in Angola," the speaker says, "and the English may go in on the wrong side as it spreads." The panel is winding up. The crazy increasingly rambunctious. Ethel gives him a cigarette. She addresses him as a rational, a friend, a person. The moderator hurries trying to make announcements, like a schoolteacher before his pupils escape. Crazy stands before the platform now. Has put on a paper hat, a folded newspaper like a child's toy tricorn. People giggle. Moderator says keep it peaceful, the last meeting ended in five hundred pounds of damage, a shocking waste of money. Paper hat leaps on stage, pissing hot to talk. Some prophetic message. But all he calls out is FREE LITERATURE. Ended up not really doing it, his crisis past, his figure shining in a spotlight. The paper hat glittering like a star. Is he peace or chaos?

A reporter tells me he's really Bryan Mattisson. A Cambridge don once an authority on political science, next a computer expert. The story transforms the figure before me, clothes him in a white coat, a savant till he dropped out, wiped his mind in acid. After his brother was jailed and tortured in South Africa. Mattisson concluded his academic career by informing the Master of All Souls he was God. As the reporter talks, making the crazy a man insane with grief, with suicide, with drugs, with insight beyond the logical that we have listened to all morning, the thing becomes harder, more terrifying.

The reporter continues describing the life inside apartheid. The full implications of house arrest. South Africa grows and comes alive like a ghastly hell of the future. For a second I become one of them, seeing the police arrive to arrest me. Helpless years in jail. My face is the one that opens the door as the officer arrives with the envelope. The condemnation papers passing into my hand. I cannot bear to go on imagining it. Craziness is one response. Is there another? The documentary has been running as we talk, black and white footage stolen on a bishop's visit, the cameraman presenting the innocuous camouflage of clergy in order to smuggle this fierce terror away and let us see the lines of bodies, killings, the wreck of black lives programmed, curtailed beyond any possibility for human participation in life. Slaves. The mines. And the dockets. Cards, papers, registration forms, my reporter friend keeps talking on in clipped sentences, BBC English, but with the soul of a man who has lived there five years too long. He says one goes mad there—so in excess of what can be borne. Explaining the last details of fact and imagination, just what it is like in their prisons, the entire area and society one vast insufferable jail.

We group our way to a pair of seats for the second film, a technicolor documentary on the revolution in Mozambique. The two kinds of soldiers, the white Portuguese and the black guerrilla faces, talking out of green jungle backgrounds. Mondlane and the cult of the hero. The black army is a good army. Black. It teaches its soldiers with dances. The men look happy. They have an army. Their own thing. Smiling faces in training, calisthenics, marches. More dances together. They look wonderful.

There are no women in the army, or so far one sees none. Only a few even take part in the dances. Most only look on, babies on their backs. They are indoctrinated in the villages. Colonial women, the subjects of subjects being taught the political line by men. Joachim making a speech. Unexpectedly the movie presents women who are in the army. You see two black women grinning in army green. Then men helping with tasks, grinding cereals, women's work. There are still very few women in the pictures. Are they marginal? More political lessons. Couples are split up by revolutionary duties. Child-care centers for the fighters' kids, orphans, men and women both seem to be doing it. Pedro Jama explaining cooperative farming. Women seem far better off now than in either colonial or traditional tribal society. Next there are shots of building schools. Children sit learning how to read, a gentle man instructing them. You see the gun in the grass next to him. The mounted gun gleaming in a child's eyes. The proudest thing owned. The gun a flag of freedom. Maniacal. Comprehensible.

Then the other side. White faces again. Explanation of how Western capitalism aids and abets. Then South African whites training in guerrilla warfare. They really do look fascist. But the young Portuguese boys look like our own in Vietnam, unwilling conscripts. Paul was just telling me about meeting one of them on a trip, the kid had gone AWOL but they got his mother. Then the black guerrillas again. They know what they're about. The revolution is their new life, groups of them singing. The film closes in shots of nature. I recall Felix Greene's film on China, how that last shot of the boy playing a flute on a water buffalo against a range of mountains makes one's mouth water to see the place, China itself. A propaganda film? No. They are right of course. But war? Women. Guns. Black faces in the green.

I am in trauma through lunch. Cheer up, this is only England, you still need not choose between violent revolution or the everyone-says-empty stance of pacifism. Just decide between two kinds of salad, both nobly radical, equally repellent, and slide your tray along, make jokes with the volunteer waiters and try not to lose your bag and the movie money. And hurry, 'cause Caroline is on in a minute. Cordial again in the hall, Caroline has completely forgotten our altercation and wants to be sure I hear her speech.

Caroline is all brothers and sisters. Then to business. Polaroid got its start in South Africa. With worldwide monopoly on instant photography's magical patterns, Polaroid prospered. Year after Polaroid invented the quick picture, South Africa invented the Passbook. Your photo laminated into indestructible plastic all in two minutes and you are identified forever. But starting off in the cambridge plant Caroline and other factory workers began talking, fussing, asking questions. Factory hands, they had nothing concrete on South Africa or Polaroid, they just knew intuitively as blacks that it was wrong.

Caroline waxes militant, I catch her phrases intermittently between Bryan's bizarre exits and entrances, seize the time, death to the pigs. The first rallying cry for the strike, pamphlet or something. Polaroid said it was inflammatory rhetoric. Workers at Polaroid who had been there for thirty years had no information on the South African connection. The corporation lies like a god: Polaroid explains it didn't sell its indentification equipment to South Africa, it just sold it to the army. And *they* sell it to South Africa. Bryan outside talking hard. Protesting shrilly in the corridor.

In Caroline's rap Polaroid is now denying its connection to South Africa, deprecating its business there, just hobbyist stuff in department stores. Moreover, it argues there are five hundred U.S. companies in South Africa and Polaroid's the best of the bunch. Caroline insists liberalism is merely a degree of racism. Polaroid's own donation of twenty thousand dollars to black cultural events was simply a bribe. Her strikers should get half and send the rest of it to the liberation army in Africa. No more goddam ballet and basket-weaving, guns and bullets are a higher priority.

Next Polaroid offered to study the situation with a handpicked committee of stooges. They got Caroline and another black militant by mistake. But one of the committee was the company vice-president who sold the apartheid state the machine to start with. The rest of them are fronts. Caroline and the other black were put in to pose for the news photographers. Polaroid bought ads to tell their fellow Americans it's all O.K.

and Polaroid will "work through the system" for change, donate little bits of bread to native education. When the committee gets to South Africa they run around and find a few black South Africans to tell them it's a paradise. Would have their throats cut if they said otherwise. All the time nobody had figured on Caroline.

Leaving South Africa, Caroline outlines the political dangers of Polaroid to the rest of the world: Trudeau's martial law in Canada is now negotiating for the process, Berkeley already labels its young at the moment of their college entrance, but other schools in California start at thirteen. Must carry it on their persons at all times. Voters are already ticketed in some places. In Cambridge, Mass., every driver has one. In Birmingham, England, they already do it to the bobbies. "Who will be next?" she shouts.

Computerized face print will be the next step. You can alter your fingerprints but not your face. Caroline goes on rapping, a chaotic version of technological fascism. She crescendos. Is photography the devil? But the revolutionary movie was also on film. All the Americans arrested this May Day were photographed with a big swinger camera on black and white film. That was fifteen thousand people, young people, the middle class. It is all coming closer as Caroline rises to her peroration. May Day kids are filed now forever in the FBI computers, which correspond with all other government agency files and army information on civilians. All America's millions soon in print. Prison of the mind. Body comes later. Caroline steams on toward the finish line. The U.S. already has South African laws: preventive detention, stop and frisk, suppression of common law freedoms; you're guilty till proven innocent, Mitchell just said. We've got to unite in resistance. By Any Means Necessary. The clenched fist raised.

She winds up Power To The People. The People clap. The reporter and I stand for her. An Englishman then explains to us what she's said, converting her passion to reason, to masculine British logic. Then the local pillars of antiapartheid get down to business, naming the companies that float South Africa and what's to be done about them. Profits sometimes as high as thirty percent. All day each speaker laments the Labour Party but remains loyal. The universities' investment in South Africa; Edinburgh had one-half million invested in slave mines till the students forced them to pull out. The Church of Scotland buys South African stock, Church of England too.

Bryan back in a frenzy. Asking permissiom to talk. He is told to shut up. Black guys in sunglasses lounging near the doors look at him menacingly. But it is Question Time. They will have to let him now. Then he walks out in his bare feet. When he stood before me a moment ago I saw a spot on his shirt like a bullet hole. A priest who has been expelled from South Africa says that we must take responsibility when informed: he will take on the Church of England. Lady gets up and blows the whole thing: "All day we've talked about the working class yet all of us are middle class, we talk about investment but nobody here has any money to invest, we talk about Africa and live in suburbia. We talk about racism and have never had relationships with persons of another race. We have been doing it for years. Shall we now all go home and be depressed?" The moderator argues that no one here is even reaching out to the people whom they do know. An elected politician says we should become enlightened. Citizens of the world, etc. It is time to leave.

I must keep my promise, go home to pattern. Passing Bryan on the stairs, our eyes meet and say nothing. As I wait for a cab I see him again barefoot among the children of the Left who mock him, their idiot and saint. It is one way to relate to students. Bryan, a figure sitting alone on the cement, forlorn for a match saying again and again . . . "Does anyone smoke?" Seeking community among those who spurn him while egging him on. He is about something that is not politics. Something that is suffering and madness. I feel its old call in the gut, thankful for convalescence, measuring the steps back to health in England as it flashes past in a cab. The "Take

Courage" slogan is howling at me from a pub front. What is politics? What does change mean?

"And what did you see today at the gashouse?" Nell demands. I saw the conjunction of three things: political and economic fact logically explained, Bryan's madness, Caroline's mystique of violence. Realizing only as I say it the full mystery of the riddle. Then we pattern. Today the three of us together again over the body on the table. Winnie might wind up being the revolution. The insurrection surely, cutting Paul's face, struggling in my arms like a wild animal, fearfully strong. His face all terror coming down the crawl box. We feel like monsters and endure it with humor, close to each other. Between rounds I run the revolutionary movie in my head, cutting back and forth between its jungle green army suits and the voice of reason in the commentator. There is no other way . . . given the objective economic and military conditions . . . pacifism . . . freedom . . . politics, not change . . . roles . . . the baby on her back, the gun on his. And homosexuality? While Winnie's head rolls in our hands.

9

Paul abstains. Has ceased to eat at all. Me and O'Rourke in the land of the living at the kitchen table. Awash in talk, the movement analyzed in brilliant detail, the zeitgeist, and then the psyche, each examined with rapt affection. Transforming all our friends to saints and geniuses, believing in them, bemoaning their troubles, building their careers, rejoicing in their achievements, defending their weaknesses. And critical too. Mallory doesn't write. Vita's endless service is a rip-off. "People do have a responsibility for the way they love," O'Rourke pronounces. But at the very moment I am being excused I see my own cheapness in what I let myself take from Vita's prodigality. Another kind of thief.

"All part of the old habit," O'Rourke pounces on roles and lights the grill, its gas shrieking for our steak. "All women do it. You should see Wanda turning me into her pair of pants, crying great tears up in my office. I said look dammit, here's a check for that ticket. Go." O'Rourke's rings snap their fingers over the stove, cooking as hotly as she talks. "One bloody instant later I'm a man." Nell stands fast, looking her outrage, the green eyes wide open. Marches to the window box, smacks off a dead geranium, grabs the cream from the icebox, turns the steak. "Who wants to be a friggin' man?"

I lift a potato, checking on its progress, wondering as always if I am going forward or backward. "Nell, I'm afraid I'm not political enough." The Left accusing in my head—just a silly broad, no notion what she thinks she means. Politics is real—hardness, money, power, kill, guns, death. A man's world, don't even want it. But supposed to, supposed to be athirst for power, take over and shove utopia down everyone's throat, then you're a radical. "My book's got no politics, Nell, can't be serious, merely personal. Sniffs of the confessional." "A whiny form," she says, rolling out the whisperbox. "Daddy I'm a bad one. That will be five Hail Marys my daughter." We are hilarious intoning in unison skating on the mnemonic till we both get stuck at Blessed is the fruit of they womb—Jesus! And of course it's Winnie raising hell in the basement.

Letty flowerchild emerges from her den below stairs, rattles about the kitchen making her dinner. She takes a look at ours: "I can't believe it, the two of you really do eat potatoes." We are a freak show, half drunk and putting on the brogue. Letty reminds me today is the Fourth of July. This very night on Claire's street the whole Lower East Side erupts in an immigrant din of patriotism, Puerto Rican and Chinese ending a three-week crisis of firecracker. And the Angels in leather lurk in pinched white faces on the pavement flicking their whips

at the ankles of passersby. Forbear, Satan, do not touch
that puff of yellow hair floating through chaos like a
dandelion top blown in the wind. Why do I never mention Claire to Nell? My secret. Final vulnerability even
here. And closer to O'Rourke than anytime this high
feast of Independence, three bottles of wine between us
and a rapport so fantastic I think we are two sides of
Plato's tennis ball. Still there is a difference. Good fences?
No, a line between us invisible as experience.

O'Rourke reads me Mossman's note again. *I don't
know what it is but I can't stand it any longer.* Then
his suicide. Mossman of the BBC, all the hot spots of
the world he saw, crime, flood, agony. Vietnam too. And
honest. So they put him into the art department. But
he would still go for his man in an interview. Used the
program to get the big shots. Culture is safe but Nell's
pal Mossman wouldn't let it be. And going mad with
all he'd known and dying didn't know what to call it.
The London *Times* called him a homosexual in its
obituary. Setting a precedent of certain dubious value.
"Suffering is a heightened form of reality," O'Rourke
says, Badger on her lap. An old woman of Ireland, her
eyes keen over his lazy blink, a hand on his sensual purr.
I wonder if I had what Mossman had, and have lost it
by staying alive, getting well. Knowing I would rather
live without the panic whatever it may contribute, the
terrible energy of nausea, but is that missing the point—if
it goes, what have I left?—mediocre gray everyday cereal-
colored bland pointless. Or is there something washed
ashore, something never lost because you've been there
and come back?

Paul bursts in with TV news. Enticing us toward a
late movie. We don't budge. And he won't join us,
wishing so that he would, big shape of his back going
out the door, rejecting us. Stubborn. Back to his soccer
on the other channel. Finally I have to tell her. She has
known all along but I have to put it on the table next
to the remnants of the feast, breadcrumbs and chilling
steak juice oiled over going lard at the surface. What
after all, what if I were a viper in their midst? "You

and Paul are in my book. The rule is that it's a record.
Everything that happens to me. So you have to be in
it. But what will you say when you read it?" Will I lose
my friends by putting them in a book? Or just say nice
things? Simplify. Distort. Hoke it up. Make a valentine.
And loving my friends, how easy I would be to subvert.
I wait for her verdict, aquiver with dread and indecision,
squirming again while she grows vehement, the green
eyes aboil at the changeling in me. "Write that book for
yourself!" She says it hard. "Your truth. Not theirs."
"But they haven't written a book," I parry, "so they
have less recourse." "Their problem entirely," she says.
"Write it and send it to them, give them the option of
changing their names, tell them it's the thing as you knew
it, subjective, your experience not theirs. You can't start
making adjustments, rewriting, patching over, taking
orders, doing things their way or you'll never stop."

Write the book for yourself: she is an oracle intoning
it. "Look, who else would I be doing it for?" "No, for
yourself, not the movement. Any movement. Politics is
not about people at all. You saw that movie guerrilla,
didn't you? He's past caring about mere people. There
are only his kind and the enemy now. And the political
line is a kind of gun among all your little urban Leftist
intellectuals exchanging jargon like trading cards. If you
came out at Columbia they don't care about your mother!
They use you. Naturally. Since they need to use someone.
You're a factor only. An object, a pawn. Politics requires
that someone be used. And you're handy. That's how
it goes. Do you think Ethel can worry about Caroline
Hunter's mother? If Caroline's old lady had a stroke
yesterday antiapartheid would only have been out a
speaker. Speakers are what they need. That's politics."

The guru is high in her now. She pauses, about to
deliver a big one. "I'll tell you something more revolutionary than politics, more radical than the Left
Support. Just that, support. Sounds dotty, doesn't it?
Silly, very apolitical, but it's the biggest change I can
think of . . . giving another person total support. Never
balking, just hanging in, believing in them while they

get it together. The most you can offer another human
being. It changes things from the very bottom. More
productive than criticism because it demands something
finer. Damn rare thing these days, all this raving talk,
rhetoric thing and the other, but who comes through?"
I remember Celia's sentence that it's by what people do
that you know them. Acts rather than intentions. "We
have scads of people so interested in the patterning, lovely
idea, fine thing to do they say. And come along once.
Next time they find they just can't make it."

Late now, we ought to stop talking but we can't. Have
to remember New York; me the Bowery, Nell the early
years she lived in my city. "Slept in the window open,
how did I know everyone in the bloody place was a
rapist?" Her production of *Electra* for the ballet. Stolen
now and billed to another name, playing this week in
London. Always the tears in her eyes when she talks of
this time, her big break, huge multimedia project: film,
dancers, lights, sets, a big budget. Then the baby born,
Winnie, and when things went wrong she had to come
back to London where the world shut down on her. An
old woman of sorrows now by the sink saying she wants
to die. Her spirit broken like that day when Norman
got the job to go to Afghanistan to do that documentary
on the harem. Producer promised it to her then gave it
to Norman, very guy she'd trained and taught herself.
I sat by helpless, tears inside me to see her giving up.
She sniffs and curses. "You'll be shooting again soon,
you could start right after the next commercial." "No,
I must write first." Together we consider the problem.

And Paul bursts in, afire in a red bathrobe at both
of us, bellowing Bluebeard, "Just 'cause your boozing
buddy is here from New York, do you have to stay up
all night?" Arbitrary. Out of nowhere. Pure unconscious
without forewarning. Jealous. Of rapport. Threatened.
Fumio too, not sex but alienation of affection was what
he feared. But then it was of women who were lovers.
And Paul knows our lovemaking is our talk. Feels it,
though he would die maybe before he'd say it. Or kill.
Instead of mayhem we are sent to bed like two naughty

girls. At one-ten, really not that late. Trudging up the stairs behind him like whipped children I wonder why it did not occur to us to protest. Why not just say fuck off or join us, we happen to be enjoying ourselves? Grumbling at him, like a mean big brother, a bullying old man, some gigantic irascible father. Does he think I'm trying to put the make on his wife? Great prior claims of heterosexuality; always the man comes before the woman friend. And the two of us battered Irish kids still putting up with it. Contemptible, the lot of us.

Upstairs I rattle about in my room. Defiant bringing up another drink. Boozing buddy indeed. But of course he's right and we are a mess, all the words of my sibyl spilled upon a kitchen's stale air dead upon the morning. Wasted, never caught on paper, tape, or film. And will she go on forever with no outlet but a wine glass and the ephemera of talk? All I can give her so far is the ear to talk into. I must do better. Solve the dilemma, find people to pattern. Free her to work. Really so hard to help people, whatever you do is a little wrong somewhere. Paul has behaved like an ass. Probably fair enough to admit it sometime. Few people in the world have his absolute integrity. Loving the man, his displeasure is a blow. I am not doing too well in London. Should I just clear out? Or gamble on getting people to pattern, volunteers, recruits, blow the works, hustle everywhere in London? Gamble.

Ursula is sick. Didn't come. Today Nell stayed home from the office. We take turns with Winnie. But it's an all-day thing now, not just the four hours of pattern. I was supposed to work. Copy Chapter One on the dining room table, Selby Avenue, childhood place to study, child of the house. Child is more innocent than rival, Paul. But no such luck, there is Winnie who is a child who is not a child. Not yet. Instead he is a tyrannical force in the basement. Dominating every moment. I putter about in my mind: I am a woman. I have a child now. Therefore I am a woman. Standard definition. Begin to get a notion of what it's like, being a woman. There is no time. You cannot concentrate. You start things and stop.

We are all three caged in this house. I flew in, arriving solitary, free as a bird on my winds. And they talked to me, said they were trapped. And now it's all three of us, the rescuer too is stuck. My job was to dig them out. Preposterous meddling. Marriage is sacred. I feel its sacredness. Come off it, they aren't even married. Never mind, they are a "couple," same thing. And we are caring for a child, a noble occupation. You sound like a brochure in honor of the nuclear family. What else are you going to do with children? Leave them outdoors? There is no other way finally to take care of Winnie—just us, the only ones around who happen to be interested. And I'm a visitor, can just pop back to the U.S.A. when the mood strikes me. Ultimately, when push comes to shove, it's just them. Suddenly I remember—yesterday was Sunday. Paul was supposed to go to Cheltenham for a solution. Didn't go. The phone rings next to me. It is Paul, calling from the office. Very cheery voice. His stomach is bad. Ask him about Cheltenham, go on ask him. He is exquisitely nonchalant: "Couldn't get through on Friday. Something wrong with the lines down there." I forgive him, contrite, offer to make him my newly invented scrambled egg with heavy cream. "You know I never eat in the evening, darling. But what shall I bring the two of you?" Paul is incorrigible. And we are all so civilized, so considerate, such good friends. Meanwhile, nothing whatsoever is settled. Our deliberate and manicured irresponsibility is criminal. We are all completely unreal. And I am now infected by them, not only condone but contribute. They are defeating me.

All right, take another task, attend to your own problems. Try to book a screening and show you film to the movement here before you go home. A secretary snaps that Crown is booked until the fifteenth. My plane leaves morning of the same day. Postpone the flight? But Celia goes into The Mercy Hospital the sixteenth. Would they even let me get near her? "Irregular," the nurse will sniff, a scandalous relationship. And her parents will be there. Naturally they'll prevent me. Couldn't make it in time, won't land at Kennedy till nightfall. Always the movie versus Celia. What I really want is to see her before she goes in, alive and whole. No way. "Wait till she's mended a few days. Send flowers. Ring her up in New York day before the operation," Nell advises. Yes, call transatlantic like a kiss for luck, energy, strength to live. Would she let herself die? So near it the last time. Feel the sidewalk and the dark in New York, the Soho lofts, her friends in the car restless. Observed in the headlights. I didn't tell her. Proud, stubborn, afraid to say it. The last time I saw her. And dreading here in London that it might be.

Then with Nell to the basement and Winnie. The masks to strengthen his breathing, the gags to teach him reflexes, the noise on the tape to help him hear. We wake him from a nap in order to watch him struggle in plastic, all three of us hating it. When the pattern is over it is my turn at sentinel. Winnie's having a fit. I must pay attention to him. He bangs his big head into my face. So that I will stop writing he has cut my mouth. When I do he ignores me to play idiot with his birthday card. The stare. When I start again he screams and throws himself on the floor. Bangs his head. Needs all my attention so that he can discard it the moment he's grabbed me. I stop. Put the notebook down. Defeated by Winnie the determined analphabet and philistine. At this moment I hate him. The noise machine plays its own mindless Stockhausen in the background. This room is a nightmare. I give up all hope of writing and Winnie plays quietly with his toys.

Nell's turn at guard. I attend to reality via the telephone. Setting up a screening at the Regency Grand. The secretary assures me it has "the finest acoustical equipment in London." Could she possibly have listened to it? Downstairs in her office with the fact of that hideous sound projection safely removed. Even I know it's terrible. Nell has tipped me off. Everyone agrees, all of the London film world laments the Regency Grand. But there is no option, the Paris Pullman's booked, and that

place in Kentish Town we could get for free is too far
for people to travel. The screening is a present for the
London women. Will cost money that the movie can't
really afford. Already I doubt if I can pay my bills. But
I love presents. And why should they pay? My sisters.
A night screening on projectionists' overtime is more
accessible for the mothers and working women. That
lovely Irish girl at the Women's Center, Una, said they'd
take up a collection. Nell said no. Stick by making it
free. The Irish become grander as they go broke.

Now hustle for Nell. Explain to Una about Winnie.
The patterning. Put everything into it, talk as hard as
you can. We need volunteers. Una is receptive. I zero
in on the satisfactions of creating a child, watching intelligence form where there had been no possibility of
it so long. Una will write a blurb in the newsletter. Interested in this stuff herself, has read a book on brain-
damaged children. It is like grace to find someone who
cares, who won't come down hard and righteous, lecture
me that our women have problems of their own, etc.,
with child care so inadequate how could they help an
individual? All true of course, but so without mercy.

Nell hangs fire in the kitchen while I make my pitch.
Afraid to ask them all these months. What is her im-
possibility I do in high gear. It is always easier to ask
for others. My scheme is taking shape: first the plug in
the newsletter, then I'll go to the Women's Center, plead
in person for volunteers. Put all my credit on the line,
be eloquent, bet everything I can scrape together to get
this set up while I'm here. And there are so few days.
My film is already in the lab. What if it's not done in
time? Daily confab with Jim Hutton, kindly paternal figure in charge of my grading. Gives off the reliable feeling
of a family dentist but doubts it can be printed on time.
Extend the plane ticket? Impossible, there is Celia on
the sixteenth. Even if you don't see her, it is keeping
faith with an idea. Risk it. Then back again to Winnie.

Nell comes down to join me. We light cigarettes. "Very
hard not to hit him," I tell her. "Damn right, especially
if you're Irish." Both our childhoods are in this, our

hatred of violence and its habituation, our bitter rage for gentleness pitted against the long haul with Winnie. In a glance we exchange our exhaustion in today's despairing tedium. "Such a great cause to think about, such a damned bore to live." Nell collapses on the floor stubbing out her cigarette, "I pulled his hair today. Just did it. He was pounding his head on the floor and I had to stop him." It is painful to listen to her. "Pulled his head back by the hair. We've never struck him, but it helped when I learned to yell back." We look at each other. Demoralized.

End of a long day. We drink wine in the garden, two tired commandos. Paul comes home. "I've scored," his voice that rare gleeful conspiratorial flavor I have heard only once before. That day he got a military print for a fraction of its value on the Portobello Road. Actually walked us all to a pub and bought us drinks. Repeating over and over that he was "chuffed, terribly chuffed, chap didn't know what he was selling." And again today, his moustache in a grin, unwrapping china from newspapers. Nell calculates them with the eye of one paying cash. She made only two commercials while I was gone. Paul crows over "a remarkably beautiful stipple in the glaze." Finds a star mark on the back of a platter and runs upstairs to check the pieces against his books. I go inside in search of privacy to curse his damned blue and white. Standing at the dining room table making note of my irritation in Blick.

Paul comes into the kitchen next door to fetch something. Sees me writing, pinned over my malediction. I am caught in the act as he leans in the door. "What are you doing?" "Just making a note," I tell him, rattled, but at least not lying. Terrified before the judge in his eye but neither closing the book nor stopping. Paul goes away. I have leisure to repent. I am a traitor. Here I am in the man's own house criticizing him for extravagance. This is ridiculous, I am taking sides. What if he was wasting her money? Paul is an expert on china. Someone is asking him to collaborate on a definitive

work. Maybe he'll end up getting that series of art film
for Christie's. They are dickering now. All up in the air.
Like Steven Runciman. Like Nell's brainstorm scenarios.
Remember you are here to help and not to judge.

At dinner we play. I demonstrate my eggs. Paul unbends
and informs me that he is actually St. Francis and has
eaten the eggs so that I would feel an "inner peace."
I find Paul's pronunication of the phrase irresistible.
He is a genius at poker-faced parody, and the ultimate
mark of his art is that he permits himself a margin to be
serious, deriving the full benefit of a phrase both in the
light of its thesis and antithesis. Sarah stops by and gives
us an account of the new sex shop in Tottenham Court
Road. "Lovecraft, it's called. Whole atmosphere flaw-
lessly antiseptic. Everything in its plastic wrapper. Lots
of items, each item overdisplayed so you'll feel easy
in your mind. Buy one, there are so many, there'll be
plenty left. One whole wall is Tampax. There it is,
revealed as if it were an exotic. Large stock of dildoes.
Variety of colors, mostly red, rubber blood dripping off
certain ones. Bumps on others. Even hooks. Thoroughly
repellent idea if you consider how uncomfortable they'd
be." Objects for men to buy imagining dykes buy them,
I think, as Sarah hastens on to the pièce de résistance.
"You must listen to this, they had an electric vagina—for
the single man." Paul promises to write a polemic on
the myth of the electric vagina and become famous.
Nell decides to go into business and market the item as
a glove puppet. We contemplate visions of flying electric
vaginas and compose short stories of men eaten alive
by them. Sarah lends me her pen to keep track of our
titles. *My Night with the Dentist. The Solitary's Companion,* etc. I am bold and obvious about Blick, I will not
hide my crucible. Paul can watch me stoking it in ink
at the kitchen table right before his eyes. No, I do not
want to "roast" you, Paul, your delightful wit bestirring
yourself to entertain us as we go from one wave of
laughter to the next, enjoying the miracle of being silly.
It is a rare occasion, Paul will even go out with us.

Fine evening for a stroll and a visit to the pub. In Paul's company the neighborhood is transformed into a nest of antique stores and houses up for sale, a series of lovely Georgian squares. But when we get to the pub he refuses to enter, loathes pubs, will not join us. Prefers to walk around by himself. We are three ladies lined up along the bar under the smart Gay Nineties decor. Nell takes charge and beguiles the bartender into making us some terrible thing she has recommended, looks like a fruit salad. Waiting for our drinks we titter, feeling girlish, doing something extraordinary, going out on the town for an hour. But at our table outside we grow moody watching the evening. Dampened by Paul's absence. I look up from under the table's umbrella at an old Victorian brick wall and see a window open into someone else's life. A figure comes to the opening. Looks out. I set about inventing nostalgia, history, motives, everything for this stranger in an undershirt. Feeling London outside the tight house in Islington. Every now and then Paul comes into view and disappears in the foreground of our vision, looking urbane and unruffled as we catch a fleeting sight of him winding in and out of shops, strolling with a cigar in the evening, at regular intervals emerging from one or another of the lanes spread out around the pub. Nell praises him. We admire. A figure handsome and determinedly alone in the twilight. Stubbornly aloof. Withholding himself while his shadow beckons around corners and up streets. And finally circles toward us to say only that he's going home. There's rugby on the telly. Sarah must study. Nell and I will have another drink at the King's Head. We walk back with Sarah. Nell walks with her hands in her jeans pockets as if it's fun to be out of the house. A man whistles at me. We laugh, I tell him he has just made me feel permanently young and even beautiful. Then I thought I heard O'Rourke say yes and so you are. Curious remark. Curious too how boyish Nell feels beside me in her denim outfit. At this moment one could imagine her single, even something outrageous like Lesbian. Imagine it as easily of her as of me. More so. See how she stretches out her legs when she walks. See how she seems to take charge and escort the two of us. Sarah says good-bye. We sashay on for the King's Head, Nell's long dungaree strides fancy free. It is good for her to be away from Winnie and the responsibility. Late and extravagant as it is, this will be a spot of cheer at the end of a long dull day.

But it is no good when we get there. Nell waits impatiently for me to finish my Scotch. We walk home, boring ourselves with an earnest discussion inspired by the London Council health poster abjuring all to avoid venereal disease. When we get to our door some kids running by make a crack. I couldn't hear it but Nell took it to be a dig at her age. She is crestfallen. I am sorry we ever tried the experiment of going out independently. In the King's Head, surrounded by arty bar pictures of New York prizefighters and theater queens, I was uneasy lest the people spot me for an outlaw. It would reflect on her. We cannot go out alone.

They do the first pattern without waking me. Paul's kindness with coffee, instant with plenty of milk, coming in each day at eight to murmur, "Good morning, lovely," his soft voice so gentle under the moustache while I sit up and he hands it to me in bed. "You and Nell do the next two patterns. I'm for the office." Nell and I stay home to cope. Ursula has called in the news that she'll be sick all week. Collapsed at the end of Winnie's tether with a serious infection. Between patterns we have another cup in the kitchen. Nell tells about shooting the Durham Gala, its crowds of miners from all over England ". . . come in wagons even. Four days of music and all those batty dances you never heard of. The great event of their lives." The time she made the trip to the North and Yorkshire. "People up there are alive, a different kind of English, older, harder. Work like slaves in those mines, but they know how to play." She passes on to the boy from the North Country who stopped by the night she was sick. "Didn't know he was there. Paul should have told me. I would have gotten up." Regret in her voice and nostalgia. How can I focus her attention on the real problem? Indulging her because she needs it, impossible to refuse that need. But there is the problem of Winnie, of Paul's imminent defection, and maybe bankruptcy ahead. Dressed to the nines, looking like a trendy pimp in a striped shirt and white tie, Paul has gone to the banker today to beg for more time. And now Nell is dragging me upstairs to hear this singer lad's record. We grin at each other over the words, song of a man got him a wife she's the bane of his life. And dumb enough to get another, minute she dies. The refrain gets us both—O I wish I was single again. Laughing in guilty complicity, making his bitterness our own. I feel the lure of him this red-haired footloose boy who has come around beckoning her to Durham. And this weekend the Gala again. Nell in her predicament, the fast eyes going everywhere. "Could get a crew together, do it again. Must be why he stopped by." We are late to pattern the third time.

Paul is home at noon. Vomiting. I watch him while we watch Winnie. I want to tell him what I think it means, the vomiting, what I remember of it. But he insists it's his ulcer and refuses to admit it's in any sense psychological. I venture toward the women's workshop. My hopes for volunteers. I watch his suffering, suffering to watch. Surrounded by his pain. He hardly listens. I cannot help because he refuses help. Renders me impotent. Does not even wish me to see. So I leave. It is his afternoon on duty.

Nell and I forgather in the kitchen. "To hell with guilt. Instead of being tortured by things, do them. I made *Bea* for myself. When I was finished I took to bed. Had nothing to hide behind any more. Up till then I could hide behind modern art or the Ku Klux Klan. But not with that film. Don't you see, I'm Bea. My crew said I was a sick chick. It was an honest film. Banal too. Don't leave out the banal. Life is not heroical."

Launched now, she's telling me, the green eyes maniacal with force, "They have taken our anger from us, it's the biggest crime perpetrated against women. Got in touch with mine through that group therapy business.

Men and women behave differently in group therapy, you know. Men discover their fear. Women their hostility. Paul was physically attacked in the first group we joined. Look, learn to get angry, stop being humble and calling yourself queer. There are dead people shouting inside you. You have got to shut up your mother. There she is, quivering away inside you, screeching at you." I hear her voice on the phone, hear her voice at thirteen. "The family is a dead area inside our skulls," O'Rourke resumes. "Drop your endless capacity for punishment. Let yourself. Do. They cannot punish you, the voices inside. Stifle them."

We have planned a lunch at the King's Head, where there's to be a matinee. I get the drinks from the bar while Nell fights for table and chairs. Seated we must then fend off the amorous attention of two seedy toffs equipped with working-class accents known to be irresistible to peculiar dames like these. They linger on the edges of our conversation, itself a remarkable cacophony of "I want to shoot you." "No, I want to shoot you." "When you get to America." All this time O'Rourke has been insisting that she's coming to New York next week to renew her work permit. Can't believe she'll ever escape. "Really ought to shoot you here." "We could shoot each other."

Taking wing into a scatter shot of movie notions, ways to capture the living present. Preserve the life we know, reinterpret, present in our own terms as women. "I'm so tired of the old one-dimensional notions of things, the media, even the square historians, they catch nothing at all. Once I saw an old photograph, early feminists, looked like a tribal dinner, each one of them grim as hell. I know they weren't like that." "Of course not, must have been real people, sense of humor, complete, equipped with fire, imagination, some spark, dammit." "If we go down that way, just boring stuff for librarians, I'll choke."

We bounce back to our men. Agreeing we need opposites. Paul's taciturnity the very antidote to big hat now all high and hoarse making Irish grand schemes on second martini. Then she remembers I could do the two of them a "massive service" if I brought Paul some of that chocolate cake from Harrods—"It's the only thing he can bear in this condition." I remember Fumio's solitude at the farm: "What's fine about him is that he's always real, even when I'm not. And he stays with me times no one else can. How do you ever leave someone like that?" "You don't." "So I'm not going to." "Look, you should rent your place in New York," O'Rourke says, suddenly practical, "you are spending too much money." "No, I need the Bowery to write. I need the city too. And the women I love are there. I have two lives. One in each place. But how do you lead two lives in a society that is not so keen on your having even one? Either one." The strain of being what I am gets to me in the middle of a London pub lunch, salad unspeakable hamburger nothing else on the menu, din of glasses, talk, pictures on the walls of old places in my own town. And its fallen heroes. O'Rourke and I are only hot air. Surprised by terror in the midst of our giddiest movie talk, "One more martini," she says while I cast a wary eye toward the reality principle and the clock. She must not miss the bank.

Running toward it, trying to keep up with her long legs, both of us shouting opinions of Bergman full tilt along Upper Street until we are safe in the arms of Barclay. Cashing checks before the old-fashioned window, little bell on the side to summon three-piece suit if he malingers over pointless papers, a young man his whole day's summer lost in this morgue.

Then out into the rush of afternoon, Nell to her errands, I to the top of the 73 bus, where you can smoke and see Dickens's London at King's Cross, the vast pile of old brick appearing to be the biggest building in the world. There is *Time Out*'s store front. Get off and file an ad? Or stay on to Liberty's? I get off. Mind the stove and be sure that screening notice is in. Off again at Regent's Street, having to ask the newsvendors which way is Liberty's. Feeling a tourist for not having been here since Oxford times. Even the summer I was a kid

from St. Paul waitressing in Glacier Park we went over
the Canadian line to buy Liberty scarves. Dreaming of
Banff at Calgary in time for the rodeo and hitching rides
with Indians in battered trucks. It is Nell's idea to get
fabric for a dress in their fine strong upholstery cotton.
I survey them, bolt upon bolt of William Morris patterns.
Makes me a Victorian scholar again just to look. I want
to buy them all, the pink, this green one. And the blue
one too. Delicious black flowers in that one. Eyes greedy
for hundreds I settle for five. More than I'd meant to.
While the one man, a West Indian, measures and cuts,
and the other, the Englishman, remains staid in the face
of my elation, the three of us thoroughly aware that this
is eighty bucks she shouldn't spend. But how irresistible
is everything here, finding two more splendid pieces of
cloth on sale. No, stop here. I write the check, vibrating
with excitement. How grand they'll look, sweeping to
the floor these five new dresses. Last me the rest of my
life. Already I'm late, clinging to my instructions for
the dressmaker's. I exit carrying two big bundles, my
treasure. It is closing time at Liberty's. And I am a lady.
Elevator man all smiles. Inside Liberty's elevator it smells
like lemon soap and leather. The Yardley's we used to
buy. Or English lavender. All utterly comforting feminine
things, snug as a fur coat. High on the bourgeois mystique
as we drop gently floor by floor. Elevator and I infatuated
with each other and with all the ladies who step on at
the intervening floors. Till I am deposited, no longer the
apple of every eye, but only a foreigner with something
like twenty pounds of fabric to carry.

In the morning Nell has a hangover. Last night in my
yellow bed I was lonely for everyone. Spent the evening
with American crony carousing in a little passageway
off St. Martin's Lane, then a women's meeting where I
could find no volunteers. My prospects as an organizer
dimming. Perhaps a mistake to be here at all. Got up
and called Fumio. Frieda is at the farm. It is such a relief
that he has her back, hurting so long in his stoic gloomy
way from that rejection. I feel a ton of guilt removed.

I do not sin against him loving others if he loves another too and is loved. Then it's fair. Otherwise it's not fair. Then the vague stirring of annoyance that he did not tell me at once she was there. Hedged. How sad if he is afraid of me. Perhaps his secretive self moves slowly. Clearly time to leave him alone for a while.

Going back to bed a moment's terror that some chick's going to rack him up someday, steal him into marriage, discover he's the most charming man in the world and imprison him in a cupboard. Want to own him. So there will be no Fumio left for me. Relax and remember this hardly gives him credit for much deciding on his own. Still lonely so I did the ultimate and wrote letters. One to Celia just too admit the love I wouldn't say before, repaired now in the thin blue paper of an air letter. Do not place any other object inside, it warns.

And this morning O'Rourke cannot stir from her bed. Paul is her cavalier servant, a lover with a tray. I am Cinderella in the basement with the dynamo. I sit on the floor with Winnie. He throws my glasses away again right across the carpet. Head bent over his red train. Whistling his idiot whistle. Regressing. Now he giggles in the crawl box and won't move when we try to shove him down it. This is better than the screaming rage when he refuses to move altogether, beating his head against the sides. But it is not progress. Paul is desperate. I'm afraid he'll hurt him. The big arms hanging on to patience. Breathing hard behind his moustache. Letty croons American optimism at the end of the chute: "C'mon, Winnie." The crawl box lined with its ironic Morris-patterned contact, the grace of hope. Paul comes down from the kitchen, bringing the cocoa made for his stomach and the Mariners ashtray. The Mariners ashtray is not art nouveau. It is the only vulgarity in the house except Winnie's toys. I love it, flicking an ash in the purest affection. And look at Paul. It is insoluble. Winnie makes it insoluble. I want to hug Paul, but he is immovable. Hanging in. Beyond comfort. When he woke me this morning I tried to cheer him with Una's optimism and the volunteers we expect from the newsletter. "We'll get them." "Fantastic," he says. His voice friendly but not fantastic at all. "I am counting on it." But Paul will not count on things. We are not sure when Ursula will come back, if ever. "We'll get through it," I say to Paul. No idea how. Sound like an idiot. And his sense of irony defeats me. I want to ask what the two of them plan to do. They probably don't know either. See it through? Split? Give up the noble experiment to a foster home? Paul said the only hope was in some form of separation. Nell sat in the garden describing the new floor they would add at the top of the house. Telling Hedda. What on earth is she talking about? Paul is planning to leave her. And he never bothered to go to Cheltenham. What is he doing? When am I supposed to believe them?

I tell Paul the story I heard yesterday, nasty crack at Fumio in the *Village Voice,* called him a "visa fetishist," implication that only sorriest need could make anybody love that dyke. He is not interested. Has no comfort to give. Why extend sympathy when he gives none himself? He finishes making Nell's breakfast. The hangover. I am to bring it up. Paul seems to think I do not understand how to make instant coffee. After so many thousand cups I should have lost the knack? "How can we work it out so that she gets to the office and you do too?" "Never mind," he grunts and starts down the stairs to Winnie. "Paul, you are not using me, you are wasting my time." "Well never mind," he says. Man, you are so fucking stubborn, I howl silently at his back. Desperate beleaguered Paul running about his house. Unable. And still having to.

She is in the new brown sheets. Wild flowers on the pillow cases. Same ones we have on the Bowery, Fumio's favorites. Nell reclines luxuriously. Movie queen in black negligee. "I'm still feeling fragile." I decide they are both impossible. And the downstairs bathtub is free. I will take a bath. Stepping into the water I congratulate myself upon my maturity. This morning I told Nell about Fumio and Frieda. She thought it a good thing. So do I. Happy for him in my bath. Told Paul and he looked at me like I was mad. Why shouldn't Fumio be happy in upstate

New York? Why shouldn't he make love to someone? I'm in London sleeping alone, can hardly lay interdict on his penis three thousand miles away insisting I own it to transport via transatlantic liner crated in dry ice. It is some satisfaction to know that one of us is knowing the joys of life at this moment. Fumio's my best friend, I wish him well, sudsing up.

In miraculous recovery from her hangover Nell shouts that she needs nappies. I bring them up. Washing out the preliminary shit I gag. Not cut out for motherhood. Who is? We leave the diapers in the kitchen sink. On the stairs she tells me about her party last night. Went out. Paul wouldn't go. When she got home she read McLuhan. We drop everything to sit down on the staircase and do McLuhan. We are two friends in college. Girls reading books feeling like intellectuals. I must try for more volunteers on the phone, line up meetings. "For an academic you have the mind of a grasshopper," she says. "All part of the housewife's syndrome," I tell her, rushing down a flight of carpet, eager to save the ship.

When I get off she is sitting on a chair in the kitchen. Paul standing protectively before her. They are lining up her crew for the commerical on Tuesday. Everything is fine again. How charming to live with such volatile people. Suddenly they are efficient and thriving, but I am not getting Chapter One copied out for typing at the dining room table. I am not writing the part about New York before I came to London either. Want to do the whole book at once. So far it is just a draft for a first section that is too long. My shame already at being verbose, unorthodox. When will it ever get done in the press of living it? And how to remember it all? Every conversation of the high Irish talkers. Impossible. Well, I am spitting out the ordinary here and now at least, doubting why I write but taking notes in Blick anyway. What is England about? I cannot seize it. No longer a mere interruption, but what else beyond that?

Behind me Nell is laughing into the phone, telling it she has "the Piscean migraine and a touch of the Irish death." Ridiculing her last commerical, singing the jingle.

"Did they cut the fucking jingle into the front?" She is talking to Angus. She calls him "treasure." Form of address she adopts when she needs a favor. So phony at moments like this and so impossible to resist. We confer again around the table. Paul changes the subject, becomes an expert on films. Puts down someone's movie. Nell objects. Guy who made it's a friend of hers. They glare at each other. Paul threatens to leave but has no money. "Well piss off," she says all green-eyed rage, her voice harsh and broken at the edges. He goes down to Winnie. "Having a little trouble today," Nell admits nervously. "Bad day for a Leo. He'll come off it." I listen, wishing I were in Italy, New York, Afghanistan, even St. Paul. Or had the problem solved. Rescued finally by the breakfast dishes. Here at last is meaningful work.

Nell is on the phone hiring a nanny. Calling agencies. I wash dishes wondering why a Ph.D. is automatically considered too stupid to put marks on a card numbering Winnie's masks, gags, patterns, etc. Nell emerges from a conversation with a "certified moron in a phone booth" who has just stated categorically she's got no taste for defective children but needs the cash. I point out my qualifications. It would also save money. "No, we need a slave." I argue weakly there must be another way than slavery. And count the meetings I've lined up.

Nell has brought Winnie into the garden, little white sailor hat in the sun, splashing water in a big bowl, colored plastic toys float in it red and green. He looks like a real little boy. Happy. If the sun shone often this wouldn't be England. Winnie gurgles delighted outside the window. We are doing swimmingly. Paul pops in to announce for the thousandth time that he's the only one who is competent, the only one who knows the pattern. I lose patience: Keep on like that baby and you'll be so isolated you'll be right. Then I return to my neutrality, my role as a breakwater between two fiercely opposing currents. Of course they are both right. Nell is right giving Winnie a day in the sun. Paul is right brooding away on his timetables. His accuracy. Finally he is the only hope of scientific method that we have in this ménage.

When I have at last settled down to work in the dining room Nell appears to show me how they taught her to curtsy in convent school. I relinquish all hope of industry and enjoy her. We have the same childhood. In different editions. Nell a scholarship girl among stout tradespeople on the rise, "your promising dry goods family, and me in the same gray dress all year." We linger over our nuns. Favorite and most detested. We laugh and remember persons from our long-ago times named Sister St. Agnes, Sister Mary Theresa, Sister Margaret. And a Sister St. Edmond who taught me books, heavy stuff like Byron and Hardy, notorious, proscribed.

I will compose a list for Una. Carefully drawing charts on lined papers. All the present volunteers are listed, just a handful of names scattered across the huge blank hours that have yet to be filled. By the new candidates. Greedy, I even want a roster of extras. Ursula will become a bureaucrat, we'll install a phone in the basement, she need not even pattern any more, just stay on top of things, call everyone up and check them each day with a list of replacements for all emergencies. Pare her job down to human size so she won't get sick any more. Nell and Paul will go to the office and only see Winnie after working hours. During leisure time when they are fresh just to play with him. The exercises are done best by persons less involved, I have already seen that demonstrated. My battery of papers is arranged and in hand. Neatly laid out on ruled paper, a miracle of efficiency. I am off to the London Gay Liberation Front where for some reason or another Una wants to meet me to get the list. I make one last trip to the garden. "Wish me luck." Paul is a cigar glow of contentment. Sir Steven Runciman said yes.

Out of the black cave of a cab. Gay driver, but careful to betray no connection with this meeting. We are all secret agents. Not giving signals. Or only the most inconspicuous and ephemeral ones. The surface of London is composed again, placid a second after the question is asked. A man on the street motions that way. A sign says Middle Earth. I must go down a hole like Alice. Two girls ahead of me. They are English Lesbians—I have finally seen not one but two. They exist. No. They do not exist because the pair walk on and do not enter. Long dark corridor. Desk at the end. Here is a flyer for a demonstration at a park. Timidly ask the date. In a surreal gesture faceless man at the desk consults his watch. It knows the date.

Large circular room like in hell. And I am the only woman. Everyone huddles in groups. Talking. Know each other. I cannot huddle with them. How to pretend I am in any way different from the two guys leaning against the wall ten feet apart, also wallflowers? My sandal breaks. I repair it the usual makeshift way by grinding in a thumbtack. Fine show of nonchalance.

Write down my impressions on the back of the flyer, using steel pillar for a desk. If I am busy writing I will not look conspicious. Arm is tiring. What gimmick can I think up next to consume the time? Pillar has knobs. A T-beam. Rusty. Infernal. Frightening as the subway. Why am I afraid of underground places. Of basements?

How can I meet Una if there are no other women? Of course she must be straight and will be here for "political reasons." I am the only Lesbian. The guys look trendy, mustaches like pirates. Like Paul. Imagine them looking so like Paul. But more slender. One woman does turn up. I gather hope. Turns out she's here for the BBC. Group on the floor near me are discussing the scene in New York. I could tell them. Bring news. But I can't break in. Fellow comes by and stares at my flyer. I let him read. Details of the demonstration printed on the front. Turns it over to read my handwriting. I ask to have it back. Receive it embarrassed. We smile, but he is suspicious.

A girl. Yes, there is actually a girl here, sitting on the floor. She complains they need a magazine. "Left with that rag *Lonely,* bloody rubbish it is." Needs someone to share a flat with. "No, we still see each other. Nearly every day. Couldn't work. We're too different." Her phrases linger like the aroma of failure, still see each other can't work nearly every day too different. Hundreds of sorrows, lives, mundane New York tragedies in the words. My own, Zooey's. Still see her. Not every day because that is too much agony. But sometimes. Didn't work—how many other people I love and have now will someday be the same tedious refrain? Winters. And lives drifting different directions. Is it only timing? Great loves melting into occasional dinners at apartment houses in February. Meeting once or twice in summers. Old age a graying head in the distance at an intersection, but forewarned you turn off and avoid the encounter.

And all the brave new chatter—liberation music laughter meetings marches shouts charges—but a thin veneer to hide our essential despair. Merely human, everyone has it. Do we have more of it or less? What matters is that our euphoria is a mask, our hope finally blindness. There is no beating life. Probably we are only tawdry. Not even scribbling now, standing by my pillar dazed to discover there is no freedom. When a guy asks me am I a member of the press. Suddenly ashamed of my pen. A double agent CIA traitor caught red-handed. Guilty as Judas over my squiggles. Paranoia lives.

Charles begins the meeting. Young man in Renaissance velvet floppy hat, lovely curls and mustache. We are another age in a timeless underground. New people are to leave for orientation. Subterranean passageways grottoes and catacombs, the Early Church where mere catechumens may not attend the rituals of the confirmed. I am new; here I am new. So I leave. Ego a bit crestfallen at being a freshman again. England does this for you. Neophyte shuffling up ramps and dark corridors to a room above and to the right. All men and me. Brazen it through and sit on the floor. Finally another woman enters. The room is red scarlet fire painted. Our teachers align themselves above us in leather pirate black hat elegance. One instructor looking nearly civilian. I await them with an interesting mixture of humility and old-hand hauteur. Let's see how they do their job. Very well in fact. Reasoned, low-key on the rhetoric, diplomatic about competitive organizations, competent on law and constitutional fronts, realistic about demonstrations, image, power. The boy next to me asks about parents. The answers are human, even psychological. But his worry is deeper, more horrible than their assurances. Insists his parents could not bear to know nor he to hurt them. The leaders pause. Come up with stupid suggestions, pay a visit and leave a copy of some beef tabloid behind, etc. Calling cards for the nefarious self. I have asked we be given women indoctrinators for the two of us who are women. Black she is, all energy, force, cannot catch her name. She leans forward and talks to the boy with a greater understanding, admits the difficulties, does not batter him with formulae. Two women by the sink prepare coffee unnoticed. The woman next to me begins a tirade against the psychologists. The leaders reply in confusion.

It is all a mistake, time is going by. Una must be at the other meeting. I must find her and give her the schedule. Get out of here before it's too late. This is all very interesting but it is not my job. If I could get to the black woman she might know Una. Atmosphere of stifling tension, conformity—to get up and leave would be committing a crime. How to cross the room and ask her help? Imprisoned by the situation, this will go on all night, never escape. Pushed enough now to get up. I ask her to give me a moment in the hall. Trembling with my need to explain it. Everything. Winnie a rush out of my mouth these people need help so badly and the program works. She is not white, not English, not afraid of emotion. And has two children of her own. Takes me to Charles. They are having announcements, I could ask if Una is here. Charles listens to a calmer version of my Winnie Nell and Paul. He'll let me call for volunteers.

Someone is describing a meeting of the clergy to discuss "homosexuality." Public debate at a cinema. Gay Lib had intended to pack it but word got out and the reverend Catholic father has withdrawn. "If we went in drag . . ." one laughs, meaning business suits. It is re-

solved somehow while I swallow in the terror that comes
before a speech. No one hears my first three sentences,
voice so small and everyone talking, till finally I am my
own anonymous American voice telling them I have
come to beg a favor. Some friends of mine need their
help. Frightened but knowing I must push hard, give
everything, they must be moved, must hear me, the program, the progress we've made—it has begun to work and
you can see the human being forming. We are creating
a child. But there are not enough of us and the work
is breaking us in pieces. Unless we have help. My voice
going on in the dark of the room across faces turned up
listening. Glare of some red exit lamp somewhere on
the edge of my eyes casting a glow into the shadows
while I try harder now they are listening, beg them to take
interest and care; here are people drowning. It would
not be empty for you. Our own ideas of community, that
children are everyone's responsibility and childless we
never see them. Here is one who needs, you can do more
for him than parenthood can, more then some child-
care center just talked about, some project from a vague
missionary distance. This is immediate.

Then I stop. Wondering. Till I see the slips of paper
coming up with addresses. More and then more, a fist-
ful. My treasure spilling out of my hand while they
crowd around asking for paper. Here's a pen. The phone
number. How to get there. Can they use people mornings? Can I bring a friend? Tears of gratitude for these
men open to the troubles of a few strangers I have invented for them in three minutes. One of whom, big Paul,
may raise hell over the whole idea. And the other hadn't
liked their meeting the one time she stopped by 'cause
she was the only dame and they challenged her, was she
a Lesbian. No says Nell all squeaky voice. Covering the
event for some underground paper. In the moment of my
triumph, my sheaf of names safe in my back pocket,
I begin to wonder how they'll take this coup of mine.

But it is not Paul and Nell they ask about, it is Winnie. For his chance. And they give it. Worried already,
will they hang in, keep coming, not get sick busy bored.

Planning the shifts and the work ahead of lining them up on the phone. Nervous if I can really pull it off. Then ecstatic again at what has happened: people cared, gave help, did not turn away. This is change. The new life in a slip of paper from a boy who lisps in Charles Street.

Gay Lib crowds about seeming to want to pat me on the back, since I behave like an anxious epileptic. Or like Napoleon, far more like Napoleon in the privacy of my cab, shamelessly hugging myself with joy past grave gray townhouses, flowers, the green of grass behind the iron rail of Hyde Park. Even the hideous gasworks, which Paul invariably points out as a masterpiece of early industrial design. I stare down the "Take Courage" sign before a pub, frankly triumphant. Twice in my life I have gone to a meeting needing something, having to get it, spoke for it, and won. With the pillars of the women's movement that night when we turned the *Time* attack into a united front and manifesto for Gay Liberation. And now for Winnie. Alight with glory bobbing up and down on the leather seat of my cab. I have gone to the underworld, through its labyrinths and waiting, its uncertainty. Asked. And received. From my own people.

Now what will the others say? So high I giggle behind the driver, they'll bloody have to like it if they want volunteers. Nell will be okay. How about Paul? His son. The surge of the patriarchal graft always within reach to claim him when Winnie gets to boy. Rehearsing to myself as Nell does: Winnie is a potential person not property at all. But ownership dies hard. And the manly thing that is Paul's very beauty. Most masculine person I've ever met, despite the china and the silver bracelet that both of them wear in place of wedding rings. A circle shining on his great hairy arm as I whirl along to Islington.

In the morning I tell Nell. A flurry of being proud. Then nervous how she will take it. Grandly. But she worries about Paul. We worry in unison taking a cab to the office, where I drop her off and proceed through the morning mist beautiful in Hyde Park, an English summer filmed through gauze, to the dressmaker of Beauchamp Place. Measured with genteel disinterest by a man whose thing is men not women. Back through the park England seems less formidable, why is nature here always so much more approachable than its people? I consider the English lying about in the grass. Is it only their clothes, the mod gear, or is it that their bodies are becoming lighter, springing as that young couple darting about on the green playing tag?

Then Soho market, a storn of shopping for our house. Wanting to buy everything in sight. Snow them in steaks and chickens. The artichokes I introduced on my last visit were so successful they became a fetish. Nell and Paul ate them night after night until they were permanently sated. Artichoked for life. Get strawberries instead. Paul's butcher grows solemn on learning this pullet is for such discerning taste. Then cream and butter for our three varieties of spuds. Buying them roses from a cart. Pounding back to the office under my burdens of love I see three pigeons on the cobblestones as the light falls gray in an old passage, London and England hurting me with the beauty of centuries. Mellow forever in stone. And loved like Oxford in a sunny day of the market.

Paul will kill me, I am late to pattern Winnie. Has a screening today himself. Be back no later than four, he said, pointing at his watch on the big arm. It is twenty minutes of. A rabbit in a taxi urging us home. Then running the two blocks more into the door, he will brain me as I enter. But he only laughs at me. His screening was canceled, air of complete detachment. Yet he must care terribly. His hopes from Christie's riding on it. Stoic Paul to my butterfly. There was no need to hurry at all, they even have an extra person to pattern. I speed upstairs and onto the phone. All energy to get GLF person by person into those slots on my yellow chart. Calling the first one. He remembers. Yes, he will come. Silent prayers of benediction. Giving directions as if I were the A to Zed itself. Next one. Out. Three more out. Then the phone rings by itself. A real volunteer. Just heard about it. Will be over tomorrow. Nervous magic fingers crossed I have put us all on the line baby don't let me down. What if I fill all the slots and they don't come? What will Paul say? Paul who doesn't even know yet.

He comes up for coffee. And I tell him. Got fifteen volunteers last night, Paul. His face lights up. It's the GLF. "Super," he says. Nell's own word. Didn't bat an eye. "You're not nervous about them being gay?" "Don't be absurd," he rebukes me, soft voice very straight and together under his handlebar. I worship him and return to the wire. Two more lined up. Five more not home.

It is Gala Week in Islington. Later we should all go out and see the hoopla. But first there's a party, two American show-biz types doing it big. Paul and Nell are invited. They descend resplendent from hours of dressing. Nell all in white with her most insane T-shirt. A huge mouth its tongue sticking out in satin on her front. Paul à la mode with velvet pants and vast bell bottoms. The two of them gorgeous worldlings already practicing a number too sophisticated for reproduction. The movie industry hustler-actress out in Nell, doing a turn, her long legs arched in a pirouette, husky voice below the hat putting me on. I am charmed. A bumpkin from St. Paul agog at London smartness, style, polish. An anxious and managing Irish aunt pleased with her prodigies. Swell with pride for knowing such people, my friends. Conspiratorial laughter at how hokey they are. Paul who rarely condescends to appear in company is preening and feline, an enormous beautiful cat, phrases of the devastating wit hum from beneath the enormous mat over his mouth, thoroughly conscious of his powers in these moments he'll deign to expose it. The lucky people at your party. But perhaps they will all be spectacular. All of London's glitter there tonight. Each moment I am more relieved to be spared this excursion. Nothing striking to wear. And no sharp sayings at hand.

They run back for extra trimmings. Then enter the dining room hand in hand. Bow regally and take their leave. They are my parents out to a ball. In adoration

watching Daddy doing his tux. First the black tie. Next
the studs. Waiting on him like a page. Then he claims
my mother, a little thing in lavender gauze transformed
tonight as he is. Not a mouse. A lady. And him. Not
a construction worker mud on his big yellow boots even
if he is the boss and twelve pearl buttons on the fancy
work shirts ordered direct from Canada. Not that but
a gentleman in a tuxedo. My own father a prince until
I cannot bear to watch him, so in love I challenge him.
And he cracks me against the wall plaster turquoise
painted kitchen under the clock. Hoping I would die
pass out and show him. Might feel remorse. Or notice
me. But I am just a heap crying on the floor. His daughter more like a son, too little to fight the big one and
win. A neuter too young and impotent to go out. Must
stay home. Odd I should remember that night so many
nights ago, St. Paul in London. How silly to confuse
good Paul with my old man. Is it the contagious quality
of Nell's mental virus? Nell now playing the Queen
Mother upon his arm.

Let them paint the town while I stay home virtuously
hustling faggots on the telephone for the sake of a child.
As if all things for children were not for oneself, once
a child and still hurting from it. Like O'Rourke herself
the battered child of the Dublin beatings. "In the beginning it was both of them beat me, democratic and without
distinction. After Mother left then it was him, the old
bastard himself, turning it into a full-time job. Had to
stand in for my little brothers, keep him off their backs."
And when she had a child of her own not to beat but
to atone and compensate her whole childhood for—it's
Winnie. Cheated. As few mothers could be though any
would be. So that she can barely look at him sometimes,
the bitterness too great. Cannot bear to hear him scream
while we impose the pattern, maniacs forcing a child's
body down the crawl box so he may be a child someday.
If we win. Whereas Paul is reason, thank God someone
is. Following the regimen. Determination of a fanatic.
His son glowing before him like the Promised Land. Or
perhaps only an utterly dogged moral impulse to save.

Maybe stubbornness. Maybe habit. Maybe all of these. "Men do these things better," he tells me arrogantly, using the camouflage of humor. At moments I suspect he's right.

Now on the phone wheedling and hustling one gay man's voice after another. They will have muscles like Paul. Sensibility like Nell. And none of them parents, remembering Paul's agony when we took Winnie on an outing to the garden show, lady at the turnstile asking his age. Under three he's free. Lady thinks he's an infant. "He's four," Paul in choler putting down the money. Grandeur of his pride humiliated. But for these men it will be easier. Less ego and property sense over another's child. Only the future hope that all children are. Winnie the most crucial test of all—care for him and you have transcended what family means and found the individual, rough in the potential stone.

Just to prove my perfect disinterest I rip off a can of Winnie's own pork and beans. Do a little dance about the kitchen, having lined up four more steadies. All coming this week. Letty emerges from her basement. I see Paul in extremis sweeping out her room that day we fixed it up for Berda's arrival, the Irish nurse who lasted only two weeks. How long will Letty stick? Calculating her on behalf of Winnie. Yet liking her for a good American kid—it's a hard way to earn your keep. We have a chat in the garden where I presume to lecture her. What hell it is for Nell and Paul, their beautiful endurance now breaking. Could she throw in one afternoon a week besides her evenings? And Pete? Her little beau lurking in hallways or marching boldly out the door in full sight of our congregation. Hinting that if he chipped in a bit of help no one would mind his living there all summer rent free. Afire for another recruit. Carrying on like a Bible salesman. Fill another slot. Need forty-seven people. Now up to thirty. But it appears Pete is too delicate to pattern. Tears him up just to hear Winnie yell. Yes, I understand, the whole thing struck me as bizarre too at first, appeared cruel. "But Winnie's change is wonderful, you've seen it yourself." Sounding like a member of the faculty. Or a cat paused over a mouse. But she is slipping from my grasp. I feel her go. A student who cannot be forced. Admirable. Having it her way, as she should. I catch sight of Nell and Paul through the window and casually abandon Letty for more impressive loves. Shouting to them my total cast of volunteers.

They must have come back to pick me up for the gala. But they have been there already. It was boring and the party was trivial. Except for John someone and Mary someone who broke a water bed, one hundred and fifty gallons all over the floor. They forgot to come back for me. I am crushed at their neglect, orphaned at home while they grow so irresponsible and self-absorbed in their new freedom they forgot me. But how good it is that they do. Out of their trap at last. "We bought a present," Nell says. For an instant I hope it is mine. My consolation prize. A turquoise set in silver gleaming on Paul's big arm. A bracelet. Then I realize it is his. Suits him. He poses, playing sugarman, purring, his wrist against his cheek displaying it. Her gigolo while she gloats over her prize, long legs butch in her white pants. I laugh at both of them in my vast relief that I never gave myself away. Knowing them is present enough. And seeing them together tonight out on the town. Careless. Young in summer. Lighthearted with Winnie under the auspices of the GLF.

I report phone calls like a first-rate answering service complete with glosses. "A Lady Somebody called about Antiapartheid. Never talked to a lady so I enjoyed it." My landlord at Oxford was a rake named Colin Merton-Taylor. His mother was Lady Merton-Taylor but I thought she was the cleaning lady the day I moved in. Her head in a towel sweeping out cupboards. What else could she be? So I treated her with kindly condescension and tipped the moving man five pounds, getting it confused with dollars. Frowzy old dame looked on, turned up her eyes. Ten minutes later I realized I had tipped the guy fourteen bucks. But not until I'd discovered the little body I thought was the char was an English Lady. "I've never been very sure of myself over here ever since." They laugh and we go upstairs together, both of them kissing me good night. I am the dunce who came through to get an Oxford First and solve Winnie with the GLF.

It is a beautiful morning. Nell is alive and well and not her usual dragged-out preluncheon self. She is full of schemes. Making a film at the kitchen table. All grays and greens. A dream she had last night. A huge soft tunnel . . . she chooses the fabric constructing her set. Padded it will be. And vast. I see dead subways. Nell's dream takes a sharp turn to the left and ends in a ditch. It is Dante's landscape of the mind, throwing in further ditches from Hardy, from Minnesota, from Tennyson's *Maud,* the Inferno's dark wood, the brown air and the windswept plain. A dream of promise with terror beckoning behind it. "Shoot it. Film what no one has ever seen before," I say, "I want to see it." That's why you do things—in order to see them. A sculpture always a photograph behind my eyes tempting me to build it. So I may see it and be done. "It will be a womb and then like a hangar, hell of a thing to light . . ." But she breaks off. Not because of Paul, who sat through her film, his face turned up to her searching. She breaks off because there is the story board. Tuesday's commercial.

Last night they rehearsed how you shoot the little man behind his cactus squeaking about chocolate while Cadbury's new product explodes in his mouth like trick cigars. British notion of Wild West. Nell her small face the wan white of an orphan, a communion wafer while Paul priestlike draws frame after frame of the cactus, putting in arrows for the camera angle. Now he does it again while she trembles. I fidget, wondering if this is my movie teacher, this incompetent female dependent upon the all-powerful male father figure to get her through a bad scene in a nitwit commercial she does not even get to direct. Some moron writes them so she is reduced to a machine, a technician operating on camera angle. Sordid as life itself to watch them intent upon these little squares. Paul's art history erudition mobilized to sketches of a cowboy hat behind a cactus. Nell's crazy imagination having to follow the little boxes neatly drawn across the page. I want to sob but I dare not. To acknowledge the waste would be cruelty itself.

Nell disappears into her arrangements. Paul serves me a homily upon the fatal gene. Behan had it. "For a while another chap and I shared a flat with him. Time Behan was doing *The Hostage* here in London. Fine opportunity to observe the gene at work." Trips over to Dublin, Behan in the money, buying drinks for the whole bunch of Irish talkers living in McSomething's bar on the Liffey. Pub built right over the water. Same types occupying same seats for years. Talking. All they ever do. "Squeezing life's essence into the vaguely inebriated wit of afternoons." "Yes, Paul, I know the gene. I am its daughter." Does he say all this to warn me or to blast my future? Dark prophet like the French editor in his Paris office reciting failure upon failure. Sat before him barely concealing the secret that he need expect no other book. Smiling vaguely when he mentioned it. His eminence on a swivel chair saying Durrell drinks continuously now and lives in a camping van. Mary McCarthy is through. Miller is simply an old man. Senile. Even dared to put down de Beauvoir. Wanted to throw the desk at his head and shout damned bourgeois what have you ever done, does a happy marriage and an infant son in your fiftieth year make you grander than these artists whose lives' blood you've dealt and sold and now tell me you have drained and discarded? Your husks have been our food. Growing up on them in places like St. Paul. Paul goes on describing Behan's trip to New York. "Brendan thought he'd do television, get a free trip, after all, he'd never seen the States." Ed Sullivan show. "And they kept him drunk the whole time, their clown while he withered inside from contact with the electric hell of showbiz America." I want to argue Behan needed to be drunk, it's one way to survive. Paul forestalls me, explaining how Brendan couldn't survive. And the wife estranged since his success coming to harry him. And then the end of the man. Paul putting in all he feels for Joplin too, his horrified fascination with her exploding death. Now he has really got me scared. Why tell me this stuff? I'm a punk, not in their class. And no drinker anyway. The Milletts drank for me. I did not spend fourteen years with an alcoholic father and twenty-one with a teetotaling mother to end up anything else but iron moderation. And that no matter how many bouts I permit myself. But does he talk of Nell and not to me? His eyes fixed upon me in a mixture of solicitude and malevolence I can never comprehend. As if I were already legend not life because Paul has withdrawn himself from being now and will convert all doers into symbols. Like a dilettante. Worrying our destruction because it is the pattern, the usual thing, history.

They are both at the office. My own afternoon a waste of sordid hustle. Seamy side of the art world. What Fumio calls the "swimming." Had put all my chips on Winnie and didn't intend to push the film. But with a large screening it seems extravagant not even bothering to try. At least owe it to the company to make a plunge into the BBC. Racquet between secretaries and offices. Boss out of town. So tell the film to secretaries. Each time I describe it diminishes further. At each stop chipped down a bit. Too long. Too short. Just about women. Too dull. O Women's Liberation. Awful. An abomination. An obscenity. A bore. Keep trying to say it's not propaganda, human document, etc., phrase so pretentious I choke on it.

I am my mother selling insurance to people who didn't want it. Her voice fighting their sullen scorn in its humble dignity, gagging when they hang up and gallantly trying the next number while I try to study in the next room. Seething over some volume of poetry my heart hanging on each click and spin of the dial turning. Her sales formula a prayer for all of us, her own self-sacrificing need and the requirements of two proud children. My fierce love striding in and pulling the phone from the wall, fantasizing superman, I will take care of you. But hanging on to my chair instead. Because I know I can't support us and she must. Must plug on call after call, from mailing lists, newspapers, phone books. A spy to the world. A nuisance to persons on their days off. Families with too many bills to pay. Snobs who despise insurance salesmen. Kind persons who pity and let her come. Then don't buy of course, but waste her evening. The slipperies who sign and never pay the premium on this stuff Mother sells with perfect conscience. One of the true believers in the business. "Quality insurance," she says and means it, selling only the solid sort, kind you get very little agent's cut on. My mother begging the world on the telephone.

Watched *Salesman* once sitting next to Mother, her great love the theater finally come back to the twin cities with the Guthrie. Like watching an assassination next to a Kennedy. Just back from Japan, America fresh and garish as the raw hate-love edges in Albee. The Salesman our other emblem. In Willy's slow descent my mother's future. Like Martha that big woman in the office that they chucked.

"But you never tell people I was a success in the insurance business," she says. "You make me look like a fool who couldn't earn a living." Mother I know that side of you too, swelled with pride at your portrait, little lady in sequin specs in the trade magazine, "Man of the Year," they wrote under it. Let me sing your praises. President of the Women's Quarter Million Roundtable. Three years running. One of the most successful women in insurance in the country. Mention your name to agents anywhere and expect instant reverence for your fame. They do not always respond. Even your company, which compels your devotion second only to the Catholic Church. "Back of your independence stands your insurer." Picture of Independence Hall on the logo. Tightwads who wouldn't pay you a salary because you were a woman. Bright young men starting out given a nice sum calculated on the wife and kids number of cars style of living. For you it was straight commission. Six hundred dollars your first year of sales. But you kept us alive. Daddy left us in the road. But you sold life in-

nd we made it. They you sold more and got
portant. Invited to conventions. Your cronies
the other big-shot ladies. All fifty-five of them. Now
dying. Sylvia Franklin raped at seventy in a parking lot.
Natalie's cancerous months in the hospital. Irene's fleeing
middle age into marriage. When she gave up her name
we argued over it. Where are they now? What has life
given you in friendship? You live alone. The Church
frowns on remarriage. Your relatives too. You were
cheated. By life. By motherhood. We are bad daughters.
And I the worst of the lot. When you die will we fall
apart in quarrels, argue over the spoils of house and place
and silver? Your little treasure you assign and reassign
as if the will were to be read tomorrow. I dread it, fearing
the end of our wild alliance, our tribal blood, the memory
of being four women carrying on alone in the house on
Selby Avenue without a man, head, pillar, social validity.
Will we meet again when you are gone, three weird sisters
always at each other's throats, primitive as savages?
When you are dead, the ointment of our wars, the
peacemaker, the tie, rope, ball and chain that has held
us together. Our noose. We will cease to be a family.
And the house will be sold. The three of us adrift in the
world. Finally adults. Persons without roots. Mother,
my whole life is an evasion of yours. Not to repeat. Not
to be you. And then I am anyway. Fooled men, never
loved or believed them, avoided them, trifled with them,
heard them say they loved and twisted a smile inside
to hear them lie. I would never be caught. But I found
women instead to break me, reduce me to the abandoned
woman who was you always, bereft. I found your faith-
less Milletts in Celia. In JayCee. Even my poor broken
soul-mad Zooey. Managed even that one so that she was
the one to desert.

And my day in the sun with the thesis. Being the
scholar you'd started out to be, an English major at the
U of M and then a teacher. Sally got further. But she
stopped too. Husband and children both of you. And
they take all, you are fed into little mouths and wived
under a man. But I went the course. First Ph.D. in the

family on either side. Either side being immigrants and before that Irish illiterates. And wrote a book. Dream of your life, Mother. And for a few moments famous in magazines. Then a hate object while you wept in St. Paul because the neighbors heard *Time* say I was queer, my life's shame home at last. While my star fell. Not man of the year but a scandal. All your pride in me deflated to scandal before the great steel eyes of St. Paul. And the Milletts. The papers printing nasty things about Daddy. And then he died. A cold winter, Mother. Your daughter bringing it all down on your head and cowering now like you do before the world. My own self forged long and alone on the Bowery crumbling into the essence of fear which is my heritage from you. Hoping always to convert you, lead you my way. Hope gone then too, my faith melting away to expose the final scared animal we both are.

That the world is pitiless and its ingratitude a cold stone, you taught me those kitchen table nights, nights when you rhapsodized back your four years at the U. The Harvard prof who taught you writing. "Never waste a word, forget you even know the big ones." I put all the big ones in my thesis. That huge vocabulary you taught me, words we doted on, favorites like "perspicacious." Our little vocabulary quizzes nights he doesn't come home for dinner. Training each of us in language. Driving us to be your writers. Reading me poetry before I could even speak. Mother tongue I write for you, across the great space between us this perilous bond. And you preached me the lessons of this young cock from Harvard twenty years ago, lessons twenty years before laid down to you, the rules for all of us. "If you can't put it into English you don't know it, haven't thought it, don't have it." And tales of the red-haired boy you loved, the footloose boy in theater, a Minneapolis intellectual. But you married Dad instead, my wild father and his sisters. I didn't marry Rick, a guy like Dad who never went to college but dropped out into a packing house, a prisoner like Dad, big Jim forever upon the road in mud heroic. I married Fumio. And didn't even marry him.

Mother settled on the one good chair demanding we do it and when we did it was only the immigration. We are lovers not married not friends. You will never understand. And now the women, sin of all sins beyond theological it is a social crime in St. Paul. A Lesbian. And the book stopped selling. Thought it odd at first. Controversy's supposed to be a capitalist aphrodisiac. Then I was relieved, it seemed right somehow, had sold too much. The money confused me. If it stopped the Left might stop biting me with its guilt about success. Fail and they hate you less.

Just as you would have predicted. When I dialed Granada Annabelle had left. Of course they must have fired her, smart young man in her job never heard of me says it's frightfully nice to ring up doubts he can make it to the screening however he's delighted to have word good-bye. And then the strangest thing. They called back. Chief editor himself. Reynolds who took me to lunch asking me what book I'd do next. I said something about gay and straight, my eyes looking into his cool blue ones while he coughed and recommended something on ecology, that's a good topic these days. My head whirled. My God he thinks I'm topical. Knowing in my own sure loser's bare rock of instinct I was through.

And here he is on the phone asking me to dinner. Of course he'll come to see the film. Patrick will come too. And Annabelle, who's now in another department, will scare up the press people. Her voice on another line accomplishing this. I climb down from the phone's euphoria. Saved. By the human beings within capitalism. Mother could be wrong. The radical in me, flinthearted enemy of all business, is perplexed. Even in Granada's huge pointless combine swallowing what once were publishers like Rupert Hart-Davis, fine old names on the spines of books at Oxford, even in that holocaust of honor there is something left alive. People not a company.

Paul walks into the garden. "Go to Africa. You could test your pacifism against the guerrillas there while you watched a revolution happen." "Yes . . . to see a place where they're trying to do it." "And Russia, now there's a society in process of change over fifty years now." I make a face. "Not enough has changed." "Oh, the superstructure." I go on to state my terms, the changes I'd like to see. Political and economic structure of course, socialism of course. But more. Change in personal dynamics, in group life and community, in sex roles, in the self released. "What's that mean?" "I don't quite know. But I think it's change in the attitude of force, power, authority. Change in the treatment of children, for example, since the brutality practiced on them is the first sort of violence we learn."

"Revolutionaries in backward countries have to think first about what people will eat." "Sure, but don't confuse survival or an old idea like nationalism with revolution. Of course, there are economic priorities, but what does it cost to make love, have communal child care, or free speech? And what economic determinism justifies social hierarchy? If a tribe had only ten dead bones it could divide them equally." "Ah, but that's not politics. Politics is a science built on fact."

"But it is all human relations, Paul. 'Politics' is a mirage between persons and their fate, individuals and their needs. We've made it so complicated." "But it is complicated." "Then bring it back to the human level. It's the GLF and Winnie. It's you and Nell. Or just managing to enjoy ourselves on a summer evening. The revolution as we call it is not necessarily an uprising in the streets or the old business of seizing power. Though the Left has always imagined it was. The revolution is change. Not merely rearrangement, but a deep emotional type of transformation that must also take place inside us. It's a better way to live. So it's more basic than the machinery of force, bureaucracies, institutions. It's . . ." But Paul is making objections. We have ceased to be a conversation, we are me preaching at him. He is arguing that one must gain power to bring about change. I am arguing that in pursuit of power we must necessarily contaminate ourselves with what we despise, rationalize methods common to the injustice we opposed. We become the enemy, what we sought to replace because its use of power was corrupt. Why not go further and discover power itself is corrupt? Corrupting. That power over others is a presumption emotionally and logically so criminal that we must transcend it and find another way.

"Nonsense, one must have power even to enunciate this," he counters. Not power but influence I say, believing they are different. Hoping they are different. "And repression?" he asks. "Remember that power resists change." "But change is fluid," I argue, "although it produces new behavior it's essentially of the spirit, an attitude. It insinuates. It's oblique. It evades the forces sent against it. It doesn't break laws, it challenges them. Calls them into question. Demonstrates they are impossible to justify or enforce. It's state of mind so it's got to be resourceful. Outwit rather than respond. It doesn't strike back in anger or revenge. It doesn't confront where it will take losses or prejudice the issue by morally ambiguous behavior. It's not suicide or despair. That's the lesson of the Panther. Or the . . ." Paul is bored. He is off to the kitchen to get some coffee, leaving me to go on arguing to myself. Struggle between Left and Right as good and evil. Left commits evil coming to power, commits more to stay there. History. How to go it one better? How to discriminate, make grounds of choice not ideological but wiser, more flexible, moral, humane? Without the anxious orthodoxy of cult thinking. The choice between stasis and change being that between what is and what could be.

Still fumbling about in my head. The heavy English twilight, the sadness of backyards. A little giddy. I have just dared to risk my notions in Paul's presence. What an egotist I sound. And what a fool. Remembering the winter prancing about on airplanes. Forced to play the pundit before students, university audiences looking up, their faces draining me like a stein of beer while each week I know less, am more devoid of ideas. More uncertain. More sure I am unsure of everything. Longing for the year's retreat I promised myself reading Gandhi in January. Hankering to be penniless and disappear. Anonymous. But instead the whore of students' essays at Bryn Mawr, my own ideas simplified into idiocy, parodied to comedy. I should tell anyone how to live? And be mimeographed into a hazy futuristic blurb in the minds of the young? When I could not live it out myself. The disaster of Celia Fumio Miriam. The glimpse of life beyond the revolution. Failed and gone. Disproven. Odd subjectivity of course to imagine a taste for loving a pair of musicians and a Japanese sculptor could constitute proof of anything, failed or successful. But it was my own living in your gut or nowhere version of possibility. Spoiled, I suppose, if I *had* gotten it, snug self-satisfied utopia. "So you start with yourself," Claire said. "Put that together right and you might be ready for other things."

Paul comes back. To talk about Winnie. His hopes. His passion. One feels them, though Paul will never be exuberant enough to speak aloud. One must infer them from his understated manner, seek them out through his slaughtered despondency. Paul is not really a Canadian at all but a Yugoslav who grew up in the loneliness of fishing boats. Weeks at sea. The steel determination of wreckage in the calm of his moustache. I am going to suggest something. It is dangerous. It risks a great deal. But I dare to trifle. And with stuffy tact, with elaborate gentleness begin to challenge his possession, his fervor. Winnie will not be Paul's now. He will be with the GLF, who will bring him into himself if he can get there. And face Paul someday but not as an owned thing.

Paul wants to go inside. We will join Nell, and the three of us will stand at the table while I ask them, so in love with each I am terrified asking. But I must. Can they be sure or at least question themselves hard that it's Winnie—his chance rather than their child that we struggle for? Remembering that I began by seeing Winnie as their problem. To be solved because I loved them. Only later saw it was Winnie's own right that was the issue. Emerging into humanity as a child with a child's

full human claim. Perhaps claims whether human or not.
Even full ones. But it is at the child we aim now. This
moment like a consecration to that. Frightened when
I have asked, hoping it is not an outrage. Even telling
Paul how Sarah and I both find him overbearing to work
with, too obsessed with his own prowess as master of
the pattern. He permits me. I hear him sigh, his arms
leaning on the table. Ashamed and fearful I have hurt
him. The wood of the table shining brown between us
in the dark of the kitchen not yet lit for evening. And
they say they know. They have thought of it a long time.
And one other thing, an idea someone mentioned the
other day: what if Winnie did make it and grew up a
man? How much would he owe you two? Would it be
too much for him to bear? "The others make this
different," Paul says. "He would be indebted to so many
it will be no obligation at all." For this I could adore
him on the spot, but only hug him. We are all three
moved. O'Rourke brings out the wine. We talk of their
own work. I am jubilant and noisy. The will have it now.
The way is open, I say.

Then Paul gives me a peculiar warning. Hearing him
I know I will always be haunted by it. "You must not
think all life is to produce," he says. "It is also to live.
You cannot forever package it into art. This cheapens
it to product. You burn out your fire or you die."
O'Rourke seems to agree. Places change and again I am
their younger sister, though only Paul is my senior. Their
student, each in their different ways keeping me to the
mark. Respecting them with the honor I learned in Japan
is due an elder or a *sensei*—teacher master sage.

It is bedtime and we observe the hour. Paul has already
gone upstairs. Nell and I joke about the Church. And
what it's done to us. The morass of piety. The grief of
guilt. Giggling at it. Furious. Saddened. I try to penetrate
the shield of her frigidity with Paul. Hesitant to mention
it. But he suffers so. And I know that suffering. "I will
not be bullied," she says. Cantankerous to think of it.
"I will not have someone on top of me giving orders."

"O'Rourke the Church is still in your head. And the family." But she insists, finger jabbing into the table, weeping almost like a child weeps being beaten. She will not give in. Bullied. Nell the termagant lib talker switching always into Paul's womanchild, finally after outrageous testing and tantrums obeying when he shouts. Leaving me flat to be carried off on his great arm, the admiration in his eyes, the Mickey Mouse shirt twinkling on her long-legged tough-girl self. All the cameramen in New York thought she was a sport. Nell in the wind of her change, her moods and variety still finding shelter in Paul. Choosing man over woman. Because it is the thing to do. Then hating him.

As we wash the dishes turn out the lights start up the stairs she mentions some street downtown. I see Claire's Fifth Street. The Angels and the urine. The tenement room full of pictures. And her figure at the desk reading interminable years of books. 1969 for psychology. 1970 for philosophy and history. 1971 for space and science fiction. Books like stalagmites climbing off the floor in piles. Reading systematically as people haven't read since the nineteenth century. And the great blond head like a baby's, wise, serene, her figure solid behind a crack in the door as I mount the stairs exhausted by the fourth floor. And revived with a smile. The door always open to me. Bookie everyone calls her. I call her Bookie too when we are fellow students. Claire when we are lovers. A distinction blurred in friendship.

What does her passion mean? Head back in ecstacy, a great sensualist calling herself an ascetic and reading the nay-sayers of the past. Her passion and my fear of it. Her precarious control. Why am I afraid to talk or even think of Claire? What finally do I know of her except her reading, her jokes, her warm steady glow of encouragement? Which I forever suspect. Because it is food. And she is so beautiful I am afraid. What is so gratifying must be sinful. Rummaging through my radical catechism. Confess me, Father Marx, for I have sinned exceedingly and love a woman. A blonde at that, who tells me I am "an extraordinary human being." "Like myself," she says, finger to her chin before she bursts into laughter. "And in moments of particular trepidation you must remember I am your eternal friend; you are also, poor thing, the great love of my life, an idea which doubtless bores you to tears and runs counter to all your revolutionary theories. But I am at least as stubborn as you are. And just as much an egotist."

Bit drunk in my London bed wondering why I'm not letting myself write the mind's voice in Blick. Denying myself. Laziness. "Not laziness," Lila insisted. "There is no such thing as laziness. It is something else always that keeps us from work." Like the fear of failure? I said. "Sure, but deeper than that." Groping about in the dark with repression and fear, the American dilemma of success and failure. We kill ourselves that way. Surely I was sick with ego all winter. And wanted to die. So kill that self and live another. Resurrected in spring behind the Steembeck, working my tail off to turn celluloid into movie. "You are best when worried to death," Nell said. "That's the side of you I like. Your anxiety. Working." But then she's Irish too. Even tempted me to continue the quest for Celia.

Night and morning reverie merging. Light and birds. Nell saying last evening, "But she could die." Meaning Celia. Glistening knives and surgery, my mind like a pigeon now checking into The Mercy Hospital. And Nell saying she could die. "Don't you realize they'll be looking for cancer this time?" I said that's Irish melodrama. "What should I say, that it's not possible?" Her green eyes wide. Emphatic. O'Rourke, I have thought of it myself.

10

There is sun in the basement. Ursula is back. I see her thin arms, wondering how long it can last with her, the struggle for Winnie. "We have help," I boast, field marshal, fellow conspirator, political analyst, maniac. "We have the London GLF. Now if they'll just hang in we're set." Ursula has never heard of the GLF, wants to know what it is. "Oh, it's the Gay Liberation Front." She asks what gay means. "It means homosexuals." I pause and wait for the bomb of ridicule. Ursula is a black South African. Prison, centuries of slavery, exile in the cold English summer. Missing home she said, the only part that hurt was the land. Never seeing it again. So I wait in fear. "Homosexuals getting together? Good idea, probably about time too." Reprieved. Go on to beg her unnecessarily to be supportive, "We are said to be sick diseased depraved, should never be with children. These men may be nervous, taught so long and so well to despise themselves." And surely we all do it, regard the child as moral arbiter. If Winnie kicks me I am judged before the world a creature unworthy to live. Ursula smiles at my neurosis and prepares the inevitable instant thin water slop. Brown mugs and a cigarette. It gets late. They do not come.

I race upstairs to cover the damage. Voice at the other end of London says they've left already and are on their way. Paul hovers. I am on the carpet. They are letting me down, my people. Must've had second thoughts. Got lost. Forgot. Paul paces while my mind pleads silently for mercy, indicts long defenses, transposes blame, haggles for a shorter sentence, grovels, wheedles, dances, shuffles, invents lame little jokes. Stalls for time. Paul leaves for the office. Nell lies abed two floors above. Enough of us women to cover if the guys fail to show. Downstairs again for the next round of coffee, nervously repeating my speeches to Ursula, rubbing my hands like a maître d'. A car salesman with rabid clients while Detroit is on strike. A pusher dealing salt, baking powder, crushed aspirin. And waiting for the knife to fall.

Then the knock arrives upon the door. And two young men stride in fresh from an accident. Car hit a bus. "Bit of a delay," one of them all ready to start, his hands still shaking. Ursula and I come on with coffee and methodology. She teaches them, lectures on the brain, the body, exercises, masks, gags. Even the silly peanut butter and the business of holding the child upside down for one minute twice a day. Her slim brown arms swinging Winnie, who thinks it's a lark. Nell enters in full regalia, makes them welcome, then off to the office in a flurry of costume. I propagandize and make coffee leaning on the service angle. But hanging back to watch them do the first pattern by themselves. They are men and women at the same time. Strong when Winnie fights being put in the crawl box. Both of them taller, bigger in the arm can handle him more easily. But they touch him with all the gentleness of women while performing their parts with the objectivity of men. Wise in not over-identifying with his child's rage or pain. Ursula is perfect. The young men are enjoying all of it. "Getting Winnie for themselves," as Fumio would put it. Playing with him between patterns. Admiring him, learning him. When we see them out I have yet my entrepreneur's eye for the main chance, hanging like a hollyhock on its stalk, "Tell the others." And the pillar who ran the meeting in his velvet hat will be here tomorrow. Vamping around the dining room hugging my success. Mentality of a Fuller Brush man. Not a saleswoman's daughter for nothing.

Now in the morning I stand a long moment in the door between dining room and kitchen, looking out the big sunny window to the garden hearing a voice, a woman's voice, grand and querulous. Denunciatory. Another voice squabbles back in a strange tongue. From the buildings whose backs are across the way. Speaking the language of the South. Suddenly my London garden, the big roses across the wall, the geraniums in the foreground window box, the orange narcissus in urns, suddenly it becomes Spain. No, Italy I thought as I wrote it down. For a moment not here but there in the languid southern earth, its mystery of heat, the Mediterranean. The light pours down on the roses, Winnie's mechanical tape operates in the basement, the huge clock ticks in the hall, striking eleven, one hundred clocks tick or fail to tick throughout the house.

Time hovers while I notice the wet of the floor. Having found my efforts inadequate Nell has rescrubbed. Watered down by America's five generations my Irish never the real thing, I lack the true touch. So she has scrubbed again. Saying nothing of it. But I see a cleaner, fairer image in the quiet tiles. Brown and black vinyl. Examine them amused to find one Yankee note in an English house and then feel the South pull again through the garden. So many countries at once can claim you. Yesterday English Magda, Magda Bernstein, just back from Italy the warm bubble of it all around her: "Why not make a stop there on your way home?" And I saw Venice as it looked that first morning standing on the Stazione bridge with my suitcase, Venice in the dawn rose while I stared. Gasped to see it from a hundred pictures the vulva of mist on its sky and waters. English Magda, her frank brown eyes offering to type my manuscript. What will she think when she reads another Magda's name? Paranoia jumps another knot tighter in my throat. Did she hear the other Magda's name in Italy where our Magda is busy organizing in Milan each summer, a California vintner's daughter grown like an orphan in their convents. American Magda once my lover. Till I failed before her beauty. Terrified by its perfection. My own unworthiness. One must be peers in all things. But I felt her inferior just there where she had

been hurt most. And flinched making love, didn't reach
the goal of orgasm shining ahead in her dark hair.
And knew that instant she would discard me. Sinned another sin as well. I fell, or just about, into love. Tottering
like a cockroach on the fine edge of a saucepan. And
that scared her. Being adventuresome was making love
in the afternoon on Fifty-eighth Street with the rain
falling in the courtyard. But it could not be caring. So
Magda went back to men. Loving was too much. She
said women clung and depended. I knew what she
meant. I knew Naomi and Vita. I did not have that in
mind, going to her those two afternoons for comfort.
Friendship, a bottle of white wine and some talk when cut
and diced to Celia's vegetable. And Magda was kind.
Gave comfort. Sat next to me and said we should be
lovers, being friends so long and loving each other already. And kissed me, pushed me, gesture like grace
itself, down on the carpet and took my clothes off. I held
my breath dizzy as she made love to my poor beauty
while her own shone like power above me, the great courageous fire of her eyes. After that we were casual and
polite. I would not embarrass her with hounding.

But I will not see Italy this time. Angelo's Florence
that he gave me once, grave young doctor of art pulling
me from church to church until my feet bled and I'd
seen them all. As he would have it, a fanatic. Then his
studio the toilet in the hall you squatted. I was Isabel
Archer and the young Oxonian just finished the Honours
Schools, soon to ride down the High with JayCee, our
bicycles whirling against the wind till I saw my name
printed fair among the Firsts. But that was later. After
the Viva Voce and Italy on my own. Where I met Angelo
and fell in love with art, even the new pictures. Hunting
the new canvases down Roman streets like a bitch in
heat. But that was later. Angelo I met first. In the Ac-
cademia in Venice. Picked him up. Your usual American Daisy Miller gets herself an Italian lover. Mine had
this difference that we were correspondents still two years
later till he lost my address and I no longer needed him
as teacher. Graduated. A sculptor then myself. His pupil.

And it was wonderful when he leaned me against the wall, old room some seven hundred years of art, long high windows through a courtyard, touched me and I came. But no good in bed the flies biting us, the stench of his unwashed socks, the pain of his cock ramming me with some terrible hatred one never saw other times in that somber face. First gentle man I'd ever met, I thought, touched by his poverty, the purity of student lunches, the worn copy of Dante read every day like a Bible. Wanted to buy a bronze but he said no, you cannot afford it. Which was true. And the last day he had no money for milk at breakfast time, I said, "Be fair, you've paid for everything, let me treat you now." His mouth furious with pride. Angelo his Florence. Or Oxford. Sarah asked me the other night would I go up there again this time to visit. Perhaps I am not strong enough. Or cannot spare the time from Winnie. But if I had to see Oxford I would be there.

In Sarah's question I felt the pull, go up to Oxford, get a bedsitter, remember those years moment by moment. Eleven Stanley Road and JayCee. So I said no, perhaps I'll save something, leave one cupboard unopened. In case I should ever want to write again, might have something left to say. For I have split myself in this book. Prodigal. Then a fear of being emptied. The peasant holds a few things back. For next time.

And as I jiggle along scribbling this it occurs to me to issue a warning: I didn't get them. The people, especially Nell. You won't get all there is of them. Neither will you know them as I do. In the round. You will hear tin echoes, see feeble sketches. This is not literature. Though of course I had hoped for that. And relinquished my ambition in bitter disappointment. Only when I knew that further attendance upon the shades of giants would starve me out of words and into madness. I had the ambition of all who haven't started. I wanted to excel all those who have finished. The book of books. Folly, even to remember it aghast. But that's how it is before you take the plunge. Just to start I must prune my sights to near drivel, swallow hard and enunciate my lifeless diction. Just to speak at all. Had to play with paper as if it were cheap as air and words required no more patience to follow than the wind of a drinker.

Still giddy. Jumping upstairs to dress. Strutting about in this shirt or that. Trying on outfits in Nell's full length. With what blouse shall I astonish the world today? Indulge in a bath. The only one home except for Ursula cooing to Winnie in the basement. Splash in the master bathroom. The roses thrive in the garden. The sun shines in every room. I have nothing to do but make merry springing from garden to kitchen to bath. Have the whole day off. And don't want to work. But do anyway. Putting the pieces of the beginning into the tape recorder helter-skelter and with infinite care and timidly and with trepidation after endless hesitations turning off the machine and starting it up again while I read the tape slowly and carefully for the Magda here. Where did the shot in the back at Bryn Mawr go? Why are there two versions of that first trip to Oxford? Read them both in and choose later. Frantic over a missing link. The order forming itself and then lost again. Should I change a word? Do. And find it less satisfactory. Stick by the original. Have faith in the notebooks' first feel of it. Can Magda finish typing it before I'm out of England? So little time now.

Floor a litter of papers on its discouraging brown carpet. Trunk top unsatisfactory. Paul's hussars eyeing me from the walls. Bookcases staring down a disapproval of real books printed sewn edited approved. Conceived by rational minds not this mouse scurrying between phone calls and flat language. How will I appear? Just fuck it and read it all in. You can always revise later. Already guilty knowing I won't revise enough. To be saved in the end by vanity? Precious she is about what appears over her name. Her style! Dear God, as if she had one. Like a nylon with runs. Just do the thing and you'll be lucky. Time flying past and still not finished. Sarah and I have a date for the Folly. Tonight we see Danny La Rue and confront the last specter in England.

Then I'm off, tape under arm to deliver. A neighbor will receive the first tape, pass it on to Magda, expected there tonight for dinner. We are an intrigue over precious cellophane very likely to be pointless. But we pretend. I hasten to the place of assignation. Sensible Englishman receives my burden. He nods. Sane in contrast to my eccentricity. Now I must find my way to Upper Street and the bus. But by devious methods. Trying new streets. Exploring the neighborhood. Deliberately getting lost so I can find myself. An Islington tourist.

Here is a fire. Held in my behalf. So that I may admire a fireman, seeing him through a charred window six feet of English blond. Adam Bede. Lawrence's Captain. My own movie hero adventurer. His is the mystery beyond a broken archway, a blackened wooden frame its panes gone. He moves. I hold my breath in adoration, our eyes meet and the spell intensifies then evaporates in my embarrassment. Shameless to infatuate upon the spot, kneel to him, go down on him, thrash about pinioned to the floor of an abandoned house. Or become his muse or his mother or the companion of his soul. Wondering in some dim corner of my cave if he isn't Claire too striding in her heroic mood. Then he is just a fireman and there are other firemen, the moment passed into ordinary life again. And I ask the captain in my jaunty not quite American but I can do that for you too if it amuses you—what's up? And where's the bus? I have overdone my adventure and am really lost. Captain plays Daddy calling me girlie, another charade also fun to play since life is momentarily dream and game. While Adonis looks on I skirt hoses in my trousers, my sandaled feet American as Allen Block's on Fourth Street Greenwich Village. In New York.

How beautiful men are. Headed back toward Upper Street and the number 19. Till I pass one utterly ugly tattooed like a Hell's Angel. And another sadly walking dead of everyday British depression. But then there's Winnie with his Italian painting angel head grown up to be a man. Someday walking right up to me standing taller than me on the pavement while I wait for the bus.

The landscape of Upper Street confronts me. Saying
motion is illusory, change a mirage of my own. An insurance broker, a police station, radio shop, candy store,
loan society. Sutton Place Slums. The air of depression.
North Thames Gas, Huge Bargains in Furniture. But
it *is* depression. O'Rourke says the depression is of
course depressing. In every way. Not poverty but futility.
Sense of static ugliness without hope of change. Satisfied
with itself. Unconscious. Atmosphere of prams and family and Sunday. Weeklies full of soccer and religion.
Drab loyalty to a drab past and the gray establishment.
The fire department passes. A red truck heroic with great
wooden wheels.

Then I met Fumio on Upper Street, getting on the
bus with me in his straw hat striped shirt chirping voice
making all my favorite errors in English. Like the way
he says, "I am boring," when he means he is bored. We
snuggle nicely in the top deck and proceed to admire
the ads as I explain the puns and kiss his ear when we
approach Bloomsbury. I drone on to him about Virginia
Woolf and her circle, next proceed to interpret Gray's
Inn. He flies out the window when we take a turn. And
before I have salvaged or replaced him we are smack
in Cambridge Circus. Opposite the bank, which is closed
and therefore inoperative and without the threat it held
each time I cashed a movie company traveler's check
daily closer to the end, incompetent female playing with
business forms momentarily expecting the strong arm
of the law to descend upon my shoulder—young lady
you do not have sufficient funds to be a movie company.

Danny La Rue at the Palace. Could run as long as *The
Mousetrap,* warns the *Daily Express* from a poster. "The
return of glamour and all that word suggests in terms
of razzle-dazzle sparkle"—other words cry out from the
wall. Curious texts in pink and yellow ominous tinsel.
"Danny is Superstar Class." Term has a piquant nausea.
"Star" so unlike Claire's astral bodies in their charts
ringing out like bells pure white and terrible in the night

sky. We will look up and make love in furious passion coming to the galaxy. But here and now the pavement and the line of Bradley Coaches. Through each window simulated leopard-skin seat covers. They disgorge middle-aged British ladies from the Midlands. Native tourists come to gobble up the family entertainment. Big fat sensible shoes and hosiery.

Sarah says the GLF are packing the galleries. Last we ever heard of them, swimming in the sea of respectability down to the plush Victorian bar. Red velvet. Danny stares at us with his empty non-person eyes from record jackets first in his masculine then in his feminine self. Like Rosalind in *As You Like It?* Like Woolf's Orlando? But not at all. Because they were real, were the freedom to change sex and be either. And Danny is paper, a tawdry less actual than make-believe.

Whole first floor is women. Middle-aged housewives. It is not a show about homosexuality, we decide. Not even a safe version of queer. It is a displacement. Something other. We nod at each other wearily, looking over the house. Danny appears after fanfare, revealed like God. "He equals she," the chorus bellows at us from stage, kick dance cancan and so forth. In artificial joy they prepare us to behold a man over six feet tall dressed as a woman, continuous patter to remind us incessantly he is a male. Posing as a female. The whole point is that we have both factors in mind simultaneously. And do not believe in either one. "You can't tell a Jack from a Jill," they trumpet. We are to be overwhelmed with ambiguity. Does this relieve the Briton? Satisfy an impulse? Tease or terrorize a precarious sexual identity?

Danny is a vision in white. No prose but the sublimity of ladies' mag can describe him. Clichés come to mind with the ease of nature. He is loveliness in immaculate samite, a swoon, a sward of tulle. He is a wedding dress with lovely shoulders six sizes larger than life. Whose life? He has a very male voice. He refers to his manly bosom. Nice Camp and bawdy. He is Liz Taylor, he announces. "There is very little difference. Don't worry, I won't show it." The ladies are enraptured. They adore his jokes dirtier by degrees the smuttier the better. If he is a revelation, they are more so. This morning they buttered scones for children. Last night they denied their husbands for the twenty-eighth day in a row. Tonight they are sucking Danny's mighty cock. Because he wears a gown more beautiful than their wildest dream's breathing ecstasy overweight in elastic girdles. Their superior in every way. With a cock to make him better, the scepter concealed in his dress. And the dress my dear is a vision. Of all they have ever failed to be as women. So they drink him in while he rubs salt in every wound of the lives they never lived. A celebrity. With the figure of a goddess. And a prick on top of that. My dear, it's irresistible.

After an innocent interval of children's film Danny rejoins us to parode the Prime Minister. At first I am amused, serves him right the old fuddy-duddy. Then the other side gets it too. Nice impartiality, I reason. Then I realize nothing is meant but random hostility. Malice only. Bitchery, a kind of madness that has nothing to do with ideas, an infantile destruction, every antisocial impulse. A belief in nothing but show business. And his own ego. One begins to have compassion on his victims. Ridiculing Tories more Tory than all, epitome of the open snob always lurking behind the coat of failure we call Camp. Chief executioner Danny murders every name in England. Then I hear him handle a friend's name. Yoko. Now a joke for fools. For television and tabloid, a target face for the unfulfilled masses close enough to spit, alienated enough to do it. Objectify and dismiss, objectify and applaud, objectify and slaughter.

Intermission arrives like relief from sentry duty over a whiskey at the bar. Sarah says the women respond to Danny out of their fascination with punishment. I tell her how my tobacco lady in Nishi-Ogikubo lined her room with the magic dyke faces of the Takarazuka gleaming down in gold-toothed smile seducing her while she exchanged ten Shinsei for one hundred yen, the tin coin on the glass case as the neat packages below grinned back, fresh and clean in their cardboard and cellophane.

What were the Takarazuka to her? A dream. A schoolgirl recess permitted because as I watched her man emerged from the *kotatsu* behind stage, carrying the child in a quilt. I could scream your wife lives in a fantasy of Lesbos. But I would not. Because it was only fantasy. A vulgarity never even permitted to rise into art, cheap versions of kabuki enacted by an all-woman cast, the swordplay of these heroines with gold-capped teeth who decorate her wall. Lower by far than the *oiyama,* kabuki "women" who are actually men but suffered as grave mysterious beings, carpenters in the top tiers shouting at their entrances, "Matchimashita"—we've been waiting for you." The Takarazuka are lesser persons. But what are they doing on your wall, Mrs. Tanaka? What obscure impulse throbs for them in your eyes, half awake most of the day? Selling tobacco gives one great leisure for reverie. And the baby sleeps, not interrupting. The man lives elsewhere too, never intruding.

Sarah treats me to a whiskey. We haggle over who will pay. We are becoming friends. Affection for the strangely bruised look in her eyes. And we grope our way back to Danny, the great farce awaiting us, the mechanical god on stage. His next number is Miss World. Sarah whispers that London Women's Liberation broke up the Miss Universe contest this year. A few got busted. Everyone had fun. Danny's contest parodies the parody. Nationalism in a bathing suit. A tourist's view of geography, an airline poster, a pretty girl becomes Switzerland, Holland. He challenges us to discover what personality the candidates have. "If any." The ladies love it. Their masochism roars at the sadist in his bathing suit before them. He is enormous. Shoulders of a football hero. Smooth padded crotch. He is Miss England looking American. If only foreign policy depended upon this spectacle. Danny is the perfect vehicle of diplomacy. "Drill your own hole," he gives notice, "have tool." Everybody loves it. They are the jokes we giggled over hysterical with guilt and naughtiness at thirteen. Adam and Eve in the Garden. He dug her hole. Floss McCarthy and Marianne Schwartz shrieked while Jerome McMann told it. We shook with scared laughter, knowing God and the nuns and our mothers lay in wait to thrash us. Tonight I watch grown and elderly women at the same four-letter titter. Like seeing one's own mother masturbate. Stupefaction.

Danny is enshrined in the eyes of ten thousand English women telling castration jokes. The humor of repression. Cute references to whores. Swinburne and the English disease. Long rows of one-liners for the whip types, the leather types. Nasty-faced back-up man's abusive clichés about wives. A sea of wives lap it up. Sarah and I have stopped looking at each other. The ladies are in an ecstasy. The hall bristles with a terrible sexual hostility. Diffused so perfectly, muscled so gracefully. That no one need notice. The labyrinthine course of humor, a pinball always in motion, so devious that no purpose need emerge. No one will ever have to see. Eyes understanding would confront a face perceiving truth, its lines changing in realization. Instead it is a rouged skin cracking grimace of laughter.

Jokes against hippies, the modern age, the young. Good old days sex. " 'How did you find it, Grandaddy?' 'Instinct,' he said." They laugh obediently. Jokes against blacks. How good they feel laughing. Jokes on uppity young women who don't wear bras or undies. The ladies concur. They want iron pants, their girdles expanding in laughter. Jokes on frigidity. "Wife wanted Mars Bar so he let her take one to bed. She still didn't want it." The ladies are hysterical. He has hit a nerve.

Then sentiment—the other side of an old currency. Nostalgia numbers, top hats, hits from old movies. Safe innocuous Camp. Garbo and then Dietrich submitted to Danny's superior impersonation. The last number is simply an ad. Danny is glamour. And will play the Palace forever. All sequins. The last dress. The victims applaud each dress. So beyond their capacity even to hope. The chorus girls, real women therefore second-raters, sing sweetly to us that the show is over. The straight man grades us ten out of ten. We are successful pupils. Danny in the very last dress. Everybody is asking us to come back again and again. Danny at the Palace forever. One believes it.

Cowed only by Jill's titanic blue jeans railroad jacket with insignia and yes the American flag sewn upon her arm. Telling me I'm thirty minutes late. During which time she has alerted them all, set enmity even between us and the bartenders. Long dark room at high noon full of tough guys who go there for lunch since this is still a man's bar. Invaded by superdyke in full regalia. I take another tack, try my inoffensive person, but just to get a martini one must cringe before the Welsh bartender here, hates women so much I've really got to ask him why. No answer and the drink takes ten minutes longer. No peaceful smile disarms him. In his one body I find the perfect antidote to nonviolence. Or humor. He begins to fascinate me. Such conviction is hard to resist. Patiently waiting for this bastard to have been arrogant long enough, punishing me for my accent, my sex. Until he is satisfied. But will not even grin when sated. A hard case.

Jill and I sit opposite. And begin our little dance. It is not a conversation. It is a chess game. A minuet, a duel. The bourgeoisie sit perilously close at either side. A jowly man and his lady. They will be subjected to us just as we are victimized by their proximity. The light through a stained-glass window is darkly religious. Jill shrugs it off, the shoulders in her insignia, the talismans upon her arms hold Britain at a distance. We might be comspiring to bring about the Boston Tea Party.

Jill sits across from me saying there is not enough opportunity for heroism over here. I am late coming into this mean old bar full of Americans. Too early for a martini but I have one anyway. Jill is eating a sandwich. Heroism is suspect, I say. She frankly wants to be heroic. "Admit it, you do too," she says. I do sometimes. Not now. Now it just seems deluded. Because she has said it out loud.

I am fidgety listening to her. She says women are up-

tight. Always want to love, whereas they really ought
to be free to screw like guys. She is describing me. I am
unliberated. Will she notice? I wonder if she might be
right. What about my temple prostitute trip? Love all
the women in the world, etc. But Jill is butch. Which
turns me off. My crime is snobbery. Which doesn't want
to love all the women in the world at all. It desires only
where there is beauty, intelligence, humor. I am checking
Jill out on these qualifications. While her crap detector
is mining away at my underpinnings, putting the make
on me through theory. "Women have always been the
victims of sentiment," she says. Smelling my sentimentalist. I squirm, a femme on the side of women.
Too intimidated to argue, I fall into moralizing. Love
is the obligations of friendship. You owe it forever to
anyone with whom you share intimacy. So what about
Vita? No, it's all right. I love Vita now. In England.

Jill describes her adventure. Last night at the Gateways.
London bar dykes all live in cliques, sit there being dull
in their tweeds, suits and skirts, won't talk to outsiders.
A woman from Boston got sentimental over someone
she came with. Broke a glass. While Jill recites the crime
I relax in my shirt. Relieved I wasn't there. "Here are
three of these Boston chicks living in a commune," Jill
says outraged across the table while our neighbors cough,
"and this woman's posssesive!" At least I'm not possessive, I think. My elbow loosens a muscle upon the
table. I focus upon the belligerence of her Levi jacket
and remember she was too shy to take off her shirt at
DOB. Jill is my enigma.

Because she is so positive of everything. Can it be so
much easier for her? She has no doubts. We talk about
coming out. Her Lois Lane piece I so admired. The one
Voice I heard after *Time*'s cannon. Reassuring then
frightening again. Has the guts of a lion, I thought,
reading it. Then out of nowhere she produces St. Louis.
Throws it into the clear water of my martini. Has two
kids there. Husband she put through medical school now
a righteous citizen remarried. Won't let her see the
children. Older one a boy. On her side. Goes to school

and teach assigns the *Village Voice*. Lois Lane is his mother. Daughter is younger, too far away, feminine, on her stepmother's side. Jill rants on, contemptuous of women. I listen, on their side. The thing always between us on the table, the feminism I've been trying for weeks to get into her head. And why does she always pretend things are not hard? Because they are so hard. I never knew about St. Louis.

Jill wants to rush upon the media. She has the courage of desperation. "The revolution is going on right now, the magazines are just a bullhorn." I believe her. Then I don't again. Not a bullhorn. A muffler. Confuse everyone, make causes ephemeral, each lib craze a bubble bursting in copy. Swallow it all up. "We are devoured," I say. Jill is raring to smash herself upon the flames, be Joan of Arc. Garbage, I argue, I prefer to stay alive. Martyrdom's a bad number. Vicious. Lets off steam. Everyone commits murder and feels better for weeks afterwards. They kill people so that nothing can happen. It's spectator sport. Change is harder than this, goes deeper, must move in everyone. Jill's thrust of ego. Its gallantry. Its mania. Urging herself in the pain of the pariah, fame its reward. And still hungry. A difference of appetite. I threw up and went crazy. She thinks that's a put-on. Who wouldn't want all they could get of it? And Jill's fame is finer, more crafted, solid, built up in her own town over years of writing, respected by special friends in art. My course was different. Unknown sculptor to media nut in a matter of weeks, all because of a doctoral thesis. Different routes, reputation versus notoriety.

And now I must renovate my interior. Winnie helps. And Nell. I tell Jill about Winnie. It does not interest her. I try harder. But she is not to be interested. We talk gay again. Our bond. But I have other places. Never queer enough for the fanatic. Confused with straight people because I know Jill. Confused with Jill because I know straight people. And Winnie. But I cannot live with Winnie either. And have to be myself. Wondering who this is. In a London bar.

We are off to the movies. My movie. Showing it to Mrs. Fenimore today. Jill has consented to watch. Through Soho with our legs swinging. Right along Greek Street and into Montage Films. Swinging through the door. We are important persons. I have an appointment. Acting significant while I check to see if the film has been delivered by the lab. Of course it hasn't. Voice on the phone rather bored saying they did put it on the van. Might be there sometime this afternoon. Here I am with a real English distributor willing to sit through a screening and they can't come up with the damn film. Upstairs we discover the film has already arrived in Mrs. Fenimore's office. However, she has forgotten the appointment. We are the very opposite of important persons. We are two very peculiar American dykes in dungarees. Jill gives me the what the hell are you waiting for worm let's get out of here look. But it is not her movie. I become a rigid object. Assisted by the company who function as one great recriminating mother, giving orders that you don't walk out in pique when it's business. That the seller has no right to vanity. Even pride. Anyway, Bella Fenimore is obliged to keep her appointments. So I keep my seat. All amiable determination. Mrs. Fenimore suddenly finds time at five. It is four. We will be back.

We have an hour. What shall we do? Jill would have us go to a strip show. Why not? I have been running an imagined one in my head for months, now, thanks to thousands of Soho poster come-ons. Try the real thing and see what the case may be. We find a sleazy fellow in a booth. Pound apiece, he says. Fifty new pence, Jill bargains. The thing is done. We wait for him to open the magic doors of vice. Elbowing each other for daring. He will of course decide we are depraved females, but the hell with what he thinks.

Instead he leaves his little booth. Gruff voice, follow me. We look askance at each other behind his back. Shrug our shoulders, being brave. And follow. One block after another. Till we are scared. Passing a garage I fantasize the warehouse murders out of some movie on Forty-second Street eating popcorn with Fumio in the balcony. Blood flows in technicolor. And James Bond or Jimmy Brown plays samurai surrounded by killers knocking one off at a time. In no mood for this, thank you. Jill has had it too. Whatever movie she's playing, our reels have run out at the same moment. "Now look mister where the hell are you taking us?" Prudent U.S. tourists. He scarcely deigns to turn his head. We are touts going along behind the pimp. This is getting on my nerves, I'm quitting. Then he turns into the first gray breast of London. How providential. My own magic mystery theater. Home at last. Brazen it past the lady who holds the curtain. Thoroughly ashamed of ourselves until we see the crowd. Little gathering of weirdies. Spending the afternoon in similar fashion. Don't get righteous libby, I repeat to myself, sliding into a chair embarrassed. Only other woman here is with a middle-aged mustache up front. Jill and I struggle to preserve our difference during the long wait till something happens. Remind myself I am pursuing education. Gathering data. Feeling like a heel.

"This is probably the oldest form of human entertainment," Jill philosophizes in a whisper, seat on my left. We grow wise and tolerant over British repression, probably helps people like this. Why deny another's need, pleasure? And so forth. So much for the client. Likely to pay better than other jobs in Soho. So much for the "girls." Always they are "girls," I sotto voce, griping about the cops and their jailhouse familiarity with prostitutes. Artists and models, we muse. Till shushed by the man in the back. Less than a paragraph's repartee left before we'll get kicked out. And the show not even started. We agree to keep silent. Waiting still in the glare red light of sinful. How many fleas? Our knees up on the seats before us empty. Defiant outsiders. "Have two women together ever visited this joint before?" "Yes, I expect they get everything." Pretty soon a hard dame selling beer. Then orange soda. When does the popcorn arrive? But it never did. Instead they start the show.

Patience rewarded in the sight of a bored girl with a green scarf.

Scratchy phonograph plays snake dance. Paraphernalia with scarf while she takes off her clothes. Slow dancing the while, slithering the scarf. Supposed to diddle herself with it. Male fantasy of lonely chick masturbating in sad need of him. The unforeseen takes charge, her record slows from 33 to 18 rpm. Catastrophe sets in, the audience unable even to titter. Green scarf can't dance anymore, wobbles around, makes faces desperate in annoyance, signals to guy offstage—get that damn thing to work. First thing you want to do is laugh. Usual instance of technology's subversion of the arts. Then you can't laugh. Same way you can't enjoy the lovely body. Because of the face, so alienated shattered wretched. Speed down to about 7 rpm now. She stand there not moving, not even trying to move. Alone on the stage. Naked to the outlines of gents in the audience front rows ahead of us. Green rag in her hand. Perfection of her solitude, mocked by every circumstance. Humiliated by life. Curtain closes. Got their money's worth.

That's when I whispered to Jill, "Let's neck." If we were to sit there necking in our back seats. Knowing that only by necking, the two women of us, kicked out maybe but only by that could we defy, negate, lay waste the place. Scared suggesting it. Afraid she'd take me up on it. Might have the nerve for it if she did. We didn't. Next stripper looks like Lila. And smiles. I thought this would be better. But it isn't, it's worse. The sporting attitude in it only furthers the hurt. The last woman in red, cold pure and British. Her icy Saxon look defiled by masturbation to the anticipated and calculated relish of the myth. The stomach watches weak with anger. Thought I heard Jill sob in her seat. Hair over her eyes, face in profile. Do I imagine or does she have a cold? Out of the basement and back to the movies.

Lionel Rogosin is in the building. Will I let him see my film? Flaherty's heir, and will I let him? Big meek man in white hair, soft like a woman, quiet. So we are four when the little screen lights up. Tensing before my first lookers. I can feel them seeing. My hope trying to carry each point into their minds through eyes watching in darkness. Jill on my left, her energy, Lionel and Mrs. Fenimore back of us where I cannot supervise. The eyes in my back along the shoulders, guiding, worrying over them. But unable to control. Jill either. Be damned with it then, let it be their movie. Watching Mallory. All there really. When she's real. When she's phony. Integrity, fantasy, pathos, bitchery. All her fetches and glances. Voices and faces. Winks a big left eye at you—"You see I thought we were going to live some place like Paris or Rome . . ." Then broke and sad. Then Camping it, "But you don't know my poor husband!" Or soap opera—"He was desperate to keep me." "And here I am in New York City," the curtain blowing orange life behind her, "a wicked woman who lived this wicked life in Hollywood. And what did I want with this child? What did I want with her anyway?" The question stark and homely as life. Then in the black and white another version, "Motherhood is the moment when you really lose your freedom." And her childhood, the part we fought over most. I had wanted her to tell my childhood. But she had her own. "My father left when I was eight," Mallory announces out of the movie. Mine left when I was thirteen. Mallory wringing her hands across the screen. Like me. Like Mom. We all squeak. Superfeminine panic gesture. Mother a mouse all those years. How easily I despised her. Till I went mouse myself that winter. Now Mallory up there complaining. How good we all are at griping. The other side of our don't-hit-me racket.

Mallory does her pouting game. Family beauty. "I got to a point in Manila where I felt so idle." Camera moves across the curtain the way Betty and I spent six tense hours of cutting to make it move, just that way. Mallory goes on, realizing she has gotten to be twenty-five, "My God, it was so easy to get to be this age. Another little while and I'll be fifty or fifty-five. And sit around at the country club with other women who have rich husbands and say you know when I was twenty I wanted to . . . And I always thought that was such a pathetic thing to hear." Nell and I never got through that part without wincing. Looking at each other each time we ran it through the Steembeck knowing Mallory had put her finger on time and what you get done in a life. Never enough even if you scramble. How much if you are trapped like Nell?

"Robin told me about a job driving a hansom cab," Mallory introducing the grit and circus of her waitressing. "I was fired from fourteen jobs. Now you just try to *find* fourteen jobs. Fired for everything from not fucking the boss to . . ." she rolls her eyes in the force of her vulgarity, the staying power in her tough broad human self. Mallory is stronger. Can outlast anyone. Then high on herself, ". . . to just not showing up for work. After all, my life is fascinating." There is one dishonest second, her mouth wrong on "had to borrow to pay the rent last month, which I *do* not like to do."

Then the last beautiful sequence on her loft. One shot pure as Eisenstein. Her long rap on what the loft has meant. Making it on her own at last. "Going from everything neat and tidy and American clean to living in a loft near the Bowery. Building my own whole new life." A fire engine starts up across the street. Mallory's genius weaving it into her speech, sitting on the bed in her work shirt. "I would go down that elevator. And there would be a bum. In his own vomit and piss and shit. And I would look at him and know what it means to give up." The camera on her hands. How fine of Delora to give up the face this one most important second, not do the obvious but instead watch those frantic pair of hands.

"All I think about is money . . . All I can think about in the city of New York is money." My sister's face staring at me in her desperation. Voice catches, "And you *know* that no one you'd go up to and ask . . . why, they'd look at you like a piece of shit. . . . And when I say that what I've been through has been hell, I don't mean I wasn't happy." Bravery of hysteria in her voice.

"He can go away. You don't need him. He can go away forever." All paradox. We hear what she means. Meaning it to be true. Yet still isn't.

Then Lillian. Little mystery story. Two women. One on camera, another one off. The second speaking as the picture freezes, telling the other side of herself she won't tell the camera eye. What do you do with a subject who won't talk to the camera? We froze her and played the wild sound version of herself against the sync. Our ultimate solution. Having no choice if we were to make sense. Running the wild sound, the relaxed version given to us as people sitting around just taping. In opposition to the "adjusted woman" reserved for the camera. The immigrant home, the tyrannical father she still so loves and admires. "I had to beg my father to go to college," serene remembering it. And the beaten mother whose superstitions she carries still, putting down the old lady as a frigid woman, "There were many of them in her generation." Then telling you that sex is like pissing for guys, "Like going to the bathroom," Lillian pronounces, all unaware what she is saying, the damage that line represents. A woman my mother's age never guessing she is her own mother still. The hard-won freedom of education begged from her father and surrendered to her husband, a chemist. Gave up her chemistry for his. In the interview a thousand justifications. She was not good enough. Didn't have the dedication of a great scientist. Does he? No. But he did have a nervous breakdown. That's some revenge. For one or the other. Index of what it costs to stifle a life. The black water pounces across the screen, my own crazy night visual in his. "What caused it?" Her voice trailing off. Still not comprehending it.

Then Robin hippie radical talk mouth. Catching herself in her own lies' truth. A tough searching mind. A political jesuit. A put-on with her nonsense about magic or astrology. Next second telling you it's all bullshit. A cynic hiding the scars of a sentimentalist. The hurt kid thrown out of the house always pretending that she moved out. Kicked out, a kid in the Brooklyn snow with a flare for histrionics but still a child in the street penniless. Dad won't endure queers. The bleacher scene, showing off. Hell no, she doesn't want to get a job. Would rather rip off the world. Finding her freedom a vacuum. Still alive after that summer on drugs. "Bullshit kind of killing myself," demeaning even her own suicide. Still not telling you why. Robin in her cages so much like my own. Both of us sculptors. And Robin a prodigy, director, actress, writer. Her "very portable cage." Her Hell's Canyon story. The fun Ellen and I had trick-cutting this. Delora's shadow shots to fool around with. And the cross-cutting during the exercises where Robin directs the company. Herself the director of a successful repertory at twenty. Then left it flat. They made her "weird."

And finally it starts, the scene in the toilet, Robin's come-out. Nice Jewish girl from Queens. Ran away to summer stock. Long three-stand narrative. We just trimmed it and kept the form of her own three-way pounce: reading *Well of Loneliness* while her roommate laughed, exploring the boardwalk and met a freak in the night. Harmless gypsy dwarf. But afraid. Her love of water and adventure roaring at you like the waves. Carnivals and freaks. Lastly the boy brutally fucking her in cold blood. "I learned a lot when he did it to me," never even letting it add up. "I have to just work. Go. I don't have time to think." Then my own voice telling her, "We're halfway through the roll." "So what do you want? . . . Cut," she orders. Screen goes blank while we fight in the basement of a real loft in a real toilet. Should have left that part as was. Too raw, I thought. Watching it now wish I'd been braver. To hell with form. Let them sit there in the dark and bear reality even without pictures.

On screen again, Robin the defensive homosexual. The world can drop dead. "There's the word—LESBIAN." Making a face at us, demonstrating its absurdity. Gives notice she will not be boxed in. Lectures you. Pleads. Bullies. Tells us our fears. Her own. More fights with camera, with crew. Sticks. Robin telling me to shut up. "Finally they make you insane." "It's true, you make yourself grotesque." At last explaining the repertory company. "Either ball them or ball no one. So they made me weird." And at last, head down among the big wooden spools, that final sad surreal shot. Voices saying Robin Robin keep quiet. Like after a rape. Yet not that either. Robin all the time wise and careful she would be seen only on her terms. Nobody's movie Lesbian. Telling you again after the credits that she's someone else now. An epilogue on time and change, speech I wrote for her on the cutter, composed like a Scrabble game from the wastes of language.

My attention reaches back for the figures watching behind me. Lost them with that pause before Robin. The lab didn't have a show reel long enough for the whole thing and the projectionist must rewind in awkward silence while I curse the unprofessional look of things. Mrs. Fenimore ventures a remark on how my characters echo their parents' lives. As I had meant them to. But she sounds disapproving. "They speak of their fathers," she says. I am defensive, not really answering, just enduring until the third reel is shown, then get out of here. Grinding through Robin without hope. Mrs. Fenimore's formulating the little speech that says it's all very nice indeed but not suitable, no we can't use it. Composing myself for graceful rejection, but just as she begins it Lionel slaps his knee, shouts it's a great movie can he distribute it?

How to avoid fainting upon his trouser cuffs, slobbering upon his shoelaces? By focusing upon what he says, yes Bleecker Street Cinema, of course he owns that. My movie schoolroom these past ten years. Dear old firetrap movie shrine. And Lionel has a college circuit thing too, explaining it all four times since I can hardly listen because I have got an American distributor by accident in England and here is Mrs. Fenimore even changing her mind. A man said the movie was good. Now she is undecided. Her husband must see it. All of us standing by the staircase being inefficient, should a print be left here, when to pick it up, I leave so soon. Jill is bolting already. And Lionel, must have a moment with him, the two of us rattling down Greek Street bemoaning the distribution racket. How it fucks up the filmmaker. And the radicals always wanting your movie free even if you went broke making it. Jill holds aloof. Doing my own business on her time, she resents this. Lionel and I effuse over our favorite filmmakers. Then I praise his documentaries and he praises my first flick. Approval of a master, Lionel saying I should make more films, bathing in these words the unbelievable sweetness of it. That someone liked my movie. Jill of course would not venture that far, liked Mallory, a good-looking chick. But Robin wasn't good enough since Robin has to be Jill, the gay standard bearer. And no one is good enough for that. Jill hostile, impossible to please. Scolding me for Robin's smart-aleck toss-offs, remarks like "Books are pretty trivial." A remark Jill now takes to be the summit of my own philosophy.

Then Lionel is off. I must pack up my exhilaration and talk another whiskey to Jill. Who wants to talk about our images. "They're magic. When JERRY RUBIN walks down the street people see that. He alone knows it's only jerry rubin. This is how revolution works in media. You make yourself a myth." But I object that myths are dangerous. And besides, it's hokey. But she says I'm being unrealistic—"Anyway why not enjoy it?"

She enjoys being Jill Johnston, looking the part in this bar but also an aging woman living in a mirror on her reflection given back as food by those she feeds also picking her bones in the process. "And when you wake up alone who are you then?"—I say, dreading winter. She doesn't answer, not listening. Running on in my own privacy, no I will go on trying to be real, leaving the silvered surface behind only mercury dull in daylight go down below the waters of the glass and try to grow a soul. "But there you are being serious again," she says. "You think you really are the women's movement, don't you?" Habitual put-down. Teetering before it, grip the table, wait for the third and final whiskey and consider saying, "Why not be very serious, Jill, what I meant to be is not that political idiocy of newsprint." But how can I say what it is when I am so ashamed to word it, say that I would like to be a catalyst and give my life to help somehow, if I could grow enough, find, hack, wait, build, space inside to know more, of course not to perfect but invent improve . . . the sunlight through the window hitting Jill's hair, lighting its gray then beating afternoon into my eyes . . . if I could go on and do and become no, not fine, the rays lighting each strand, . . . but finer anyway than I started, that fool cowering in upon her night. The golden glass is empty and we go.

11

I manage it up the stairs. A full case of Valpolicella. And the bottles of Scotch. Restocking the larder because tomorrow I fly. The office door is locked. Have to wait here on the landing till Paul has parked the car. It is my last day in England. Driving to the office they played the cassettes and I finger-popped in the back seat. But Nell sat rigid under her hat. Passing under the railroad bridge at St. Pancras a billboard shouted "Cystic Fibrosis." Medical intelligence of Celia. Everything is magical today because it is the last day. We passed a theater offering Shaw. Literature has lost its violence for me. I observe with equanimity an old play mounted wondering vaguely even why they do it. The sense of emergency has passed. Paul stops the car and lets me out. Waiting with his exquisite courtesy while I get down before he drives on to the parking lot. I have spent my ten minutes with luxurious economy, revitalizing the office bar and dragging the whole conglomerate purchase up the four flights. Past the shady businesses on landing one, the desolate employment agency on landing two, the peculiar French cooking outfit that is always locked or full of Germans on landing three. And now I must wait in front of our big English door locked. Wishing I had not yet turned in my key. There were mornings once when I was first to the office, waiting for Betty in a fury of fear ... how to turn this mess into a movie. Driven over the pages of transcript, rearranging the blocks, cutting, pasting a new arrangement on paper. Frantic waiting to see it cut into film and run through the Steembeck. Would it work? And tonight it is screened in England. Today I pay my bills.

I lean my cardboard case against the door and rest. There is something huge about this day. Hard too, like leaving home, the three of them Nell Winnie Paul. The office in Soho. The house in Islington. At least they'll have booze. Winnie has the GLF. If Nell ever gets to New York she can shoot film again. If only Paul could get work. If the Joplin thing came through. But here he is, full majesty climbing the stairs, amused at the sight of me under my burden. "You could at least put the bloody thing down." "I was thinking, Paul, how sorry I am to leave." "Well, never mind. Let's have some coffee."

I fix the last cup of watered instant and we start on the bills. At first it seems possible. I'll make it. Only eleven hundred something. I have that much in traveler's checks. Spreading them on the floor. The American faces looking up at us, Presidents of the dollar. Paul adds more figures. Translates currency. His huge shoulders bent over the pieces of paper. Back from her vacation, Betty dashes in and out, feeding the fire with further invoices. Opticals. Labs. Rentals. I remember Nell estimated fifteen hundred just for the printing costs. And hold my breath. We are up to seventeen hundred now and I am over my head. Could send him a check from New York tomorrow, very moment I arrive. But no, I don't want to leave owing money. Paul has given me full use of his credit. And their company is broke now, the bank manager insistent. I imagine their interviews. Paul grand as a duke requesting time, the manager some small figure from real life presenting him with creditors. No, I cannot leave England owing them money. But we are up to twenty-three hundred dollars now. The last huge bill for the masters comes in. We have just passed three thousand.

My head spins in Paul's elegant office, the leather chairs, the glass tabletops, the antique camera mounted like a sculpture, Hedda's paintings. The heroic photograph of Paul shooting an Ariflex. The still more heroic shot of Nell behind a full-scale 35 mm big as a building. Paul dusts his cigar and begins translating pounds and dollars. I no longer follow the figures. He is more honest than I am and a far better mathematician. This frees me to pace the room and have a really good handwringing. How to find three thousand dollars in an afternoon? I look at Paul dumbfounded.

He is nonplussed. Has probably been in this bind a hundred times. Whole movie business runs on credit. I must be the only filmmaker alive who pays each bill in cash as I go along. Girl from St. Paul, I titter in semi-hysterics. "Call your publisher," Paul says as if this were not an amazing thing to do. "Granada gives my royalties to Doubleday, who gives them to me only twice a year in New York." "Ask them for a loan." Voice of reason. "They don't have to make loans to itinerant authors who run up movie bills. They'll just say it isn't policy and all that rot." "You can try." I must get on the phone. Mortified that the first thing I do after thanking the women at Doubleday for their kindness and dinners is to hit them for bread. Barbara Noble just laughs and asks how much. I repeat the awesome figure. Her voice, lower now, says give me a bit of time. "I doubt we have that much in our London account. I'll need twenty minutes or so to call Garden City, New York." I hang up in a daze. In twenty minutes she means to find three thousand dollars. Paul comments on the notorious reverence with which the Briton holds all writers of books. I am nearly prepared to agree. But I know it is a miracle. The miracle of Barbara Noble. Meanwhile I tread on air and chew my nails over the income tax. The phone rings, three grand, she's got it. We plunge through the labyrinth of capitalist machinery to find a way to the bank before closing time, a certified check for the lab before they shut in the evening. Even Paul is impressed by this process and grows dubious. "You may have to stay on a few days." But there is Celia's surgery. Nell wouldn't let a few obstacles like banks intrude upon sentiment. Neither will I.

A good ten minutes late for lunch with no less a person than Doris Lessing. A thought that reduces money to its rightful insignificance as I churn out of the office leaving Paul to rumble. I astonish myself today. Waiting for a cab at Charing Cross I am Mary Marvel. A mere word and my blouse will explode revealing the mystic thunderbolt. I am an American comic strip heroine. Full tilt from broken wing to superwoman. Efforts to control my euphoria succeed not at all. Give in and live it, life has so few days like this. The cab obeys my supernatural signs. A great black beast at my command all the way to this great lady.

Roses in front and cheerful wallpaper. Impossible to be more extraordinarily ordinary. Nothing is more impressive than the commonplace situations that surround great persons. Like de Beauvoir's pedestrian rooms hidden behind the most unassuming white stone front and a draconic concierge. I call up the stairs and she shakes my hand. Today a day so beyond possibility that I am flowing through it like a fairy tale. Or an acid trip. Or what you will. I feel like Anthony returned from the wars as I behold the strawberries she has actually washed with her own hands in my honor. "Lily white," we joke. "Isn't the racism of language amazing?" I am grateful as any undergraduate having lunch with the professor of his soul but we chatter like any two women over recipes. The room where she writes spied through a half-opened door. Inner sanctum of paper confusion. How reassuring that she's not neat. And wait with my gin in the living room friendly in its rather tacky orientalia, Persian this and thats and rugs and curtains and cushions. The soft clutter of an English room, homely as the grace of her hair in a bun.

Confess my agony of last time. How absurd not to tell her of *The Golden Notebook* that I couldn't write. "But now you can," she says. Bright, maternal. "Do you worry you will lose writing?" "No, I know now that I can do it." She says it simply. Just that command is what a lifetime has given. Then she astounds me. "I know I can do it. My problem is wondering why I should." "But you are making literature," I protest. Lifetimes of libraries and scholarships, vigil lamps, envy, admiration, idolatry. Six years of graduate school. My God, to make literature and wonder why one does it. Of course she has made a grimace over "literature." "And if I were? What does it accomplish?" I have never thought. Art is of itself surely. I am dumbfounded by such a question. "Your book does things," she says. Doris Lessing is referring to my poor damned thesis. Its humid rhetoric. The pedestrian tirade. "Books like that make change," she insists.

"Just think of what *The Golden Notebook* has meant to the thousands of women who read it." "But I've no idea. When I came to New York they thought it meant something else. We had a terrible time." I laugh, remembering the fiasco at Kaufmann Hall. Movement heavies coming to cheer Lessing as their heroine, but she infuriates them by saying she doesn't hate men at all and finds other world conditions—peace, poverty, class—all far more pressing than the problems of women. "Let me tell you what it meant to me. In a detail you may find ridiculous. It's the moment your heroine shall we say," we smile, "finds herself in a toilet at the outset of her period. In St. Paul we call it the curse." We smile again. "And the blood is running down her legs while she struggles with toilet paper. Kleenex. That sort of thing In a book! Happens every month of adult life to half the population of the globe and no one had ever mentioned it in a book." There is a passage in Mary

McCarthy where the heroine so-called does the sub-
limely stupid thing of getting drunk on a train and
spends the night in a berth fucking some character she's
picked up. It's the sort of harebrained thing we've all
done and hated ourselves for afterwards. But she had
the guts to admit it. Was honest enough. "Of course that
is just the sort of thing one blushes to write," she laughs.
"But the most curious thing is that the very passages that
once caused me the most anxiety, the moments when
I thought, no, I cannot put this on paper—are now the
passages I'm proud of. That comfort me most out of all
I've written. Because through letters and readers I discovered these were the moments when I spoke for other
people. So paradoxical. Because at the time they seemed
so hopelessly private . . ."

"It is the expression of the self in women now that is
most interesting," she goes on. "I have been getting it
in the mail and hearing it in rumors from the most peculiar places." And she tells me people write her from
loony bins. And she writes back. Virtue like this is
too great a reproof to a noncorrespondent. "I cannot
cure this woman's mind but I do read her manuscript,"
Lessing chuckles. "And it is fascinating. The whole thing
pours out of her. So I suggested she write a book. Now
I can't wait to read it. In fact this is the only sort of
thing that interests me now. What people write about
their lives. I want to see what you do too."

"But I'm always embarrassed. Have so much to be self-
conscious about. Doing it in the first person which seems
necessary somehow, much of the point is lost in my case
if I didn't put myself on the line. But feeling so
vulnerable, my god, a Lesbian. Sure, an experience of
human beings. But not described. Not permitted. It has
no traditions. No language. No history of agreed values."
"But of course people wish to know," she interrupts.
"And you cannot be intimidated into silence. Or the
silence is prolonged forever."

I am lulled by her kindness and the strawberries.
Slender maternal figure before me in her chair as I sit
on the floor. Primed with my greatest confusion. Mother.

"You see if I write this book my mother's going to die. She has already given me notice." Lessing laughs. "Mothers do not die as easily as they claim. My own announced her intentions with every book I wrote. And I went on hoping eventually I might manage to please her, that I could finally make her proud of me. Only to produce another funeral. Women who write books have a particular obstacle in their mothers. I suppose it is universal." "There's Colette and Sidonie." "Ah, but they never quite convinced me. In any case I did not have their luck. My mother finally did die, for reasons of her own. But I find she never quite went away."

With coffee we turn to politics and why it is not enough. Or never quite the right thing. "You'll get it from that angle," she warns. "I already hear you damned for a pacifist." "I plan to atone for my sins with a course of study. Bury myself for a year in the country under volumes of Marx." "You will be doing the Left an honor They never read Marx themselves. But the irritating thing is their general inhumanity. If becomes the question of how to the exclusion of why. And the how grows more and more ugly. I did not join the Party till much later in England, so my real political activity was out in Rhodesia, where politics was something terribly real. The situation confronting us every day in is full horror and injustice. But when I came to England I found the Left could mean dull persons shouting at meetings. Boring me to death with their egos. With words. Verbiage more outrageous the less it meant. They hated art. In time I came to fear that they hated people as well. Living lives of frenzied emotionality based on the sufferings of other persons in other countries about whom they seemed to care very little except to find them convenient for certain neurotic needs and schemes of their own."

I suddenly remember something from the news. "Did you notice in yesterday's paper, Mideast oligarch arrests ten who plotted his assassination? What if this guy let them go? Showed mercy, and depended upon it as a tactic. Who could bring about his overthrow if he displayed such confidence in his powers to bring better

rule than the other types? And if he can't why doesn't
he quite? Imagine what a nightmare it must be to be in
power. He'd enjoy his existence so much better as a
private citizen." While I am conjuring up a situation
where the tyrant reforms in a great fanfare of trumpets,
she notifies me that by today's paper the despot has
already dispatched his victims. "No one ever exercises
any imagination," we laugh, a laugh like a sigh.

"What is truly depressing," she moves in her chair,
"is to see men you've known, given shelter, fed, housed,
helped once when they were radicals, outlaws, revolutionaries, returned to England now as powers. Ministers
in African states. And have to listen while they describe
their murders, rationalize their purges, excuse their
crimes because they were necessary to stay in power."

We are naïve and moralistic women. We are human
beings. Who find politics a blight upon the human condition. And do not know how one copes with it except
through politics. And more directly through change,
liberation, small personal things, subjective exercises
appropriate only to persons with enough to eat, residence
in one of the supposedly advanced, namely developed,
capitalist and imperialist nations. Who if they made
certain inroads upon their own society could redirect
it even to the advantage of the others upon whose neck
it stands.

"But in seven years we have not even stopped the war
in Vietnam," I argue. "No, you have not. But you have
begun something else more remarkable if less efficacious.
A great pendulum of social force, a charge, a movement
among millions of Americans spreading now abroad too.
A potential. Beginning at home, or in the area upon
which one has control, effect, knowledge." I catch her
meaning and see even why one begins with the self. All
one has claim to finally. And change is a spiritual
discipline one practices, waiting in hope. Starting with
you and those around you. Knowing it takes time and
that change is deep, is living, is a force formed within.
Then projected, supported by others, feeling it too. A
communion. No, not mystic or if so, surely not bullshit,

evangelical, deluded, or irrational. But real and measured in acts, in reality as well as in the psyche, as real, often, as the objective world. It is another way to live, to act, to feel, a transvaluation of values and of the very forms of apprehension. A reorientation of attitudes. A revolution is not the overturning of a cart, a reshuffling in the cards of state. It is a process, a swelling, a new growth in the race. If it is real, not simply a trauma, it is another ring in the tree of history, layer upon layer of invisible tissue composing the evidence of a circle.

Whatever else was said upon that second cup of coffee was unimportant since that moment held upon a spoon whereby we have communicated our hope and kissed good-bye. But still the walk to the station. No cabs. And the tube, she claims, is quicker. Watching her, a middle-aged English lady troubling to guide this brash American to a train station. Effusive in thanks, but it is insolence somehow to thank the great. And a poignant little hug no humility could honor.

Crazy American lady bowling down Oxford Street. Rogosin waiting at the office to make the contract. Will he help Nell and Paul distribute their films? Tearing along in search of Wardour Streeet into Soho. A black man said two turnings down. And here it is. Soho's street of film. The big ones standing shoulder to shoulder, Rank and Universal Pictures. Vast plate glass displays porno, *Estelle's Secret*. Science fiction in seven colors. Wonderful wars in panorama, fifteen thousand extras to impersonate the "Jap" army. Real movies out of real money.

Upstairs to Nell. Magda's on the phone saying the manuscript is already half typed, she'll finish the rest in time for the plane. Nell under the big hat, same black mood of this morning's doldrum. I am leaving England tomorrow. Tonight is my first public screening. I cannot leave if she's angry. And tonight the screening. Nell in a sandpaper mood, cutting her new footage with Betty. I look at the big 35 mm frames. Color. Flawless shooting. Lovely woman with a little girl running in the woods at Hampton Heath. It is a fine still. A dream. They are flying a kite together. In three days it will be covered with talk about candy bars. All its liveliness will become pointless, lost. Nell is angry at Magda. Didn't say good-bye when she left the house the other day. "That's probably my fault. You were downstairs with Winnie when they had to leave so I just showed them out without bothering you. Of course she said good-bye, but I forgot to convey it. Be mad at me. Not Magda." Nell is in tears now. "I'm not angry with you. Or even Magda. I'm angry at everyone. Here I am, stuck with this damned lousy commercial." Crying now, in her crying I can fill in the rest—Here I am with this damned lousy commercial and there you are with a film and a distributor and a big screening tonight. She is crying in my arms and I am crying while I mumble good-bye I'll see you there. "Please be there tonight Nell, don't let me down." And forgive me too, I am saying. But not out loud. Because she is stuck here and envious but will not be envious because she wishes me well and has helped me to get these things, things she wanted for herself. And somehow I must help her get them too.

I am a figure in white clothes in Cambridge Circus before Danny's great palace. Scrambling for a cab. As they hurl about me not stopping. I am to be punished for my glamorous life. Today of all days, today when I can borrow three grand in twenty minutes, have lunch with Doris Lessing, and throw my first screening. But for want of a cab will blow the whole thing, miss the check, fail to pay the lab for prints, the screen will be empty at the screening. All for lack of a cab. As a brash man seizes a cab from an old lady I have leisure to wonder if I would have had courtesy enough to give her mine. But there are none. No more. Never. In Cambridge Circus in my best white ice-cream pants and Mexican shirt. A figure in the center of chaos. Swimming in a desperation to live and do better, prevail. Will one never come?

Then speeding to the Regency Grand. Scene of dull wedding receptions, British bar mitzvah, company banquets, red velvet carpets, brocade wallpaper shtick.

Enough to retch at just getting up the stairs. The movement here? All those English women in Yankee overalls and stompers, radical gear, trendy people in this mausoleum? They will refuse to enter. No one will come. I will sit there alone and watch my movie. *Citizen Kane*. Even Paul had promised to come. Saw the first assembly of Mallory and went humph. Tonight I was going to show him it wasn't as hopeless as he thought. Top of the stairs it says "Disney" in large letters. My people will see that and leave. Disney is screening on my time. My people will have to wait hours till he stops. Disney and fans, most awful people I ever saw, all over the place. Door opens to a view of the screening room. Hideous. I hate it. Dreaming in the toilet at the office this afternoon I heard applause. Huzzahs. My English sisters loving my movie, loving me. No one will ever applaud in this room.

No one will even collect my damn film. I will have to leave it here in the corridor to be stolen. A man jumps through the window. The projectionist. Senile, with impossible eyesight. Takes my cans of film and disappears, saying they have only one 16 mm projector. Means they will have to stop my movie in the middle and rewind. I jump through the window, trying to pursue this malevolent idiot along a narrow catwalk. Remind him not to lose my film. And check to see what he's done with it. Busy reading his comic book, never even looking at the movie going on. Poor Disney, banging through the window after me, both of us fifty feet in the air, Disney yelling full force Hollywood voice *Put that in focus or I'll strangle you I have backers in there you are ruining me*. Projectionist scarcely misses a frame of his comic book. "Who are you?" I ask the Disney guy. "I'm Disney." "Disney's dead years ago. Right after *Fantasia*." "There are a million Disneys." We exchange a hypnotized American intelligence composed of Hollywood and movies, money, cigars and childhood, philistine hatred and patriotism.

As I come down the stairs I see the crowd. It cannot be for my film. But they raise a yell when I come out.

Heavens, I'm heroized, how embarrassing, trying to find a familiar face in the mob. O'Rourke screaming, "By Jesus you're late and they won't let us in. Get up there again and make them open those damned doors." It is still funny, so I laugh plunging through the horde of overalls knapsacks full redical fettle. Now grumbling at me. "Really I'm terribly sorry they've got this Disney thing on, overbooked their lousy theater and so there'll be a slight delay, forgive us." Grim-faced lady at the door in no mood to reason, still less for humor. "Who are these dreadful people?" "My guests, madam." Someone from the press is furious and actually screaming at me, she will never do this again for anyone. And goes off in a huff with Lady Somebody who can't wait a moment longer. I am sorry but unable to do anything about it. And the movement waiting outside outraged that media persons in straight clothes are permitted to enter before them, the management in collusion with the respectable-seeming among my friends who were able to talk their way in. Everything is going wrong. I have just arrived, had nothing to do with the favoritism, but am going to get flogged anyway. The movement yelling that even men have been permitted to enter! Why am I letting men in? Because they have been invited. But it is not fair, they'll use all the seats! Somehow I must get them all in, even the men. Because they are guests. Uncivilized to invite and then exclude. But there may not be enough chairs. And the bloody management will not even open the doors yet. Lady in charge wants me to hurry up and go inside.

I refuse. Will stay outside with the movement until we are all permitted inside. More dressed-up persons pass by, leaving in pique. The movement gets uglier noisier more impossible. Enjoying themselves hugely. Righteous. Converting themselves into an army, liberate this joint with fire and sword of radical rhetoric. Volume of their grumbling reaches a fine pitch. Wonderful, I think, Disney will precipitate the revolution by running overtime.

Finally here are the Disney crowd in exit. Stand back

and let them pass. Willing to give them my shirt for a carpet. Anything to get them out of there. And us in. Then the crunch as my irate comrades swarm the theater, five of them at me like gadflies. Will I permit the men to sit, to stay? Let's just see how far the chairs go. Then we may have to make a decision. Perhaps we can ask them to stand. To sit on the floor or give up their seats? Giggling at how much it sounds like chivalry. And rushing through the alternatives while five very intelligent women gone banshee insist on total exclusion. Imagining Paul's face if they kick him out. Mr. Reynolds and Patrick, my guests from Granada. Not to mention the movement's own boyfriends. All innocents who in the course of things have been invited and have bothered to come. Humiliation of being ejected from a theater by a gaggle of screaming females. But the nightmare ends. There are just enough seats. Finally the violence subsides. Everyone will be served. I am not going to be torn limb from limb. Now if that projectionist will get his shit together back there and start before they tear the place apart in impatience. The crowd now yelling for air. I find a side door and open it. Stand in its cool air one full claustrophobe moment wishing I could follow that staircase and escape. Never come back. How much cash do I have on me? How far could I get? Grinning at the idea.

Back to my seat. Next to Paul, who's next to Nell. I would like to sit between them. He is not letting me. Then he gets up and I take his seat. Between them I can both observe Paul's reactions and whisper with Nell over audience response. Now the lights go down. The titles come up over an American ocean and three women. Mallory starts her rap. The images flicker huge upon the screen. I sweat and hanker after the dim light coming through the door in the corner. Gray as fate. Paul chews. We smoke. Mallory goes out of focus. She is talking one frame too slow. Nell sees it too. Paul does not notice. It is getting worse. That crazy idiot is reading his comic book. "Go back and get him to fix it," Nell whispers. I crawl along the floor. Then hurl myself to the door and out the window. Would love to shake him but then he'd really mess me up. Being polite, though I could choke him, aghast at my own fury. While he argues. Makes excuses. Mystifies me with technology while I insist he get it right. Change the frame speed. Totally uninterested in anything but his child picturebook, he is exercising the power of life and death over me, ruining one year's work absentmindedly, sabotaging a film two hundred and forty persons have wasted a London evening to see. And not seeing it. Scarcely aware yet they are not seeing it. Just frowning, unaccountably bored because the tiny images go one frame per second too slow and the voice they hear cannnot command their attention because it is ever so slightly distorted. The projectionist, an old man who hates his life, relents at last, says he'll change it. Back like a rat scurrying to my seat. To wait on in a terror of nerves wondering what he will do next till Nell holds my hand and I relax.

Paul breathes hard on my right. Nell breathes hard on my left. The audience breathes in my back. I can feel them seeing my film, actually feel their comprehension, their concentration, know when a sequence succeeds. When it fails. When it was too subtle. When it was confusing. When it is too slender to work, not oversophisticated, just not meaty enough. Mostly it is working. The gray light from the door filters through the corner of my eye. The film, so dead because so overfamiliar, lives again in their vision. Already I know I can only see it with others from now on. Through them. And that will not last much longer either. But tonight it lives hugely, breathing in their breathing, laughing in their laughter, cheering in their cheers. Of course my oblivious enemy the projectionist takes a full ten minutes changing reels. Diminishing all the psychic energy the first two reels have generated. I hasten him and return. My other self yearning into the thin gray light, that remote corner where a door beckons. And the light falling gray summer evening. Robin comes on. It takes longer than it should to involve them again. But they have humor and realize she is funny. Enjoying themselves, laughing hard at the right parts. Till it is over. And they applaud thunderously.

A man from the BBC documentary section introduces himself to say that my film is a very poor one, indeed it is not even a film, merely radio. Quite hopeless for any purpose of theirs. Indeed quite hopeless altogether. And he knows I will appreciate his frankness. Huge monster, his head towering down at me all candor and insult. Stunned, I actually thank him. Why not? What purpose is served competing with someone so outrageously abusive and self-important I am nearly laughing over the bullet hole in the stomach. Projectionist sets up a mike at the right front. I thank them for coming. No one listens. I sit down and wait. Paul says this is the hard part. "You were a fool to book these extra twenty minutes. They will go to get you now." Nell says be brave. "They'll roast you just the way they roasted Nell for the film she made. Petty bitchery," Paul mutters, cursing radical spite. I look over the crowd, trying to look confident. It would be nice if they praised my movie. But I'll be lucky if they just don't trash me. My legs shake in my white pants. The seem so ridiculously optimistic now, the pants. Ashamed of the panache they represented. Wanted to look good. That too appears to be a crime. I announce that if anyone would like to stay to discuss the film they are welcome. The lay audience departs. The movement stays. Nell makes a gesture to remind me that I should only answer questions. But already a young woman is denouncing me from the back. "Your film is not about Vietnamese women!" It is such a remarkable statement. Did we print the notices incorrectly? I am saved by the memory of one of Nell's favorite answers, "You're right. That's another movie." She demands to know why I filmed the women I did. "Because they are people I knew, women accessible to me who would agree to be in a film. One of them is even my own sister. It is just because they are persons usually ignored that I wished to put them in a movie. Rather ordinary women, women rather like most of us."

And there of course I made my fatal error. It is just because they are like her that she hates them. Denouncing Mallory now. "Sick chick, indulged middle class."

Spewing Marxist slogans in her own middle-class intelligentsia's accent. Vietnamese women are better. They are involved in a revolution. They are superior persons. We are inferior persons, unworthy to be in films. The impracticability of filming Vietnamese women is irrelevant. Their lesser relevance to these London counterparts of the women in my film is irrelevant as well. I let her go on. Destroying my film inch by inch, the celluloid in a rattle of blood and loss at her feet. I have given her my film and she has murdered it. I wonder as the next one takes up the theme if possibly she wants to make films herself. Nell said she was interested in films. Why doesn't she let me help her make her own movie? And let me keep mine? Then there would be two movies. We would each have one. But when she is finished there is no movie for anyone. Nell watches from the vantage of her déjà vu. Paul groans and puts out his cigar.

A crazy lady with a shopping bag full of odds and ends takes over the mike. I sit down. She makes a speech which is incomprehensible. Everyone listens in respectful silence for at least eight minutes. They imagine she is the proletariat. They imagine she is the final answer, the most oppressed woman of all. She denounces everything, then veers off toward some children mysteriously taken from her. I inquire for legal assistance. No one is interested in helping her. She continues. They grow tired of listening. She does not entertain any more. They will turn her off now. I try to find someone who will take care of her. Two women volunteer to see her home if she has one. My assailant is one of them. I stop trembling long enough to admire her.

Someone argues for the film. Someone argues against it. Everyone is getting bored. It is not even interesting to trash any more. Magda makes an eloquent speech explaining the audience to themselves and ends up telling them that they are absurd. Naturally they are infuriated. But they don't listen to her much either. The projectionist says we are out of time. He is roundly booed. It is a nightmare I am delighted to end.

As we go out many of the people come up to shake my hand and say how much they liked the movie. I ask one why she did not say so during the discussion. But her eyes explain her intimidation. And her despair. I have felt it myself, never speaking out against the class workshop motion on writers at the Congress last year. Sat through hours of foolish and totalitarian debate. And did not speak because I was afraid. It is for our moments of silence we are most culpable. At the door the Lesbians hand me a bag. They made a collection. To pay for the hall. Handing the bag heavy with coins. I am embarrassed. The screening was supposed to be a gift. But they are so pleased with themselves that I cannot give it back. How right it should be the Lesbians who answer the occasion with affection. With good will. Even with love. Someone in England having done this for me.

Hedda has invited us for a drink. Paul relents and permits it. Brooding on the trashing I have need of solace and thank the brown bear in him as we climb through a rose garden to white wine in an old house. Hedda's studio looks like Florence, the great windows of Angelo's place. It is the comfort of an artist's world. Its spartan light and chill. And Hedda is kind tonight, a fellow artist while we grumble at the politicos, their envy narrowness intolerance. And I worry, is it only the hurt and fickle animal in me that draws its ease now from Hedda's sympathy. Hedda who has envied and hated me at times too perhaps. But tonight regards me as victimized, a fellow artist treated unfairly. Hedda with whom I quarreled over art and politics, contradicting her when she said every work of art is revolutionary.

She describes her weekend at the nudist colony. Hedda went to one with her therapy group. Credibly funny that first awful moment when you have to take your clothes off. All the bodies standing there tense, who will do it first, who will look, do I dare? We stoke her with questions, do people get erections? "Yes, you've no idea how absurd it was on the dance floor." Skeptical

and challenging her when she describes a fat man no
one would dance with. Because he was so fat. Had the
bad grace to keep asking people to dance. "He annoyed
us. He imposed himself." She has no care for his predicament. I am on his side. He is Fosta. He is me being my pretty sister Mallory's fat older sister even though
I am not fat any more. "Why shouldn't he be able to
dance?" "He could dance with himself," Hedda reasons.
"But he wanted someone to dance with him. Hadn't any
of you the kindness to do that? Are you all such body
snobs? Think what courage a fat man has to go to a
nudist colony." "He's fat by his own fault," she counters.
"Of course. I agree with you completely. But till he gets
unfat shouldn't he have help and support?" "He was a
bore, you don't understand." She dismisses him. Goes to
ask Paul about the Joplin film, will he ever be able
to get it out of Canada and finish it. He explains the
labyrinth of red tape customs and finance. The haggling.
The months now years of waiting. I stop listening and
return to my wounds. Out of the hurt of the trashing trying to comprehend it. Savage rite invented by Weather-
men of the manly Left. Yell you down, violate your
freedom, your right to speak. Like all tyrants of the
Left through history, if you hold opinions or disagree
you're out of line, unorthodox. But of course being
women we keep it down to our specialty, our culturally
assigned role of psychological violence. Maternal sham-
ing. Womanly complaining. And humiliate the victim in
public, using the force of the situation, the many against
the one, the classroom rebellion of an audience. And
the curious sex role sadistic ritual of trasher and trashed.

Time to go home. Rather disconsolate the three of us
this last ride together, Islington in the sad light of arc
lamps. Waiting till we are nearly in front of the house
until I cannot wait any longer. And ask Paul what he
thought of my film. I never did get around to seeing
Paul's own films. And I should have. Had I needed to
I would have found the time. Knowing right then,
words out of my mouth, that I shouldn't have asked.
Since he offered no opinion. Haven't I known this un-

easiness a thousand times myself, forced to comment on someone's work I disliked or could not respect? And now I have done this ugly thing of pushing him. Paul the honest man. He hums and prevaricates. Then says he does not believe my method is the correct one to portray the human condition. For a moment I want to laugh. It sounds so pretentious. But on second thought I had in fact wanted to portray just that, the human condition for Godsake. I get out of the car wondering what method is adequate. Will I hit closer to it if I write? I ask him what method is correct. Closing the door. He says he doesn't know. We all kiss good night.

When I saw Jill it was already America. The long white night past. Past Celia's voice sweet brave sassy, "Of course I'll be okay. They'll just shave off my pubic hair and starve me. When I wake up it will be all over." Voice behind the phrase wondering how much over. "Come see me Saturday and help me cope with the hysterical females who'll be surrounding me." Past the strange voice from Vita's place, young male hustler and said to be diseased, talking mysteriously about some letter Vita's sent, sounding very ominous. A death warrant? Wanting to know did I get it? His voice an interrogator's—the association with Vita has had its effect. What has Vita written me?

"Why take charter flights?" Jill demands. "Cattle cars. Steerage. Organized masochism." Today I'm a member of the Long Island Beach Club, signed it, legal document. Jill is right. She has bought herself a leather notebook. "Most expensive one they had, a writer cannot be too self-indulgent." I get mine for forty-five cents. No place to buy another and Blick is full. The nice American kid who was going to make it all right about my ticket becomes Judas Iscariot. Careful structure of my good nature becoming unhinged. Who will harbor the bulk of my master prints, suitcase, the shopping bag of this book? Carefully numbering the packages. A Harlem kindergarten teacher responsible for life. Choosing which child will die, come the emergency, book or movie?

"Zelda had twice the genius of Scott." Jill is putting me down, artist to mere graduate student. "But you must admit it was Scott who actually got it on paper." "Bullshit." Jill turns toward me, "My God, that bag. Only someone from the Middle West would run around dragging an object like that." I have never liked her better than this moment.

And I chose the shopping bag over the movie cans. Let the movie melt in vinyl liquid over some strange floor. I grow old searching in lost-parcels departments, dull brown cloakrooms, the dark tunnels of parochial school. Last night, Paul appearing middle of the dawn on the staircase. "Did you call me, love?" "No dear, good night." Ringing off from America the phone made a beep, woke him up. His great beautiful hairy legs hanging out of the scarlet bathrobe, that marvelous body, one feels its balls and sex protected only by the terrycloth he holds modestly before him. Beautiful man unloved in his beautiful body. Some dame should call you. But not me, O'Rourke's best friend. And am I letting my feeling run on with Nell, friendship spilling over into the great forbidden else? Taking Fumio in the arms of my mind this last night in London. The dawn already coming summer morning.

Jill is broke in England, so I give her fifty of my last, her old rock integrity will not accept a hundred. Does me in when I say over coffee I'm scared of editors, editing. "Oh, are you still back there," her face making the expression that lets you know you are a hopeless case in high school. But she trusted me to finish her column and deliver it to the *Voice*. Then in Epping Forest alone on the bus I felt her touch my breasts. A Lesbian fantasy in full view of the regulation American mother bullying her two sons with naggle. And them so rude back at her, the three savages so wretched it ought to be against the law but isn't. So where are we? Paraded by cheery English hostess across a desert of service roads, macadam, hangars, to temporary building for the prefabricated lunch. I respond to undergraduate questions like a bandit, putting on four youngsters who think I go to college someplace. Finally confess I am overage for youth fare. They try to cheer me up, condescending to my senility. I revenge myself by saying I am a schoolteacher.

I drag my boxes the two full city blocks to the terminal, a college boy helping me. Assigned by the authorities to my peculiar case. And finally bought a Dunhill. Fumio's brandy. The last waiting room a bar. Yellow balloon floating over plastic chairs attached to a black six-year-old and he alone among us free in his mind, America, while the rest of us sizzle and wilt. You bought your ticket you had your choice. Because we are now eight hours late for takeoff. They couldn't find an airplane. Then spent four hours turning it around to point in the right direction. The fighting spirits are on the line now. Ready to jump for seats. It will be a subway war. I have my martini and my film, the true pacifist drinks sitting down. High as a D-47 on sleeplessness. And going home. New York by midnight.

The speed coming up it's England goodbye in the golden evening's yellow green fields. Couple on the right. English. Smug nose. Sun gold on his moustache and forelock. Reminds me of D. H. Lawrence. But she's drab and mouse. Knitting some pink thing. Mod young clothes but a face that obeys. Looks beaten for all her serenity, her youth already full of the wife thing. Ahead on the right a bold lad, wild as a Welshman, winking. Perky lady journalist waking me up again to know if anatomy is destiny—has a bet on with the American girl next to her. Up the aisle an American cozy-quilt young mother in homemade skirt. Her baby's feet dandling over the arm. Would be fun to sculpt them in wet Kleenex. Round soft fat. What if Celia had been a mother? Tomorrow they remove the possibility.

Under the murk America, beginning with Bangor. Nixon has blacked it out. America is now invisible. The international bureaucracy comes on with its forms, filing us into its bins of petition. U.S. blanks refer to us all as family members. I cannot give names and relationship of my accompanying family members. Is it an oversight or an error in judgment? The inference is clear that one should never go out alone. The United States Government reserves the right to search me. Pawing through my underwear in public. Bag nice and full today, hope they have trouble in closing it. Let them try to seize my movie and I throw over nonviolence upon the instant. Scratch me don't scratch my master print.

"Excellent bird's eye view of Boston," a cockney voice announces from the front. We all stood to see land, my Claire's Boston. Shameless, New York below us now doing its number down there, fireworks of light along the water. Do my friends still exist or have I invented them? Improbable that the fantasy I was living before England could support itself over time. A figment. Fictive. Most of all I inquire of myself in the earsplitting pressure of landing, feeling very New Yorker, most of all, am I gonna get laid?

And then I can't find the papers. Letters written so carefully months ago swearing that this footage was shot in America and need not be inspected by customs. My reprieve from confiscation. So I need not lose the movie after this year's work the very moment I bring it home in triumph. And now I've lost the damn papers. New York is gone while we preserve a holding pattern over New Jersey in a heavy rainstorm. Searching frenetically through pocketbook's junk filing cabinet. Grinning in open throttle crisis through my rubbish. Throat closing while I paw through unanswered mail, haunting reminders of all my failures, each rumpled paper a memo of airplanes, letters, bills, all the things that went wrong or crazy the thing too big for me too fast. Cancerous paper of our lives, the guilt of things we didn't do or should have or were too late. Hurry find it we're landing. I can't find, the letters just aren't there. All's lost, relax.

A suitcase falls on a lady's head three seats forward, the plane in a storm of dark now. Hearing her sob and scream that her head is broken, calmly awaiting the end—just as well, I've lost the film to customs can't go home again in any case. But furious at the stewardess, who is furious at the lady for bleeding, "Really, how she

does carry on." Scolding her for making a fuss merely
because she is scared out of her mind, her scalp cut and
shattered. And might make trouble for the company. The
plane hitting ground hard, way too hard. Then the lights
go out the fans off. And the door will not open. Claustrophobia is a real thing. And death. Because the thing
might blow up now and we cannot escape. Because the
others feel it. "Jammed," the word is whispered down
the aisles. A woman screams and faints, seat back of me
on the right. All the passengers standing, asking questions, trying to get out, pushing in the dark. My heart
begins to attack, gathering its forces to strangle me.

It is near pitch here but you can see them the way you
can see things in the dark. Menacing silhouettes filling
the aisles, killing all chances of escape, space, air, with
their full bodies. That is for us sitters. For themselves
they are poised to flee upright push and trample each
other to give rise to madness, that terrifying passage in
Tolstoi, the chaos of violent anarchy. Outside the windows
the lights of Kennedy and home. But we will never see
it. Blow up on a runway or strangle here in airless tomb
finally all of us screaming and pummeling each other
till we die. People are shoving. It is going to get ugly.
I make the effort you finally make when you have to
and suggest in my best manner that we should all be less
afraid if we sat down to wait.

Lawrentian man to my right, testy in a tantrum calls
me a bossy bitch, he knows my kind, domineering cunt.
It is like a blow to the back of the neck. I reach my hand
to the Welshman's elbow. "Would you just talk to me,
I'm claustrophobic and occasions like this are . . ." He
smiles. The passengers sit down. The Welshman, editor
and journalist, struggles with wartime humor till we are
RAF movie chin up, beating it. His infinite goodness
to me these moments.

Time stops its breath and waits to live. Forty-five
minutes the throat labors to keep the heart and lungs
in place. To stifle madness, its cries and whispers, its
flailing arms and rage to smash all and everything for
mere air. When it is over I have died and been reborn.

In home and myself, the disease of years, if not broken the back of it then at least a major rung up on its grip, my used body shaken. Let it happen, if this is the moment to die try doing it in style, don't lose your mind as well. Indian-wrestle your claustrophobe's panic and win this thing. Till I am ready even, oddly composed. It is easier when you don't struggle, eyes closed and the other passengers trying probably just as hard, harder, silent now either fainting or cardiac or praying or whatever one does, the range of possibilities before death. All quiet now, some embracing, some weeping in arms. Hotter and hotter in here. All quiet now except a few children's full terror sounds, loud, the proper response to situations over which we have control. But not these. Lawrentian man and his woman in his arms tense. But he is more afraid than she.

Years in moments. Until my ears like all our ears starve for the sound in blackness of this last trap of all, the noise of delivery. The door is open. The air coming down the aisle like grace. I apologize to Lawrence, had no intention of being domineering, was only afraid, terribly afraid, subject to this fear of enclosed places. And I actually thought it would be easier to wait sitting. He cannot say anything at all. But his eyes get better and he moves. Recovering himself in his burdensome mission of his woman and his fine new boots and traveling cases. Gracious at the very last. We are all too worn for radiance, but we are alive. New York.

PART FOUR

TRAJECTORY

ASCENT

It's Vita at the barricades. Her in her hat and her red
suspenders. The purple trousers and a grin. After the
great blank wall of glass, my America's stare into the
eyes of entrants. Now my own eyes racing back and forth
across the overhead panel at Kennedy empty of faces,
there is no one. Pacing before it, waiting for the packages
to come up the conveyer belt's iron wheels oiled big as
a hand, guarding my movie and my book. No American
currency, how will I get home? Or through customs. Not
even a match. My eye falls on a black man, eternal
alliance. And he is a customs man as well, taking his
break on an old bench, looks tired middle-aged and kind.
I will try. So just tell him I've lost the letters and now
may lose the film to customs. He has a match and doesn't
think they'll get me. Sits me down like a warm father
on his bench, "You're tired honey," and tells me the
news of our town. "Little bit wilder every day and it's
been hot."

I assemble my junk and await my fate. But am waved
through with nothing to declare. Declaring to myself I

could have fifteen hundred pounds of heroin in here and Sam has just let me slip through his fingers. That easy. Did my matchman give a nod? I'll never know.

Then Vita at the barricade leaning over the armpit-high beam stenciled "Do Not Cross," yelling my name, one ear cocked out below her hatbrim makes you want to tuck it in and kiss her like a six-year-old. Remembering myself with an ear that folded always under the felt hat leggings to match my aunt gave us years we ate stew but had hand-tailored winter outfis, Easter dresses from Saks. Rich relatives provided embroidered bodices while Mother worried about the oil burner, the storm windows, the utilities, repairs on the house. Vita's off finding the car while I wait, my victory all about me in parcels. Home to the romance of neon Holiday Inn and the cab rank. Will she have lost it again? At last backing it into the curb full sight of police force Carey busmen and all. A scandal as we giggle and throw everything into the truck—my God, you've cleaned it. Of course. But its cracker is gone, its traveling slum with blankets, empty Coke bottles, random samples of last fall's leaves, the full range of emergency preparations, the moving auto hospital of old oil cans, funnels, jump cables, antifreeze. And the Kleenex box. Because you can't have a wreck like this without a whole box of tissues some nasty color once white but stained forever with crankcase drippings. I can hardly believe the Anglo-Saxon order, the meticulous Vita detail imposed upon it actually agreeable to see, even the padded mat on the floor of the trunk, probably laundered it. Stray gift of *Life* Magazine years ago, they borrowed three sculptures to photograph and broke every one of them. I asked for damages, backed up by Plexus folk who knew about such things. Would never have occurred to me to dare. *Life* made threats, said they wouldn't print the pictures after all and make my mother proud in St. Paul. Then paid me five hundred for the loss of three sculptures and six thousand to the uptown photographer who broke them. And threw in the mover's blanket for a bonus. Afterwards they said their insurance only covered losses over six hundred dollars, and if I'd made a bigger claim it would have saved them money. I decided they were crazy. One of my first real insights into money.

"Did you get any tickets?" "Of course not, I kept it in a garage. Fred's space is available now that he's gone to New Mexico." Marveling again at Vita's methodology. Probably is easier to pay for things. "Did you get my letter?" While she drives, the big trouble comes and squats over us, hooding our open car. "It sounded scary, Vita. Lethal or something. I'm glad I didn't get it." Our voices have landed us back in a rut. Hers tired, mine frayed, about to erupt in a rough edge and cut someone. No, I will not let it happen, I'll resist. Humor her, talk to entertain, it always worked with Mother. So I convert my customs man into a magical encounter, fictionalize myself, "I was shameless with the Irish charm and beclouded his vision," carrying on as if we had defied the federal government together and should have adjoining cells in Sing Sing. Till she laughs. Then I begin a diatribe on charter food, "Would you believe the poor limeys had the cheek to offer us hot dogs more depraved than our native product? Never believe we have a corner upon the inedible, sausage in it looked for all the world like a dead dog." "I know," gleeful at the wheel, she rivals me, "the roll was yellow rubber and had a worm in it." And then I love her when she will laugh, forget the invoices of love, the receipts and unanswered mail, the business world of the heart and give away a joke, repeating nonsense verses to me as we cross the Triborough Bridge, having nearly missed that quick chute into Manhattan and come up with a quarter for the tunnel. Still not lost, still magically running on the strength of a Minneapolis Honeywell sign huge red as Christmas neon top of a building off below a rampway telling me there is a home and hometown way here in the east of Manhattan's bitchy city, and thermostats to warm or worry you, the farm has one like Selby Avenue had and I wring my winter hands at its expense the way my mother did. Trailing the sign for hope until it is lost behind us. Anxious all the way to

Forty-second Street's canyons of buildings. "Grand Central!" they used to call it on the radio, some soap opera when I was a kid listening in the lair of my bedroom for the moment I would escape to New Yrok City and hear on waking in a berth to freedom, a grownup, a girl who left home, something unheard of in St. Paul or heard only in stunned silence, awesome, the voice of a black porter stride like the god Poseidon along the cement shore "Grand Central Stashunnn!" "Kyoto, Kyoto," they always call it soft when other mornings coming back from knapsack and temple beds adventure home to "Tokyo!" They say it hard 'cause it's a big town like this one.

No place to eat. Past midnight now. She didn't shop, hasn't any liquor. "How much I would like a bath food sleep. In that order." "The bath I'll give you. As for the rest we'll see what's open." Sensible Vita reminding me the world is not a toy even if you imagine you're the return of the native. Odd, though, that she made no preparations. Kind of thing I so love to do, prepared JayCee's arrival in England for something like six weeks, an apartment, a car, two bicycles, champagne, steaks, and a red leather edition of Fielding. But Vita is very busy working for Joe Kaplan. I wait for her outside the Finale. No, they are closed. We will try Verde's.

Who have a garden and who feed us. Even a martini. I revive and do wonders of transporting O'Rourke the Great. Bragging up my movie teacher till suddenly Vita is actually yelling at me I must never put down Joe he's the Greatest. Who is this guy, Vita? What does he mean to you, okay look I'm sorry, I'm sure he's wonderful, stop having a tantrum.

In the temporary truce Vita mentions that my old Zoe is in her group now. Wonderful if the movement could save her. Last hope. The shrinks and the loony bins couldn't. So I paint Zoe in huge strokes over the table, doing her wonderful nudes black ink on brown paper ten feet high, all the Bowery walls were hung in them she had a great draftsman's hand for women the whole tragedy of her loss come back again. Washing her brushes now at the table like in the old days when I tried to help her paint. "But the ego was broken before I ever met her, Vita." "Shut up." "But I tried so hard." "Shut up we're going home it's late."

My talk, which had been my gift like a plate of spaghetti shoved back into my mouth, Laurel and Hardy pie in the eye. All right, we'll go. Why couldn't it have been some high-flown come home happy meal, surely she is not jealous of a girl I loved over ten years ago who went crazy after I went to Japan after she left me. Goodbye mart in its glass and candle in its crystal chimney guarded from the wind but no wind tonight, perfect summer outdoors garden trees and my town's bewitching night to glow in. Follow Vita. Down the hall they never got around to fixing and onto the mattress on the floor. Her prisoner in her eyes commanding me to perform the lover. Had wanted to. Driving past the Bowery had wondered paused a moment would this be the more enchanted spot? No, try her place, it has stronger electrical current cable fence vibes to conquer with the win of love. But lost it now as she puts the hex on me. And I say, "In the morning, Vita, really I can't." Begging off. Because the eyes so still accuse and bully. And Nell teaching me not to be bullied.

In the morning it is different, taking the long and small of her girl's body, such pretty breasts against my arm. And feeling her stir and churn in me, that particular haul-my-ashes thing at last no longer with us. For I want her too, not just getting laid myself and then thank you no, for which she has hated me rightfully, for my indifference leaving her high and dry or falling into sleepiness and inattention a second before she could have come and is furious not getting her orgasm. A woman scorned and cheated. My sins of chill and impotence topping the costs of Fred's debt over the years. At least all this has not happened. And after our first success we smoke the cigarettes of dawn and talk as friends and lovers. As the early butts quash carefully on the good broad boards she tells me of her adventure. Went out and picked up a black man in a bar. Went back to his hotel. And it was nice. To do that once. Yes, going through the race wall I remember it, the free cool shock on the other side. "But you have friends who are black, why make it with a stranger?" "It had to be this way." "Of course, because it was." And haven't I done things like this? Of course, and it was an encounter. "And he was nice to me, interested in cameras. Went back to his hotel and picked up his Nikon to show me. Came back to the bar with it so I could trust him." "Was he kind?" Worrying that he would revenge his race and class on her and hers, like prick gun Cleaver. "Yes, well it was lovely." Grinning at each other the approval she needs. I feel a bit bereft but no right to, so forget it, making love again, keeping the ardor for her loins the lovely slim of waist. And going down, the full homage of it.

On the next cigarette it's Tom. How he is so wonderful. "Has the soul of a woman." When we say that, we are hooked. "Why didn't you ever tell me, Vita? Why make a secret of sex and when did it start?" "It must be secret!" Swearing me to a hundred forms of it while I puff and tease her. "Why the amazing secrecy here when you're delighted to publish our thing?" "Because of his wife." "And so?" Remembering now how she had flown off the handle when I quoted someone who saw Tom as a man trapped by a bourgeois wife and her notions of the costs of the kids' educations. So he couldn't really paint. "Those responsibilities are sacred!'" Vita sounding like the soul of convention, foaming at the mouth, the absolutely uptight wife and mother. "And his wife doesn't know?" "Of course not, he can't tell her, it would break her heart." "And she'd break his neck. So would I at being deceived. Why doesn't he tell her and keep faith?" Vita regards me as an innocent. A nitwit. "Vita, my father did this to us six years and yes I forgive him, he hadn't as many options. But Tom needn't live like Catholic St. Paul twenty years ago when it's now." "I don't want to talk about it." "All right don't."

I go to the toilet for a change of scene. The inquisitor's toilet amid labels for flush, labels for hot and cold and

turn off the faucet, all stamped out in bright paint and
metal from a neat little writing machine, Vita's
pathological habit for detail that she claims was a way
of teaching the children to read in the toilet. The toilet,
here where I first met my crime, morning after that first
night. And knew I had made love without love.
Congratulations, things are better now. Rocky road and
so on. But real progress. I love Vita now, habits and all.
So when I am back in bed I tell her Celia's operation.
Happening now in New Haven. This very morning she
may die and I can't go there till tomorrow. Maybe too
late, who knows, there is always some danger in surgery.
Celia. Hit with tears and suddenly shaking in Vita's arms,
sobbing to her all Celia had been to me no matter what
and that I will never know what lost her, still obsessively
going over each possibility, jealousy over Miriam, over
Fumio, over work, or my hateful dependency frightening
her, or my hateful notoriety doing the same, but give
up motivation between gasps and just howl full out-loud
crying uncontrollable fit while Vita holds me like a good
mother, that Celia was my teacher of life. Taught me
to enjoy. Music, flowers, the road. And the new life's
other branch of love, the thing of loving your friends—
wow, did that backfire! And we both laugh wonderful
conjunction of snot and tears snuffling a big throaty sniff
then laughing again. "Surely it must be ill bred to mourn
another lover in your bed." "So shanty of you to see
it that way," both of us in fine humor making love with
the decks cleared now, the third and best time of all.

Then it's time to get up. Get on the phone and arrange
a screening for the company. Vita says Jonas Mekas will
let us show it at his place. His voice on the phone, this
patron saint of all undergrounders, years reading him
in the *Voice,* Jonas will encourage anybody trying to
make films yes he'll let us. So it is not just an ordinary
day when Vita has to go to work and I have to type my
piece for the *Voice* and deliver it with Jill's. Because
the word has come already that O'Rourke arrives tomorrow and will stay here at Vita's house. It is the
perfection of every possibility that all my friends will

know each other, what greater gladness? Heaven is not utopian socialism after all, just the bliss of friendship. Typing in Vita's immaculate office each paper clip filed and labeled into absolute order, yes here is bond paper here an envelope. Here is breakfast. "Let's see if you can finish it for a change," getting me just when I thought I had got her, a reformed self who can type her own stuff. But she had the sly wit to cook breakfast for me between phone calls from her lovers Ruth Claudia and Tom. You are a remarkable woman, Vita, how are you managing with each today? Getting progress reports on her emancipation efforts. Only six short months ago housewife mother of three. She grins her swallowed the cat along with it, then launches into Frederick's language, which was his father's who was a professor, all about relating to and achieving understanding with and acquiring insight into. She has just written a piece on her childhood. Joe insisted she do it. And gives me to read. The beach, the ferry boats and the aunts and Vita at six. They had a fire, not their own but someone else's house, another part of the beach and Vita hid from the family, vanished from the tribe until they discovered they had lost her. Several hours later. Self-orphaned on yellow paper. Next she heaps on Joe's film scripts printed in mimeo, his literary side really so talented. But there is not more time to read. Because it is Joe himself now, Vita afire to get there, even a volunteer she must never be late for work and disappoint him.

And Joe himself is an easy guy no work to do drinking white wine, "Come on, let's see that movie." Am I an eager adulteress showing it to them even before the company see it? But since Vita's the heroine of the struggle, she must have a special screening. So we lace up, Joe threading it in from the back of the office, blinds drawn wine arranged and cigarettes within call. Roll it for Vita, who scuttles all over the room, nudging me for one cut, Joe for another, forever with the wow and golly and the irrepressible scooting about on her ass like Winnie. Midway strangers, friends of Joe pop in making me paranoid at interruptions. They'll walk on our concentration, this screening is in honor of Vita. But no they stay quietly and watch. And Joe's praises at the end, now how can I resist that? Will buy me a drink of congratulations. Getting to like him even better at his annex the bar across the street.

Bar dark Manhattan uptown five o'clock the world is all talk. Some newsclippings Joe's got what the *New York Times* said about "women's lib" today and trading stories with the other two, turns out the guy's a filmmaker . . . when Vita says call the hospital. Of course. How could I forget what good Vita remembered. Crammed into a phone booth where it's all just happened, Celia dead forever in the hesitation of a woman's voice very officialese can't find her listed, they will have parked her in a cart deserted hallway only the ticket on her arm and my memory? But no, west wing room something, then she's disconnected. How does one proceed through the lines of long distance, the complicated change of quarters and dimes, who has another nickel that life may go on, till a black operator takes me in charge a real loony at my end of the wire. And the strangling in this coffin at the bottom of the bar, will the door jam? No, she's still in surgery. But they finished at one o'clock. Whereas I conducted my operation at eleven in Vita's arms, sobbing sympathetic magic as in primitive tribes where the man goes through labor too, yelling under a banyan tree at the wrong moment I find, my own crises never smart enough to outguess Celia. At one o'clock today I was parking my car delivering copy to the *Voice* or stuck in the trivial heartburn of traffic on Eighth Avenue past the Port Authority cab rank. No way to endure major surgery. And listen kindly lady receptionist, it is now four o'clock, why does she still lie sheet over her face in limbo of postoperative room? "Perhaps there were complications," her voice no more reassuring than the Internal Revenue. I can bolt out of this coal bin relieved then that Celia lives. Or in tremors that she only lingers. What else to try? Her surgeon, that guilty party steel-edged rapist villain turns out to be a very busy lady doctor, you can try later. My fellow conspirator at Bell wants me to go home and take a rest. I settle for a second martini and the jitters.

In the cold light of day's street again, an insistent message relayed through Vita that I go up to Columbia, there's that conference on abortion, they want you to talk five minutes at the kickoff. "Will you come with me?" No, she'll go downtown to Tom, who needs her so much, anxious little mother between two charges, choosing the boy child weaker sex in Tom's guilty softness. The time two summers ago when she had an abortion not another child and Fred brought her over to the Bowery. Both back from California someplace, had sat Zazen and found the way or part of it. Vita an odd kind of peace like someone back from crazy, very keen on the abortion issue then. But now it's Tom who needs her. Thinking of the two of them as I drive off, I foresee them. Dinner and then her place to rub his back hear his troubles how much like my own recuperation and it gives comfort, blessings then with some reservations as I spring along, the hood gobbling those Broadway streets each more familiar until you see Columbia the big brick masses and those black gates presided over by Greek male Scientia and very allegorical lady who was Artis years before they admitted women. The still more implacable iron wall of Barnard. And no place to park. Wonderful how nothing changes. Gives you a notion of the power of institutions. The evening bringing back the other time I ran into the door of Macmillan under the stone gaze of Science in a rush back from Washington very tedious luncheon Democratic wives but met Gene McCarthy's Abigail dressed polite gloved ladylike establishment politics. And scuttled through the door, so glad to be home I said. No, we're in trouble Sidney whispered the bunch putting it on are all very uptight because the Radical Lesbians are going to zap us tonight. Then Teresa Juarez. Then *Time*. Then the dark nights of winter, Celia.

Remembering it all in the very posture of the chairs when I speak. Their red velvet tacky long stretch of backs and the gallery above, another time is now when I begin again with a joke. Always get in trouble when I come up to Columbia. Used to work here. On to business, repeating all the points I've given to enunciate in the past twenty-five minutes, running from the women who are the conference sponsors with one point of view, consensus on abortion repeal nationwide campaign, to the dissident groups upstairs, mostly gay women with another thing to say on the issue of sexual liberation, and an audience of just plain women come from all over, don't even know if they approve of women's liberation, a few still smelling a burned bra, but sure that abortions are something to talk about and then do what? The weekend ahead of them to decide. While I try to put it all in context, trying even harder to bring the factions together, foreseeing the splits that can come up over class (one group demanding free abortions above the usual call for legal repeal), and the gay movement tipping the problem into the far more controversial area of sexual freedom for women, not just the usual rhetoric demanding the right to control our own bodies. Upstairs a group called WISE said their demand was for freedom of sexual expression. "What's that mean?" I asked. They didn't quite know but it could cover the gays. And the child molesters and the rapists too. No qualifications. "Why not make consent the issue?" "Well, it was the best we could do, the only phrase we could all agree on within a short time and it's more radical than the other proposals." "I like to be radical too but you are obscure," feeling they probably would be my club if I were into joining one. But that's not my job tonight. And the job itself very confusing indeed. My sympathies torn between the groups, not well enough informed, have been in England while this was planned and now trying to give the help they ask, an enthusiastic welcome. Trying to do two jobs at once, a perspective on the abortion campaign itself, national now and involving women who were until now outside the movement, but also to stress the implications of a freer sexual culture, the perhaps disturbing but important questions that will be raised by the vanguard groups from the City and New Haven. Urging most that, in the two days they have to work out strategy, they find not only the issues but the sentiment to unite. Then taking off hoping they will but I can't stay because I have another meeting.

Wunderbar, we are doing orgasm when I get there. So good to be home I have to say it though I disrupt the mediations of Fosta, Ruth. "We have made enormous progress in your absence and are now discussing the most bedrock topics of all." Behold this England! I apostrophize snuggled into my very own nest sitting across from Claire. Fosta returns to the question of do we give or are we given orgasm. Delightful problem. Nice shiver down the back just leaning hand on chin to follow. What of power is involved? What of gratitude? I'll never know though I tried so hard to discover. "Have a Pepsi, we are concentrating without alcohol nowadays." O,Flynn next. About finding a stranger and going home with her and she's black. "Am I communicating or are we pawns in the order of things?" And faking an orgasm what does it mean? The purity of O'Flynn, graduate student in Classics having dropped out to produce the revolution and pondering tonight, not the eternal other and its social effect, but her own experience. "Everyone's done it with guys, why do we do it with each other, this tedious goal setting?" her voice ending up in querulous scholastic doubt like her neat small head, a figure like a page boy dressed in knickers.

It is my turn, and there is something I want to say. That it's mystic, trying to say what it was with Celia. But Claire is looking at me, well say it anyway, not Celia but that the experience can be transcendent. Making a great fool of myself spitting it out I feel and not giving them well-wrought words, language frigid before the fact of love, its power like a drug higher and higher till floating have seen God in the carvings of Indian temples they were lovers every conceivable posture it was holy. And if there were a thing to worship though there isn't, it might be this sacred really, looking at my hands, ashamed stumbling while they put up with my bumbling phrases, but surely she listens, her eyes on me like searchlights, great open truths of green. Under the mop of gold hair her head is too big, she is one great head staring at me. Afraid. No hope of talking for effect, no just in terror to get this across, I have found something that astonished my very soul held at the throat bliss nearly annihilating, something in the eye of love. And perhaps it was a mirage. No, Claire, for all your boring theologians or whatever hermits starving in their deserts going pop off in furtive left over love damned up to poison them, no, I tell you no, God is love, sweet Eros. Not a pincushion. Back then and off the polemic, last try humble to say it is exquisitely beautiful and the closest to truth, I did not understand but knew its force and will say that mystery is not an unlikely word for such a thing. My hands tire of playing church steeple. And give up.

Too sleepy to dance. Though they are raising hell tonight. Just lie here, friendly old platform DOB must use for something. I will use it for a bed, home with O'Flynn rubbing my head. Claire next to me sometimes. Then wandering off again. Has probably hidden a book somewhere like an alcoholic for little nips beneath the counter. I have been through the last telephone crisis in a neon phonebooth Italian bar and street lamps of Soho like that last sad time we stood by the headlamps while I harangue the operators and lose my quarters, find out if she's still alive ready to kick the box apart, the door really is stuck. Then a hand on my shoulder. I turn to commit mayhem or save myself from knife point of some maniac. But it is only Claire come down to see how I'm managing the great indifferent world. Full of peace and quarters. The voice in New Haven says all's well. So I am nodding between waking and watching the figures move in the dance because the movie is safe and the key to a cheap English trunk full of the master prints a little silver thing is sleeping in my pocket. And Miss Celia Tyburn is sleeping peacefully after surgery in Room 608. The girl who assaulted me for a celebrity once is here and says she wants to make movies, so I introduce her to Claudia. Then she wants to write books, so I introduce her to Claire. How she is mollified now she is getting what she wants. The business of nobody. And somebody. What a lot of crap it is. But how can you say that till you've been there and were astonished at the emptiness. How can you say that to somebody who wants to go. Bags ticket carefully saved bread. Dying, killing, to arrive. How can you dare mention that being somebody you become nobody but worse. Not even who you were when nobody because that was somebody namely yourself. Treason to bring it up. To say in a barely audible whisper that the return to self was exhausting not to mention ridiculous. And you are still barely sure you're back. Arriving full of wisdom and good will between sleeping and waking. And I will just see if I can manage to dance one minute or so before Claire makes me go home, which will be so agreeable everything is so very agreeable going or staying, O'Flynn stroking my hair or Claire while I am the African Queen herself reposed upon a cushion just before final exhaustion, it must be days since I have slept or eaten. And euphoria. All the terrible energy, my demon that appalls everyone I know, leaked out now upon the floor just a puddle on my dais so unutterably happy to be home in a minute with Claire.

At the corner of First Avenue and Second Street waiting at the stop light I hear but do not quite understand yet that she has been ill, the asthma, night's anxiety so intense she went to St. Vincent's, told them she was having heart attacks. They sent her to a shrink, who blames it on her reading, declares it a frequent event when you start "really getting into mysticism." Joanne Sontag the local faith healer who lives in Sidney's building, all our friends go to see her. Claire still talking when the light changes, "So she tells me anxiety is on the side of the angels. I have to pay ten dollars to hear that!" We laugh. "No, listen it's all witless, terrifying. It happened once before

when you were in England the last time, I think I
despaired you did not come back for so long. I took acid
with French and Sandy Merman. And came home alone
at dawn—I could see how pointless things are." When
we are in her sanctuary she is still trying to describe it,
but I do not understand, this hideous thing at the center
of life."Nothing but a void like a glass milk bottle just
air colorless without substance, I can't sleep any more.
And the city is madness, so much anguish gathered in
one place bellowing. And no relief in sight." Her
description punctuated with laughter because it is all
so funny, but it's not. What does her terror mean, is it
mine or her own, the optimism crumbling? Bookie forever
telling me it's our job to make hope. "And pass it out
to our generation like joints?" Dubious while she argues,
"What else finally beneath the ruckus but an impression,
only a chance maybe, but something beyond the reason
and event you insist on, your disbelieving reality principle." Her hand grabbing under her arm. "Now I go
around in my new neurosis clutching my side armed for
the attack." And I look, it's true she's doing it. "Stop."
The two of us staring at the guilty and compulsive hand
grabbing her side just below the armpit. "My clutch,"
she says. Laughing into passion, kissing at last after so
much restraint, at times I think we dement ourselves with
holding back. Superior to sense again and moving away,
resorting to talk. Our endless talk. "Now tell your heroic
exploits, I'd like to hear about England, do you want
some eggs?"

Suddenly I want eggs more than anything. And the
glass of milk, long white plastic cup full of magic.
Healing. Luxurious. The blue and white plate for me.
Very imitation English. Swiped from a Chinese restaurant. Her good plate. There being two. I being the
guest, "Will there be enough forks?" heckling her because
otherwise I might be forced to weep at her generosity.
She had caused Mahalia to sing "God Bless America" full
tilt from the phonograph while I wash my face in the
kitchen sink seeing in the bathtub next to me all three
forks two knives and one teaspoon stored where the dishes

drain among the cockroaches when not in use. I give her England and Winnie. And get high marks. The movie home. And get a compliment—what I like about you is you finish things. Deciding on the spot to make it my life motto, watching her try to make coffee, finally never knowing if she flatters or only teases me because I do not know her at all. But sure she is teasing when I see the coffee she produces. "You will have to endure this without cream."

We sit with our feet up on the old office desk that tries to be a kitchen table but won't permit any leg room, adamant that you bark your shins on its bookshelves. "Let me read you my space chapter. Rosemary said it's completely boring." Does she tremble when she's got her yellow sheets together firm hand of the Flair pen words aggressively marching across the page only to be knocked down or crossed out? Started over. Bookie the better workman. Doing her own critique before she'll even read it. "It's too adstract. What I need is something human. I have an idea of several other paragraphs interspersed, the wistful things of the planet like a chrysalis, a barrow, games. Pets even." I don't like pets am down on pets, hope she keeps pets out. But the thing she reads is grave, beautiful, and difficult to follow. So very sleepy now, straining after the language, which is generally right but never easy.

"But I want it to have snap." Now she is carried away. "I want the reader to *leap* from paragraph to paragraph." *Leap* she says, eager young egotist so very beautiful utterly exhausted watching her. "And I want to sleep in your bed." Intending to do just that, but proximity inspired the energy of one sad beautiful set of love. Crying as she takes, enters me, so long away from that storm in me her fingers make far within, definitive as a hand grabbing the back of my neck shaking the very core of me. And the rich impossible good of her nipples, the gift of her wet upon my hand when I reach her that first touch open welcoming, invariable. Nothing I could accomplish in life is such cause for pride, a gratitude straining the heart to watch her come, great lovely head back in ecstasy. Arrogance hubris humility all in one tenderness and surprise.

Then darkness till the sun wakes through the ivy new-made light green summer day. Saturday. The day I see Celia. Telling her this, telling her Celia, what it meant, why it went away I do not understand. Then crying again for the hurt of the loss, this is awful, second time I've done it but where else to find comfort but with friends? Claire a big serious head looking down at me, the light doing things to her hair strange marvelous radiant and along her white body lying on its side, so curious even her pubic hair is yellow, reclining her great beautiful thighs stomach sticking out like a child's and breasts large as mine, thank God no inferiority complex about boyish figures. Celia's breasts were small precious nipples you could push them in and they stayèd. Then kiss them out again like a game. And the head so grave now, her expression just saying you should learn to defend yourself, never get in a situation like that again. It is so astonishing that she cares, a little hard to believe. Accept that. "But it wasn't fair to Celia either," I insist, "putting the hex on her that couldn't write or live without her blessing like a curse." "Of course," she answers, the whole seven thousand dollars of psychoanalysis clinking in her voice. But the years of reading too, the deliberate solitude that makes me most admire what she knows. How does one finally know anything? The Celia I tell her is all she gets. There is Celia's side too, you know, and it must be very different. But she doesn't talk. Playing advocate and defense to Claire because we do talk, always our hope that we keep trying to say it, figure it out and say it between laughing at it, which is another hope. Or is it just the final defense against everything? In any case it is time to leave or nearly. And love, to drink it in again at the mouth is more nourishing than breakfast.

But there is also breakfast. She is going off to the store for a big breakfast, cream and all. Before that we can sit on the edge of the bed and talk about what we'll do in Provincetown. Urgent, already shining in my mind, fresh as the first eye of ocean caught behind the front row of houses when you drive along the dunes, the excited feeling in your feet when you go down Commercial Street, heads and shoulders bobbing in T-shirts the streets packed. And Mrs. Sylva's lobsters in the evening. All the summers in the world. Enjoying it all now beforehand, Claire crowing that this way we get it three times, before during and after. "We have economy and humor, Bookie, that's a start." "We need restraint. And distance," she says. "All this when you are as great a need to me as food." It humiliates me listening. That she might mean it. A woman. And actually love me. From Fumio I can take it. He's a man. Old friend these ten years by now it's customary to know he loves me. But from this radiant girl her head lighting like sunlight a moment past and now in the dark kitchen finding change for the store with just a Fifth Street forty watts to do it by. No. A trap. All gone in the morning. No more. Like Celia was gone. You can't trust that sort of thing. You'd be a fool. Embarrassed because embarrassment is the most embarrassing thing of all. Because she actually respects me, believes me, admires me. How of course outrageous, one cannot rely on that sort of thing. Snare and delusion.

Copying out the Rilke quote again because I lost it the first time, how works of art always spring from those who have faced the danger, gone to the very end of the experience, to the point beyond which no human being can go. The further one dares to go, the more decent, the more personal, the more unique a life becomes. "What's the reference?" "No reference. Found it in one of my poetical scientists. And this time hang on to it. But you are also welcome to your little inferiority complex too. Hand wringer . . ." "You have a penchant for the grandiloquent, Bookie, fancy diction scares me shitless." "Of course it does because you were brought up on those dopey new critics and finished college. My Ph.D." Then silent looking at me. "I adore you." Helpless, all right, give in to the elevator running in my gut who the hell cares what ironists or gossips or all people who cannot and never will see the glory bullying triumphant in her eyes, the pure beauty of her face the power of her head like thunder. Have it your way, mind already gone with her tongue in my mouth and wanting to feel the wet fresh of her welcome on my hand trembling now for hers. A delirium of hot pants in my jeans, the heat climbing my legs till my mind begs her voice to order me out of them.

First I must balance my soul upon the icebox. The lights have all blown out forever, "Capitalist Pigs" Fumio yells at General Electric each time one explodes in blue that awesome second when you turn it on. And the icebox needs defrosting. While it melts I will shower, pay the bill, clean my conscience with Fat Harry and get enough light bulbs to write forever. Looking around at the roaches who have taken over. Smug, have even forgotten how to run. Bowery a pigpen. Slipping since I did somewhere last fall, then bang in winter a sludge still in spring and off to England. My haunted house just a glance at the filth, no time now the hospital you can see her today at last, hurry forget the dirt run guilty into the shower and scrub hard. Simultaneously ironing a dress, one of my nighties to be seen upon the street. Hottest day of the year a long dress nothing under might be mighty cool. Finding excuses for a dress. Bumping into the real reason. Celia said in one batty letter I treated her like a mistress. See this floorlength, know who's mistress here, slouch hat baggy trousers, you're very welcome to be the fella if that's going to make it all right. Worked then. The early days she flattered me upon a lute courting. But not that day she had on her town dress Connecticut kind of woman despite the absurd big Provincetown straw hat, watching the first movie rushes and I wanted to take her hand. Reached for it then saw she was seeing the others see. And reached for her hairbrush fancy variety pure natural bristle, "You should get this kind, your own ruins your hair." And one day a long time too late in Montreal I put down twenty-five dollars for the correct model. Remember to bring a hairbrush today your wild hair wilder from the drive to New Haven, "looking like a old Indian crone," Mother says. Outwoman the bloody world in this nightie, by God you look a sight. What does the mirror say? Dubious. Needs a washing. No, it's O.K. Wear it. Dare.

Today the big risk itself. Almost too frightened to drive the long way there, the mind racing yet trying not to exceed the limits, my slow reflective driver's mind reaching to every corner of the world and all times at once, can hardly afford to speed. Driving, which is— look at that nut risking life to beat a light—just a form of capitalism naked or a game that one plays, Celia saying once that when you are in tune with the rhythm of the lights along the boulevard you have discovered how to live. Kind of insubstantial remark that might make sense if you were in the right mood and stuffed it full of instinct and prescience. What's going on today? My magic side fiddling with the mind's old footage of Celia and New Haven. Cut it in here or use it earlier? The night we left Brookfield, the kids sobbing their frank adoration of Celia, radiating more juice of youth even than they. And we all wept. Celia did her monologue to cheer us up. Spartacus in the manner of some prep school farce. Her nipples in open glee bursting through the yellow jersey in the exuberance of the piece, playing all six voices, every part of the Roman Empire, jumping from chair to table. Her naughtiness, Fumio called it. Her tomboy. Whole gang of us strangling with laughter. Then we made popcorn and drank the rest of the whiskey. Fumio telling us the custom of water-drinking farewells in Japan, when those who part know they will never meet till death. Not for us. The whole bunch of kids came down to town next week for the book party. But by then our end had set in. Celia standing on the street as I raced from the Bowery door to Hilly's Bar the TV waiting and raising hell one crew already left, publishers frantic, can't let my editor down. Celia seeing me already at a distance, did say of the long purple, my first long dress, you look beautiful she said. It went right through the stiff Mexican cotton into my flesh, pierced by what I so wished she'd say, the words a knife across the distance between us on the pavement.

A sign welcomes me to Connecticut and I feel welcome. And then the labyrinth of New Haven. My landmark the Dunkin Donuts. Guided first by a garage mechanic on the highway, one greasy finger finding Yale. Does his good humor accept my mission? You sound innocent asking your way to a hospital. But stay on guard, you have no time to lose getting lost here in this enemy burg, because moments taking the wrong turn are moments without her. The next guide a black man, compassionate, vital, heroic, best of guides, halfway into the city. Knew just where it was and wanted me to get there. Careful at an intersection asking again, this time a professorial type. In this guide the power of the academic establishment against my love, although he is cheerfully superior, points to it just ahead of us, as absolute as Marcus yet unaware of my treason because I have asked with such guile, long rose-colored dress elaborately displayed upon my cheek-hot leather seats, freshly laundered hair shining in open convertible to deceive him.

Then I see it like a squatbug. Big enough, as the scholar said, not to miss it. Hideous pile of concrete full of victims, my Celia caught in that hell box worse than K's castle, six times more confusing. I will wander from room to room, each airless artificial metallic, in search of her forever. They will of course do unspeakable things in a place like that. Cement ant looming upon the landscape right out of science fiction. One waits to see King Kong crunch it holding fair maiden aloft. Jesus they have imprisoned her here. What ominous thing to have by accident hit upon, I will never touch her within these walls. All a mistake. All unlucky. To park now, tacky little lot, man and boy all teeth but no possible notion of where you could buy a flower. Of course I must find some, seeing their fingers point back there—crisis of decision making—to the loop I've just escaped, actually finding the hospital trap without mishap. And now I can brush my hair sitting right in the car, eccentric in full view, becoming presentable amid the debris. But of course the bristle hairbrush lost long ago, wonder maybe it was England. Its wooden handle transformed again into the clear plastic one I always had, never lost, like my final unacceptable self.

Which will not be enough. I must bring flowers. The decision reached, I'll go on gambling. Rehearsing what I say when I present them to her—"Acknowledging all you taught me, flowers." Which do not exist in all of New Haven, though a plump young man next to a woman selling cigarettes glares at the sight in a long dress on an ordinary afternoon in this small town, and thinks there might be some behind the shopping center. While his mother like his wife looks on in sour disapproval. Nice enough about letting me have cancer but flowers are another matter. So it's Temple or is it Church or is it Chapel? Circling the hateful Commons they have where you take this street and get to Celia's old house or the other and get to nowhere under a railroad trestle and the highway says go back to New York. But it's the wrong highway and you're not going to Celia's house ever again, she's moved, lives in the West Nineties little apartment with Ann. Who will be there today and her mother. Miriam and all the claimants. Brushing that aside in noble resolve like the next crushing disappointment, all the injustice in the world, for no amount of cajoling will open the florist, the only one I could succeed in finding if I dedicated a life of research to it. Glass window shut just five minutes ago in the only hotel they seem to have in this town. And the guy's gone home, bellhop truly sorry. While I am myself at my last reserve of willfulness, deciding as the long outlandish dress trails absurdly through gray cement underfoot and overhead like a bad dream, back to my car parked so very illegally, deciding there will be no flowers. And tip a wink to several rowdies in an old white Cadillac. Who simply think I'm a nut. So do the hospital ladies at their front desk, where I bitch the whole town, not one flower in it, how do you manage? They reply with the yellow pages, phone numbers. One merchant even delivers. But I am past interest, just get

up there let's stop fooling around it's late hurrying the
elevator, teeth set against hospital stench's equal parts
of butchery and bureaucracy.

There is no sound in the room. A body white as its
sheets, confused with them and victimized by tubes. Probably pumping blood in one arm, food in the other. But
it's to no point, she'd dead for sure. Top of that,
Ann's here. Vigilant I do not make a noise and wake
the sleeper, have my great projected embrace, hear her
name my name. All the carefully labeled joys I came
this long way to garnish. The scene booming into a vacuum in the sight of Celia merely a very sick body in a
bed. Vanish, Ann, let me have my turn. But she won't,
stubborn as a bedside table. Then vanish anyway and
let me stand beside her, only look at her. I would shield
my eyes if the love in them offends. Trying by mere force
of admiration to wake the dead. The white face still as
a coma, even her eyes rolled back, it is too horrible for
tears. They happen anyway while it seems I'll stop
breathing so hurtfully I love her, so hurt here in this place.
Come away, Celia, wake out of this soulless huge piece
of glass, fly out beyond the gray industrial mess they
picture-windowed for you. A view like this would force
anyone to recover. Wake so I can tell you that and we
can laugh.

But the notion is unthinkable before Ann's tight piety,
prim in her chair. Celia must on no account be distubed
she is in great pain and spends the time knocked out.
Terrified like last time that she'll die, I'll bet. But shut up
about that and join Ann on a chair. Disguising shock
behind sunglasses and figuring out how not to borrow
a Kleenex. Until my great intellectual reach perceives
the toilet. And then resumes the watch in whispered so-
ciability. No matter how charming we are to each other,
Ann is not leaving this room. It is her first occasion to be
free of mother and Miriam. I compose schedules in my
head, trying to hit upon the vacant moment when they'll
all be gone. Trying not to tread upon Ann's time, her
prior right. Very willing to be a sport. Juggling the hours

ahead so I can leave her a full half-hour by herself.
Munificent. Now let her get the point and go out for a
cigarette. But no she can smoke right here. She does
however think it unwise we do so. Has she no sense of
the elastic? Look, at this moment I need nicotine. Finding that I don't. Or not as much as I need to comprehend
why Celia did not say hello when her eyes opened and
I saw them see me. And would not register, recognize.
Celia, I came all the way from England, at least be
civil. It's diabolical. Her eyes point my way but care
not to see me. Ann has the amazing grace to contradict
the facts and say that Celia has been looking forward
to my visit. How nice she has a spokeswoman. Do the
dirty work, say things in her behalf she'd never condescend to utter in person. By all appearances Ann actually
believes this statement. Perhaps I should. Grateful to this
kid next to me, whole thing must be very trying for her.
Waiting up two nights while I've done other things. Because I am not Celia's Ann but her importunate lover
arriving with absurd hopes in a big rush and this crazy
dress. Celia mangled with bandages looking like a very
ordinary sick woman, her long hair braided hanging
down like an elderly New England invalid utterly
neuter, no color even in her face, yet ethereal somehow,
and despite the drab more beautiful than I have ever
remembered it. Then her doctor, fearless soul barging
in to wake her while I envy that another, hundreds of
others touch her.

Her eyes. Quietly I am found in them. Known and
remembered at last. But no great scene after all, both of
us shy while I say whatever stupid things I can think of
and she says she's glad I've come. Rewarded in the
sight of her gallantry, Celia serenely dignified upon her
potty. Which Ann brings, sole nurse and competent. I just
a worshiper more struck by the unruffled poise than anything. Then when it won't happen I have sense enough
to leave the room. To come back later and find her sitting up reckless with anal humor. And just before I leave
permitted to help with something trivial and earthshaking
about a water glass. The perpetual sips of liquid, she

has had much trouble breathing. As I hand it back she gives herself. Kissing me while I feel her fear in the moment of my joy. "You have been afraid, haven't you?" Her head against my cheek nodding in my arms, the two of them straining to give off such force of life energy shameless health and yet so gently do it without disturbing an atom of her flesh, which is still so very tired shock ridden from the knife. Ann miraculously vanished during this unorthodox conversation. One does not ask such questions in a hospital. Only Celia and I might understand how important it is for her to say she has seen death. I can taste it in the sweetness of her kiss. And my plugging life to bring her all the way back across the line. Celia, this here is the other side of the tunnel you'll have to live now. The worst is passed, your audience demand it think of the bunch of them hanging around. You have only this tedium to put up with the next few days. And the view. Knowing how she thirsts for the country. "I expect you have noticed that view?" But her eyes, frightened to laugh and break stitches, pick out her legs instead to demonstrate. "Not to mention these." And she shows me the ridiculous elastic stockings. "Very Chaplinesque, no?" She smiles, trying not to laugh. Saying good-bye, my own stitches ripping as I get to the door. Scattering blessings upon nurses along pointless corridors to sick persons I don't know and would have cheerfully annihilated but a few hours past.

In the North Terminal I scrunch into a bench and wait for Nell. She is delayed three more hours. I have taken the road that said to Kennedy. Rather than the one that said West Side Drive to pick up Vita first. With efficient and comfortable excuses of being just in time, why bother Vita with the trip, etc. Surprised to discover I do not want to share O'Rourke with anyone. So I enjoyed her in absentia all through a long stately dinner. Scribbling against the waiter's disapproval I re-created the myth of my fabulous Millett aunts in solemn splendor. My Aunt Christina must have done this for forty years. Butler, fire, brandy, and all. So keep it down to scale and call it one night's occasion in honor of O'Rourke the battered Irish child miserable in some sky on her charter flight. We stood on the lawn at the garden party watching the children in the window and big hat said to me, tonight a lady and without the hat, "What must it be like to grow up a kid in such a house hearing music like we've just heard?" Our noses born on the wrong side of the glass. What do they hear who grow up on the right side?

Further waiting in the bar, blue laws closing bartender eyeballs grab boobs in long dress. Wore it for Celia. Men engorging it. Funny they are. Glad you like it, flattered by your attention, but the peremptory feel of your stare deprives me of my self. I have been beautiful to please a women, visiting the sick's a cardinal virtue. But the thing got out of hand. Further waiting in the snack shop, getting high on Coke making Nell the great hallucinating patron of my madness for Celia and the cult of the new life business. Waiting for Nell mad instinct knowing I was right. Despite what they all say, even Fumio who has been bitter against Celia. But the relief in his voice when I said that she lived. Right whatever half-assed reality, it's mine. Right to hold out because there could be survival but no life till Celia. Stubborn pupil insisting the teacher never recant. Celia a new life en route to New Haven station when she said she lived for friendship and the very joy of living now that she had died already once upon the table. Bold in her boy's cap daring to say she loved me. A stranger. Wanted my friendship forever. Driving along said she sleeps with her friends and has more than one friend. Bluffing, I ask if she limits herself to gentleman friends, my answer on the ready some not very witty cop-out in case she blew the whistle on me. Celia kissed me at a stoplight and I became her disciple. On the train already praying into a tape recorder letter of love rhapsodically composed jolting down to New York, moving when porter or pop star with guitar case disturbed my outpourings.

Transporting O'Rourke along to the Ladies. Last

refuge of patience. To observe the new and wonderful rapport among women. Sitting through a long rap on purse snatchers with a Puerto Rican mother and an Italian hooker in yellow pants and the attendant powder make-up peroxide woman, very type who used to scare me, judge of my academic pug hair hornrim spectacle of earlier self, accusation unfeminine. Under it always the terrible charge of being queer. Tonight goofy glamorous in my long dress no longer vulnerable, I notice she's scared too in her false eyelashes, talisman to protect her from the world.

Justifying myself conversing the while with O'Rourke, Nell still hovering along in her skies, playing the great potato conclave over again in a notebook. So I say to O'Rourke holy mother Ireland bless me for I have sinned. Showing her my sin. The roguish exploitation of Vita. "She has made a thing of serving me and I have been weak, lazy, and so forth enough to permit it for my own convenience. Now she is spreading guilt on me like lard. I am a stinking turd. I am viscous with it. I am a sandwich spread through the grinning chopper. I am sticky with peanut butter. I am a wreck a wretch sinking in quicksand. She rebukes me with the sorrowful glare of exploited typist."

Says Nell to me in all wisdom, "Tears like whine. When you exploit if you did. When she manipulates if she does. We are all women in this company. But we learn our behavior from most people."

Having gotten this far I notice I am running along in unconscious imitation of Joyce's Baby in the Kitchen, conscious imitation of all British literary stylists. And on to the King's Head feast of learning. Big hat and I in fervent historical imagination taking each other seriously. Power, she says, is the second step in Don Juan's system. Him of the Indian wisdom. "And after that?" Me asking the way. "To learn to deal with death." She says it ominous grand, of course. Since the bank closed at three-thirty the King's Head symposium took place within rigid limitations of time. Medium of writing and music as light is in film. Memory sending messages back from when it happened. Straining in my disordered mind for the sound of her raspy voice.

Over a coffee urn, single concession to comfort, really Alexandrian decadence thrown in by the corporation only in dire emergencies, aged King Lear pilot tells an inquisitive tourist that the plane went down in Maine. "Passenger with a coronary." Not Irish heart for Christ-sakes? No, a man. Who couldn't bear his captivity any longer, just died on their lousy plane because they made him spend twenty-seven aggravated hours waiting to take a seven-hour voyage. Fatigue. It's the waiting on plastic chairs that does you in.

Then all is off in a whirl and O'Rourke is landing, barreling through the door yelling with some British in-valid novice first time in the States and O'Rourke is helping her find her luggage. Shiny yellow cans of film, "just brought it along," she says. My mind groggy now in the sunlight, it's already day, they keep telling me I can't park my car here lady. I'll just be a moment. Till we are all collected and the convertible gleams gorgeous in the rising sun we're off.

And arrive at the Bowery, having deposited O'Rourke's charge at Pan Am headed for Dallas. "Just get here and already I'm somebody's man," says Nell in her jeans and dungaree jacket as we come to where the road could make a mistake and take us to Queens or Long Island or still further like Vita's Montauk day, O'Rourke says, "Did it ever occur to you Celia grows tumors instead of babies to appease her mother? Maybe you went crazy but she went rotten inside and had to cut it out." I argue that is magical Irish horseshit. Drive on, she says. And when we got to the Bowery in golden dawn three junkies two faggots and one transvestite comment extraneously as she gets out on her side in jeans and me in the great big dress, "Which one's the guy?" They laugh in unison. Welcome to the U.S. Poor O'Rourke my neighborhood offends you.

There is however one sovereign remedy. She pulls it out, the perfect bottle of Scotch, rare old kind malt or something. This is no hour to drink. But we are putting off bed. Since there is only one. How lovely if we didn't go to Vita's, yet what if O'Rourke slept with me? Trusted me that much. Or what if O'Rourke slept with me and didn't sleep? Reached over and got what she wanted, wanting it. Myself wanting that, after all I love her, love her as well or better than any, with what other human being have I known such rapport? Sex is but another dimension in friendship, glowing fanatic in the wild light of my theories. But then rehearsing, as she fills the glasses, all the reasons I have always invented for not wanting her. Her red hair. Told myself it was scrawny. Easy, since she thinks it is. Fancy having to invent something as silly as that. To preserve Paul's wife and Winnie's mother. All divested now in America. Where something might happen. And if it did just how would I manage? No problem, I won't have to. She will. I'll never initiate one damn thing, just fall quietly asleep. Or will I? Hours tossing to and fro coughing in frustration. And so forth. No thank you, hand me my glass I'll drink booze at any hour, babble about the three basic and four fine degrees of Irish sloven or whatever. To divert the mind.

"I have left my immaculate London house immaculate and never want to see the place again." Talking as if she'll stay forever, go back into the antique business over here, ship stuff from London, showing me some brochures. First thing in the morning she's going off to hustle Bloomingdale's. Kind of scheme I nod and listen to, discounting most of it as a never-happen. Bring her back to the reality of my dirty floor. Common ground for our Irish sensibilities. "Does my squalor offend you, the roaches have taken over in my absences. Someday I'm really together I'll scrub it." Which reminds her of childhood, a scrubber the whole tribe getting the place dirty, she was Daddy's little wife with lots of brothers. "And certain mornings I lost interest in waking up. What, after all, was the point?" her green eyes opening in exclamation marks. The bed she slept in like a torture cell narrow blue and canvas. I see it as she speaks it. "Touched myself up. Then one would call the others

reporting, till they were all up and whacking me."
Listening, trying to tape her in my mind. How finky
movie makers are, how calculating, but how else could
others ever see the accusation in her eyes rolled back
a bit wide open and terrified? Could she do this part
again for camera, a kid lib movie, the child beaten still
within the adult woman? Drinking whiskey at eight A.M.
telling me she wants to shoot me while she's here. I am
embarrassed. Shoot, but why me? Dead in front of the
camera. No, anything to help her work.

But she changes the subject, wants to know what Vita's
place is like. I'm getting more ice cubes. "Lovely old
penthouse but they haven't fixed it up much." "And kids
do mess up a place," she says understanding it all. "I
think you'll be comfortable there, lots of room, Fred and
the kids are out West, most of the creeps that occupy
the commune thing have bugged off. You and Vita have
the place to yourselves. Nice neighborhood."

"Look, Nell," trying to pin her down, "What shooting
schedule do you have? Can we get all this film through
a camera while you're here?" "Everything that is meant
to happens," she dodges. "Ethel calls this grade school
existentialism." "And by the way, Ethel needs that fifty
dollars you pledged." "I'll send it first thing tomorrow."
She pours herself another and does the last sit-in at South
African House. "Didn't want to go, you know. Not my
cause. I decided I would have a cold. Then a backache
just to be sure. And that morning it was raining. Greatest
backache of my life. But I went. Never seen police go
wild before. I could see what blacks see. You only get
one turn."

Since it is already broad daylight the phone starts
ringing. "Learn to take it off the hook," she says, getting
ready to sleep. "But it talks back." And now it's O'Flynn
calling from Columbia, "You've got to come up here."
"Why, when I haven't slept in days?" "Because everything's falling apart they're all at each other's
throats." "What do you want me to do?" "Peacemaker,"
she says, my worst vice, pushing the exact button to make

me come. One eye on O'Rourke getting into bed wondering if she is appreciating me while I talk like a founding mother of Columbia Lib. The other eye closing in exasperation, such a pity they blew the whole conference in walkouts, how many last night, yes lovely, tell it all to the press they adore stuff like that, bitches fighting in public, have been doing that to blacks for decades— write up their quarrels help rip them apart. Okay, I'll be there as soon as I can, how late can I sleep?

Doing just that. Nell doing it already. The feel of the sheets wonderful foam mattress soothing not one thought till pure unconsciousness. For maybe three hours when I hear O'Rourke swishing about in her green silk meaning it's time to get up. And grouchy. Why is she so irritable when I am serene, able to congratulate myself on the pure disinterested quality of my friendship? We are late to Vita, who has invited us to breakfast. Cooking scones for O'Rourke. Scots blood ancestors old world roots. Clearly a big deal so we must go.

Claire is on the phone to give the weather report. "The Atlantic coast is sinking at the rate of five feet per year, in five hundred years there will be no Provincetown. We must hurry and live, the *New York Times* said so this morning." Parodying herself in high gear now, the chuckle bubbling through each of her batty phrases until it erupts in her laugh. "It'll be glorious, I'm going up there Saturday with Barbara and my sailboat." "Then is it my turn since you have your lovers in shifts?" "All I know, Katsie, is that you are the brains and I am the spirit of the revolution." I am still laughing when I hang up. "Who is this Claire?" O'Rourke demands. "I love her." "Why haven't you told me about her before?" "Because she's impossible to describe. You'll meet her when we go to the farm. Hurry or Vita will have a fit."

Vita is in her elevated kitchen. Her throne of industry. The altar of her stove a personal achievement, designed it all herself that this technological wonder be center stage, so modern you can't even tell if it is on, great way to burn your hand on its innocent look of a tabletop.

She is making the scones. Has been making them for hours. O'Rourke's scones. I am late to Columbia. Bacon neatly fried waiting on its paper towel. Vita addresses Nell, little mother speaking of troublesome childman. "Kate is so difficult to bake for—she scolds." I listen in astonishment. My head buzzes and turns a criminal scarlet. Accused before a judge no less than Nell, whose face is stolid. Nell who was to be edified by our nicely adjusted model Lesbian relationship is hearing all this instead. Wonderful. The scenario conveyed in Vita's tone is full of vivid incident. First frame Vita arises at dawn chops wood starts ancient stove bakes daily bread while I lie abed until I stomp downstairs big boots to beat her on the back with a stick of kindling wood. My projection of what she is saying. Her own projection is based on that day at the farm she bought the wrong kind of flour going to bake real bread like a prize schoolgirl but it came out like a rock and we teased her, Fumio and I trying to soften the disappointment with a joke.

I put down my glass of milk. "Wash it yourself, this is a commune not a hotel." My face is redder now. Stung. "I did not think it was a hotel." She laughs at me. I am humorless. Vita's joke. I no longer understand anything, only that the floor refuses to open, swallow me, remove me from Nell's gaze upon me from the rattan swing in the corner of the living room. I can say nothing, knowing I have lost Nell's good opinion forever. She will of course have seen in this one moment the whole sorry character of my relationship with Vita. And sided with her against me. Green eyes burning at me while she swings, idle lady of leisure. Celia's swing too. Odd they should both pick it. Same spot. Affinity? Never mind insight, you are late to Columbia but must eat scones first. The table set with real strawberrries. Actual sit-down food, Vita is taking this brunch very seriously. I must stay until the end, finally explaining the abortion thing uptown. Would they like to go, maybe help, at least tell me what to say. I'm not as qualified, they both have children or abortions? But no, they plan to be busy.

"Why didn't you get here sooner, where the hell have you been?" a woman yells as I run in the door. Mac-Millan again and a voice accusing me. Because I had other things to do, forget your guilt rap, lady. Under my breath. While a bit further back in my head I'm hearing her loud and clear, first holding up Celia's ashen bedside then O'Rourke's middle of the night arrival from London. Then Vita's scolding scones. None are sufficient. And the fact that I was never invited to stay for this conference, just do us a favor make the kickoff speech little thing five minutes long we don't need you after that. But this won't do either, her voice already a staircase behind me still bitching and joined by ten others of different persuasion briefing me on what has happened last night, two hundred walked out claiming they were feminists the others were frauds. Because they lost the vote on free abortions and the issue of sexual freedom was shelved, too controversial. "Well, you lost the vote," I say. "It's not because we lost the vote it's because the whole conference is a gimmick run on phony procedure masterminded by SWP." "What's that?" "Socialist Workers Party, they control the entire staff and run their votes through like clockwork, the body of the meeting has no idea what's going down it's all a fix." I look at them. Am I to believe all this? Ruth had warned me to stay away from the whole thing to start with. Well, what to do now? You are listed as a sponsor. "Withdraw your support," they urge. "How can I withdraw my support from a conference on abortion," I ask when I've finally got the mike, organizing staff saw me coming and adjourned the thing with the speed of a high-powered machine. Fifty voices yell me down. "You'd better not withdraw." "Let her talk." "Who do you think you are?" I'm not so sure myself. If I'm an ego-tripping star they have every right to go on yelling, throw me off the stage or whatever. If I'm a name used for sponsorship I have the right to withdraw. Problem is I don't want to. So I will hedge. Because I want them to heal their fragments and come to agreement. But it's too late. The conference is over. Yes, but the fighting will go on forever, can we

get representatives of both sides to sit down together?
The seats empty, most everyone has left now, the out-of-
towners innocent, apolitical, their first meeting come to
this confusion, to see floor fights, walkouts, quarrels. How
disappointed they must be. The real victims of the war.
Their idealism dirtied by the yelling. Because a few from
each side are now having it out on the stage. Let's sit
down in a circle and talk in turn, let's lower our voices.
With the limitless patience for abuse you must have if
you step into a dogfight, are fool enough to try to mediate
anything at all, let along this. And I haven't been here
through it, scarcely understand. But the fighting I know
is no good for us. Trying to give off the affection and
good will I tried to give them last time. Feeling a bit
of an ass, presumptuous but what else can a pacifist do?
I have a half-hour before I must go to the hospital. Irene
Rosenberg stands next to me, pointing out the Party
members. In the eye of her paranoia they are robots.
She nudges me, "Look how they signal each other with
their eyes, look at how they smirk." On stage it is lunacy,
but at least the volume is lower. They are sitting down
in a heap, accusation falls over accusation. Could one
person talk at a time? The staff make a good case, the
meetings were orderly, the votes were good majorities,
if you lose them and walk out you should admit it as
fair play. Then the other side charging subversion, the
women's movement exploited for political ends by an
outside party looking for a protest issue safe enough for
the establishment to swallow, therefore no talk of free
abortions, no nonsense about queers, the sodomy laws,
sexual freedom.

I listen but I don't know. Abortion seems to be the
thing for this conference to work on. Gay Liberation
should cover its own issues. But that is the old split between gay women and straight. Why continue to fumble
here? And what real difference does it make what
demands they set? You might as well ask for everything
you want since that way you are likely to get more of
the some the system will concede you, always so little.
A black woman is saying the vote satisfied her. "Why

not a free abortion demand? White middle-class women
can afford abortions, but can you?" "Honey, if we just
got repeal we're doing fine." I don't know. Do they?
But they are not thinking, their proposals have turned
to cement on each side, they are fetishes by now, magical
formulae identified by alphabet names, WISE versus
WONAAC. As in all warfare you are for one group or
another by now, forget what they stand for. And you
talk and listen only to your side. You signal them. They
signal you. When you call on the next person after bun-
dling your rhetoric and holding the floor as long as
possible you call on your own side. The other side is
not people but forces, not women but agents. There are
twenty minutes left. Now that you have differed what
will you do in the future? Denounce each other, hold
press conferences. Feminists will warn women against
the party. The staff will continue to carry on the coalition
authorized by the votes. It is impossible for them to entertain further demands because they are not entitled
to act without the body. Who have disappeared leaving
only its leaders, who are too democratic, etc. There are
ten minutes left. Is it possible you could agree to disagree
and regard each other if not as friends then as other
women doing their thing not yours but why vamp on
it? What need of a press conference? The noise getting
softer, more like human conversation, my eyes drift off
into the pit of the red chairs. Still hearing Teresa Juarez's
voice accusing me in the other voices today accusing me.
Nothing is good enough. I am not good enough. Late
and remiss because I did other things. They are right.
I have not said anything for a while because they are
at last talking to each other. It's time to leave. Probably
too late for New Haven. Two-hour drive and turned away
when I get there. I did not do a good enough job with
the peacemaking but it is all I can do.

That woman on the staircase. All the way to New
Haven I hear women's voices. The voices that demand
all your time, though they themselves are often too busy
to attend. Or when you next run into them they've lost
interest altogether and look upon their involvement as

a phase. They are back in school, have a better job, are thinking of leaving town, need a vacation. But you mustn't. You must serve continuously because they think you're no not a leader just some asshole created by publicity—a star. So they need your name and presence whenever they need it. And a check would be handy too. And when they have used you they denounce you. You are a piece of shit, you are a star. De Beauvoir said *étoile*. Sounded so funny in French. The Left's exploitation and manipulation of *les étoiles*. A degenerate thing, she said. Her voice with its impeccable moral force. But still more moving the pain in her face inflicted by a few thoughtless youngsters who urged her to find all the celebrated signatures in France and publish in the papers that they had had abortions. Defy the law. Risk arrest. Persons vulnerable by visibility. Or persons protected by it. Carefully alphabetized together with the ordinary citizens they themselves enlisted. Then insulted her for her efforts, she was an elitist, a star. Why exploit the famous if you hate them? Just because you need them and must hate them. Act out your outrage upon them when you can come within spitting range. So they are right, the shrieking voices. And right too, de Beauvoir her annoyance, no it was worse than that, a real sorrow, which could drive her as Nell as driven right away from the movement. Of course the whole thing is a terrible botch on all sides. Vicious. Inhuman. And inexpedient as well. Yet somehow horribly necessary. Keep it up and we may destroy the concept, even the reality of fame and an elite. Is it my masochism only, my guilt feelings that tell me I need that woman's voice? Why? Is it because I'm some consecrated silly? Yes. No. Perhaps it's because I owe a debt to her. For your income? My money comes from a publisher. You are not salaried by the movement. But the book sold because there was a movement. So have other books. By persons less committed, even pop nonsense. Every week I receive another plagiarism in the mail. And yet I am in debt. Why? For this dreadful new identity? Come, are you taking yourself seriously as Kate Millett of Women's Lib? I hope not. That media-elected leader is now my worst enemy, would have me ousted from a movement I worked in six years, long before publicity entered to mess it up. But you are an artist. You have other work to do. You have a life of your own. Your friends go to the hospital or arrive from England. Are you a pawn? Do you belong to the movement not yourself? I hope not. Damned little good to it if I'm not my own woman first. Who are you then? I am all the things I am. One of them is a woman in the movement. What is your life about? About change, I think lately. And if you change your mind? Then I am a fool. Who changed her mind. But I think I won't.

Welcome to Connecticut. A fool. You were certainly a fool to go up to Columbia today. Should I have ignored O'Flynn's request? So urgent. Then she wasn't even there herself. So I have learned something. And did not harm, the battle was over before I got there. Didn't do much good either. I learned something about war and peace, hostility and good will. Is the world your kindergarten? Will you put it in your book what an ass you were with that microphone? It is supposed to be a record of what I learned. And I did learn not to make statements at the end of rows I was too distracted to attend. Or too busy. There is never enough time. Or too disinterested. Yes. What's with this lesson plan? Because Gandhi said it, his experiments with truth. How else am I going to learn without role models? What if he is both a pietistic old fuddy-duddy and an untouchable saint truly wise great man? Monotones can listen to Beethoven.

Cheer up, you have Vita to teach you your evil. Replaying her kitchen remarks five thousand times in variation. Each time I have something more wonderful to retort. More insightful, pompous, cutting, vindictive, powerfully exculpating. Pick up her whole guilt load and hit her on the head with it. Very violent person for a pacifist. Watch that pedestrian or you're a homicide for sure.

Out of gas. Inconceivable idiot, why didn't you remember to fill the tank? Distracted by a mother. In full ingratitude blaming it on Celia's mother, who was there today and didn't bite me. A frightened fragile little woman whose daughter is in the hospital next bed to an Italian lady who is having the priest. Surgery tomorrow, confession today. He won't give her absolution because she's remarried. Excommunicated because the first man abandoned her with two kids and the next one came along and took care of them all. Mortal sin. Facing the knife. Too old to have more children, afraid of pregnancy and now tying her tubes. But the good father her parish priest won't help her out. We considered the problem. Celia and her mother staunch High Church Episcopal probably find Catholicism a disease of the lower classes but certainly don't show it. I am outraged at this moronic pharisee and would like to pitch him out the window. But don't show it. It is Celia who comes up with the answer. We'll get another priest from Yale. The Newman Club, I said, suddenly remembering.

Afterwards a little drink with Mrs. Tyburn, though she generally doesn't drink. And is worried if her car will be all right. The two of us bumbling through New Haven on a Sunday, she knows a place but now it's gone, changed management into a scruffy little bar, she says it will be fun. An adventure in jukebox blue lights over the bartender and six truckers glued to their stools. What will I say to Celia's mother? That I have an illicit passion . . . One does not say these things. So I don't. Instead we talk about aesthetics. In no time very absorbed in a conversation on the different narrative techniques of the novel and film—look up for an instant see my own face flash on TV. Big color box above the bartender. Must have imagined it. But I could swear. Some news footage of the year in pictures, it could be possible. How disgusting, won't it go away and leave me in peace with Celia's mother, who must find me embarrassing enough. But she is infinitely kind. "You must have found it hard at times," she ventures. To explain would take too long, and it is more interesting to hear what she's doing. She's been playing tennis, which makes her feel fit, has to pick up a new racquet today. And has quit teaching drama. Now teaching art instead at a high school. And likes it very much, watching the kids grow. Vastly pleased with ourselves by the second martini, she's so much like my mother in a good mood same size just as timid I'd like to hug her. Then Mrs. Tyburn thought we ought to go, worried about her car, which is all right on the whole but gives her some trouble. A brave little lady in pitch-black parking lot, all my protective impulses spring to attention. Also the supplicatory calls for absolution. Her little honk saying good-bye. But in three minutes I had managed to get off the course she set me and onto a road heading north. Huge signs and lights advise me of my mischance. The road is over there. A hundred feet in the air and flying fast. With great finesse and full powers of concentration I achieve the miracle. And go on making movies in my head at a sedate fifty miles an hour, brain ablaze with a new project call it *Roll Your Own,* first sequence in Vita's kitchen full screen of splendid grimace, then both of us in next frame floating like a Chagall across the room.

Then suddenly the sputter. Meet a mother go to pieces had it in mind to buy gas then got to thinking about movies. Deserted highway, utter darkness, open car—do you realize you are at the mercy of any crazy who stops? Sitting by the side of the road, realizing fully but too late. So obviously ridiculous, why we even had a good time together, that I laugh. Laughing alone in the dark on an empty tank, infallible sign of madness. Laugh again, will now have to ask help of fellow man, let's hope he's not a rapist. But he's nothing at all. Whizzing by time after time. More embarrassed must now signal him, stand in the road and beg, how will you have the nerve to say you actually ran out of gas, totally humiliating oversight only a guaranteed idiot . . . In the morning by daylight perhaps I'll be less conspicuous. But there is a huge station wagon. I await my fate, remembering how it was a cripple, the only man who would stop when we had that flat on the trip to Vassar organizing for the Cambodian War strike.

Expecting to see him limp. But he doesn't. Preparing utterly self-abnegating little apology for taking up his time. Snug in his car to the filling station, trust him. Then he says the oddest thing, that he's glad to do someone a favor. After the day he's had. Look over by light of dashboard see he's fifty maybe gray hair handsome probably professional man looks Jewish reminds me of Jacob wonder if he's a physicist too. Though he might as well be a plumber, somehow it seems superfluous to introduce ourselves with what do you do, his charity so actual it asks no explanation. Well, ask him, he's giving you a ride. Like hitchhiking in France with JayCee. I had to do the talking in French to pay for the ride. But the truckdriver threw our suitcases out on the road at our heads when I said stop you bastard, his hand pawing over my breast. "What sort of a day was it?" thinking of my own. "My mother was assaulted beaten and raped today in New Haven by a man who broke into her apartment. She is seventy-six years old." Jesus how very sorry I am I say, knowing never in my lifetime would I be able to say how utterly sorry I was. Seventy-six years old and raped her. How insane with misery you would be to inflict that on an old woman cowering blood all over her face in the basement apartment, discovering I have made it a basement myself.

"This happened to you today and you want to do another human being a favor?" and found a woman, me there's irony in that but never mind, then aloud, "But you realize of course that most people who have suffered so would have as their first reaction to go out and harm, retaliate somehow." Thinking that he has broken the chain, as Mallory calls it, when you do not react to violence with more of it. Thinking how most of the really contemptible atrocities are commited by people who have just heard or been lied to that one of their own kind is raped or cut into pieces or whatnot. Not only in war but the whole Middle American Right is responding to a mind rape by the Left, the youth the broads the queers. All of us stomping on their world.

His mother. And what if it were mine? Or Celia's, how does one bear such thoughts? Forget it. Listening to him tell it, his calm, his stoicism, his fortitude beneath this meaningless catastrophe. Can she speak of it, bumbling ideas about therapy, just to discuss it with someone not necessarily a psychiatrist might be very useful after such a trauma and at her age so probably worse, a greater affront to her human dignity violated so piteously. Still trying to ease his pain and never knowing how but letting him talk. And admiring his incredible statement that it was important to him when hurt this way to help someone. Our journey to Emmaeus in the dark of not really even a highway just a country road in pitch to where my car sits useless and foolhardy before his lesson, this amazing man I will never meet again, seeing the license plate recede unrecorded. He has left his mark behind substantial, and changed me forever, this chance meeting upon a road.

She is there with the door a bit ajar to show the light of her with the light behind through the window's ivy. Magnanimous about the errands we must run before we find O'Rourke in an Irish bar. At last these two to meet. And will they like each other? Will Claire go silent, be shy, hide her light? Watching them, watching Claire really as she follows me at a distance mounting the steps in the restaurant. Expensive place uptown and we are in old clothes. Downtown clothes, going-to-the-country clothes. But O'Rourke is high upon the afternoon's town, drinking she will keep us waiting still longer.

We have stifled doubt by having first visited the stationer for notebooks. The clerk is sympathetic to my requirements, big but not too big. And cheerful colors. We are writers. We will fortify ourselves with paper. New notebooks will protect us from headwaiters and executives, Madison Avenue eaters and drinkers at fancy places. Claire lights on a small brown one, priced right. Still needs eight cents. Promising as always to repay, keep track, borrows but keeps her credit. Nearly legendary with her rigor over sixty-cent loans. Puerto Rican money orders no one can ever cash.

We hug the paper and enter. Past the dragon with his glasses pointed toward our clothes. Do we look gay? Do we look ragged? Where did Claire go? Here I have mounted the steps and shook hands. But Claire has disappeared. No, slowly, with the slowness of fate or disappointment, she is climbing the little steps up to the table. I would like you to meet my friend Claire Bookbinder. And the big hat reaches a ring. They have touched. Claire, her slouch elegant among tablecloths, the swing of her hips cotton trousers riding low seat very flat, turtleneck sweater, hand plucking at its collar then gripping for her arm. Shy but being brave. Smiling at them not afraid but gallant taking Nell's hand. Then talking, voluble with Joe Kaplan, another whale-freak who can begin a conversation with a fly, progress to an elephant, supply her with references on dolphins. And then arrive at the inevitable sea beast as she grows confident and secure the sweater coming off. Safe now, her beautiful head alight over the naked and glowing shoulders of her usual tank top. One martini turns into its second, I can relax and listen to O'Rourke telling Joe the film she has just shown him, her pop star flick on BBC commission, is garbage commercial dribble yet technically such lovely Roxy, "I blew every trick I knew into it." Joe her first teacher too demure to criticize whereas Nell is now the woman of the world hotshot movie director, a relentless critic of herself. But off the tough whenever she turns to Claire, gentle as one might be with innocence.

Listening. When O'Rourke is pried from her bar and Joe is left behind us. The three of us on the road to the farm. Nell lying prone, whole back seat to herself, taking little naps or looking up at the trees. Like an infant in the back seat indulged, her eyes in outlandish blue sunglasses. Listening to Claire describe the telescope she wants to buy, one hundred and eighty dollars, can save up get another job at Bloomingdale's like the sailboat took. O'Rourke listening as Claire wonders aloud if there's any point in purchase, since the robbers take everything. Each year at Christmas her mother replaces her phonograph and the typewriter. Hardly seems worth bothering unless the thief holds off till summer, "And lets me type through spring," leaping off into her laugh, which fills the landscape bringing all the trees of summer down on our heads. I am luxuriously happy. Propagandizing Nell the Taconic is a lovely highway, that man was a genius, landscape artist planning each cluster for our eyes to pleasure on, consider his infinite kindness. "Got trees in England too. I need rest. America is crazy." Slipping back to the doze of one resolutely unimpressed by nature.

Listening while under the light of the tulip, dinner at the farmhouse, eyes loving them both and finding Fumio's so long away and home at last while O'Rourke's eyes study Claire camping herself on the search for charity, "Got very enthusiastic reading Bonhoeffer during my Christie period, I let this bum live with me. Had two beds then. His and mine. Got along fine till the bedbugs left his territory. He never did. Just the bugs. At that point I gave up the quest."

Rich beyond speech or memory. All my beloveds about a table under one roof. And Fumio. But holding back, we meet later when we are alone. After the fire and the last nip of whiskey in the little blue and white cups. O'Rourke has of course the best bedroom, self-appointed and settled in great lady splendor rustle of her dress. Our movie queen, Fumio winks at me. Claire declares her independence, will sleep in her sleeping bag under the stars. Saying as I bend down to kiss the yellow head stuck out above the blue flannel lining with its pictures of animals printed loud and vulgar for the thrifty, her blessed head's gold-dust like a wind of straw, the light coming from the hallway, explaining that I have not seen him in so long. And slept first with her coming home from England. She is matter of fact, then ominous—"you must take care of yourself the way you live is dangerous." "Why?" Kneeling in the grass beside her.

"Look, kid, you won't love life very much longer if you go on chasing around in that old car. I swear if you kill yourself I'll put plastic flowers on your grave. Plastic and I know where to get them. Orchard Street, in just one Saturday I could buy up the whole market. The revenge would be worth the expense." Our heads together while I bend into her bag, laughing our kisses into each other's mouth. The moon on top of us and all the stars clean as they never are in town.

After this the calm of his arms and his body his small cock larger each second in my mouth and his tongue tickling me until in peace he comes enters the long waited feel of him full inside and his eyes dark coming, the last pumping thrusts a shudder while I squeeze powerfully in my closing on him, bringing him while he is making it come in me, the sureness of it happening now both at once. Then rest tender in the quiet like sleep already so much a harbor, while we whisper children in the dark after lights out, and will she be safe there, the two big farmhouse doors thrown open the hall lights on, what if some crazy saw her from the road? Stopped his car. My mind already a tabloid headline. While he reassures, his small dark head so gentle saying we are all safe here. It is the farm.

Listening while the Texaco man fills up at the Billings Light, Claire is telling Nell the anxiety, the hand clutching her arm. Mocking her own habits of narrative making the whole thing casually amusing till she comes to the acid trip. I am in the front with Fumio, but I hear her over the hum of the gas pump, over the dialogue of oil and water. Her voice telling it to Machree. "In the dawn I was walking home along Fifth Street from Second Avenue. The sun was coming up in a dirty halfhearted way, at the end of the street there was a huge carton, you know the kind refrigerators come in. And it was moving toward me, blowing along in the wind. Walking by itself, moving enormous menacing. And the light behind it was utterly pointless. I realized, of course the evidence was irrefutable, that the thing at the end of the block approaching was there to tell me the horror at the center of the universe. How it means nothing. That's when I chickened out and started hanging on to myself." The voice losing its concentration on language, its hold over meaning, and breaking into nervous laughter. "For support, don't you see?" Turning as we all turn and see her beautiful head shining laughing back, the arm clutching as expected. Nell's eyes staring. Then her voice, reassuring as it had been in its British grunts and yesses, now drifting off to a monastery she's read about somewhere that Claire should visit. What bond have they made? What has Machree absorbed of Claire's terror so great it fills the car, forms an electric fence between us and the landscape, settling over the open convertible like a gas bubble sealing us finally from the fine high Connecticut summer.

In my shoulders too as we enter New Haven, the maze, stiffening through the turnings that could be this way or that way but one or the other and each so familiar they could as easily be right or wrong. But one of them is wrong and does not say so. Each claiming through the old recognition of error that it is as probable as its alternative. Until I feel Claire's hands settle upon each shoulder in that declivity between the bones of neck and collar and her voice encouraging me teasing of course but deadly serious, onward have confidence we are simply in the presence of the enigma.

Then we are all at Celia's bedside. The lot of us. Watching each of them, my eyes touching each face like the fingers of the blind, caressing them. Silent. I have brought them all together. Fumio, Celia, Machree, and Claire with the clutch on and holding back. Then reaching to shake Celia's hand who is bluff and hearty, and with O'Rourke grateful that she came from so far. And a silent look for Fumio who is silent. Glowing at her from his corner. Always he hangs back, but their two natures know each other and recognize that fine likeness which no longer threatens me. Rejoicing in the moment almost removed from it unless I toss the little ball of conversation and help to facilitate the dumb show of talk, its trivia of meetings and sick rooms, the banal questions of what have you been doing lately. An entrepreneur of friendship turning to the deeper waves exchanged between those I love assembled here to love each other. This moment planned awaited schemed for. A whim. A notion. A project. A hope. Seeing it as real as the hospital bed or the light out the window. Flowing now into oneness as Claire's smile melts into Celia's or Fumio's eyes on Machree a figure at the foot of the bed next to Claire.

But of course it breaks, brittle in the sound of Nell's voice already out the door, grabbing Claire with her before I hear her words—something about starving, buy food, meet you in the car. Bereaving me. Only the three of us left. As once. Fumio Celia and me. With so much to say we say nothing. But communicate in signs. Of eyes, of smiles, of a water glass. Of routine hospital jokes. Of Fumio's mute solicitude. Of my garrulous Irish ramble. Of Celia's incredible new beauty when ill, ordinary and without color. The beatitude in her new stillness, the removed and distant grandeur of her power. Like knowledge. Another self who has transcended and prevailed without losing all that she was.

The projector prepared but no Fumio. The crew raucous, why should we wait for a man let's go come on damn it, as I hold my breath a traitor to all chauvinism and convicted of caring so that he see it. Claire too. Fumio not here though we are all here, all of us here in Jonas's little coffin seats so private you cannot see your neighbor's face watching because the headrests slope around you to cut off your view. Movies rendered even more secret than their natural darkness. I hate these seats. To hell with whatever concentration they are meant to impose, I want to watch reactions. And Claire is a row ahead of me, the back of her head three seats to the right. And no Fumio yet. Saving the seat on my right for him. Send out and see where he could possibly be. The report is he's pissing. Catcalls at this proof of masculinity, how awful. Rhoda laughing above all of them.

Delora stroking my hand excited. Shirley raising hell, when does this damn thing start? Mallory in general hysteria. Robin preparing for schizophrenia. Then he finally appears to their cheering. His little chuckle apologizes and dives into his seat. The dark comes. Roll it.

But I cannot see Mallory's face, hold her hand, see her through the ordeal of seeing herself. Only a long hug when it is over. "Just too traumatized to say anything now but I love it," squeezing my arm. Then a *shhhhhh* from all sides while they devour Lillian. Then my hand on her head during Robin, "You're beautiful, baby." While she cries and they are all yelling "It's over, we did it, the film is finished." Fumio gives me the eye and a wink that means the movie's O.K. Pandemonium has set in with the rest. Relief gives way to euphoria. They approve their movie, presented and received at last. The company in bedlam whooping in the seats, and when kicked out since somebody else needs the screening room, still yelling in the corridor everybody talking at once, loving the movie and themselves. The moviemakers' high. "Wow, are we great." Jumping up and down bellowing kissing pounding on the back. Then silent just looking at each other our consummation. Rhoda barks again, "Oh that part you kept it thank God where Mallory"—but Sybil is saying, "Why didn't you use the red rooster?" and I am calm, "Yes, we tried for two days to keep it in but it wouldn't cut." Rhoda saying yes. Delora too. Robin skeptical. And Mallory grinning, shifting from boot to boot her elegant mod outfit cloche hat scarf and all, Mallory suddenly run backwards to a child's glee. That pleased-with-herself slightly embarrassed grin I love so, kid sister. Actually approving of me. And infatuated with herself. Hugging me again— you did such a beautiful job. Everybody praising everybody, "We really are the movie company, we made it." Claire her entirely serious self goes by beating a retreat to quietude, shakes my hand and calls it a "distinguished achievement." No less than the full grandiloquent phrase. Suddenly I realize it's just a movie.

We stand in the dark of the hallway. The tiles blue and yellow. The cheap silver paint on the banisters. Does every slumlord buy from the same jobber? I have not been here in a long time, not since the old days when we were friends dragging each other through graduate school, regular calls to demand one or the other write the damn thesis and get out. And once years ago picking up the portfolio for the employment committee already cursing myself for having saddled my sculpture time with paperwork. Wore my big brown Mexican sweater that night, feeling exotic till I got there. Then felt shy, red in the face, sweater too hot, my body awkward as a bear. Do I look all right, do I look feminine enough? We were two married ladies. Fumio sculpting at home, her own Mike out at a meeting, not yet absorbed by his radical politics but in the process. She will need a divorce soon. Her stark beauty numbs me, there are pauses in the conversation. Frieda, with her Swedish exactitude. She must think I am stupid, will be poor at the work. Odd how things start. Then after she cut Fumio I talked to her once on the phone. She had just been fired from State.

Fumio talks to Karl, some guy who came by to pick up the cat for the summer. Its plastic box sits in the hallway. Karl, fat in his suitcoat, buttons don't reach, hairy as a bear. The men talk art, little bantam steps. What medium do you work in? Fumio doing a put-on without meaning to by saying he draws in air. And Karl, a psychologist turned sculptor but still an intellectual, not getting it.

Frieda gives me a drink in the kitchen. We are past the worst now, seen each other, talked, all last summer's hurt gone, her fear I'd be the avenging wife hatpin in hand to strike her heart. But in the living room Frieda tells us about a course on homosexuality she taught at State last year with another young instructor. Both straight but the other one just might not be. I tease her it's a bit like black studies taught by a putative mulatto. No one willing to say. The two of them did it under cover, the university gave credit but no salary, the classes met at the instructors' houses. I tell about a course at Nebraska well hidden in the medical school that got written up in the student newspaper, big hullabaloo reaching even the legislature, who promptly considered making homosexuality a still more serious offense with mandatory aversion therapy thrown in. Karl can't understand all the fuss. Perfectly all right for people to be homosexual if they like, their business, private matter. I tell him what it took me to come out in media that torn winter. He doesn't hear me at all. I talk louder. He insists it's all just personal life. "Look you moron do you think I had any interest in making copy of my private affairs? Do you think I did that without consequences?" Talking very loud now. I've become abusive, calling him a son of a bitch, yelling how my mother went crazy in St. Paul where her neighbors read magazines. Her reality. "And what right did I have to disturb her peace?" "What right indeed," he says, "it's all private." "Look you bastard every queer in America has grief from parents, suffers from mother guilt. If no one comes out we must all hide in silence forever."

Frieda explains how breaking the speech taboo is important to homosexuals, vital to any struggle for rights to announce yourself, oppressed groups never get anywhere shutting up. I tell him, upping the ante for the sake of rhetoric, that I have now effectively lost my entire family. Mother going the way of the Milletts. Karl is solving it all for us by observing that if people are prejudiced they simply deprive themselves of good company. Suddenly I am offering to throw my drink in his face, bellowing that I loved my aunts their company my great joy in childhood, their grace and wit and beauty every good thing I ever desired now gone. One adored uncle, the uncle I wanted for a father after Dad left, telling me in the driveway end of that awful Christmas— "If you must be like this," the word too gross to utter, "then we cannot know you." Now I am sobbing, still telling Karl that I loved them, that I am deprived forever and they will die, are old now. "They aren't going without, but I am. They don't want to know a Lesbian so they're okay," knowing even when I say it that they might miss me somewhere, the favorite niece, their pride, the one they sent all the way to Oxford. Aunt Christina, adored aunt of good fairy childhood godmother, great lady in fine house went to see once with my carfare coming home from the dentist on the streetcar every week passing Virginia Avenue. And got off one brave time, went up to the door. Butler surprised. I wait in the front hall, black and white marble squares of formal entrance. Knowing the rooms that stretch beyond because I see them at Christmas and high feast days. And once she let me stay there the summer I was thirteen, a few weeks' bliss reading Poe's complete works in the cool dark library. Rare books, floor to ceiling shelves of brown leather. All the Irish authors.

Here I am trying to get some work done writing about Frieda three days ago and when I get to the library I remember the music too. That my aunt had music coming from the big Capehart in the hallway, always seemed Mozart, most perfect music. And showed me *Beggar's Opera* bawdy pictures great disrespectful songs about crooks who were not the fancy music that bored me. And when I remember the music I begin to sob with terrible pain because I realize Celia is music become as distant as this aunt my first love.

So I wait while the butler tells her. And she comes down. I think she will send me away, just telling him to get rid of me. I am eight and have braces that require the dentist and the retainer brace, but already I know you can be sent away. She comes down the big staircase, and my heart goes noisy with hope to see her crown of auburn hair curls on her head like a helmet gold. She has come to send me away. And I go. There is no reason for me to come. I was not invited. I have broken a rule of society. My reason was only my worship. She is my aunt, my own damn Millett family. But there are rules.

And when I write this I begin to sob for myself as a child, actually making a noise as I have not cried and now I cannot remember when. Telling myself I am an ass and stroking my own arm to mother me. Working it out. Then a headache and I feel better. When the door closed I had to knock again and borrow fifteen cents from the butler. My mother's house from my aunt's was so far even passion could not walk it. He had mercy. He did not go upstairs to let her know I needed money. Then the door closed, great black Georgian brass knocker. My body stood on the steps, eyes looking down Virginia Avenue toward the streetcar tracks. Lines laid forever. They took up the tracks years later. I am their warehouse, storing them inside my body.

Yelled at poor Karl. Frieda looking on said it was a good thing I did it. My encounter. Like a good stone-headed radical never going in for that sort of thing. We explain to Karl why it's important and when Fumio goes to get more ice because we're all staying for dinner and Frieda is cooking I tell Karl I am grateful to him. He chops onions into the clotheswasher and I hug him. In England finally able to tell people, but humbly, clowning it, saying "queer," the cruel word, just so servile and grateful they don't leave the room or make a terrible face. Now tonight I got mad, shouted at someone, swore, gave up the gentleness won so hard for the relief felt so good.

Dinner is confusion for me because I am drunk. Suddenly I am so drunk I can scarcely sit through Karl's good bourguignon, though it's the first time I ever liked a beef stew. But I am a prisoner of the drug, cannot see any more. Just hanging on so I won't fall off. Keeping the room from spinning. Always the test in college, lie on a bed and try to keep the room from moving. Have to sit on another chair even before the coffee. Then I can't sit. I go into the bathroom. Can't throw up 'cause I don't want to. Glance at my face in the mirror. It is gone. I am my own arms and legs in their white clothes on the red rug, stretched out on the floor of the bathroom. Pasted there. Paralyzed. I will rest.

Then I remember Fumio and Frieda undressing me, taking off my white Mexican shirt and white trousers. Who is taking off what I can't tell, too far gone for embarrassment and thinking vaguely how I never get drunk.

It's my accomplishment. I have not been this drunk since college. Then Fumio is gone. Frieda is feeding me stuff, sugar cube with some bitter junk on it. I will eat one but not two. Then they are both gone. Then I wake up. Frieda is in my arms. How did this happen? What in the devil is happening anyway? She is talking about a child, an orphan. She is going to adopt an orphan. Little war victim. Call it Orpheus. I wonder if she is drunk or crazy. She is saying that the doctors took her cervix but not her womb and she will get Orpheus anyway. I ask if they'll let you have these kids easily, remembering many times I've thought of doing it, asking people what my chances were. Smile in the dark at what they'd be now. Yes, she says, I'll get it. She is kissing me. I must be a hangover to kiss. She seems to want to. I don't know what to do. She is Fumio's friend, I think, remembering she is mine too. I can scarcely be said to be seducing my husband's mistress at this rate, the terms nonsensical outmoded and now especially silly against our friendship and the warmth that happens as she touches my breasts, though I can still hardly feel it, preventing it. But then her hand touches my flank, slides along it, reaches me and she enters, taking me surprised to the moment when the wall melts and pours forth. Now we are crying and she says she could feel it, my cervix. And she sobs for her own lost. Says it felt beautiful and I remember how Claire's felt the night before, a warmth tangible by an inch even, moving in the most remote dark. My arms hold Frieda in my gratitude to give comfort. I want to make love to her but she says no, she is not ready she is still afraid. I think of her body cut and wonder if it is a physical fear too, lest a woman know what she is not afraid Fumio knows or cannot. I say it's all right. But I am hurt and cannot have the completion of the thing. Frieda is glad she has done what she feared and wished to know. Am I her homosexual experience? I love her enough now even to forgive this, holding her.

She kneels on the floor near the bed and reads me Rilke. First the German in her lovely voice. Then the English, translating for me since she knows I have forgotten it all. Then some poems of her own and I am touched she reads them to me, showing herself to me. The *Seven Last Words* call out from the record player— *verlassen,* the word in all its beauty, its loss not lost.

In a while Karl appears, oblivious to all. Or so he looks. Sits down and starts to sketch, showing us the picture he has done of Fumio asleep in the next room. It's a bit like, but not right in the mouth. Not handsome enough. Frieda pulls the cover over my shoulder, protecting me. I am touched by her mother sister kindness guarding me. It has been dark, but finally I can make out the room, the flowered sheets. A good thing. If you have flowered sheets you like yourself. Frieda sits next to me on the bed. I see the beauty of her foot, the tan of her leg. I am alive to her now and want her, Why doesn't Karl go away? Desiring her seeing the light come Lower East Side through the red curtains and on the blue corduroy bedspread a summer morning. Fumio comes in and the three of us sit on the bed watching Karl draw unperturbed in his chair, his stocking feet up on the mattress.

To amuse us Frieda tries on a blond wig. Suddenly she is someone else I don't like. Cheap tartish not herself. "It's horrible, take it off," laughing with relief while the others laugh playing. But it was one moment ominous.

Dealing with this enormous hangover I take a shower. Karl tells us how he stole his sister's bath salts in childhood and loved it. We are all up now, sitting about in the sun of the living room so precious, Manhattan apartments always they are dark. Frieda puts on music and dances "Cecelia" to Simon and Garfunkel, doing the cancan, she is exuberance glowing brilliant black hair in the light her bronze feet lovely beneath the blue hem jumping and arching. She is flirting. She is Dietrich's young goddess. She is dancing for me. I am embarrassed for the two men, do they notice? I am also fatuous pleased. She asks me to dance with her, but I can for only a moment before the record stops, releasing me. She dances with Karl. He is a troll dancing, Russian legs in air all directions doing the *chotska*. Fumio dances his

dance where he flirts with his ass, modified Imperial Art
Academy, the fool's dance they used to do naked before
women were admitted. I love the way he dances. And
Karl. And Frieda. We are all great friends in the morning
sun dancing. Fumio in the clear of morning draws a
caricature of each of us, me with the lantern jaw the way
he always does it, Frieda like a carefree feather, Karl
like a wool animal with a grin. We drink coffee and the
moment is one of life's reserved, you may suffer or be
bored for years but you know you can remember if you
strike it deep upon the mind in light, Such light of summers.

Karl must go off to work at the museum, where he
knows our old friend Toshio. We should send a message.
Toshio the great Japanese folk singer, macho and funny.
Missed for a long time hearing him sing. Especially the
one of the San-sho Tree that he sang at the dinner Fumio
gave when we married, Toshio standing tall among the
uptight relatives from the Midwest now delightedly
plastered, their water mixing in oil of boiled artist. Toshio
singing in a great voice of lovers parted, his hands clap-
ping to the music's slow pulsing rhythm. And I tell Karl
to have Toshio sing this for him. The great party supposed to end at ten and went on till four in the morning,
its moment remembered in a photograph and Zell was
there, my mother's escort in tuxedo. Zell dead now, his
face in its elegant silver hair exploded black to white
to vanish. We had kimonos sent from Tokyo. Fumio is
in the picture with his family crest stamped on his
sleeves, looking alas very drunk. And my obi came un-
raveled and I got the flowers at the bottom dirty.
Brother Edward wore his most remarkable uniform and
looked, in some artist's phrase, like a headwaiter. Even
Edward thought this was funny, though he'd spent the
day retrieving the thing from a bus where he'd forgotten
it. Brought all the unlikelies together and they loved
each other.

Dark of bar daytime. Jukebox radiating the timeless high
of daiquiris upon all three of us. Rachel Godwin and

I compare our paranoid fate as stars in the movement and chew over today's press conference. Rachel arrived for it with butch assertion, followed by Vita pounding under a knapsack announcing in the very manner of her walk that they had spent the night together. Relief to know someone else is shouldering the load. Waiting for the media to show up, Rachel sat across from me on the grass and reeled off an entire program of intrigue and Leftist alphabets, agreeing with the majority that SWP had subverted the abortion conference up at Columbia and was trying to infiltrate the women's movement for purposes of its own. I was torn between agreeing that the movement should never be the instrument of any party and my own admiration for the conviction and sincerity of the conference staff, remembering how they had begged me not to denounce their hard work. So I sat the fence and refused to withdraw my support. Having tried and failed in the last three days to mediate the quarrels. Today we held the line against media elitism while I sat in the back of the room and refused to play star. Rachel leaned against a doorway and said we both ought to cut out. "I've written a very good poem and I'd like to go off and do another." Then apropos of nothing explains she took acid on the coast and it changed her mind about politics. "I have done terrible things, I have blood on my hands." She must mean those nasty little denunciatory essays she used to write for *Rat*. Politics is not change, I grumble, looking out over the room at the politics of alphabet groups, the distrust, the suspicion, factions, hatred, deception, politics grabbing after power so it can control.

Under the colored lights of Wurlitzer red across the paper I read her poem. About the trip to Washington last time in May marching, but it is not thank God a marching poem. It is cars and wine and friendship a moment caught shared and recognizable. Rachel elaborating now, more or less raving, about a friend, a communist the real kind, Eastern Europe or something, actually sent people to their deaths. Literal blood on her hands. Met her in California tripping on a mountain, the tripping on a mountain that changed her head. This woman has made a new start, changed her life, returned and rejoined humanity. Rachel willing to forgive even Eichmann today.

Will Vita forgive me? "There are still phone calls coming in." "Why don't you just tell them they can spread the word you are not, 'cause I do not have, a secretary?" "Do you want me to find a ladies' room or something?" Rachel stands up ready to leave us quarrel. "No stay, we could use a referee, someone sane. Last time we didn't, it was worse." And Rachel can support Vita her lover. "What it's about, Rachel, is a wonderful error. Vita needed a job so she became my secretary. Because it seemed so reasonable, her independence, an income, my laziness served in the chaos of correspondence I couldn't handle. Then suddenly it became a catastrophe." "But you two must be mad. Anyone would have realized it was idiocy to start with. After all you were lovers, and employment is scarcely a peer relationship." Vita's eyes and mine meet, humiliated. "But we didn't." Till it was too late. "We found out afterwards," I sigh. Vita insists it was a perfectly rational solution, "Just a matter of how people interpret it, or what individuals make of it." "We made a mess of it," I tell her a bit emphatic. "Having invented the situation you soon resented it and drowned me in recriminations. I am furious with myself for having been led into such a false position, and with you for having manipulated my life so it came under your moral jurisdiction."

"Don't you realize you are now turning that guilt on Vita?" Rachel's right. Apologizing, afraid I have done it already, put her in the hole where I foundered dark and ashamed these months. But Vita seems wonderfully unaffected by all our talk. The dark doleful eyes doggedly impervious. Perhaps this is how she protects herself. Rachel is fatalistic. "It's your own fault for having this effect on people. You're bound to provoke this sort of thing," she explains, polluting my future in a prediction. While I struggle in the trap, flail, deny it.

There are further more sinister revelations at the bottom of the glass. Vita has just announced that she will murder O'Rourke if she fucks up Tom. "Murder, Vita? You are a soap opera. Murder for the man you love, how exciting." "Absolutely. He's the nicest guy in the world. So if she fucks him up . . ." "And how do you imagine Nell, who is an older friend of his than you are, is going to fuck him up?" She becomes secretive, changes the subject to Fred and the kids finally leaving for the West Place to herself and Nell her murder victim. I giggle at the notion, hardly listening while she goes on to tell Rachel about the next job, another pay later if they pay at all. And mentions in passing that she thinks she has the clap. "Gonorrhea? You're kidding. How?" But of course there was her Adventure, that guy she picked up. Has she been to a doctor? "It's all taken care of," she says very tidily. "But if I have it I'm on the wagon for a month or so."

Somehow it is not until the next drink and Rachel has given me the news that however nonviolent I may be I can still get busted on a sodomy charge, "Do you realize it's actually against the law to be a dyke," "No you're kidding," "Here's your change,"—somehow it's not until the next drink that we decide because Rachel has decided that we are all going to the clinic.

How scandalous. How absurd. How ridiculous and so forth, but this is going to end up in the record. That Vita might have given us all the clap. The Adventure was Wednesday. I was Thursday. Her own gynecologist tested her on Monday. She should find out tomorrow. Rachel was yesterday. My mind labors like a computer. A sudden sour stomach like a Ferris wheel out of whack —my God there is Frieda and Claire. My own case is easy. A faretheewell. Of course I'll be delighted to take my shot and recover. Even Fumio could find it funny maybe, an irritation at most. But how are the others going to handle it? Claire the former ascetic? Frieda with her fears, her history of cancer. Vita's Adventure involves too many people. But we must be exquisitely tactful, gentle, endlessly patient. Vita does not want to go to the clinic, her eyes defensive, a naughty girl boasting who's been caught in her secret. She'll wait for her "private physician," there is no hurry. But Rachel knows a guy at the city clinic, it's free, they don't hassle you, the information is confidential, it is really irresponsible not to go. This bar is very comfortable but I think I prefer responsibility. We are two adults and one minor. We outnumber her.

Marching three abreast down Eighth Avenue my foot about to kick an apple carton and then desisted. You can't take any chances. Arguing tediously about nonviolence with Rachel, boring myself with prepared formula but euphoric enough to want to convince her even though I recognize my own phrases, "revolutionary crime precipitates counterrevolution." There, the big red fruit on the side of the box, smack in the middle for emphasis. Still amused by the notion of Vita a murderess. And besides, there's no ticket on my windshield.

Then when we are filling out the forms it is not so funny. The men looking at us. Their eyes registering our crime. Rachel's pal is one thing, it's no blot in his books, he's glad we came in. But where was I born? St. Paul and Mother Millett rising to accuse me in the bungalow on Selby Avenue, the drugstore on the corner, the iron fence around St. Katherine's College and Derham Hall. All present in this little office. My mother's horror, her mouth drawn in disappointment, scolding at me from a swivel chair where sits my inquisitor like the ghost of Christmas past. The clerk's questions make us feel guilty. I look over at Rachel. She feels it too. But Vita has locked it out. Where is she from? Not Newport. Her parents dead, not living. She is unmarried. Is Fred protected thus or annihilated? The address in the East Seventies is finally given in hesitation. Then her interviewer, kid looking like a hippie, asks is that a house? "It's a penthouse and I own it," she snaps. Then he laughs, smirking little bastard like to bust his mouth how dare he say to her now, "Well, lady, if you dance you pay the piper." Some conceited middle-class kid imagines he's a radical. "Fancy address," he comments. Look punk, it's not your job to moralize amuse yourself or judge the persons who have enough sense or honesty to come here for a test. That's how you drive people away and spread disease. Lecturing him in sudden wrath. Protecting Vita. Not to mention the public. Rachel and her pal join us and we grumble at him as we are packed into the waiting room.

We are three women on plastic chairs. Edgy, Nervous. Staring at our numbers. Four, five, six. For Rachel it is all the clinics a poor Jew ever saw, dragged through public medicine by an immigrant mother. For me it is one more impossible disgrace in a life all too disgraceful for respectable St. Paul and an upbringing aimed resolutely at genteel poverty. And missing by a mile. Later on the clinics of the starving artist days in an unheated loft several winters of bronchitis, the clinic over on Second Avenue where I used to wait all day for penicillin shots. What is it to Vita? Nothing. Or so she says.

Number one is called. A woman of the poor, nondescript, anonymous. Her shapeless dress a rebuke to our carefree scruffy, her actual trouble how different from our carefully constructed defiance. Our surreal humor rewriting tonight's news. This is better copy than the press conference: "Three members of Women's Liberation were discovered today under compromising conditions. Two of them, leading figures in the bra-burning craze sweeping the nation, warned against the dangers of venereal disease for women so politically backward or misled as to have contact with members of the male sex. The third, reputedly the Friend of Man, refused to commit herself but hinted darkly at masculine treachery." Number two is called. Then three. Now it is Vita's turn. We watch her disappear into some trauma or another. Soon discovered, my old enemy the hoisting block, "Take off your panties dearie yes of course your trousers too, hurry now spread you legs wide for the doctor." Have a care nurse or you'll break the left one, wondering what this bloke will see in the crater beneath my sheet, damn that draft on my cunt. Do they plan this thing to be the humiliation it is? What sadism motivates the builders of examination couches, the developers of pelvic routine, the collusion of male and female nurse and doctor in their heartless alliance? His glove shoveling inside me to the pained disapproval on his face plummeting my plumbing. Her face a duplication of his disgust. This I think, contemplating the ceiling while they contemplate me, this dammit must be courage. Not that I have much choice in the matter. But I did permit it to happen, stifled the normal impulse to jump out of a window. Not even barred. Did not chance life on Eighth Avenue emboldened only by a sheet. As his hand withdraws I am comforted at the end of this celluloid rape into a fulsome irony—the things one must do for one's friends. Accept dear Vita this proof of my loyal affection. Or is it in honor of Claire and Frieda? Could I have done this to my friends! Vita, you are a maze just to know, planning already how I must warn the others immediately, before the afternoon is over. Why didn't she tell me at once? Ask the question of the sphinx. Becoming one myself to the medicine man while he is remorseless interrogating FBI grand inquisitor, Monsignor Corrigan himself resurrected from a consecrated grave. Who is my contact? No one, I myself, said Desdemona, and expired. A woman, I say, and refuse to say more.

None of his bloody business, I snort, huffy into the waiting room. Rachel is called. And rejected. Back in a flash. We have become an issue. I am called for. "My god you *are* a leader," Rachel snickers as I groan and face the man. This time I am not a nameless cunt. I am Miss Millett. He has heard I am the author of a book. My heart bursts when faced with the full majesty of literature, the perfect sycophancy of readers. It was for this I was elected. The day is too exciting, it deserves a volume of its own, I decide in secret. My craftier public self accepts homage modestly. It is after all reassuring on a day when one may have the clap to find some tatter of self-esteem in having been responsible for a publication this man will never read and would most surely detest if he did. But the word "bestseller" is magic. She wrote a bestseller, I hear one clerk announce, running the news right back here to the table where I was a bushy mound of flesh, meat he's seen a million times. But suddenly now a woman. A person. By virtue of a bestseller. "What do you do if you haven't a bestseller?" I ask, actually wanting to know. He on the other hand wants to know why I think I have the clap. " 'Cause I slept with a woman who thinks she has." He smiles, derisive and superior. And in a careful is it Portuguese or Hungarian accent informs me it is impossible to contract gonorrhea from another female.

Dumb jerk doesn't understand I think, girding myself for the blow of specifics. There was sexual contact, now drag out the full horror of it, must offend his religion, probably Catholic, poor man I must undeceive you, such things happen in this world. And say it was oral-genital contact. Phrase like an amputation. Take that and endure your bestseller, alas it will be the end of his faith in books.

"Of course" he replies, "but infection will still fail to take place." I have mistaken my man. A cosmopolitan. A man of the world. A true scientist explaining first incomprehensivly in a jargon that cannot possible be Latin, I remember some, than a retake in English to elaborate that only penile contact within the vagina produces sufficient friction heat pressure to implant the bacilli. Or to contract it either. But that is not the question. We deal here only with the invulnerability of woman to woman. An outrageous advertisement for Lesbianism. An original miracle I perceive, carefully rehearsing my explanation so that I may repeat it to my friends. We are all saved, go in peace, we are clean. Except Vita, called again into the outer office. My eyes finding her eyes finding she's got it. Rachel and I are as reassuring as circumstances permit, which is not very. I give her a hug. "Look, don't worry, it's just hard luck, be over in no time. Baby, I'm sorry." While for a time too small to measure, the Waspish armor, her hopeless act of debonair bourgeois woman disintegrates. And the eyes are sorry too. And afraid.

We await her fate. With a young black woman, very pretty, keep wondering where I've seen her. She seems to do the same, asks me finally do I know Gardenia White? How I wish I did. What a name, pure transvestite hooker. Snowball in Genet's *Les Noirs*. But she's perfectly serious and so I must remember. Cause Gardenia White lives in Jersey. But I don't know her. The girl insisting then she knows me from somewhere. Then she astounds me with Bryn Mawr. She was a freshman there. Saw me on campus but did not attend my lectures. How remarkable, meet the faculty at your local VD clinic. I blush till I remember this kid is here for a reason too. Now grumbling away cheerfully together about how chilly and overfed Bryn Mawr can be, no picnic for a black. We sat across from each other at dinner the night of the Christmas dinner. This strikes us both as droll. We are enjoying ourselves, doing an informal seminar on the sexual revolution right here on location.

Vita is back and positive she's positive. "You better tell your friend." "I called him the next day. Men know when they have it. It hurts when they urinate. I couldn't reach him." "So that bastard knew he had given you the clap?" In cold blood. Or revenge. How does one understand men, I wonder. The four of us leave together but my student has to stop at the office. Outside Vita tells us that's where you go when you got it. Poor kid. I want to go back and cheer her up. We ought to take her out for a drink, she must be shaky. Eighteen-year-old kid. Rachel groans, "Knock off the endless faculty thing, if I had met my profs in a sex clinic at her age it would have been help enough."

We linger on the sidewalk. Should we go somewhere for coffee, after all it has been a trying afternoon. But Vita must find a phone booth, it's an emergency, she must call Tom. "Vita, you gave it to him?" "Maybe." "And his wife? How kind you both are to deceive her, now you can give her the clap too." "Shut up, there is such a thing as private life," she insists as Rachel and I grow weak with laughter finding her a dime while counting the number of persons whose privates she could have involved in her privacy. Rachel says it is the Pentagon Papers home style, the slow accretion of one lie into a thousand. "You are incorrigible," I say to her through the glass. Rachel shakes her head at Vita: "The whole mammoth lesson of clinic day is lost on her." Vita grins back at us from behind the glass, the dime going down, the face composing itself to meet her God.

"Do you know you are in a book?" I ask Rachel, suddenly remembering it only fair to warn her. "Of course." She blinks behind her heavy lenses. "Everybody knows you're writing a book, you never shut up about it. You couldn't possibly make me paranoid. And I defy you to be as insane as life, which is light-years ahead of art." And more pragmatic than Vita who opens the phone booth to announce that since it's six o'clock she must go home for dinner.

If that bastard would move his car I could get out of here. But what's the point? Can't make it to New Haven anyway. Too late. For a moment furious at Vita, the clap, the movement, the world, the steering wheel, all that detains me from my quest and especially the Mafia type who has finally stopped leaning against the front of the bar relishing my frenzy. And is now ever so slowly moving his car. My face studies patience like a maniac. I pretend to the gentleness of a Quaker. Is it thus that one pursues virtue? The filling station man advises caution. He thinks that the hospital will make an exception because I have driven so far. Only halfway there and already it's seven-thirty. What you get for following your scenic route, Celia whispers from the glove compartment. Exxon's final verdict is that it's not worth racking yourself up about. A thing I try to remember while my passion yelps still from my gut. The highway speaks its Connecticut welcome then rumbles into abortions and hysterectomies convincing me I'm not a woman anyway, was never pregnant. Useless the rifle I stored in Mother's closet just to shoot myself when the occasion arose. All through college and never a chamber emptied. By senior year I had lost the hammer. But could still put on a demonstration one night marvelous hullabaloo probably about why I came home at six A.M. "What can you and that boy be doing after four o'clock in the morning, everything in St. Paul is closed?" Or was it over Jay-Cee and the final indictment? You cannot be a pervert, can you? And got out the gun threatening suicide, laughing while I fitted the pieces together. Mother of course bananas by now. Mallory yelling let her do it serves her right good riddance. Grinning over the absurdity of it all while I make impressive noises. Really that kid's a brat, just listen to her. Discovering beforehand how I'll be missed and deciding it's not worth going for. Tom Sawyer had the right answer, cake and eat it too, keep tight lipped and don't miss your own funeral.

And slide finally past guards notices nurses doctors elevators as inconspicuous as the paint on the wall yet already I hear them a knife in my back, stop you—it is after visiting hours. And reach the room, empty but for her. Long awaited just the two of us. Privacy. How she'll love clinic day. And then don't even get to tell her. Because we talk about England. In the gray room twilight just our hands warm in each other's. Celia will go back with me. To England. Next summer. It is too much to give. Over the lid the pleasure spilling. It could not be a promise? Are we then what we were, the grand old days our high and arrogant love? But different now, paler, wiser as she is.

I will leave of my own accord, not even wait for the nurse, rich enough to be generous by fifteen minutes because I am a millionaire loved again. Celia like home upon my shoulder. And tired. Saying good-bye so gently I will give her all my health like a gift through my hands. Like energy, here I have too much take all, if I could bleed my strength for you. As determined I will triumph, my desire now bigger than the entire New Haven Mercy Medical Complex to do all manner of good services, magical dry cell Eveready battery of love.

Then like a carrier pigeon to New York. Until that moment Celia predicted, that sharp little turn just at the end of the bridge it's hardly marked you must watch carefully. Dives right down to the West Side Highway. Without warning I suddenly flash on the night at Vita's bargaining over her salary. Feeling that artificial grave, her cotton red bedspread treated to look like velvet, the fabric over her bed and sofa, a mattress on the floor. No chair so had to sit on it, leaning my back against the wall while her eternal incense burned and the light of a Wonder Bread sign beams across the East River, a neon blight high above us, saying nothing. While I felt the dark, my own fear she would demand more than I could afford. No, she wants a regular stipend. So it's an actual job, doesn't want to be paid by the page, she is even thinking of farming out the typing to a friend. She'll be an editor and eighty's not much, yes I know, shall I make it more? But she settles and shakes hands. It's going to be fine. Then my God I remember now that later that night we made love, Jesus what madness of prostitution had we both some secret corner of our minds consented to? Recalling in confusion the odd excitement I felt that afternoon looking forward to the discussion, having the salary settled, did I ever imagine that night O God I have missed the turn. Punished by and for the pure fucking unconscious all the way into New Jersey, this is the bloody George Washington Bridge, I'll be late to read the Pentagon Papers for WBAI. Vita you have taught me my own evil. Now wandering the wilds of Passaic Kerouac's pasture and Ginsberg's Paterson next on the line. Thrown back into the fifties twenty years of my life will be lost on this highway frantic for an exit. But there will never be one because I am my sister's keeper and have kept her keeping at me forever because in some crazy way Vita is woman herself. Her eyes a neverending judgment that no love is enough. And no good intentions excuse bad faith a lifetime does not forgive an instant's calm superiority. But was it? Even the breath of suspicion guarantees it will be paid forever without stint. Or diminishment of interest. Capital never dipped into at all. Look, this is silly. But not entirely. For there is always Vita. What she is. Finding the exit at last and safe past the danger spot at Raleigh Warehouse. Still carrying Vita, who is me too. All of us. Like a stone my own nature she is all women she is why we have the movement.

And nearly kill a pedestrian on Eighteith Street. A woman too. The idea that it could have happened. The very moment, one never knows it, springing from behind a car in the dark. Stop and apologize but she is too angry to listen or accept. Too shaken to notice she is unreasonable and by traffic law in the wrong. But in the dark I could not see. Stunned to realize it's my blue glasses I wore for vanity and they are darker than the ordinary type I ought to be wearing at this hour. Very much my fault. And nearly hit someone. I must stop driving, here is Vita's house I'll rest, use the phone.

Vita like a wraith appears in the kitchen. Of course she knows the number for WBAI. Her eyes like the holes in a high school Hamlet's ghost sheet announce that O'Rourke is with Tom. Getting the clap? She couldn't reach either of them. Nell was gone when she got home. Vita has reached the end of intrigue. Finally. I have reached the end of this moment's interest while beholding life's complexity in the toilet at the end of the hallway. And leave.

If I do not get there I do not know Jennifer. Because she is Claire's past. Two years of living together in New York after college. Jennifer who was older as JayCee was older. Jennifer who wears a long dress looks different tonight from last time, no longer a heavy woman in dungarees but beautiful, appalled to discover I am approving a face so like my own. Jennifer who is me because I am older. Jennifer who teases Claire as I do. Watching her be who I am, must I be that cynic, challenging Claire's optimism continually, dismissing her enthusiasms for passing fads? Has Jennifer lived through them then, how many? Knowing Claire since she left school. Claire whom I scarcely know, discovering that. Am I taken in by a fraud? The ground shifting under my chair. Where does Bookie disappear? Into the cheap lampshade, little tag hanging down says "Practice Non-

violence." Into the sappy Christmas carols she threatens
to play for us now in July. Bold under Jennifer's barrage
of, "Oh no not Andy Williams, do you still have Dorothy
and the Wizard of Oz?" "Perhaps you should freshen
up your collection," I venture, excusing it as the junk
she gathered in college and has been too poor to replace.
Claire needs no justification, opposing us to the hilt,
drives in her own wedge, a mythified version of Oz, a
parody of lit crit. "Look you creeps the tornado is
Dante's storm that gets you into the dream vision
business. And Dorothy's a long philosophical quest more
recondite than Godot, 'cause you find at the end the
wizard God himself's not even a humbug, nothing but
a radio voice going dead, no answer left to enunciate.
Except that you'd better look after yourselves, I've run
out."

"And what are you reading these days, what nos-
trum?" Jennifer catechizes while I tremble for Claire.
Protective watching a younger sister policed. Let there
be no more younger sisters I beg inside, remembering
how my head could explode at a sniff from JayCee, a
frown against some title, the very paper of a book
scorched by her disapproval. Jennifer now is lost in her
singleness in New Orleans, though I keep insisting she
look up my friend Sherman down there, great tragic drag
Joan in jeans and white shirt striding along downtown
Village streets until she became a legend. But to me she
was the evenings on Sixth Avenue, the smell of oil paint
and the grace of her kind hands while they moved as
she talked to us novices, Zoe, sometimes Bertha and
Janey, quiet hours and candles listening to Billie Holiday.
Then later Sherman would play Handel on the flute, the
everytime of it I learned from her solitude, music, craftsmanship. Learned from her what it meant, the artist's life.

And what has Jennifer been to Claire these years after?
Sleeping in her bed tonight, the annual visit of a few days
every summer when she flies up from New Orleans. Once
her lover, how does Jennifer bear to watch Claire resolute
upon the floor in her sleeping bag. Where does desire
go, I wonder, wondering if it will go too from us, such

boon companion lovers. "Eternal comrades in the search for truth and beauty," Claire boomed at me that first time. "Where did you pick up that corny phrase?" "From Plato, stupid."

Jennifer is telling a story. About a rabbit in the lab where she works. Before dissecting they pump a bit of air into its veins, usually dies easily in an instant. This time the presiding doctor blew it, and it took minutes. And the animal screamed it seemed so viciously long a time till she could take over, do a proper embolism to the brain, then silence. But the scream obsesses her stern Quaker upbringing and all the logic of her father's science. "Immortalized in a worm," she laughs. "They named a worm after him, his life's achievement." Even her own reason was shaken by this scream, which she breathes now, why I cannot imagine, into the warm soft lighted sanctum Fifth Street photo gallery to pound against the Etruscans and color gravures of the Kennedys, a hairy ape his fairly appealing face scratching lice, Rodin's thinker properly constipated in the toilet. And Casals intent above the tub. The scream ricocheting against the ice box and Katie Hepburn's photogenic smile, the sight of the Negro poor displaying a flag while Bobby's corpse chugs by on a locomotive or Van Gogh puzzles through his portrait, with and without the ear, a scream bouncing against the works of man and nature. Each curious facet, history and human life cut out and Scotch-taped, the seconds of time trapped in the camera's black chamber. Or supplied by the *National Geographic,* the Space Agency, the caves of Lascaux, the magical bull of Crete, a smiling Roman face, the wall of time hearing a rabbit yell while we fall silent.

And the future is a week hence, the sea. And Claire mine until I am Jennifer always. Perhaps there is no solution but forbearance. Even the room outlasts us, knows others coming as it has known the ones who went before, permanent its stench of urine, the roaches too are older, will prevail. While we have but words and memories. To stop them.

DESCENT

At the end of an afternoon I see it in a pile of family mail. Old photo wallet size, Mother's scratch on an insurance memo says "It's Jim at his best you were about four years old we still lived on Princeton Avenue I think." My father and myself in an old picture. The past saved on a few inches of paper. He is standing, watering the lawn in flannels, white shoes of summer evening. A tall young man and handsome, the kind they call black Irish. I am next to him, staunch at his legside. He holds the hose in front of him, his hand just below the nozzle, relaxed looking at the stream. An ad for phallic power. I am tied to his leg holding the hose below his hand uselessly helping. An ad for penis envy. I stand there mesmerized by the important work he is doing, my body rigid. I look as possessive as Vita. Definitely a nudge. Head tucked in concentration, pigtails, sunsuit, sandals with those perforations and straps. Intent, negative little face ending in a hairbow. I find myself thoroughly dislikable, recognizing a horde of neurotic adults in my childhood fierceness. Then I suppose I forgave myself because I am seeing the thing through tears, the picture thirty years old, paper out of light in a box making real that he was and I was once on that grassy suburban street 1930s cars in the background, small-town trees and front-porch houses. Square of paper summing up my childhood. I never had him so I hung on his hose, always remote glamorous guy wanting his separateness, not noticing this four-year-old's passion seething at his side, a huge man, I don't even reach to his waist. Way above me his troubled face, or is he only watching the stream of water?

He always looks frightened in his pictures, probably he was, three kids and a job with the highway department, his marriage flat on him already maybe. Thought he was a Titan still ten years later when he slapped me against a plaster wall in the kitchen on Selby Avenue, sure my jaw had broken defying him. And then he was gone forever. Just one kind and pointless visit at the end, that May before he died in January. And we never talked.

Holding you in that long-ago summer, leaning on the picnic table in the farmyard. Having you still or later or never. How to bring back the loss of it? I show the picture to Fumio. "You should call your mother, she wants you to." But I postpone it a bit, chattering about the day with Celia, having a drink across from each other the sun setting for us dramatically across that lonely hill behind the farmhouse. Celia. The words strain out of him, hitch in his chest, admitting at last that he always loved her. And I confess how I was jealous, wanted her to myself, afraid to share because she might so much prefer him and he her that I'd lose all, both of them. Terrified the nobles would club together and shut me out. But no longer afraid, I can say it. Asked him this morning driving over to Connecticut, my hand reaching over to squeeze his arm on the blue leather seat back, the convertible top down, feeling his skin warm in the sun. Pressed the flesh of his arm, said you did always love her didn't you? And he looks at the sun and the green going by all the farmhouses, derelicts here and there we spotted on this road last summer, the three of us making plans then to restore one. We have not driven this road since then. And that first time we went to Milton and it turned out to be Open House Day in eighteenth-centuryville. Each untouched old New England place a Brahmin trove of China tea trade relics, porcelain gleaming in the somber light of old rugs. Mahogany. We were two radical bigots shitting rhetoric on her hometown, Fumio refusing even to look. We were embarrassing, Celia that day a part of this curious rite, scheduled to play hostess in a modern house full of Klee and Calder. Coming in to meet her we were caught by a society lady who's hitting us for ten dollars and the minute we paid it Yoshimura refused to cooperate further. I am part peasant and when I pay ten bucks I'm going to get my money's worth. I am for the tour. He is not. He will sulk in the car. It's a very hot day. We are bedraggled bohemians in the midst of starch. Then he changed his mind, decides the whole place is really Kyoto, contrite for affection's sake, decides we must, as friends, respect Celia's heritage. If it's Kyoto it's okay. So he goes about quietly offering to straighten them out on a name or a date. Art historian and gentleman. They found him charming and he was.

Now finally admitting his love. But I saw it today, reticent as he stood back by the radiator cover in her mother's long music room while they sang for us again. Miriam's voice with Celia's like two kites playing tag in air, a flirtation of sopranos. Exquisite pain of the past restored. Performing for us *di camera,* we two their only audience, friendship's music. But Miriam would not sing well, so it grew tedious. Ann leading them always toward academic things, overexquisite scraps, not the strong and simple ones the other two do so well together. Ann's viola da gamba played well and with passion. But it drowns out the lute.

When we got there the house was so crowded with lovers each needing audience that I gave up for a while and walked out onto the lawn, remembering how I played baseball better than she did, vexing her when I pitched hard and hit too far. How I must have hurt her last summer with the hellbent rush of me. There was a horse here that day over there through the trees. Celia proving her courage, grabbed it. I was afraid of its hooves because we wore sandals. Wishing now that she were with me up here looking down over the trees, the moments coming back in jolts. But of course not. She is ill. So I will walk back by the garden. And then I see her coming toward me, a weak progress in the silly terrycloth robe, her legs bare and white. I go to her and she leans on my shoulder, pointing out the corner where she started to redig her father's pond before the operation. Explaining about dahlias. I don't know about dahlias. We walk toward the trees and the bank falling away above them. I can entertain her with clinic day, the miracle of Lesbian security. Then we walk down the drive and I tell her about Claire, her strange goodness and beauty. "Claire said you have a beautiful face." Celia likes that. We pass near the woods where I imagined us lovers in the grass, night of the Persian rug and the day I bought the car. Remember one summer in another, happy now as then.

Celia frets over Ann and Miriam, always their tension in the room, waves of electric energy debating each other. We discuss abstractions, possession, security, groping toward the past. Celia is calm and reasoned. "It's hard to change, both of us made mistakes last summer." "It got out of control, Celia," I answer, feeling it is really too hard to mend. "So you make mistakes and you learn what not to do next time," she pronounces. There is hope.

We are back in the garden again. Celia is a convalescent dependent on my arm and describing her operation like an old lady in a nursing home. We are laughing and I ache with loving her. Now she needs a Kleenex. I fetch it exuberantly. Celia standing in her noble and unshakable dignity wiping the blood between her legs, the wound still bleeding. Again I am cut for her, mangled with knives, a primitive condemning doctors for their steel intrusion into her beloved self, this chubby body in a terrycloth bathrobe. Her feet in the glass like a child's, pudgy, somehow distinguished, elegant in their unpretension. Defenseless, naked. Sick, she came out to me. Made a gesture and a sign. Gave me something she did not even give the others. And gave it when I had left, not asking. It has made me proud. I came from England and now I am not empty-handed, her weight on my arm when we go back. And they played music, fetching the lute from the hallway where her bicycle, the Yellow Peril, is parked useless.

Fumio and I sit at the picnic table, talking as the sun goes down all colors. Our favorite subjects, food and friends. How odd Miriam was today, not coming back with us for dinner. Could not need to see her new man so much it couldn't wait till tomorrow, when we haven't seen her in months. I could drive her back to town in the morning. We feel rejected by her schoolteacher's self-denial, wouldn't let herself come with us. Some humor to it after all, maybe she felt awkward about spending the night, lover to each of us before dumping us both. "Miriam's a middlewesterner, you know, we have an admirable reality sense." The one flyspeck of irritation in a golden day, that she would not come back with us, old friends who love her, wanted so to show her the farm. "Some other time, drive me to the Watertown bus station." On the road it began to rain. I had to stop to put the top up. Then coming into a sad little New England town, drugstore and flags, a few stray hippies forlorn in an old place. The hope for a new life damp and lost as I find in the rear view mirror the desolate shape of a bus reading "New York" on its front.

Then the phone rings. Mother. "Mary says your movie's done." Mother naturally ignores any changes Mallory may make in her name. "Is it awful? Will it have all that stuff about Ronny in it?" "It's about Mallory, Mother, so it'll have Ron when she talks about him." She was married to him about seven years. The only place it's likely to be shown in Minnesota is out at the U. But we're having an opening in New York just like a real movie, critics even. Telling her people have said it was good, "Rogosin called me a filmmaker, Mother," repeating his name, explaining his movies. Searching for certification. Of course she ought to see it. Go the whole way, invite her out for the opening? But that would be too early, the book wouldn't be finished. I did not want her to come East till I had gotten it on paper. But already she's asking about it. Can read my mind on the phone. "What are you writing now, dear?" Voice of doom on long distance. "Another book, Mother, a little crazy, it's about me. No, well, not quite an autobiography." "You're not going to put that awful stuff about Lesbianism in it?" Hit finally. At last. There it goes, blown. Fragile hopes, all my well-laid plans of showing it to her in September, going home with the manuscript, presenting it to her. Mother reading it on Selby Avenue while I rummage through childhood remembering Summit and the elms, the river road, the desk I grew up at, my own bedroom smaller each visit, the geraniums in the window box, the French doors onto the balcony in her room, the peace and calm of her house now in summer, the way she took baths while one of us sat on the toilet seat or the edge of the tub and chatted with her. Mother in the leisure of her tub, her breasts deformed from nursing us, and the lovely scent of her talcum, the soap, the fluffy towels she has now. She will cook meringues and spoil me. I will take her to the movies. St. Paul I think, the words savored like the light in summer elms. But it is also the bleak of winter's naked branches spread over the power lines, the defeated little houses out the window. It could be wrong. A down. Maybe St. Paul's not the right place to read a manuscript like this. Better at the farm, in the East, away from the neighbors who are St. Paul. "Katie, you are not writing about that Lesbianism, are you?" She is a terrier after a bone now. To hell with memories. She is banging the emergency button. My throat tightens, waiting for its bullet. Guilty as in childhood. I am a freak. "Well Mother, that has to be in it because it's part of my experience." Now there is just her nervous wail. "But one part, remember, not all of it." She escalates to moaning. I am a freak. One queer drop queers it all. The whole book is a livid cancer. I begin to tremble in her vision, my own voice getting shaky. Then I gamble everything. "Mother, I want you to read it when I'm finished 'cause I want you to know me. I'm your daughter. I want you to accept me. This book is myself. Could you accept even this because you love me?" So long rehearsed, this demand for unconditional love, so fatuous it sounds after I've said it. Her voice repeating my name, an accusation. What crimes do I commit, remembering vaguely as I say it that Rachel Godwin says we're on the books as sodomists, a term too

outrageous for my mother to acknowledge, the civil law
never having covered sin adequately. "I don't steal money
and I'm not killing people in war." I'm killing her, she
says. I tell her Doris Lessing said mothers don't die as
easily as they claim. Now she's just crying. So am I. The
mad optimism of family acceptance collapsing under
her misery. I have imposed it. "You are not hurt if I
touch another woman's body, Mother, I can't live with
this guilt any more." But my mother doesn't know what
on earth I mean by guilt. "You should be ashamed."
"Mom, it will go on forever, all this agony on each side,
unless people start telling the truth. You have known
this about me since I was thirteen." But it's not the
knowing, it's the telling she objects to. "Why should you
give them the evidence, all those magazine people?" "If
I do nothing wrong it isn't evidence, Mother." "But my
clients, people here in St. Paul." She is crying. "We are
only free when we tell the truth. If you really let people
know you aren't at their mercy. I do not live a life I'm
ashamed of." She weeps. "Stick by me, Mother." Un-
furling the whole manic scheme that I would dedicate
the book to her. That we could survive any attack if we
hang together. Wondering if this is all the heavy drug
of bloodkin or the stratagem of a fox. To keep her safe.
She is weeping now that the neighbors will know, she
will have to move. Long tirade on the neighbor's dog,
neighbor on the other side never speaks. Neighborhood
deteriorating. "Mother, get off real estate for a second.
What is it, is it St. Paul? All your life you have been
run by that small-town narrow-ass provincial opinion
and the Catholic Church. Not to mention your relatives.
Respectability is death, Mother." But she is just crying
now. Me too, for all my propaganda. Gay Liberation
formula, tell your parents they must value you blah blah,
what do you say to your mother's pain? Then a last
desperate justification, telling her how much the book
cost me, going crazy, having to do it or give up writing.
Mother, I want to be a writer more than anything. "Yes,
dear, I always said you wrote beautifully, but why do
you have to write about this kind of stuff?" "Mother,

I have to write. And I couldn't do another academic book. Look, I tried. Finally all I had was who I am." Running on to Zell's death, stopping everything in the middle of tears catching up, she hadn't heard, Zell her escort in New York taking her to hear the Modern Jazz Quartet at Carnegie, an elegant black man in a tuxedo with a little middlewestern lady, sequin glasses, pillbox hat and veil. Five feet tall in her dignity, pleased, smoothing her dress at his attentions. "Zell's dying made me realize you have to do things while there's still time, Mother. They didn't give him that, so he didn't finish." Stop for a while to diatribe on the plight of black artists till she admits the obstacles. Crying again for Zell, her, me, everything. "Why don't you let me call Jane Larson, Mother, what you need right now is a friend, someone to talk to after all this." "Oh don't be silly, I couldn't think of telling her."

The big front doors are closed. The farmhouse doors that I keep open to watch the trees while I talk on the phone. I'm left to stare bleakly at the desk I'm supposed to write on. How will I ever do it now? I hear Fumio in the kitchen starting dinner. The drink he made me has melted on the table. His noises are sympathetic, disturbed for me. Appealing to authority, Mother wants to talk to Fumio, does he know about all this? "I have never lied to him, Mother. Daddy's life taught me that. Fumio knows, has always known." "That Celia." "Yes, Celia." Mother's X-ray eyes met Celia once, had it all psyched out in three minutes, and what—hated her, feared her, envied her? I'll never know. Celia drove her back to the hotel after I had exposed my mother to Myrna Lamb's *Mod Donna,* a monumental error in educational diplomacy, Mother very rude to Celia and furious at a play that had immoral triangles, "Language like that," she kept saying, outraged at the characters for having acknowledged at one point that people fucked each other in the ass. Daddy sat through it, bemused, on his visit. Afterward he looked old and lonely as a gang of us sat squabbling over what the play meant in a restaurant,

Myrna with us, trying to explain. The two different worlds banging into each other and here I am finally telling her who I am on the phone. Crazy, then out with it all, surreal buzz in my head. "Yes Fumio knows. He has other lovers too. Women, Mother." Oh my God she thinks it's adultery. "We think it's friendship, a new way to live, no, we don't think we are married. It was for the Immigration, Mother. And last summer we unmarried ourselves, Fumio lost his ring at Fire Island, I stopped wearing mine. Mother, I adore him and you know it. If I want to love other people it doesn't mean I stop loving him. Yes, he agrees with me, and sometimes he says I am full of theoretical crap, but that's when some lady's giving him trouble. Right now he's very happy, yes she came back. He needs the love of other women besides me. Sure, I've been telling him he's beautiful for ten years and he still hasn't heard me. Don't you see how another woman . . . Yes, he's here."

Fumio's voice on the phone, sweetly calling her Mother, loving her as he does his own, a good son. "Yes, Mother I read some of it, it's not that bad. Well, she must do what she thinks is right. Artists have to work, Mother. She has some typed out and I been reading it, not so bad, little bit romantic though." Will you tell her you've been reading it on the toilet, Mother, where you do all your serious reading? I stumble into the kitchen trying to find a drink, my head reeling back to when I gave him the first paragraph to read in handwriting. Trying to find a coffeepot while he puzzled over it. Then reading it aloud to him since he couldn't decipher and wouldn't admit it.

Then it is over. As if it had never happened. How could it? Thirty-six and I have never been honest with my mother since I was an adolescent. An obliging daughter. She never wanted to know. Questioning me about Zoe or JayCee on visits home, driving to Farmington to see her people, the old farm. Where the road lay along the river to Redwing she asked about Zoe. Wanting me to deny it for her. And today I told her.

Eating dinner outside. The wind bells echo in the dark. We eat steak. The candles blow out and I relight them, determined not to give in, eat in the unromantic indoors. We are getting tight. Perennial and friendly solution to the day's dread all these years of our loving and being each other's accomplice in life. Somehow we'll manage, he always says. Even Mother, the shock still numb. "Trouble is your mother thinks you are the historical landmark. That makes her nervous. She thinks you are the statue who wrote a book. But for me you are more interesting. The pubic hair I find floating in the bathtub after you've left." "How flattering." "It's my love, darling, I can tell your kind that's different from mine. Curlier. I found one on the staircase right after I'd painted it white. It had to yours 'cause it wasn't mine. Mine are shorter," he muses, intent upon his topic.

"Let's go to the drive-in movie and *neck,*" I tease him. "You know why I have so many friends?" Fumio on his tangent, since he never quite replies. "It's because I'm not horny. My friends are all the women." "So you are a rooster then, surrounded by hens." "But I am not ejaculating machine," he counters. "What is the purpose of this conversation?" "To entertain you, darling," he replies serenely. Dylan sings Minnesota voice from inside the house. Melancholy over Hibbing's failing mines or a South Dakota farmer's suicide. It is a beautiful feast. Midsummer night in the wine. Why don't we make love on the grass? "I am a farmer now," he replies primly, "I do not do the exotic things like the outdoor fucking." "If you were really a farmer instead of a samurai transported into upstate New York disguised in an undershirt—you would. Bird, you are phony," I say, caressing his crotch with a foot. He giggles at me in the dark. The candles keep blowing out on the picnic table. Dylan remembers my homeland from the house, Dylan at the University with Mallory.

Fumio lectures. "If you would love Celia you must learn to withdraw. It is a delicate thing. I am more stubborn even than you are, can wait sixty years. But you must be careful the sex. It is still dangerous. Everyone uses it for the weapon. I am off from that. I am getting myself. Living here alone. I am my work. I have a religion for the hands. It is not spectacular to be artist." He next recites Frieda's new recipe for baked fish. Then suddenly he switches to the war. His general ran away with the rice, the day they surrrendered. "I watched him going. He took everything. Why didn't I shoot him?" The idea overcoming him like something forgotten, then off into a tirade. That general is all of Them. Like Nixon and the West Pakistanis, the bastards. Entering upon one of his off-with-their-heads perorations, harmless as the Mad Hatter, delighted with his dinner, the night around us soft as its darkness, mild time held midsummer rich and tenuous as the candle flame wavering against the black around it, lighting his face which is home.

We look at each other. Both hearing the screams offstage. "Vita is doing something," Nell explains. "Vita is doing something with Rachel Godwin, who is seeing herself through something. It's all very mysterious." Another animal rasp horrible desperate yell. This time we avoid each other's eyes. Rachel screams, Maybe it's a good thing, that strangled sound, wondering what it could possibly look like. Maybe it's madness. Vita playing matron, daft herself. Maybe it's none of my business. "Should I go in and see it, Nell?" "Please yourself." Noncommittal, but the snap of her wrists on a camera case have already spoken their disapproval. Disastrous idea, putting her up here at Vita's. Crossing the hall I catch sight of Rachel in one of the children's rooms, her face choking, tears and sweat in a bunk bed. "Sounds like you'll cough up your gut," I say, weak appearance of the casual. I sit on a little stool next to her, wondering is this my colleague the Leftist terror? "I'm discovering my irrational self and letting it out. I am sick from a lifetime of reason," she informs me. Hmmm. Then she dives into another conniption, Vita pounding into the room, her special loveless posture of head nurse, announcing, "I'm here get it all out you're safe." Wondering while I watch their peculiar charade just how safe

Rachel might be. But how dare I carp when Vita helped me? Believe.

Yet I cannot believe this. Are they in utter innocence following some hearsay version of that Primal Scream guy Yoko was so hot on? Sent me the book from L.A., but I haven't read it either. So I don't know. It's their thing, not mine. One last glance at Rachel's convulsions, Vita's mother earth elation crooning to her that it's all right, all right, all right. Like the ritual murder of the bed last month, Bici's divorce. And just like then I feel queasy before such headlong pursuit of ideas. And go back to Nell.

You have got to get me out of here, O'Rourke's back is saying. Her hands zipper a suitcase. "Shall we just step out and have a drink?" I suggest the Cedar Bar through Rachel's shouts, vomiting. "We mustn't go far," Nell orders once she is in the car. She has decided to make a film that is Vita's front room. What it sees. What happens in it. What it knows. Only the room, its intelligent experience, the people who pass in and out merely appendages to the life of the room, which is a life in itself. Good, I think, a crazy idea but good. Already she has borrowed a camera and started shooting. Now she will not need me. "Why are you going so far, there must be bars all over this neighborhood." "I want to go to the Cedar Bar, it feels like the right place."

To hear O'Rourke tell me Vita is a cat sitting on her chest. Smothering her. She can't bear to live there another minute. "A cat on my chest!" Odd she should have the same image of Vita I once had. Is Vita really impossible then? Could it be an objective fact rather than my own subjective perception? I try weakly to defend her. O'Rourke will have none of it. Snug in our booth, drinks gleaming between us on the table. Nell has given up the movie of the room. I watch it snuffed out in an ashtray, mourning its death twenty-six minutes after her mind has borne it for me, O'Rourke in her sudden jerk of mood annihilating the room's unseen future. "I cannot do the room. Vita invades it, she permeates the house, her feet pound upstairs even when she is not down there with me, I must listen to her sound violating my silence. Or put up with her like a troublesome child. "Nell, show me how it works . . ." fiddling with the camera, the tape recorder. "I guess she's just eager to learn," I say, excusing her. O'Rourke's index finger stabs at the tabletop. "No, it's a pattern. She will never stop doing it. I can fancy how her father suffered, fathering such a child in his old age. Can't you see him squinting over his blueprints, gritting his teeth to hear those feet banging away at him without mercy?" "We never forgive those who will not love us," I venture.

"Your problem maybe, not mine," O'Rourke hits me with it. "You have crossed the line with Vita, I never did." "True enough." "There are three ways to do it. Sexually, economically, artistically. If I let her work with me . . ." I hear Nell, knowing she's right. I crossed on all counts. I gave in, am obligated. Culpable. "She stands there beckoning, inveigling me. But I won't budge," O'Rourke insists. "Well O.K., I admit I crossed it." "Precisely," she says it without pity, judging my folly, my guilt, then dismissing the way I persist, Vita's friend on Vita's side. "Catholic bullshit," her hand smacking the table, rigor and authority of a greater Jesuit old world Paddy ruling on my sense of obligation, caring, yes sisterhood even, transcendence, Vita the final test—"More of your idealistic nonsense."

"All right, you have found Vita out. She is a cat. She does smother. But why flee her?" Tom crosses my mind. "Listen, this is not some personal thing, I'm just leaving." I listen, thinking it is not the same for her, she has never crossed the line. Blessed be the discreet for they will escape Vita. As I never will. Indiscreet enough to plead still for her, to remember her. "Look, Nell, there are her good times too." "Your experience, not mine," she settles me. But could it be that they are fighting over a man.

"All right, then, where will you go? What do you want to do?" Up at the bar now, transported from the Old Cedar Tavern, even the bartenders came with it. Clinging to the rail. There is Big Peter who threw me out one night for defending Billy. Called him a Nazi bastard and he chucked me out into the road. Won't have no niggers here with white girls. Blackballed days of my girlhood, this bar was my art school, my college of manners. They still got Tony, the sexy one. And a few of the old guard, compulsive barstool warmers, Roberts and that sculptor who never works. And the big Greek who pinched bottoms, felt breasts. "Something authentic," O'Rourke says. It is her password today for art, the world just beyond the window. How can I help her get there? How can I serve a friend in art? How do you help people? How do you do them well, wishing it so much? And afraid to end up only hindering. Interfering or making new bondages of dependency. The weight of it sitting on me while I straddle my stool. Out the window University Place. When we drove up Nell threw her peach pit in the gutter and glared at the young man who picked it up, all gentleness, suggesting she put it in the litter can. "America is changing," I said. "You are all crazy, nothing here is real." "No, we are only different. Different even from last time." And wanting now to give her the Old Cedar of my youth, but how could I? Or why interrupt while she searches, frantic as I have been so many times? For the thread. What to do. "Will you shoot film or write? Or both?" Wanting everything, all of it for her, as she fumbles, "If I had some neutral space and quiet." I try to catch the drift, reinforce, give her hope, confidence, what Claire is always doing and Vita, yes Vita, had done once. It is why we have friends in art, what we need from them, just the underpinning even if it's bullshit, someone believing can get you most of the way there, then you can pull through the rest somehow yourself, since by then you believe it too. "I will go to the Chelsea," she says. "I will drive you."

Then I am alone, waiting while her figure crosses. Lean as a knife across the street, a sweep of decision over what chasm of fear? Frightened and hoping I am doing the right thing. "Let me give you five hundred because your money's running out." "You haven't got it," she argues.

O'Rourke who will never take. "Five hundred could keep you here a couple weeks, it would be a start till we could find something else. You'd be into a book then and you could stay in someone's apartment. Take the five hundred now." "You don't have enough." "Well, I'm kind of broke till I get my royalties in February. But I can get it." "How?" "I'll rob Uncle's piggy, I'll turn a trick and make a speech. Something will happen. I'll find it, don't worry." Watching her go. Betting on her, this tall gangle of a woman in velvet bellbottoms and that crazy orange hair concealed by a hat. Crossing through the risk of traffic. One thin line before the bloated and balconied façade of the Chelsea. Where so many people write their books. And a young man walks out onto the balcony. Superb black man in an open shirt above the plaque about Mark Twain on the wall. Taking the air, brute beautiful cool with a cigarette between his fingers. My mind hovers over possibilities, smoking break while he writes the great American novel, a pimp displaying his finery or watching trade, the janitor on his lunch break? Whatever, he appears secure, sure of himself. While we are two women in a dilemma, ninnies behaving like conspirators, the one waiting outside, the other marching in the door to put ten dollars on a room, two silly females wasting money on the writing of a book.

"We will return the camera," she orders. Back to Vita's, entering the house feeling like thieves to find her gone but foreknowing Nell's exodus has left a note requesting her keys. Pretext of a meeting there tonight, prior arrival of a roomer will let the rest in, etc. Complex, Byzantine, oblique. And for me another note. Vita's attempt at gracious heroine bids a relaxed adieu. "This seems a good time to return keys. Here are yours. Do not mistake this for a dramatic gesture." I read it, piqued over my enforced reprieve, even saddened, showing it to Nell, the two of us share a bitter amusement at Vita's gift for denying the obvious. I am being dismissed. Should I take the big tape recorder too? Ugly massive machine that made our movie duplicates. Vita typed the whole transcript off this expensive monster. Standing before it all the hours of her suffering come back, long labor of love. I begin to pack it, securing the top, my hair falling in my eyes, need something to tie it with. Next door I hear Nell dismantling the camera, the tripod, the legs, I have lost that yellow ribbon in here somewhere, looking over the immaculate objects upon the desk. Was it today or last year I slept here? A mere week already another life. Vita has stolen it, bewitched it. She will conjure me by it, burn me in effigy, she has kept it in spite. Where would malice secret such a thing? Or sentiment? Under the pillow. My hands actually looking despite the chuckle in my head. Suddenly I'm caught redhanded. By myself. Idiot, I whisper, you are behaving like a savage. Do you believe in magic? Or why have you made Vita a witch? How treacherous a mind is, crazy. Ultimately we have no control. Fool, will you suppress this moment in your damn book? Paranoid as a loon. And for a ribbon? To doubt her after all this, to deny her reality, abandon her to Nell's sweeping condemnations. Take care or Nell will take charge. You are torn between two women tearing for a man. You are torn between two friends and in danger of losing one if you do not insist on your own way, keeping both. Stop being influenced or you will lose yourself again. The hell with the ribbon. Yes, and I'll leave the tape recorder. And the keys to the Bowery as well. A risk I take, must really, because trust is what it's about. Writing her a note, "Nell's key should be sufficient for the meeting, therefore I do not return my copy until you do ask more dramatically." Noticing Vita's Bowery keys, the ones she meant to return, are tied with a very short bit of yellow ribbon. Wrong length, of course. There are so many bits of ribbon in the world, I decide, placing the three keys to my kingdom on top of the note as Nell, corner of my eye, has fitted the camera in the case. We're ready to load.

Packing and schlepping we work like pros, each object, lights, Nagra, tripod, baby legs, handled with firm and exquisite care. Guarded each moment. Nothing is easier to steal, more likely to disappear in the turn of a back. We move fast, faster the two of us in unison than the nine of my company ever were, always then the shirking and griping, the counting who's carried what. But not with Nell, the two of us tight like the two hands of a sculptor, the cooperative expertise of lovers. Till it is all loaded. With the camera in her lap. I look wistfully at the rig, so precious and give it back? Greed, some of it my own, lingering over the opportunity these boxes represent. With this camera I could film O'Rourke too, catch her before she goes. "Why return it till the two weeks are up?" "Because it is the man's dearest possession," she barks, "and I have nowhere to keep it." "The Chelsea?" "Never. They'd see me bring it in, be gone first time I went out for cigarettes." I wait outside the house while she goes in. First she'll ask him about the jam, some occasional little trick of the machine. Check to be sure it's returned in excellent condition. Waiting with the top down in Sheridan Square among junkies still chewing the problem, why couldn't she keep this rig a bit longer, if there were some place safe she could shoot out all the film she brought over with her. And go home when she feels like it but with something under her arm. The moment she leaves slamming toward me like a brick wall toward a skidding car or a hand squeezing my own throat. Sure, write at the Chelsea, but she could, if she kept that rig, do both. Or is it only my own greed for records? She comes out from the building. Has left the camera inside. Sits next to me, smoking furiously. "He's looking it over, thinks he can fix that little bug." "Would he let you keep it a little longer?" "Where is it safe?" Not the Bowery we agree, though how sweet to work there alone the two of us, one could guard while the other went for food. But we would be prisoners. "The farm? It's safe up there. You could shoot or write. You'd have a lot of space. Fumio works in the barn, you can do anything you like." She pauses and considers. "You could rest there." Seeing the hunted soul in her eyes. New York has been her nightmare. "I could get out of this bloody city . . ." Already I see the morning asters in the lens of her eyes. She goes inside again. Already I wonder if I have erred, taken from her the fine independence of the Chelsea. Because I saw she was afraid. Do I do the right thing suggesting flight at this moment? Today she is not the usual so definite-seeming Nell. She is indecision itself. What if this trip—I hoped so much from it and she must have as well—turned into nothing? A bummer. And go home to the house in Islington, Paul, Winnie, the commercials, emptyhanded? No, let her take the camera, shoot it till the end of the loan. Then write. The Chelsea can wait till she's out of film. A junkie walks by, tells me not to look so worried, the weather's perfect. Then a panhandler, past master of liberal guilt, staying to the last drop of change working on the third cigarette when I tell him, wonderful sweetness, to fuck off. They are coming toward me, the young filmmaker who loaned her the rig has got it fixed, showing her how it's a bit slow on the uptake here but you do it this way. Gentle bemused face in a beard. Will see what he thinks, telling where we'd like to take the stuff, he can call us the moment he needs it back. And he trusts us.

So we are off upstate in the almost dark. But first a hamburger for the road. I get them while she guards the car and its treasures. One more malted. "Only decent thing they make here," she says, going back for another while I watch out for our gold. Fifteen thousand so movable beautiful black and silver dollars filling the back seat. Then driving as gingerly as a moving incubator all the way to the farm to burst in on Fumio. "We have captured Hollywood, this is a movie company." O'Rourke plays impresario, Fumio admires each piece unloaded. We sit around the table under the tulip lamp, safe from the world.

Driving with rigid care and by maps. Checking devoutly mid-highway just below the Cloisters. There will be a forkoff to Connecticut. Yes. Then little roads. Stop again, invite no error. Yes. Highway 7? Recheck again with a filling station attendant. Do not neglect the gas tank. Through the windows watching him wash the view, wondering do I see men only through windows? Do we all now, are we separated from each other? Surely it is not fair, not how we would wish it to be. But there is Fumio. There is Paul. Do not impose your subjectivity upon the world. Why not? It can stand it. What else have I? But there must be some better way, realizing I have turned a bridge into an enemy because of one false turn. Operating from magic and longing finally back on the road again. The way now. To Celia. All her stillness and beauty crushed into a fine afternoon mist through valleys. The perfect Connecticut hills. And somewhere among these hills is Celia. My very hope flying right over the top to find her in the poem outside the windscreen. If it were only so simple. Sick again with love at a crossroads. Passionate to find the so nearly invisible road, here it is, that sharp left by a supermarket, then gravel through woods. Past the funny lady who grows huge numbers of marigolds. Left again. More trees. The wonder of entering a forest. Until I see the house, brave eighteenth century, parking my old car right behind hers. The sight of her trim blue roadster keen as if it were herself.

I run back of the house and see the lawn. She is not there. She is not where she promised, her promise already broken. But of course not. She is ill. She will be resting. The music room with Ann. Very well, so it will be the three of us. Celia still in the terrycloth. Her color back, how wonderful she looks. A freshness blooming in the center of the room that puts us in shadow. Her nurse seems sallow. Ann the timid attendant, hovering yet insistent. I admire her poise, unshakeable before the family and intruders like me, my smile trying to reassure her. Being my best self, modest seeming but actually preening while they interview me. The movie. The *Prostitution Papers*. All my projects. They are making me who I would be but am not. My real self merely a suitor under the disguise, my hand somewhere in my shirt pocket holding my heart still so it will not jump and disturb our gracious afternoon. Celia sitting up, her long braid riding upon her back, does the hospital: "Student nurses," she grins, "one especially. Been there another week I would have taught her about friendship." Her eyes flash at us with the old lotharian glitter. "Bit of a macho, aren't you?" I tease her gently, careful not to give offense. But meaning it. Under her laugh just a nub of pique perhaps. Or do I imagine? How she hated my criticism telling her New Haven days she was a snob. Spoiled. Had never suffered. I cringe, remembering that arrogance. And have I done it again?

Nephews wander through the room. The pure towhead youngest, Ned, how splendid he looked last time sitting on Fumio's lap, the contrast of worlds in their two heads, the child's nestled against the man's hair, so fair and so black. The child next to the man, but both heads boy shaped, that exquisite dip in the back Fumio still has it, my hand shaping the curve down along toward the neck, tracing the line with a finger on my jeans as I watch the child across the room enveloped in his composure. Then his brother, Celia's favorite, little Reg. Boisterous, definite as her own adored brother Reg this namesake's father. They dispute, the youngest losing as he always will. "No, the guitar belongs to Reg, it's his, I gave it to him," Celia judges. Ned's bitterness like that of children always, inconsolable, permanent. He will not permit me to comfort him, his eyes recognizing me as one too much like himself, bad news.

I will change my clothes, dungarees and denim shirt crumpled from driving. Not good enough. Hoping it will not be commented on too archly that I have pleased myself to find clean striped pants in the car, another shirt crisp laundered, enjoy the full bourgeois elegance of Mrs. Tyburn's bathroom, soap towels shower. Scents even. Making myself at home. Taking yourself a bit for granted really, I say into the mirror. Easy and pleased like one accepted, sitting with them through the afternoon. Julia comes home from the golf course, Reg's wife. Mistress of the house during summers while Celia's parents are in Maryland. Reg and Julia the real people, married, with children, a status and authority we seem to lack. How assured their presence, greater somehow, more solid than Celia and Ann. Who are what? Surely not another Mr. and Mrs. Tyburn? And I of their camp but still further off, an intruder. We are the unmarried ones, women living in peculiar relationships. Known, tolerated, accepted even, but unspeakable because not spoken of. And I, a suitor of some malodorous notoriety, less a reputation than a disgrace. It is Reg's wife Julia who asks me to stay for dinner. No one else. Ann and I pool change and concoct a menu. Celia does not deign to invite. The timid, the wavering are already disqualified in her view. One assumes or one is out, down, done for, beaten. So I assume. Julia wants steak. Does she remember last year we came with Celia from Brookfield three boon companions Fumio and I dashing to the best butcher, steaks and we played chef to a disaster? Reg was angry at life, no one would sit down, eating like gypsies on the porch with the plates on our laps before a television set. Tonight we can repeat and take away the curse. I am getting to like Julia as we make peanut butter sandwiches for the boys, who are too hungry to wait. She lets me feed the baby, a nightdress in the Sweet Pea stage, all smiles and delightful to hold. "How sensual they are," we laugh, the child's body like warmth flesh grace itself in my arms, turning me on, how pleasant I think. Really this is fun and they are all such likable people, this family. Reg whom I feared always is home now, a tired man trapped in a bank who loves his children. Reg freed into sneakers, a drink to take away the taste of his day, this still handsome young man who used to sing a perfect tenor, Celia always says.

I notice the child on the cover of *Newsweek,* his stomach bloated into my eyes like a shot. I am here for cigarettes. Just a quick hop over to the supermarket then back to the calm of Celia's music room, the echoes of our talk and laughter, why should the day be fractured by a picture of a child in Bangladesh dying of starvation? But one cannot avoid reading the picture all the way back, its full horror sickening the day. The bucolic Connecticut evening glows upon the lawn as I return, placing the dark paper child on a ledge of rock. Careful that he does not insist too much, scream rhetoric or guilt but waits a moment till registered. His intrusion in this so different place, such other children. Then reading the article by myself, its unbelievable print jumping in sharp little points moving through paragraphs, the unconscionable atrocities. Famine, starvation, rape, the most savage and wanton murder of survivors, even children. Shooting kids, they must be insane, my gut angry at what I read. Such things are unthinkable, savage, barbarous. Like the *Life* photos in the bookstore at Oxford, the Hungarian Uprising, they had thrown a Russian colonel naked upon a hook like a side of beef, the thing felt even in my genitals. Do we register shock there, is cruelty obscene or sexual because its portrayal is taboo? The pictures of Hiroshima hidden always deeper than pornography. Why are we secretly thrilled at the brutal, does our savagery persist because protected from sight like the parts of the body also said to be dirty? Have we coupled fuck with kill? Uncoupled here surely in this child his belly pregnant with death. A woman's breast dry of milk the baby dying in her arms. While the camera clicks. The man who takes it, the man who sees it. Hardly sexual or is it? Or a frisson here too? How when these creatures pictured are so plainly man but a sick animal, hungry at the last shred of civilization, our clothes of life ripped, all dignity gone in this reduction to prey? Who then is the beast? Why do the soldiers rape twelve-year-old girls dying of starvation? Who then is the beast—word misused, what animal would condescend to this criminal insanity? Criminal, but not insane. Insane too is wrong. The mad are not so. How does one talk of a bad dream? What language is appropriate to a nightmare carried on by respectable institutions, government and war?

"What's it about," Celia asks, her face hit by the pictures mid-sentence. "All about the burning question of who's a Muslim and who's a Hindu," I answer, angry. And what can you do? It is a question without answer, the last frustration that we must know it and be powerless. Still more angry that the one facile almost dishonorable thing I can do, send money, might be futile.

Furious to read that Nixon sends ten boats of—no, not the food we've paid for, but more arms to kill the rest of them. So write a check and cross your fingers it arrives as food, fearful it may rot in a warehouse somewhere and never reach them. Of course, in my mind burning to ask the others to send money too. But refraining. Dare I coerce them with my world, which is theirs just as much? But Ann insists on diverting us with a story. Seems a preliterate tribe discovered recently had lost their numbers to some contagion a generation back, the mere twenty who survive live in trauma, scarcely possess language now. The moment is passed as the two sit next to me, philosophical over man past future and to come. The child is discarded to die its paper death upon the floor.

The rain begins even before dinner is over. Heavy terrible deluge. Lightning. Ned is frightened, the thunder sends him screaming after his elder brother, bravely showing off, trying to prove to him it will not hurt you. I should call the farm, perhaps I ought to stay over. Julia again my ally. Reg too. Kind to me as he is to his son, cradling the boy in his arms while he sobs. I sit on the other side, holding the terrified child between us. Drawing the pain from his body into my own. Reg soothing him with a father's kindness. The child's sobs so powerful so blasting they will last forever. Reg telling me he cried so at the rain once but his father did not touch him. It is what Celia says too. That he was cold, their resentment always a bond between them unrelenting as steel. The wild smell of the rain. Celia sits down next to me. It pleases her to do so, the gesture gratuitous as all her gestures, surprising, indeed marvelous, outrageous, she holds me as I hold the child, her arm about me for Reg to see. Is it a fetch, I wonder, hardly caring because wrapped in her scent, the force of it filling in me again in her arms and the soft of her cheek on my temple, hardly breathing while we are four in a row along this absurd plastic love seat, riding out the storm around us pitch and terrible.

It is just the three of us now, I think, rummaging through the liquor cabinet. Reg and Julia and the kids in bed. If only Ann would get lost for a few minutes I could tell her, Celia, because I must now. Talk to her finally. This house owes me a drink, boorish and quarrelsome with its master absent. Then penitent, grateful to the viola sounding in another room. Ann is practicing, leaving us alone. A toast then to Mr. Tyburn, a man I never met, your health, in my fool's courage my legs shaking as I cross the patio's flagstones and over the threshold to where she sits, a queen with the naked legs of a child, that foolish bathrobe. "Celia, I had a very hard time of it last winter." "Yes." "Somewhere in the middle of it my father died." She is grave, listening. "I panicked. I had never been so afraid, even now I hardly understand. Gone all the time, living in airports," should I clown, describe how you can live in the Dallas one the rest of your life, it has everything even a shoe repair, "I went crazy." "Yes," she nods. "Somebody told me I don't qualify as a legitimate nervous breakdown 'cause I didn't quite break down, couldn't afford to. And besides I never missed a speech," Camping it for her, smiling over the rim of the glass. Too much bourbon, be careful. "Celia it was awful it hurt so, thinking I could never work and wanted to die the future was too boring to wait for." I am crying, a fool. She hands me a Kleenex without emotion. I would dive into her lap and sob, home at last and never mention this again, grateful to forgive. But she is so removed. Sitting across from me almost knee to knee. Her eyes regard me slowly from her broad face. Showing nothing at all. Be careful now. "Look, I don't want to lay a trip on you, but I think it would have been different, easier maybe if you had stayed in touch." The word abandon bellows in my throat, murdered for its melodrama. Hang on, be gentle, can't you see she's sick, it's not her problem if you go berserk. She does not move, her eyes, her mouth will not smile, will say nothing. It is closed. "Of course I was an ass, Celia, an idiot. The sun rose and set on Celia Tyburn." "Of course I couldn't bear that," she speaks finally. "Yes, it was monstrous of me, I was infatuated. I learned from it. I could do better now." Her mouth registers nothing. She hands the second Kleenex like a doctor. Clinical, giving no sign. Has she concluded this interview? It is impossible she feels nothing, does not feel at all. The viola slows. "But we were friends too, you might have called. Tell me how it was for you, what happened?" And now I have gone too far, feeling her tense, withdrawing. The viola stops. It is over. Now I want to waive all accusations, seize her, become tender, contrite, fall at her feet for forgiveness, any sign, noise, something. Click of the viola case. She rises looking tired.

When I come back from the kitchen they handed me two candles. There are no lights on the third floor. Only these candles burning below the sloped roof where a summer ago she found me, her hand stealthy along the black tights I slept in. Lusting now for her. Yet pure it seems, only to hold her, kiss the places where she had been hurt so gently and the tiny nipples that fold in at her breasts. She could take me, my cunt howling for the feel of her hand entering me as I open, fantasy primed to the point I can hardly bear it. Out the light then and lie in the dark, wanting her as I have never wanted her before this much past bearing. Then find matches have another cigarette, let the ice melt in the glass, useless to drink. Do it yourself, how empty, no dammit I will hold the trembling in my legs. For never then. Leave now, do not wait for morning. There will be no sign. It was a lie that we should go to England. Folly imagining you were loved. The old enigma that she lied or never loved at all never from the beginning, never gave a damn. A liar then, why love her? New Haven those first days she said she loved. Yes then maybe, but people change. Celia someone not worth loving, all that agony over a shallow soul? Cold comfort of morality and common sense. But New Haven those first days she said it, she loved me. Something you'd say to someone you sleep with after a few good days in bed. But people change, even if you insist that you won't you have already. No, she is not like that. Celia is no coward being polite, saying the words I said to Vita. Think of Vita. Has she spent nights like this looking at a candle? These things are inexplicable, just have another cigarette, be civilized. And leave after breakfast.

Learn patience from the flame, red gold in the darkness. Time will not come again. The next room's empty. Where she slept last summer. Go. Or stay and fuss over the knotty pine or the bedspread and how people can spoil a fine old house with remodeling. Complain, grumble, but stay in your den. Do not create a scene. Behave yourself, this is not a movie. You shouldn't even smoke in bed. Smoking as the fire between my legs cools in its own dampness. So wet for her so open. Well, that's just grand. The wonders of biology. Life isn't like that. It's the objects on the desk, coffee table relics, something about gardens or Spain in photographs. As random as this, as disinterested. Some old textbooks. Why not amuse yourself with literature? No, print is anathema. Well, then you needn't read. And stop thinking. Put out the light, learn fortitude in the dark. Let go.

The morning has certainty. There is no hope by the toaster, the egg-beater, Julia and the baby's breakfast cereal all over her mouth. "It's wonderful that she lets you feed her. She's never let a stranger do it." Ann and Celia are not up yet. "We spent the night quarreling, never got any sleep at all," my princess grumbles her way into the kitchen. "Then Ann left the cat in. It ate all of Mother's dried flower collection, ten dollars an ounce." "Why Ann? You could have remembered the cat yourself." Her face is sullen, fat, not even pretty today. Petulant oversized head of a spoiled girl above that infernal terrycloth.

But then she is different again, seeing me to the car, so vulnerable her bare feet on the gravel, her head exposed a second to the light rain. I bless her for risking herself, her tender nakedness under the light cloth. But when I open the door she fools me, pops into the back seat. I sit behind the wheel. Always outmaneuvered, I must turn around to talk to her. This last little talk I have begged for after saying good-bye to Ann, a tired kid still in bed. Her face bewildered, so dependent it is useless in the minute we have to suggest she love others too so she would not be so at Celia's mercy. But she would have it no other way.

"Shall I tell you how Elizabeth Barrett got married?" Celia pipes at my elbow. "Seems Browning brought her violets one day. So she put them on a chair and forgot them in the excitement of his proposal. While he's talking she sits on them unawares. After such a faux pas there was no going back. She consented out of sheer embarrassment." Anecdotes, I think, my throat closing in fury. I could strangle her for these little feints, ways to avoid the overwhelming question, where do we go from here? But she answers it ahead of me. "I do not want to be lovers. Not now." Her voice wavering at the time specified. "If I were not so bloody nice I might have come downstairs, thrown Ann out the window, and . . ." "Not without consulting me you don't." "I realize you've had an operation." Her face is startled. "Look, I didn't mean that." But how can I say what I meant, that I wanted only to be gentle, tender, nurse her. And that I wanted to give myself. How do you tell someone to want you when they don't? When they have just said it. "I do not want to be lovers." The door closes now, flies down like a shop window. Final. I am helpless. Checkmated. There is no move for me now. She has done it again, landed us in the same rut. Back to square one, last August.

"It is about power, Celia," I say, knowing it does no good to argue. I should agree, say fine we should not be lovers, I'm of your mind, concur exactly. Lie. But I will not, though by being honest I lose all. Come on, it's lost already in the pit of your sick stomach. Hell, tell her. "You do this to control. You draw a line, make one thing paramount, forbidden it grows out of proportion, becomes obscene actually." "It's always about power," she says. "Everything. And it's about size, who's

bigger or smaller, younger or older." "Like the boys?
Like you and Ann then?" "Yes." "Then be good to her."
"Don't lecture me," she snaps. "You offer so many op-
portunities." I smile, trying to make her smile. But she
is gone already in the last final awkward silences while
I say it is all a mistake, wanting to run the whole thing
over, make it yesterday, do it differently. Forbear now.
Do not lean on her. Vow you will love her in any way
she'll have it. Or if she'll have it not, love anyway.
Transcend the real Celia here and now whom I do not
even like at this moment. Exchange her for one better,
living in my mind, my memory, or the one last look at
the dear face behind the screen door, a face hardly
bothering to say good-bye. And then the rain, steady
futile back and forth of windshield wipers, their thud
and sweep over my tears, the pathetic fallacy gone
mechanized, am I lost on country roads, deliberately?

Till it is real and Kent may be Morris, may be the way
back to the farm or just the opposite. Cursing her and
turning around. Through Milton again. Stop and consult
the map. Should I go back, pretext of asking directions,
confront her, now or never, "Look I will not be treated
this way." What I wanted to do the nights driving to
New Haven and she was never there. Bang, nice suburban couple have just put out my headlight, backing their
nice new car. No it's just fine, forget it. Not realizing until
I am parking my car in the driveway off to the side where
Reg usually parks that they were legally obliged to exchange names and fix the thing. The rain on the canvas
roof like fate. Indecision. Hold on don't go entirely crazy,
call O'Rourke she'll know what to do. Go in there get
slaughtered or take the remains of your self, a little pride
please, and go home? Sweep through the rain into the
house, meeting no one. I can just reach the phone. Julia's
cheery "You're back." "Yes, excuse me I must call the
farm collect, forgot something." "Well how was it?"
Nell's voice like a crotchety hag, a warm feast of comfort. "A catastrophe. I started to leave and then came
back. I want to make her talk to me, force her." "No,
you don't. That would be disastrous. You don't cross

their lines. Not that kind of people, known them all my life in England. Get the hell out of there. Come home." Yes. Of course she's right, I'll go back to my own kind, running like one from danger past Julia's bewildered face through the rain, pumping adrenalin like a burning building. Just escaped in time.

Through the long drive home each landmark—old houses, hillside, country stores—another stab. Blew it. The windshield wipers echo while I talk out loud, cry baby and hassle it's all over. I am Vita to her. My eyes the same beggars. It is like this then. Just pecking order. As I am to Vita so Celia is to me? Got what I deserved. No, nobody deserves it. It's war then and the little one loses. Tough shit. You were asking for justice? Mercy perhaps? Compassion. I was kinder to Vita. Or was I? Is Celia's chill finally more kind? Permitting no hope, even withholding friendship. Sex fucks it up. Best way to ruin a friendship. Fumio is right. But I wanted her to love me. "Everyone wants to be loved," favorite sentence of freshman English classes. Used to write on the margin that it's a cliché. But it's true they always argued. Everyone deserves to be loved. Fat lot of good it does you. It don't go by deserts. That's life, kid, like it or lose it. And Provincetown ruined. Won't be able to write. Done for again. She's blitzed me, without Celia I cannot work. Of course she hates me for that. Who wouldn't? What a trip to lay on someone, make them your damn muse. Ridiculous. I am contemptible, I deserve her contempt. No one deserves contempt. Now you are righteous. Didn't you feel some towards Vita? Bitterness. And tears till I am really right off the end of the dock whispering Celia you didn't want me, affronted when I mentioned coming to you last night, outraged female, tyrannical lady, nobody's sex object. Well I'll be your sex object. I'd be delighted, your whore, anything you want, slave yes that too, cunt, go ahead take me. The grave eyes staring back their disgust. Puzzlement even at such behavior while I snivel, hopeless. Blow your nose, it's running.

Barge into the farmhouse ranting against Connecticut Women, marching from room to room bellowing insult and laughter. Quite another tune, make it funny, dead Custer returned from the wars foaming like stage Irish. "By God next time I'll stay away from the fisheyed British, hearts like frozen artichokes, the Pope's nose to them." Mallory laughs and hugs me. Nell looks on, her eyes a wise woman's full tilt green enormous over her cigarette smoke. They are kind, they give comfort. "Celia, it is all she can do in her blasted power game to pull the sex bit," I thunder. "All she could take from me, having all that she envied in the world. Even a better friendship with my younger sister, have you any idea how much Celia envies that?" I ask, my arm around Mallory's shoulder. Mallory resists the temptation to resist my mood. For once she does not contradict. No one preaches wisdom, that this is folly or sickness. Even that it is different, Lesbian, is not referred to. We do the Irish thing and sit around the dining room table drinking early. I pound my fists and belt whiskeyed eggnog. Someone rolls a joint. Fumio gives a wise smile at intemperance and goes to the barn. They are wonderful, echoing each denunciation, O'Rourke describing the coldness of the moneyed WASP with a flick of her bracelet. "Afraid of feeling, terrifies them, can't handle it at all." Mallory assures me I am well out of it. Nell agrees. "But of course I don't want to be out of it, don't you see I loved her, wanted her more than anything?" crying openly in front of them. All delusion, Mallory intones, echoes of her sage Krishnamurti poured like treacle on my wounds. Has given me the paperback three separate birthdays and I can recognize every word of him without ever having read it.

We go to the store for more eggnog. Mallory drives. When we are back in the farmyard she delivers her diagnosis. "You wanted something back." "Yes. I wanted to be loved in return." "Well, that's wrong." "I'm only human, Mallory." "But you can't do that. Don't you understand love has got to be unqualified? And besides she's still sick, don't you realize you are not yourself for months after major surgery like that? When I had my Caesarean . . ." And she is off on her Caesarean while I number my sins. I have done it all wrong. Mallory says Celia was still sick. I don't know enough about operations. She seemed well enough. And I wanted something back. Love is not wanting something back, it is all giving. I sit in the back seat realizing this while Mallory holds forth in the front. She knows everything. At the dining room table we resume our philosophy. Nell is taping us on her Nagra. We are an experiment in communication. We are an authentic Event. Maybe she can use us in her movie.

"People like that you don't need," Mallory lectures. She is all wisdom today, all compassion. She has decided I am a victim. I have been through such strain, everybody bitches me out, I am surrounded by envy, I have radical guilt. I should do as I like, live my own life, and if no Celia, then damn her. "People like that are false, fickle, don't know how to love anyway, soon as you've cared they put you on the shelf. You're worthless, an object. Philip was like that." Now off on Philip. Celia is Philip. So damned glad to be rid of him, a blessing he got his ass off to England. "The same kind of hell. Exactly the same. Treat you like dirt, minute they got you you lose your value entirely, you're refuse, you're expendable. Expendable. Man you're shit, that's what."

It bores me. Philip is not Celia, did not have to be locked out of the house as she says Philip did, mind blown completely by then, Mallory afraid to call for help. "He had to go, I'm not going to let some guy terrorize me, it gets to be like Mother and Dad." I jump in, "Yes, you were repeating them, don't you see?" "Of course I see, that's why he had to go." "But I didn't have that sort of thing with Celia. You see, it's entirely different with women." "No, it's not. It's all the same thing. Love is garbage, it's a trap, you lose yourself. I'm glad he's gone."

"Philip's a bastard, you're well rid of him." "Philip's not a bastard, he's a beautiful human being." "Well, he's

a very sick boy by now. Let him get well on his own."
"You never understood Philip." "He was insufferable
to me." "That's because you hurt him." "Hurt him?
He treated me like a piece of shit, Mallory, with his little
games about who's cool, he bullied and insulted me every
time I met him." "No, you don't understand. Philip's
very sensitive," she says aggressively, "you hurt him,
he hurt back." "How in hell did I hurt him?" "When
you wouldn't let him shoot that time in Philadelphia,
the Panther thing." "Look, Mallory, that was our movie
company, it's just women remember, our thing, I'm not
buying film for that kid to learn off." "But you should
have let him shoot," she insists. Wondering, but not
admitting, perhaps I should have. Maybe she's right. Seeing again how he cried like a child in the back seat. I was
driving, said look, Philip I'm terribly sorry you didn't
understand when you came but it's Women's Liberation
cinema, we can't let you. "You're a sexist," Mallory
shrills. "You let Celia shoot." "No, I did not. Remember
she had her own camera and film just a Super 8 and
could shoot stuff just like anyone else, she was on her
own." "Well, you wounded Philip." "I know and I'm
sorry. I told him a thousand times since but he's never
forgiven me. He has been deliberately obnoxious ever
since. Does he imagine I have no feelings?" "Yes."
"Well, he underestimates his own power." "He can't
believe you feel pain." "That's his problem if he makes
me into some monster." "But you're bigger than he is."
"No, I'm not. I'm just a woman he puts down as hard
as he can whenever he gets the chance. And I'm sorry
'cause I used to like him a lot." Brother Philip, remembering how fun it was to have a younger brother, his often
amazing insight, his cleverness, his grave respect, his shy
affection. "But he hates you now. Don't you see he has
to? You have everything he wants and can't get."

Back off now. Watch it, you're near a quarrel. And
you don't want to quarrel with her. "I see what you
mean, Mallory, but he's also a white boy who could get
it himself if he made an effort. Why didn't he ever finish
his movie?" "He couldn't get the money." "I hustle for

mine, he could have too. Why didn't he ever get a job?" "Oh, wow, you don't even understand, the world just isn't run by the puritan ethic any more." "O.K., Mallory, maybe he'll put himself together and come back." "I don't want him back. It's over. When things are over they're over," pounds her side of the table while I think well, at least she had him, lived with him loving that beautiful young body. Eating meals with him every day, sleeping with him at night. A year of it. All the things I never got with Celia. Their world in her loft, its soft light, great empty space, the big stereo speakers in solitary grandeur middle of the room. So different. How could I tell her what Celia was, the terrror of her eyes stealing my soul? "Maybe it's always the same. No, with a woman it's different. I know both of them. And be damned if I'd live with a man who bullied me ten full seconds." "So what did you have with Celia?" She's got me. "Nah, same sado-masochistic thing, only you do it with words." "I can't explain, it was an idea I loved, a vision she gave me of how to live, but we couldn't." "Bullshit, more of your boring theories." "Or maybe it was just that Celia was the most delightful person I'd ever met, the greatest joy to be with, the most laughs. It was summer." "What do you think Philip was, just that, we had the most wonderful times, it seemed I'd never been so happy before." Yes. We look at each other. We are sisters. That was what it was like.

Sometimes. Then the other times. Our laugh is harsh and bitter. "Well, it's over, you make your own life." She wipes her hand across the table. "Anyway, that's what I am finding out and not gonna let anybody the movement or anybody tell me what to do. It's all bullshit and rhetoric. Like Male Chauvinist Pig. I hate that phrase, we've got to stop using it." "I don't use it anyway, Mallory." We should write a book together, I suggest, trying to get her to change the subject. She is going to write an essay on why one shouldn't use that term. "Male Chauvinist. It's fascist." "Did you write about that strip joint you told me about?" "Not yet,

but I did write something." "Read it." She reads her
essay to us. It is *Sex Pol* in mimeo, précis, condensed
to three pages with a utopia worked out in the last two
paragraphs. It reminds me of my students at Bryn Mawr,
of my lectures. When she is done I say I think maybe
it's a bit too polemical. "You think it's too abstract?"
she asks, brave as hellfire before criticism. Nell recommends expanding it. I recommend the strip joint. "It's
too expensive, six fucking dollars to get in there." "Call
it a writing expense. I want to read from my book. Can
it be my turn now?"

Scared and excited, making an explanation that I'm
writing a different way now, want to show them. "Did
you listen to the tapes I made for you, Nell?" "No, it
turned out I liked reading better than listening." She
is noncommittal. I wait for her to say something. "Oh,
it was very interesting." She pauses, there is a hitch. "But
I agree with Fumio. It's too romantic." "What does that
mean? What part seemed romantic?" My face red with
shame and fear. Must know, must fix it, I want it to be
good. "Well those little bits about Vita the guiding light,
utterly phony." I am humiliated in front of Mallory,
who took criticism like a hero. Instead I wiggle, justify
myself. "Well, I'm not done yet, I'm going to add more,
I'll have to fill things in." "You better fill in plenty."
I will redeem myself, play the tape about having dinner
at Frieda's. But it will sound funny, it has the punctuation read in. They will find it ridiculous, Mallory will
laugh. O'Rourke will say it's idealistic. But they listen.
O'Rourke decides I found something out about myself.
Mallory says Celia looks like Aunt Christina. "Just like
her, I couldn't believe it the first time I saw her." I say
Celia is shorter, but she doesn't hear me. "You've got
a genius for finding your own poison, don't you? Wow."
She is leaning on me. "You are infatuated with the past,
that's what's wrong with you. You can't grow up. And
Mother too. You're into a real thing with Mother. It's
stupid. Not me, man. I don't bother, I know she's never
gonna understand. It's ridiculous to let people run your
mind like that, you're not even your own person, Kate,

you're a puppet really. You know you never call me, you just hang out with those friends of yours. You're getting peculiar." "But Mallory, I've been very happy lately. I'm living in the movement. I have a lot of friends." "Why don't you ever call me? I don't like the people that you hang out with."

Getting up to use the toilet, not really listening to her. "Those people, all into that totalitarian head. It's fascist really, fascist." Suddenly she's calling me a fascist. "I'm not a fascist," I yell back, sitting on the toilet. "You are too." "No dammit Mallory I'm not." "Yes you are, I know you." Getting angry listening to her. "No, I am not a fascist how dare you say that," mad enough to shoot her I kick the door open my dragging pants still unzipped. "You are Hitler," she bellows. "I am not Hitler," I bellow back, Hitler enough to garrote her whatever that means, wondering about the word and repeating it in my head still pounding with anger, this is absurd, dammit, here I am trying to be nonviolent and this is as far as I get. "How dare you call me a fascist." "Sure you're a fascist, everybody's a fascist, me and Nell, every human being is capable of fascism." Mallory's Sermon on the Mount. "Well, if it's a general condition it's meaningless." "No, it's not, don't you see that's just what I mean? See how violent you were just now?" "I kicked a door, Mallory." "Man, that's not all." "All right all right." Mallory would teach patience to the saints of the calendar. But she doesn't stop, off on her platform, holding forth to O'Rourke, who merely watches. We are two creatures in her movie.

It is awful. My high is going down. Is it the booze? We are quarreling. Yelling. It is then. Again. The old insults, Mallory throwing them, her voice furious, slighted somehow. I have wronged her. Mother. The bunch of them. I fuck everybody up. Done all that with my book. Mallory is abusing me. I am a star. A prima donna. Also a fanatic. She has found my worst dream and is announcing it as reality. Like the attacks in the papers, she knows just who I don't want to be and says I am. I am on trial. And losing my life in her charges. I am spoiled, the oppressor. She is oppressed. Poorer, has less of everything. So she must be right. She is Celia. She is Teresa Juarez, all of them younger, closer to the truth. Like all the younger sisters in the movement who hate me for the media trip, ambitious themselves but purists, quoting the line, sticking me for it. Is she right after all? Can I be this bad? What am I after all, losing myself. Shouting at her now. I did not want to shout. I do not want to fight. And now I am fighting. I don't want to be here any more. I must go to New York, the group meets tonight. Friday. It's at my place.

Fumio walks through, finding something. "Don't go, your consciousness if just fine, don't raise it. Anyway, you're drinking too much." Now they are all saying stay. "Listen to Fumio," O'Rourke urges. "Don't go." "No, I'm expected, and I want to tell them what's happened, they'll understand." Worrying as I say it that maybe the group will make it worse, encourage my delusion, perpetuate the romantic agony. O'Rourke has run out of tape. Mallory is yelling I'm a gay chauvinist. She understands me just as well as they do. Better. O'Rourke joining her, has lost her neutrality. She was supposed to be the umpire, a noncombatant. Why has she turned against me and teamed up with Mallory? She was supposed to be objective, an artist, but now she is furious. "What have they got we haven't got here?" "I can talk to them about Celia, they're gay, it's a different experience." "Bullshit." "No it isn't, Nell, really. You can understand to a point, but it is not the same really," feeling priggish. But now they are both shouting at me. And I am talking the line, saying these are my own people, have been through the same things. "Then go with Fumio," O'Rourke orders. "He can drive you." "Why should he? He can't go to the meeting. He'd have to sit around someplace, a bar or something, for hours maybe, complete waste of his time." "But he loves you." She says it like an accusation. She is making me a wife. Why all these conventional assumptions? Surely she knows Fumio is not some starched husband but a friend that I love. Nell making me a wife. She is getting odd.

I can't stop her, pushing me, like a tree fallen on me I can't budge her, her notions were there first. A wife for Godsake, as a wife I'm a disgrace. Standing next to Fumio while two women survey me. What can I do, they are all at me now. But Fumio separates himself. Back to his barn. I go on drinking while the two of them keep yelling. Why are they so angry? Then I am saying, "You come with me, O'Rourke," following her into the old kitchen, reaching for her shoulder, "You drive down with me." The idea like a worm pushing from the soil dark place somewhere in my mind we could sleep together in the Bowery, maybe she'd want to. Excited, hoping. How wonderful, since I love her this would be completeness. But she is quivering with rage, her eyes popping open preaching that I have hurt Fumio's feelings, I have humiliated him. Now I can't go till we straighten that out. My God I am drunk have I made a pass at Nell I must be crazy. Calling Ruth to say I'll be late, would you put a note on the door saying I'll get there at eight and could people wait for me next door at Hilly's?

I should stop drinking. I should get out of here. It must be the pot, "makes me depressed sometimes," I say to Mallory. She sneers, "It shouldn't." I have profaned her religion, it's not cool. Trying to explain why I should go to the meeting, how supportive it would be. Both of them jump on me now. Why on earth are they so angry? Hearing through their simultaneous denunciation strident voices proclaiming they love me I should stay with them. "But you're straight, you don't really know what it's like." Odd, the more they scream their love for me the more I feel their hatred. Have I frightened them somewhere by being queer? And their hostility is making me ashamed, slimy. They go on yelling. My face is hot with shame; damn straight women, I am thinking like the bigot they accuse me of being. "It's not the same," I insist. "Does it make it different if someone sucks your cunt?" O'Rourke screams at me, I see her bare foot on the floor walking back another drink. Her words stay in the air an instant then hit me. A crack across the face. Is that what she thinks it is, is that all? Is that what I have with Claire, this obscenity, sucking cunt? I look my astonishment at her, "A low blow, O'Rourke, that's cruel." "The hell it is what the fucking hell do you think I am? I'll tell you—I'm a cocksucker, that's what, that's me." I don't understand her. Is this some uninvited information, some unsought admission about her favorite sexual practices? Not the way she says it. Such a wealth of self-disgust. What does it mean to see yourself that way, what is she trying to tell me, my head spinning in booze and pot and the sound of Mallory's fishwife. I will leave.

Outside I look at the car. I could make it with the top down, the wind in my face. Be sober by the time I got to the highway. But there's only one headlight. Fake it. No stop, you look like a maniac insisting you drive in this condition. Stop. Stop being an ass. Of course they may forgive, being kin and mad Irish too. But don't fiddle with the reality principle, steel, concrete, has Celia made it impossible again to write I'm staggering. Now they're after me yes pull me inside yes I've decided not to go. I'll call Ruth.

But when I am off the phone they are not interested. When I have chosen them they ignore me. Go outside feel the grass lie in it how pleasant will feel the dew on my face will cool my body through my clothes but it keeps jumping around, the ground doesn't stay under my feet it shifts how ridiculous I have fallen down. No one even looks out the window. They don't give a damn now that they've won their point.

We sit at the breakfast table. I apologize for my remarkable behavior. "The combination of marijuana and bourbon whiskey is lethal," O'Rourke rules solemnly. "If I was crazy, came on or something," I sputter, "if I was ugly, O'Rourke, forgive me. Your friendship's my dearest possession." She nods, too gritty to permit such sentimentality to continue. "But why were you two so angry?" "Because you were saying you had suffered more than we have." I look at her and remember Winnie. "But I didn't mean that, only meant it was different. Not

more." "It sounded like more to us. You cannot say that
to anyone. Ever." "Yes, I know." By the second cup
of coffee I must say it. That I am ashamed of yesterday's
self. "Don't use those tapes to rip me off, O'Rourke."
"Am I a rip-off artist?" She is angry. "No, but they could
be edited so I'd come out a monster." "Do you think
that's how I edit? Do you want them back? Are you
paranoid? Are you Vita demanding back that mewling
garbage about her childhood?" she demands. "Is this
phony? Is this some scenario for Hollywood?" She
imitates Hollywood. "No, I trust you, O'Rourke." My
gut relaxes. What she asks of me I have asked of other
people. The people in my film. They were not being their
worst selves but their best, the ones they wanted to be.
What O'Rourke wants is more real than this, her ultimate
authenticity. "Did it not happen?" she reminds me. "Of
course it happened. But I hate myself when I fight with
Mallory." "It is not yourself anyway, it is two people
not listening to each other. It has nothing to do with
either of you. It could be any two people trapped in a
pattern. A pattern where we don't give each other what
we need. We don't hear each other crying for approval,
so we hold back, refuse to give, torture each other, deny
each other." "Yes, each time it happens I feel it taking
over like a nightmare. I want to yell no stop it—it's all
a mistake—it's all going wrong. But it builds, gets worse.
I try so hard not to shout, not to play the game. But
my resistance weakens, I start reacting, fitting into my
part of it, finding my lines. I can't get out. I can't stop."
She holds up a finger; wait for the camera. We will work
today. Shoot film. Watching and acknowledging the
miracle of her bracelets running both the Nagra and the
Arriflex at once. The one-woman company sets up. I
am her subject. All I have to do is talk. Sitting in a long
dress the first one come from England this morning, just
sit still and queen it. Mallory lies on her towel outside
the window. Sunbathing. Nell asks me questions. I see
the shape of Mallory's shoulders how skinny they are.
Like a child's. It is the polio that made them never grow,

nearly killed her, reliving our terror to lose her ever after the nervous beloved child saved.

Mallory petulant when I ask her to go out and buy film in Poughkeepsie. "We could shoot some of Nell today. She'll set up the Arriflex and show me how to run it. You already know how to do sound." "I'm not your errand girl," she says, adjusting her halter. "Mallory, I can't go myself because Nell needs me." "Well, I need to rest, that's what I need," she snaps. "This is my vacation, I never get out of the city and here you are wanting to work. Why are you so crazy to work all the time? You should learn how to live, Kate. You're a complete compulsive." Settling herself back on her towel, adjusting her sunglasses, oiling her skin. Absolute contentment. Doesn't she realize it is exciting to make movies? I swallow my annoyance. I'll have to do it myself or there will be no footage this trip. But you can't buy 16 mm film in Poughkeepsie. Trying every place in the phonebook. I give up and work for Nell.

"Explain what it means to you, to love women." But I do not explain well. I am stiff. The camera is black glass between us. Am I overemphatic when I describe the energy, the sense of release when I let myself be? Do I sound like some convert? Do I exaggerate? What was it that gives me such power lately, the sense I can do things, finish what I start? What held me back then from doing? Do I overestimate the force of repression, like stuffing an animal in a suitcase? Nell must stop to change the tape. "Before you said it was stuffing a coat in a suitcase, it works better." All right a coat then, wondering if I am accurate as I tell it. I did not miss women so much those years, complete with Fumio. What was it I missed? The sense of being able to do things. To accomplish what I set out to do. To fix something, the electricity for example. Or sculpting on a large scale. What made everything so hard then? Why is it easier now? Telling Nell who is not the media but just a friend behind the great black eye, her own buried and removed from me, trying to tell her accurately but still dissatisfied with what I say. It is too pat. The camera would make me feel important.

My words, my image repeated. Thank God we are running out of film. Finally one is only an important ass.

Then she shoots us together. Mallory wears her hat. We are laughing. We are great buddies. We try to say clever things but I can't think of any. Mallory is better, more relaxed. She looks wonderful. She is beautiful. We are who we want to be. We have transcended the circumstance of being sisters. Escaped the family. The feuds. Become friends. It is what we want to be. But we are not yet. The picture is a lie and the truth. It is our good times when we have them. But not the rest. The savagery of our love bumping against the inarticulate or the forbidden. How much of lust is there in my impossible affection? How much of revenge in her denial? How much of greed to be each other in each of us? Mallory wants my substance. I want her glamour. The safety of her carefree. And its righteousness. I am helpless before her judging eyes, I am a bug splayed upon the floor, needing her approval to go on crawling. The one thing she must withhold. Because her eyes had imagined an eagle, Mallory proud and loyal before her greatest disappointment.

After dinner we are a cabal discussing the sexual revolution, a flock of higher theorists. It's about freedom, I say, loving more than one person's a good thing multiplied. Mallory says that's capitalism. On the contrary, I argue, you stop seeing people as property. Mallory says that's impossible. Fumio says it's risky and people are still ridiculous about sex. He stays long enough to announce his position and qualify my own with his skepticism. Then goes to bed pleased with himself. To get out of monogamy is hard but it's worth it, I say. Jealousy is so many-sided, a boy in my experimental college spent a year trying to figure it out, said he thought it almost unbeatable. But we must learn if we're going to live in communes, Nell muses. Mallory says I'm naive. I say that sex, if you have friendship, completes it. And if you rule out a whole sex, half the world from this acceptance, you are as deprived as if you could not cross the lines of race or class. Nell thinks bisexuality is in the future. But not her future. Mallory announces that all she wants is to establish a relationship with one man. Just that and she'd be satisfied. I would like to say I've done that and want more but I had better shut up. Nell says maybe I've got something, lessens the dependency on one person if you spread it around. Her voice tentative . . . "Cooper says that too." I am aglow now, receiving support. The authorities are on my side. Mallory says I am promiscuous. I say I am not. She says I am. "You don't understand the word," she shouts. I am careful not to shout. She is stubborn enough to find the dictionary. Quoting my own Webster at me, had it since college. My god do I have to listen to this, I wonder. Mallory would make anyone the Mahatma, I think, keeping very quiet. Then telling her again I am not promiscuous, "It means fucking around like some crazy, that is not how I'm trying to live." "Shut up," she thunders, the dictionary in her hands spread out like a choirboy over the Bible. It says, "consisting of a heterogeneous mixture of persons or things." "I'm not heterogeneous, Mallory, just bisexual." "Read the next definition yourself." It says "indiscriminately distributed, applied, granted, etc., as promiscuous blame, intercourse." "See?" I remain calm, my voice so low I can scarcely be heard. I am choking in the effort not to yell at her. "Have you no idea how insulting you are?" She bangs the book on the table. "I did not mean the second definition but the first!" I keep quiet with supernatural effort.

She knows all about it, she assures me. Understands the whole problem. Has seen a lot of life. Recognizes all the symptoms of promiscuity. As for Lesbians, she understands them too, has known some, been around the thing. "Are you serious, Mallory?" "Of course I'm serious." "Where, Mallory?" "In Manila, they did everything. It's a decadent society, y'know. Everybody screwed everybody. They had a whole scene going. Not my scene, but I couldn't help knowing about it. The whole place was a party." "Parties, Mallory—that isn't what I meant." "Yeah, well it's the same when you get down to it." "Do you realize you dichotomize sex and friendship?" "So what, everybody does it, it's a sexist society, how do you think we got our start?" Switching over to the offensive. "You're not so smart with that multiple relationship stuff, you're no big success, you're just indulging yourself."

I am on trial again. This time for promiscuity. I am fucking up Fumio. I have ruined his life. "Did he tell you that?" I plead with her. My voice is a whisper. In a minute I will lose it altogether. I look to O'Rourke for support. She withholds it. Mallory continues, merciless. I destroy everyone I meet, I am a plague. I look at O'Rourke. "Please tell Mallory I can't take any more. If she doesn't stop I'll go crazy." "Well, if you won't listen to reason, good night." Mallory kisses both of us, goes cheerfully to bed.

Nell wants me to go to bed with Fumio. I will in a while. She also wants me to stay up and drink with her. I'll do that for a while too. We sit across from each other at the table. I am sick of drinking. Just the smallest shot of Jack Daniel's to keep her company. I will start with Mallory. "Bananas isn't it, the way she divides the two things, sex and affection. Is that necessary? I have a great affection for you, Nell. We could be lovers. But I think you wouldn't want it." "No, I wouldn't." It is that simple. I am rejected. It hurts but not as it used to. Do I dare to ask her why? "Is Estelle that much more attractive, you said she turned you on." "Yes, but I don't trust her so it will never happen." "Do you trust me?" "Yes." "So it will never happen?" "Right." "Isn't it odd?" "Maybe, but you don't turn me on." Hard words to listen to, and treacherous, really what does turn us on? Remembering all the devices I had to be sure O'Rourke was beyond reach, her funny hair, scraggly, maybe it wouldn't work in bed, etc. Nonsense, all phony, preventive measure to be sure I wouldn't want her. Wanting her now and sorry. Give in, maybe she's right. "What we have, our friendship, it's not worth taking risks," I say to her, reconciled.

She goes into the kitchen. I follow for a last drink. "Why do you and Mallory still yell at me?" "Because you are asking us to follow you and go places we don't want to be. Aren't now, may never be. And you may be dead wrong. But the badgering us to follow makes us savage." "Badgering? I was defending myself. Maybe I was badgering before, but I'm not now." Raising my glass, "Peace to both our ways." She nods.

Perhaps we are saying good-bye. She sits in the rickety kitchen chair, tired. Suddenly she is transformed. She looks as old as the world. "Claire is a saint." "Really, Nell." Her eyes are enormous. Bloodshot. Her words magical as a holy card. "Claire is purity," she insists. "Right there on Fifth Street in the middle of that madness and untouched!" What if Nell rockets back to England while I'm in Provincetown? This may be the last time we meet till one of us crosses the water. The book may end before I see her again. She preaches to me I must love Claire. It is her farewell sermon. "It is an awful thing you did, bringing her with us to see Celia." I am thunderstruck. Have I caused Claire to suffer, not knowing what I did? "She seemed all right to me. Why did you two disappear at the hospital?" "The poor child was in agony," O'Rourke declares. "Well, I'll ask her when I see her. She's up in Provincetown now with Barbara. I thought she agreed with me about jealousy." "Who could agree with your nonsense?" she demands. How old she is tonight. Looks fifty, my grandmother. Old crone, she is wisdom itself lecturing me. "Love Claire. She loves you." Her voice incredulous. "And take care of her. Love Fumio." "But I do, Nell." "Then go to him. And when he reaches toward you do not turn away." I want to laugh. O'Rourke sounding like a Victorian marriage manual, waving me to bed with the gesture of the old queen herself. I have received her blessing.

Fumio is half awake. He snuggles up to me, his prick stiffening as he rubs against me. Does he feel horny, I wonder hopefully, since I have had this in mind for the past three hours. But it is so late now, five in the morning. Maybe he'll be too sleepy. I should never have stayed up so late. Leaving in a few hours. But now I want him so, open to him as he slides in, so comforting. The ease of it. The gentle familiarity. Then we chatter and compare armpit hair. "Yours is just the chicken shit," he boasts. "Was it you who farted or me?" I ask him. We smoke cigarettes, the only ones awake in the house, whispering like conspirators. Then it is time to get up, just the two of us. He waves good-bye to me in the driveway. "Have a good vacation." "Work lots." "Give the Claire a hello for me." "Good-bye." The slight figure waving its arm as I turn the corner.

PART FIVE

LANDFALL

PROVINCETOWN

F-51 is there. Right next to me in his flushed red trousers, Lawrentian legs. And a white T-shirt. On his biceps a flower engraved. Mom + Dad, it says. The flower splatters relish on its mile-long hot dogs. Two with, two without. Coke floating in the ice of paper cup. Ketchup on the French fries. Salt. Then the arm floats the whole gleaming tray, flying it easily but carefully to the station wagon off to the right side of the parking lot. Full of kids. Maybe five. And the wife. F-51.

I am F-53. Waiting in the sun before the screen window, dancing impatiently. There is one more order to be filled. When mine arrives it is hideous, onion rings their color gritty with old fat, perfectly artificial food. I do not like my mile-long hot dog. Have to get out of the car again to put mustard on it, ketchup for the dirty onions, oiled looking like a set of piston rings. The mess on the seat next to me, smelling in the heat, the paper wrinkled. Bumping obscenely as I drive. Cigarette ash falling into ketchup of onion rings. Still so far to go. The radio delivers astronauts to the moon. "Wow," says an army voice from the lunar surface, articulate with government wonder. Could do the whole thing in a studio somewhere in Texas, so vividly do they represent the miracle of space. These buffoons who command Claire's adulation. The station wagon, which she calls the "adult" car, in contrast to my convertible, is a sardine can in this heat, a movable broiler with its boat rack on top. Fumio has been to it. Neighbor Baker loaned us his rack. All things and all friends conspire to get me to Provincetown. Further than the moon.

Already I have made the turn, a long arm to the right, Highway 6, remembered with the memory of place. Turning here years ago with Olga, the first trip. Didn't want her much but came anyway, Bowery artist not really able to pay the rent on the fancy cottage. That summer I went to Japan. Passed her shop on First Avenue last week, scrunching my shoulders in the car not wanting to be seen. We played a game sitting on the beach at Staten Island. I said well it didn't matter anyway, we'd never been in love. But then she hit me with it. Said she was. Now I was caught. The first game was the usual, everyone played it. It was New York. Win or lose. If you care you're the loser. I never did well, was not a good player. So I thought I was losing that first time, supposed to go to a seafood restaurant in the Village, drank a whole bottle of Cutty Sark instead and never got there. Waking up in a hangover after sex thinking I cared on the green couch by the partition we'd built, the private entrance that went up to Janey's loft. Proud when I saw her next morning in her uptown lady rig, high hat and heels. Off to be a biologist somewhere on Madison Avenue. Then she quit to be a potter, clay and glazes, lathe and little tools in her mother's place over in Queens. Mother hysterically never wanting to know things, night I was there. Ten years living together in protective deceit, probably still thinking she'd marry, give birth to grandsons. The soft sound of maternal slippers wanting to make us breakfast. But when I knew her, I did not love her need. Olga clung and I did not have enough compassion for the tight pretense of her life. Dull as the big yellow apartment house over in Queens, having arrived at security. Or the pottery, which arrived at good taste. Made a beautiful gold bowl for me. My vanity convicted in its meaning, the maker had put our initials inside the rim. I used it for its own sake two years in Japan. Then gave it to Mori-San when I left. Just because she asked for it. A bauble. I lacked courage to keep it when she wheedled, Oriental custom to give whatever is admired. And she had been kind to me. But so had the other. Gave it and betrayed.

But I went to Provincetown anyway, balancing the sea against the lie, going up together this time of year bundled into her little Dodge. My first trip out of New York in three Bowery summers. I had not counted on the tedium of ten days in bed with someone you don't love. Affection cannot respond to that demand. A phony even when I carried off the sheets for special laundering, the landlady just as queer as we are but appearances are very important. No one talks about it. And they ran their eyes over me at the gay bars when I stood there trying to look like I knew someone, big red Mexican sweater kept me from freezing Bowery winters, slept in it. Neat white shirt, hair braided in my Minnehaha thing. The same gig I wore to the Cedar Bar where I was shopped and counted too. Janey coming home would tell us what they'd said, artist guys laying bets on us, Zooey and me, whether they could lay us. Up to a dollar and a half one night. At somebody's loft I danced with Franz Kline and he said he hoped I was happy the way I was. How was I? But another time when Pauline and JayCee came in from the country and went to the Cedar he grabbed JayCee's breast, called her a Lesbian. Everybody heard. He was asking why. Along the bar each head turned, listening. My mind went numb. Kline a kind man buying drinks for the kids, young artists without the fifty cents you need for a beer to stay there making it last all night. An intelligent humorist, witty for a whole table laughing at his generous urbanity. And when he got drunk he sang some song about Peoria. Someplace in Illinois, was he from there? We loved it, laughing at our fathers. He and

De Kooning, his beautiful woman's face shining in dark of bar-light gentleness, the two patriarchs, never tired of chasing twenty-year-old skirts in their old age. Success when they could no longer use it, recognized as great painters too late. Kline's last shows, powerful tearing slashes like the iron fire escapes on a New York tenement face.

Olga showed her pottery at Washington Square, selling it on the street. I quailed in my snobbery but turned at Route 6 anyway, off to the right the road to Provincetown remembered. Other times I have been here. Will the place jinx me again this time? Last year's trip was no better. Couldn't fulfill the long-promised vacation with Celia, kept shooting the movie. So I came up later with Naomi. Fighting at the Hawthorne Circle. Actually stopped the car in the dark and went for each other. My hands going toward her throat and she started to strangle me. I felt my mind breaking. Then we stopped, ashamed. We are friends and writers who have become this nightmare couple. She has transformed me into the man at the wheel, ignoring road signs, never even bothering to read the map I plead she follow while I steer. Told her I was very sick, help me, take care of me. But she couldn't, hardly better off herself. At dawn the long punishing drive and I just could no longer. Pulled the car off to the side and slept. Top down in the screaming sunrise. Hoping it would be better when we woke, but the dream went on worse every moment. Midst of the media stuff, running from town, asked the publisher to find a place to work. Quiet. Some place in Wellfleet. Rented by phone. But when I saw it I recognized it immediately for a suicide trap. Tawdry, isolated, overpriced, depressive. Someone will die here. We left after ten minutes. Summer greed refunded the money most reluctantly.

Then ranting on to Provincetown reduced to a vulgarity that cost more than the Hilton, smack in the middle of things, noisy, pretentious. Still fighting in the middle of a huge lobster dinner cooked without joy till I am the bully my father was and Naomi is dropping her coy child front to become that weeping neurosis, her mother.

We resented each moment the other wrote. Pushed the beds together to scandalize the management. But I slept like an animal, not giving. Working on the *Prostitution* tapes in the bedroom, technology driving me madder as the battery failed. At night I refused her but she did not ask, stayed up in the kitchen typing. In the morning I wrote a prospectus for another book, calling it *Yak,* being that person I am so glad went crazy and died. There was no peace so we left, becoming one of the sad cars coming towards me now, long trains of them, the very metal disappointed at the end of summer, driven home to the city's false reality. But I am going forward. I am going toward Provincetown, not away from it. Behind me now the ugly confusion of New Bedford's slums and ahead the long hard pull up the peninsula. Thought I was there already after the bridge. Then a sudden signpost at a turn: Provincetown, seventy-three miles. And nearly despair. So far still. The first glimpse of the sea. Miles of afternoon. My passion such a slow driver. But now the dunes swelling on the right, little cracker boxes lined up on the water at the left. When you see that you know you are there. Finally the turn to Provincetown Center, the big silly tower looming, old quiet streets narrow. There are no people yet till you reach Commercial, thronged with the summer mob, always too many others come here too. Avaricious little shops, the hustle. But the people are gentle, bearded, helping me gingerly point the car into the town landing. An address right next to the Playhouse. Right in the middle of things. Bump a trash basket not hurting it three times. No one laughs. Pedestrians walking all over, surrounding the car. People, their vulnerable skins. So frightening to have a car in the sea of them, the far of hitting one delicate human body. Suntanned, the ease of their flesh is not the machine and my highway tautness. The car settles in the sand, looking at ocean. At last.

But there is no Claire. A woman on the porch. Finally recognize it's Molly. Part of our group in New York. But dropped out early. I do not know her. So slow, vague, must be stoned. Where is Claire? Doesn't she live

here? The slip of yellow paper I have held like a talisman
never lost in the mess of my portable filing cabinet, had
the phone number too. Some guy sitting there on the
porch never heard of her. Molly saying she's glad I came,
I can stay in the cottage. Where is Claire? Are we supposed to stay here? Molly will help me find her, showing
me the cottage, beautiful Provincetown house all jerry-
built, posters all over the walls, painted floors, properly
aged. Wonderful light, so many rooms, the bedroom a
place of joy. Windows all over, deck in the front looking
to the sea. Swim right there. Even a pool next door, she
says. I can hardly stop to look. I must find Claire. Has
she gone back to New York with Barbara when I didn't
get here on time? Supposed to be here at noon, now five-
thirty. On the road all day, so much farther than I
thought. Did she give up and leave?

Everything is collapsing in my fear. Molly feels it,
telling me it will be all right, she'll go with me, find
Claire, probably just out sailing somewhere. So we back
the car out, the people stopping, letting us. To French's
shop, French in her leather apron knows where Claire
lives. Parked in a towaway zone. Let them have the thing.
I'll find Claire. Then I see her. She has her glasses on
and is laughing at me. I had the wrong address. There
were two yellow papers, both of them Provincetown
addresses. But I never understood that one was Molly's,
her invitation that first time we met, come up anytime
you want and visit. Claire shows me what she's rented.
One dark room our home. Landlady at the head of the
stairs. Shake hands. Gray-haired woman named Margaret.
Claire must come with me to get my stuff, unloaded all
in Molly's cottage. When we get back there Claire sees
it too. The light and space. But we've already rented
the other place. She's wary. Had asked Molly to stay
at her place once before but Molly said no. "Don't get
involved. Favors. We owe the landlady." "So we pay
her. We needn't stay there." "You can write here but
I've got to live up there." Molly's voice from her studio
next door, would we like a drink? "Claire, we should
accept, she even went out to buy orange juice." I solve

the fridge problem of frozen trays with a sculptor's strength. We are all laughing. We are safe. Big sunny studio, chrome yellow doors one full side of it. Claire goes to get her boat. It seems settled that we'll stay. Molly and I go out for groceries. We see a hippie being arrested for playing the guitar. Even in Provincetown it is forbidden to sing. But I am too happy to care. I buy everything for breakfast, loving to buy groceries. Orange juice coffee eggs. A man hands me the bacon from inside the case. It is playing house. So much more fun than keeping house. Carrying big bags, the store-bought ice, cream to make my special scrambled eggs. Over these eggs Claire offered to marry me. "If you weren't married already," we laughed one Bowery morning she stayed over. But that was the morning of her turnoff, the mother father child speech. How to escape the roles, how to stop being other people? Or be them for a game, changing all the time, so nothing gets stuck.

Claire is coming into the shore, a red sail. I wave back walking down to the beach, wanting her to land for me. A crown of yellow hair above a lime-colored sweatshirt. One of her classic landings aground. As she gets out she is making a speech about her humble abode. She'll stay there. Never mind the grin, she is serious. It's her identity. Everything falls to pieces in the water. Forget Molly's place, you came here to be with her. "Can't I stay there too? With you?" "Anywhere you want." "We can be both places." "Like the Rockefellers." It will work out. Relax.

Molly comes down with drinks. Cigarettes. Claire wants to sail us. To show off. It is all very wonderful till she tips over. We are in the water in our clothes. Drowning. Then standing up. This is a hell of a way to start out in Provincetown. Is it an omen? After we have reclaimed my sandal and fished out her glasses Molly's had enough.

Claire sails me, the wharf speeding by while I lie back on the deck open to her, looking my enormous desire at her eyes. Her head the gold of her hair against the sky, evening, the tower that makes it Venice in Provincetown at once—with snatches of American Florentine thrown in too. And the fishing boats, lobster pots, "Keep Off" in big letters, the lights of the houses on the shore. I am Cleopatra languorous on her barge. It is terrible how I want her. The background revolving from shore to ocean to pier as we whirl out here, her head and shoulders always before my eyes. She is shy and asks me not to stare at her or she'll make a mistake, worried the boom will hit me. But I am lying down, it can't. My clothes are soaked, the stripes of my pants vivid with the water. I can feel my legs and the shirt wet on my breasts. Nell said that Claire loved me. "That clutch, the way she grabs at her side under the armpit, that's dangerous. Help her, be gentle, I think maybe she's crazy." But Nell thinks everyone in America is crazy. "Do you remember that first day we met at Albany, how we talked about going to Provincetown? And we did it." "That's right, Katsey, convert your daydreams to fate and you can control reality, run the universe." Humor her defense against sentiment. "Shall I tell you my latest vision? I walked on the shore coming back from Race Point. We'll go there. It will be a historic moment, closest spot to England or Ireland. But it took so long to sail back that I asked Barbara to take the boat and walked along the beach." Now she is serious, really telling the story, the Donald Duck tone disappears. "There were thousands of sea gulls and I walked among them. They started to fly all around me and I felt they were recognizing me when they all suddenly took wing and called out, acknowledging me for a higher spirit, one with mind. As if they knew it when they saw it, that mind was something they didn't have but wished to pay homage to." Listening I grow sad. They all say she is getting odd, a bit too mystical. Maybe she is crazy. The wharf going by, poles in the water, dark lines, the ocean smell. I sigh for the ambition, the will to power in Claire's vision. Her awful aspiration to sanctity like some terrible height of grandeur that she cannot find yet, wearing herself out with the search.

Then we are turning and I see the tower behind her

head, gray in the blue of the sky, and the soft yellow
of her hair, her face, the green eyes on me. I am in pain
with desire. She hauls my leg between her knees, our
feet touch on the wet floor of the cockpit, the warm
water. We will go back now.

When we are ashore she fears for the boat. Wants to
return it to her place. I am cold and wet. I'd like a
shower. Warmth. A drink. "I have a pair of your pants
at my place . . ." Her voice trails off. I know she wants
me to go there. Molly's cottage calls with its light and
comfort. The choice is important. It is is even more important than the boat. "All right, we'll go to your place.
Our place." She thanks me in a way I must remember,
short and strong. I laugh, telling her I'm a good friend
and we start back out into the harbor. Around the wharf.
I am crew taking up the centerboard. She deprecates
her sailing, the great joke of her incompetence. "If you
wonder why we're going the wrong way it's only because
I'm trying not to run into something or other." When
we get there she kisses me, taking my head in her hands.
I ask are we giving scandal, not seeing the people on
the beach till later. But it doesn't seem to matter. The
landlady fusses over her. Worries over the boat. "The
child hardly knows how to sail. She has lost three hinge
pins already." Clucking her affection. I explain the
situation. That I fell into another place, bigger, better
to work in. But Margaret can't rent our room to anyone
else now. It's too late. So we must keep faith, pay
anyway. It is Claire's way to do things, her New England
straightness, better.

The shower is wonderful. Hot, heavy pressure. Claire
makes me cocoa. All the joy of being a sick child. We
each drink three glasses of milk. Her ass is so elegant
and her legs in her jeans. We are campers, and I go out
for cigarettes wearing her wool plaid jacket, my hair wet
and tangled. Walking in the Provincetown night, the
romance of the place, old houses, the crush of summer.
Living it hard in a few days. Prices too high, arty stuff
in the stores, Washington Square fake art all over.
Walking home to Claire I doubt Nell would find the place

"authentic." But I forgive it everything, love even the hype. Art snobbery over portraits and sketches of ocean shacks all gone in the musk of the streets, watching people who must save all year to be a week in the Provincetown summer. A gay town. An art colony. And the art is not so hot. All the amateur gay artists I have known here and in the city, their work never reaching across the gap in their lives, not strong enough. Derivative. Yes, and inauthentic. Arty through lack of concentration. Other people making the new art, somehow connected, while they hang about the crumbs of tradition, doing pastels. But it doesn't matter. Tonight I accept. When I open the door I discover her under a dryer. She is only a lady at the hairdresser. For a moment it is incredible. My bookworm unmasked. But how funny it is. How lovable, this last immodesty. I sit down to enjoy it. And when she takes the plastic lid off—curlers. She laughs in her superb nerve, triumphant at having shown me the most ridiculous thing in her life. I have seen it. The great yellow hair is curled in springs and rollers, unbelievable metal objects discarded one by one into a pile in the gray artificial cap now thrown upon the floor. She is bagging it up in its child carrying case, her dignity intact. "Sort of thing you never have to deal with when you live alone. If I don't do this I look like a poodle dog," her hand removing the terrible objects, freeing each wonderful swatch of hair like a chunk of taffy stretched.

Finally it is time. We clear the studio couch, the two of us moving objects, towels, glasses. She holds me now, looking in her eyes. I am afraid. There is so much feeling jumping from my throat shaking me. So glad to be here. We make love coming before we have even taken off our clothes. I tremble in her grasp, almost crying.

She tells me she won't go with me to the nonviolence panel. "I'm afraid to fly. And I doubt I'll learn anything." "I was hoping you'd teach me, you've studied so much longer." "There are so many violences," her head is beautiful lying on its side, her eyes teaching me. "It's a way of life to be nonviolent. There is a possibility of a new vision." Her fantastic hope claiming there are people now doing this. If it's a way to live it's nearly beyond reach. I could not reach it with Mallory's crescendo going fishwife, digging into me, never able to stop, tearing all the time until my stomach could brook no more patience. Claire looks at me, glowing in the soft light. "The nonviolent are here to absorb the anger of others like a sponge." I remember last winter. Hatred screaming out of magazines, the black print like knives. The malice in the eyes of students yelling from audiences. That Texas boy standing toe to toe ready to strike me for pacifism. I was poisoned and going mad. "If you have a faith you can piss away the stuff after you mop it in." I groan. "It's not about religion," she laughs at my distaste, "I mean another faith." "Like?" "Well, once I saw this movie about King marching through Chicago on a rent strike. The people were turning their hoses, their garden sprinklers on him, hundreds of them, shouting fantastic obscenities, hating him, thousands of them filling the air, the screen full of their hatred. Then later he was up in a little plane and they asked him, very good documentary really, there he is hanging his head out of the door of this plane, his face, and they showed it, hurt, confused. He said he didn't realize, and everyone of course thought he'd known, have to know that there was such hatred, that of course he'd realize. He said he didn't know if nonviolence was the way, wasn't sure. All the people in the movie house knew, had figured it out a long time ago, half dead laughing at him."

"The most important thing we can do, the one significant thing," she is grinning, "is to try to give hope. Someone has to do this, insist even monotonously to people that change can come." But while she talks I remember last August twenty-sixth, the great mass of people in Bryant Park, body to body close as a sea of flowers in the evening light. Friedan's speech after mine so cogent and full of details, facts, matter. I was ashamed, listening. When it was my turn I said we had a movement now. Really all I said, just expressing the spirit of how we felt being fifty thousand people in the streets. But I was so vague. Betty had it on the nose with employment figures, abortion demands, all the substance. "That's her job," Claire argues. "Yours was different. It's to make people believe. That's something else. Spontaneous, imaginative, to give hope."

But I felt another thing, very dangerous. Media men had been with us all day making themselves a nuisance. And the marchers were angry, we don't stage rallies in their honor and so forth. Women feeling their power a first time in their lives shouting at the men reporters to sit so we could all see, turn off their blinding lights. When I'd been marching I'd felt the pride too and the same annoyance. Though afraid even then it might come to trouble. Then they are calling for me, I have to speak, dizzy at the prospect of talking, so many people. Real people, alive, no television millions behind the vacuum of a lens. Then speaking. Time becomes the buzz in my head. "Suddenly everyone stopped listening, the lights flare on some poor moron standing up with a sign, says we'll castrate him. There he is in trouble, this demented overlighted ghost asking for it. And reminding us. The media love it, if he's stomped to death it will be news. No one is listening to my speech any more. Of course I'm a bit deflated. Everything has stopped and is hanging midair over his head. I cannot talk any more. Now they are watching me. But I knew then that if I said kill him they'd do it. It is sickening to know that. Makes you know Hitler's squares and the banners, marching, everybody just alike, all those damned flags, swastika ranks turning and rolling in perfect file salute power. I knew too that if I said the obvious pacifist thing they would not listen. And it might make it worse. So I had to be funny, humor the thing away till attention diverted itself. For his sake I could not speak the obvious truth that if a hair of his head were hurt we were all invalidated. This creature lost in the middle of strobe lights, this challenging, insanely moral figure with his cardboard. So how do you give hope when most of it is chaos?"

"I'm glad you remind me. Your reality is a nice balance to all my visions. My joy in a plastic bottle business," she laughs. "But it must still be done even

if we're wrong or crazy. First we must all learn to be
gentle. For this you risk being ridiculous." She bursts
out laughing. I'm laughing too, realizing we are lovers
discussing nonviolence in bed. I hadn't noticed, so
appropriate it seemed. As her tongue searches my mouth
I decide to study sensuality these slow summer days when
there is endless time to try everything and drown in
feeling, relishing, savoring each second. Here are the joys
of peace. Historians call this effete, remembering San-
som's beloved storybook of Japan. Every time a dynasty
settled down to court life and art he clucked that they
were going womanish, the martial arts decaying, about
to fall to another wave of real men, a new shogun's steel
people fierce to grasp, then grow civilized and lose to
the next lot pouring in cries and horses, arrows sticking
out all over like they do in Mifune when he's Kurosawa's
fallen Macbeth.

War is a serious masculine affair, but we choose to
be ladies discussing our wardrobe. Claire shows me her
minidress. It is a silver handkerchief too small to wear
in the city without being mobbed. I ask after the long
blue dress, a wonderful color for her, that I gave to her
one night she slept at my studio. "I took it to the laun-
dromat." "Have you ever heard of dry cleaning?" "It
did come back looking very funny." "But you ruined
it." "Well, you see it's simply a material object." "I can't
wait till you see my astonishing English dress." "Describe
it." "It's at Molly's, you'll see it tonight." We are ladies
discussing our wardrobe. Or lovers eating clams out of
a cardboard box on a long wharf looking over the water
and behind us the lights in the town and the tower. A
sailor walks by and asks if we are having a party. The
lights shine on our festival. We are exclusive. Wanting
only ourselves as we pass Molly and two friends on the
deck, going straight into the house. I make a drink at
last. Luxuriating in my creature comfort, thinking as I
crack the ice that I am older now and like my ease
sometimes. The voices on the porch stop talking and go
away. I will not bother Claire with my dress, she is a
child asleep in bed, lying on her stomach. Going quietly

to join her I manage to knock over the lamp. Not once
but twice. Get up and trip over the cord all over again.
Confusion. I can't find where it plugs in, have spilled
orange juice on the rug. I am a Viking destroying the
place. Claire solves the electricity while I mop up the rug.
Then we are lovers again and she a beautiful woman
struggling with passion her body so lovely when I kiss
her hip admiring the rise of it slightly plump in the
stomach, a nude with character in the pose I am fondest
of, lying on her side, a full length of leg rising to the swell
of hip then down along the line of side to rise again in
breast and shoulder.

"I've junked my Starmaker," she sighs. "He got too
abstract. I'm devoting this month to the Buddhists. Got
a whole stack of them." She snuggles next to me, my
face drinking in her neck. And the last thing I remember
falling asleep is the temples in Kyoto, sitting in the dark,
silk curtains flapping into quiet, great black and white
stripes, sometimes red or green, vibrant colors in the
dim silence before the bright outdoors. Staying in temples
'cause they were cheap and got to like them, the priest's
two little girls coming to recite English lessons after
breakfast. Tanaka-san, a name as common as Smith. Arrived at night in a rainstorm cab lost all over Hyakumon-
ben, the priest a bit overwhelmed by this *geigin* with
knapsack using full repertoire of courtly phrases to convince him I should stay. Once when we were friends and
the daughters had ripped off lots of free English lessons
he showed me his best room. Kanō school screens and
doors. The wood three hundred years old. And the time
I went with Fumio to Kyoto we spent a whole afternoon
before a much finer Kanō, a cherry tree the whole wall
of a temple, sitting on the mats in ecstasy of choice between gazing at the painting or the garden. Our sacred experience. And I know the golden tree grows still in the
eye of his mind, Miroji our mountain temple. I
photographed his head against the pagoda we loved, the
grin on his face with me after he left. Hoarded on my
bedroom wall the months he was gone in America. His
mother came upstairs to help me measure for a new

futong. And saw it though I tried to stand in front, hide in with my body. Her perfect wisdom knew and yet approved. Her stoicism when Yoshiko died. Little figure rigid in pain, *shikataganai,* it cannot be helped. I banged my hand on the doorframe, furious for a friend lost in youth, the stupid waste of her life. No, Obaachan said from her old woman's face, that will not do. You must learn when things cannot be helped. The day I left she stood there, a miniature in a Western dress. So hot that day. Flimsy wash dress. In kimono always she looked stately. A connoisseur of silks. But that day she was old in the rag of a dress. And frail. It hurt to see. Asking me to take good care of him. So acknowledged I was in her understanding. We used to get tipsy and go to baseball games together till she gave up gimlets, too old for the aftereffects. So small she was in the doorway when I left, waving her hanky. Nor will I break faith, still and always loving him. She allowed for a magnum of craziness, after all I was a *geigin.* I doubt she would quarrel with me now, though in her whole life she never knew sensuality. My second mother. The last thing I remember falling asleep on Claire's breast.

In the morning even before she wakes I am at the ocean. It is cold. Almost too cold. Unless you try hard. A man watches from the shore. Does he see my ugly black bathing suit or my cowardice? It doesn't matter. How different one day is from the next. I have stopped caring, am free not to go into the water. The calm of this place another world entering the long sweep of sea, the clean new day rebounding off the blue of the water. Life is fresh. It sparkles. It holds forth every promise. It is the first day of a vacation.

After breakfast, after the bread and butter in the sunlight looking toward the sea, the newspaper and the coffee, I am alone. I look at Molly's floor. She has painted rugs on it so one needn't bother to clean them. How can I hold this day, this time spent wondering over time held in the hands, a quivering bird. Always there

are lice upon the feathers if you look closely. I will fail.
My people mere shadows, I have not captured their
speech. The summer will end before I have finished.
What will come in the winter? It is too hard, I cannot
hold on. After breakfast, after the long lazy coffee, then
Molly came over. Gave me an art book to read, flattered
me in this kindness, remembering I am a sculptor. We
talked of Rimbaud. "Write today. Show me your vision,"
she said.

But now the light is gone. The windows boarded now
in winter, the voices of last summer. Still in the rooms
if you listen. No light falls through the big windows high
in the wall. No light or little. Winter now. I have come
back to finish and to find the past.

I look up to see it return. Claire stands by the doorway. "I have an exquisite Anglo-Saxon face." Really?
I said to her then. "Yup, lady on Wall Street said so.
'You have an exquisite Anglo-Saxon face, which would
be a great asset in our front office. Unfortunately you
lack stenographic skills.' " And that first day I wrote of
my arrival on the day before. Writing it hot after happening, no time to ripen. Reading it now I despise
its shallowness. Failing again in the January disorder of
Margaret's empty house, here again without peace and
surrounded by workmen, their boxes filling the room,
Heating Model R7050-A complete assembled units,
pipes all over the floor. And five cats. Now.

In the evening I await her coming. Then. It is the
summer when she comes, the people thronging the streets,
an army in the uniforms of peace, vacationers as eager
as we are to live. I buy Portuguese bread. Then back
inside our alley to the quiet of the sea, the satisfaction
of a meal earned. "Claire, where did you get those awful
sneakers?" "There's a man on Second Avenue sells
sneakers. This year his judgment slipped. He bought
thousands of orange sneakers. For no reason, just a tragic
error of decision making. I was going by his little thing
there, basement really, not a store. Does a side business
in plants. Very unprofitable. The Lower East Side is not
ready for flowers. I'm looking at his blue and white

sneakers when he comes up. Suggesting the orange. Right away I knew what happened to him."

The lady next door has got the bugs. She is there in the back through a window with her flashlight trained on the wall. Has millions of something. Claire asks what. No one knows, lady goes to find out. Back in a moment demonstrating, pointing to her open palm. Claire tells me the story while I light the fire for steaks. "So I took one off the wall and showed it to them. There it is in my hand. Now it's not frightening them any more, they're all crowding around it, curious. Little black thing with wings, so very fragile it even interests them. They begin to understand it's a creature with life." She is standing before the fire, her hand shining in it as she tells me, the moon behind her in the sky, luminous. There are people on it tonight. "So did they stop killing them then?" She turns around and then spins back, laughing at herself. "No, they're out buying more insecticide. Cans of it. Victory does not come at once. We will have the pleasure of foretasting it."

At dinner everyone teases her, their affection rocking her saintly boat. French asks her what she has forgone lately. "Bookie's always off something, sex or booze or cigarettes. Perfecting her human spirit. One day I stopped by and she's crawling around the place looking for a joint. On all fours, mind you." And the laughter subsides French persists. "What new wonder is it this week? What ism are you reading?" It is how they deal with her, with what is foreign, even strangely menacing in her idealism. It is also how they show admiration. Sometimes I worry for her, but she understands them and is merrier than they are. "Bookie," she says, "as in Gandhi."

After dinner we do not go with the others. Claire is reading her newspaper, withdrawn from them, bored by their talk. I sit on the bed wanting her. All through dinner wishing the others would leave. Why does she invite them? Why don't they go home, leave us our dying fire, our string of Christmas lights on the porch facing toward the sea, proclaiming our good fortune. And safe inside our house, its bedroom trumpeting delights, a king's feast of hours in the days ahead, making love in sunlight the day frank on our bodies. One afternoon I stroked her flank daylight on it gold, hearing again now her cry when I entered her, my hand intent. But we talk instead, always talking when we should be silent. Our friendship one grand interminable dialogue where talk interrupts love, postpones it until we are too tired or grown cross with waiting. Not taking what we need until our nerves are tense from anticipation. Wondering, my mind only half intent upon the argument, King the Kennedys does the martyr system make everything worse, a safety valve the citizenry enjoy the murder and the funeral televised, wondering will she deny me? Begin the asceticism thing again now? Always a threat lingering in the background to destroy my peace. The saintly nonsense taking on terrible life against me. "But they made a great light," she insists. "A beacon really, gave us a notion of how things could be.". "Comets burn out," I argue, "leaving it darker," the thing burning in my stomach, frustrated will is it merely? Or expedience calculating my chances? Yesterday she was willing, gave herself. What of to-morrow? Will it go like Celia? This week become a nightmare? Losing her I'll run out of chances. No, it must work. We have so little time. We will make love for a while, then join them at the bar. The dancing, a few more drinks, there is so much to live. All of it. We will do both. "Bars, monuments to impermanence," she says. "And gay bars the worst." "Then we'll stay home," I say smiling at her. Coaxing her stroking her, my enemy the *New York Times* crinkling underneath, then sliding to the floor. But if she is loath it is hopeless. Even now giving in to me, raising herself upon her side her hand finding me, always she wishes to take me first, serving me. I am slower to heat, whereas she is always ready, open to me. I must doubt it, even this, her hand on my breast will she touch the nipple with exquisite care, feels like it connects to the clitoris begins the heat between my legs. Should I not take her first, give myself time? Shouldn't we take turns who is first? Though she laughs at me, "Do you want to keep score on the wall?"

"Equity," I would lecture, but her tongue whispers in my ear, "Shut up. Take your clothes off." How I adore her orders, loving to be bullied by her. What sick thought is this, or is it that final safety with her, bewildered at the joy in her hand searching me, opening to her fingers upon the lips of my other mouth wet making little noises, silence to be filled with her tongue while she sifts me, reams, files, selects, and plays upon the nerve like a button pressed all heat flooding out I open wider to receive her will split myself take her whole up to the elbow, straining in hope. I love the way you move as I move dancing under your hand's power deep in me shaking when you press hard fast against the wall deep like a storm in me. I must stop breathing, so fierce you are. So powerful. Coming, dragged even, making no effort, believe only in what she does, cease to give directions from your mind spoken or strained in thought ESP of the will give over and follow be taken, hurled by a hand shaking the fear one hopes for, away from the Ferris wheel, then when it plummets terror you are the uncontrolled, taken to the place beyond thought or knowing. And I too a tyrant over her, sure she will come never failing, I can play take my time wring cries pausing even before I enter, lingering upon the tangle of hair lose myself in it like a field of wheat ripe in August. I will make her crave me, writhe for my coming, then slowly by degrees pushing while she is in a rage for me, cunning to make that first finger touch higher hotter more relief parched in the wet for me she has this greeting reserved unto me, prouder for this than anything in the world. That she is wet and open for my touch coming then at last still playing on the ledge of her, she orders me, begging really for my power is everything, come inside. To the known way of her now master in charge, sure of the volcano, I plunge stoking it for its cries, can they hear us, as she nearly bellows her coming like the lion fierce herself. Now if ever and I feel her power gone beyond me into a force, her own, past me now for an instant, no longer, seconds even until she returns in tenderness from that long place near death. And time has played its trick. Too late now for bars, talk, the others. We have had this instead. Regretting, a moment petulant that one does not get it all. Then seeing in her body naked and imperfect all one does get, like reality like everything call it enough and know your riches. This if I do not lose it, the dark thought lying in wait at the edge of my satisfaction.

Study sensation, the sea food light the senses in the moisture of the flesh. Body's mouth open in the friction even of a stray hair feel it pulled or rubbed upon the clitoris. Its pain is pleasure better understood. I lie as her hand plays upon me, the words repeating themselves inside my skull, study the senses these days live in your eyes in your skin give yourself to experience the present. Give yourself as you learn, become her teacher so she will never leave you, the joy of the flesh so great it can never be forsworn nor I who taught it. Give yourself like a Persian forgetting goals, coming is the end not an end sought for. It finishes therefore postpone the convulsion divert the mind, try other tricks insert tongue into the cleft waiting each nerve listening and alive as the nub of tongue licks and points itself upon the other nub hard stabbing softly and rhythm mounting. While my fingers sly finding another hole in her shy to enter pecking at the entrance for admission granted. Softly and with infinite gentleness turn over on your stomach rejoicing to look down and see them round waiting me while she lies below me the cheeks of her ass such lust I feel and firm, tenderness in my finger moving slowly gently in its rhythm in her, back and forth steady until she rolls away and cannot bear it. And did I hurt you struck with sorrow trying again my mouth watering her first tongue licking the place fill you with water with rain like watering a plant, I will bring all liquids to our rescue that there is no pain or friction bringing wet of her cunt too then enter easy slipping she is opening it for me for our pleasure. Only the sight of her below me, such kindness I feel for these cheeks such greed feeding upon her given and open defenseless vulnerable, but I shall never cause her harm careful to relish our abandon to savor each thrust as she does and my hand ever so slowly deliberate moving her closing on my finger's steady in and out, feeling her feeling in my own anus contracting as hers does the secret joy of it found at last.

For we can do anything. Everything. Nothing is forbidden us, all ways are open. Watching her suck me, the round of her cheek next to the round of my breast, the very sight watched excites me. As it does her too when I feed upon her, sucking hard till she erects in my mouth grows stiff as a lilac bud while I pull in the pride of it knowing she sees. Complicity so close we are each other's cunts. Feeling the hot cold rush when I touch her clitoris imagining I have her finger on my own, dizzy with the very sensation which I give her so real it is to me, our two bodies one I can no longer separate them. Her cunt from mine, feeling her fingers filling me while mine fill her and thrust against the wall inside her, feeling the pull in my own gasp while I probe the cervix like a flower hanging upside down, my fingers searching around its turrets. While I give I am given. The same storm, the same upheaval. One never has this with a man, his experience hidden as mine is. But two women have the same nerves. The merest flick of my finger on her clitoris hidden like a pearl in its folds alerts its head and my own throbs touched as surely as by a hand and my legs grab hers between them in a vise, roll then opening to the strength of her leg so satisfactory I can bring myself to a fever upon it while she shoves it hard against me, pleased with herself the pleasure she brings me gasping now as we come together one shaking cry. But I am still greedy to touch her, ringing changes upon the clitoris, this most sensitive moment after you've come. And touching it so insidiously the warmth slowly spreading upwards from her toes till it becomes a chill she can no longer bear it but bear further until you are faint with it you can always go on beyond to the next wave and further. So much further than you thought, such exquisite torture nearly you grow dizzy in stoicism further still further. And break off. Rest, she says. But I will not rest, my tongue shall bring her further until she cries out

surprised and comes again, the long difficult ecstasy of
nerves shuddering as after a shipwreck she lies within
my arms, passion and innocence.

We smoke in the stillness heavy around us as our intimacy. Becoming our other selves. Reach me a cigarette,
they're on your side. Each moment passing changes us,
we are becoming different, more apart.

"This is the cigarette that makes it impossible to give
up smoking," I say, watching her light it and flick her
ashes. She smokes like a kid. The defiance of it still in
her gestures. "I'm giving it up soon," she threatens. The
words could mean anything. Then without warning she
kisses my hand kissing herself who is in its odors so
precious lasting afterward, "Manual labor," she laughs,
"proper work for a sculptor." "Odd isn't it how people
despise it yet we do everything with our hands. We have
created civilization with them, no other creature has
them." Her eyes look at me straight grave as a child's,
direct. "Put your hand in me as I am falling asleep, it
is such comfort." In our tiredness I obey, contentment
in the wet of her, energy in the thrust again, alive to me
coming softly into sleep.

What nonsense it seems. A press conference. So far away
now, writing about it in Provincetown, this other world
looking toward the sea. Ocean makes it all seem so
boring. I thought again when I woke this morning, how
irrelevant. Could it possibly be important enough to write
down? I walk into the water, the tide too low to swim.
Wandering off my track. Then come back. Maybe this
is relevant, not quite understanding as I write it down
anyway. It passes the time till a sail appears. And since
it doesn't, since it avoids me, today looks like a day I'll
have to work. My own life merely the passing of time
till she returns. This bright youngster I would hold like
time itself, her head like the sun's warmth, light to me.
How I am fallen into idiocy. Dependent. A relative being.
She must never discover it. Guarding my secret as she
walks towards me. Putting the lobsters on the table. A

scramble inside their paper bag. We sit on the porch. I chatter. I am an animal disguising a wound.

Like fatality, the idea of showing her some of my work steals over me. Should I risk it? It is my self I expose. Would she push it away? If she despised me there, I would be done for. And what is good enough to show her? What is done? The part about Frieda, liked it so when I wrote it. But what if it were stale now? Read it, try to read it well, stop your voice from shaking. But now she says nothing. Looking at me. I will save our embarrassment. Sit away from her on the other side of the bed. My back to her discovering I am a coward, suppressed her name when I read it, did not say it was her I remembered making love to, her cervix, feeling it in my hand. Had the courage to write it but not read it. Did she intuit that? Is it that which makes her silent?

Then she comes to me, sitting on my side of he bed while I sit on the floor, excusing it, after all it's just a record: "The rest of you are too busy, everybody else has the sense to just life. I'm the only one watching the stove, trying to photograph things." "Yes, and it's a fine thing you're doing." She is perfectly serious. "There is nothing more useful than to give an account of human consciousness. It's your job. It's the present. My job is the future. It is beyond who we are to what we'll become." My God what is she saying, that we are two generations and I'm already passé, that puts me in my place nicely, but she is still talking, her voice going on—"To be like Saint Francis," she says. "The mystic sees beyond things, and now there's a new consciousness coming toward us, other forms of intelligent life will change our limited understanding, will stretch and break us into other insights. All that we knew will be irrelevant. It is for this moment I live, my whole life a preparation even if I do not live to see it come I will direct my entire energy into the course of its arrival." I can't listen to her. I am hit by knowledge as by a hand—Nell was right. She is crazy. I do not hear, her words come in fragments, just shards of her madness. She is ranting. Of course Nell was right. She is crazy. I can listen and surrender, realize she is lost. Or I can hurl it at her, grabbing for her soul. "What do you think you are? What are you doing with St. Francis and the space age?" "Our ways are very different," she says, her calm a source of irritation, deluded. "They will get more different, they will diverge. Sometime. I don't know how soon."

"So you are going to give me up? Transcend me? Like a bad habit or something?" I stare at her, my face close to her. "I must, to fulfill myself, withdraw from people again. Yes. Become as ascetic." "You are crazy," I tell her, terrified. "All my life I have wanted to see God." Her eyes are terrible. Green, wide, pitiless. They no longer see me. Already I have disappeared. It is power she seeks. I am an object to be lost, meat hurled into the gulf of her ambition, this overweening pride. But how do I know? Fighting not really on the fair ground of disagreement, but simply in my need of her now. Fighting for my life in her. "I am sorry," she goes on, not even listening to me. "It was a mistake. I have been trying to make Barbara see this." Poor damn Barbara, I think. A week of this stuff. "Do you realize how you sound?" I am fighting for her mind. I will use everything, save her. "It's spiritual pride, the worst of sins," believing for an instant in all the sins. And this the worst. Her eyes flicker. I have tripped her, now I will charge home. "You must stop wanting all, you must settle for what you can do. Write. Finish your book. That is real." But she is adamant. "Writing is delusion not wisdom, the vanity of reviews, the little puff of fame." "It's a difficult book even to publish, you will not be elected hero," I remind her. She is not even listening. Nor am I. Only my body lying on the bed. Stretched out exhausted. I have lost. Could my despondency invite her? If we could make love we would be together. But it is just this that she refuses. Taking herself away. Sitting crosslegged on the bed to my right, her beautiful face awful to look at, the gold of her head deranged and dim now like ashes. It is over, I hear in my skull. Over, it all ends here in this crummy room, we are two lunatics. I see my own foot at the end of my body. Then the lamp. The lamp is ugly now. The posters on the ceiling are not gaiety. They are ridiculous. The pictures on the wall are foolish. We are sordid. The bedspread is cheap yellow chenille. Hateful. All gone flat. The time ahead collapses as surely as the precious time gone already. Tomorrow I leave for New York. The nonviolence panel. After it is over do not come back.

I lie on the bed. I am weak from struggling. Try again, seize your happiness. Don't be robbed, a sluggard watching it go without a struggle. But I am too tired to fight any more. Already I know it is lost. Hopeless. It is Celia again. She will escape me. Like Celia. If not this time, then soon. Useless to resist, to protest, to hang on. Let go then. Taking all my nerve to say it: "Do what you think you must." The breath stopping then, I have done, my hands let go at my sides, fall on the bed useless. She goes outside. I hear her on the porch. In a while I will get up. Right now I want to lie here knowing it is over. Asking myself am I mad again? Relinquishing her, let go and did not hold. Whispering to myself you can't hold anyone, they will evade you, slip out of your grasp. Then it coming back, like nausea, the joy lost, there would have been so much of it here. Most bitter the sea now, hateful. She has bought us lobsters, the sight of the meat white when you open it and the butter repellent now. What shall we have for dinner? "Hamburgers," I said when I climbed out of the boat. "I'm nearly broke, I'll get some more money in New York." "I'll get it," she shouted, angry, showing off again, a stranger watching us quarrel. And came back with lobsters. Insisting on them when she doesn't have the money, is too poor. Well, it would never work out anyway. Too many differences. In a moment I will find the strength to get up. Mix a drink. Put a good face on things, do not show you know you are lost. Everyone hates the accusation in a beaten face. Do not let her despise you.

I am careful. Smiling at her over a glass. She takes the cigarette and grins. "Tomorrow asceticism," lighting it, "Maybe I'll put off sanctity until next year." "Then you can give me up for a New Year's resolution." Our badinage always the floor with which we cover our desperation. Her mood is light. Is it hope or does she trifle with me? "I've thought about it, Katsie, you're right, I've been a little crazy. Waited too long for this vacation, the city was making me weird. You're right. It is ambition, this hating life. I will finish my book. It's real. It's something the right size, it can be done." I listen. She has changed course again. Believe her or pretend? But already beginning to believe, confessing how I could not write before because it had to be so good, good as my heroes Beckett, Genet, or why bother? At that rate one writes nothing. "You must give up vanity, be grateful finally to write at all, humble enough to see any sentence in your joy at just being able to speak." "Yes," she agrees with me. Yet I watch her, leery it will come again. But it all goes my way, she is agreeing with me, "The ancients, those creeps that write books, all the mystics insisting asceticism is a prerequisite." She holds the idea up for me to smash with contempt. "Who needs to be an imitator?" "Surely you can do better." Am I only feeding the fire of her madness, both of us making sport of it, in the usual manner, the one everyone accepts, just a joke, "Bookie's got it into her head to be a saint no less," a whole table of friends laughing their affection. Her charming eccentricity.

Molly comes over. We roast the Christians. "Barbarous," Molly says, "Despising themselves they've made us all miserable for centuries. Consider their crimes, the pain they inflict, the sufferings still with us." "Morbid they are," I join in, hauling forth my convent, its sickly sensuality, the whole place seething with repressed sexuality, most of it queer and gone dangerously sour. Betraying it, all its fragrances of sentiment, its urchin's feast of the heart, loving a senior, the Virgin, some favorite nun—all one in the candles and the chant. But this I do not say, that it was the rise of pain in my chest seeing them, these heroines, because I would not be childish, live in the old mist of the emotions with me still. Bravely forward for the life of reason. Ganging up with Molly's outraged common sense, her greater care

for humanity smashing the wooden doctrines that cause
the soul to shrivel. Siding with Molly, I am cheating
Claire, for I only parody what I will not admit.

Dishonest too about her dinner. "Oh you have invited
other people, your landlady, how nice." Pretending not
that convincingly that it is. But even my sarcasm imperfect, since once they are come I would not permit
them to leave, one portion of me wishing them in hell,
the other aghast they might disappear, leave me bereft
of persons to serve, to feed, to talk to. Their presence
once established is fine rare luxurious, as necessary as
the night air. Holding forth on my porch. The big talker.
To Roz whom I like. Roz sporting as a tennis player,
black and gay, the manager at the theater. And Claire's
landlady, Margaret, with whom I resent sharing this
lobster. Scandalized to remember it, sitting before the
fire of a Franklin stove in Margaret's house this cold
January night. It is now.

Then it is then again, that summer night when I didn't
know her yet. She is interviewing me, has just heard I'm
a "famous person." I cringe at the phrase. She mocks
me. Yesterday I was another paying dyke, eighty dollars
worth of nobody. Now she has heard I'm a somebody
it's all different. Ordering me to recite what I plan to
say tomorrow in my speech, give her a précis. "It's
so pleasant to hear distinguished people express themselves." The high-flown sentiment hits me like the voice
of conscience—the nonviolence panel, so important, the
most important thing all summer, but I haven't written
anything yet. Don't even know what I'll say, already
very worried. "Excuse me I'll just see if Claire needs
some help, the lobster." Claire cooking for a change.
Generally she announces herself, maintains her status,
peers or be damned—by being waited on. "Go back and
appease Margaret. Her diction is driving me mad. She
keeps calling Roz's job a position." "Don't be a snob,
it's her way of being brave. Margaret's a little insecure,
but very kind." "All right, you handle it, I'll manage
the lobster." Heating the butter. I will take over. The
sensualist must be a cook above all. The butter melting,

the great sea beasts out of their glaring red shells exposed. Now find cups in which to serve the butter. But it spills and I am just myself, not a celebrity, not even a sybarite, just a frantic woman mopping butter, nearly half a pound of it, off a dirty kitchen floor deciding it can't be saved. Even to think of saving it is knavery. Start over. Damn the extravagance. Sculptors and painters know how to cook, I am always lecturing her. Part of my course in the senses. And cheating on the exam while more butter softens now safely. And the whole mess can be served. Don't forget the wine. Feast them, toasting my own little secrets.

Margaret is an old-timer. Provincetown in the winter, wood fires, solitude, it is better then, come back and see. Once you get past the diction she is a good talker. A fine traditional type who talks to entertain. Holding forth on history, how the Pilgrims landed *here* of course, not Plymouth. How the lobster fishermen have depleted our food in their greed to feed us for gain. "Just a few more years and Provincetown lobster will be a thing of the past." The big fisheries have scraped the bottoms, destroyed all the young. Roz reports that the theater has lost money. The townspeople, it had been her hope to involve them, but they will not come. "These jive ass arty plays turn them off. And who needs more O'Neill? But whatever they need we ain't got it. We're going down six thousand bucks." I fear my own failure in hers, accepted with such certitude and grace now at the end of the summer. Margaret asks if we have read the *Playboy* interview of Tennessee Williams. "It sounds like Tom, so honest." I shiver for anyone honest with the media. Tom she calls him. Wanting us to know that she knows him. Liking her by now, I ask about it. "Oh he's very happy now, rises early, swims, then composes for a few hours. Strict schedule, no drinking. Lives with a boy who adores him, simply adores him." I groan for him, how hideous to be adored by a youth with whom you may finally have nothing in common. You own home a sanitorium. How trapped all his life. The mother, then the sister. Now this. Still living it out, his guts in public.

Playboy no less. Remembering that desolating preface that describes waking up famous. The morning after *Streetcar*. His life ever after a not so slowly decaying ruin. America has eaten him alive. Now *Playboy*. "What a horrible life he has had," I say to her, suddenly loving the man. "Oh there was a time after Frank died, he was wretched, poor dear, but not now," she assures me. She saw him just recently, he told an awfully funny story about an ingenue coming to see him with champagne. "He rewarded her with a Wellfleet lobster. Just one." She bounces on to gossip about O'Neill's widow, how they say there are still some manuscripts. My soul protests.

How lucky they are, the people who dissect writers over dinner. The spectators who watch our scapegoats faded into dusk, starved themselves for the change they tried to make, but the artist caught so young because observed, bottled by the public in what their lives were dedicated to escaping, bleeding so long and obviously in the very ditches they spring from, their own early ruts. Scott and his booze, Williams and his faggotry, Mailer and his mania. Bonfires of themselves so fascinating everyone sits down to watch. And never notices the hand in the flames points in another direction.

Voices divert us into music. Two girls from the theater showing off in the dark singing duets by the water, their hair wet from swimming, their bodies young, shy as foxes when we all to them. Sing for us. And slowly with coaxing they come, their faces the same patrician Saxon cast as Celia's. The one named Katey is Celia fifteen years ago, the eyes as frank the voice as sure and then uncertain, singing Shakespeare's songs an echo upon the water of time in summer night perfection. But then I notice everything has gone all wrong. Claire is gone, the shadow of her feet naked in the sand under moonlight. Does she recognize that air? I follow, walking the beach to find her. But she is lost. Nowhere. Gone from me while I fidget, enforced hostess, my mind searching everywhere for her, frantic they should stay, as frantic they should leave. Then she returns as mysteriously. One cannot ask

her why or where. Reborn with relief and listening
politely to one girl's school joke, Prinderella and the
Cince she calls it, doing the whole recitation not once
but twice because someone was incautious.

When they are gone the last of them and the wine, lobster
shells a clutter upon the table will draw flies in the
morning, but tonight at last it is ours. The house the
safety of it ours, like the time awaiting us. Then I must
ask her, know my chances. Prepare my exits. Does
another door shut? She is evasive, perhaps unsure.
"People should make love on their vacations, it would
be a pity not to." Her voice trails off. I must push on,
take the risk. I will begin with Williams, using him as
a pretext. I talk of patterns and breaking through, insisting we can transcend the welts and scars of youth,
the deprivations of our childhood setting up eternal patterns we only repeat. But with a new and if necessary
heroic effort, the insight, the determination we must have
won by now, we can beat them, escape. Sighing at the
end of my tirade. Claire's voice booms at me from the
bathroom, "Right on Katsey, you solve the problems
of the world for a few minutes. I'll just have a shower."
I realize slowly that Mallory's boil, or is it Claire's now,
has reappeared under my arm. Mallory's boil, the interesting psychological outburst that flowered after
Mallory had lived with us a month when she first came
to New York. We fought continuously. I fell behind a
full chapter on my thesis and developed the boil.

Claire comes out of the shower and lights a cigarette.
And when we slept she wanted me. Her hand finding
me like a balm to my ravings, peace deep in my center
it will all stop hurting stop happening even. The whirl
of lights ceases. Comes to a halt. And listens. To the
nerves at the core throbbing for the touch of her finger
the sight of her head between my legs what honor in that,
it is what is done that speaks louder than mere words,
the gesture speaking that I am loved she will not forswear
me. Not this night.

We talk in the dark. In a rush I realize how little I

know her. "Tell me the people you have loved." And she tells me of Jennifer the two years in New York. Boredom, the thing gone dead, sitting alone in Russian bars playing the jukebox. Jennifer's brother a chemist she's convinced will be important someday, "And I loved him but Jennifer loved him more, it was incestuous. I was caught between them, they used me as a pawn. Finally I had to break away from both." Then the race car driver, her college chum now so in love with death, a stud transfixed by her purity, the one girl he couldn't have. And then her cousin, the sly cruelty of his lust. And finally solitude. Give them all up. There is no health in persons, study the mind instead five lonely years in analysis. Until a kind of peace disturbed by French. "French changed things. After that I could no longer hide. I let her crash at my place when she came down from Maine. Every night she was out in the bars, meetings, DOB. I would look up from reading Huxley's *Evolution* and there she was bringing the world through the door." As she talks I can see them, French as she was yesterday vital and butch, all the aggression of the Left in her pounding up the stairs on Fifth Street. Claire a student under the lamp at her desk, the big book spread before her, a dropout turned scholar, clinging to paper against the terrors of life. French changed things.

I am overcome with shame to see how little I have known her, almost a stranger to me, this remote girl lost in the years after school. Burned, picked over by people, and the time going by until you set yourself up alone somewhere in a coldwater flat and do some work. And try to call your soul your home, wondering always if it is. I make love to her past, its hurts, taking them in my fingers to solace them. Can I be of any help to one so tired of lovers? Stroking the soft inside of her thighs as if life itself depended on my effort to bring life new in her, the woman blooming as yesterday when I rushed from store to store buying her presents, a long lavender dress. Shy in it she put it on and lovely as now, her head thrown back its fine brow and curls dear to me, eyes closed in the press of coming my hand sure now it can give her joy, these few seconds out of time.

Now. Remembering then. In a stark white room seeing snow on a blank wall next door. Provincetown now in winter. Not Margaret's place today but another refuge. Because the workmen won, drove me out. And I cannot find the sea through the neighbor's walls. The notebook says when we woke I made love to her, realizing I am always the first to be taken. Insensitive. What was it like that morning, gray perhaps as this one? Thinking then it might be the last time. Don't come back. Stay in New York. Don't fly back after the panel. Provincetown over in this last time of love. This then might be the end. The evanescence of sex. One time fades into another. One cannot hold it. Always I think I shall remember this time always by the spot on the wall, by the stain on a sheet, by a particular and unmistakable cry she made. Or he. Fumio often cannot remember even the next day, says men never remember distinctly. But women? I do. And then again I do not. Remembering only an ache when they are gone. Or a generalized warmth when they are here. The joy of knowing I will get what I want, that it will not be withheld from me. As if acceptance in the flesh were all acceptance. And who can prove that it is not?

I put down my pencil to watch a cat shit carefully in a green plastic dishpan, the turds emerging like well-planned sausages, the animal aghast he should step in it, wretched that he cannot cover it, scratching distractedly at the newspaper underneath. Give up, you will never finish this book. Never pin down the past. Watch the cat. Yes, enraged as I am fighting with time and the dirt of myself, this book but a leaving off. How glad I will be when it is shed, the ego kicked off like an old pair of shoes, the phrase used in one of Claire's koans. Push on, it is not over. Make it then again.

The sadness of a rainy day in Provincetown end of summer. Intimations of age and death, the failure of love. The hopeless character of romantic infatuation, its terrible strivings. Cooking eggs this morning knowing disappointment even as they bloomed into aroma, perfect in their color and consistency. Claire will always find some way to be beyond my reach. This morning's crisis over an airplane, will she go with me, will she stay, the thing still not settled, only the inevitable neurosis of our condition. Then Fumio's voice on the phone, hearing its loneliness as the people troop by reflected in the window of a glass telephone booth, Fumio dejected. Raining too at the farm. Nell went back to town. "I will be a hermit," he says, "I only live in my work. Probably I'm adolescent. Just like you are. I think I just discovered it." I try to laugh at him, he who is always reproaching me with this. "How you are the great adolescent," he comes back, his voice thin, flat, toneless. Never has any resonance on the telephone. Today it is particularly tuneless, hurts so. The summer people course by, reflected double, two men in blue jerseys, two women in white hats. I am filled with remorse, a fool—all I have accomplished is the sorrow of this beautiful man, wanting me with him. But I am here. When does his emptiness fill? Or mine? "You are doing what you have to now," he absolves me partly. "But you will have to come down, get back on your system." Already he knows there will be September at the farm, on my system as he calls it, the final discipline of finishing my manuscript. His own work goes so slowly, the wooden typewriter creeping to a completion he does not even see yet. Could I give him energy and hope? Often when we are together he is at peace, yet lethargic, bored, needing other people to shine. Frieda is gone now to Mexico. A torn man, a retrograde planet spinning back toward monogamy.

I stand on the porch taking comfort from Molly. Her own past bouts with grief permitting me. He will be all right, she says, he is getting his stride back in solitude, "getting himself," as he calls it. But when I sit here looking at the sea, the dull melancholy wharf, long-haired kids in the foreground, must be eighteen inches those mops above their old clothes, like young animals casually eating in a circle around an upturned boat, my folly comes to a crisis in tears that are beyond guilt. I am failing. I am not doing well. Wrong, and have brought harm.

Private property is dead, I told Vita in the meadow after the march. But how do you cope with want, with Fumio being alone? Or my own dizzy impulse back to self-destruction? Claire repeats Celia. Admit it is neither of them at the last. Only your own genius at finding a way to be rejected, blind instrument cunning in its ingenuity, unconsciously maneuvering the most innocent situation until it is a trap your own past has built. Realizing, waking in anguish, lunging surprised down a corridor, astonished in the darkness. Recognized in panic. Too late.

Shall I say then that I have failed? Stop here. Give it all up, admit my fatal mistake. I must leave for the plane in a few minutes. Then it will all be over. I will stay in New York and not come back here.

The ballpoint drops from my hand. Look out to sea. And the young people sitting on a battered boat make me old. My eyes on a dull gray afternoon waiting for a red and white sail. Why will she not come? Catch the plane with me. Come at least to say good-bye. Is it deliberate cruelty? Unconscious resentment? Is it an act to know her by? This nothing, this vacuum, this negative gesture of not coming. Hurry, there is so little time. But she does not hurry. She does not come. I am blundered into the final folly. In love now—the very phrase is fatuous—and cannot escape, captured in the void. The treachery of the self's betrayal. I have let this happen to me. My mind hinges perilously on the appearance of a sail. Which will not come. The sea vast gray empty before me. It is inconceivable she could treat me this way. Always so direct and honest.

My faith runs out in the minutes. She has deceived me. Really false after all. Now when I have no choice any longer, I learn it. What is there to live for now? Death will be a rest, an exit from this shame, the sickening terror of love. Idiot, would you kill yourself over a girl who

won't show up in a sailboat? How I could murder her
with scorn, hot with anger, leaving her a note. I will not
come back. But the car? All her stuff, your own clothes,
notebook. You have to. Return quietly and do not see
her then? The parking lot in the morning. Steal away
without a word. Here, and not see her again? Unthinkable. How could I resist? Even the temptation to
tell her off in person. Rather than on paper. The note
starting—because you did not care, etc. No, tear it up.
Just the fact of departure, its very blankness a rebuke.
Does she want me to miss the plane? Will she ruin the
thing we have talked about so often? The nonviolence
panel, so crucial, the most important thing of the summer.
Doesn't she care? Is she resentful some corner of her
being, resentful that I go, that they asked me to talk?
It's not like her. Only twenty minutes left. Dressed now.
The wound in my armpit worse, Mallory's little namesake
violent in its swelling. Cursing Claire while I inspect
myself in the mirror, vain over the lavender shirt, the
immaculate white ducks. I will love myself. Hating the
image in the mirror though approving it. Then noticing
some verses framed next to the bed: "You are a child
of the universe, be at home in this world." Sort of stuff
Claire would dig. Odd, comes from a seventeenth-century
English church. Should one pay attention, forget anger,
recover peace? Ashamed to remember where I am going.
A hypocrite full of rage on her way to preach gentleness.
Why have you done this to me?

Staring at the sea. Please, please I whisper. But she
will not come to me. Go over to the theater. Check the
time. She has taken time from me, my wristwatch, spoiled
it in the sea the day I came. Giving me peace, I thought,
surveying the ruined thing, Fumio's old ticker carelessly
borrowed half a year till he got one of his own. Now
I see it was sabotage. For this, that I might miss a plane.
I am a crazy woman staring through the cashier's window
at their clock on the wall. Only fifteen minutes left. Roz
peeks out. "I got to catch the plane for New York, is
it easy to get to the airport?" "No problem at all, just
follow the signs." "That's fatal in someone with my

directional sense." "No really, it's simple. You're coming back?" I pause, caught by the question. "I'm just going down to be on a panel. We're debating violence in the women's movement, all the heavies. It's a family affair. No media. It should be fun." "Will Gloria Steinem be there?" "Yes, I think so." Roz makes a face. "What's she like?" "Not just the pretty lady you think she is. Very decent person."

Claire is gone. There will be no sail. Save yourself now. You have a job to do. Make your notes for the speech. This last act of faith. Doing it without faith because she was my faith, my teacher defected. I am abandoned to say these futile things alone. To insist on hope when there is none. Because she is gone who was hope. Surely this is not politics, change, or any actuality whatsoever, subjective fool, what has it to do with anything that a sail will not come? This angry, you can't even believe in an idea. You are full of hate, how can you talk for peace, say even that nonviolence is a way of life, when you can't live it? Five minutes left. Is she doing me a favor? Is she doing this to let me work? Yes, her better wisdom must have planned it this way. I have slandered her. Not understanding. Check the time again. Across the sand to the theater. How I wish I could find her, the old woman, I forgot her name, the fine elderly pioneer woman who started this theater. How good it would be to see an old face now. Could she help me? But just the clock staring back, emptiness in its face. What if it's wrong? Run to the street. A hip shop. No clock. Then to the druggist's. Through the alley. I will not come back to Provincetown. It is already past the time. Run. Just get out of here.

And almost miss seeing her, the boat floundering in the shallows, she cannot land it, fool of a sailor I curse her, hatred bumping into my joy. Her face is beautifully impassive. "I lost the rudder and had to go back." "Drag that damn thing up here, let's go." Watching her in fury hating even her beauty, my great treasure it was, as her legs flounder through the water. Like a stupid adolescent I think, silly toy of a boat. But dangerous if she goes

with me and leaves it here—might float away. Someone
might steal it. The two of us dragging it onto the beach.
"Ask those people to guard it," I order, afraid to ask
them myself. Circle of bearded prophets disdainful of
us two women. Would they laugh and watch it disappear,
this precious boat?

We walk along not speaking, my anger is silent, hard
against her, all over my body a plate of iron. She
apologizes matter-of-factly. It is the first time she has
ever had to apologize. But in no time she has found the
humor in it. "Isn't it interesting, we're having our first
little lovers' quarrel." Merry and unaware of the fury
in me. Has no idea what she has done, will never understand. This thing she has so carelessly jeopardized
mattered to me more than anything. My work, and she
sees it as a game, chuckling along beside me. "If you're
still mad, go on, punch me, punch me right in the
mouth." She stops. We are at the corner. She is barefoot,
the pavement is steaming. It is pointless for her to go
any further. She will lose her boat because of it. Her jewel
must not float away because of this. Then everything
would be lost. A total waste. The thing she slaved for
weekends at Bloomingdale's to buy. No, she ought to
lose it, I think, merciless, for what she has made me lose.
Then she would understand. I look at her face. Innocent,
not caring, not even worried. While the knowledge runs
yelling to my head the plane is already missed. I can't
make it. She has cost me all I had my work and my love,
how can I forgive? But you must forgive. You cannot
leave her this way. You cannot leave, hating her. We
both stop abruptly. "Call me the worst thing you can
think of," she invites. "Jackass." I say the word, it explodes between us like a jumping toy, a jack-in-the-box
merely ridiculous, "Couldn't you think of anything better
than that?" We laugh, standing still on the pavement.
The absurdity radiates in a circle around us like a smile.
"Go home and save your fucking boat."

Now I am on my own. Straight ahead, the parking
lot must be in the three hundred block near Margaret's.
I cannot remember where it was, we were talking, we

went from Margaret's house then back to Molly's, on
a hill somewhere. Suddenly realizing I do not actually
know. Sun burning the blacktop. Hot smell. Too hot
to walk and running. So many blocks, it's not here, fool
you have lost it now you will never get there. First the
car then the road then the plane. Already it is after four.
Now it becomes the worst. It is running. All lost now
the plane the speech the purpose. Claire you have cost
them all, yourself too. Because you are gone now. You
have cost me my work, I cannot let anyone take it, finally
all I have, myself, found in it—when all the people go
you have only your work. And I have thrown it away
on the love of a girl she is not even a woman no better
than a child in her whim. Watch it, you have found
another dangerous person who's sabotaged you. You
are back in the void again. This time robbed even of the
dignity of your work. Keep running. You can't go back,
tell them you missed the plane. Eat and sleep tonight
in Provincetown? No, never. Head running forehead hot
the actual heat the asphalt smell banging the lungs cannot
hold longer. Ask. Give in and ask. Where is the parking
lot I've lost my car? Like a moron. Stop or lose more
than that, arrogant nitwit.

Asking in the filling station they say the lot's that way
but it can't be, they are pointing at the city hall. It's not
that way it's at the high school. But they have turned
away. It must be this way I am right they are wrong.
Just a block or two more. No, they said the other way,
seemed sure. Back down the hill running I can no further
will faint in the heat. Of course they are wrong. It is to
the right up a hill and again nothing. The tedium of lost.
The repetition of it. Asking them again and they say back
there. But I go the other way. Then back exhausted. It
cannot be that way. I have looked. "Listen lady it's that
way now don't bother us we're busy. Either take our
advice or." "I have a plane to catch I am terribly confused I will miss it. Please help me." Throwing myself
at their mercy, a madwoman. "Well whadya want?"
The one winking to the other. Some dame. Must be out
of her head. "Can you drive me? It's an emergency, it's

terribly important. I'll miss a plane." It is just one human asking another human to help. "Just to the parking lot. Or to the airport, I'll pay you." "We got no cars free here, we're not a taxi company, lady." "Where can I get one?" My hands shaking my voice begging them never will I need something so badly. He spits on the floor and turns his back. "Phone there, lady. Use it if you got any sense left." Calling the cab. Then not waiting. I cannot wait. They will come. I will be gone. Running from the place their contempt laughing in my ears. "Crazy cunt." Yes, that is what I am. A nut bounding along the road to the next filling station where a man points that I am going in the right direction. The hill again? Not up that way. The real nightmare of lost. The nightmare awake. The heat, smell of the tar. My mind cannot hold. Lost. Everything. Now I am crazy again. Not up that way. Straight ahead. But there is the town hall. They keep thinking I want the town hall lot but it's the high school lot I want. Man on the street says two more blocks, then right up the hill, I will never get there. Lost again, another hell. Cars but not my car. Then I see it. Too late. Get in anyway. Drive. The airport. Somewhere. Rest, sit down, drive carefully. Then the highway, follow the signs. Airport. Yes. Right here. But it is not here. Further then in the sand scrub pines the sad beach forest. Lost in the woods. Race Point. Go on. But I must have passed it. I am crazy again. It broke. The mind just snapped like a rubber band. Try. Keep trying. Ask the cyclists. No, sorry, no idea where the airport is, keep on. No, I am back where I started. The supermarket. Give up then. Rest. You have just lost your mind, this deserves at least a cigarette break. No. Calm down go back please please, the sign around the observation deck. It points to the right. Back up, watched, don't hit that car, they said right, look right, no sign never find please Jesus mad crazy missed it turn right they never wait stop lock run the door swinging the counter mind life my hands shaking before him on the counter. "Girl, you missed that plane twenty minutes ago."

Yes of course that is how it is. Life goes by a schedule.

You miss it you are lost. There are rules. With timetables. You miss it, just too bad. There is plenty of time still. You can easily get from Provincetown to New York in the space of three hours during the twentieth century. There are airplanes. But that is not how things work. Planes, boats, they don't wait for individuals. Their purposes are larger. Like governments. One or two strangers in this little airport sitting about like brochures on the desk, neat in their little tin display trays, like maps folded into their chairs. That's how it is. Two men are using the phonebooth. Wait quietly until they are through. It is all over now but the explaining.

Then I am just a woman in a phonebooth. Calling New York a bit demented again, number after number, the mind's still there, enough of it to try this number look under Wallace, home and office. One busy. Other doesn't answer. Then Levine. She's the other organizer for this thing. Getting a man, says she's left. Try Wallace, the home one again. Perhaps she left early. Scramble of the pages and numbers, the shame of it still ahead of me. I will have to tell them I'm a fuck-up. Can't get there. Yes, it is ringing. Anticipating the disappointment in their voices, steeling myself for the inevitable recrimination of the people who depend on speakers to show up. And sometimes they don't. Get drunk in bars or something. A thousand times I wanted to. But this was never me. Now my case even more absurd. Missed the plane because Claire—but they think we are such great friends. How could I speak her defection? But of course not, it's all my fault I got lost. The surprise in their voices. Preparing what I'll say, yes I'm terribly sorry you'll have to get along without me. Well, they have plenty of speakers. Won't miss me after the initial shock. Then it hitting me. That none of this matters. That it's only that *I* wanted to be there. Wanted it for myself. Crying when I tell Anne Wallace, furious. "It's only four-thirty here, so it is possible to get there still but the plane has left, it was the last one out of here." "How about driving to Boston?" "It can't be done. Not time enough. I would need a plane and I lost it. Idiotic that this should have happened, I got lost and missed the plane." But I will never be able to tell her how much I wanted to be there. This will not interest her, she clocks the talkers, they show or they don't. Shrieking nearly, try to explain how important it had been to me. Then a man interrupting me knocking on the glass. Leave me alone. I am just this lost crazy woman long hair disheveled you can bloody wait. "Do you want to get to New York?" His voice coming through the glass. "Just a moment, Anne, there's some guy outside." "Yes, I had to make a speech. But I missed the plane." "Well, if you need to go you can charter one." Unheard of. It sounds suspicious. Expensive. Who cares? "Anne, he says I can get to Boston by the six o'clock plane. I would be there before it's over." "Fine. John will meet you." "Now he thinks I can make the five o'clock." "John will be at Kennedy as soon as you get there."

I follow him like a dog. He has seen me. He came out. The other guy told him this broad is supposed to be making a speech tonight, out there in the booth carrying on like a loony. He had an idea. One plane is just sitting there. She could charter it. Fourteen extra dollars. "What about this Bookbinder? Where is she?" "Not coming." I announce her betrayal calmly. No one notices. "O.K., we take it out of her ticket. You can cash in the rest at New York," they tell me, unaware good has come out of evil. And the organizers will get a refund. Then I'm following him again. To the airplane. This odd reedy little man, my savior.

It is as if there were a reprieve. From everything. There is mercy, I think dumbly. As if all the machines were for us. Just there to be used. For people and what they might need. As if time and space were things you could just calculate, and if possible, with the wonderful power of the machine—like flying—do it. It is as if there were cooperation. As if common sense, kindness, and imagination took over. Waived the rules. As if by a miracle the timetable were broken. Ignored.

It would be silly to thank him. Trying anyway. This man who has done the unthinkable. Doing even better by calling Boston, he'll go with me, see me onto the plane. Why? I want to shout at him. Why would you help me? Desert is out of the question. People who miss planes deserve nothing, not even good manners. But he wants to talk, of all things, about chivalry. Don't I believe in chivalry? Like a television question, "Hmm, well, I think it's more like good will, uh shouldn't we have it for everyone?" I would like to sort this all out but I am too busy. My hands shake in my gratitude. "You know I saw you come in. And you seemed pretty upset. So while you were out in the booth I asked the controller what's wrong with that lady? 'Seems she thought she had to get to New York, something about making a speech.' These fellows you get nowadays, they don't have much imagination." He leans toward me, nodding like a fellow conspirator. "Didn't occur to him to think of a solution. Lost his initiative the day he got the job. Then I remembered we had one more plane. And Pat here can drive. So I thought why not help her out." He jumps up around the cockpit, helping me some more by calling Boston again. "Yeah, we got her here, one of your passengers, we'll land her right next to your five o'clock." He is whimsical, delighted with his own ingenuity. It is as if everything is a game to him. There is time, there is distance, there is the machine. And the mind to play with them all. Toys real or abstract in the service of persons. He is the most astonishing man I ever met.

It is like flying when you lift in a small plane. All the excitement of how it used to be before the big ships and the companies. Here again fresh, the dangers of takeoff, the exhilaration of being in the sky, walking running through the clouds, big now the wings over them. Look down see houses like pieces in a Monopoly game. The power of it, the risk and the beauty. People, man has achieved this.

He leans back across his seat. "I was thinking about you the other day," he laughs. Astonishing sentence. Doesn't know me from Adam and thinks about me. "How do you know me and how come you think about me?" Humoring him. "Well, I was walking along Commercial Street with the wife. We saw a sign, said no female customers allowed. Seems that old codger runs the preserve store, jams and jellies don't you know, got so tired of lady customers he put up this sign. We had a good laugh about it. The wife, she's one of your fans, said Kate Millett would sure raise hell about this." I laugh with him, sick to be a folk figure to some curmudgeon, some bigot. Am I expected to hatchet the guy's windows? And how did he know my name? "Oh, we heard you were using the line last month when they made the reservations for you. But I didn't know it was you till I saw your name after I rebooked your ticket. You were just some lady in distress don't you know, some person, I guess you're right, maybe it isn't chivalry, just somebody needing help."

He looks like Mr. Luger who lived up the alley of my childhood, righteous Catholic father of six. But Bernadette drank and took morphine. Our neighborhood scandal, Bernadette the only living soul in the block, though everyone said it was a shame, Ernest Luger's such a good patient soul. And outlived her. Remarried. You can see him every Sunday at church. "I'll see you get on the plane," he calls back as we ready to land. Still looking like Mr. Luger, very sort of man I usually find so impossible to bear. Skinny bespectacled like Mr. Luger. This new father of mine. But he's not Mr. Luger at all. He is Mr. Van Arsdale. He is a novelty, a businessman who digs imagination, a member of the middle classes who would help someone in a phone-booth, a man with the power to do it who would break the rules and make an exception. Hugging him as he puts me on the plane.

Do I have enough for a drink? Yes, and twenty-five cents extra. The hostess fusses about being wife mother sex object nurse, every conceivable human need at once. She can tuck me in and they'll take off. The last seat is the first. Between two crewcuts. One is Contemporary Mathematics. One is Sports Illustrated. They are alive. I am alive. We are all fifty of us alive, having risked oblivion in a take-off, now living together in the sky. It is as if all rancor falls from me, discarded and thrown down upon a Boston runway, floating with my fellow men saved in the sky. We survive, foreigner or American, a community going from one place to another. Human beings. It is so simple. I can say it now. Having been through the madness again. I am alive with love. But take your pulse, check your condition. After the time in the dark lost. Did you kill anyone? No. Was not violent. Or only to myself. But that is its beginning. It was there, but just at the inception, someone intervened. Showed mercy. Showed what mercy was. A second chance. You have just been reborn in an airplane, breached in an aisle over Boston Airport. Rest now. Van Arsdale has saved you from yourself.

Consult the magazines for diversion. Here is a teacher who touched children. Now the country wants to hang him. His crime that he fondled their backsides, thought he was a father, loved them to the point of skin. Village in an uproar. Got a little girl to play patsy, turned him in, now all the children confused, betraying him. Within a week the entire town is lying so hard with accusations and rebuttals no one knows any more, truth disappears like before the witches. The man fighting for his life in teaching spends two years and a fortune to get back what he was. But it's gone. Here's Teddy Kennedy. Would you like him for President? Why not? That girl is why not. But we might have a better chance. A Kennedy, hope again in this place. They always give us that before the gun takes them. Would he be game enough to run? Made a speech at the Gridiron Club. A professional job. Politics. I'll just lift this quotation he has lifted from Aeschylus, touched by the words of a tragedian reprinted in *Look* Magazine. And lean out of the magazine's Irish romance power glamour to see Manhattan Island stretching like fingers in its wharves toward the sea. Then in glory the skyline in a haze of sun dying around the wings, flying right past the windows, its collection of towers like big blocks. It has never looked so dramatic in a landing. Proud with the burst you can have every now and again. To think I live in this town.

And John there on the ramp, I fall into his arms, both of us bewildered and glad. We could so easily have passed each other, the plane an hour earlier than he'd expected. Then driving, our talk speeding the highway. "Someone in the movement should be filming this tonight." "Yes, it really is a pity. But we made these rules to keep out the media. We expect Ti-Grace, you know, it's a real occasion." "Probably never happen again, all the heavies together." Maybe we ought to have taken ourselves seriously. We grin at each other over history at an underpass near the East River. John watches the car while I get us hot dogs. Consoling an old black woman who got mustard by mistake. Then off downtown. To the evening pavement outside. Everyone sitting on the curb in front of P.S. 41. Waiting for it all to start.

They are all there. All my old friends. There's Barbara, do you want some coffee? Here's Sidney and Ruth. Here's Sue Schneider, Peg and Louise. No, Bookie didn't want to come. The bubble of it all. How pleasant it is to greet people. Someone else has a beer. I know everyone. I kiss Gloria, some photographers hanging about, we mug for them. The two of us sit, leaning against the wall. When I move away someone bugs me about the picture with Gloria. Why did I let them take it? I don't know. Look blank. Why not, I guess. The voice bitches again, "Gloria's a star. All that star stuff. How come you go along with that?" "Gloria had her picture in the *Times* with me the day of the gay press conference. She got hell from a lot of people for that. Maybe that's why." The voice goes on scolding about the media, they're following Gloria around. "Tonight she's it." "Well, how do we keep them out?" In the foyer I ask a woman reporter not to take pictures inside. She promises.

Outside there is a hassle on the street. A strange-looking woman frantically struggling in a circle. A man drove her down from Massachusetts so she could attend this. She wants him to get in. The meeting is closed to men. He glowers at us from his car. Excluded. He must feel it is unfair. I remember that we are letting John inside. And realize that he's right. The woman is screaming at us. Women are shouting back at her. It is hopeless. They will not waive their rules. I put my hand on her shoulder to give her comfort, but she strikes it. A panel on violence and already we are committing it.

I go down the ramp to the auditorium. Frightened as always. Loathing the stairs to the stage. Prominence. Do not be a coward. You are with your friends, peers, the best minds of my generation and so forth looking along the table. Flo Kennedy, Anselma Dell'Olio, Gloria Steinem, Myrna Lamb, Robin Morgan. Martha Shelley at the end. Then out at the audience. How small it is. Disappointed. This topic should have done better, drawn more, but it wasn't advertised. Whisper campaign only. To avoid the elitism of media and stars we have ended up with the elitism of being in the know. The women here tonight are the core of the movement, the Feminists, the Radical Feminists, the Redstockings, members of consciousness-raising cells, the organizers. They are not likely to put up with being a proletarian audience very long. How nice it would be if they took over. Made it a general discussion. Then I wouldn't have to make a speech. Is this the room where we had the Congress? How fitting, one year later, to assess the damage we have done to each other since. We shuffle for who goes first. No one wants to. I am hoping to be last. It's up to Flo. "At my age and in my condition I may die before the rest of you get through," she starts off. Always the toughest. Her black wit booming them into joy. But she hedges on the issue, violence itself. Impossible to contradict or even follow, off in her usual metaphoric ramble, which defies logic or morality. Flo who has more wit, the most soul, the greatest generosity. The real mother of us all. "Everyone's sucking and licking, and I know how dangerous it is in a prostitute society to bite. Women live longer than their husbands 'cause they do the cooking. All that chocolate-covered bullshit. Baby, violence like power is in the hands of the establishment." Then the black line about any means necessary. Then to the point. Laying out her theory of horizontal hostility, how like all oppressed peoples we are masochists hurting only each other, underdog eat underdog. How working out our anger laterally we get nowhere. "Think vertical. Learn to piss up." Flo is all style.*

Gloria looks at violence from both sides. Listening, I admire her honest uncertainty. Are women disadvantaged because not acculturated into physical violence? Or, reading a passage from de Beauvoir, is violence an expression of the self too long denied us? Anger suppressed may be a kind of death. Then becoming personal, how her own ideas of violence were formed in the Toledo slums, a whole society built upon brutality. "You bowled on Tuesday, played pinochle on Wednesday. And beat up your wife or the nearest available black on Saturday. The ordinary way of expressing your masculinity. The Chicago police were really the boys I went to high school with. One can scarcely blame them for living out the ethic in which they grew up." The audience groans. Flo shuts them up. Gloria goes on. "The violence of America is not primal violence but systematic, institutional violence, the health system, the schools, the draft." Laying into the bureaucratic. "Remembering my childhood and having first rejected violence on visceral grounds, I was attracted to it for intellectual reasons as the means to an end. But I rejected it at last as something I cannot justify." She qualifies, uncertain again, "Unless one's life is threatened." Hesitant and moving as she finishes, "Somehow we must save the executioner from being the executioner as well as the victim from being the victim."

Then Myrna. Her face always like a woman lifting her head after a beating. Grateful at the applause. Her long isolation since the play failed, the spiteful attacks made on her made larger always by her suffering. A woman who has had so little. Marriage at seventeen to

---

The speeches of the other panelists are not recorded at length or even with accuracy. The following is simply an impressionistic reconstruction from notes taken at the time.

a soldier, four kids, six years of night school getting
through college. Finally writing plays, getting produced.
Then Joe Papp did her *Mod Donna*. And then it collapsed, because we let it, the movement wouldn't come.
Or not enough of us. "We are the violated," she begins.
The audience love it. Admitting that she feels violence
herself. "Less on a global than on a personal level, violence toward other women. Women who will not accept
me." She has hit a nerve. It is not popular. It is real.
Telling of a moment in childhood betrayed by her
mother before an unsympathetic father. The old man
called her queer. Her mother connived, turned her face
away. "I wanted to kill her, the knife in my hand." Her
voice shakes. "Now my father saw his chance, joyfully
he beat me unconscious. Why didn't I turn the knife on
him instead? That has been my problem. It might be
yours too." There is understanding, but it is confused.
She reads from her work, a passage in the *Mod Donna*
where one woman falls upon another in rage. Now she
sums it up. "The worst we can do to the cold woman is
to fall out of love with the man." Great applause. But
one has the feeling she is still not being understood.

Anselma Dell'Olio reading nervously from her typed
papers. So hurt still. Her hands trembling in her courage.
The violence women in the movement have done to each
other. The essay is tense, lucid, but ultimately pointless
in its despairing recommendation that we turn our violence outward. "Because there is no alternative." She
makes a reference to the paper she read at the Congress, her voice bitter with the memory of it. "The kan-
garoo courts, the juntas where we sit in judgment, the
violence we solemnly and righteously practice upon each
other. We have failed to change ourselves. There is no
solution."

Martha Shelley says she's violent. They applaud, delighted. She presents them with a rolling pin. Hilarity.
She entertains them with her Weather trip, her days and
weeks of guilt over not having blown anything up.
"Dynamite is elitist, it costs money. I had no backers. I
read the *Anarchist's Cookbook* before bed, but it re-

quired too much chemistry. I took karate and hurt my back. After one street fight I gave up the sport. He won. We both got arrested." Then Martha gets down to business. "Tonight I'm starting an anti-rape squad." Long rigmarole of organizational tactics, calls for volunteers.

The microphone is passed to me. The notes trembling in my hand. At this rate I might as well abandon them. No, don't chicken now, the faces looking up, waiting, I must reach them, say this thing I came to say. There's still Robin. She'll speak for violence. I want to be last. If Robin follows, violence will have the last word. I also want to be last because I am afraid. Telling them that, asking them if they are often afraid. The question sounds odd, invading, too personal. Response is quizzical, spotty. I am in for it now, I have to speak. Hoping so that I can say it. Opening every vulnerability to admitting how I got lost today and nearly didn't make it, how I was helped by unreasonable kindness. Wanting to shout like a cheerleader, Van Arsdale saved me. From the void, from the madness of my own self-violence. But how could they understand? I must say it in the terms they know, in a voice they can hear. Mentioning how when I first read the leaflet I thought it said violence *and* the movement. Big current controversy, the political question of the Left. "Then I looked again, it said violence *in* the movement. I was relieved. Here was something I really knew about." They laugh, understanding. "Look, I have seen my friends savaged in this movement." It is not a nice thing to say. "By other women, and we have all done it. We have done too much of it." They are annoyed hearing this. "And it hurts far more to be hurt by women." Their voices rumble, protesting. "Hurts more than the abuse of men." There is an echo back, rejecting my words. "Men are the enemy," I hear from a few voices. "I have been hurt more by women because I love women more." And the protest subsides. I go back to the Congress last year, "Nothing so debilitates or immobilizes as hatred. I have seen sisters, friends I have worked with for years in this movement rendered incapable, no longer able to work.

Our trashing each other began then. Women shouted each other down. Free speech was not permitted. But what I heard behind the shouting was the voices of men, our boyfriends in the Left who cooked up the idea that trashing is the true revolutionary form of discourse."

Wondering as I say it, do they also feel that we are past this, that a new spirit has come to us in the spring? That we are ending this long winter's totalitarian chaos, that we have had our fascist era and that it's over now. A woman heckles me, "Do you know what fascism is?" Flo annihilates her in a snort. But I register her objection. Of course she is right. I had meant only verbal and emotional fascism. So we haven't executed anyone in the flesh. But isn't the mind and its reality where things begin?

Shaky, going on, "I should like to take this occasion to come out." Laughter while I camp it. "Look, this isn't a rerun. I've got *Time* Magazine to publicize my sex life. So it's not that I'm gay. Today I'm admitting to something still less socially acceptable. A pacifist." I wait wondering how they will take it. The word so hated in the Left. To the hecklers, "All I can do is to ask you too to be human to me. To listen." Finally I have said it, still afraid but moving now into the sentences. "I want to speak in favor of and as an advocate for nonviolence." The worst is over now. I have taken my stand, drawn a line between myself and the other speakers. None of them went this far. "I want to say that it is a way of life. Something I can imagine, but cannot live in yet. I am always on my way and always failing . . .

"My deepest commitment to nonviolence comes from having suffered violence as a child. Where violence begins. Violence begins with how we abuse children. And growing up, these children perpetuate the violence they've known upon other children. There is a kind of panic, a terror when you're a child being beaten that can make you kill one day. Later. That can make men into soldiers. It can also make one into the psychologically violent species women are. The violence done to children is the root then, the first imprint learned that makes war or atrocity possible. I believe there's a killer in all of us. I know there's one inside me. When you know the killer in you and you know also that you do not want to kill, you have to set yourself upon a course of learning. Not to kill that killer then, but to control it. To accept the responsibility of your knowledge that killing other human beings is in fact easy. A possibility. But not what you want to do.

"Take this then at the political level. Consider the current discussion on the expediency of revolutionary violence. The question of violence and the movement. The idea of armed revolutionary violence begins with a peculiar idea. That there are two kinds of human beings in the world—them and us. If they hurt one of us, it's bad. If we hurt one of them, it's good. This is essentially inhuman because it denies the humanity of the other, now an enemy. Once begun there is no logical termination to violence. After you've killed the first, why not the second? How does one decide? In a society which is racist or capitalist or sexist how much of a racist or capitalist or sexist do you have to be to get it in the head? I'm one. You're one. What is the safe percentile? How do you stop ideological crime once you've started it? How do you preserve the purity of revolution when you have already committed crimes in its name? How in the name of justice will you attain the justice you went out to get? With the first act of cruelty committed in the name of revolution, with the first murder, with the first purge and execution, we have lost the revolution."

Some agree. Some don't. Flo bitches them. I ask the people who are impatient to hear me out even though they disapprove. "Your forbearance," I beg, terrified of their unthinking anger. "I've been talking about politics. Where the means corrupt and prevent the end. Politics is repetition. It is not change. Change is something beyond what we call politics. Change is the essence politics is supposed to be the means to bring into being. The argument for change is an argument for the end of violence. Of all kinds. Economic, psychological, political, social, physical. We are women. We are a subject peo-

ple who have inherited an alien culture. We have never
taken the initiative. It will be difficult. But as outsiders
we're somehow fortunate in having the opportunity to
do something not only very grand but very different. To
discriminate carefully and select from among the possibilities of the past. Better yet, to invent. As women we
have already begun to develop a new social dynamic,
challenging the traditional hierarchy of station and place
in meetings, the conventional notions of leadership, authority, and talent. More than that, we are challenging the
traditional separation of the public and personal, those
segregated categories of life we've inherited from the
past. In discovering the vital integrity of all human experience, we've reintegrated and subsumed these artificial distinctions. In all these ways we are forging a new
politic. Or rather we are transcending what is usually
called politics and arriving at change. And the first prerequisite is to transcend all the violence we feel toward
each other and the world. I'm recommending something
that I know sounds extreme, something about which I
feel continual doubt and ambivalence. I'm saying that
we must invent then a new method for the conduct of
human life."

I stop for a second, winding up. Then wanting to say
it, to make it happen for them as it has for me today
in a vision. Van Arsdale. Claire. Lost. Then found. Hitting on the quotation printed before me. "Aeschylus defined it this way, 'Our purpose must be to tame the sav-
ageness of man, and make gentle the life of the world.'
If we are to succeed, if change is to come there must be
mercy. There must finally be love."

Stopping. Realizing I have not said it. For a second I
was transformed by what I had spoken. Living it. This
strange euphoria, this boundless affection. But what is it?
And why did I fall back on the word mercy? Chris-
tianity, love, why are there no new words? Humiliated. I
have failed. Hearing nothing. Vanity of the applause
meter. Then it starts. Just a few, finally all, perhaps they
are being sporting. I had asked them to love me, loving
them. So happy to hear their approval. But wait, are you

grandstanding for yourself? Have you really fulfilled the
mission you came on? That is above the applause.
Doesn't even mean anything, only a performance carefully wrought? Politics as drama as an art form, if you
would win their judgment, sway them, you need the best
command of language. I should have written it down.
What does it matter anyway, Mallory was right, yelling
at me up at the farm that it was silly to debate. One believes or one doesn't. But I came here with an alien view
knowing I was an advocate for the unpopular cause.
Well, I'm lucky they sat through it. Now Robin concludes with the argument for violence.

She begins with a trick of rhetoric, turning the question on its head. "Will someone please explain what
could justify nonviolence?" The crowd is pleased. She
continues with riddles. Mothers are required to be violent
on behalf of their children. Otherwise they are not "real"
women. But in our own behalf, violence is begrudged
us. "If we developed a violence of our *own* it would be
more witty, more deadly." Appealing to their chauvinism. More applause. "But our violence is toward each
other, toward kids, toward ourselves. Because it has nowhere to go." Growing excited now. Stirring them more.
Then Fanon, violence is purgative. Then moving into
paranoia. All men are violent, are rapists, the FBI's training infiltrators for the women's movement. Cheap humor
—NOW thinks it's groovy, it'll get women some cushy
job. Pandemonium. Robin is moving into a poem. But
first an odd prologue that we should all rally round
"when the shit comes down, and it will come down."
Usual way to stroke the flames. The audience in raptures. Then pain in her voice. "We are not healthy.
This poem is one last word to the men." Listening I
realize it is not a poem but a slice of her flesh. Bitter and
eloquent, an appeal to Ken and the child. A labyrinth of
ambivalence. A wealth here of jealousy, Robin's rage
locked out by the menacing figures she sketches for us
at the kitchen table, Ken and his male lover, while their
boy-child sleeps a room away. And the time the child
saw her naked and laughed, called her a "monster." His

fancy caught by some caricature from television, furry as
a woman is furry. Monster. Her shock rocking the
poem, the sting of it, a mother's body rejected. Female.
The cry comes from the poem of a woman strangled.
Dying, going crazy. Hallucinating being killed, killing.
Wanting her words to become bullets. Monster. Saying
that we may have to kill even kill men into their freedom. "Beautiful!" a voice yells from the audience.
Robin goes on, predicting the loss of her child, Ken, the
loss of herself preceding all. "How do you stop from going crazy? No way, my sister, no way." Then female
mysticism. Mysticism of violence. The word "monster"
echoing through the end of the poem. Her voice full of
tears. "May I realize that I am a monster. I am a monster. I am a monster. And I am *proud*." The audience
grows wild with listening to her finish. Shouting, standing
up. Well, she has won I think. Fitting. The laurel for a
poet. But what does it mean? Has she expressed them
best?

Then it is Ti-Grace. Late. Peculiarly late. Deliberate,
I think watching her come to the stage more than peculiar in black pajamas. Does she think she's a Viet
Cong? Ti-Grace. In so many ways our finest mind,
dimmed now, beyond us. Her face cold as it always was.
Resolute as it always was. Her whole figure rigid against
affection. Its singleness. I see fire hating warmth. Alone.
Only Flo to welcome her. She will no longer acknowledge the rest of us. She will not sit with us at the table.
Too elitist to join the elite. Standing behind the podium
lecturing as if it were Columbia again. The impossible
language of the Ph.D. candidate, too far out by now to
ever finish her degree. She congratulates the panel of
superstars—"They are legitimate experts on violence because they are its targets both in and outside the movement." Nicely put. Then the wit of magazines. Someone
has sent her a book entitled *The Power Tactics of Jesus
Christ*. "Of course I immersed it in water immediately."
Something is going wrong. I cannot hear her. The words
fast, disconnected. Does she speak in sentences? Calls
come from the floor, "Talk into the mike." Her voice

too fast. Nervous, I think. Isolated. Realizing she does not even try to be understood. She disdains them. Too afraid now to communicate. But it is brave of her to come. Out of her glittering and remote distance. Into this danger. Here in the movement itself where she might be challenged, where she cannot play the ultraradical leader of Women's Liberation. Here in the family. Here among her peers. She has been a star too long too high and too far away. I know so well how it can make you crazy. The pain of it. But I remember its arrogance too, the lighted figure in such solitude upon a platform, you come to hate the hands that clap, the faces looking up. The suckers. So remote finally you never want to come back. She is all of that, this chilly southern belle upon her way to the stake. Only that can satisfy her now. Since we were friends once and Ti-Grace my guru hours upon the phone—how she coerced one with her superiority. No ingratiation of the mind was ever sufficient, two graduate students and the brighter one playing master Leftist, could I get the right answer, pounding upon it like the dogs in seminar. Since there is that always between us I will listen with another ear and insist she make sense. Translate. I will pretend she is talking to me. I listen harder. Taking notes. Phrases I try to register, "violence is not available to us as a class," "women are a special class perceived," "men are a class positive," "men are the enemy, the oppressor or class focused upon if verbally assaulted it is mere militancy of the mouth." Her scorn. But it is so hard to hear. Then I realize she does not want to talk to me, an old friend, any more than the rest. Mumbling. I catch some phrases— "ingratiating myself by pretending this is serious." Then a sentence or two later—"violence is not possible for us. We pick targets we can hit—makes you feel better." "Why are we here, instead of leaning on St. Patrick's? Why don't we go up there and hang around?" Then a tirade against Catholic University. "Like a fortress—blue, they were—I was violence just walking in the door." This is where she was attacked, I think, her life threatened, that's what's on her mind—say it. That you are afraid for your life. I fear for it too. But she swerves and digresses into parody, feminist marchers are about hoof and mouth disease. We are all mouth. If we were going to do violence would we sit here talking? Then another switch. We are rebuked for not being involved in the Italian-American civil rights struggle. Why aren't we working with them? "The Mafiosi are real—they're not about writing poetry." Unkind cut at Robin, who shouts at her hysterically, "Yes, they're real, they're about killing and making money on prostitution." Never flustered by disagreement Ti-Grace does not hear. She unrolls a poster. "O God, her visual aids," someone groans. It's a picture of a man dying. A bullet in his head. "That's violence," she shouts, suddenly clear. "You've been talking about these things. Now look at them." It is "sister Joe Colombo," she taunts them. Jeers and catcalls. The audience come alive out of sleep and erupt into hatred.

She is brilliant, I think—she is the best teacher we have —she will give us the hardest case, a Mafia boss, and impose his humanity upon us. Rub our noses in his bullet wounds. Teach us humanity. The rest of us used words. She is more perceptive. I am a sculptor and a filmmaker but I did not remember how better a picture than mere words. Abstractions. Verbal emptiness. She reminds me. Always the brightest of us, the farthest out.

But now she is off on a wing again. Catholic University. For a full ten minutes she is perfectly unintelligible. Myrna and Anselma begin to break out in nerves. "Will she never stop." The word is whispered along the table she's been talking thirty minutes. If she isn't turned off soon the audience will kill her. Must have a good forty-five minutes of this left in her and she is completely incomprehensible. Suddenly Ti-Grace is screaming "Who is going to protect us when violence comes down on us? If you want to change things they'll kill you. The black movement had heavy casualties. It's ugly. People groove on you till the shit hits." Now she puts Colombo before us. A man struggling to learn. She tutored him. I writhe, remembering how she taught Hegel at DOB. She is obsessed with Colombo's assassination. "It

was a case of political violence." She is equating him
with the heroes of the Left. The audience protests. It is
an outraged voice. An animal force against her. Anselma is ready to go berserk in public. Myrna an exhausted heap. Ti-Grace will go on forever. "I told her
to stay home," Flo rumbles. The audience scream that
Colombo was a thief, a pusher, a man who prostituted
women. Flo leaves for another meeting, mailing two letters with one stamp as it were by telling the audience
she is protesting the fact that no one listens to the
speaker. Ti-Grace calmly announces that Cleaver and
Malcolm were criminals too. Rapists and pimps.

Then she nails them. "You are saying he's a criminal,
therefore you do not care if he lives. And you tell me
you care about human life?" Brilliant, I think, cheering
for her, how wise she is, how much the best of us, demanding the best. But then another crazy move—her
assassination fantasy returns like an attack. "How many
people when Malcolm was shot . . ." Does she think
she is Malcolm? The audience is shouting her down.
They should listen. Have respect. Hear her out. But that
presupposes she wishes to be heard. Talks in English.
"When the shit comes down you're alone." Is she that
determined to be killed? They are throwing things
now. Paper balls bounce on the stage. She must stop.
She will be hurt. They will damage her forever. Already
so damaged. She should stop. Be stopped even for her
own good. In a moment they will be upon the stage. Run
her off. Hurt her. "At Catholic University they had guns
in there but I wasn't hit 'cause we only burn bras."
Then you're safe, I grumble. Why must you court danger? "What people do for you," she screams, "what he
got was three bullets in the head. I'm saying relevant
people do—now if you want to write it off. Mrs. Bozell hits
me"—Martha Shelley calls for questions—"raises her
hand for the second blow, a black man shot Malcolm"
—her voice lost in the bellowing against her. They have
shut her up. She is there alone on the podium, still sputtering. She can no longer be heard. I go up to her. "Give
up, they will not listen." Taking her hand. She rips it

away. Strides out of reach. Leaving. Stay, I plead, stay, talk, don't leave us. But she won't. Cold and obdurate to the last. Theatrical in her exit.

Phony, I think, sitting down. Angry with her. But more with the ones who would let her egg them on, baiting them to hurt her. Making executioners of them. Taking this vast amount of so many people's time and patience—the ultimate insult—she refused to communicate. And they went for her. How boring it is, this eternal collusion of the prey and hunter, boring in its eternal misunderstanding of how things need be. So obvious it seems. But in a crowd no individual bothers to acknowledge common sense, rage takes over and jeers. No, it must stop, I think, for once it must stop. The floor is lining up for questions. She is gone. No one seems to care. Suddenly I remember. But of course, they couldn't hear her. So no one got the point. She was careful to make herself utterly unintelligible, first in her prose, which I went mad just deciphering, and then in her delivery, done so that not one word in ten ever registered over the microphone. Ti-Grace who has made hundreds of speeches. Why on earth did she do this to us? "Could I say something?" I butt in. "I also found it hard to follow Ti-Grace. But I've known her for a long time and I was sitting closer so I think I got some of it. What she was saying to me was that she's afraid, has already been threatened with death and knew someone who has just been destroyed. Colombo. Perhaps all this was apparent. I found it very opaque. Underneath she is telling you she's in danger, needs your support. Her feeling of danger has so mesmerized her that it has become real. She is in fact in great danger. There is a way one provokes danger." Trying hard to convince them she is the most hurt, the most isolated. Feeling the danger so imminent to her, urging them to reach out to her in person by mail by phone in the immediate future. How odd it sounds. Who would bother to carry it through? Will I tomorrow, when I feel normal? Feeling already it is doomed, it is in the things left undone that we commit crimes. Realizing that in her cold and curious way she has asked them for her life. Asked them to love her in a way perfectly calculated to provoke their hatred. Understanding suddenly by a prescience as powerful as Ti-Grace's own specter of her death that yes, it *could* all happen. That she could go on this way till somehow she were hurt. And then it would be too late. Understanding suddenly her solitude and how it invites violence, how alienation is fascinated with its own death, preparing by a thousand subtle machinations its perfect proof. Unless there is intervention. But by now it would require force to bring Ti-Grace back to us. Because she will not come. But having given us so much, we owe it to her. And to ourselves that we do not become accomplices, traitors to what we meant to do, avoiding the martyr's lust and our own guilt to follow, having permitted her.

Gloria explains how Ti-Grace got in with Colombo. A scrub lady complained of her circumstances to the Human Rights Commission. Fired. Went to the women's movement for help. Ti-Grace gave it. Wrote and upbraided the union. The union spit on Ti-Grace. But the union is scared of the Mafia. Ti-Grace goes to the Mafia. Colombo gets scrub lady her job back. And then Colombo got shot. "This is her experience, she identifies with him." Robin reports loudly that she's been firebombed and she also feels unsafe. "But all women are unsafe." As for Colombo, all this doesn't make her feel any pity for "a man who put millions of women into prostitution, some of whom bleed uglier deaths"—screaming, hysterical, now banging the mike. The crowd goes mad. Colombo is settled. He isn't human. Ti-Grace has lost.

A woman speaks from the floor. Heavy in a striped shirt, an old Radical Feminist. I remember her. She hissed Anselma at the Congress. She says the stars whine. "And we are pretending that differences are personal which are merely political differences after all. Sisterhood is nonsense. All women don't love each other, that's crap." She was knifed last weekend. Wants us all to get guns. Anselma zeroes in. "How long has she been in the movement?" "Three years." Anselma's been in five. The audience raises hell. I cringe for Anselma, who is losing her temper. Myrna solves it all by suggesting the "political reasons" are often sibling rivalry. Describes her own agony being attacked as having made it off her sisters' backs. "I never made a fucking thing," she sobs at them. "All my writing came out of my gut." Then her voice despairing, "We can kill each other, it's easier really." A Leftist in a workshirt informs me the working class cannot transcend violence as I recommend. Martha becomes our expert on the working class. The next woman wants to become violent, beat men at their game.

I am still hearing the previous exchange. The quarrel between stars and the anti-elitists. Then a kid in a plaid shirt says she's going to put in on the line. "We're attacking the panel because they've done what we haven't." Her example not a superstar situation at all but some humble little committee organizing for the Christopher Street march. She and a friend did all the work for it till its leisured members decided they had been elitists. Her outrage still fresh. "That we had volunteered and worked. And got dumped on." She has to fight for each sentence. No one will sympathize. I remember how Joan Brown used to be trashed just for talking well. A registered nurse with a kid. Worked on the night shift. Her crime only her eloquence. Of course it is unfair. The girl still trying to be heard. She is right. But the ones who shout her down are right too. In a minute they will annihilate the panel, plunge their superstars, so loved and so hated, into interminable oblivion. Because they ought to. Yes, we have done what they wanted to. Talked. Written. Got it together. And they will never forgive us for it. And why should they? But yet how odd. That is how it started. It was for their right to express themselves that we expressed ourselves. But it is not the same. We have done it. Now we have made it. They haven't. Why don't they leave us alone, let us do our thing? Why must they take from us our hard-won identity? Why must the pen be torn from my hand? Because they never got one. But why so rigid? Why either or? Why not both? You do your thing, I'll do mine.

But they cannot do their thing. Why? Money. Time which is money which buys freedom. Or just the confidence to do it. That furthest beyond, that above all because if you have it really together in your head you could write *War and Peace* on the subway. Confidence. Believing in yourself. It is another kind of opportunity lost. Which we must find together. As hard for us now, the star-crazies, as it is for them, the star-crazed. Because we are as necessary to each other as black and white, rich and poor, two halves of the dichotomy forever at war over the wrong bone. Our own tragic failure to cooperate. To help each other accomplish. Deluded into believing that there is a limited supply of paper in the world, of art, of achievement, of recognition. But there's the rub. The supply of recognition is limited, regulated by the system. If you believe in it. And they have. We all have. Stars and antistars together we believe. How do you make everyone famous? By killing fame? Not by killing the famous, noticing suddenly how hot it is up here. I want to get off.

Megora diverts us now with the ultimate paranoia. The SWP will kill us all. Megora the female minister of a gay church, Megora the soul sister in a dog collar. At this moment off her rocker and raving about our imminent destruction while the entire audience yawns and wants to go home. A note is passed along. There is a party. I admire Megora, am enormously fond of her, but I cannot believe a word she is saying. "The SWP are bumping sisters off in Boston." One terrible story after another. No one listens. It is over.

Alone. And going back. The plane lifts with the same uncertainty that lovers know. Yet I knew this morning when I woke. In the bald light of a Brooklyn apartment. Seeing in my own daze the figure of a girl on a couch. Someone else who slept over. Waking at nine to find a clock, knowing it was already too late. Everyone had already missed work. The party went on till five. When I fell asleep John promised he would drive me to the airport at seven. Of course it was impossible. But there will be other planes. And there's no real hurry. Because I know I am going back. Now it is only time until I am with her. Calling to say I'll be late. Margaret's voice then Claire's, with its usual crabbed edge of the higher spirit who despises machines. But do I detect relief? Had she feared I might not come back? Relishing my power. "We stayed up too late and I've missed the plane." Noticing how I have missed a plane and feel cavalier about it—does it even our score? Have I heard or do I imagine the slight pause of disappointment? It is enough. Already I am hurrying to be there. Can get back before noon.

It is only time. And a little patience. Enduring Marsha's eggs. Her job at the back of a shoestore among receipts where no one ever comes. Her parents need the money. Detecting my own animal self in the trap she describes. Gathering myself to jump. So back to the sea. Get out of this fetid city. Its lines of traffic in the heat. Suffered through with John on the desolate overpasses in Queens. Ahead is the airport. And John, this kind young man driving me, is a man strangling in an advertising agency. Wanting to be a lawyer. In the gray dirt of a railroad crossing he explains degree requirements. The ghost of my pedagogue returns for a moment to give him recommendations. Wendell Johnson at Hunter might help him.

The plane in air now. And the voice begins in my head. My tormentor who would write. Muttering about the other book, the one in your head that you don't dare write down. Why? Have you less confidence in it than in this one? Or is it too disparate? Mere tidbits of thought, memory, grasshopper trivia. Are they things you protect from invasion? You who have murdered privacy. Your crime. So what do you protect now? A fantasy self in Mexican shirts thinking she's glamorous and hoping women will love her, bit of a character, always carried a large disheveled bag, drives an outlandish old car, is tickled when people discuss it. They indulge her. The great fault in her character, this insatiable thirst for affection. Does things people are not going to love her for. And then insists on being surprised when they hate her instead.

And the worst vice. Wanting to be thought well of. "A particularly nice person." Odious phrase. Reaching to protect this self with irony. Take that young sniper, if you're there. How long could you go on keeping the book in your head before it got longer and longer and burst through the skin, wrenched out the hair? But you will never remember it all. There you will fail for sure. It will never be the exact copy, the documentary you have projected. Authentic, as Nell would insist. Don't neglect the banal, she advised. Surely there is enough of it.

Back to this vice of wanting to be a good person. Few notions are so repellent. Bookie's "exceptional human being." Perhaps everyone in the world harbors this ambition. I'll bet millions share the same sneaky desire. Could it be a general malady, this last nasty proclivity? What the devil is goodness? You might try another word. Virtue? Sounds like Spenser and Milton, that puritan rot of chastity. No. Who then is good? Gandhi. But he's not sexy. Not only a vegetarian, but a sexual abstainer. But that won't do for you, you're a hedonist, a lover, want to have a good time, laugh, booze, make love, talk all the time, play with your friends, run around from place to place. Fly, stay high, living it. So you will have to think of something else then. Keep chasing it. Perhaps it will be another word. Freedom? All these nouns sound tired, frayed at the edge from overuse. "Good" is still there. You learn it in childhood. It is strong, English. But it gets mixed up with other things, Sunday school, righteous behavior, the reality of respectable persons. So it is more like liberation? But that sounds like rhetoric. No, it is a way of inventing the self. Striving toward one you can live with. Like the feeling I had that night I just stayed home alone and scrubbed the floor. But is it a private thing finally? And you lose it when you are public. Lost it by writing even if writing helps you find it. By publishing you may get lost again. Belong to other people again. And be lost another time? I read *The*

Golden Notebook at a low ebb in the months after I came home from Japan. And knew Lessing. Not because I thought the book was about her. It was about me. Too naïve then, a graduate student, didn't know yet that all books are about the people who write them. But she has always the protective coloring of fiction. And no wonder people have kept it so long.

There are writers of books on this airplane. Editors. Members of the intelligentsia. Behind me a guy who could be somebody like Barney Rosset is talking about the young writers. I wuld like to meet him. But I'm too shy. He is a celebrity. I begin putting him down in my mind. He talks too loud. Sounds like Mailer and the fight mystique. Cigar in his mouth. Rosset had my friends arrested when they sat in at his publishing house. Since I am too timid to introduce myself I can invent a thousand calumnies against him. How petty I am. How delightful it is to shit on a big shot. A name. Of course people enjoy it. A minute ago you were blabbing away about wanting to be good. But look over here, see that reverend old man walking down the ramp now. Surely he is an illustrious person. Everyone treats him with great deference. He must be some saintly man of letters. I should like to kiss the hem of his jacket. He is met by a serene woman who embraces him. Her lovely face calling out his name. But I miss it. Should I ask his name of the stewardess? No, I will make him a mystery.

I insert the key in the back window. It rolls down. My face disappears. There are wild flowers in the parking lot. Turn the ignition. The voice will stop when the engine starts. You're not expected to write while you drive. A safety hazard. Think about other things. It must cease. Take that pen out of your mouth, you're driving. And there is the bend and the sea. It is still here, stretching crisp white sand under the perfect sky. It dances. It glistens. One long line of sea opens to me. A red sail. I am back.

Damn you, Bookie, where are you? I have come back. Only to find you gone. Wasting the precious time in mere waiting. Forever waiting on my porch for a sail. Stranded in Provincetown with nothing to do but wait. I have tried swimming but there is no water. A whole ocean and not enough water. The tides have taken it away. One walks out for miles but it's still only up to the knee. I have had a little lie on the beach, exposing my poor boil to the sun, agonizing in my hideous thirties tank suit. A far cry from the imperious beauty telling you to get out of that boat and walk. That was yesterday. A lot of Millett in me, can be like the towering aunts when I'm up to it. Which is not often. You were in your bathing suit. You looked stupid. Such a lousy sailor. A bathing suit so you'd be sure not to have to go to New York at the last minute, change your mind. So I lay on the beach and decided that since I am neither a glamorous nor romantic person but merely myself looking tacky in this lamentable black rag of a swimming suit, the boil in my armpit baking in the sun—that you would be sure to show up.

But nothing is sure. You still evade me. I have been stoic and covered an English muffin with peanut butter. But you still make me wait. You are not here. Nor at the other place. The phone rang unanswered. Do you still maintain that totalitarian schedule you invented the first day? Disappear after breakfast to read and sail and don't come back till nine at night for dinner. I wrote twenty-five pages that day. You looked a little wistful. Did it hurt you to stay away? But now you're good at it. Abandoning all the pretensions of style today, just blathering on. If I read books as you do I'd occupy myself more constructively. At the party last night Ruth said that one is either a consumer or producer of books. I liked that. Some people are water skiing. Never had the nerve to try it.

When I drove into Provincetown I saw a red sail in the harbor. Was it yours? I parked the car. Fixed upon your sail I crossed the street. Sign said "Private Staircase." I called your name across the water. A voice answered, I thought it was your voice. I waited. But it was some kids further down the beach. And the sailboat too far away. Whoever rode on it couldn't hear. All Provincetown beach stretched clean clear blue yellow in the sun. Just washed. And still you do not come. Or is that your sail there now? I've waved twice, you must be able to see me sitting her on my desk. Why are you sailing away behind the wharf? Is this some test of will? Tack, you idiot. All right, have it your own way. At least the little girl next door was glad to see me back. I have much leisure for self-pity and she is now chattering in my ear busy at her cake-baking project, putting sand in a flower pot. Wants to know if I'm going to the circus tonight. I am a clam. This morning I called again, shouting your name. Claire. The sound stretching over blue of water clean. Were you too far away to hear? Walked up the rocks, fought back by the private staircase. Supposed to be a radical, scrambling around on these blasted rocks out of respect for private property.

When I got back to the road I noticed the A&P. This would be a great opportunity to buy peanut butter. The little cutthroat stores on Commercial Street all stock the blue label. Creamy. My love is crunchy. The red label. I will console myself with material goods. I will shop up a storm. Beautiful lettuces, oranges, lemons, limes, red tomatoes all nestling in steel basket. Grinning at me. I am so shamelessly in love with the way food looks I often buy it just to look at it. And experience only slight twinges of conscience when my still lifes go rotten before they're et. Cornish hens: two bucks, why not? Make a chicken Kiev too. Long moral struggle over the price of a steak. Six dollars is really shocking. Your existential poverty will never endure it. And it is dishonest to remove the tag. Am I an old woman buying love? But the difference in our ages is less than that between mine and Fumio's. Among the broccoli I do arithmetic. Fumio is nine years older than I am. Why is it that he always seems the same age, maybe younger? Go ahead, buy thick-sliced bacon. Food is living. The shopping center is a festival of love. We'll have feasts each remaining night. I run around the aisles getting instructions from men who all claim they don't work here, are just filling the shelves. The manager scolds me for leaving my handbag in the shopping cart. Needn't worry about it, since he is right there carrying on like my mother. Everyone's a thief, he declares. Despite the evidence. Still trying to find the oil for the chicken. I have always wanted to write a poem to the supermarket. A ramble through vegetables and brand names. Ginsberg and Whitman pursue me through oranges, Sunkist with tradition.

When I am back in my house I arrange the fruit in a basket, lemons, onions, and apples. Their colors. The tomatoes. The strawberries in a big flat white plate. They glow at me. Preparations for a lover.

And still you don't come. Or is that a sail? Yes. Now you are walking toward me from the water, your eyes on me. Your foot now on the porch. Coming in your power. Like a god, something fierce in your beauty. In the gleam of your hair and the green eyes, nonchalant, steady, sure.

"How was the conference?"

"Amazing."

"Did you get an A?"

"Claire, you made me miss that plane."

"But you came back."

"I had to."

"After I called the airport here and found out what happened I was afraid you'd stay in New York."

"I thought of it."

"I lied to you. It wasn't the rudder. I fell asleep."

"But don't you realize what it means, falling asleep?"

"But it was unconscious."

"Don't you see what you were doing to us? And to me."

"It was unconscious. You must understand that. I would never do it on purpose."

Her eyes are so direct one has to trust them. And what choice do I have?

We rehearse the reasons she did not come. Her fear of flying. The budget. "Anyway, the conference couldn't afford it," she argues. Then I ask her, afraid, but I must know. Asking it while she is changing her clothes in another room so that I need not see her face. "Is it because you did not want to be tagging along?" Now I am standing in the door. Watching her button the shirt. "Yes." She admits it. The air is cleared enough for me to realize she had waited all morning with breakfast things, then went sailing with two orphans from the boardinghouse, people she had met, acquired in her taste for strays. We can laugh now over the loss of the day and go out upon the water. Life is not a tragedy.

We sail. Claire is at the helm. Smoking a Tiparillo. Talking big in the Boston accent, giving orders. A blonde playing Teddy Kennedy. Our minds rub each other like young animals, cubs sporting in the sunshine across the sea. The wind will carry us around the wharf. "The flight back was beautiful, I love to fly." I am announcing myself. "I hate it," she counters. "Terrifies me. But I did fly back from Boston the last time. Fastened my seatbelt, sent off a little prayer to Krishna. I did however mention to the stewardess in the course of things that the wing was falling off." "A lie," I charge. "A fiction," she replies serenely. "I make myself interesting. Waiting for the time when I will bore you." Suddenly she has found me, opened a door and shown me her dread.

"Whose print did you eat while I was gone?" "Devoured all the Buddhists." "Thought you lost them." "Found them under the bed." "Are they the answer?" "They don't appear to be." "Write, Bookie!" "Pusher!" "Write. You're a writer." "I don't seem to have found my way in the world." She looks away. We are silent then in our temporary joy. Why wonder at permanence when the evening is our ocean. Finest time of day to sail, we agree together. The water bringing us conjunction. Our love now a satisfaction in itself. Found in time, in the perfect evening.

The sun in a communion wafer in one sky, the moon in another, the two present at one time like a miracle in different colors. A great red disk floats to starboard, another, paler, stranger still on the other side. They lean over us, confederates of our love. She describes the moon, the flight, which makes it ours now. Mankind's. I object that it is woman's planet, our tides, our blood in all the old religions. Now planted with the flag, ground under the heel of government issue. "Bigotry," she smiles. I subside and watch the two strange planets. Then we watch each other. One pair of eyes inside the other breathing. It is her sun and moon, our sail. The government has departed. The harbor is hushed while we commune. All time ceases, or is present together aloft in the sky like the two incongruous lights sinking and rising but arrested now as we are while we laugh or gaze or smoke, repeating our endless litany of love. She recites Emily Dickinson. I reply with this is no country for old men the young in one another's arms. We are lovers reciting verses to each other across the space between us in a small boat in Provincetown harbor. We are lovers to whom the banal is original. I remember the line from Millay's Renascence that Mother taught me when I was small. Claire doesn't like it. Which was not the point. Only my gratitude to an aging woman far away who read the tracks of poetry into my mind when I was three. Claire's eyes are on the sea. If I speak they return to me. We come about. The planets remain steady over the water. I'm sailing now and she's teaching me. But I would rather watch her captain in her glory, so I give back the tiller. She looks me full in the eyes. "What does the word Claire mean?" "Light." She answers just the one word. So simply. Looking away again.

And when we walk back to Molly's along Commercial Street, arms about each other, in this gay town you can do that, a man stops to smile at us. Are people admiring two beautiful women? For with her I am beautiful, the dark woman mated and at peace with the fair. Or do they admire lovers, the sight of us causing them to remember joy? When the fussy man in the grocery store sees her he sees serenity. When his old mother sees her she sees goodness like a sunny child, its very presence making her smile. I am at her side hurrying to announce myself, appended to this wonder. We stroll together like two queens. We own Commercial Street. The fudge store, all the dress shops, the man who sits on the front porch of his pretentious boardinghouse dreaming it is Tara. The tawdry places where they paint your portrait. The sitters all sitting for us. Then a window on the left compels us. Here is a splendid leather jacket. I will be bold and try it on. Too small for either of us. It would fit Fumio. It could be a present. How fine he would look in his striped legs and neat boots topped with this. How he would strut, the coxcomb in him, the dandy. The part that he denies that I love so well. We discuss it past the place where you take tours on the dunes. Rent a plane, buy a ticket, the girl calls to us. But we only smile back enigmatically. Not even buying candy apples. Intent upon the topic. How well Fumio looks in macho clothes, lumberjack stompers, the tan pants of Caucasian bulk somehow remarkably elegant reduced to his slender size. Claire sums it up by saying that his is a beautiful existence, everyone must feel it who meets him. Our contentment is infectious. It has turned the world to summer, reflected in all the passersby. Their evening glowing ahead of them in just the same way, because ours does. Then. Remembering it now. In winter.

I go down the steps. Into French's den. Smell of the leather, the stains, and the oil. The basement room is old rafters and brick. It resists light and is somber. The legs go by outside still in daylight. Only five o'clock in the afternoon for the tourists. But already here it is night. French is a curmudgeon Vulcan, a vast bosom behind her leather apron at odds with the face above it, the face of a schoolgirl. If Claire were here she could enlist her favorite word and call it "wistful." No one's buying leather, French complains. The summer's a bust. I will buy some then. Plunking down my tacky old bag. Let's replace it. This is a great moment, I think, a turning point. I am disposing of a friend. Will the new one be as accommodating? Will it sit through meetings patiently ready to produce an address? Will it repose steadily on

barroom floors while I wheel and deal in my amateur
exercises in politics? We measure. Nine and a half inches
high. Eleven inches wide. Four inches deep. If she notices I buy because she needs the money, will she resent
it? Finding another bag. Throw this in too. And the belt.
Then enough business. Caroline takes care of the sordid
details of trade, French hating it all by now. At the end
of the summer and broke. Caroline, a girl who has run
away from her husband to cater now to a woman. In
French's den smoothing the cat, the dog, the economy.
French's bearishness.

We will drink gin and orange juice. Claire will be here
in a moment. To tell Caroline her spiritual crises while
I must listen to French talk politics. But I want to hear
every word Claire says. If I overhear the word asceticism
I tremble. It may affect my chances. I am never safe.
And I do not want to play the husband while they play
wives. Why don't they talk to us? I have nothing to say
to French's heaviness. Why should we pair off like this?
As if, odious thought, we were two couples. I will engage
Caroline in conversation. She is from Minnesota too.
Realizing with a start I have fallen for it, find her name
slipping away from my memory. I too imagined French
the more significant being.

Smoking pot and getting higher. Claire and French
and Caroline all say they can feel it now too. We are
dissipating. What is Claire saying, I wonder? Huddled
with Caroline. Exchanging meditations like recipes. Will
she leave me, withdraw again? But her arm is about my
shoulder warm. Yes I feel very high the music now we
should dance to it. But she is so high she cannot hear
the beat, is out of step. I lean against her, my voice
teasing her my lips on her throat that lovely place between the collarbones. The round of her arms in the tank
top. Our breasts touch for a second like recognition.
"You're not really dancing." She stops. Have I hurt her?
She is sitting down. Now it is Saint John of the Cross,
now it's yoga, special foods for vegetarians. Ridiculous
I think, unhealthy. But she is holding my hand, her head
on my shoulder. We are floating in our own place and

hear nothing. Caroline dances with French. It is good to watch them. Then Claire dances with French to show me she can dance. But not with me, refusing to try again. I have hurt her. This warm proud boy that she is sometimes. Then a girl, then a woman, then a child, then her mother, how her mother must look, every day becoming her more as we all do inch by inch growing older we become what we came from and left.

Higher in her arms my head in her lap, can the chairs accommodate all this? "Things of the spirit," she is grinning at me. "Dull gospel diction," I sneer. Our eyes are laughing at each other. "Then metaphysics at least," she holds out, "Hot gas, Bookie, what's it all mean?" "Just relax, I'll let you know the moment I find out." "Of course there has to be something beyond the political roar," I venture. Conceding. "Or even our own remarkable bliss," she replies. Greater concession. She has stopped laughing just long enough to get her tongue in my ear. "You're the spirit I'm the flesh. No, damn it, I got it backwards." "Listen, I got a proposal. We'll get a federal grant and apply in triplicate. Undertake to resolve yin and yang, the old dichotomy of spirit and body. You'll put in all the big words." "Sure, kid." Sure, kid—how I love it, her pretentions to toughness. "And since you're a big shot you handle the public relations end of it."

We are higher and higher. Playing the same records over and over. They are not loud but this high you can hear every note in the music. Certain things of the Beatles or the Simon and Garfunkel we've heard a hundred times together, all the glistening sounds made now in her honor. Sail on, silver girl, your time has come to shine. Suddenly a bang from the upstairs. Bang again, the ceiling's falling. A broom is coming through the floorboards. Two of them are already broken. It is funny and somehow obscene. The landlady has gone mad. Our happiness gives her agony. She bellows we are degenerates. "They have seventeen dogs in that place upstairs," French whispers. "Of course they're crazy." "Turn off that music," the termagant voice from upstairs shaking with a strange unnecessary rage. French wants to keep it on. I'm stoned, daydreaming of universal peace. It's time to go home, it's the end, Claire decides. I stay to help French keep face, but when she says Claire is a coward, always leaving when things get rough, I lose patience and go home too.

Running after her. I will catch her up past the post office, the shell shop. Not finding her till I fall on her at last, my hand reaching out in the dark. But we are too high now. This stuff is supposed to be an aphrodisiac, Claudia swears by it, why are we falling asleep? There is no point in it. Wait till the morning. The long pleasure of a kiss. "Love you." "It's good to be back." "Good night." Falling asleep in the luxury of knowing it is not necessary, knowing as we do the paradoxical release from the mythos of love, moments when we are just friends not even lovers. Feeling her warmth like an animal, the comfort of it. Like the bump of her stomach.

In the morning I am afraid again. I examine the kitchen. Knowing it. That I will fail. I will not get anyone right in the book. Claire especially. She will vanish like my memory for her repartee. Why do I not write it down when she says it? Why don't I tape everything, then later work from transcripts. Some way to hold onto the words as they fall. Do they echo still in that room? The sounds like dust in the air, falling. Then. I am anxious now as I listen. Now remembering then. The windows boarded in the winter here. There is no light in Molly's cottage. It would be dark and cold. No point even in going by to see it from outside. I wished it to be music like our summer days that were huge skies of sun and laughter. But then too I felt the panic. That it would slip away. Molly appears in the doorway. I give her coffee. Then, that yellow morning. "Why *not* use a tape recorder? It's like sand in a painting. If you need it you put it in." But I have used people I know. Pacing the place alone talking to myself. Putting my friends into a book, capturing them. Even if the likenesses are faulty the people themselves are stopped midgesture like people in old photographs. Their paranoia is just. Those who admit to it and those who do not, proudly refusing to be self-conscious. Each is harmed by the thing known, made larger by print. Even when I sing their praises, loving them, I wrong them with my grasp, the vise of my hand on their ankle through time.

Why not take the day off? Go for a sail. We could sail as far as the lighthouse and the island. Bring Molly too. She has bought kites to fly from the boat. They are there on the table in the sunlight as unexpected as all of Molly's kindness. The three of us shoving off. Our skin delighted by the water. "Have you got everything?" Claire booms at us. "Your cigarettes, your books, your booze, your dinners." "All, I want all," Molly says it for me as well, the two of us Dionysian accomplices against Claire, who is discipline and order. We are folly and joy. We go fast. We skim along in the pureness of water and sky. It is all before us. In a moment I can stand and sail the kite. "You must put it in your book," Claire orders. "It's historical fact that we sailed a kite from a sunfish in Provincetown harbor today the sixth of August. Then you'll have the comfort of one true statement, if nothing else." I stand, launching the kite. It is red. It is a plastic bat. Its string is an excitement flashing out of my hand while it is a red flag upon the water, rising grandly while we cheer it. Then it falls. "Sit down," Claire orders. Stern. Meaning it. We chase the kite but it is gone. A red slip fragile as paper under the wake. Later when we tack I can try the blue one. Molly lights cigarettes. Now we can go ahead, try the blue one. I stand again with our luck in my hands. Will it fly? No then yes then its line is caught in the sail. Sitting while we turn to retrieve it. Then it is up and running bravely behind us. The other boats watch, they are sails and faces gazing under the sails. The people are waving. Our kite is brilliant for an instant. Then extinguished.

We will save the last one for the island. Turning to other entertainment. Claire becomes the *African Queen*, both Hepburn and Bogart, by turns the lady and the tramp. "God has not forsaken this place, Mr. Allport, you must remember that my brother is here," she intones. "It's perfect." Molly laughs. "You are incredible, how did you manage to memorize every line?" "I have seen it twenty times. But the last two times at St. Mark's Place they cut it. Whole scenes omitted. Shameful." She is in her glory. She is the class actress. She is both of them, the man and the woman, the quest, the stubborn hope good enough to fix a machine and find the way back. "Chaaarlie," she minces for us the way Rosa says it at the last, giving herself. Then we are landed.

Here where the rocks stretch away and no one has ever lived, only the gulls in their thousands, the ruined tower like a fortress blind and pitiless, here then is the last kite. The black one. Molly holds it for me. It will fly. Already a speck ahead of me to the right of the lighthouse. I nod to Mrs. Woolf.

Claire lies on the boat deck. She is contentment as pure and light as the air in sun and water. The kite is bravery booming at the end of its line. Climbing still. In a moment I will give the line to Molly. But she does not want a turn. "It's yours," she says. If it's mine then it's a wish. The kite is all my hopes, my self, my future. Will it fly? Dipping now, hurry, use all your skills, remember Sunday afternoons on the Sheep Meadow with Fumio the master kite maker, what you do is work the line. Working in the heat of the sun, pulling hand over hand, the line falling at my feet, the extra footage like film on a cutting room floor. The kit holds. It hovers like death, the fortress next to it a blind eye like Childe Roland saw, desolated by the sight of it. Now it is going out fast and I let it run until the bewildered instant its string has snapped. This can't be. Yet it's happening I see it happen as Molly gasps and Claire sits up to watch it go like a meteor for heaven. It will never stop until eternity, the wonder of it free. Freed before we meant to. But then with a bound fated helpless unhooked it falls, plunges into the sea, a star broken. For an instant my heart too was with it, my self, until almost by surprise I accept its death.

"Come on we'll find it," Claire springing up in the

boat, a savior bent on heroism shoving us off the sand, we will run after it. But then we begin to talk. She is telling of her book that she will finish as soon as she gets back. Her space chapter, the one that's been giving her trouble. "I want to end it with all the things of earth, all things young and taking comfort in the warmth of life, the young and yet to be born." She describes her chapter on Thompson the businessman who wanted to buy immortality and thought the display case in the Museum of Natural History a good bargain. Walking back and forth noticing the dedicatory plaques, brass, the donor's name permanently engraved. Three thousand for a New England scene. But the one from Wisconsin has bigger animals, you get more for your money.

No one remembers the kite. It is lost freely and without regret. While we sail over the water, still around us the sail peaceful as the time after dusk. Hungering for asceticism Claire makes life a sacrilege. "All I do is sail and eat. And repent after lovemaking. Fuck Buddha, Barbara said last week." Delighted with her own indignation. "Friends like this, you see how far I'm likely to get." Molly invents a movie, cheerful Hollywood spectacular of Claire's spiritual crises. As the devil's advocate I advance the master's cinema. Dreyer's *St. Joan.* Artaud is in it, his face so strangely ascetic. And Joan in her flames calling out. The heart stops, seeing it. And the rout that follows is chaos, horsemen flailing the crowds with chains, the peasants beaten back, the people who have seen her die and would rise now merciless in a terrible fury of mad incoherent destruction, put down by still more pointless force. Terrible to look at, like war. Joan is gone. We have run aground. All around us the dead squid float, poisoned. Claire grows pale and leans over the side. What on earth is she doing? Will she have to do it here? But quietly and with great delicacy she vomits over the side. Our captain. With her hangover. Watching with a crush of tenderness, my extravagant admiration as she smiles back. Never was she braver or more lovely. The squid float about our legs in the water, helpless and empty. Our kites are gone. Landing the boat, we walk through the dead. The corpse of each squid makes us more alive.

I must call Nell. Go to the hotel where they have a pay phone. Fumio will know where she is. But his line is busy. Young man behind me would like to use the booth. Nice young fellow, gay, a comrade. One of ours. A holiday maker with his necessities. I am all courtesy, beckoning him to take my place. I'll just have a cigarette and wait. Then I'll make my call and join my friends. Tonight is our last feast. Molly will need the house tomorrow. It is rented. Our time is up here. We must move to Margaret's. Tonight is our farewell. They wait for me on the deck, drinking in the evening and watching the moon rise. I finish one cigarette and begin a magazine. Chap takes a lot of time. I light the next cigarette, looking through at him in his booth. I point gently at my watch. He is talking about money. Needs to have it sent, making arrangements, bargaining, begging. Excited. Now angry, now pleading. Fellow's in trouble, one must be patient. I will sit down. Not bother him. By the time I finish this cigarette he will have of course vacated the premises.

But when I look again he is in no hurry. Goes by the law of possession. Rich inside his booth. Look, fellow, I have to use the phone. His face doesn't give a damn. This is too much. I have friends waiting. This time is precious to me. Seeing them lined up at the railing. Molly, Joyce, Claire. They are waiting because I am waiting on this creep in his bloody booth. Get out of there. Doesn't stir. Complete in his concentration he annihilates me. I have no rights, no existence, no claims at all. Bastard, I whisper. At war with him, his enemy in wait. His avenger rising in a heat to repay centuries of callow injustice. I am past charity, whispering obscenities, wallowing in bigotry, slandering him with faggot. I commit acts of calculated meanness. I resort to sabotage, I disconnect him in New York. Unruffled, he continues to talk. Passing the crisis I abandon nonviolence with a bound to strangle him in several positions. My mind doing it quietly and with relish through the glass. I experience the forgiveness of Jesus and sit upon a chair. Then the wrath of Achilles motioning to him, you have got to give up this booth it's over half an hour. The patience of Job, my gorge rising, I pace conspicuously before him. The crimes of Attila, doing the unspeakable and knocking on the glass. The stare of the hopelessly poor eating hatred in a poster. The fury of a witch staring at a hotel banister until it becomes invisible. But my powers fail me when I turn toward my tyrant. He is insensible self-possession winding down a war . After many years he opens the door. "I was talking to my mother," he announces as if it were every justification. "Big deal." "But I haven't spoken to her in eighteen months." He is shaking, hysterical. "If you called her more often it might not take so long"—how much I would love to say it, pointing the phrase like a paper glider right up between his eyes. My party doesn't answer.

"I abandoned the true path and committed homicide in the phone booth." They laugh at my defection. My petty rages. "The world is full of ill nature," Claire concludes, handing me a drink. We begin by being silly. Joyce and Molly have prepared a schedule. They will give a birthday party for a dog, Molly's incontinent old Iggy. "Just what you need at this point, a little whimsy." Joyce rules. She has written it out like a happening, the language calculated, plasticene, impersonal. "Various treats shall be arranged but certain austerities observed as well. Molly may not hump Iggy during the day of the celebration." "Does she hump her dog?" I sputter. "That will remain forever dark." Joyce's voice is oracular. "Marisol the cat may not participate in the festivities. There shall be an ascent of balloons at the climax."

My irritation falls from me in our frivolity, the benign influence of the moon shedding its light across the wide of the waters. Molly and Joyce disappear to rest before the ardors of the feast. Claire sits next to me. Her presence wrapping me with assurance like a warm coat settling over my shoulders, available always but as yet almost unnoticed. It is Hiroshima, the sixth day of August.

Other nights, two of them, those sacred times I drank to peace with strangers, drinking in the neighborhood sake bars of Tokyo, astonished past tears that they would toast with me, eager and forgiving this one night from chaos saved for hope. We watch the moon. Strange tonight and red. It beckons radiant with a new age. Mars hangs near it. "Nearer to us tonight than it has been since the time of Shakespeare," Claire says, her voice grave in its sweetness. Warming to the topic, ripe with it now, the galactic point of view. I am left to be the opposition, testing her always, finding how much there is to believe in her philosophy.

"It's Hiroshima night. The blood on the moon cries out against the Americans who have just left its surface." "No. It's past that, it's a new beginning," she says, her voice quiet. "We're no longer alone in the universe. It's a change as great as Galileo's when we ceased to be the middle of things. We've seen our own planet from a distance. And know we are all brothers flying in the void together on this one stone." "But unless we find our own explanations . . . why should we go on journeying to dead places far away and at great cost, cold when we reach them?"

"Human nature is no longer the standard. You can't be a humanist any more. It's an immoral position." "Why not?" I ask, sure of my stance. "Who does the humanist harm? Give me your case." "The lobster fishermen in their so human greed to make a living have killed a species. The humanist is a fool killing for himself. Put a pencil through a spider's web—he won't know you wrote a book with it. The humanist disregards all things not human, the very place he lives finally. And now we see it's all we have. If life is sacred how do we decide which life to lose, which to save? We must give up our irrational preference for our own kind." She is irrefutable. I will resort to irony. "You are quoting yourself," I badger her. "But of course, I never pass up an opportunity." She is delighted, she has won.

We are two persons in happiness. Our figures dwarfed black shadows before the great red light of Mars. The

huge and pulsing moon always full these nights. And red
as if to mark the time from heaven, a portent, the magical correspondence of two worlds. Like in an old play.
Macbeth. "What do they think Mars is like? This year's
opinion." She rolls out her science, not only this year's
opinion but the earlier opinions on its satellites, Deimos
and Phobos. The latest theories of Venus. What is said
of Saturn. And what of beyond where her hope lies, the
outer rings. Other galaxies. The black holes in the sky.
The vast time span between the stars. Each a sun lighting
itself to us so long after. Light shed perhaps by its own
strange former life, dark now behind it. Side by side with
this world's darkness around us, here in our place at the
edge of America looking to sea and at one with each
other, with all, past present and to come. Hiroshima night
with Mars to signal the new age. The old dying. And the
next coming to be. We watch, expecting a miracle. It is
already before us in the great terrible blood red light of
the moon. Loud upon the water from heaven this night.
Light beaming toward us in its eerie color. Harvest signal of the time gone. The time to come. Awaited in a
red rush of light on water. A bonfire like the coming
of peace. And then calm, serene in its distance, perfection. A kindness like the powers of the mind. Meditate.
Do not forget.

I have made havoc of the kitchen. Followed by order.
The wine waits quietly in the glasses. The bread shines
on its plate. The butter gives off a light of its own. The
bird is golden, ready. The feast is laid. We drink our
toast to friendship. Claire extends our thanks to all the
"creatures in the galaxy who have made this occasion
possible." Joyce preserves her vegatarian position. The
rest of us present our apologies to the chicken who has
given his life to become our Kiev. It is a feast of conversation where we exchange work and friends, enemies
and fears, parents and childhoods. The lives we have
observed set in the tracks of their tragic absurdity. Molly,
describing her mother, a woman who stayed up all night
fending off sex, too tired in the daytime to trudge through

the little sphere of her housework. Mine was a woman intoxicated by a man who one day ceased to love her. They are another generation but within us are the same fears. "Like a third eye," Molly says, giving it a name. "When I go to paint there is another eye looking at me, criticizing, preventing. When it speaks it talks in a distinctly masculine voice." "So does mine. He is a reviewer of books." "The eye has been with me all my life, spoiling it somehow," she continues. "Like a voyeur, it has made even sex impossible." Claire astounds us with a speech in praise of the flesh. "Whatever gives joy lights up the planet, makes it run and sing," she concludes to universal congratulations. But what is joy? Molly is skeptical. "Last year my sister came to stay and produced her life. A series of photographs spread out on this table. Husband. The first child. The second. The third. Then she was finished. All she had. We had not seen each other in years. There was nothing, ultimately, to talk about. Only her pictures. I wept looking at them, spread out like a pack of cards. She was not in them." Joyce observes us like a grave child sitting by the older woman at her side. The two are repeating the sorrows of all mothers and daughters in their love.

"We are all searching for a cure," Claire says. "We never tire. Running continuously. Humanity's like a lunatic after remedies, seizing on panaceas. Billy Graham or Zen. As long as it's encapsulated. Americans have created twenty-eight flavors of ice cream to console themselves for living on the earth." We are lyrical and silly, philosophical and trite. Talking of a painting or how a child grows. How teaching is done. Claire describes her nephews at breakfast. "The younger one spills the jam and brings down his father's wrath. The elder brother's confirmed forever while the smaller one becomes increasingly incompetent. The damage building and setting a course." I think of my own nephews. Or Celia's. How one brother is set above another, scheduled and programmed so early, each family member vehemently denying the obvious, imagines it is some God-given proclivity that one is steady, the other sensitive, artistic,

or an outlaw. Claire goes inside. I sit on in the moonlight
with Molly. We are two women in our ripe after-dinner
mood. I have great admiration for the sanity Molly has
won from madness, the kindness wrung out of suffering.
Grateful for the comfort of her incorrigible optimism
these days here, realizing I have fed and lived upon it.
This strange middle-aged woman with her still beautiful
body, her bobbed hair, and a broken tooth. Her odd
deep voice like a slack and weathered drum, but somehow
restful. "There was a time this place was hateful to me.
Winters I lived here alone furious at solitude. One night
I smashed a dozen glasses against the wall of a bar. I have
known terrible rages. But time has cured the madness
in me. Given me peace."

Will you teach again, she asks me. I pause, not
knowing whether to prefer my freedom to my love. She
tells of a friend's long dedication to her pupils, disturbed
children who consumed her like a disease until she quit.
And found life empty without them. Listening, I realize
that I too have lived upon the young. Made them my
hope. "What will the winter bring?" I ask Joyce. But
she has no answer.

I go inside to find Claire in her book. I make my notes.
Doing a little dance because I am learning to do it better.
Becoming more workmanlike. But I am still not accurate.
When the time comes to write it out the words of the
others will have dissolved in air. I tell Claire the problem.
"Tape it then if you're so fanatical." "Do you know how
radicals feel about tape recorders?" "So they're paranoid
and we're not," she reasons, making coffee. "You could
bug yourself and carry the silly thing with you all the
time. Why not? Everywhere I go I carry my hinge pin.
There's no reason you shouldn't be just as eccentric. My
mother uses walnuts. With every wave of frustration she
bangs one against the dashboard."

The idea has seized hold of me like a devil. The mind
cannot remember enough. It is spongy. The machine only
is truth. Exactitude. Excitedly I set it up. Aiming at
greater precision. Avid for accuracy. I will plug it in.
Our only working plug. Next to the bed. "Even the

bedroom," I call back at her. She comes to the door. Her eyes register their patient amusement. "Think I'll sleep at Margaret's place tonight." "No, you don't. We're going to use this." It's a game. But it's serious. I will capture her in the tape. Counting a test. Five, six, seven, eight. "What will you say to it?" I call out to her. "That you missed your ice cream for all eternity by trying to record it." Our voices laugh into the machine. "I hope you appreciate the efforts I go to." But then it seems she has nothing to say to the black box. Settles into her pillows, like an owl in her reading glasses.

"You're always trying to make speeches. Here I give you a chance and you shut up." Egging her on. She giggles. Tempted. "What will you say?" "I'll give my speech, the one I'm always making in my head." We are playing. Yet it's serious. If she hears herself, I wonder. If she listens to herself she may back down on her messianic pretensions. Mad myself wondering if she will see her own madness. She takes up the microphone. "Now I want to give a few of my speeches which I have contemplated in the course of my studies." Then she stops to laugh at herself. "This will be bad for my career but I'll do it anyway just so I'll be a bit different in my maturity. The first thing I say is—WOMEN AND MEN OF EARTH! Hmmm, I've wondered a long time what my opening would be. Thinking about ladies and gentlemen. But I concluded this was more resonant." Booming it into the machine, our laughter with it. I stop to make a test, belaboring her with O'Rourke's achievements in technology. Her voice cuts in, "Is it on now?" "Yes."

"Will you let me continue my speech so I can go to sleep? WOMEN AND MEN OF EARTH!" Her laughter like music. "Isn't this amazing? I forgot the whole speech because I have this damn machine confronting me. Say it every day. Recite it when I get up in the morning." "Then tell it to me," I urge her, insidious. "This is very important, stole it from Saint Francis his Revelations, I'm sort of converting it to my own uses. God supposedly spoke to Saint Francis and said GO AND REPAIR YOUR WORLD for it is fallen into decay and you have been chosen from all eternity. Well, He didn't say that. God never seems to say a word. But imagine He did. Now what I say is—WOMEN AND MEN OF EARTH, GO AND REPAIR YOUR WORLD FOR IT IS FALLEN INTO DECAY AND YOU HAVE BEEN CHOSEN FROM ALL ETERNITY to transform mankind into humankind." Her voice breaking into hilarity at the sound of herself. "And I think I'm sick of that phrase. Used it a hundred times—transform mankind"—her laugh is sudden hearing herself. "Decided today that I'm going to say transform a dangerous unpredictable animal into a lover of life." Her voice severe, judicial. "I think that's better." I am kicking my legs against the mattress, delighted with my experiment.

"And then I have another speech I could work into this one. It would be all one speech when I finish it." I am critical, objective, amused. "Shut up and play it back." She bites her lip listening. "It's ridiculous." She is crestfallen. "It's not that ridiculous," I say, letting her down gently. Am I cruel to be kind? Or only cruel? But she is fascinated now. "Is it on?" We are both laughing now at her vanity. "No, it isn't ridiculous. I'm learning. When you're becoming one of the heroes of your time you need a little patience. Take *time* to command the attention of the world." "Well, it is a little grandiose," I drawl. She is undaunted.

I must tell her. I begin tentatively. "Look, the machine records it. It's real. You play it back and you hear yourself for the first time. You have never listened to yourself." "Who would want to?" she argues. "It's so incoherent and rambling and maniacal. I'm just a maniac. Not even a religious fanatic. Just a fanatic. It takes a long time to command the attention of myself." "There's still something quite real in what you're saying," I argue. "It would be less maniacal if it were all real. If it were all happening." "Yes. Exactly," she agrees. Then is silent. The tape spins on empty. Then she goes on, "What must happen is you must transform your daydreams into fate, your daydream meaning your inner life. And fate meaning the real presence of yourself in the world. And if I can make my fate, I mean my inner life," laughing again.

"THIS MACHINE! Anyway you understand my point. What we have to do is transform the world into our world. I listen. "Oh dear, I don't have any more to say. If I think of something particularly brilliant I'll wake you up." "Shall I turn it off?" I offer. "Yes. But play it back first."

She listens again. "You're right it is ridiculous." She stops. "No." I refuse to believe that. It's only that my fantasies are, hmm extraordinarily imaginative . . . No, I will not give in. I am the only one I know, the only one in my peer group who is looking out for metaphysics. Spirit is emerging from matter. You can have all the action you want. But it's the metaphysician who weaves the rug into a pattern. You can have all the threads—no, I don't like that metaphor, don't use it. Without the metaphysician the revolution is nothing!

"All right, here's my vision in a nutshell, a walnut. Taking after my mother. On all the different worlds in all the different galaxies there are creatures. Each creature sometimes pauses looking up at its own sky with its own sun and configuration of plants. And wonders with the sorrow and the gratefulness which I believe is at the heart of the universe, wonders about this awful helpless silence that sometimes you can hear when you listen to the night or the sky. The race is entering a new age where it sees all life with new eyes, from the smallest to the most significant forms. Realizing that all life is valuable. It is the task of the human personality to protect and sympathize, to give shelter to the creature life force. On this planet. On our home. Because there may be so many homes. And we don't quite know yet how we fit in.

"So now let's recite The Battle Hymn of the Republic," she explodes into laughter. She has had enough of herself. But I press home and the argument continues. She will give up being a saint. And become a prophet. Impose her cosmic vision upon the world, recommending humility to the species. I laugh. "This is humility week," I tease her, shouting with laughter. "All week from Monday to Sunday." "All right, you've caught me. I am not humble. But it doesn't matter.

Because I have an idea of what I can do with my life. Because I want to give confidence and hope, a sense of exhilaration and joy." Her voice soft, thoughtful. "Will you be Churchill and give out cigars? Or FDR and buy a dog?" "Shut up. I'll just stick by my cross, thank you. I have the rest of you to keep my feet on the ground. But you're right about the hot air."

The tape has got to her, she has heard herself. And doubted. Now she doubts me as well. I tell her how I trusted Nell. She is thoughtful. "It is about having to accept who you are." "Yes, you have taught me something," she says. "It's as if you've healed me." "It was a risk I had to take. Life itself is a risk, but it gets riskier somehow when it's canned. Preserved. You get caught in time."

Suddenly terrified I might be frozen in time. I lie face down repeating what Robin said in the film, the closing lines, her spell of protection against time. Saying the words like a prayer, exhausted. "We shot this in just two days. You know a couple of things about me. And the things you know about me are valid. And the things you know about the other people are valid. But nothing stops. A point on a line doesn't exist. You make it for yourself. The line goes on forever. Off into nowhere."

Will I be caught here? I wonder. Trapped in this book forever?

And then we talk, propped in our pillows. I am full of all my schemes, hopes, projects. That I would make a film of Nell. That I would sculpt again. Released from my usual terror at the bad magic of being held to a word spoken. Pinned by it as by a rash promise. And later, having to make it good. We are safe in our privacy. High on the night and our closeness. This last test passed. I have shown her herself and she could bear it. Was gallant. She has taken a look at the ledge where she stood. Rock she had thought it. And discovered a landslide. But she will not go back, she will go forward. And I, her skeptic, having tried to demolish what I thought was her folly, must now admit it is her foundation, her beginnings.

Now that we have made our pact we are lovers. Her hand reaches into the wide sleeve of my dress. Waiting for her is the first moment in flying. She approaches up the tunnel of my sleeve. My arm is a wing for her. As she nears me I feel an air pocket. When will she reach my breast? Hurry. My nipple waiting, standing up to receive her. Like a little old woman waving a handkerchief. How pleasant it is to begin with some clothing, the preventive of cloth, a garment, something to remove, some step to excite and then overcome. "It would be a pity to wrinkle it," she whispers, her hypocrisy open and frivolous. Our bodies come together and meet at the base. There the hairlike brush on two small hills. Meet and set each other on fire.

But I hang back. There is still my fear. And I must have her assurance. "Molly said something tonight that made a lot of sense, how one must above all avoid being controlled by negatives. Your imminent asceticism is this sort of thing. A threat. It controls me. Will you keep it up?" I have brought it into the open. Sex, the mystery of our lovemaking. It sits between us like a last unsolved problem. She protects herself with laughter. "I've degenerated so far I can't live without it. Every day. Somehow it appears to be habit-forming. An addiction." "Look, don't be so pious about it. Are you going to keep on threatening me?" She will hedge. She will keep me on the broiler forever. But her voice comes back humble with what it says. "I could never give you up or making love with you. It's a need now." Her pride nearly gone admitting it.

She has never really looked at me. Never looked me straight in the eyes when we've made love. That long full look, the sex of the eyes in sex. Tonight I will ask this of her. I lick along the soft gold hairs on her cheek. Being in love is saying the same name over and over. It is the touch of her quivering for me. The soft slide going in. Cry of it. The tenderness. The throb of it. Living. Soft. Moving. The lick of a tongue on a secret place. Rolled back to reveal a pearl. Sliding away. Catching it. It is the adoration of this act. The beat of it.

Hips moving. Hard to hold on. Greedy for it. Taste of salt. Catching it in my mouth. A thirst to suckle it. Loving. Her cries. My triumph. So much, loving. Hot. Wet. Good. How long feeling the lust of her. Hurting for loving. Very small thing, tender shoot jumping on my tongue. Pain of tenderness. Yes. The world is here. In a fingertip of flesh. Fire. The vulva a sun setting behind trees. A tongue stabbing in the tenderness of loving. Make, come for me. Always. Do not go away. A leg moves. The beauty of her foot on the sheet. Devour it. Preserve. Hold. Have always. Remember.

Here I am, she whispers, moving within me. You are home. Flesh in my flesh. In this act we are married. How can I give you joy? Her mouth drinks in my throat. Look at me. Eyes searching for. Commanding. Here I am. You are inside me, the voice coming as if softly. Only the two of us. The near pain of it a grandeur. When you stand at the Highland Light and look down on the hundred feet to foam the sea roaring at you is such pain. Here it is gentleness again, a quiet voice, how good you are to me, lover. Then crying, how you move me, moving within me a crisis of beating wings. Coming. The cries of it like birds filling the room. With this mystery. Birds full of wings, sound, in this hallowed air. An arm around a shoulder breathing hard. Eyes too covered to see. Blind with all of it.

Our bodies are spread out between us. They are friends. We are seeing the sunrise on the world as it comes over the edge of the sea, ephemeral as time, as summer. But as sure. The world has so much beauty, flying as it does, and because it flies, more holy, more pinching in its greatness, the glory of it hurting one's side to watch. Crossing the sky I'll see her, a light against the light, the golden sphere of her head warmed by the greater sun behind her over all. Light. Buoyant. Diaphanous. And of the spirit.

Her body has risen from the sea beyond the window, all air and water, purity and freshness. It has escaped matter, the inert, it is only the essence of love. In her eyes too there is concentration only. Imperious as the god of love, magisterial Eros, his power in light. "Turn over." And she takes me as I had so long hoped, ashamed to ask it. Slow. Fervent. The end of it sinking always to a sob like pain but more terrible in its joy. Until I am filled and emptied, weak. But there is more. Every orifice. The softer one now with a richness of her flesh in mine. And the nerve at the top. That too. And then in other ways and again in all ways exploring every region every possibility of awe and terror. Brushed and pushed powerfully like a spring till I am crying out, turning back out of frenzy to see her face serene behind me, riding me. Unperturbed. Essentially innocent. She kneels over me in her beauty naked. Grave as the green of her eyes. They have never known deception or shame, never been surprised in servility or compromise, never abandoned their freedom. Over me her head now, the sun its echo filling this room. I am sure of her at last.

It is for this reason that I asked her. All the others in my odyssey pass before my mind at once. Vita, Fumio, O'Rourke, Mallory. And Celia. My head buzzes with the fear of it. But I can no longer bear it, the thing that saved me now driving me mad. Do I dare to ask? But it has been a night of strangeness. The sun is rising behind her head glorious. She has said to me, "I want you when you are with me in a room to know that you are so valued, priceless." She has given me now everything. And I must ask her this foolish thing, this shame. Trusting she has the courage to refuse. Then I say it. That she could release me. "Help me."

"How?" "I can't live in this book any more." "Small wonder, it must distract from your privacy considerably." "No, it's worse than that. It has become the voice inside my mind, starting me on madness again." "Then end it." "I wanted to end it with Celia." "And?" "And I find I don't want that any more. The heart relinquishing her slowly, in grief and with regret. "But it was a moment in her eyes that captured me. I could beat the system . . ." my voice falls off ashamed realizing already I have asked her to be Celia. Or what Celia was. "Ask then," she says steadily. "I am ashamed," ashamed still, writing it. Her voice is slow, "Loren Eiseley says somewhere we're all our lives like children saying please please, tugging at a sleeve, but then the children go on too long unanswered, and so when someone finally turns around and says what do you want, they only say 'Never mind.'" Her voice as desolate as an urchin's. How like her, showing this exquisite mercy, to have refuge in a quotation.

There is the last shame now to conquer, to say that it was while making love. Trying to tell her, to show her. But she enters me too quickly. I had wanted her to stay on the edge and look at me, our eyes meeting as mine were fixed in Celia's. And now finally these other eyes coming. But the moment is a different one as she is different. There is not the magic or the terror. Something else more solemn. We are at last without irony. The excitement of fear is gone. And betrayal. I miss it for an instant, then let it go. These are other eyes. Celia's go out. Not replaced because nothing is replaced. Never the same. The new spirit enters, entering as she enters. But her soul remains her own. She does not exchange it. She is there like a dazed and golden youth, woman and lover, touched by the sun full now in its heat. All the summers of the world are in her eyes. All the summers of my life. She has taken me, accepted me, did not throw me back, shut me out. She will not close the door on me. No matter how I inveigled, maneuvered, schemed, I could not lose her to my self. Because she wanted me that much, it was enough. And have I betrayed her asking her this? But she cannot be betrayed, would not permit it. And now in full sunlight commanding me finally I come to her.

Did we sleep? I am washed up on her breast. But the fury is still in my head. I have not slept, not rested. And the book goes on talking in my head like torture. The hippies on the beach in full view out the window. Will they kill us, suddenly terribly afraid, Manson popping into my head. The violence of sex ignites people in such uncanny ways. Have they seen us? Seized by a panic, sitting up terrified in bed, shaken, the very thought of it, dying in this moment our love perfect, all lost to some casual insanity. Running to the window, having frightened her as well with this sudden crazed paranoia. Pulling the shades but realizing even as I do it that they are the gentle ones, these long-haired children of the beach. They will not hurt us. We are forever safe now. With all the little safety one has.

And now we must leave. Resenting for a moment that this place of discovery, given gratuitously, must as freely revert. We must load the car now, but first I will clean the place. The cheerful Irish scrub-lady preparing to evacuate her palace. "It is not even dirty," Claire objects. She is sullen at leaving. Devouring a Jesus tabloid. "Why are you reading that garbage?" "It's the nearest available print. Some nut in the alley's giving them out free." "Why don't you help?"

"What is this book about?" I wonder out loud, imitating a reviewer. "Broad goes to Provincetown and gets laid." Claire abandons her paper in disgust. "Garbage, really garbage. If you say you got laid by a Jesus freak I'll never speak to you again. But do mention that my aunt had the largest gladiolus farm in New England. She developed a black gladiolus. One form of immortality." I can see the floor through my tears, scrubbing in an exstasy of gratitude to Molly for having given us the place. "Why don't you help?" "Will you scrub the ceiling too?" she asks archly, "surely you carry it too far." "Ethnic trait," I snort, furious she will not lift a finger. "You're a creep," she says, watching me. Clinical. Detached. "I'm only one quarter Irish, the rest is sane. I'll wait for you in the car." When I join her she is still pouting. "Molly could do it in no time, she said it was no trouble." "And would you let her do our work?" I turn on her outraged. She repents. "I must confess that for a moment you reminded me of my mother who always keeps me waiting. One last transference."

I turn to see the cottage through the car window, to see it vanish, and cannot drive for my tears. "You will have to do something about your sentimentality." Then we both stop to realize Molly is up and awake and is saying good-bye. Her kindness seeing us to the end of the alley, waving us on.

The bed is beautiful. It is gold sheets, a blue and white flowered spread, like a Cornish cream pitcher. But it's in two parts. One half slips out to be six inches lower than the top. Count on Bookie to pay twenty dollars a day for a place with a crooked bed. We must sleep on different levels. She gives me the top and slightly wider side in honor of my debilitated condition. Molly's picture has accompanied us to the boardinghouse, an old woman looking out from the wall at us, secure from a thumbtack. Claire praises me for having thought to hang it. We discuss the satisfaction of liking our friends' work, the relief when you do because you want to so much and are afraid you might not. But this is good, a good drawing. Molly's own goodness in an old woman posing at the Art Students League in an ancient dress, her face so much like Molly's own I gaped from one to the other when she gave it to me. I have noticed the fruit Claire has piled in a bowl on the table. She has put it there for us. This is our place now.

We are quiet. Our two heads lie here black and gold on the gold of the sheets, but as the sun enters Claire's hair the sheet becomes inert, merely a color. She recites from her oracle the *New York Times*. Science has just decided apes descend from man. A reversal of the standard version illustrated by a nice Pop-Magritte, a large monkey walking down the tree via his human ladder to earth. The Victorian divines rejoice in the heavens—right all along. Next item. They have found a crucified man in a cave in Palestine. Intact, even the nails in his feet. "Probably crucified thousands of guys in those days, only your man in the street victim," Clair grumbles, "but still, consider the possibilities." And her final item. Venus could have the atmosphere of Earth and support life if we transplanted algae there to give it oxygen. Scientists are working on the idea. "Take forever," I tell her, not having the slightest idea how long it would take to re-create evolutionary process. Claire explains the stages. "Long time before you get to anybody interesting." "No, we'll speed it up."

Now she lies exhausted from the effort of keeping on top of the universe, the past and present daily available to the imaginative reader of a newspaper. The full woman of her spread and mingled with the exhaustion of a tired child. Lying on her stomach, the great aureole of her hair shining like a miracle in my eyes, my head turned toward hers. I turn the other way to sleep and hear cars going by outside in summer streets. The sound of motors strangely aged, like the engines of the thirties. I see them in my head, old black sedans of my childhood summers, slowly passing in hot August's sunlight streets. When the book is finished I must die. It is myself stopping, held in time there, not going on. The voice in my head slows to a buzz. There is a throb of silence, loud with no talking in it. Over at last. Then it starts up again, insanely yammering, will never shut up. Thinking of my mother, dedicate it to her she will receive me at last who I am. Everyone comes back all my friends, mumbling their names like a chant, Fumio Nell Vita Mallory Celia. I cannot sleep unless I know about Nell. I will never sleep, go crazy again, sure to be dotty in a number of hours if I can't sleep. Maybe I am resting and don't know it.

I turn to see her shining next to me, the fire of gold in the gloom. She is a big woman stretched on a bed, faded raspberry of her tank top below the golden hair. A Marilyn spared the murder of locker rooms, cunt for American smut dreams till it killed her. Marilyn martyred to our sickness. I read her death in Tokyo's subway sandwiched into *Native Son,* becoming a complusive murderer reading it becoming the murderer with him as you have to with Raskolnikov too, looking up to see other passengers recognize the guilt in my eyes. Then I opened the English-speaking newspaper and found Monroe whom I had hated, our reproach because we were not white blondes pin ups for me in parking lots, garages, under the lids of tool boxes, Marilyn I hated till I knew her dead naked on her bed. And understood at last who she was. Too late. But not this time, and never again. Safe the big blonde on the bed next to me my lover. Not lovers clutching each other, going down till drowning we break for life. We are two individuals now, each in her own space. We are two women lying here, black and blond reconciled at last. Her golden hair, hardest to accept of all now accepted. And her great beauty, the gift of her whole womanhood. I will stop squirming around and trying to lose it. I can say yes. Once Claire was a sunny kid, deep Baptist home, a fanatical grandmother, no one noticed her. So she got pious. They paid attention. Still doing it. Can my love keep off the saint craze, her kite string holding her down to earth? She must know her own passion now as I do, seeing her head on the pillow and turned upward in a rage of orgasm these many times furious with a joy astounding us both, hurting my hand with her force, gushing then a balm washing over tightened muscles, her senses' teacher so surpassed. And if I go up the urine stairs of Fifth Street she will always open the door to me, the slam of childhood overcome now. We have healed each other here in Provincetown. But still there is no rest.

Later she sits on the porch waiting for her astronauts' return, ear attached to the little radio like a slum dweller afraid of silence. "My Puerto Rican radio," she chuckles, her back toward me going to the door, her ass and legs walking beautiful in white ducks, her ankles tan and her feet lovely shapes on the boards, strong. Her sunglasses sit on the chair. They are dime store, like the curlers, the cracker in her most lovable of all, the poor white abstracted by the stars, crazy after the spirit in tedious volumes of mystic philotheology. Clutching Einstein and the Sutras as she slops around in bedroom slippers.

I lie on the beach and pretend to sunbathe. Just my luck to fall asleep here, wake up an emergency case. If I could stop the voice in my head. Two boys launch a rowboat, gentle, their sounds soft and protective. I will click it off in my head, stop the book like a tape recorder. Click but it does not stop. Hateful insidious machine out of control. Remember to put it in, that moment Fumio stood at the top of the red stairs, opening of his big show at the Pennsylvania Academy, stood looking so oddly sophisticated in a suit. Slight figure at the head of that long staircase. And he swept the place with a gesture, the huge kites, the bouquets of wooden bicycles. As if he made them all to give me. Remember the red of the stairs. The lady in the room above us keeps interrupting our radio, flying around in a net dress like a parakeet who cannot be quiet as we strain for the announcer's words. "Think how excited they must be to be home. To touch earth." I stifle the cynic's voice: expensive space program, earth still a mess, Nixon's advertisement for the flag while he ups the war. Entering her mood tolerant and forgiving to feel their gladness. The one time I actually cared for them, that time they nearly didn't come home, something went wrong. Imagined them spinning into the void forever bodies already dead a million years never buried in earth, never to rest they cannot cease to move encased in steel falling to infinity. Chaucer's old man groping in the dirt for solace, for a way back into the earth, "leve moder" he calls it in the Pardoner's tale. Claire blocks out everything with her supreme concentration, catching the radio words. They made it. The moon had come back to Planet Earth. It is a satisfactory morning. I cannot sleep till I have called, found Nell. This is the seventh day of August. She might escape to England, today is the date on her ticket. So tired but I must try if I can help her one last time. Call Fumio. He will know. Sidney answers. Her dog has wet the rug and dug holes in the back yard. She got there last night, this morning they have mild hangovers, it will be an easy day. Fumio's thin little telephone voice chirping long distance from the farm. "I am well at last, I have ended that awful book." Is he disappointed I did not end with him? "It just couldn't go on any more, I was getting crazy from it, the strain." "You are living exaggerated life," he says "Well, sometimes that's necessary," holding on to my way of seeing. "My life is not so spectacular but I am on my schedule, my typewriter is growing in the wood." He is himself. He does not know where Nell is, she disappeared, never called after she left, went back to the city. "I am coming up to the farm and just live quietly with you and write it. You are my best person to work with." Suddenly, idiotically sobbing in Japanese that I love him, adore him. He laughs his embarrassed way and says he's glad. When I ask will he come to Provincetown with me he says he will. He would like to sail a boat because at Lake Nogiri twenty years ago in summer he sailed with a girl. But she hurt him, led him on and then went after his friend Ojiko. A strange girl dancer with an ambitious mother pushing her daughter into love and art, extensions of her craving self. Even Fumio my sane adult has old ruts still bleeding to heal. "We'll sail then. We can use Claire's boat. Somehow we'll figure out how to run the thing, put up the mast. Someone here will show us. And I would never hurt you," weeping to him my joy that he will come here with me later. September.

Dialing again, try Rosemary. Nell said she might stay there while Rosemary's in Italy. But it's Rosemary's voice that answers in New York. No idea where Nell is. Offers to help but it's too complicated. My mind is in the Chelsea Hotel where Nell is writing her book next to the balconies where all the writers have stood looking down at Twenty-third Street. Provincetown operator infinitely patient with my nervous exhaustion. A last and final call to the Cheslsea Hotel. "Charge it to my phone in New York, it's unlisted no one is there, Millett M-i-l-l-e-t-t," spelling it. "D?" she says. "No, two t's." "Kate Millett? Did you write a book?" I am embarrassed. We make jokes against Ma Bell. "What are the chances of organizing the telephone operators?" How do people know who I am, some special common property, some pet incompetent they take care of as she does now, holding on, getting New York information. The New York operator on the line too. All of us spelling Chelsea together like demented children, three women in three different places.

But the voice of the man at the desk says there is no Nell O'Rourke at the Chelsea Hotel. And hangs up. I see him in a white suit like an old movie, a Tennessee Williams villain before cubbyholes, keys in boxes. A roll-top desk efficiency declares the nothing. Things turn out as they will, but if she had stayed she would be writing there. Did I ruin it by not letting her off there the first time? Saw the cameras, thought of the waste, giving them back so soon, she had brought film too. Things happen when it is their time. And there is the future also. I had wanted her there, doing that when it ended. But she is herself, I must remember that. Help but not help too much when it is not what is wanted. Help by getting off. Leaving alone. I could call other people too, but it's not the time. Celia should be left alone now. Vita too. To be a friend is to learn timing. I am learning a little.

"You should brag more," Claire says. "Then you could be less ridiculous, always holding your potato whining away asking forgiveness of everyone till you come out smirking with the shred of assurance you were sneaking up to get in the first place." We are amused she has caught me, my tactic transparent. "It is absolutely necessary to laugh, most life is frankly insane, it's pathology, witless. And to have patience." Listening to let her preach at me, can never remember exactly what she says, only the curious attraction of her goodness, so real whatever saintly nonsense she blunders into, driven by her aspiration, not an evil ambition, only her neurotic fear she will never achieve, trying to be herself finished when she is still so young, just starting. Thinking softly of Celia, whom I will always love. Maybe better now. Patience for her fear of passion, her pout resisting me with all its own integrity. Can I learn to ask nothing back unless it's given? Perhaps one day, with all lovers, Fumio too. And Vita, her thoroughly exasperating perverse childish will against every growing up. She said maybe we would be better friends not being lovers. Surprised to discover she's right. Hoping for a friend's patience while she goes on hurling herself through the changes of her life. Wondering idly if she is over the clap. Tomorrow I will find the energy to walk down the street and buy Fumio's leather jacket, irrelevant what it costs, the fun of doing it. Looking to sea, already anticipating his black hair, the face sundark over the oiled leather clinging to his slender body, exuberance of his dandyism released for a moment from that glum regimentation of his own making. If Sidney is with him at least he won't be able to live on Spam the whole time I'm gone.

Idle chatter, the sea before us, evening coming. Claire making dinner admits her fear of being told to serve anyone, proud and angry when I asked her to make coffee. "I cooked your breakfast, why not? And you love ordering me to sit down in the boat." Laugh, having found her out. We are learning to live together, to ask favors without ego or umbrage, the shin-breaking over who is important. And how wonderful she is to insist on her self, never letting me put her in my shade. Then a peculiar thought. Does Claire look like Cousin Colleen? Colleen that awful Christmas the Milletts laid traps, invited me only to send me away their exile ever since. One aunt slapped me. She was kindest. Among us a blow was caring of a sort. Contact. Recognition. The rest were Brahmin and chilly, my uncle saying they couldn't know me any more since I was "like that." They waited till Colleen was gone back to Washington before they started on me. Protecting her from the knowledge of my crimes, my peer, same age, best friends in childhood, only other Millett cousin in that generation. Colleen my fair-haired cousin, an heiress working after Smith at Katherine Gibbs, fitting college graduates into secretarial slots, a young executive. On the way back south I was broke, driving through Washington and it started to snow. So I called her in a pay phone at a filling station, do I have enough left for gas? My cousin's voice sounding distant in her nice apartment, she has tickets tonight for the symphony. She is engaged. If I could stay over we could visit at breakfast. She thinks the Hotel Roosevelt across the street is quite comfortable. They must have called her, warned her. Does she think I am a rapist, will contaminate the very sheets with my perversion, leak it onto the rug? Never saw her, just hung up and drove on south. Two years later I danced at her wedding in a black dress, acting like some sort of tart from downtown trying to look sexy. I would caricature straightness. Only me and the men who already knew the Twist.

"You are not my Cousin Colleen, you don't even look like her. Of course the yellow hair but her hair was longer and very straight." "They really worked you over, didn't they?" Her eyes steady watching me and I am ashamed of this last broken-wing story, putting down my potato at last. She shows me the children next door playing in the yard before the sea. I had not noticed them. She is telling me a story. "Once I saw a man and a woman looking into Saks' window at Christmas time. They had a child with them standing there on the sidewalk, just disregarded there behind them, all the people walking by bumping it. Then I saw the child at the center of a series of concentric circles reaching out each one bigger expanded, all through the universe. That kid was a bull's-eye."

She walks down the stairs to the beach. Walking alone in her heroic mood like the photograph with her head bent in the wind striding through woods, one of the pictures on the wall at Fifth Street. She is alone, herself, with the green stuff on shore that may be algae and the sea at low tide along the gray expanse of sand. I see her separate at a distance and respected. Her identity. I watch the neighbors. There is a child next door, a little girl squatting in the dirt, playing alone. Incredible but her name is Katie. She is me then when I look at her. When I was eight Mallory was three and broke my sand castle. I punched her in the stomach. Hard. For a moment she turned blue. My dear little sister bellowing because I had hurt her. Dad spanked me. A violent man then. I screamed. We never broke the circuit. This Katie has a brother and a father who walks out of this house down below me, gray haired, looking like an intellectual on vacation, not very physical fellow. Claire is a figure in the distance walking on the shore looking down at things like the dead squid, her trousers rolled up over her knees. The father takes his son's toy and spins it. A launching rocket. But the thing is unpredictable, the plastic suddenly vicious in the air, exlodes, hurling a jagged part at his eyes. He is hit. Blood of the cut. He goes into the house and comes out with a handkerchief. It is hard to keep your manly dignity when a child's toy has nearly blinded you while some female in blue glasses is observing you from a balcony. But he has not lost it. Nor his temper. Gentle as his little girl rushes to him, comforting him. In their two bodies hugging now I have overwhelmed my childhood. Free of its patterns finally. Sometimes watching Claire walk in her independence upon the shore, herself alone while I am alone, sometimes watching only the blue enormous empty sea.

We cleared the table, and when I went outside to get the plates the whole sky was evening. Pink Titian clouds like cotton candy on Commerical Street. The boats, a whole fleet of them. And the water reaching toward a rowboat, its own rose color spread on it thin like gauze. Gulls going by. A girl walks out on the balcony of the cottage ahead and to the right. Her hands clutch the railing. The fleshline of her arms along the wooden two-by-four of the railing is the very expectation of life, its urgency. There are sails way out beyond the shallows, tall ships. The people upstairs had to paddle home today the tide was so low. And a young man in white clothing walks out below me on the grass. He looks clean and fresh. He is tall and has yellow hair. Like Bud Weber when I came back from Japan landing in Los Angeles, a big Caucasian man frightening me and speaking English again, his eyes the strange color of green. My own race. In two years I had nearly forgotten it, hating the tall *geigins* strutting in the Silk Hotel at Yokohama looking down on the dark heads of the Japanese like bugs. But Bud was kind, letting me stay in his place by the sea. I woke to find white curtains and a frame window six over six. It looked so like New England my chest hurt lying in bed the early sun coming through it. I was home.

Now gulls squealing, squadrons numbers turning strange white faces on them. The people next door talking about the spaghetti they had for dinner. Just sounds floating past. One of the children had two helpings. There is success in the sound of it. The gulls screaming. Turning turning in their curves, the sky graying. Like the sparrows on Second Avenue at dusk. The only birds I ever watched before. All the Bowery years, going to the store around suppertime. Gulls so many of them I try to count them but they split and break I cannot place and order them in the sky. Flying in a haze of wings noises cries. Chaos and serenity together.

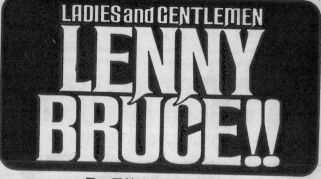

Contents

Introduction

This book is an exercise in crowding angels on a pinhead, or students into a telephone box. It is deliberately the shortest book in which I could possibly squeeze a book's-worth of information. Conversely it holds as much information as I could possibly squeeze into a little diary-format book. Hence no prose: the whole work is played staccato.

Its arrangement is intended to be as helpful as possible when you are buying a bottle, whether you are on the nursery slopes or an old hand with a bad memory. You are faced with a list of wines or an array of bottles in a restaurant, wine merchant or bottle store. Your mind goes blank. You fumble for your little book. All you need to establish is what country a wine comes from. Look up the principal words on the label in the appropriate country's section. You will find enough potted information to let you judge whether this is the wine you want.

Specifically, you will find information on the colour and type of wine, its status or prestige, whether it is usually particularly good value, which vintages are good and which are ready to drink—and often considerably more . . . about the quantity made, the grapes used, ownership and the rest. Hundreds of cross-references help you go further into the matter if you want to.

The introduction to each national section will help you to establish which label-terms are the ones that count. In many cases you will find you can look up almost all the words on the label: estate, grape, shipper, quality-rating, bottling-information. . . .

For your browsing moments the introduction contains important background information about grape types; the first of all determining factors for the quality and essential flavour of any wine.

Note on the 1980/81 Edition

If wine stood still for a moment it would be a less fascinating subject. Being a living thing it is constantly in flux; maturing, growing or diminishing in stature, growing old, being replaced. This new edition tries to reflect the state of maturity of wines which may be currently available, and includes quality notes on the (generally very good) 1979 vintage. The whole book has been revised and new entries squeezed in wherever possible, even if sometimes I have had to resort to telegraphese.

How to read an entry

The top line of most entries consists of the following information in an abbreviated form.

1. Which part of the country in question the wine comes from. (References to the maps in this book.)
2. Whether it is red, rosé or white (or brown/amber), dry, sweet or sparkling, or several of these.
3. Its general standing as to quality: a necessarily rough and ready guide based principally on the following ascending scale:

   * plain, everyday quality
   ** above average
   *** well known, highly reputed
   **** grand, prestigious, expensive

So much is more or less objective. Additionally there is a subjective rating: a box round the stars of any wine which in my experience is usually particularly good (which means good value) within its price range. There are good everyday wines as well as good luxury wines. The box system helps you find them.

4. Vintage information: which were the more successful of the recent vintages which *may* still be available. And of these which are ready to drink this year, and which will probably improve with keeping. Your first choice for current drinking should be one of the vintage years printed in **bold** type. Buy light-type years for further maturing.

The German vintage information works on a different principle: see the Introduction to Germany, page 62.

Acknowledgements

This store of detailed recommendations comes partly from my own notes and partly from those of a great number of kind friends. Without the generous help and co-operation of every single member of the wine trade I have approached, I could not have attempted it. I particularly want to thank the following for giving me material help with research or in the areas of their special knowledge.

Martin Bamford	Tim Marshall
Anthony Barton	Patrick Matthews
Jean Claude Berrouet	Christian Moueix
Michael Broadbent M.W.	Reginald Nicholson
Sheila Cavanagh-Bradbury	David Peppercorn M.W.
Fiona Cowell	Alain Querre
Jan Critchley-Salmonson	Jan Read
Len Evans	Dr. Bruno Roncarati
Francis Fouquet	Steven Spurrier
Jean-Paul Gardère	Keith Stevens
Robert Hart M.W.	Serena Sutcliffe M.W.
Peter Hasslacher	Hugh Suter M.W.
Tony Laithwaite	Bob Thompson
Michael Longhurst	Peter Vinding-Diers

Grape varieties

The most basic of all differences between wines stems from the grapes they are made of. Centuries of selection have resulted in each of the long-established wine-areas having its favourite single variety, or a group of varieties whose juice or wine is blended together. Red burgundy is made of one grape, the Pinot Noir; red Bordeaux of three or four: two kinds of Cabernet, Merlot, Malbec and sometimes others. The laws say which grapes must be used, so the labels assume it.

So in newer vineyards the choice of a grape is the planter's single most crucial decision. Where he is proud of it, and intends his wine to have the character of a particular grape, the variety is the first thing he puts on the label—hence the useful, originally Californian, term "varietal wine".

A knowledge of grape varieties, therefore, is the single most helpful piece of knowledge in finding wines you will like wherever they are grown. Learn to recognize the characters of the most important. At least seven—Cabernet, Pinot Noir, Riesling, Sauvignon Blanc, Chardonnay, Gewürztraminer and Muscat—have memorable tastes and smells distinct enough to form international categories of wine.

Further notes on grapes will be found on page 126 (for California) and in the sections on Germany, Italy, central and south-east Europe, South Africa, etc.

The following are the best and commonest wine grapes.

Grapes for white wine

Aligoté
Burgundy's second-rank white grape. Crisp (often sharp) wine, needs drinking young. Perfect for mixing with cassis (blackcurrant liqueur) to make a "Kir". Also grown in the USSR.

Blanc Fumé
Another name for SAUVIGNON BLANC, referring to the "smoky" smell of the wine, particularly on the upper Loire. Makes some of California's best whites.

Bual
Makes sweet Madeira wines.

Chardonnay
The white burgundy grape, one of the grapes of Champagne, and the best white grape of California. Gives dry wine of rich complexity. Trials in Australia and eastern Europe are also successful.

Chasselas
A prolific and widely grown early-ripening grape with little flavour, also grown for eating. Best known as Fendant in Switzerland, Gutedel in Germany. Perhaps the same as Hungary's Leanyka and Romania's Feteasca.

Chenin Blanc
The leading white grape of the middle Loire (Vouvray, Layon, etc.). Wine can be dry or sweet (or very sweet), but always retains plenty of acidity—hence its popularity in California, where it rarely distinguishes itself.

Clairette

A dull neutral grape widely used in the s. of France.

Fendant

See Chasselas

Folle Blanche

The third most widely grown grape of France, though nowhere making fine wine. High acid and little flavour makes it ideal for brandy. Known as Gros Plant in Brittany, Picpoul in the Midi. At its best in California.

Furmint

A grape of great character: the trade mark of Hungary both in Tokay and as vivid vigorous table wine with an appley flavour. Called Sipon in Jugoslavia.

Gewürztraminer (or Traminer)

The most pungent wine grape, distinctively spicy to smell and taste. Wines are often rich and soft, even when fully dry. Best in Alsace; also good in Germany, eastern Europe, Australia, California.

Gros Plant

See Folle Blanche

Grüner Veltliner

An Austrian speciality. Round Vienna and in the Wachau and Weinviertel can be delicious: light but lively. For drinking young.

Italian Riesling

Grown in n. Italy and all over central eastern Europe. Inferior to German or Rhine Riesling with lower acidity, but a good all-round grape. Alias Wälschriesling, Olaszriesling (or often just "Riesling").

Kerner

The most successful of a wide range of recent German varieties, largely made by crossing Riesling and Sylvaner (but in this case Riesling and [red] Trollinger). Early-ripening; pleasant flowery wine with good acidity. Popular in RHEINPFALZ.

Malvasia

Known as Malmsey in Madeira, Malvasia in Italy: also grown in Greece, Spain, eastern Europe. Makes rich brown wines or soft whites of no great character.

Müller-Thurgau

Dominant variety in Germany's Rheinhessen and Rheinpfalz; said to be a cross between Riesling and Sylvaner. Ripens early to make soft flowery wines to drink young. Makes good sweet wines. Grows well in Austria, England.

Muscadet

Makes light, very dry wines round Nantes in Brittany. Recently some have been sharper than they should.

Muscat (many varieties)

Universally grown easily recognized pungent grape, mostly made into perfumed sweet wines, often fortified (as in France's VIN DOUX NATURELS). Muscat d'Alsace is alone in being dry.

Palomino

Alias Listan. Makes all the best sherry.

Pedro Ximénez

Said to have come to s. Spain from Germany. Makes very strong wine in Montilla and Malaga. Used in blending sherry. Also grown in Australia, California, South Africa.

Pinot Blanc

A close relation of CHARDONNAY without its ultimate nobility. Grown in Champagne, Alsace, n. Italy (good sparkling wine), s. Germany, eastern Europe, California.

Pinot Gris

Makes rather heavy full-bodied whites with a certain spicy style. Known as Tokay in Alsace, Tocai in n.e. Italy and Jugoslavia, Ruländer in Germany.

Pinot Noir

Superlative black grape (see under Grapes for red wine) used in Champagne and occasionally elsewhere for making white wine.

Riesling

Germany's finest grape, now planted round the world. Wine of brilliant sweet/acid balance, flowery in youth but maturing to subtle oily scents and flavours. Successful in Alsace (for dry wine), Austria, parts of eastern Europe, Australia, California, South Africa. Often called White, Johannisberg or Rhine Riesling.

Sauvignon Blanc

Very distinctive aromatic, herby and sometimes smoky scented wine, can be austere (on the upper Loire) or buxom (in Bordeaux, where it is combined with SEMILLON, and parts of California). Also called Fumé Blanc.

Semillon

The grape contributing the lusciousness to great Sauternes; subject to "noble rot" in the right conditions. Makes soft dry wine. Called "Riesling" in Australia.

Sercial

Makes the driest wine of Madeira—where they claim it is really Riesling.

Seyval Blanc

French-made hybrid between French and American vines. Very hardy and attractively fruity. Popular and successful in the eastern States and England.

Steen

South Africa's best white grape: lively fruity wine. Said to be the Chenin Blanc of the Loire.

Sylvaner

Germany's workhorse grape: wine rarely better than pleasant except in Franconia. Good in the Italian Tyrol and useful in Alsace. Wrongly called Riesling in California.

Tokay

See Pinot Gris. Also a table grape in California and a supposedly Hungarian grape in Australia.

Traminer

See Gewürztraminer

Trebbiano

Important grape of central Italy, used in Orvieto, Chianti, Soave, etc. Also grown in s. France as Ugni Blanc, and Cognac as "St-Emilion".

Ugni Blanc

See Trebbiano

Verdelho

Madeira grape making excellent medium-sweet wine.

Verdicchio

Gives its name to good dry wine in central Italy.

Vernaccia

Grape grown in central and s. Italy and Sardinia for strong wine inclining towards sherry.

Viognier

Rare but remarkable grape of the Rhône valley, grown at Condrieu to make very fine soft and fragrant wine.

Welschriesling (or Wälschriesling)

See Italian Riesling

Grapes for red wine

Barbera
One of several good standard grapes of Piemonte, giving dark, robust, fruity and often rather sharp wine. High acidity makes it a good grape for California.

Cabernet Franc
The lesser of two sorts of Cabernet grown in Bordeaux; the Cabernet of the Loire making Chinon and rosé.

Cabernet Sauvignon
Grape of great character; spicy, herby and tannic. The first grape of the Médoc, also makes the best Californian, Australian, South American and eastern European reds. Its wine always needs ageing and usually blending.

Carignan
By far the commonest grape of France, covering hundreds of thousands of acres. Prolific with dull but harmless wine. Also common in North Africa, Spain and California.

Gamay
The Beaujolais grape: light fragrant wines at their best quite young. Makes even lighter wine on the Loire and in Switzerland and Savoie. Known as Napa Gamay in California.

Gamay Beaujolais
Not Gamay but a variety of PINOT NOIR grown in California.

Grenache
Useful grape giving strong and fruity but pale wine: good rosé. Grown in s. France, Spain, California and usually blended.

Grignolino
Makes one of the good cheap table wines of Piemonte. Also used in California.

Merlot
Adaptable grape making the great fragrant and rich wines of Pomerol and St-Emilion, an important element in Médoc reds, and making lighter but good wines in n. Italy, Italian Switzerland, Jugoslavia, Argentina, etc.

Nebbiolo (also called Spanna)
Italy's best red grape, the grape of Barolo, Barbaresco, Gattinara and Valtellina. Intense, nobly fruity and perfumed wine taking years to mature.

Pinot Noir
The glory of Burgundy's Côte d'Or, with scent, flavour, texture and body unmatched anywhere. Less happy elsewhere; makes light wines of no great distinction in Germany, Switzerland, Austria; good ones in Hungary; generally dull ones in California.

Sangiovese
The main red grape of Chianti and much of central Italy.

Syrah
The best Rhône red grape, with heavy purple wine, which can mature superbly. Said by some to come from Shiraz in Persia; others say Syracuse in Sicily. Very important as "Shiraz" in Australia.

Zinfandel
Fruity adaptable grape peculiar to California.

Wine & Food

There are no rules and regulations about what wine goes with what food, but there is a vast body of accumulated experience which it is absurd to ignore.

This list of dishes and appropriate wines records most of the conventional combinations and suggests others that I personally have found good. But it is only a list of ideas intended to help you make quick decisions. Any of the groups of recommended wines could have been extended almost indefinitely, drawing on the whole world's wine list. In general I have stuck to the wines that are widely available, at the same time trying to ring the changes so that the same wines don't come up time and time again—as they tend to do in real life.

The stars refer to the rating system used throughout the book: see opposite Contents.

First courses

Aïoli

A thirst-quencher is needed with so much garlic. ★→★★ white Rhône, or Verdicchio, and mineral water.

Antipasto (see also Hors d'oeuvre)

★★ dry or medium white, preferably Italian (e.g. Soave) or light red, e.g. Valpolicella, Bardolino or young ★ Bordeaux.

Artichoke

★ red or rosé.

vinaigrette ★ young red, e.g. Bordeaux.

hollandaise ★ or ★★ full-bodied dry or medium white, e.g. Mâcon Blanc, Rheinpfalz or California "Chablis".

Asparagus

★★→★★★ white burgundy or Chardonnay, or Tavel rosé.

Assiette anglaise (assorted cold meats)

★★ dry white, e.g. Chablis, Graves, Muscadet, Dão.

Avocado

with prawns, crab, etc. ★★→★★★ dry to medium white, e.g. Rheingau or Rheinpfalz Kabinett, Graves, California Chardonnay or Sauvignon, Cape Stein, or dry rosé.

vinaigrette ★ light red, or fino sherry.

Bisques

★★ dry white with plenty of body: Verdicchio, Pinot Gris, Graves.

Bouillabaisse

★→★★ very dry white: Muscadet, Alsace Sylvaner, Entre-Deux-Mers, Pouilly Fumé, Cassis.

Caviare

★★★ champagne or iced vodka.

Cheese fondue

★★ dry white: Fendant du Valais, Grüner Veltliner.

Chicken Liver Pâté

Appetizing dry white, e.g. ★★ white Bordeaux, or light fruity red; Beaujolais, Gamay de Touraine or Valpolicella.

Clams and Chowders

★★ big-scale white, not necessarily bone dry: e.g. Rhône, Pinot Gris, Dry Sauternes.

Consommé

★★→★★★ medium-dry sherry, dry Madeira, Marsala, Montilla.

Crudités

★→★★ light red or rosé, e.g. Côtes-du-Rhône, Beaujolais, Chianti, Zinfandel.

Eggs (see also Soufflés)

These present difficulties: they clash with most wine and spoil good ones. So ★→★★ of whatever is going.

Empanadas

★→★★ Chilean Cabernet, Zinfandel.

Escargots

★★ red or white of some substance: e.g. Burgundy; Côtes-du-Rhône, Chardonnay, Shiraz, etc.

Foie gras

★★★→★★★★ white. In Bordeaux they drink Sauternes. Others prefer vintage champagne or a rich Gewürztraminer Vendange tardive.

Gazpacho

Sangria (see Spain) is refreshing, but to avoid too much liquid intake dry Manzanilla or Montilla is better.

Grapefruit

If you must start a meal with grapefruit try port, Madeira or sweet sherry with it.

Ham, raw

See Prosciutto

Herrings, raw or pickled

Dutch gin or Scandinavian akvavit, or ★★ full-bodied white Mâcon-Villages, Graves or Dão.

Hors d'oeuvre (see also Antipasto)

★→★★ clean fruity sharp white: Sancerre or any Sauvignon, Alsace Sylvaner, Muscadet, Cape Stein—or young light red Bordeaux, Rhône or equivalent.

Mackerel, smoked

★★→★★★ full-bodied tasty white: e.g. Gewürztraminer, Tokay d'Alsace or Chablis Premier Cru.

Melon

Needs a strong sweet wine: ★★ Port, Bual Madeira, Muscat, Oloroso sherry or Vin doux naturel.

Minestrone

★ red: Grignolino, Chianti, etc.

Omelettes

See observations under Eggs

Onion/Leek tart

★→★★★ fruity dry white, e.g. Alsace Sylvaner or Riesling. Mâcon-Villages of a good vintage, California or Australian Riesling.

Pasta

★→★★ red or white according to the sauce or accompaniments, e.g.

with fish sauce (vongole, etc.) Verdicchio or Soave.

meat sauce Chianti, Beaujolais or Côtes-du-Rhône.

tomato sauce Barbera or Sicilian red.

cream sauce Orvieto or Frascati.

Pâté

★★ dry white: e.g. Chablis, Mâcon Blanc, Graves.

Peppers or aubergines (egg-plant), stuffed

★★ vigorous red: e.g. Bull's Blood, Chianti, Zinfandel.

Pizza

Any ★★ dry Italian red or a ★★ Rioja, Australian Shiraz or California Zinfandel.

Prawns or Shrimps

★★→★★★ dry white: burgundy or Bordeaux, Chardonnay or Riesling. ("Cocktail sauce" kills wine.)

Prosciutto with melon

★★→★★★★ full-bodied dry or medium white: e.g. Orvieto or Frascati, Fendant, Grüner Veltliner, Alsace Sylvaner, California Gewürztraminer, Australian Riesling.

Quiches

    *→** dry white with body (Alsace, Graves, Sauvignon) or young red according to the ingredients.

Ratatouille

    ** vigorous young red, e.g. Chianti, Zinfandel, Bull's Blood, young red Bordeaux.

Salade niçoise

    ** very dry not too light or flowery white, e.g. white (or rosé) Rhône, white Spanish, Dão, California Sauvignon Blanc.

Salads

    As a first course: any dry and appetizing white wine. After a main course: no wine.

    N.B. Vinegar in salad dressings destroys the flavour of wine. If you want salad at a meal with fine wine, dress the salad with wine instead of vinegar.

Salami

    *→** powerfully tasty red or rosé: e.g. Barbera, young Zinfandel, Tavel rosé, young Bordeaux.

Salmon, smoked

    A dry but pungent white, e.g. fino sherry, Alsace Gewürztraminer, Chablis Grand Cru.

Soufflés

    As show dishes these deserve **→*** wines.

    Fish soufflés Dry white, e.g. burgundy, Bordeaux, Alsace, Chardonnay, etc.

    Cheese soufflé Red burgundy or Bordeaux, Cabernet Sauvignon, etc.

Taramasalata

    Calls for a rustic southern white of strong personality; not necessarily the Greek Retsina.

Terrine

    As for pâté, or the equivalent red: e.g. Beaune, Mercurey, Beaujolais-Villages, fairly young ** St-Emilion, California Cabernet or Zinfandel, Bulgarian or Chilean Cabernet, etc.

Fish

Abalone

    →* dry or medium white: e.g. Sauvignon Blanc, Chardonnay, Verdicchio.

Cod

    A good neutral background for fine dry or medium whites, e.g. **→*** Chablis, cru classé Graves, German Kabinetts and their equivalents.

Coquilles St. Jacques

    An inherently slightly sweet dish, best with medium-dry white wine.

    in cream sauces *** German wines.

    grilled or fried Hermitage Blanc, Gewürztraminer, California Chenin Blanc or Riesling.

Eel, smoked

    Either strong or sharp wine, e.g. fino sherry or Bourgogne Aligoté.

Haddock

    →* dry white with a certain richness: e.g. Meursault, California Chardonnay.

Herrings

    Need a white with some acidity to cut their richness. Burgundy Aligoté or Gros Plant from Brittany or dry Sauvignon Blanc. **Kippers:** a good cup of tea, preferably Ceylon.

Lamproie à la Bordelaise

    ** young red Bordeaux, especially St-Emilion or Pomerol.

Lobster or Crab

salad ★★→★★★★ white. Non-vintage champagne, Alsace Riesling, Chablis Premier Cru.

richly sauced Vintage champagne, fine white burgundy, cru classé Graves, California Chardonnay, Rheinpfalz Spätlese, Hermitage Blanc.

Mackerel

★★ hard or sharp white: Sauvignon Blanc from Bergerac or Touraine, Gros Plant, vinho verde, white Rioja.

Mullet, red

★★ Mediterranean white, even Retsina, for the atmosphere.

Mussels

★→★★★ Gros Plant, Muscadet, California "Chablis".

Oysters

★★→★★★ white. Champagne (non-vintage), Chablis or (better) Chablis Premier Cru, Muscadet or Entre-Deux-Mers.

Salmon, fresh

★★★ fine white burgundy: Puligny- or Chassagne-Montrachet, Meursault, Corton-Charlemagne, Chablis Grand Cru, California Chardonnay, or Rheingau Kabinett or Spätlese, California Riesling or equivalent.

Sardines, fresh grilled

★→★★★ very dry white: e.g. vinho verde, Dão, Muscadet.

Scallops

See Coquilles St. Jacques

Shad

★★→★★★ white Graves or Meursault.

Shellfish (general)

Dry white with plain boiled shellfish, richer wines with richer sauces.

Shrimps, potted

Fino sherry or Chablis.

Skate with black butter

★★ white with some pungency (e.g. Alsace Pinot Gris) or a clean one like Muscadet.

Sole, Plaice, etc.

plain, grilled or fried An ideal accompaniment for fine wines: ★ up to ★★★★ white burgundy, or its equivalent.

with sauce Depending on the ingredients: sharp dry wine for tomato sauce, fairly sweet for Sole véronique, etc.

Trout

Delicate white wine, e.g. ★★★ Mosel.

Smoked, a full-flavoured ★★→★★★ white: Gewürztraminer, Pinot Gris, Rhine Spätlese or Australian Hunter white.

Turbot

Fine rich dry white, e.g. ★★★ Meursault or its Californian equivalent.

Meat

Beef, boiled

★★ red: e.g. Cru Bourgeois Bordeaux (Bourg or Fronsac), Côtes-du-Rhône-Villages, Australian Shiraz or Claret.

Beef, roast

An ideal partner for fine red wine. ★→★★★★ red of any kind.

Beef stew

★★→★★★★ sturdy red, e.g. Pomerol or St-Emilion, Hermitage, Shiraz.

Beef Strogonoff

★★★→★★★★ suitably dramatic red: e.g. Barolo, Valpolicella, Amarone, Hermitage, late-harvest Zinfandel.

Cassoulet

    ** red from s.w. France, e.g. Cahors or Corbières, or Barbera or Zinfandel.

Chicken or Turkey, roast

    Virtually any wine, including your very best bottles of dry or medium white and fine old reds.

Chili con carne

    *→** young red: e.g. Bull's Blood, Chianti, Mountain Red.

Chinese food

    ** dry to medium-dry white: e.g. Jugoslav Riesling, Mâcon-Villages, California "Chablis".

Choucroute

    Lager.

Confit d'Oie

    →* rather young and tannic red Bordeaux helps to cut the richness. Alsace Tokay or Gewürztraminer matches it.

Coq au Vin

    →** red burgundy. In an ideal world one bottle of Chambertin in the dish, one on the table.

Corned beef hash

    ** Zinfandel, Chianti, Côtes-du-Rhône red.

Curry

    *→** medium-sweet white, very cold: e.g. Orvieto abboccato, certain California Chenin Blancs, Jugoslav Traminer.

Duck or Goose

    *** rather rich white, e.g. Rheinpfalz Spätlese or Alsace Réserve Exceptionelle, or *** Bordeaux or burgundy.

    Wild Duck *** big-scale red: e.g. Hermitage, Châteauneuf-du-Pape, Calif. or S. African Cabernet, Australian Shiraz.

Frankfurters

    *→** German or Austrian white.

Game birds

    Young birds plain roasted deserve the best red wine you can afford. With older birds in casseroles **→*** red, e.g. Gevrey-Chambertin, St-Emilion, Napa Cabernet.

Game Pie

    *** red wine.

Goulash

    ** strong young red: e.g. Zinfandel, Bulgarian Cabernet.

Grouse

    See under Game birds

Ham

    →* fairly young red burgundy, e.g. Volnay, Savigny, Beaune, Corton, or a slightly sweet German white, e.g. a Rhine Spätlese, or Chianti or Valpolicella.

Hamburger

    *→** young red: e.g. Beaujolais, Corbières or Minervois, Chianti, Zinfandel.

Hare

    Jugged hare calls for **→*** red with plenty of flavour: not-too-old burgundy or Bordeaux. The same for saddle.

Kebabs

    ** vigorous red: e.g. Greek Demestica, Turkish Doluca, Hungarian Pinot Noir, Chilean Cabernet, Zinfandel.

Kidneys

    →* red: Pomerol or St-Emilion, Rhône, Barbaresco, Rioja, California or Australian Cabernet.

Lamb cutlets or chops

    As for roast lamb, but less grand.

Lamb, roast

    One of the traditional and best partners for very good red Bordeaux—or its equivalents.

Liver

** young red: Beaujolais-Villages, Rhône, Médoc, Italian Merlot, Zinfandel.

Meatballs

→* red: e.g. Mercurey, Madiran, Rubesco, Dão, Zinfandel.

Mixed Grill

A fairly light easily swallowable red; ** red Bordeaux from Bourg, Fronsac or Premières Côtes; Chianti; Bourgogne Passetoutgrains.

Moussaka

*→** red or rosé: e.g. Chianti, Corbières, Côtes de Provence, California Burgundy.

Oxtail

→* rather rich red: e.g. St-Emilion or Pomerol, Burgundy, Barolo or Chianti Classico, Rioja Reserva, California Cabernet.

Paella

** Spanish red, dry white or rosé, e.g. Panades or Rioja or vinho verde.

Partridge, pheasant

See under Game birds

Pigeons or squabs

→* red Bordeaux, Chianti Classico, Cabernet Sauvignon, etc.

Pork, roast

The sauce or stuffing has more flavour than the meat. Sharp apple sauce or pungent sage and onion need only a plain young wine. Pork without them, on the other hand, is a good neutral background to very good white or red wine.

Rabbit

*→*** young red: Italian for preference.

Sauerkraut

Beer.

Shepherd's Pie

*→** rough and ready red seems most appropriate, but no harm would come to a good one.

Steak and Kidney Pie or Pudding

Red Rioja Reserva or mature **→*** Bordeaux.

Steaks

Au poivre a fairly young *** Rhône red or Cabernet.

Tartare ** light young red: Bergerac, Valpolicella.

Filet or Tournedos *** red of any kind (but not old wines with Béarnaise sauce).

T-bone **→*** reds of similar bone-structure: e.g. Barolo, Hermitage, Australian Cabernet.

Fiorentina (bistecca) Chianti Classico.

Stews and Casseroles

A lusty full-flavoured red, e.g. young Côtes-du-Rhône, Corbières, Barbera, Shiraz, Zinfandel, etc.

Sweetbreads

These tend to be a grand dish, suggesting a grand wine, e.g. *** Rhine Kabinett or Spätlese, or well-matured Bordeaux or Burgundy, depending on the sauce.

Tongue

Ideal for favourite bottles of any red or white.

Tripe

*→** red: Corbières, Mâcon Rouge, etc., or rather sweet white, e.g. Liebfraumilch.

Veal, roast

A good neutral background dish for any old red which may have faded, or a *** German white.

Venison

    ★★★ big-scale red (Rhône, Bordeaux of a grand vintage) or rather rich white (Rheinpfalz Spätlese or Tokay d'Alsace).

Wiener Schnitzel

    ★★→★★★ light red from the Italian Tyrol (Alto Adige) or the Médoc: or Austrian Riesling, Grüner Veltliner or Gumpoldskirchener.

Cheese

Very ripe cheese completely masks the flavour of wine. Only serve fine wine with mild cheeses.

Bleu de Bresse, Dolcelatte, Gorgonzola

    Need fairly emphatic accompaniment: young ★★ red wine (Barbera, Dolcetto, Moulin-à-Vent, etc.) or sweet white.

Cream cheeses: Brie, Camembert, Bel Paese, Edam, etc.

    In their mild state go perfectly with any good wine, red or white.

English cheeses

    On the whole are strong and acidic. Sweet or strong wine is needed.

    Cheddar, Cheshire, Wensleydale, Stilton, Gloucester, etc. Ruby, tawny or vintage-character (not vintage) port, or a very big red: Hermitage, Châteauneuf-du-Pape, Barolo, etc.

Goat cheeses

    ★★→★★★ white wine of marked character, either dry (e.g. Sancerre) or sweet (e.g. Monbazillac, Sauternes).

Hard Cheese, Parmesan, Gruyère, Emmenthal

    Full-bodied dry whites, e.g. Tokay d'Alsace or Vernaccia.

Roquefort, Danish Blue

    Are so strong-flavoured that only the youngest, biggest or sweetest wines stand a chance.

Desserts

Apple pie, apple strudel

    ★★→★★★ sweet German, Austrian or Hungarian white.

Baked Alaska

    Sweet champagne or Asti Spumante.

Cakes

    Bual or Malmsey Madeira, Oloroso or cream sherry.

Cheesecake

    ★★→★★★ sweet white from Vouvray or Coteaux du Layon.

Chocolate cake, mousse, soufflés

    No wine.

Christmas pudding

    Sweet champagne or Asti Spumante.

Creams and Custards

    ★★→★★★ Sauternes, Monbazillac or similar golden white.

Crème brûlée

    The most luxurious dish, demanding ★★★→★★★★ Sauternes or Rhine Beerenauslese, or the best Madeira or Tokay.

Crêpes Suzette

    Sweet champagne or Asti Spumante.

Fruit flans (i.e. peach, raspberry)

    ★★★ Sauternes, Monbazillac or sweet Vouvray.

Fruit salads, orange salad

    No wine.

Nuts

    Oloroso sherry, Bual, Madeira, vintage or tawny port.

Sorbets, ice-creams

    No wine.

Stewed fruits, i.e. apricots, pears, etc.
> Sweet Muscatel: e.g. Muscat de Beaumes de Venise, Moscato di Pantelleria.

Strawberries and cream
> ★★★ Sauternes or Vouvray.
>
> **Wild strawberries** Serve with ★★★ red Bordeaux poured over them and in your glass (no cream).

Summer Pudding
> Fairly young Sauternes of a good vintage (e.g. 70, 71, 75).

Treacle Tart
> Too sweet for any wine but a treacly Malmsey Madeira.

Trifle
> No wine: should be sufficiently vibrant with sherry.

Sweet Soufflés
> Sweet Vouvray or Coteaux du Layon.

Zabaglione
> Light gold Marsala.

Savoury

Cheese straws
> Admirable meal-ending with a final glass (or bottle) of a particularly good red wine.

Temperature

No single aspect of serving wine makes or mars it so easily as getting the temperature right. White wines almost invariably taste dull and insipid served warm and red wines have disappointingly little scent or flavour served cold. The chart below gives an indication of what is generally found to be the best and most satisfactory temperature for serving each class of wine.

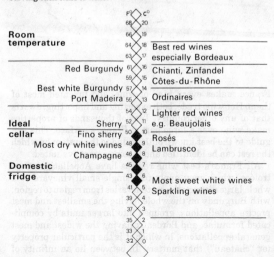

	F°	C°	
	68	20	
Room	66	19	
temperature	64	18	Best red wines
	63	17	especially Bordeaux
Red Burgundy	61	16	Chianti, Zinfandel
	59	15	Côtes-du-Rhône
Best white Burgundy	57	14	
Port Madeira	55	13	Ordinaires
	54	12	Lighter red wines
Ideal	Sherry 52	11	e.g. Beaujolais
cellar	Fino sherry 50	10	Rosés
Most dry white wines	48	9	Lambrusco
Champagne	46	8	
Domestic	45	7	
fridge	43	6	Most sweet white wines
	41	5	Sparkling wines
	39	4	
	37	3	
	35	2	
	33	1	
	32	0	

France

Brittany

Loire **Lo**

R. Seine

R. Loire

Cognac

Bordeaux **B'x**

• Bordeaux

R. Garonne

SW France

France makes every kind of wine, and invented most of them. Her wine trade, both exporting and importing, dwarfs that of any other country. Tens of thousands of properties make wine over a large part of France's surface. This is a guide to the best known of them and to the system by which the rest can be identified and to some extent evaluated.

All France's best wine regions have Appellations Contrôlées, which may apply to a single small vineyard or a whole large district: the system varies from region to region, with Burgundy on the whole having the smallest and most precise appellations, grouped into larger units by complicated formulae, and Bordeaux having the widest and most general appellations, in which it is the particular property (or "château") that matters. In between lie an infinity of variations.

Reims ●

Champagne **Champ**

● Paris

Alsace **Al**

Burgundy **B'y**

Upper Loire

Dijon ●

R. Saône

Jura

Central France

Beaujolais

Dordogne

Rhône **Rh**

Savoie

R. Rhône

R. Dordogne

Provence **Prov**

● Marseille

Midi

Pyrenees **Pyr**

Abbreviations of regional names shown in bold type are used in the text.

An Appellation Controlée is a guarantee of origin and of production method, of grape varieties and quantities produced: not of quality. France does not have a quality-testing system as Germany does. The scale of the problem is too vast and the French are too French.

Appellations therefore help to identify a wine and indicate that it comes from a major area. They are the first thing to look for on a label.

Wine regions without the overall quality and traditions required for an appellation can be ranked as Vins Délimites de Qualité Supérieure (VDQS), or (a new third rank created largely to encourage the improvement of mediocre wines in the south of France) Vins de Pays. VDQS wines are often good value, on the Avis principle. Vins de Pays are worth trying for curiosity's sake.

Recent Vintages

Red Burgundy

Côte d'Or Côte de Beaune reds generally mature sooner than the bigger wines of the Côte de Nuits. Earliest drinking dates are for lighter commune wines: Volnay, Beaune, etc. Latest for the biggest wines of Chambertin, Romanée, etc. Different growers make wines of different styles, for longer or shorter maturing, but even the best burgundies are much more attractive young than the equivalent red Bordeaux.

1979	Big generally good ripe vintage. S. Côte de Nuits suffered from hail.
1978	Poor summer saved by miraculous autumn. A small vintage of outstanding quality.
1977	Very wet summer. Better wine than expected, especially in northern côtes.
1976	Hot summer, excellent vintage. Some wines may be too tannic.
1975	Rot was rife, particularly in the Côte de Beaune. Mostly very poor. A few good wines from the northern Côte de Nuits with careful vinification. To be drunk.
1974	Another big wet vintage; mostly poor, even the best light and lean. Drink up.
1973	Again, vintage rain stretched the crop. Light wines, but many fruity and delicate. Many are already too old.
1972	High acidity posed problems, but the wines are firm and full of character, ageing well. Few need keeping.
1971	Very powerful and impressive wines, not as long-lasting as they first appeared. Most now ready.
1970	Attractive soft fruity wines, but should be drunk up now. Big crop.
1969	A magnificent vintage with very few exceptions. Small crop. The best will mature as long as any modern burgundy. The rest are ready.

Older fine vintages: '66, '64, '62, '61, '59.

Beaujolais

1979	Big crop of good quick-maturing typical wine.
1978	A very good vintage in profusion. Most now ready.
1977	Generally poor, some pleasant light wines and good Crus.
1976	Was the best vintage since 1971. Most wines are now delicious. Its best will keep for 2–3 years.

White Burgundy

Côte de Beaune Well-made wines of good vintages with plenty of acidity as well as fruit will improve and gain depth and richness for some years—anything up to ten. Lesser wines from lighter years are ready for drinking after two or three years.

1979	Very big vintage. Overall good and useful, not great.
1978	Very good wines, some perhaps too soft to keep for long.
1977	Rather light; some well-balanced and good.
1976	Hot summer, rather heavy wines; good but not for laying-down.
1975	Hot summer, then vintage rain. Whites did much better than reds. Rot reduced quantity, but the grapes were ripe and the wine can be excellent. No hurry to drink.
1974	Spring frosts reduced the crop, but the hot summer made some fine wines, now generally ready.
1973	Very attractive, fruity, typical and plentiful. Drink up.
1972	Awkward wines to make with high acidity, even greenness, but plenty of character. The best have developed into classical wines.
1971	Great power and style, some almost too rich, but the best have good balance. Small crop. Generally ready.

The white wines of the Mâconnais (Pouilly-Fuissé, St Véran, Mâcon-Villages) follow a similar pattern, but do not last as long. They are more appreciated for their freshness than their richness.

Chablis Grand Cru Chablis of vintages with both strength and acidity can age superbly for up to ten years. Premier Crus proportionately less. Only buy Petit Chablis of ripe years, and drink it young.

1979	Very big crop. Good easy wines, not for storing.
1978	Excellent wines for fairly early drinking.
1977	Reduced quantity, but typical and fresh like 1974.
1976	A great vintage. Start to drink.
1975	Very good wines maturing rather quickly. Drink.
1974	A trifle sharp at first, but lively, attractive and typical.
1973	Very good ripe and plentiful vintage. Needs drinking.

Red Bordeaux

Médoc/red Graves For some wines bottle-age is optional: for these it is indispensable. Minor châteaux from light vintages need only two or three years, but even modest wines of great years can improve for fifteen years or so, and the great châteaux of these years need double that time.

1979	Abundant harvest of good average quality.
1978	A miracle vintage: magnificent long warm autumn saved the day. Some very good wines.
1977	Very wet summer. Pleasant light wine, many better than 1974.
1976	Excessively hot, dry summer; rain just before vintage. Difficult year, but its best wine will be very good, maturing rather quickly.
1975	A splendid summer and very fine vintage, with deep colour, high sugar content and some tannin. For long keeping.
1974	Diluting vintage rain ruined hopes of a really good vintage. Oceans of disappointing light wines, though the best have good colour and have developed some character.
1973	Again, last-minute rain turned quality into quantity. A huge vintage, attractive to drink young but lacking acidity and tannin.
1972	High acidity from unripe grapes. Do not pay much for '72s.
1971	Small crop. Less fruity than '70 and less consistent. Some châteaux made outstanding wine. Most are ready to drink.
1970	Abundance *and* uniform quality. Big fruity wines with elegance and attractive suppleness. Although not tannic they are wines of great distinction for long keeping.
1969	Heavy September rain after a good summer. Mean wines lacking fruit and colour. Should all be drunk soon.
1968	This time a wet August was the culprit. Very few drinkable wines.
1967	Large; first judged to be light and for early drinking, has developed well and gained body and interest, though not always charm.
1966	A very fine vintage with depth, fruit and tannin. Still needs time to open out. Classic claret.

Older fine vintages: '62, '61, '59, '55, '53, '52, '50, '49, '48, '47, '45, '29, '28.

St-Emilion/Pomerol

1979	Big rather patchy vintage. The best better than '78.
1978	Lovely wine, to everyone's surprise. Will mature fairly early.
1977	Very wet summer. Mediocre with few exceptions.
1976	Very hot, dry summer and early vintage, but vintage rain made complications. Some excellent wines: the best great.
1975	Most St-Emilions good, the best superb. Frost in Pomerol reduced crops and made splendid concentrated wine.
1974	Vintage rain again. Mainly disappointing light wines.
1973	Good summer, big wet vintage. Pleasant: wines to drink young.
1972	Poor summer but fine for the late vintage. Many unripe wines, but some are pleasant enough. Choose carefully.
1971	Small crop: fine wines with length and depth, on the whole better than Médocs but generally now ready.
1970	Glorious weather and beautiful wines with great fruit and strength throughout the district. Very big crop.
1969	Fine summer, small wet vintage. At best agreeable.
1968	A disaster. Endless rain.
1967	Large and generally very good; on the whole better than Médoc.
1966	Ripe, powerful, round. Maturing well.

Older fine vintages: '64, '61, '59, '53, '52, '49, '47, '45.
For other areas see under A–Z entries.

Ajaccio   Corsica r. p. or w. dr. ★ NV
>The capital of Corsica and its strong plain wines.

Aligoté
>Second-rank burgundy white grape and its often sharp wine, often agreeable and with considerable local character when young.

Aloxe-Corton   B'y. r. or w. ★★★ 69 71 72 73 76 77 78 79
>Northernmost village of CÔTE DE BEAUNE: best v'yds.: CORTON (red) and CORTON-CHARLEMAGNE (white). Village wines lighter but often good value.

Alsace   Al. w. or (r.) ★★ 71 75 76 77 78 79
>Aromatic, fruity dry white of Germanic character from French Rhineland. Normally sold by grape variety (RIESLING, GEWÜRZTRAMINER, etc.). Matures well.

Alsace Grand Cru   ★★★
>Appellation restricted to the best named v'yds.

Alsace Grand Vin or Réserve
>Wine with minimum 11° natural alcohol.

Ampeau, Robert
>Leading grower and specialist in MEURSAULT.

Anjou   Lo. (r.) p. or w. (sw. dr. or sp.) ★→★★★ 69 70 71 73 75 76 78 79
>Very various Loire wines, incl. good CABERNET rosé, luscious COTEAUX DU LAYON. Maturity depends on style.

Appellation Controlée
>Government control of origin and production of all the best French wines (see France Introduction).

Apremont   Savoie w. dr. ★★ D.Y.A.
>One of the best villages of SAVOIE for pale delicate whites.

Arbois   Jura r. p. or w. (dr. sp.) ★★ D.Y.A.
>Various pleasant light wines; speciality VIN JAUNE.

Armagnac
>Region of s.w. France famous for its excellent brandy, a fiery spirit of rustic character. The chief town is Condom.

Auxey-Duresses   B'y. r. or w.   ★★   71 72 75w 76 77 78 79
>Second-rank CÔTE DE BEAUNE village: has affinities with VOLNAY and MEURSAULT. Best estates: Duc de Magenta, Prunier, Roy, HOSPICES DE BEAUNE Cuvée Boillot.

Avize   Champ. ★★★★
>One of the best white-grape villages of CHAMPAGNE.

Ay   Champ. ★★★★
>One of the best black-grape villages of CHAMPAGNE.

Bandol   Prov. r. p. or (w.) ★★ 70 71 72 73 74 76
>Little coastal region near Toulon with strong tasty reds.

Banyuls   Pyr. br. sw. ★★ NV
>One of the best VIN DOUX NATURELS (fortified sweet red wines) of the s. of France. Not unlike port.

Barsac   B'x. w. sw. ★★→   ★★★
>Neighbour of SAUTERNES with similar superb golden wines often more racy and less rich. Top ch'x.: CLIMENS and COUTET.

Barton & Guestier
>Important Bordeaux shipper dating from the 18th century, now owned by Seagram's.

Bâtard-Montrachet   B'y. w. dr.   ★★★★   69 71 72 73 74 76 77 78 79
>Neighbour and almost equal of MONTRACHET, the top white burgundy. As rich in flavour as dry white wine can be.

Béarn   S.W. France r. p. or w. dr. ★
>VDQS of local interest.

Beaujolais   B'y. r. (p. w.) ★ 79 D.Y.A.
>The simple appellation of the big Beaujolais region: light short-lived fruity red.

Beaujolais de l'année
>The Beaujolais of the latest vintage, until the next.

Beaujolais Primeur (or Nouveau)
> The same made in a hurry (often only 4–5 days fermenting) for drinking 15 Nov. to the end of Feb. The best come from light sandy soil and are as strong as 12.5% alcohol.

Beaujolais Supérieur   B'y. r. (w.) ∗ **76 78 79**
> Beaujolais 1° of natural alcohol stronger than the 9° minimum. Since sugar is almost always added this makes little difference to the final product.

Beaujolais Villages   B'y. r. ∗∗ **76 78 79**
> Wine from the better (northern) half of Beaujolais, stronger and tastier than plain Beaujolais. The 9 (easily) best "villages" are the "crus": FLEURIE, BROUILLY, etc. Of the 30 others the best lie around Beaujeu. The crus cannot be released 'en primeur' before December 15th.

Beaumes de Venise   Rh. (r. p.) br. sw.   ∗∗∗   NV
> France's best dessert MUSCAT, from the s. Côtes-du-Rhône; high-flavoured, subtle, lingering. The red and rosé from the co-operative are also good.

Beaune   B'y. r. or (w. dr.) ∗∗∗ **71 72 76 78 79**
> Middle-rank classic burgundy. Négociants' "CLOS" wines (usually "Premier Cru") are often best.

Bellet   Prov. p. (r. w. dr.) ∗∗
> Highly fashionable, much above average, local wine from near Nice. Tiny production. Very expensive.

Bergerac   Dordogne r. or w. sw. or dr.   ∗∗   **78 79**
> Light-weight, often tasty, Bordeaux-style. Drink young, the white very young.

Beyer, Leon
> Ancient Alsace family wine business at Eguisheim.

Blagny   B'y. r. or w. dr.   ∗∗   **71 72 73 76 78 79**
> Hamlet between MEURSAULT and PULIGNY-MONT-RACHET; affinities with both and VOLNAY for reds. Ages well.

Blanc de Blancs
> Any white wine made from (only) white grapes, esp. champagne, which is usually made of black and white.

Blanc de Noirs
> White wine made from black grapes.

Blanquette de Limoux   Midi w. dr. sp.   ∗   NV
> Good cheap sparkler from near Carcassonne made by a version of the MÉTHODE CHAMPENOISE. Very dry and clean.

Blaye   B'x. r. or w. dr. ∗→∗∗ **70 75 76 78 79**
> Your average Bordeaux from e. of the Gironde. PREMIÈRES CÔTES DE BLAYE are better.

Bollinger   NV "Special Cuvee" and **64 66 69 70 73 75**
> Top champagne house, at AY. Dry full-flavoured style. Luxury wines "Tradition R. D."; and "Vieilles Vignes Françaises" (**70** 73) from ungrafted vines.

Bommes
> Village of SAUTERNES. Best ch'x.: LA TOUR-BLANCHE, LAFAURIE-PEYRAGUEY, etc.

Bonnes Mares   B'y. r.   ∗∗∗∗   **66 69 71 72 73** 76 77 78 79
> 37-acre Grand Cru between CHAMBOLLE-MUSIGNY and MOREY-SAINT-DENIS. Often better than CHAMBERTIN.

Bonnezeaux   Lo. w. sw.   ∗∗∗   **67 69 70 71 73** 75 76 78 79
> Unusual fruity/acidic wine from CHENIN BLANC grapes.

Bordeaux   B'x. r. or (p.) or w. ∗ **75 76 78** 79 (for ch'x. see p. 47)
> Basic catch-all appellation for low-strength Bordeaux wine.

Bordeaux Supérieur
> Ditto, with slightly more alcohol.

Bordeaux Côtes-de-Castillon   B'x. r.   ∗   **70 71 73 75 76** 78 79
> Fringe Bordeaux from east of ST-EMILION, and not far from some St-Emilions in quality.

Bordeaux Côtes-de-Francs B'x. r. or wh. dr. ★ 75 76 78 79
Fringe Bordeaux from east of ST-EMILION. Light wines.

Borie-Manoux
Bordeaux shippers and château-owners, incl. Ch'x. BATAILLEY, HAUT BAGES-MONPELOU, DOMAINE DE L'EGLISE, TROTTEVIEILLE.

Bouchard Aîné
Famous and long-established burgundy shipper and grower with 60 acres in Beaune, Mercurey, etc.

Bouchard Père et Fils
Important burgundy shipper (est. 1731) with 200 acres of excellent v'yds., mainly in the CÔTE DE BEAUNE, and cellars at the Château de Beaune.

Bourg B'x. r. or (w. dr.) ★★ 70 73 75 78 79
Meaty, un-fancy claret from e. of the Gironde. CÔTES DE BOURG are better.

Bourgogne B'y. r. (p.) or w. dr. ★★ 76 78 79
Catch-all appellation for burgundy, but with theoretically higher standards than basic BORDEAUX. Light but often good flavour. BEAUJOLAIS crus can be sold as Bourgogne.

Bourgogne Grand Ordinaire B'y. r. or (w.) ★ D.Y.A.
The lowest burgundy appellation. Seldom seen.

Bourgogne Passetoutgrains B'y. r. or (p.) ⟨★⟩ D.Y.A.
Often enjoyable junior burgundy. ⅓ PINOT NOIR and ⅔ GAMAY grapes mixed. Not as "heady" as BEAUJOLAIS.

Bourgueil Lo. r. ★★★ 71 73 75 76 78 79
Delicate fruity CABERNET red from Touraine.

Bouzy Rouge Champ. r. ★★★ 69 70 71 73 75 76 79
Still red wine from famous black-grape CHAMPAGNE village.

Brédif, Marc
One of the most important growers and traders of VOUVRAY.

Brouilly B'y. r. ★★★ 78 79
One of the 9 best CRUS of BEAUJOLAIS: fruity, round, refreshing. One year in bottle is enough.

Brut
Term for the driest wines of CHAMPAGNE until recently, when some completely unsugared wines have become available as 'Brut Intégrale', 'Brut non-dosé', 'Brut zéro' etc.

Bugey Savoie w. dr. or sp. ★ D.Y.A.
District with a variety of light sparkling, still or half-sparkling wines. The grape is the Rousette (or Roussanne).

Cabernet
See Grapes for red wine

Cabernet d'Anjou Lo. p. ★★ D.Y.A.
Delicate, often slightly sweet, grapy rosé.

Cahors S.W. France r. ★→ ⟨★★⟩ 70 71 72 75 76 78 79
Very dark, traditionally hard "black" wine, now made more like Bordeaux but can be full-bodied and distinct.

Cairanne Rh. r. p. or w. dr. ⟨★★⟩ 76 78 79
Village of CÔTE-DU-RHÔNE-VILLAGES. Good solid wines.

Calvet
Great family wine business, originally on the Rhône, now important in Bordeaux and Burgundy.

Canon-Fronsac
See Côtes-Canon-Fronsac

Cantenac B'x. r. ★★★
Village of the HAUT-MÉDOC entitled to the Appellation MARGAUX. Top ch'x. include PALMER, BRANE-CANTENAC, etc.

Cassis Prov. (r. p.) w. dr. ★★ D.Y.A.
Seaside village e. of Marseille known for its very dry white, above the usual standard of Provence. Not to be confused with cassis, a blackcurrant liqueur made in Dijon.

Cave Cellar, or any wine establishment.

Cave co-opérative

Wine-growers' co-operative winery. Formerly viticultural dustbins, most are now well run, well equipped and making some of the best wine of their areas.

Cépage

Variety of vine, e.g. CHARDONNAY, MERLOT.

Cérons B'x. w. dr. or sw. ** 70 71 75 76 78 79

Neighbour of SAUTERNES with some good sweet-wine ch'x.

Chablis B'y. w. dr. ** 74 75 76 77 78 79

Distinctive full-flavoured greeny gold wine. APPELLATION CONTRÔLÉE essential. Petit Chablis is less fine, but often good.

Chablis Grand Cru B'y. w. dr. ｜****｜ 69 71 74 75 76 77 78 79

Strong, subtle and altogether splendid. One of the great white burgundies.

Chablis Premier Cru B'y. w. dr. ｜***｜ 71 75 76 77 78 79

Second-rank but often excellent and more typical of Chablis than Grands Crus.

Chai Building for storing and maturing wine, esp. in Bordeaux.

Chambertin B'y. r. **** 66 69 70 71 72 73 76 77 78 79

32-acre Grand Cru giving the meatiest, most enduring and often the best red burgundy. Many growers.

Chambertin-Clos-de-Bèze B'y. r. **** 69 70 71 72 73 76 77 78 79

37-acre neighbour of CHAMBERTIN. Similarly splendid wine.

Chambolle-Musigny B'y. r. (w. .) *** 69 70 71 72 73 76 77 78 79

420-acre CÔTE DE NUITS village with fabulously fragrant, complex wine. Best v'yds.: MUSIGNY, Les Amoureuses, Les Charmes. Best grower: de Vogüé.

Chambré

At (old-fashioned) room temperature; normal for drinking red wines. Modern room temperature is often too high.

Champagne

Sparkling wine from 55,000 acres 90 miles e. of Paris, made by the MÉTHODE CHAMPENOISE: wines from elsewhere, however good, cannot be Champagne. (See also name of brand.)

Champagne, Grande

The appellation of the best area of COGNAC.

Champigny

See Saumur

Chanson Père et Fils

Growers and traders in fine wine at BEAUNE.

Chante-Alouette

A famous brand of white HERMITAGE.

Chapelle-Chambertin B'y. r. *** 69 70 71 72 73 76 77 78 79

13-acre neighbour of CHAMBERTIN. Similar wine, not quite so full and meaty.

Chapoutier

Long-established family firm of growers and traders of Rhône wines, particularly HERMITAGE.

Chardonnay

See Grapes for white wine

Charmes-Chambertin B'y. r. *** 69 70 71 72 73 76 77 78 79

76-acre neighbour of CHAMBERTIN. Similar but lighter wine.

Chassagne-Montrachet B'y. r. or w. dr. *** 69 70 71 72 73 74w. 75w. 76 77w. 78 79.

750-acre CÔTE DE BEAUNE village with superlative rich dry whites and sterling hefty reds. Best v'yds.: MONTRACHET, BÂTARD-MONTRACHET, CRIOTS-BÂTARD-MONTRACHET, Ruchottes, Caillerets, Boudriottes, Morgeot (r. w.), CLOS-ST-JEAN (r.).

Château

For all Bordeaux ch'x see pp. 47–61.

Château-Chalon Jura w. dr. ★★★

Unique strong dry yellow wine, almost like sherry. Ready to drink when bottled.

Château Corton-Grancey B'y. r. ★★★ 69 70 71 72 73 76 78 79

Famous estate at ALOXE-CORTON, the property of Louis LATOUR. Impressive wine with a long life.

Château de la Chaize B'y. r. ★★★ 78 79

The best-known estate of BROUILLY.

Château de Panisseau Dordogne w. dr. ★★ D.Y.A.

Leading estate of BERGERAC: good dry SAUVIGNON BLANC.

Château de Selle Prov. r. p. or w. dr. ★★ D.Y.A.

Estate near Cotignac. Well-known and typical Provence wines.

Château des Fines Roches Rh. r. ★★★ 71 72 73 74 76 78 79

Large (114 acres) and distinguished estate in CHÂTEAUNEUF-DU-PAPE. Strong old-style wine.

Château du Nozet Lo. w. dr. ★★★ 76 78 79

Biggest and best-known estate of Pouilly (FUMÉ) sur Loire.

Château Fortia Rh. r. ★★★ 71 72 73 74 76 78 79

First-class property in CHÂTEAUNEUF-DU-PAPE. Traditional methods. The owner's father, Baron Le Roy, also fathered the APPELLATION CONTROLÉE system.

Château-Grillet Rh. w. dr. ★★★★ 76 78 79

3½-acre v'yd. with one of France's smallest appellations. Intense, fragrant, expensive. Drink fairly young.

Burgundy boasts one of the world's most famous and certainly its most beautiful hospital, the Hospices de Beaune, founded in 1443 by Nicolas Rolin, Chancellor to the Duke of Burgundy, and his wife Guigone de Salins. The hospital he built and endowed with vineyards for its income still operates in the same building and still thrives, tending the sick of Beaune without charge, on the sale of its wine. Many growers since have bequeathed their land to the Hospices. Today it owns 125 acres of prime land in Beaune, Pommard, Volnay, Meursault, Corton and Mazis-Chambertin. The wine is sold by auction every year on the third Sunday in November.

Château-Gris B'y. r. ★★★ 69 71 72 73 76 78 79

Famous estate at NUITS-ST-GEORGES.

Châteaumeillant Lo. r. p. or w. dr. ★ D.Y.A.

Small VDQS area near SANCERRE.

Châteauneuf-du-Pape Rh. r. (w. dr.) ★★★ 69 70 71 72 73 74 76 78 79

7,500 acres near Avignon. Best estate ("domaine") wines are dark, strong, long-lived. Others may be light and/or disappointing. The white is heavy: at best rich, almost sweet.

Château Rayas Rh. r. (w. dr.) ★★★

Excellent old-style property in Ch'neuf-du-Pape.

Château Simone Prov. r. p. or w. dr. ★★

Well-known property in Palette; the only one in this appellation near Aix-en-Provence.

Château Vignelaure Prov. r. ★★ 70 71 73 74 75 76 77 78

Very good Provençal estate near Aix making Bordeaux-style wine with CABERNET grapes.

Chatillon-en-Diois Rh. r. p. or w. dr. ★ D.Y.A.

Small VDQS e. of the Rhône near Die. Good GAMAY reds; white mostly made into CLAIRETTE DE DIE.

Chavignol

Village of SANCERRE with famous v'yd., Les Monts Damnés.

Chénas B'y. r. ★★★ 76 78 79

Good Beaujolais cru, neighbour to MOULIN-À-VENT and JULIÉNAS. One of the weightier Beaujolais.

Chenin Blanc
> See Grapes for white wine

Chevalier-Montrachet B'y. w. dr. ★★★★ 69 71 72 73 75 76 77 78 79
> 17-acre neighbour of MONTRACHET with similar luxurious wine, perhaps a little less powerful.

Cheverny Lo. w. dr. ★ D.Y.A.
> Light sharp Loire country wine from near Chambord.

Chinon Lo. r. ★★★ 70 71 73 75 76 78 79
> Delicate fruity CABERNET from TOURAINE. Drink cool when young.

Chiroubles B'y. r. ★★★ 78 79
> Good but tiny Beaujolais cru next to FLEURIE; freshly fruity silky wine for early drinking.

Chusclan Rh. r. p. or w. dr. ⏺ 78 79
> Village of CÔTE-DU-RHÔNE-VILLAGES. Good middle-weight wines from the co-operative.

Cissac
> HAUT-MÉDOC village just w. of PAUILLAC.

Clair-Daü
> First-class 100-acre burgundy estate of the northern CÔTE DE NUITS, with cellars at MARSANNAY-la-Côte.

Clairet
> Very light red wine, almost rosé.

Clairette
> Mediocre white grape of the s. of France.

Clairette de Bellegarde Midi w. dr. ★ D.Y.A.
> Plain neutral white from near Nîmes.

Clairette de Die Rh. w. dr. or s./sw. sp. ★★ NV
> Popular dry or semi-sweet rather MUSCAT-flavoured sparkling wine from the e. Rhône, or straight dry CLAIRETTE white.

Clairette du Languedoc Midi w. dr. ★ D.Y.A.
> Plain neutral white from near Montpellier.

La Clape Midi r. or w. dr. ★.
> Full-bodied VDQS wines from near Narbonne. The red gains character after 2–3 years.

Claret
> Traditional English term for red BORDEAUX.

Climat
> Burgundian word for individual named v'yd., e.g. Beaune Grèves, Chambolle-Musigny les Amoureuses.

Clos
> A term carrying some prestige, reserved for distinct, usually walled, v'yds., often in one ownership. Frequent in Burgundy and Alsace.

Clos-de-Bèze
> See Chambertin-Clos-de-Bèze

Clos de la Roche B'y. r. ★★★ 69 70 71 72 73 76 77 78 79
> 38-acre Grand Cru at MOREY-ST-DENIS. Powerful complex wine like CHAMBERTIN.

Clos des Lambrays B'y. r. ★★★ 71 72 73 76 78
> 15-acre Premier Cru v'yd. at MOREY-ST-DENIS. Changed hands in 1979 after a shaky period. Being replanted.

Clos des Mouches B'y. r. or w. dr. ★★★
> Well-known Premier Cru v'yd. of BEAUNE.

Clos de Tart B'y. r. ★★★ 71 72 73 76 77 78 79
> 18-acre Grand Cru at MOREY-ST-DENIS owned by MOMMESSIN. Recently much improved.

Clos de Vougeot B'y. r. ★★★ 66 69 70 71 72 73 76 78 79
> 124-acre CÔTE-DE-NUITS Grand Cru with many owners. Variable, sometimes sublime. Maturity depends on the grower's technique and his position on the hillside.

Clos du Chêne Marchand
>Well-known v'yd. at Bué, SANCERRE.

Clos du Roi B'y. r. ★★★
>Part of the Grand Cru CORTON; also a Premier Cru of BEAUNE.

Clos St Denis B'y. r. ★★★ **69 71 72 73** 76 77 78 79
>16-acre Grand Cru at MOREY-ST-DENIS. Splendid sturdy wine.

Clos St Jacques B'y. r. ★★★ **69 71 72 73** 76 77 78 79
>17-acre Premier Cru of GEVREY-CHAMBERTIN. Excellent powerful wine, often better (and dearer) than some of the CHAMBERTIN Grands Crus.

Clos St Jean B'y. r. ★★★ **69 71 72 73** 76 78 79
>36-acre Premier Cru of CHASSAGNE-MONTRACHET. Very good red, more solid than subtle.

Cognac
>Town and region of w. France and its brandy.

Collioure Midi r. ★ **75 76** 78 79
>Strong dry red from BANYULS area.

Condrieu Rh. w. dr. ★★★ D.Y.A.
>Unusual soft fragrant white of great character from the Viognier grape. CH.-GRILLET is similar.

Corbières Midi r. or (p.) or (w.) ★ **76 78** 79
>Good vigorous cheap VDQS reds, steadily improving.

Corbières de Roussillon Midi r. (p.) or (w.) ★ **76 78** 79
>The same from slightly farther s.

Cordier, Ets D.
>Important Bordeaux shipper and château-owner, including Ch'x. GRUAUD-LAROSE, TALBOT.

Cornas Rh. r. ★★ **69 71 72 73** 76 78 79
>Small area near HERMITAGE. Typical sturdy Rhône wine of good quality from the SYRAH grape.

The Confrèrie des Chevaliers du Tastevin is Burgundy's wine fraternity and the most famous of its kind in the world. It was founded in 1933 by a group of Burgundian patriots, headed by Camille Rodier and Georges Faiveley, to rescue their beloved Burgundy from a period of slump and despair by promoting its inimitable products. Today it regularly holds banquets with elaborate and sprightly ceremonial for 600 guests at its headquarters, the old château in the Clos de Vougeot. The Confrèrie has branches in many countries and members among lovers of wine all over the world.

Corse
>The island of Corsica. Strong ordinary wines of all colours. Better appellations include PATRIMONIO, SARTÈNE, AJACCIO.

Corton B'y. r. ★★★★ **69 70 71 72 73** 76 77 78 79
>The only Grand Cru red of the CÔTE DE BEAUNE. 200 acres in ALOXE-CORTON incl. les Bressandes and le CLOS DU ROI. Rich powerful wines.

Corton-Charlemagne B'y. w. dr. ★★★★ **69 71 72 73 74 75** 76 77 78 79
>The white section (one-third) of CORTON. Rich spicy lingering wine. Behaves like a red wine and ages magnificently.

Costières du Gard Midi r. p. or w. dr. ★ D.Y.A.
>VDQS of moderate quality from the Rhône delta.

Coteaux Champenois Champ. r. (p.) or w. dr. ★★★ D.Y.A.
>The appellation for non-sparkling champagne.

Coteaux d'Aix-en-Provence Prov r. p. or w. dr. ★ NV
>Agreeable country wines tending to improve. CH. VIGNELAURE is far above average.

Coteaux de la Loire Lo. w. dr. sw. **★★★** **71 73 75** 76 78 79
Forceful and fragrant CHENIN BLANC whites from Anjou. The best are in SAVENNIÈRES.

Coteaux de l'Aubance Lo. p. or w. dr./sw. **★★** D.Y.A.
Light and typical minor Anjou wines.

Coteaux de Pierrevert Rh. r. p. or w. dr. **⬜** D.Y.A.
Minor southern VDQS.

Coteaux de Saumur Lo. w. dr./sw. **⬜** D.Y.A.
Pleasant dry or sweetish fruity CHENIN BLANC.

Coteaux des Baux-en-Provence Prov. r. p. or w. dr. **★** NV
A twin to COTEAUX D'AIX, sharing the same VDQS.

Coteaux du Languedoc Midi r. p. or w. dr. **⬜** D.Y.A.
Scattered better-than-ordinary Midi areas with VDQS status. The best (e.g. Faugères, St Saturnin) age for a year or two.

Coteaux du Layon Lo. w. s./sw. or sw. **★★** **71 73 75 76** 78 79
District centred on Rochefort, s. of Angers, making sweet CHENIN BLANC wines above the general Anjou standard.

Coteaux du Loir Lo. r. p. or w. dr./sw. **★★** **64 69 71 73** 76 78 79
Small region n. of Tours. Occasionally excellent wines. Best v'yd.: JASNIÈRES. The Loir is a tributary of the Loire.

Coteaux du Tricastin Rh. r. p. or w. dr. **★★** D.Y.A.
Fringe CÔTES-DU-RHÔNE of increasing quality from s. of Valence.

Coteaux du Vendomois Lo. r. p. or w. dr. **★** D.Y.A.
Fringe Loire from n. of Blois.

Côte(s) Means hillside; generally a superior v'yd. In ST-EMILION it distinguishes the valley slopes from the higher plateau.

Côte Chalonnaise B'y. r. w. dr. sp. **★★→★★★★**
Lesser-known v'yd. area between BEAUNE and MÂCON. See Mercurey, Givry, Rully, Montagny.

Côte de Beaune B'y. r. or w. dr. **★★→★★★★**
Used geographically: the s. half of the CÔTE D'OR. Applies as an appellation only to parts of BEAUNE.

Côte de Beaune-Villages B'y. r. or w. dr. **★★**
Regional appellation for secondary wines of the classic area. They cannot be labelled "Côte de Beaune" without either "Villages" or the village name.

Côte de Brouilly B'y. r. **★★★** **76 78** 79
Fruity, rich, vigorous Beaujolais cru. One of the best. Leading estate: Ch. Thivin.

Côte de Nuits B'y. r. or (w. dr.) **★★→★★★★**
The northern half of the CÔTE D'OR.

Côte de Nuits-Villages B'y. r. (w.) **★★** **71 72 73** 76 78 79
A junior appellation, rarely seen but worth investigating.

Côte d'Or
Département name applied to the central and principal Burgundy v'yd. slopes, consisting of the CÔTE DE BEAUNE and CÔTE DE NUITS. The name is not used on labels.

Côte Rôtie Rh. r. **★★★** **69 70 71 72** 74 76 78 79
The finest Rhône red, from just s. of Vienne; achieves complex delicacy with age. Very small production. Top growers include JABOULET, CHAPUTIER, VIDAL-FLEURY, Jasmin.

Côtes Canon-Fronsac B'x. r. **★★** **70 71 73 75 76** 78 79
Attractive solid reds from small area w. of ST-EMILION. Ch'x. include Bodet, Canon, Junayme, Moulin-Pey-Labrie, Pichelèvre, Toumalin. The appellation can be simply "Canon-Fronsac". See also FRONSAC.

Côtes d'Auvergne Central France r. p. or (w. dr.) **★** D.Y.A.
Flourishing small VDQS area near Clermont-Ferrand. Red (at best) like light Beaujolais.

Côtes de Blaye B'x. w. dr. **★** D.Y.A.
Run-of-the-mill Bordeaux white from BLAYE.

Côtes de Bordeaux Saint-Macaire   B'x. w. dr./sw. * D.Y.A.
Run-of-the-mill Bordeaux white from e. of Sauternes.

Côtes de Bourg   Appellation
Appellation used for many of the better reds of BOURG.
Ch'x incl. de Barbe, La Barde, du Bousquet, de la Croix-
Millorit, Eyquem, Font-Guilhem, Lamothe, Mendoce,
Mille-Secousses, Domaine de Christoly, Domaine de Taste.

Côtes de Buzet   S.W. France r. or w. dr. ** 76 78 79
Good light wines from just s.e. of Bordeaux. Promising area
with well-run co-operative. Best wine: Cuvée Napoléon.

Côtes de Duras   Dordogne r. or w. dr. ⌐*⌐ 76 78 79
Neighbour to BERGERAC. Similar light wines.

Côtes de Fronsac   B'x. r. ⌐*→**⌐ 70 71 73 75 76 78 79
Some of the best slopes of FRONSAC, making considerable
slow-maturing reds. Ch'x incl. la Dauphine, Mayne-Vieil, la
Rivière, Rouet, Tasta.

Côtes de Jura   Jura r. p. or w. dr. (sp.) * NV
Various light tints and tastes. ARBOIS is better.

Côtes de Montravel   Dordogne w. dr./sw. ⌐*⌐ NV
Part of BERGERAC; traditionally medium-sweet wine, now
often made dry.

Côtes de Provence   Prov. r. p. or w. dr. NV *→**
The wine of Provence; often more alcohol than character.
Standards have recently been improving.

Côtes de Toul   E. France r. p. or w. dr. * D.Y.A.
Very light wines from Lorraine; mainly VIN GRIS (rosé).

Côtes de Ventoux   Rh. r. p. or w. dr. ⌐*⌐ 78 79 (D.Y.A.)
Fringe s. Rhône wines, fruity and light.

Côtes du Forez   Central France r. or p. ⌐*⌐ D.Y.A.
Light Beaujolais-style red, can be good in warm years.

Côtes du Fronton   S.W. France r. or p. ⌐*⌐ D.Y.A.
The local wine of Toulouse.

Côtes du Haut-Roussillon   S.W. France br. sw. * NV
Sweet-wine area n. of Perpignan.

Côtes du Luberon   Rh. r. p. or w. dr. (sp.) ⌐*⌐ D.Y.A.
Improving country wines from northern Provence.

Côtes du Marmandais   Dordogne r. p. or w. dr. * D.Y.A.
Undistinguished light wines from s.e. of Bordeaux.

Côtes-du-Rhône   Rh. r. p. or w. dr. * 78 79
The basic appellation of the Rhône valley. Best drunk young.
Wide variations of quality due to grape ripeness, therefore
rising with degree of alcohol. See CÔTES-DU-RHÔNE-VILLAGES.

Côtes-du-Rhône-Villages   Rh. r. p. or w. dr. ** 76 78 79
The wine of the 14 best villages of the southern Rhône.
Substantial and on the whole reliable.

Côtes du Roussillon   S.W. France r. p. or w. dr. ⌐*⌐ 75 76 78 79
Country wine of e. Pyrenees. The hefty dark reds are best.
Some whites are sharp VINS VERTS.

Côtes du Vivarais   Prov. r. p. or w. dr. * NV
Pleasant country wines from s. Massif Centrale.

Côtes Frontonnais   See Côtes du Fronton

Coulée de Serrant   Lo. w. dr./sw. *** 64 69 71 73 75 76 78 79
10-acre v'yd. on n. bank of Loire at Savennières, Anjou.
Intense strong fruity/sharp wine, ages well.

Crémant
In Champagne means "Creaming"—i.e. half-sparkling. Also
high-quality sparkling wines from other parts of France.

Crémant de Loire   w. dr./sp. ** NV
High-quality semi-sparkling wine from ANJOU and TOURAINE.
The leading brand is Sablant.

Crépy   Savoie w. dr. ** D.Y.A.
Light, Swiss-style white from s. shore of La. Geneva.

Criots-Bâtard-Montrachet B'y. w. ✱✱✱ **69 71 72 73 74 76** 77 78 79
>7-acre neighbour to BÂTARD-MONTRACHET. Similar wine.

Crozes-Hermitage Rh. r. or (w. dr.) ✱✱ **72 73 76** 78 79
>Larger and less distinguished neighbour to HERMITAGE.
>Robust and often excellent reds but choose carefully.

Cru "Growth", as in "first-growth"—meaning vineyard.

Cru Bourgeois
>Rank of Bordeaux château below CRU CLASSÉ.

Cru Bourgeois Supérieur
>Official rank one better than the last.

Cru Classé
>Classed growth. One of the first five official quality classes of
>the Médoc, classified in 1855. Also any classed growth of
>another district (see p. 47).

Cru Exceptionnel
>Official rank above CRU BOURGEOIS SUPÉRIEUR, immediately
>below CRU CLASSÉ.

Cruse et Fils Frères
>Long-established Bordeaux shipper famous for fine wine.
>Owner of CH. D'ISSAN.

Cubzac, St.-André-de B'x. r. or w. dr. ✱ **75 76 78** 79
>Town 15 miles n.e. of Bordeaux, centre of the minor Cub-
>zaguais region. Sound reds have the appellation Bordeaux.
>Estates include: Ch. du Bouilh, Ch. de Terrefort-Quancard,
>Ch. Timberley, Domaine de Beychevelle.

---

*The curiously inefficient shape of the traditional shallow champagne-
glass known as a "coupe" is accounted for (at least in legend) by the
fact that it was modelled on Queen Marie Antoinette's breast.
Admirable though that organ undoubtedly was, it was not designed
for dispensing sparkling wine. Champagne goes flat and gets warm
almost as fast in a coupe as it would in your cupped hand. The ideal
champagne glass is a tall, thin "tulip".*

Cussac
>Village just s. of ST. JULIEN. Appellation Haut-Médoc.

Cuve Close
>Short-cut way of making sparkling wine in a tank. The
>sparkle dies away in the glass much quicker than with
>MÉTHODE CHAMPENOISE wine.

Cuvée
>The quantity of wine produced in a "cuve" or vat. Also a word
>of many uses, incl. "blend". In Burgundy interchangeable
>with "Cru". Often just refers to a "lot" of wine.

d'Angerville, Marquis
>Famous burgundy grower with immaculate estate in VOLNAY.

Danglade, L. et Fils
>Shipper of St-Emilion and Pomerol, now owned by J-P MOUEIX
>of Libourne.

Degré alcoolique
>Degrees of alcohol, i.e. per cent by volume.

Delagrange-Bachelet
>One of the leading proprietors in CHASSAGNE-MONTRACHET.

Delas Frères
>Long-established firm of Rhône-wine specialists at Tournon,
>v'yds. at CÔTE RÔTIE, HERMITAGE, CORNAS etc.

Delor, A. et Cie
>Bordeaux shippers owned by the English Allied Breweries.

Delorme, André
>Leading merchants and growers of the CÔTE CHALONNAISE.

De Luze, A. et Fils

Bordeaux shipper and owners of Ch'x. CANTENAC-BROWN and PAVEIL-DE LUZE.

Demi-Sec

"Half-dry": in practice more than half-sweet.

Depagneux, Jacques et Cie

Well-regarded merchants of BEAUJOLAIS.

Deutz & Geldermann   NV rosé **71 73 75**, Blanc de Blancs 73 and **64 66 70 71 75**

One of the best of the smaller champagne houses. Luxury brand: Cuvée William Deutz. Also makes SEKT in Germany.

Domaine

Property, particularly in Burgundy.

Domaine de Belair

A light-weight branded red Bordeaux of reliable quality made by SICHEL.

Dom Pérignon   **62 64 66 69** 70 71

Luxury brand of MOËT ET CHANDON named after the legendary blind inventor of champagne. Also occasionally a rosé.

Dopff "au Moulin"

Ancient family wine-house at Riquewihr, Alsace. Best wines: Riesling Schoenenbourg, Gewürztraminer Eichberg.

Dopff & Irion

Another excellent Riquewihr (ALSACE) business. Best wines include Muscat les Amandiers, Riesling de Riquewihr.

Doudet-Naudin

Burgundy merchant and grower at Savigny-lès-Beaune. V'yds. incl. BEAUNE CLOS DE ROI.

Dourthe Frères

Well-reputed Bordeaux merchant representing a wide range of ch'x., mainly good Crus Bourgeois, incl. Ch'x. MAUCAILLOU, TRONQUOY-LALANDE, BELGRAVE.

Doux   Sweet.

Drouhin, J. et Cie

Prestigious Burgundy grower and merchant. Offices in BEAUNE, v'yds. in MUSIGNY, CLOS DE VOUGEOT, etc.

Duboeuf, Georges

Top-class BEAUJOLAIS merchant at Romanèche-Thorin.

Dujac, Domaine

Perfectionist burgundian grower at MOREY-ST-DENIS with v'yds in that village, ECHÉZEAUX, BONNES-MARES, GEVREY-CHAMBERTIN, etc.

Echézeaux   B'y. r. |***| **69 71 72 73** 76 77 78 79

74-acre Grand Cru between VOSNE-ROMANÉE and CLOS DE VOUGEOT. Superlative fragrant burgundy without great weight.

Edelzwicker   Alsace w. |*| D.Y.A.

Light white from mixture of grapes, often fruity and good.

Entre-Deux-Mers   B'x. w. dr. |*| D.Y.A.

Standard dry white Bordeaux from between the Garonne and Dordogne rivers. Often a good buy.

Les Epenots   B'y. r.   ***

Famous Premier Cru v'yd. of POMMARD. Also spelt Epeneaux for the 12-acre Clos des Epeneaux owned by Comte Armand.

Eschenauer, Louis

Famous Bordeaux merchants, owners of Ch'x. RAUSAN-SÉGLA and SMITH-HAUT-LAFITTE, De Lamouroux and LA GARDE in GRAVES. Now controlled by John Holt Vintners, part of the Lonrho group.

l'Etoile   Jura (r.) (p.) or w. dr./sw./sp.   **

Sub-region of the Jura with typically various wines, incl. VIN JAUNE like CHÂTEAU-CHALON.

Faiveley, J.
Family-owned growers (with 250 acres) and merchants at NUITS-ST-GEORGES, with v'yds. in CHAMBERTIN-CLOS-DE-BÈZE, CHAMBOLLE-MUSIGNY, CORTON, NUITS and MERCUREY (150 acres).

Faugères Midi (r.) (p.) or w. dr. ★ **76 78** 79
Isolated village of the COTEAUX DU LANGUEDOC making above-average wine.

Fitou Midi r. ★★ **73 75 76** 78
Superior CORBIÈRES red; powerful and ages well.

Fixin B'y. r. ⟦★★⟧ **71 72 73** 76 78
A worthy and under-valued neighbour to GEVREY-CHAMBERTIN. Often splendid reds.

Fleurie B'y. r. ⟦★★★⟧ **76 78** 79
The epitome of a Beaujolais cru: fruity, scented, silky, racy.

Frais
Fresh or cool.

Frappé
Ice-cold.

Froid
Cold.

Fronsac B'x. r. ⟦★→★★⟧ **70 71 73 75 76** 78 79
Pretty hilly area of good reds just w. of St-Emilion. CÔTES-CANON-FRONSAC and CÔTES DE FRONSAC are the appellations of the best wines. For ch'x see these entries.

Frontignan Midi br. sw. ⟦★⟧ NV
Strong sweet and liquorous muscat wine.

Gaillac S.W. France r. p. or w. dr./sw. or sp. ★ NV
Generally dull but usually adequate everyday wine.

Gamay
See Grapes for red wine

Geisweiler et Fils
One of the biggest merchant-houses of Burgundy. Cellars and 50 acres of v'yds. at NUITS-ST-GEORGES. Also 150 acres at Bevy in the HAUTES CÔTES DE NUITS and 30 in the CÔTE CHALONNAISE.

Gevrey-Chambertin B'y. r. ★★★ **71 72 73** 76 78 79
The village containing the great CHAMBERTIN and many other noble v'yds. as well as some more commonplace.

Gewürztraminer
The speciality grape of ALSACE: perfumed and spicy, whether dry or sweet.

Gigondas Rh. r. or p. ⟦★★⟧ **69 70 71 72 73 74** 76 78 79
Worthy neighbour to CHÂTEAUNEUF-DU-PAPE. Strong full-bodied wine.

Gilbey, S.A.
British firm long-established as Bordeaux merchants at Ch. LOUDENNE in the MÉDOC. Now owned by International Distillers and Vintners.

Ginestet
Third-generation Bordeaux merchants and former owners of CH. MARGAUX.

Givry B'y. r. or w. dr. ⟦★★⟧ **76** 78 79
Underrated village of the CÔTE CHALONNAISE: light but tasty and typical burgundy.

Gouges, Henri
Leading burgundy grower of NUITS-ST-GEORGES.

Goût
Taste, e.g. "goût anglais"—as the English like it (i.e. dry).

Grand Cru
One of the top Burgundy v'yds. with its own Appellation Controlée. Similar in Alsace but more vague elsewhere.

Grand Roussillon Midi br. sw. ** NV

Broad appellation for muscat and other sweet fortified wines of eastern Pyrenees.

Grands-Echézeaux B'y.r. **** 69 71 72 73 76 78 79

22-acre Grand Cru next to CLOS DE VOUGEOT. Superlative rich burgundy.

Gratien, Alfred and Gratien & Meyer

Good smaller champagne house and its counterpart at SAUMUR on the Loire.

Graves B'x. r. or w. *→*****

Large region s. of Bordeaux city. Its best wines are red, but the name is used chiefly for its dry or medium golden-whites.

Graves de Vayres B'x r. or w. *

Part of ENTRE-DEUX-MERS; of no special character.

Les Gravières B'y. r. ***

Famous Premier Cru v'yd. of SANTENAY.

Griotte-Chambertin B'y. r. *** 69 71 72 73 76 77 78 79

14-acre Grand Cru adjoining CHAMBERTIN. Similar wine, but less masculine and more "tender".

Gros Plant du Pays Nantais Lo. w. ⟮*⟯ D.Y.A.

Junior cousin of MUSCADET, sharper and lighter; made of the COGNAC grape also known as Folle Blanche, Ugni Blanc etc.

Haut Comtat Rh. r. or p. ** 74 76 78 79

Small appellation n. of Avignon. Sound strong wines.

Hautes-Côtes de Beaune B'y. r. or w. dr. ⟮**⟯ 76 78 79

Appellation for a dozen villages in the hills behind the CÔTE DE BEAUNE. Light wines, worth investigating.

Hautes-Côtes de Nuits B'y. r. or w. dr. ⟮**⟯ 71 72 76 78 79

The same for the CÔTE DE NUITS. Rarely seen outside France.

Haut-Médoc B'x. r. **→*** 66 70 71 73 75 76 77 78 79

Big appellation including all the best areas of the Médoc. Most wines have château names: those without should still be above average.

Haut-Montravel Dordogne w. sw. * 75 76 78 79

Medium-sweet BERGERAC.

Haut Poitou

Up-and-coming VDQS area s. of ANJOU. Co-operative makes good whites, incl. CHARDONNAY and SAUVIGNON BLANC.

Heidsieck, Charles NV and 66 69 70 71 73 75

Leading champagne house of Reims, family-owned, now merged with Champagne Henriot. Luxury brand: Cuvée Royal Champagne.

Heidsieck, Dry Monopole NV and 66 69 71 73 75

Important champagne merchant and grower of Reims. Luxury brand: Diamant Bleu (1971)

Hérault Midi

The biggest v'yd. *département* in France with 400,000 hectares of vines. Chiefly vin ordinaire.

Hermitage Rh. r. or w. dr. ⟮***⟯ 66 67 69 70 71 72 73 76 78 79

The "manliest" wine of France. Dark, powerful and profound. Needs long ageing. The white is heady and golden.

Hospices de Beaune

Hospital in BEAUNE, with excellent v'yds. in MEURSAULT, POMMARD, VOLNAY, BEAUNE, CORTON, etc. See panel on page 26.

Hugel Père et Fils

The best-known ALSACE growers and merchants. Founded at Riquewihr in 1639 and still in the family. Best wines: Cuvées Exceptionnelles.

Imperiale

Bordeaux bottle holding 8½ normal bottles.

Irancy B'y. r. or (p.) ★★ **71 76** 78 79
Good light red made near CHABLIS. The best vintages are long-lived and mature well.

Irouléguy S.W. France (r.) or w. dr. ★★ D.Y.A.
Agreeable local wine of the Basque country.

Jaboulet, Paul
Old family firm at Tain, leading growers of HERMITAGE etc.

Jaboulet-Vercherre et Cie
Well-known Burgundy merchant-house with v'yds. in POMMARD, etc., and cellars in Beaune.

Jadot, Louis
Much-respected Burgundy merchant-house with v'yds. in BEAUNE, CORTON, etc.

Jasnières Lo. (r.) (p.) or w. sw. ★★★ **69 70 71** 73 **75** 76 78 79
Rare VOUVRAY-like wine of n. Touraine.

Jeroboam
In England a 6-bottle bottle, or triple magnum; in Champagne a double magnum.

Juliénas B'y. r. ★★★ **76 78** 79
Leading cru of Beaujolais: vigorous fruity wine.

Jura See Côtes de Jura

Jurançon S.W. France w. sw. or dr. ★★ **72 73 75** 76 78 79
Unusual high-flavoured and long-lived speciality of Pau in the Pyrenean foothills. Ages well for several years.

Kressman, E. S. & Cie
Family-owned Bordeaux merchants and owners of CH. LATOUR-MARTILLAC in GRAVES.

Kriter
Popular low-price sparkling wine processed in Burgundy.

Krug "Grande Cuvée", NV and **66** 69 71 73
Small but very prestigious champagne house known for full-bodied very dry wine.

Labarde
Village just s. of MARGAUX and included in that appellation. Best ch.: GISCOURS.

La Cour Pavillon
Reliable branded red and white Bordeaux from GILBEY, SA.

Lalande de Pomerol B'x. r. ★★ **70 71 73 75 76** 78 79
Neighbour to POMEROL. Wines similar but considerably less fine. Ch. BEL-AIR is well known.

Lanson Père et Fils NV and **66 69 71** 75
Important growers and merchants of Champagne, cellars at Reims. Luxury brand: Red Label.

Laroche, Domaine
Important growers of CHABLIS marketed by the house of Bacheroy-Josselin.

Latour, Louis
Top Burgundy merchant and grower with v'yds. in CORTON, BEAUNE, etc.

Latricières-Chambertin B'y. r. ★★★ **69 70 71 72 73** 76 78 79
17-acre Grand Cru neighbour of CHAMBERTIN. Similar wine, but lighter and "prettier".

Laudun rh. r. p. or w. dr. ★
Village of CÔTES-DU-RHÔNE-VILLAGES. Attractive wines from the co-operative.

Laurent-Perrier NV and rosé brut and **64 66 70** 73 75
Well-known champagne house of Tours-sur-Marne. Luxury brand: Cuvée Grand Siécle.

Léognan B'x.
Leading village of the GRAVES. Best ch'x.: DOMAINE DE CHEVALIER, MALARTIC-LAGRAVIÈRE and HAUT-BAILLY.

Leroy

Important burgundy merchants at MEURSAULT, part-owners and distributors of the DOMAINE DE LA ROMANÉE-CONTI.

Lichine, Alexis et Cie

Successful post-war Bordeaux merchants, proprietors of CH. LASCOMBES, now controlled by Bass Charrington Ltd.

Burgundy: a grower's own label

MISE EN BOUTEILLES
AU DOMAINE

NUITS ST GEORGES

LES PRULIERS

APPELLATION CONTROLÉE
DOMAINE HENRI GOUGES A
NUITS ST GEORGES, CÔTE D'OR

Domaine is the burgundy equivalent of château.
The Appellation Controlée is Nuits St Georges.
The individual v'yd. in Nuits is called Les Pruliers.
The name and address of the grower/producer.
(The word propriétaire is often also used.)

A merchant's label

SANTENAY

LES GRAVIERES

APPELLATION CONTROLÉE
PROSPER MAUFOUX
NEGOCIANT À SANTENAY

The village.
The vineyard.
The wine qualifies for the Appellation Santenay.
Prosper Maufoux is a Négociant, or merchant, who bought the wine from the grower to mature, bottle and sell.

Lie, sur

"On the lees." Muscadet is often so bottled, for maximum freshness.

Limoux Nature Midi w. dr. ⋆ D.Y.A.

The non-sparkling version of BLANQUETTE DE LIMOUX.

Lirac Rh. r. p. or (w. dr.) ⋆⋆ 74 76 78

Neighbouring village to TAVEL. Similar wine; the red becoming more important than the rosé.

Listel Midi r. p. w. dr ⋆ D.Y.A.

Estate in the Camargue making pleasant light "vins des sables". Domaine du Bosquet is a fruity red.

Listrac B'x. r. ⋆⋆

Village of HAUT-MÉDOC next to MOULIS. Best ch.: FOURCAS-HOSTEN and FOURCAS-DUPRÉ.

Loire The major river of n.w. France. See under wine names.

Loupiac B'x. w. sw. ⋆⋆ 67 70 71 75 76 79

Neighbour to SAUTERNES with similar but less good wine.

Ludon

HAUT-MÉDOC village s. of MARGAUX. Best ch.: LA LAGUNE.

Lupé-Cholet et Cie

Merchants and growers at NUITS-ST-GEORGES controlled by Bichot of BEAUNE. Best estate wine: Château Gris.

Lussac-Saint-Emilion B'x. r. ⋆⋆ 70 75 76 78 79

North-eastern neighbour to ST-EMILION. Often good value. Co-operative makes "Roc de Lussac".

Macau

HAUT-MÉDOC village s. of MARGAUX. Best ch.: CANTEMERLE.

macération carbonique

Traditional Beaujolais technique of fermentation with whole bunches of unbroken grapes in an atmosphere saturated with carbon dioxide. Fermentation inside each grape eventually bursts it, giving vivid and very fruity mild wine for quick consumption. Now much used in the Midi.

Machard de Gramont
 Family estate in Burgundy with cellars in NUITS. Recently enlarged with v'yds. in NUITS, SAVIGNY, BEAUNE, POMMARD, CLOS DE VOUGEOT. Traditional wines for laying down.

Mâcon B'y. r. (p.) or w. dr. ★★ 75w. 76 77w. 78 79
 Southern district of sound, usually unremarkable, reds and tasty dry whites. Wine with a village name (e.g. Mâcon-Prissé) is better. POUILLY-FUISSÉ is best appellation of the region. See also Mâcon-Villages.

Mâcon Supérieur
 The same but slightly stronger from riper grapes.

Mâcon-Villages B'y. w. dr. ★★ 75 76 77 78 79
 Increasingly well-made and excellent white burgundies. Mâcon-Prissé, MÂCON-VIRÉ are examples.

Mâcon-Viré
 See Mâcon-Villages and Viré.

Madiran S.W. France r. ★★ 70 71 72 73 75 76 78
 Dark vigorous red from ARMAGNAC. Needs ageing.

Magnum
 A double bottle.

Mähler-Besse
 First-class Dutch wine-merchants in Bordeaux, with a majority shareholding in Ch. PALMER.

Maire, Henri
 The biggest grower and merchant of JURA wines.

Marc Grape skins after pressing; also the strong-smelling brandy made from them.

Margaux B'x. r. ★★→★★★★ 66 67 70 71 73 75 76 78 79
 Village of the HAUT-MÉDOC making the most "elegant" red Bordeaux. The name includes CANTENAC and several other villages as well. Top ch'x. include MARGAUX, LASCOMBES, etc.

Marque déposée
 Trade mark.

Marsannay B'y. (r.) or p. ★★★ 76 78 79
 Village near Dijon with excellent light red and delicate rosé, perhaps the best rosé in France.

Martillac
 Village in the GRAVES appellation, Bordeaux.

Maufoux, Prosper
 Family firm of burgundy merchants at SANTENAY.

Mazis-Chambertin B'y. r. ★★★ 69 70 71 72 73 76 78 79
 30-acre Grand Cru neighbour of CHAMBERTIN. Lighter wine.

Médoc B'x. r. ★★ 70 73 75 76 78 79
 Appellation for reds of the less good (n.) part of Bordeaux's biggest and best district. Typical but light wines. HAUT-MÉDOC is better.

Ménétou-Salon Lo. r. p. or w. dr. ★★ D.Y.A.
 Attractive light wines from w. of SANCERRE. SAUVIGNON white; CABERNET red.

Mercier et Cie NV and 62 64 66 69 70 71 73 75
 One of the biggest champagne houses, at Epernay.

Mercurey B'y. r. or w. dr. ★★ 71 76 78 79
 Leading red-wine village of the CÔTE CHALONNAISE. Good middle-rank burgundy.

méthode champenoise
 The traditional laborious method of putting the bubbles in champagne by refermenting the wine in its bottle.

Meursault B'y. (r.) w. dr. ★★★ 69 71 72 73 74 75 76 77 78 79
 CÔTE DE BEAUNE village with some of the world's greatest whites: rich, smooth, savoury, dry but mellow. Best v'yds. incl. Perrières, Genevrières, Charmes.

Meursault-Blagny See Blagny

Midi   General term for the south of France. When used of wine is often derogatory, though standards have risen consistently in recent years.

Minervois   Midi r. or (p.)   [★→★★]   76 78 79
Hilly VDQS area with some of the best wines of the Midi: lively and full of flavour.

mise en bouteilles au château, au domaine
Bottled at the château, at the property or estate. N.B. dans nos caves (in our cellars) or dans la région de production (in the area of production) mean little.

Moët & Chandon   NV and 64 66 69 70 71 73 75
The biggest champagne merchant and grower, with cellars in Epernay and sparkling wine branches in Argentina and California. Luxury brand: DOM PÉRIGNON.

Moillard
Big firm of growers and merchants in NUITS-ST-GEORGES.

Mommessin, J.
Major Beaujolais merchant and owner of CLOS DE TART.

Monbazillac   Dordogne w. sw.   [★★]   71 73 74 75 76 78 79
Golden SAUTERNES-style wine from BERGERAC. Ages well. Ch. Monbazillac is best known.

Monopole
V'yd. in single ownership.

Montagne-Saint-Emilion   B'x. r.   [★★]   70 71 75 76 78 79
North-east neighbour of ST-EMILION with similar wines.

Montagny   B'y. w. dr.   [★★]   →★★★ 75 76 77 78 79
CÔTE CHALONNAISE village between MÂCON and MEURSAULT, both geographically and gastronomically.

Montée de Tonnerre   B'y.
Famous and excellent PREMIER CRU of CHABLIS.

Monthélie   B'y. r.   [★★★]   71 72 76 78 79
Little-known neighbour and almost equal of VOLNAY. Excellent fragrant reds. Best estate: Château de Monthélie.

Montlouis   Lo. w. sw./dr.   ★★ 64 69 71 73 74 75 76 78 79
Neighbour of VOUVRAY. Similar sweet or dry long-lived wine.

Montrachet   B'y. w. dr.   ★★★★ 67 69 70 71 72 73 74 75 76 77 78 79
19-acre Grand Cru v'yd. in both PULIGNY and CHASSAGNE-MONTRACHET. The greatest white burgundy: strong, perfumed, intense, dry yet luscious. (The "ts" are silent.)

Montravel
See Côtes de Montravel

Mont-Redon, Domaine de   Rh. r. (w. dr.)   ★★★ 73 74 76 77 78
Outstanding 215-acre estate in CHÂTEAUNEUF-DU-PAPE.

Morey-Saint-Denis   B'y. r.   [★★★]   66 69 70 71 72 73 76 77 78 79
Small village with four Grands Crus between GEVREY-CHAMBERTIN and CHAMBOLLE-MUSIGNY. Glorious wine, often overlooked.

Morgon   B'y. r.   ★★★ 76 78 79
The "firmest" cru of Beaujolais, needing time to develop its rich flavour.

Moueix, J-P et Cie
The leading proprietor and merchant of St-Emilion and Pomerol. Ch'x. incl. MAGDELAINE, LAFLEUR-PETRUS, and part of PETRUS.

Moulin-à-Vent   B'y. r.   ★★★ 71 76 78 79
The "biggest" and best wine of Beaujolais; powerful and long-lived when not unbalanced by too much added sugar.

Moulis   B'x. r.   ★★→★★★
Village of the HAUT-MÉDOC with its own appellation and several good, not top-rank ch'x.: CHASSE-SPLEEN, POUJEAUX-THEIL, etc.

Mousseux
> Sparkling.

Mouton Cadet
> Best-selling brand of red Bordeaux.

Mumm, G. H. & Cie NV "Cordon Rouge", rosé, Crémant and **69 71 73 75 76**
> Major champagne grower and merchant owned by Seagram's. Luxury brand: Président René Lalou.

Muscadet Lo. w. dr. ⟦**∗∗**⟧ D.Y.A.
> Popular, good-value, often delicious dry wine from round Nantes in s. Brittany. Perfect with fish.

Muscadet de Sèvre-et-Maine
> Wine from the central and usually best part of the area.

Muscat
> Distinctively perfumed grape and its (usually sweet) wine.

Muscat de Beaumes de Venise
> The best French muscat (see Beaumes de Venise).

Muscat de Lunel br. sw. ∗∗ NV
> Sweet Midi muscat. A small area but good.

Muscat de Mireval br. sw. ∗∗ NV
> Ditto, from near Montpellier.

Muscat de Rivesaltes br. sw. ∗ NV
> Sweet muscat from a big zone near Perpignan.

Musigny B'y. r. ∗∗∗∗ **66 69 70 71 72 73** 76 77 78 79
> 25-acre Grand Cru in CHAMBOLLE-MUSIGNY. Often the best, if not the most powerful, of all red burgundies. Best growers: DE VOGÜÉ, DROUHIN.

Nature Natural or unprocessed, esp. of still champagne.

Néac B'x. r. ∗∗
> Village n. of POMEROL. Wines sold as LALANDE-DE-POMEROL.

Négociant-éleveur
> Merchant who "brings up" (i.e. matures) the wine.

Nicolas, Ets.
> Paris-based wholesale and retail wine merchants; one of the biggest in France and one of the best.

Nuits-St-Georges r. ∗∗→∗∗∗ **66 69 70 71 72 73** 76 77 78 79
> Important wine-town: wines of all qualities, typically sturdy and full-flavoured. Name can be shortened to "Nuits". Best v'yds. incl. Les St-Georges, Vaucrains, Les Pruliers, Clos des Corvées, Les Cailles, etc.

Ordinaire
> Commonplace, everyday: not necessarily pejorative.

Ott, Domaine
> Important producer of high-quality PROVENCE wines.

Pacherenc-du-Vic-Bilh S.W. France w. sw. ∗ NV
> Rare minor speciality of the ARMAGNAC region.

Palette Prov. r. p. or w. dr. ∗∗
> Near Aix-en-Provence. Aromatic reds and good rosés.

Pasquier-Desvignes
> Very old firm of Beaujolais merchants at St Lager, BROUILLY.

Passe-Tout-Grains
> Light red burgundy made of mixed GAMAY and PINOT NOIR.

Patriarche
> Popular firm of burgundy merchants in BEAUNE.

Pauillac B'x. r. ∗∗→∗∗∗∗ **66 67** 70 **71 73** 75 76 78 79
> The only village in Bordeaux (HAUT-MÉDOC) with three first-growths (Ch'x. LAFITE, LATOUR, MOUTON-ROTHSCHILD) and many other fine ones, famous for high flavour and a scent of cedarwood.

Pécharmant Dordogne r. ∗∗ **76 78** 79
> Slightly better-than-typical light BERGERAC red.

Pelure d'oignon

"Onion skin"—tawny tint of certain rosés.

Perlant

Very slightly sparkling.

Pernand-Vergelesses B'y. r. or (w. dr.) ★★★ **69 71 72 73** 76 78 79

Village next to ALOXE-CORTON containing part of the great CORTON and CORTON-CHARLEMAGNE v'yds. and one other top v'yd.: Ile des Vergelesses.

Perrier-Jouet NV, **69 71** 73 75 76 and rosé brut 73 75

Excellent champagne-growers and makers at Epernay. Luxury brand: Belle Epoque.

Pétillant

Slightly sparkling.

Petit Chablis B'y. w. dr. ★★ **77 78** 79

Wine from fourth-rank CHABLIS v'yds. Lacks great character but can be good value. But frost severely reduced '77 and '78.

Piat Père et Fils

Important growers and merchants of Beaujolais and Mâcon wines at MÂCON, now controlled by Grand Metropolitan Ltd. V'yds. in MOULIN-À-VENT, also CLOS DE VOUGEOT. BEAUJOLAIS and MÂCON-VIRÉ in special Piat bottles are good value.

Picpoul-de-Pinet Midi w. dr. ★ NV

Rather dull very dry southern white.

Pineau de Charente

Strong sweet apéritif made of white grape juice and Cognac.

Pinot

See Grapes for white wine

Piper-Heidsieck NV, rosé 75 and **66 69 71 73** 75

Champagne-makers of old repute at Reims. Luxury brand: Florens Louis Blanc de Blancs.

Pol Roger NV, rosé **71 73, Blanc de Blancs** 71 and **66 69 71 73** 75

Excellent champagne house at Epernay. Particularly good non-vintage White Foil.

Pomerol B'x. r. ★★→★★★★ **66 70 71 73** 75 76 78 79

The next village to ST-EMILION: similar but more "fleshy" wines, maturing sooner, on the whole reliable and delicious. Top ch.: PETRUS.

Pommard B'y. r. ★★★ **66 69 70 71 72 73** 76 78 79

The biggest and best-known village in Burgundy. No superlative wines, but many warmly appealing ones. Best v'yds.: Rugiens, EPENOTS and HOSPICES DE BEAUNE cuvées.

Pommery & Greno NV, NV rosé and **66 69 71 73** 75

Very big growers and merchants of champagne at Reims.

Ponnelle, Pierre

Well-established family wine-merchants of BEAUNE.

Pouilly-Fuissé B'y. w. dr. ★★→★★★ **75 76 77** 78 79

The best white of the MÂCON area. At its best excellent, but often over-priced. Buy it domaine-bottled.

Pouilly-Fumé Lo. w. dr. ★★→★★★ **76 78** 79

Smoky-fragrant, fruity, often sharp pale white from the upper Loire, next to SANCERRE. Grapes must be SAUVIGNON BLANC. Good vintages improve for 2–3 yrs.

Pouilly-Loché B'y. w. dr. ★★

Neighbour of POUILLY-FUISSÉ. Similar wine.

Pouilly-Sur-Loire Lo. w. dr. ★ D.Y.A.

Inferior wine from the same v'yds. as POUILLY-FUMÉ, but different grapes (CHASSELAS).

Pouilly-Vinzelles B'y. w. dr. ★★

Neighbour of POUILLY-FUISSÉ. Similar wine.

Pradel

Well-known brand of Provençal wines, esp. a dry rosé.

Preiss Zimmer, Jean
Old-established Alsace wine-merchants at Riquewihr.

Premières Côtes de Blaye
Restricted appellation for better reds of BLAYE. Ch'x. include Barbé, l'Escadre, Menaudat, des Petits-Arnauds.

Premier Cru
First-growth in Bordeaux, but the second rank of v'yds. (after Grand Cru) in Burgundy.

Premières Côtes de Bordeaux B'x. r. (p.) or w. dr. or sw. *→**
Large area east of GRAVES: a good bet for quality and value, though never brilliant. Ch'x incl. Laffitte (sic).

"Noble rot" (in French pourriture noble, in German Edelfäule, in Latin Botrytis cinerea) is a form of mould that attacks the skins of ripe grapes in certain vineyards in warm and misty autumn weather.

Its effect, instead of rotting the grapes, is to wither them. The skin grows soft and flaccid, the juice evaporates through it, and what is left is a super-sweet concentration of everything in the grape except its water content.

The world's best sweet table wines are all made of nobly rotten grapes. They occur in good vintages in Sauternes, the Rhine, the Mosel (where wine made from them is called Trockenbeerenauslese), in Tokaji in Hungary, in Burgenland in Austria, and occasionally elsewhere—California included. The danger is rain on the pulpy grapes when they are already far gone in noble rot. All too often, particularly in Sauternes, the grower's hopes are dashed by a break in the weather.

Primeur
Early wine, like early vegetables; esp. of BEAUJOLAIS.

Prissé See Mâcon-Villages

Propriétaire-récoltant
Owner–manager.

Provence
See Côtes de Provence

Puisseguin-Saint-Emilion B'x. r. ****** 75 76 78 79
Eastern neighbour of ST-EMILION; wines similar—not so fine but often good value. No famous ch'x. but a good co-operative.

Puligny-Montrachet B'y. w. dr. ******* 69 71 72 73 74 75 76 77 78 79
Bigger neighbour of CHASSAGNE-MONTRACHET with equally glorious rich dry whites. Best v'yds.: MONTRACHET, CHEVALIER-MONTRACHET, BÂTARD-MONTRACHET, Bienvenue-Bâtard-Montrachet, Les Combettes, Clavoillon, Pucelles, Champ-Canet, etc.

Quarts de Chaume Lo. w. sw. ******* 69 70 71 73 75 76 78 79
Famous 120-acre plot in COTEAUX DU LAYON, Anjou. CHENIN BLANC grapes. Long-lasting, intense, rich golden wine.

Quatourze Midi r. (p.) or w. dr. ***** 76 78 79
Minor VDQS area near Narbonne.

Quincy Lo. w. dr. ****** 76 78 79
Small area making very dry SANCERRE-style wine of SAUVIGNON BLANC.

Ramonet-Prudhon
One of the leading proprietors in CHASSAGNE-MONTRACHET.

Rasteau Rh. (r. p. w. dr.) or br. sw. ****** NV
Village of s. Rhône valley. Good strong sweet dessert wine is the local speciality.

Ratafia de Champagne
Sweet apéritif made in Champagne of ⅔ grape juice and ⅓ brandy.

Récolte

Crop or vintage.

Remoissenet Père et Fils

Fine growers and merchants of burgundy at BEAUNE.

Rémy Pannier

Important Loire-wine merchants at Saumur.

Reuilly   Lo. w. dr. ** 76 78

Neighbour of QUINCY with similar wine; also good PINOT GRIS.

Richebourg   B'y. r. **** 66 69 70 71 73 76 77 78 79

19-acre Grand Cru in VOSNE-ROMANÉE. Powerful, perfumed, fabulously expensive wine, among Burgundy's best.

Riesling

See Grapes for white wine

Rivesaltes   Midi br. sw. ** NV

Fortified sweet wine, some muscat-flavoured, from e. Pyrenees. An ancient tradition still very much alive.

La Roche-aux-Moines   Lo. w. dr./sw. *** 69 71 73 75 76 78 79

60-acre v'yd. in Savennières, Anjou. Intense strong fruity/sharp wine ages well.

Roederer, Louis   NV and 64 66 69 70 71 73 74 75

One of the best champagne-growers and merchants at Reims. Excellent non-vintage wine. Luxury brand: Cristal Brut (in white glass bottles).

La Romanée   B'y. r. **** 66 67 69 70 71 72 73 76 78

2-acre Grand Cru in VOSNE-ROMANÉE just uphill from ROMANÉE-CONTI owned by Bichot of BEAUNE.

Romanée-Conti   B'y. r. **** 66 67 71 72 73 76 78 79

4½-acre Grand Cru in VOSNE-ROMANÉE. The most celebrated and expensive red wine in the world, though seldom the best.

Romanée-Conti, Domaine de la

The grandest estate of Burgundy, owning the whole of ROMANÉE-CONTI and LA TÂCHE and major parts of RICHE-BOURG, GRANDS ECHÉZEAUX, ECHÉZEAUX and ROMANÉE-ST-VIVANT (under Marey-Monge label). Also a small part of Le MONTRACHET.

Romanée-St-Vivant   B'y. r. **** 71 72 73

23-acre Grand Cru in VOSNE-ROMANÉE. Similar to ROMANÉE-CONTI but usually lighter.

Ropiteau

Burgundy wine-growers and merchants at MEURSAULT. Specialists in Meursault and CÔTE DE BEAUNE wines.

Rosé d'Anjou   Lo. p. * D.Y.A.

Pale, often slightly sweet, rosé. Cabernet d'Anjou is better.

Rousseau, Domaine A.

Major burgundy grower famous for CHAMBERTIN, etc.

Roussette de Savoie   Savoie w. dr. ** D.Y.A.

Pleasant light fresh white from s. of Geneva.

Roussillon

See Côtes du Roussillon

Ruchottes-Chambertin   B'y. r. *** 67 69 70 71 72 73 76 77 78 79

7½-acre Grand Cru neighbour of CHAMBERTIN owned by Domaine A. ROUSSEAU. Similar splendid long-lasting wine.

Ruinart Père et Fils   NV and 66 69 71 73

The oldest champagne house, now belonging to Moët-Hennessy. Luxury brand: Dom Ruinart.

Rully   B'y. r. or w. dr. or (sp.) ** 76 78 79

Village of the CÔTE CHALONNAISE famous for sparkling burgundy. Still reds and white light but tasty and good value.

Sablant   Lo. w. dr. sp. ** NV

Brand name for high-quality CRÉMANT DE LOIRE.

Saint-Amour   B'y. r. ** 76 78 79

Northernmost cru of BEAUJOLAIS: light, fruity, irresistible.

Saint-Aubin B'y. (r.) or w. dr. **★★ 71 72 74 75w. 76 78 79**

Little-known neighbour of CHASSAGNE-MONTRACHET, up a side-valley. Not top-rank, but typical and good value. Also sold as CÔTE-DE-BEAUNE-VILLAGES.

Saint Bris B'y. w. dr. **★** D.Y.A.

Village w. of CHABLIS known for its fruity ALIGOTÉ, making good sparkling burgundy, and hillside cherry orchards. See also Sauvignon-de-St-Bris.

Saint Chinian Midi r. **★→★★ 76 78 79**

Hilly VDQS area of growing reputation. Tasty reds.

Sainte Croix-du-Mont B'x. w. sw. **★★ 67 70 71 75 76 79**

Neighbour to SAUTERNES with similar golden wine. No superlatives but well worth trying. Very reasonably priced.

Sainte-Foy-Bordeaux B'x.

Part of ENTRE-DEUX-MERS.

Saint-Emilion B'x. r. **★★★→★★★★ 66 67 70 71 73 75 76 78 79**

The biggest top-quality Bordeaux district; solid, rich, tasty wines from scores of ch'x., incl. CHEVAL-BLANC, AUSONE, CANON, MAGDELAINE, FIGEAC, etc.

Saint-Estèphe B'x. r. **★★ 66 67 70 71 73 75 77 78 79**

Northern village of HAUT-MÉDOC. Solid, satisfying, occasionally superlative wines. Top ch'x.: CALON-SÉGUR, COS D'ESTOURNEL, MONTROSE, etc., and many good CRUS BOURGEOIS.

Saint-Georges-Saint-Emilion

Part of MONTAGNE-ST-EMILION. Best ch.: ST-GEORGES.

Saint-Joseph Rh. r. (p. or w. dr.) **★★ 71 72 73 76 78 79**

Northern Rhône appellation of second rank but reasonable price. Substantial wine often better than CROZES-HERMITAGE.

Saint-Julien B'x. r. **★★★→★★★★ 66 70 71 73 75 76 77 78 79**

Mid-Médoc village with a dozen of Bordeaux's best ch'x., incl. three LÉOVILLES, BEYCHEVELLE, DUCRU-BEAUCAILLOU, GRUAUD-LAROSE, etc. The epitome of well-balanced red wine.

Saint-Laurent

Village next to SAINT-JULIEN. Appellation Haut-Médoc.

Saint-Nicolas-de-Bourgueil Lo. r. **★★ 71 75 76 78 79**

The next village to BOURGUEIL: the same light but lively and fruity CABERNET red.

Saint-Péray Rh. w. dr. or sp. **★★ NV**

Rather heavy white from the n. Rhône, much of it made sparkling. A curiosity.

Saint Pourçain Central France r. p. or w. dr **★** D.Y.A.

The agreeable local wine of Vichy, becoming fashionable in Paris. Made from GAMAY and/or PINOT NOIR, the white from CHARDONNAY or SAUVIGNON BLANC.

Saint-Sauveur

HAUT-MÉDOC village just w. of PAUILLAC.

Saint-Seurin-de-Cadourne

HAUT-MÉDOC village just n. of SAINT-ESTÈPHE.

Saint-Véran B'y. w. dr. **★★ 75 76 77 78 79**

Next-door appellation to POUILLY-FUISSÉ. Similar but better value: dry white of real character from the best slopes of MÂCON-VILLAGES.

Sancerre Lo. (r. p.) or w. dr. **★★★ 76 78 79**

Very fragrant and fresh SAUVIGNON white almost indistinguishable from POUILLY-FUMÉ, its neighbour over the Loire. Drink young. Also light PINOT NOIR red and a little rose, best drunk very young.

Santenay B'y. r. or (w. dr.) **★★★ 66 69 70 71 72 73 76 78 79**

Very worthy, rarely rapturous, sturdy reds from the s. of the CÔTE DE BEAUNE. Best v'yds.: Les Gravières, Clos de Tavannes, La Comme.

Saumur Lo. r. p. or w. dr. and sp. ★★→ ★★

Big versatile district in Anjou, with fresh fruity whites, good-value sparklers, pale rosés and occasionally good CABERNET reds, the best from Saumur-Champigny.

Sauternes B'x. w. sw. ★★→ ★★★★ 67 70 71 75 76 78 79

District of 5 villages (incl. BARSAC) making France's best sweet wine: strong (14% alcohol) luscious and golden, improving with age. Top ch'x.: D'YQUEM, LA TOUR-BLANCHE, SUDUIRAUT, COUTET, CLIMENS, GUIRAUD, etc. Also a few heavy dry wines which cannot be sold as Sauternes.

Sauvignon Blanc

See Grapes for white wine

Sauvignon-de-St-Bris B'y. w. dr. ★★ D.Y.A.

A baby VDQS cousin of SANCERRE from near CHABLIS.

Sauzet, Etienne

Excellent white burgundy estate at PULIGNY-MONTRACHET.

Savennières Lo. w. dr./sw. ★★★ 67 69 70 71 72 73 75 76 78 79

Small ANJOU district of pungent long-lived whites, incl. COULÉE DE SERRANT, LA ROCHE AUX MOINES, Clos du Papillon.

Savigny-lès-Beaune B'y. r. or (w. dr.) ★★★ 71 72 73 76 77 78 79

Important village next to BEAUNE, with similar well-balanced middle-weight wines, often deliciously delicate and fruity. Best v'yds.: Marconnets, Dominode, Serpentières, Vergelesses, les Guettes.

Savoie E. France (r.) or w. dr. ★★ D.Y.A.

Alpine area with light dry wines like some Swiss wine or minor Loires. CRÉPY and SEYSSEL are best known.

Schlumberger et Cie

Excellent Alsace growers and merchants at Guebwiller.

Schröder & Schyler

Old family firm of Bordeaux merchants, owners of CH. KIRWAN.

Sec

Literally means dry, though champagne so-called is medium-sweet.

Sèvre-et-Maine

The *département* containing the central and best v'yds. of MUSCADET.

Seyssel Savoie w. dr. or sp. ★★ NV

Delicate pale dry white making admirable sparkling wine.

Sichel & Co.

Famous Bordeaux (and Burgundy and Germany) merchants, owners of CH. D'ANGLUDET and part-owners of CH. PALMER.

Soussans

Village just n. of MARGAUX, sharing its appellation.

Sylvaner

See Grapes for white wine

La Tâche B'y. r. ★★★★ 62 67 69 70 71 72 73 74 76 77 78 79

15-acre Grand Cru of VOSNE-ROMANÉE and one of the best v'yds. on earth: dark, perfumed and luxurious wine. Owned by the DOMAINE DE LA ROMANÉE-CONTI.

Taittinger NV and 66 69 70 71 73

Fashionable champagne growers and merchants of Reims. Luxury brand: Comtes de Champagne (also rosé).

Tastevin, Confrérie du

Burgundy's colourful and successful promotion society. Wine carrying their Tastevinage label has been approved by them and will usually be good. A tastevin is the traditional shallow silver wine-tasting cup of Burgundy. See panel, page 28.

Tavel Rh. p. ★★★ D.Y.A.

France's most famous rosé, strong and dry, starting vivid pink and fading to orange. Avoid orange bottles.

Tête de Cuvée
    Term vaguely used of the best wines of an appellation.

Thorin, J.
    Fine grower and major merchant of BEAUJOLAIS, at Pontanevaux.

Tokay d'Alsace
    See Pinot Gris under Grapes for white wine

Tollot-Beaut
    Excellent burgundy grower with some 20 hectares in the Côte de Beaune, incl. Corton, Beaune Grèves, Savigny (Les Champs Chevrey) and at Chorey-lès-Beaune.

Touraine Lo. r. p. w. dr./sw./sp.
    Big mid-Loire province with immense range of wines, incl. dry white SAUVIGNON, dry and sweet CHENIN BLANC (e.g. Vouvray), red CHINON and BOURGUEIL, light red CABERNETS, GAMAYS and rosés. Cabernets, Sauvignons and Gamays of good years are bargains.

Trimbach, F. E.
    Distinguished ALSACE grower and merchant at Ribeauvillé. Best wines incl. Riesling Clos Ste. Hune.

Vacqueyras Rh. r. `**` 71 72 73 74 76 78
    Up-and-coming village of s. CÔTES-DU-RHÔNE, neighbour to GIGONDAS; comparable with CHÂTEAUNEUF-DU-PAPE but less heavy and more "elegant".

Valençay Lo. w. dr. `*` D.Y.A.
    Neighbour of CHEVERNY: similar pleasant sharpish wine.

Varichon & Clerc
    Principal makers and shippers of SAVOIE sparkling wines.

Varoilles, Domaine des
    Excellent estate of 25 acres, principally in GEVREY-CHAMBERTIN.

Vaudésir B'y. w. dr. `****` 69 71 74 75 76 77 78
    Arguably the best of the 7 Grands Crus of CHABLIS (but then so are the others).

VDQS
    Vin Délimité de Qualité Supérieure (see p. 19).

Vendange
    Vintage.

Vendange tardive
    Late vintage. IN ALSACE equivalent to German AUSLESE.

Veuve Clicquot NV and 64 66 69 70 73 75
    Historic champagne house of the highest standing. Cellars at Reims. Luxury brand: La Grande Dame.

Vidal-Fleury, J.
    Long-established shippers and growers of top Rhône wines.

Vieilles Vignes
    "Old vines" – therefore the best wine. Used for such wine by BOLLINGER and DE VOGÜÉ.

Viénot, Charles
    Grower and merchant of good burgundy, at NUITS-ST-GEORGES. 70 acres in Nuits, CORTON, RICHEBOURG, etc.

Vignoble
    Area of vineyards.

Vin de garde
    Wine that will improve with keeping.

Vin de l'année
    This year's wine. See Beaujolais.

Vin de paille
    Wine from grapes dried on straw mats, consequently very sweet, like Italian passito. Especially in the JURA.

Vin de Pays
    The junior rank of country wines (see Introduction).

Vin Doux Naturel ("VDN")

Sweet wine fortified with alcohol, so far from "natural".
Common in ROUSSILLON.

Vin Gris

"Grey" wine is very pale pink, made of red grapes pressed
before fermentation begins, unlike rosé, which ferments
briefly before pressing.

Vin Jaune Jura w. dr. ★★★

Speciality of ARBOIS: odd yellow wine like fino sherry. Ready
when bottled.

Vin nouveau

See Beaujolais Nouveau

Vin vert

A very light, acidic, refreshing white wine, a speciality of
ROUSSILLON.

---

*Paris has one wine school that offers individual amateur as well as
professional courses. L'Académie du Vin, 25 rue Royale/24 rue Boissy-
D'Anglas, was founded by an English wine merchant, Steven
Spurrier, in a little mews near La Madeleine in 1973. It has become a
centre for the fashionable pursuit of comparing the best wines of
California with those of France.*

Vinsobres Rh. r. (p. or w. dr.) ★★ 76 78 79

Contradictory name of good s. Rhône village. Strong substantial reds which mature well.

Viré

See Mâcon-Villages

Visan Rh. r. p. or w. dr. ★★ 76 78 79

One of the better s. Rhône villages. Reds better than white.

Viticulteur

Wine-grower.

Vogüé, de

First-class burgundy domaine at CHAMBOLLE-MUSIGNY.

Volnay B'y. r. ★★★ 66 69 71 72 76 78 79

Village between POMMARD and MEURSAULT: the best reds of
the CÔTE DE BEAUNE, not strong or heavy but fragrant and
silky. Best v'yds.: Caillerets, Clos des Ducs, Champans, Clos
des Chênes, etc.

Volnay-Santenots B'y. r. ★★★

Excellent red wine from MEURSAULT is sold under this name.
Indistinguishable from VOLNAY.

Vosne-Romanée B'y. r. ★★★→★★★★ 66 67 69 70 71 72 73 76 77 78 79

The village containing Burgundy's grandest Crus (ROMANÉE-
CONTI, LA TÂCHE, etc.). There are (or rather should be) no
common wines in Vosne.

Vougeot

See Clos de Vougeot

Vouvray Lo. w. dr./sw./sp. ★★→★★★★ 64 67 69 70 71 73 75 76 78 79

Small district of TOURAINE with very variable wines, at their
best intensely sweet and almost immortal. Good dry
sparkling.

"Y" (Pronounced ygrec)

Brand name of powerful dry wine occasionally made at CH.
D'YQUEM.

Châteaux of Bordeaux

Some 300 of the best-known châteaux of Bordeaux are listed below in alphabetical order.

References to their classifications into "growths" (crus) can be confusing. The following may help.

Only the Médoc châteaux have been classified as first- to fifth-growths, followed by Crus Exceptionnels and Crus Bourgeois. The 1855 order is still official. But today it helps understand the prestige of the châteaux more than the quality of their wine.

In St-Emilion, "Premier Grand Cru Classé" (the top rank, roughly equating to the top three ranks of the Médoc) has been translated as "first-growth" and all the rest as simply "classed-growth". Pomerol has no classification. The Graves châteaux are either "classed" or not (for red or white or both); there is no pecking order. Sauternes is effectively classified into two ranks below Château d'Yquem, which is given a class of its own.

General information about the quality and style of vintages will be found in the vintage charts on page 21. The particular information about the relative success and maturity of each vintage at each château is incomplete, for obvious reasons. It has been supplied by many friends in the wine trade whose impartiality I trust, supplementing my own notes, but since no one person has ever tasted all these wines it should be treated with a modicum of reserve. Further information about each village or appellation will be found under the general entries.

d'Agassac   Ludon, Haut-Médoc r.   ******   75 76 78
    14th-century moated fort with 85 acres. Same owners as Ch'x
CALON-SÉGUR and DU TERTRE and a growing reputation.

L'Angélus   St-Em. r.   ******   66 70 75 76 78
    Well-situated classed-growth of 65 acres on the St-Emilion
Côtes w. of the town. Recent vintages have not been exciting.

d'Angludet   Cant-Mar. r.   ******   66 70 71 73 75 76 77 78
    70-acre British-owned Cru Exceptionnel of classed-growth
quality.

D'Arche   Sauternes w. sw.   **   69 70 71 73 78 79
    Substantial second-rank classed-growth of 120 acres. Ch.
d'Arche-Lafaurie is its lesser wine.

Ausone   St-Em. r.   ****   66 67 70 71 75 76 78
    Celebrated first-growth with 20 acres in a commanding posi-
tion on the Côtes and famous rock-hewn cellars under the
v'yd. Off form in the sixties but first class since 1970.

Balestard-la-Tonnelle   St-Em. r.   **   64 66 67 70 71 75 76 78
    Historic little classed-growth on the plateau near the
town. Mentioned by the 15c poet Villon and still in the
same family.

de Barbe   Côtes de Bourg r. (w.)   ******   70 71 73 75 76 78
    The biggest and best-known ch. of the right bank of the
Gironde. Good full-bodied red.

Baret   Graves r. and w. dr.   **   75 76 77 w. 78
    Little estate of good quality, better known for its white wine.

Batailley   Pauillac r.   ***   61 62 64 66 70 71 72 73 75 76 77 78
    The bigger of the famous pair of fifth-growths (with HAUT-
BATAILLEY) on the borders of Pauillac and St-Julien. 125
acres. Firm strong-flavoured wine.

Beaumont   Cussac, Haut-Médoc r.   **   75 76 78
    Considerable Cru Bourgeois, well-known in France for full-
bodied, consistent, not brilliant wines.

Beauregard   Pomerol r.   ******   66 67 70 71 73 74 75 76 78
    30+ acre v'yd. with pretty 17th-century ch. near LA
CONSEILLANTE. Well-made typical "round" wines.

Beauséjour-Bécot   St-Em. r.   ***   69 70 71 73 75 76 78
    Half of the famous old Beauséjour estate on the w. slope of the
Côtes. 20 acres. Restored from serious decline since 1969.

Beauséjour-Duffau-Lagarosse   St-Em. r.   ***   66 70 71 75 76 78
    The other half of the above, in old family hands and making
traditional wine for long maturing.

Beau-Site-Haut-Vignoble   St-Est. r.   **   70 75 76 78
    Well-regarded 35-acre Cru Bourgeois near Ch. CALON-SÉGUR.

Belair   St-Em. r.   ***   70 75 76 78
    Sister-ch. and neighbour of AUSONE with 30+ acres on the
Côtes. Steady improvement in recent vintages.

de Bel-Air   Lalande de Pomerol r.   ******   73 74 75 76 78
    The best-known estate of this village just n. of Pomerol, with
very similar wine. 30 acres.

Bel-Air-Marquis d'Aligre   Sou-Mar. r.   **   69 70 71 73 75 76 78
    Reliable Cru Exceptionnel with about 35 acres.

Belgrave   St-Lau. r.   **
    Obscure fifth-growth in St-Julien's back-country. 100+ acres
Recently acquired by DOURTHE.

Bellevue   St-Em. r.   ******   75 78
    Well-known little classed-growth on the w. Côtes.

Bel-Orme-Tronquoy-de-Lalande   St-Seurin-de-Cadourne (Haut-
Médoc) r.   ******   66 69 70 71 75 76 78
    Reputable 70-acre Cru Bourgeois n. of St-Estèphe.

Beychevelle   St-Jul. r.   *******   61 64 66 67 70 71 73 74 75 76 77 78
    115-acre fourth-growth with the Médoc's finest mansion.
Wine of great distinction and more elegance than power.

Le Bourdieu Vertheuil (Haut-Médoc) r. ★★ 75 **76** 78
> Cru Bourgeois with sister ch. Victoria known for steady typical middle-Médocs.

Bourgneuf-Vayron Pomerol r. ★★ 75 76 78
> 20-acre vineyard on clay soil making good rather heavy wines.

Bouscaut Graves r. w. dr. ★★★ 70 71 **73** 75
> Neglected classed-growth at Cadaujac brought back to life by American enthusiasts since 1969. Bought in 1980 by Lucien Lurton, owner of Ch. BRANE-CANTENAC, etc.

du Bousquet Côte de Bourg r. ⟦★★⟧ 75 76 78
> Reliable estate with 100 acres making attractive solid wine.

Boyd-Cantenac Margaux r. ★★★ 66 70 71 74 75 76 78
> 60-acre third-growth united with Ch. POUGET to produce attractive soft wines. The best are sold as Boyd-Cantenac.

Branaire-Ducru St-Jul. r. ⟦★★★⟧ **61** 66 70 71 73 74 75 76 77 78
> Fourth-growth of 110 acres producing notably flowery and flavoury wine: attractive and reliable.

Brane-Cantenac Cant-Mar. r. ⟦★★★⟧ **61 64** 66 67 70 71 73 74 75 76 77 78
> Big (180 acres) well-run and reliable second-growth. Round, smooth and delightful wines. Same owners as Chx. DURFORT-VIVENS, VILLEGEORGE, CLIMENS, BOUSCAUT.

Brillette Moulis, Haut-Médoc r. ★★
> 75-acre v'yd. whose pebbly soil is said to "shine" – hence the name. Reliable rather country-style wine, improving.

A Bordeaux label

CHATEAU GISCOURS
GRAND CRU CLASSE
APPELLATION MARGAUX CONTROLEE
MIS EN BOUTEILLES AU CHATEAU

A château is an estate, not necessarily with a mansion or a big expanse of v'yd. Over 200 are listed on pages 47–61. Reference to the local classification. It varies from one part of Bordeaux to another—see p. 26. The Appellation Controlée: look up Margaux in the France A–Z. "Bottled at the château"— becoming the normal practice with classed-growth wines.

La Cabanne Pomerol r. ⟦★★★⟧ 71 73 75 **76** 78
> Highly-regarded 20-acre property near the great Ch. TROTANOY.

Cadet Piola St-Em. r. ⟦★★⟧ 70 71 73 74 75 **76** 78
> Reliable little property (17 acres) on the plateau just n. of the town of St-Emilion.

Calon-Ségur St-Est. r. ⟦★★★⟧ **61** 62 66 67 70 71 **73** 75 76 77 78 79
> Big (145-acre) third-growth of great reputation. Often the best St-Estèphe but has had off-moments. '78 and '79 suggest a return to excellence.

Camensac St-Lau. r. ⟦★★⟧ 66 70 72 73 74 75 76 77 78
> Re-emerging fifth-growth neighbour of Ch. BELGRAVE, re-planted in the '60s with new equipment and expert direction. Fine vigorous full-bodied wines.

Canon St-Em. r. ★★★ 66 70 71 75 76 78
> Famous first-classed-growth with 45+ acres on the plateau w. of the town. Conservative methods; impressive wine.

Canon-la-Gaffelière St-Em. r. ⟦★★⟧ 66 70 71 75 76 77 78
> 50-acre classed-growth on the lower slopes of the Côtes.

Cantemerle   Macau r.   `***` **61 62 64** 66 **67** 70 **71 73** 74 75 76 78
Superb estate at the extreme s. of the Médoc, with a romantic ch. in a wood and 50 acres of vines. Officially fifth-growth: in practice nearer second-growth. Traditional methods make deep, longlasting, richly subtle wine.

Cantenac-Brown   Cant-Mar. r. `***` **61 62** 66 70 **71 73** 75 76 78
Formerly old-fashioned 72-acre third-growth, now well run and making classical wine for long development.

Cap de Mourlin   St-Em. r. `***`
Well-known 40-acre château n. of St-Emilion making reliable, if sometimes rather light, wine.

Capbern   St-Est. r. `**`
80-acre Cru Bourgeois; same owner as Ch. CALON-SÉGUR.

Carbonnieux   Graves r. and w. dr. `***` **64 66** 70 **71 74** 75 76 **77** w. 78
Historic estate at Léognan making good fairly light wines with modern methods. The white is much the better.

La Cardonne   Blaignan (Médoc) r. `**`
Large Cru Bourgeois in the n. Médoc recently bought by the Rothschilds of Ch. LAFITE.

Les Carmes-Haut-Brion   Graves r. `**` 75 78
Small neighbour of HAUT-BRION. Nothing special.

Caronne-Ste-Gemme   St-Lau. (Haut-Médoc) r. `**` **73** 75 76 78
Substantial Cru Bourgeois of 80 acres.

du Castéra   Médoc r.   `**` **70 73** 75 76 78
Beautiful property at St-Germain in the n. Médoc managed by LICHINE. Fine, longlasting wine.

Certan de May   Pomerol r.   `**`   **70 71 73** 75 76 78
Neighbour of VIEUX-CHÂTEAU-CERTAN. Tiny property with fine rather hard wine, needing time to mature.

Certan-Giraud   Pomerol r. `***` **71 73** 75 76 78
Minute (8½-acre) property next to the great Ch. PETRUS.

Chasse-Spleen   Moulis r.   `**`   **64 66 67** 69 70 **71 73** 74 75 76 **77** 78
12-acre Cru Exceptionnel of classed-growth quality. Consistently good, sometimes outstanding, long-maturing wine.

Cheret-Pitre   Graves r. (w. dr.) `**` 75 76 78
35-acre property at Portets making full and meaty wines.

Cheval Blanc   St-Em. r. `****` **61 62 64** 66 **67 69** 70 71 **73** 74 75 76 78
By reputation the best wine of St-Emilion, rich and fullblooded, from an old family estate of 80 acres on the border of Pomerol. 70, 71 and 75 are outstanding vintages.

Cissac   Cissac r.   `**`   **66** 70 **71 73** 75 76 **77** 78 79
Small Cru Bourgeois with dynamic owners. Traditional methods and style.

Citran   Avensan, Haut-Médoc r. `**` 70 75 78
One of the better Crus Bourgeois at present. Full-bodied tough wine. Same owners as Ch'x. COUFRAN and Verdignan.

Clerc-Milon   Pauillac r. `***` **70 71 73** 75 76 **77** 78
Unimpressive little fifth-growth until 1970, when it was bought by Baron Philippe de Rothschild. Now 75 acres and new equipment are making first-rate wine.

Climens   Sauternes w. sw.   `***`   **62 67 69 70 71** 75 76 78 79
Famous 80-acre classed-growth at Barsac making some of the best and richest sweet wine in the world. Same owners as Ch. BRANE-CANTENAC.

Clinet   Pomerol r.   `**`   **70 71 73** 75 76 78
17-acre property in central Pomerol making elegant wine with more finesse than force.

Clos l'Eglise   Pomerol r.   `***`   **71 73** 75 76 78
13-acre v'yd in one of the best sites in Pomerol. Excellent wine.

Clos Fourtet   St-Em. r. `***` **67** 70 **73** 75 76 78
Well-known 33-acre first-growth on the plateau with cellars in the town. Not quite up to its (v. high) reputation recently.

Clos des Jacobins St-Em. r. ⭐⭐ 74 75 76 78
>Well-known and well-run little classed-growth owned by the shipper CORDIER. Matures rather quickly.

Clos René Pomerol r. ⭐⭐⭐ 61 66 67 70 71 73 75 78
>Leading ch. on the w. of Pomerol. 30 acres making powerful wine, which matures to great delicacy.

La Clotte St-Em. r. ⭐⭐ 66 70 71 75 76 78
>Small Côtes classed-growth with attractive "supple" wine.

La Conseillante Pomerol r. ⭐⭐⭐ 64 66 67 70 71 73 74 75 76 78
>30-acre classed-growth on the plateau between PETRUS and CHEVAL BLANC. At its best gloriously rich but less good in the sixties than its position would suggest.

Corbin St-Em. r. ⭐⭐
>50-acre classed-growth in n. St-Emilion where a cluster of Corbins occupy the edge of the plateau.

Corbin-Michotte St-Em. r. ⭐⭐ 66 70 71 73 75 76 78
>Well-run small property making attractive and reliable wine.

Cos-d'Estournel St-Est. r. ⭐⭐⭐ 61 62 64 66 67 70 71 72 73 75 76 77 78
>140-acre second-growth with eccentric chinoiserie building overlooking Ch. LAFITE. Usually full-flavoured, often magnificent, wine.

Cos Labory St-Est. r. ⭐⭐ 66 70 71 73 75 76 78
>Little-known fifth-growth neighbour of COS D'ESTOURNEL with 40 acres. Typical robust St-Estèphe, said to be improving in quality.

Coufran St-Seurin-de-Cadourne (Haut-Médoc) r. ⭐⭐
>Coufran and Ch. Verdignan, on the northern-most hillock of the Haut-Médoc, are under the same ownership.

Couhins Graves (r.) w. dr. ⭐⭐ 76 77 78 79
>25-acre v'yd. at Villenave-d'Ornon producing one of the best dry white Graves.

La Couronne Pauillac r. ⭐⭐ 67 70 73 75 76 78
>Small but excellent Cru Exceptionnel under the same direction as Ch. HAUT-BATAILLEY.

Coutet Sauternes w. sw. ⭐⭐⭐ 62 67 69 70 71 73 75 76 79
>Rival to Ch. CLIMENS; also 80 acres in Barsac. Said to be slightly less rich but certainly equally fine.

Couvent des Jacobins St-Em. r. ⭐⭐⭐
>Well-known vineyard of 20 acres adjacent to the town of St-Emilion on the east.

Le Crock St-Est. r. ⭐⭐
>Well-situated Cru Bourgeois of 80 acres in the same family as Ch. LÉOVILLE-POYFERRÉ.

La Croix Pomerol r. ⭐⭐ 70 71 74 75 76 78
>Well-reputed little property of 25+ acres. Old-fashioned tough wine; matures well.

La Croix de Gay Pomerol r. ⭐⭐⭐ 71 73 75 76 78
>One of the larger Pomerol v'yds. 27 acres in the best part of the commune.

Croizet-Bages Pauillac r. ⭐⭐ 61 64 66 70 71 73 75 76 78
>50-acre fifth-growth (lacking a ch.) owned by the same family as Ch. RAUZAN-GASSIES. Sound sturdy wines without flair.

Croque-Michotte St-Em. r. ⭐⭐ 66 70 72 75 76
>Small but well-known classed-growth on the Pomerol border.

Curé-Bon-la-Madeleine St-Em. r. ⭐⭐⭐ 66 70 72 75 76 78
>Small property among the best of the Côtes; between AUSONE and CANON.

Dauzac Lab-Mar. r. ⭐⭐ 66 70 73 75 76 78
>Substantial but somewhat neglected fifth-growth near the river s. of Margaux. In new hands since '79. 100 acres.

Dillon Haut-Médoc r. `**`
Often very well-made wine. Run by local wine college of Blanquefort, just n. of Bordeaux.

Doisy-Daene Barsac w. sw. and dr. `***`
Forward-looking estate making crisp dry white (incl. Riesling grapes) as well as traditional sweet Barsac.

Doisy-Védrines Sauternes w. sw. `***` 67 70 71 75 76 78
50-acre classed-growth at Barsac, near CLIMENS and COUTET and only slightly less fine.

Domaine de Chevalier Graves r. and w. dr. `****` 61 64 66 67 70 71 72 **73** 74 75 76 77w. 78
Superb small estate of 36 acres at Léognan. The red is stern at first, richly subtle with age. The white is delicate but matures to rich flavours.

Domaine de l'Eglise Pomerol r. `**` 66 67 70 71 75 76 78
Small property: good wine distributed by BORIE-MANOUX.

La Dominique St-Em. r. `***` 70 71 73 75 76 78
44-acre classed-growth next door to Ch. CHEVAL BLANC.

Du Breuil Cissac, Haut-Médoc r. `**`
V'yd. with a 10th-century castle producing full-bodied stylish wine, generally ageing well.

Ducru-Beaucaillou St-Jul. r. `***` 61 62 64 66 67 70 71 73 74 75 76 77 78
Outstanding second-growth; about 100 acres overlooking the river. The owner, M. Borie, makes classical long-lived but not harsh wines with noticeable oak flavour.

Duhart-Milon-Rothschild Pauillac r. `***` 64 66 70 71 75 76 77 78
Fourth-growth neighbour of LAFITE under the same management. Wines tend to typical Pauillac toughness rather than Lafite's elegance.

Durfort-Vivens Margaux r. `**` 66 70 75 76 78
Relatively small and obscure second-growth owned by M. Lurton of BRANE-CANTENAC and not far behind it in quality.

Dutruch-Grand-Poujeaux Moulis r. `**` 75 76 78
Rising star of Moulis, making typically hard tannic wines.

L'Eglise-Clinet Pomerol r. `***` 66 70 71 74 75 76 78
Highly ranked little property; typical, full, fleshy wine.

L'Enclos Pomerol r. `***` 64 67 70 71 73 74 75 76 78
Respected little property on the w. side of Pomerol, near CLOS-RENÉ. Big, well-made, long-flavoured wine.

L'Evangile Pomerol r. `***` 66 67 70 71 73 74 75 76 78
30+ acres between PETRUS and CHEVAL BLANC. Impressive wines. In the same area and class as LA CONSEILLANTE.

Fargues Sauternes w. sw. `**` 75 76 79
50-acre v'yd. in same ownership as Ch. YQUEM. Fruity and good but much lighter wines.

Ferrière Margaux r. `**` 66 70 75 78
Little-known third-growth of only 12 acres. The wine is made at Ch. LASCOMBES and sold to a chain of French hotels.

Feytit-Clinet Pomerol r. `**` 64 70 71 74 75 76 78
Little property next to LATOUR-POMEROL. Has made some fine big strong wines. Managed by J-P MOUEIX.

Fieuzal Graves r. and (w. dr.) `***` 64 66 67 70 71 72 73 75 76 78
40-acre classed-growth at Léognan. Changed hands in peak condition in 1973; now making some of the best GRAVES.

Figeac St-Em. r. `***` 61 62 64 66 67 70 71 73 74 75 76 78
Famous first-growth neighbour of CHEVAL BLANC. Superb 70+ acre v'yd. gives one of Bordeaux's most attractive full-bodied wines maturing fairly quickly.

Filhot Sauternes w. sw. and dr. `***` 67 69 70 71 72 75 76 78 79
Second-rank classed-growth with splendid ch., 120-acre v'yd. Very good sweet wines.

La Fleur-Pétrus Pomerol r. ★★★ **66 67** 70 71 **73 74** 75 76 78 79
    20-acre v'yd. flanking PÉTRUS and under the same MOUEIX management. Very fine rich plummy wines.

Fombrauge St-Em. r. ★★ **70** 71 75 76 78
    Major property of St-Christophe-des-Bardes, e. of St-Emilion. Reliable, if never great.

Fonbadet Pauillac r. ★★
    Well-known Cru Bourgeois with 70 acres next door to Ch. PONTET-CANET. Same owner as Ch. GLANA.

Fonplégade St-Em. r. ★★ **71 73** 75 76 78
    35-acre v'yd. on the Côtes w. of St. Emilion in another branch of the MOUEIX family.

Fonréaud Listrac r. ★★
    One of the better Crus Bourgeois of its area, selling mainly in France and at the cellar door.

Fonroque St-Em. r. ★★★ **66 67 70 71 73 74** 75 76 78
    50 acres on the plateau n. of St-Emilion, the property of another branch of the ubiquitous family MOUEIX. Big dark wine.

Les Forts de Latour Pauillac r. ★★★ **66 67** 70 75 76 78
    The second wine of Ch. Latour; well worthy of its big brother. Fetches the price of a second-growth Château.

Fourcas-Dupré Listrac r. ★★ 74 75 76 78
    A top-class Cru Bourgeois making consistent and elegant wine. To follow.

Fourcas-Hosten Listrac r. ★★ 66 70 71 **73** 75 76 78
    Reliable Cru Bourgeois of the central Médoc. Changed hands in '79. Rather hard wine is typical of Listrac.

Franc-Mayne St-Em. r. ★★ 70 71 **73** 75 76 78
    Small but reliable v'yd. on the Côtes w. of St-Emilion.

La Gaffelière St-Em. r. ★★★ 61 66 67 70 71 75 76 78
    Excellent though not always reliable 50-acre first-growth at the foot of the Côtes below Ch. BEL-AIR.

La Garde Graves r. ★★ 70 71 **73 74** 75 76 78
    Substantial ESCHENAUER property making reliably sound red.

Le Gay Pomerol r. ★★★ 70 71 **74** 75 76 78
    Well-known 14-acre v'yd. on the northern edge of Pomerol.

Gazin Pomerol r. ★★★ 66 67 70 71 75 76 78
    Large property (for Pomerol) with nearly 60 acres. Well known but below the top rank.

Giscours Lab-Mar. r. ★★★ 66 67 69 70 71 72 **73** 74 75 76 77 78
    Splendid 200-acre third-growth s. of CANTENAC. Dynamically run and making excellent wine for long maturing.

Glana St-Jul. r. ★★ **66** 70 75 78
    Big Cru Bourgeois in centre of St-Julien. Variable quality.

Gloria St-Jul. r. ★★★ 66 67 70 71 **73** 75 76 77 78
    Outstanding Cru Bourgeois making wine of vigour and finesse, among good classed-growths in quality. 100+ acres. Ch. Haut-Beycheville-Gloria is the same property.

Grand-Barrail-Lamarzelle-Figeac St-Em. r. ★★ 66 67 70 71 72 **73** 75 76 78
    Substantial property near FIGEAC. Well-reputed and popular.

Grand-Corbin-Despagne St-Em. r. ★★ 70 71 75 78
    One of the larger classed-growths on the CORBIN plateau.

Grand-Puy-Ducasse Pauillac r. ★★ 66 70 75 76 77 78
    Well-known little fifth-growth recently bought, renovated and enlarged to 70 acres under expert management.

Grand-Puy-Lacoste Pauillac r. ★★★ 61 64 66 67 70 71 72 **73** 75 76 77 78
    Leading fifth-growth famous for fine full-bodied typical Pauillac. 70 acres among the "Bages" ch'x. s. of the town, recently bought by M. Borie of DUCRU-BEAUCAILLOU.

La Grave Trigant de Boisset   Pomerol r.   ★★   66 70 71 73 75 76 78
Verdant ch. with small but first-class v'yd. owned by a MOUEIX. One of the lighter Pomerols.

Gressier Grand Poujeaux   Moulis r.   ★★   66 70 71 72 73 75 76 78
Good Cru Bourgeois. Fine firm wine.

Greysac   Médoc r.   ★★   74 75 78
Small elegant property whose wine is well-known in the U.S.A., though scarcely exceptional.

Gruaud-Larose   St-Jul. r.   ★★★   62 66 67 69 70 71 72 73 75 76 78
One of the biggest and best-known second-growths. 190 acres making smooth rich stylish claret. Owned by CORDIER.

Guiraud   Sauternes (r.) w. sw. (dr.)   ★★★   61 67 70 71 75 76 78 79
Large classed-growth of top quality. 150-acre v'yd. Excellent sweet wine and a small amount of red and dry white.

La Gurgue   Margaux r.   ★★★
Small well-placed property with fine typical Margaux sold mainly to private customers in France.

Hanteillan   Cissac r.   ★★
Large v'yd. recently renovated. To watch.

Haut-Bages-Libéral   Pauillac r.   ★★   75 76 78 79
Lesser-known fifth-growth of 50 acres recently bought by the CRUSE family. Should improve.

Haut-Bages-Monpelou   Pauillac r.   ★★   70 73 75 76 78
Cru Bourgeois stable-mate of CH. BATAILLEY. To watch.

Haut-Bailly   Graves r.   ★★★   64 66 70 71 73 75 77 78
50-acre estate at Léognan making one of the best red Graves: attractive smooth and perfumed wine.

Haut-Batailley   Pauillac r.   ★★★   61 64 66 70 71 73 74 75 76 77 78
The smaller but currently better section of the fifth-growth Batailley estate: 45 acres owned by M. Borie of Ch. DUCRU-BEAUCAILLOU. One of the most reliable Pauillacs.

Haut-Brion   Pessac, Graves r. (w.)   ★★★★   59 60 61 62 64 66 67 68 70 71 73 75 76 77 78
The oldest great ch. of Bordeaux and the only non-Medoc first-growth of 1855. 100 acres. Splendid firm reds, particularly good since 1975. A little full dry white.

Haut-Marbuzet   St-Estèphe r.   ★★   70 71 75 78
One of the best of the many Cru Bourgeois of St-Estèphe.

Haut-Pontet   St-Em. r.   ★★   70 71 73 75 78
Well-regarded 12-acre v'yd. of the Côtes.

Houissant   St-Estèphe r.   ★★
Typical robust well-balanced St-Estèphe Cru Bourgeois, well known in Denmark.

d'Issan   Cant-Mar. r.   ★★★   66 69 70 71 72 73 75 76 78
Beautifully restored moated ch. with 74-acre third-growth v'yd. well known for round and gentle wine.

Kirwan   Cant-Mar. r.   ★★   75 76 77 78
Well-run 100-acre third-growth owned by SCHRÖDER & SCHYLER. Recently much replanted: worth watching.

Labégorce   Margaux r.   ★★   75 76 78
Substantial property with rather old-fashioned long-lived wines.

Labégorce-Zédé   Margaux r.   ★★   70 71 72 73 75 76 78
Reputable little Cru Bourgeois on the road n. from Margaux. 35 acres. Typical delicate wines.

Lafaurie-Peyraguey   Sauternes w. sw.   ★★★   67 69 70 71 75 76 78
Fine classed-growth of only 40 acres at Bommes, belonging to CORDIER. Excellent wines, though not the richest.

Lafite-Rothschild   Pauillac r.   ★★★★   61 62 66 70 75 76 78
First-growth of fabulous style and perfume in its great vintages. Off-form for several years but resurgent since '76. 200+ acres. Usually known simply as "Lafite".

Lafleur Pomerol r. *** **66 67** 70 71 **73** 75 76 78
Tiny property of 10 acres just n. of PETRUS. Excellent wine of the finer, less "fleshy" kind.

Lafleur St-Em. r. ** **70 73 74** 75 76 78
Very small but well reputed Côtes estate.

Lafleur-Gazin Pomerol r. ** 71 **73 74** 75 76 78
Sound small estate on the n.e. border of Pomerol.

Lafon-Rochet St-Est. r. *** **61 64 66 67** 70 71 **73** 75 76 77 78
Fourth-growth neighbour of Ch. COS D'ESTOURNEL, restored to prominence in the '60s. 50+ acres. Typical dark full-bodied St-Estèphe. Same owner as Ch. PONTET-CANET.

Lagrange Pomerol r. ** **66 67** 70 71 75 76 78
Small v'yd. in the centre of Pomerol run by the ubiquitous house of MOUEIX.

Lagrange St-Jul. r. *** **62 66 70 71** 75 76 78
Rather run-down third-growth remote from most of St-Julien. 120 acres of the big estate are vines.

La Lagune Ludon r. *** **62 66 70 71 72 73 74** 75 76 77 78
Well-run ultra-modern 130-acre third-growth in the extreme s. of the Médoc. Attractively rich and fleshy wines.

Lamarque Lamarque (Haut-Médoc) r. ** **66 70** 75 76 78
Splendid medieval fortress of the central Médoc with 100 acres giving admirable light wine.

Lanessan Cussac (Haut-Médoc) r. ** **66 69 70 71 73** 75 76 77 78
Well-known 60-acre Cru Bourgeois just s. of St-Julien. Same owner as PICHON-LONGUEVILLE-BARON.

Langoa-Barton St-Jul. r. *** **66 67** 70 71 **72 73** 75 76 78
Fine 18th-century ch. housing the wine of third-growth Langoa (about 40 acres) as well as second-growth LÉOVILLE-BARTON. The wines are similar: Langoa slightly less fine.

Larcis-Ducasse St-Em. r. *** **66 70** 75 76 78
The top property of St-Laurent, eastern neighbour of St-Emilion, on the Côtes next to Ch. PAVIE. Rather heavy wine.

Laroque St-Em. r. ** **73 74** 75 76 78
Important 100-acre v'yd. with an impressive mansion on the St-Emilion côtes.

Larose-Trintaudon St-Lau. (Haut-Médoc) r. ** **70 71 73** 75 76 78
The biggest v'yd. in the Médoc: nearly 400 acres. Modern methods and reliable full-flavoured Cru Bourgeois wine.

Laroze St-Em. r. *** **67 70 71** 75
Big v'yd. (70 acres) on the w. Côtes. Relatively light wines from sandy soil. Sometimes excellent.

Larrivaux Cissac (Haut-Médoc) r. **
Small Cru Bourgeois respected for high standards.

Larrivet-Haut-Brion Graves r. (w.) **
Reputable little property at Léognan.

Lascombes Margaux r. (p.) *** **61 62 64 66 67** 70 71 **73** 75 76 78
240-acre second-growth owned by the British brewers Bass-Charrington and recently lavishly restored. Good vintages are rich for a Margaux. Also a pleasant rosé from young vines.

Latour Pauillac r. **** **61 62 64 66 67 69** 70 71 **73 74** 75 76 78
First-growth. The most consistent great wine in Bordeaux, in France and probably the world: rich, intense and almost immortal in great years, almost always classical and pleasing even in bad ones. British-owned. 140 acres. Second wine LES FORTS DE LATOUR.

Latour du Haut-Moulin Cussac (Haut-Médoc) r. ** **73** 75 76 79
Little-known Cru Bourgeois making classic old-style claret.

Latour-Pomerol   Pomerol r.   ★★★   **66 67** 70 71 73 74 75 76 78 79
Top growth of 20+ acres under MOUEIX management. Rich, fruity but firm wine for long maturing.

Laujac   Médoc r. ★★
Cru Bourgeois in the n. Médoc owned by the CRUSE family. Well known but scarcely outstanding.

Des Laurets   St-Em. r. ★★ 75 76 78
Major property of Puisseguin-St-Emilion (to the e.) with 66 acres on the Côtes.

Laville-Haut-Brion   Graves w. dr.   ★★★   70 71 73 75 77 78 79
A small production of one of the very best white Graves made at Ch. LA MISSION-HAUT-BRION.

Léoville-Barton   St-Jul. r.   ★★★   61 62 64 66 67 70 71 **73** 75 76 78
80-acre portion of the great second-growth Léoville v'yd. in the Anglo-Irish hands of the Barton family for over 150 years. Glorious classical claret, made by traditional methods at the Bartons' third-growth Ch. LANGOA.

Léoville-Las Cases   St-Jul. r.   ★★★   61 64 66 67 70 71 73 74 75 76 77 78 79
The largest portion of the old Léoville estate, 140 acres, with one of the highest reputations in Bordeaux. Elegant, never heavy wines. Second label Clos du Marquis.

The highest price ever paid for a bottle of wine—so far as anyone knows—was $31,000. It was paid for a single bottle of Château Lafite 1822 at a Heublein wine auction in San Francisco in May 1980.

Léoville-Poyferré   St-Jul. r.   ★★★ 66 67 70 **72** 75 76 78
At present the least outstanding of the Leovilles, though with famous old vintages to its credit and some recent ones promising well. 100+ acres. Second label Ch. Moulin-Riche.

Lestage   Listrac r. ★★ 75 78
100-acre Cru Bourgeois. Fine wine in best vintages.

Liot   Barsac w. sw.   ★★   **71 72 73** 75 76
Consistently fine fairly light golden wines.

Liversan   St-Sau. (Haut-Médoc) r.   ★★   **73** 75 76 78
Small Cru Bourgeois inland from Pauillac. Recently much improved by its new German proprietor.

Livran   Médoc r. ★★ **76** 78
Big Cru Bourgeois at St-Germain in the n. Médoc. More consistent than extraordinary.

Loudenne   St-Yzans (Médoc) r.   ★★ 70 71 **73** 75 76 78
Beautiful riverside ch. owned by Gilbeys since 1875. Well-made Cru Bourgeois red and a little excellent "modern-style" dry white from 90 acres.

La Louvière   Graves r. and w. dr.   ★★   75 76 77w. 78
Big estate at Léognan with the same director as Ch. COUHINS. Good dry white and agreeable red.

de Lussac   St-Em. r.   ★★ **73 74** 75 76 78
One of the best estates in Lussac-St-Emilion (to the n.e.).

Lynch-Bages   Pauillac r.   ★★★   61 66 70 71 **72** 74 75 76 77 78
One of the biggest and most popular fifth-growths. 140 acres making old-style rich robust wine: delicious, if never great.

Lynch-Moussas   Pauillac r.   ★★   66 75 78
Neglected little fifth-growth bought by the director of Ch. BATAILLEY in 1969. The 12 acres are being expanded and better wine is expected.

Magdelaine   St-Em. r.   ★★★   66 67 70 **72** 73 75 76 78
Leading first-growth of the Côtes, 25 acres next to AUSONE owned by J-P MOUEIX. Particularly good recently.

Magence Graves r. w. dr. ★★ 75 77w. 78

Go-ahead property at St Pierre de Mons, in the s. of the Graves, well known for distinctly SAUVIGNON-flavoured very dry white and fruity red.

Malartic-Lagravière Graves r. and (w. dr.) ★★★ 64 66 70 71 73 75 76 77 78

Well-known Léognan classed-growth of 50 acres making excellent solid red for long maturing and fruity SAUVIGNON white for early drinking.

Malescasse Lamarque (Haut-Médoc). r. ★★ 73 75 76 78

Renovated Cru Bourgeois with 70 acres in a good situation recently bought by M. Tesseron of Ch. LAFON-ROCHET.

Malescot St-Exupéry Margaux r. ★★★ 61 64 66 70 71 72 73 75 76 77 78

Third-growth of 55 acres with the same owners as Ch. MARQUIS-D'ALESME-BECKER. Rather hard, long maturing, eventually classically fragrant and stylish Margaux.

de Malle Sauternes r. w. sw./dr. ★★ 67 70 71 75 76 78

Famous and beautiful ch. at Preignac. 90 acres. Good sweet and dry whites and red (Graves) Ch. de Cardaillan.

de Marbuzet St-Est. r. ★★ 73 75 76 78

The second label of Ch. COS D'ESTOURNEL. (The actual ch. overlooks the river from the hill n. of Cos.)

Margaux Margaux r. ★★★★ 61 66 67 70 71 75 76 78

First-growth, the most delicate and finely perfumed of all in its best vintages. Changed hands in 1977 and much improved since. Noble ch. and estate with 160+ acres of vines.

Marquis-d'Alesme-Becker Margaux r. ★★

The smaller (20 acres), less famous and less fine of twin third-growths. The other is Ch. MALESCOT.

Marquis-de-Terme Margaux r. ★★★ 66 70 71 75 76 77 78

Old-style fourth-growth making fine typical Margaux, tannic and harsh when young. 125 acres. Sells principally in France.

Martinens Margaux r. ★★ 75 76 78

50-acre Cru Bourgeois recently much improved.

Maucaillou Moulis r. ★★ 70 71 72 73 75 76 78

60-acre Cru Bourgeois with high standards, property of the shippers DOURTHE FRÈRES. Full fruity wine.

Meyney St-Est. r. ★★ 66 70 71 74 75 76 78

Big (120-acre) riverside property next door to Ch. MONTROSE, one of the best of many good Crus Bourgeois in St-Estèphe. Owned by CORDIER.

La Mission-Haut-Brion Graves r. ★★★★ 59 61 64 66 70 71 74 75 76 77 78 79

Neighbour and rival to Ch. HAUT-BRION. Serious and grand old-style claret for long maturing.

Monbousquet St-Em. r. ★★ 70 71 74 75 76 78

Fine 70-acre estate in the Dordogne valley below St-Emilion. Attractive early-maturing wine from deep gravel soil.

Montrose St-Est. r. ★★★ 61 62 64 66 67 70 71 72 73 74 75 76 77 78

150-acre family-run second-growth well known for deeply coloured, forceful, old-style claret. Needs long ageing.

Moulin-à-Vent Moulis r. ★★

Small property making efforts to improve its rather hard, typically Moulis wine.

Moulin des Carruades

The second-quality wine of Ch. LAFITE.

Moulin du Cadet St-Em. r. ★★★ 70 71 73 74 75 76 78

First-class little v'yd. on the Côtes managed by J. P. MOUEIX.

Moulinet Pomerol r. ★★★ 70 71 73 75 76 78

One of Pomerol's bigger estates; 37 acres on relatively light soil.

Mouton-Baronne-Philippe Pauillac r. ✦✦✦ **61 66** 70 **73** 75 76 78
Substantial fifth-growth with the enormous advantage of belonging to Baron Philippe de Rothschild, 125 acres making gentler, less rich and tannic wine than Mouton.

Mouton-Rothschild Pauillac r. ✦✦✦✦ **60 61 62 66 67** 70 71 73 75 76
Officially a first-growth since 1973, though for 20 years worthy of the title. 145 acres (90% CABERNET SAUVIGNON) making wine of majestic richness. Also the world's greatest museum of works of art relating to wine.

Nairac Sauternes w. sw. ✦✦ 73 75 76 78
Newly restored Barsac classed-growth.

Nenin Pomerol r. ✦✦✦ **66 67** 70 71 **74** 75 76 78
Well-known 50-acre estate: good but not outstanding quality.

Olivier Graves r. and w. dr. ✦✦✦ 77w. 78
60-acre classed-growth, run by the shipper ESCHENAUER, surrounding a moated castle. Well-known, if not exciting, white; less-known but serious red.

Les Ormes-de-Pez St-Est. r. ✦✦ 66 70 71 75 76 77 78
Popular 65-acre Cru Bourgeois managed by Ch. LYNCH-BAGES. Reliable full-flavoured St-Estèphe.

Padouen Barsac w. sw. ✦✦ 76 78
Sandy soil. Good light wines. Australian-owned.

Palmer Cant-Mar. r. ✦✦✦✦ **59 60 61 66 69** 70 71 **73** 74 75 76 77 78
The star ch. of CANTENAC; a third-growth often on a level just below the first-growths. Wine of power and delicacy. 100 acres with Dutch, British and French owners.

Pape-Clément Graves r. and w. dr. ✦✦✦ **62 64 66 67** 70 71 73 74 75 76 77 78
Ancient v'yd. at Pessac, now 65 acres in fine condition making one of the most attractive red Graves.

Patache d'Aux Bégadan (Médoc) r. ✦✦ 70 71 75 76 78
70-acre Cru Bourgeois of the n. Médoc. Well-made wine.

Pauillac, La Rose Pauillac r. ✦✦
The wine of Pauillac's growers' co-op. Membership is dwindling as small growers sell out to big. Generally good value.

Paveil-de Luze Margaux r. ✦✦ **69** 70 75 76 78
Old family estate at Soussans. Small but highly regarded.

Pavie St-Em. r. ✦✦✦ **64 66 67** 70 71 73 75 76 78
Splendidly sited first-growth of 80 acres on the slope of the Côtes. Typically rich and tasty St-Em. consistently well made.

Pavie-Maquin St-Em. r. ✦✦ **73** 74 75 76 78
Reliable small Côtes v'yd. e. of St-Emilion.

Pedesclaux Pauillac r. ✦✦ 70 75
50-acre fifth-growth making wine below its full potential.

Petit-Village Pomerol r. ✦✦✦ **66 67** 70 71 75 76 78
One of the best-known little properties: 26 acres next to VIEUX-CH.-CERTAN, same owner as Ch. COS D'ESTOURNEL. Powerful long-lasting wine.

Petrus Pomerol r. ✦✦✦✦ **61 62 64 66 67** 70 71 **73** 74 75 76 77 78 79
The great name of Pomerol. 28 acres of gravelly clay giving the world's most massively rich and concentrated wine.

de Pez St-Est. r. ✦✦✦ **66 67** 70 71 72 73 75 76 77 78
Outstanding Cru Bourgeois of 60 acres. As reliable as any of the classed growths of the village. Needs long storage.

Phélan-Ségur St-Est. r. ✦✦ **66** 70 71 75 76 78
Big and important Cru Bourgeois (140 acres) with the same director as Ch. LÉOVILLE-POYFERRÉ.

Pibran Pauillac r. ✦✦
Reliable, if scarcely stylish, little Cru Bourgeois, mainly drunk in the Low Countries.

Pichon-Longueville-Baron Pauillac r. ✦✦✦ **66** 70 71 **73** 75 76 78
70-acre second-growth usually making fine sturdy Pauillac.

Pichon-Longueville, Comtesse de Lalande Pauillac r. ★★★ 61 64 66 70 71 **74** 75 76 77 78

Important second-growth neighbour to Ch. LATOUR. 110 acres. Magnificent on form: '70, '75 and '78 very good.

Pindefleurs St-Em. r. ★★ 75 76 78

Up and coming 20-acre v'yd. on the St-Emilion plateau.

de Pitray Castillon r. ★★ 75 76 78

Substantial (62 acre) v'yd. on the Côtes de Castillon e. of St-Emilion. Good lightish wines.

Plince Pomerol r. ★★

Reputable 20-acre property on the outskirts of Libourne. Relatively hard and short wines. Excellent '75.

La Pointe Pomerol r. ★★★ 66 70 71 73 **74** 75 76 78

Prominent 60-acre estate for typically fat fruity Pomerol.

Pontet-Canet Pauillac r. ★★★ 61 66 67 70 73 **74** 75 76 78

One of the biggest classed-growths with about 200 acres, neighbour to MOUTON and potentially far better than its official rank of fifth-growth. Belonged to the CRUSE family for many years, now to M. Tesseron of Ch. LAFON-ROCHET.

Potensac Potensac (Médoc) r. **★★** 66 67 70 71 73 75 76 77 78

The best-known Cru Bourgeois of Ordonnac-et-Potensac in the n. Médoc. The neighbouring Ch'x. Lassalle and Gallais-Bellevue belong to the same family, the Delons, owners of Ch. LÉOVILLE-LASCASES.

Pouget Margaux ★★

Old ch. name now used for the second wine of Ch. BOYD-CANTENAC. Sold mainly in France.

Poujeaux-Theil Moulis r. ★★

Family-run Cru Exceptionnel of 100 acres selling its rather hard wine direct to an appreciative French public.

Prieuré-Lichine Cant-Mar r. **★★★** 64 66 67 70 71 73 **74** 75 76 78

Formerly obscure fourth-growth brought to the fore by Alexis Lichine since 1952. Excellent finely fragrant Margaux.

Puy Blanquet St-Em. r ★★ 73 **74** 75 78

The major property of St-Etienne-de-Lisse, e. of St-Emilion, with over 50 acres. Wine below the top class.

Puy-Razac St-Em. r. ★★

Small property at the foot of the Côtes near Ch. PAVIE, connected with the well-known Ch. MONBOUSQUET.

Rabaud-Promis Sauternes w. sw. ★★★ 67 70 71 75 76 78

Classed-growth of 70 acres at Bommes. Good, not brilliant.

Rahoul Graves r. and w. dr. **★★** 75 76 78

Australian-owned 34-acre v'yd. at Portets making particularly good wine, 80% red.

Ramage-la-Batisse Haut-Médoc r. **★★** 70 75 76 78

Oustanding Cru Bourgeois of 75 acres at St-Sauveur, west of Pauillac. To watch.

Rausan-Ségla Margaux r. ★★★ 61 66 70 71 73 75 76 78

100-acre second-growth; famous for its fragrance; one of the great names of the Médoc, but recently below par. Owned by ESCHENAUER.

Rauzan-Gassies Margaux r. ★★★ 61 66 70 73 75 76 78

50-acre second-growth neighbour of the last with a poor record in the '60s. Said to be looking up.

Raymond-Lafon Sauternes w. sw. ★★ 75 76 78

Lesser-known but serious Sauternes estate run by the manager of Ch. YQUEM.

de Rayne-Vigneau Sauternes w. sw. ★★★ 67 70 71 75 76 78

100-acre classed-growth at Bommes with rich golden wine.

Respide Graves (r.) w. dr. ★★

One of the better white-wine ch'x. of s. Graves, at St Pierre de Mons. Full-flavoured wines.

Reysson Vertheuil Haut-Médoc r. **
>Recently replanted, up-and-coming Cru Bourgeois.

Rieussec Sauternes w. sw. *** **62 66 67 69 70 71** 75 76 78 79
>Worthy neighbour of Ch. D'YQUEM with 120 acres in Fargues.
>Not the sweetest, but can be exquisitely fine.

Ripeau St-Em. r. ** 75 78
>Above-average classed-growth in the centre of the plateau.

Rouget Pomerol r. ** **67 70 71 74** 75 76 78
>Attractive old estate on the n. edge of Pomerol. Full round
>wines, maturing well. Popular in smart Paris restaurants.

Royal St-Emilion
>Brand name of the important growers' co-operative.

St-André Corbin St-Emilion r. ** **64 66** 75 76 78
>Considerable property of Montagne-St-Emilion with a long
>record of above-average wines.

St-Estèphe, Marquis de St-Est. r. [*] **70 71 73** 75 76
>The growers' co-operative; over 200 members. Good value.

St-Georges St-Geo., St-Em. r. ** **70** 75 **76** 78
>18th-century ch. overlooking the St-Emilion plateau from the
>hill to the n. Considerable quantities of good wine.

St-Pierre (Bontemps-et-Sevaistre) St-Jul. r. *** **70 72 73** 75
76 78
>Well-run small (40-acre) fourth-growth in Belgian owner-
>ship. Attractively ripe and fruity wines.

St-Pierre Graves (r.) w. dr. **
>Estate at St Pierre de Mons making old-style Graves of
>notable character and flavour.

de Sales Pomerol r. *** **66 67 70 71** 75 76 78
>The biggest v'yd. of Pomerol, attached to the grandest ch. But
>relatively dull wine.

Sénéjac Haut-Médoc r. **
>Cru Bourgeois in s. Médoc. Small but skilful production.

Sigalas-Rabaud Sauternes w. sw. ** **67 70 71** 75 76 78
>The lesser part of the former Rabaud estate: 35 acres in
>Bommes, making first-class sweet wine.

Siran Lab-Mar. r. ** **61 66** 70 71 75
>Substantial well-run Cru Bourgeois.

Smith-Haut-Lafitte Graves r. and (w. dr.) *** **66 70 71 74** 75 76 78
>Run-down old classed-growth at Martillac restored by
>ESCHENAUER in the '60s. Now 120 acres (14 of white). The
>white wine is light and fruity; the red dry and interesting.

Soutard St-Em. r. ** **66 67 70 71 72 73 74** 75 76 78
>Reliable 50-acre classed-growth n. of the town. Wine "gener-
>ous" rather than "fine".

Suduiraut Sauternes w. sw. *** **67 70 71**
>One of the best Sauternes: of glorious creamy richness. Over
>200 acres of the top class, under promising new management.

Taillefer Pomerol r. ** **67 70 73** 75 76 78
>24-acre property on the edge of Pomerol owned by another
>branch of the MOUEIX family.

Talbot St-Jul. r. (w.) *** **62 66 70 71 73** 75 76 77 78
>Important 200-acre fourth-growth, sister ch. to GRUAUD-
>LAROSE, with similarly attractive rich and satisfying wine.

du Tertre Ar-Mar. r. ** **66 70 71 72 73** 75 76 78
>Underestimated fifth-growth isolated s. of Margaux.
>Thoroughly well-made claret matures admirably.

Tertre-Daugay St-Em. r. **
>Small classed-growth in a spectacular situation on the brow
>of the Côtes. Under new ownership.

La Tour-Blanche Sauternes w. (dr.) *** **62 67 70 71** 75
>Top-rank 60-acre estate at Bommes with a state wine-
>growing school. Wine of only moderate quality recently.

La Tour-Carnet St-Lau. r. ★★ **66 70** 75 76 78
Fourth-growth reborn from total neglect in the '60s. Medieval tower with 100+ acres just w. of St-Julien.

La Tour de By Bégadan (Médoc) r. ★★ **70 71** 75 76 77 78
Very well-run 100-acre Cru Bourgeois in the n. Médoc.

La Tour-de-Mons Sou-Mar. r. ★★★ **66 70 71 73** 75 78
Distinguished Cru Bourgeois of 60 acres, three centuries in the same family (which also owns Ch. CANTEMERLE). Sometimes excellent claret with a long life.

La Tour-du-Pin-Figeac St-Em. r. ★★
20-acre classed-growth, once part of LA TOUR-FIGEAC. Off form recently.

La Tour-du-Pin-Figeac-Moueix St-Em. r. ★★ **67** 70 75 76 78
Another 20-acre section of the same old property, owned by one of the famous MOUEIX family.

La Tour-Figeac St-Em. r. ★★ **70** 75 78
40-acre classed-growth between Ch. FIGEAC and Pomerol. Well run by a German proprietor.

La Tour-Haut-Brion Graves r. ★★ **66** 70 **74** 75 76 78
The second label of Ch. LA MISSION-HAUT-BRION. A plainer, smaller-scale wine.

La Tour-Martillac Graves r. and w. dr. ★★ **70 71** 75 76 78
Small but serious property at Martillac. 10 acres of white grapes; 20 of black. Quantity is sacrificed for quality.

La Tour St-Bonnet Médoc r. ★★
Consistently well-made and typical n. Médoc from St-Christoly.

Tournefeuille Lalande de Pomerol r. ★★ **67 70 71 73** 75 76 78
The star of Néac, overlooking Pomerol from the n. A small property, but excellent long-lived wine.

Tronquoy-Lalande St-Est. r. ★★ **70 71 73** 75 76 78
50-acre Cru Bourgeois making typical St-Estèphe. Distributed by DOURTHE.

Troplong-Mondot St-Em. r. ★★ **66 70 71** 75 76 78
One of the bigger classed-growths of St-Emilion. 70+ acres well sited on the Côtes above Ch. PAVIE.

Trotanoy Pomerol r. ★★★ **61 67 70 71 73** 74 75 76 78 79
One of the top Pomerols. Only 20 acres but a splendid fleshy perfumed wine. Managed by J-P MOUEIX.

Trottevieille St-Em. r. ★★★ **66 67 70 71** 75 76 78
Small but highly reputed first-growth of 25 acres on the Côtes e. of the town. Attractive full wines.

Le Tuquet Graves r. and w. dr. ★★ **76** 78
Substantial estate at Beautiran making light fruity wines; the white better.

Vieux-Château-Certan Pomerol r. ★★★ **61 66 67 71** 75 76 78
Potentially the second ch. of Pomerol, just s. of PETRUS, the first. 30+ acres, Belgian owned.

Vieux-Chateau-St-André St-Emilion r. ★★ **78**
Small v'yd. in Montagne-St-Emilion newly acquired by a leading wine-maker of Libourne. To watch.

Villegeorge Avensan r. ★★ **73 74** 75 76 78
Small Cru Exceptionnel to the n. of Margaux with the same owner as Ch. BRANE-CANTENAC. Excellent full-bodied wine.

Villemaurine St-Em. r. ★★
Good classed-growth well sited on the côtes by the town.

Vraye-Croix-de-Gay Pomerol ★★★ **71 73 74** 75 76 78
Very small ideally situated v'yd. in the best part of Pomerol.

d'Yquem Sauternes w. sw. (dr.) ★★★★ **59 62 66 67 68 69 70** 71 75 76
The world's most famous sweet-wine estate. 240 acres making only 500 bottles per acre of very strong, intense, luscious wine. Good vintages need a decade of maturity.

Germany

Germany has the most complicated labelling system in the world—a fact that has put most people off tackling it seriously and driven them to settle for pleasantly innocuous blended wines: Liebfraumilch and the like.

Yet those who funk its complications will never experience the real beauty of the style of wine which is Germany's unique contribution.

The secret of the style is the balance of sweetness against fruity acidity. A great vintage in Germany is one in which the autumn weather allows the late-ripening Riesling—the grape which makes virtually all the great German wines—to develop a high sugar content. What is so special about the Riesling is that as it ripens it also develops a concentration of fragrant acids and essences to balance the increasing sweetness. The resulting wine is tense and thrilling with this sugar/acid balance.

It smells and tastes extraordinarily flowery, lively and refreshing while it is young. But because of its internal equilibrium it also has the ability to live and mature for a remarkable length of time. As good Riesling matures all sorts of subtle scents and flavours emerge. Straight sweetness gives way to oily richness. Suggestions of countless flowers and fruits, herbs and spices develop.

These are the rewards for anyone who can be bothered to master the small print. They lead into realms of sensation where Liebfraumilch (with all the respect due to a perfectly decent drink) can never follow. The great German growers make wine for wine's sake. Food is irrelevant, except in so far as it gets in the way.

The Labels and the Law

German wine law is based on the ripeness of the grapes at harvest time. Recent vintages have been exceptionally kind to growers, but as a general rule most German wine needs sugar added to make up for the missing warmth and sunshine of one of the world's northernmost vineyards.

The exceptional wine, from grapes ripe enough not to need sugar, is kept apart as Qualitätswein mit Prädikat or QmP. Within this top category its natural sugar-content is expressed by traditional terms—in ascending order of ripeness: Kabinett, Spätlese, Auslese, Beerenauslese, Trockenbeerenauslese.

But reasonably good wine is also made in good vineyards from grapes that fail to reach the natural sugar-content required for a QmP label. The authorities allow this, within fairly strict controls, to be called Qualitätswein as well, but with the different qualification of bestimmter Anbaugebiete (i.e. QbA) instead of mit Prädikat. mP is therefore a vitally important ingredient of a fine-wine label.

Both levels are officially checked, tested and tasted at every bottling. Each batch is given an identifying test ("prüfungs") number. No other country has quality control approaching this. It can't make dull wine exciting, but it can and does make all "quality" wine a safe bet.

Moselle Saar Ruwer **M-S-R**

Rheingau **Rhg**

Frankfurt •

Ruwer

R. Moselle

Mittel-Mosel **M-M**

Saar

Mainz

R. Nahe

Rheinhessen
Rhh

Nahe **Na**

R. Main

Franken
Frank

Mannheim •

• Saarbrucken

R. Neckar

Abbreviations of regional names
shown in bold type are used in
the text.

Rheinpfalz
Rhpf

R. Rhine

• Karlsruhe

Stuttgart •

Württemburg **Wurt**

Baden **Bad**

• Freiburg

The third level, Tafelwein, has no pretensions to quality
and is not allowed to give itself airs beyond the name of the
village or the general region it comes from.

Though there is very much more detail in the laws this is
the gist of the quality grading. Where it differs completely
from the French system is in ignoring geographical difference. There are no Grands Crus, no VDQS. In theory all any
German vineyard has to do to make the best wine is to grow
the ripest grapes.

The law distinguishes only between degrees of geographical exactness. In labelling quality wine the grower or merchant is given a choice. He can (and always will) label the
relatively small quantities of his best wine with the name of
the precise vineyard or Einzellage where it was grown.
Germany has about 3,000 Einzellage names. Obviously only
particularly good ones are famous enough to help sell the
wine. Therefore the law has created a second class of vineyard name: the Grosslage. A Grosslage is a group of neighbouring Einzellages of supposedly similar character and
standing. Because there are fewer Grosslage names, and far
more wine from each, Grosslages have a better chance of
building reputations, brand-name fashion.*

Thirdly the grower or merchant (more likely the latter) may choose to sell his wine under a regional name: the word is Bereich. To cope with the vast demand for "Bernkasteler" or "Niersteiner" or "Johannisberger" these world-famous names have been made legal for considerable districts. "Bereich Johannisberg" is the whole of the Rheingau; "Bereich Bernkastel" the whole of the Mittel-Mosel.

As with all wine names, in fact, the better the wine the more precise the labelling. The trick with German labels is to be able to recognize which is the most precise. Finally, though, and above all, it is to recognize the grower and his vineyard.

The basic German label

The order of wording on German quality wine labels follows a standard pattern.

The first name is the town or parish, with the suffix -er. The second is the vineyard (either Einzellage or Grosslage — see introduction). The third (optional) is the grape variety. The fourth is the quality in terms of ripeness. For QmP see page 74.

For A.P. Nr. see page 66. Erzeugerabfüllung means bottled by the grower, in this case the grower's co-operative of Trier. For other words appearing on German labels see the Germany A–Z.

*Where the law is less than candid, however, is in pretending to believe that the general public will know a Grosslage name from an Einzellage name, when the two are indistinguishably similar (see any entry on the following pages). It is actually against the law to indicate on the label whether the name in question is that of a particular plot or a wider grouping. The names of all relevant Grosslages are given in this book. Note that Grosslage wines are very rarely of the stature of Einzellage wines.

N.B. on vintage notes opposite

Vintage notes after entries in the German section are given in a different form from those elsewhere, to show the style of the vintage as well as its quality.

Three styles are indicated:

The classic, super-ripe vintage with a high proportion of natural (QmP) wines, including Spätleses and Ausleses. Three of the six vintages shown, an unprecedented proportion, come into this category. Example: 71

The "normal" successful vintage with plenty of good wine but no great preponderance of sweeter wines. Example: 77

The cool vintage with generally poor ripeness but a fair proportion of reasonably successful wines, tending to be over-acid. Such wines sometimes mature better than expected. Example: 78

Where no mention is made the vintage is generally not recommended, or most of its wines have passed maturity.

Recent Vintages

Mosel

Mosels (including Saar and Ruwer wines) are so attractive young that their keeping qualities are not often enough explored, and wines older than seven years or so are unusual. But well-made wines of Kabinett class gain from two or three years in bottle, Spätleses by a little longer, and Ausleses and Beerenausleses by anything from 10 to 20 years, depending on the vintage.

As a rule, in poor years the Saar and Ruwer fare worse than the Middle Mosel and make sharp, thin wines, but in the best years they can surpass the whole of Germany for elegance and "breed".

1979	A patchy vintage after bad winter damage. But several excellent Kabinetts and better.
1978	A similar vintage to '77, though very late and rather small. Very few sweet wines but many with good balance.
1977	Big vintage of serviceable quality, mostly QbA.
1976	Very good small vintage, with some superlative sweet wines and almost no dry. Kabinetts and Spätleses can lack balance.
1975	Superb; many Spätleses and Ausleses. Perfect balance will give them long life.
1974	Most wine needed sugaring; few Kabinetts, but some well-balanced wines which have kept well. Drink now.
1973	Very large, attractive, but low acid and extract have meant a short life. Good eiswein. Drink now.
1972	Large; medium to poor; few late-picked wines, many with unripe flavour. Should be drunk by now.
1971	Superb, with perfect balance. Many top wines still need keeping.
1970	Large; good to average. Quite soft, not for keeping.
1969	Some very fine wines; most merely good. Best in the Saar and Ruwer. Now mature.

Older fine vintages: '67, '64, '59, '53, '49, '45.

Rhine/Nahe/Palatinate

Even the best wines can be drunk with pleasure after two or three years, but Kabinett, Spätlese and Auslese wines of good vintages gain enormously in character and complexity by keeping for longer. Rheingau wines tend to be longest-lived, often improving for 10 years or more, but wines from the Nahe and the Palatinate can last nearly as long. Rheinhessen wines usually mature sooner, and dry Franconian wines are best young.

The Riesling, predominant in the Rheingau, benefits most from hot summers; Palatinate wines can taste almost overripe.

1979	Uneven and reduced in size. Few great wines but many typical and good.
1978	Satisfactory vintage saved by late autumn. 25% QmP, but very few Spätleses. Some excellent wines in the south.
1977	Big and useful; few Kabinett wines or better. Not to keep. Rheinpfalz best.
1976	The richest vintage since 1921 in places. Very few dry wines. Balance less consistent than 1975. Maturing well.
1975	A splendid Riesling year, a high percentage of Kabinetts and Spätleses. The best need time to mature.
1974	Variable; the best fruity and good; many Kabinetts. Drink now.
1973	Very large, consistent and attractive, but not for keeping.
1972	Excess acidity was the problem; no exciting wines, but some presentable. Should be drunk now.
1971	A superlative vintage with perfect balance. The finest are still improving.
1970	Very pleasant wines, but no more. Huge crop. Not for keeping.
1969	All above average; the best great. Nahe and Palatinate specially good. Now mature.
1967	Marvellous; the best of the '60s; Rheinhessen made great wines.

Older fine vintages: '66, '64, '59, '57, '53, '49, '45.

Achkarren   Bad. (r.) w. ★→★★

> Well-known wine village of the KAISERSTUHL.

Adelmann, Graf

> Famous grower with 125 acres at Kleinbottwar, WÜRTTEM-BERG. Uses the name Brussele. Light reds; good RIESLINGS.

Ahr   Ahr r. ★→★★★   71 75 76 77 79

> Germany's best-known red-wine area, s. of Bonn. Very light pale SPÄTBURGUNDERS.

Amtliche Prüfungsnummer

> See Prüfungsnummer

Anbaugebiet

> Wine-region. See QbA.

Anheuser

> Name of two distinguished growers of the NAHE.

Annaberg   Rhpf. w. ★★★71 75 76 77 78 79

> Thirty-two-acre estate at DÜRKHEIM famous for sweet and pungent wines, esp. SCHEUREBE.

A.P.Nr.

> Abbreviation of Amtliche Prüfungsnummer.

Assmannshausen   Rhg. r. ★→★★★   71 75 76 77 78 79

> RHEINGAU village known for its pale reds. Top v'yd.: Höllenberg. Grosslage: Steil.

The German Wine Academy runs regular courses of wine-instruction at all levels for both amateurs and professionals, in German and English. The Academy is based at the glorious 12th-century Cistercian monastery of Kloster Eberbach in the Rheingau. The course normally includes tasting-tours of Germany's wine regions. Particulars can be obtained from the Academy, P. O. Box 1705, D-6500 Mainz, West Germany.

Auslese

> Late-gathered wine with high natural sugar content.

Avelsbach   M-S-R (Ruwer) w. ★★★ 71 75 76 77 78 79

> Village near TRIER. Supremely delicate wines. Growers: Staatliche Weinbaudomäne (see Staatsweingut), BISCHÖFLICHE WEINGÜTER. Grosslage: Trierer Römerlay.

Ayl   M-S-R (Saar) w. ★★★ 71 75 76 77 78 79

> One of the best villages of the SAAR. Top v'yds.: Kupp, Herrenberger. Grosslage: Scharzberg.

Bacchus

> Modern highly perfumed grape variety.

Bacharach (Bereich)

> District name for the s. Mittelrhein v'yds. downstream from the RHEINGAU. No great or famous wines; some pleasant.

Baden

> Huge area of scattered wine-growing. Few classic wines: most are heavy or soft. Best areas are KAISERSTUHL and ORTENAU.

Badische Bergstrasse/Kraichgau (Bereich)

> Principal district name of n. BADEN.

Bad Dürkheim

> See Dürkheim

Badisches Frankenland (Bereich)

> Minor district name of n. BADEN.

Bad Kreuznach   Na. w. ★★→★★★ 71 75 76 77 78 79

> Main town of the NAHE with some of its best wines. Many fine v'yds., incl. Brückes, St. Martin, Kauzenberg. Grosslage: Kronenberg.

Balbach Erben

> One of the best growers of NIERSTEIN.

Basserman-Jordan
100-acre MITTEL-HAARDT family estate with many of the best v'yds. in DEIDESHEIM, FORST, RUPPERTSBERG, etc.

Beerenauslese
Extremely sweet and luscious wine from very late-gathered individual bunches.

Bereich
District within a Gebiet (region). See under Bereich names, e.g. Bernkastel (Bereich).

Bergzabern, Bad Rhpf. (r.) w. ★→★★ 75 76 77 78 79
Town of SÜDLICHE-WEINSTRASSE. Pleasant sweetish wines. Grosslage: Liebfrauenberg.

Bernkastel M-M w. ★★→★★★★ 71 75 76 77 78 79
Top wine-town of the Mosel; the epitome of RIESLING. Best v'yds.: Doktor, Bratenhöfchen, etc. Grosslages: Badstube (★★★) and Kurfürstlay (★★).

Bernkastel (Bereich)
Wide area of mixed quality but decided flowery character. Includes all the Mittel-Mosel.

Bingen Rhh. w. ★★→★★★ 71 75 76 77 78 79
Town on Rhine and Nahe with fine v'yds., incl. Scharlachberg. Grosslage: Sankt Rochuskapelle.

Bingen (Bereich)
District name for w. Rheinhessen.

Bischöfliche Weingüter
Outstanding M-S-R estate at TRIER, a union of the Cathedral properties with two famous charities. 230 acres of top v'yds. in AVELSBACH, WILTINGEN, SCHARZHOFBERG, AYL, KASEL, EITELSBACH, PIESPORT, TRITTENHEIM, ÜRZIG, etc.

Blue Nun
The best-selling brand of LIEBFRAUMILCH, from SICHEL.

Bodensee (Bereich)
Minor district of s. BADEN, on Lake Constance.

Boxbeutel
Flask-shaped bottle used for FRANKEN wines.

Brauneberg M-M w. ★★★ 71 75 76 77 78 79
Village near BERNKASTEL with 100 acres. Excellent full-flavoured wine. Best v'yd.: Juffer. Grosslage: Kurfürstlay.

Breisgau (Bereich)
Minor district of BADEN, just n. of KAISERSTUHL.

Brentano, von
20-acre old family estate in WINKEL, Rheingau.

Bühl, von
Great RHEINPFALZ family estate. 200+ acres in DEIDESHEIM, FORST, RUPPERTSBERG, etc. In the very top class.

Bullay M-S-R ★→ ★★ 76 77 78 79
Lower Mosel village. Good light wine to drink young.

Bundesweinprämierung
The top German Wine Award: a gold, silver or bronze medal on bottles of remarkable wines.

Burgerspital zum Heiligen Geist
Ancient charitable estate at WÜRZBURG. 185 acres in WÜRZBURG, RANDERSACKER, etc., make rich dry wines.

Bürklin-Wolf
Great RHEINPFALZ family estate. 222 acres in WACHENHEIM, FORST, DEIDESHEIM and RUPPERTSBERG, with rarely a dull, let alone poor, wine.

Castell'sches, Fürstlich Domäne
110-acre princely estate in STEIGERWALD. Good typical FRANKEN wines: Sylvanen, Müller-Thürgau. Also SEKT.

Crown of Crowns
Popular brand of LIEBFRAUMILCH from LANGENBACH & CO.

Deidesheim Rhpf. w. (r.) ★★ →★★★★ 71 74 75 76 77 78 79

Biggest top-quality wine-village of RHEINPFALZ with 1,000 acres. Rich, high-flavoured, lively wines. V'yds. incl. Hohenmorgen, Kieselberg, Grainhübel, Leinhöhle, Herrgottsacker, etc. Grosslages: Hofstück, Mariengarten.

Deinhard

Famous old Koblenz merchants and growers in Rheingau (see Wegeler), Mittel-Mosel (27 acres in Bernkastel, incl. part of Doktor v'yd., and Graach) and Rheinpfalz.

Deutscher Tafelwein

TAFELWEIN from Germany (only).

Deutsches Weinsiegel

A quality "seal" (i.e. neck label) for wines which have passed a stiff tasting test.

DLG (Deutsche Landwirtshaft Gesellschaft)

The German Agricultural Society. The body that awards national medals for quality.

Dhron

See Neumagen-Dhron

Diabetiker Wein

Wine with minimal residual sugar (less than 4gms/litre). Suitable for diabetics—or those who like very dry wine.

Dienheim Rhh. w. ★★→★★★ 77 78 79

Southern neighbour of OPPENHEIM. Mainly run-of-the-mill wines. Top v'yds.: Kreuz, Herrenberg, Schloss. Grosslages: Guldenmorgen, Krötenbrunnen.

Dom

German for Cathedral. Wines from the famous TRIER Cathedral properties have "Dom" before the v'yd. name.

Domäne

German for "domain" or "estate". Sometimes used alone to mean the "State domain" (Staatliche Weinbaudomäne).

Durbach Baden w. (r.) ★→★★★ 75 76 77 78 79

150 acres of the best v'yds. of BADEN. Top growers: Schloss Staufenberg, Wolf-Metternich, von Neveu. Choose their RIESLINGS.

Dürkheim, Bad Rhpf. w. or (r.) ★★ →★★★ 75 76 77 78 79

Main town of the MITTEL-HAARDT. Top v'yds.: Hochbenn, Michelsberg. Grosslages: Feuerberg, Schenkenböhl.

Edel

Means "noble". Edelfäule means "noble rot": the condition which gives the greatest sweet wines (see p. 52).

Edenkoben Rhpf. w.(r.) ★→ ★★ 75 76 77 78 79

Important village of n. SÜDLICHE WEINSTRASSE Grosslage: Ludwigshöhe

Egon Müller-Scharzhof

Top Saar estate of 24 acres at WILTINGEN. SCHARZHOFBERGERS are supreme in top years.

Eiswein

Wine made from frozen grapes with the ice (e.g. water content) rejected, thus very concentrated in flavour and sugar. Rare and expensive. Sometimes produced as late as the January or February following the vintage.

Eitelsbach Ruwer w. ★★→★★★★ 71 75 76 77 78 79

RUWER village now part of TRIER, incl. superb Karthäuserhofberg estate. Grosslage: Trierer Römerlay.

Elbling

Inferior grape widely grown on upper Mosel.

Eltville Rhg. w. ★★ →★★★ 71 75 76 77 78 79

Major wine-town with cellars of the Rheingau State domain, SCHLOSS ELTZ and VON SIMMERN estates. Excellent wines. Top v'yds.: Sonnenberg, Taubenberg. Grosslage: Heiligenstock.

Eltz, Schloss

Superb 98-acre Rheingau estate with v'yds. in ELTVILLE, KIEDRICH, RAUENTHAL, RÜDESHEIM.

Enkirch M-M w. **∗∗→** 〔∗∗∗〕 71 75 76 77 78 79

Minor middle-Mosel village, often overlooked but with lovely light tasty wine. Grosslage: Schwarzlay.

Erbach Rhg. w. **∗∗∗→∗∗∗∗** 71 75 76 77 78 79

One of the best parts of the Rheingau with powerful, perfumed wines, incl. the great MARCOBRUNN; other top v'yds.: Schlossberg, Siegelsberg, Hönigberg, Michelmark. Grosslage: Mehrhölzchen. Major estates: SCHLOSS REINHARTSHAUSEN, von SCHÖNBORN.

Erden M-M w. **∗∗→∗∗∗** 71 75 76 77 78 79

Village between Urzig and Kröv with full-flavoured vigorous wine. Top v'yds.: Prälat, Treppchen. Leading grower: Beeres. Grosslage: Schwarzlay.

Erzeugerabfüllung

Bottled by the grower.

Escherndorf Franc. w. **∗∗→∗∗∗** 71 75 76 77 78 79

Important wine-town near WÜRZBURG. Similar tasty dry wine. Top v'yds.: Lump, Berg. Grosslage: Kirchberg.

Feine, feinste, hochfeinste

Terms formerly used to distinguish a good grower's best barrels. Now, unfortunately, illegal.

Forst Rhpf. w. **∗∗→∗∗∗∗** 71 75 76 77 78 79

MITTEL-HAARDT village with 500 acres of Germany's best v'yds. Ripe, richly fragrant but subtle wines. Top v'yds.: Kirchenstück, Jesuitengarten, Ungeheuer, etc. Grosslages: Mariengarten, Schnepfenflüg.

Franken

Franconia: region of excellent distinctive dry wines. The centre is WÜRZBURG. BEREICH names: MAINVIERECK, MAINDREIECK, STEIGERWALD.

Freiburg Baden w. (r.) **∗→∗∗** D.Y.A.

Centre of MARKGRÄFLERLAND. Good GUTEDEL.

Friedrich Wilhelm Gymnasium

Superb 104-acre charitable estate with v'yds. in BERNKASTEL, ZELTINGEN, GRAACH, TRITTENHEIM, OCKFEN, etc., all M-S-R.

Geisenheim Rhg. w. **∗∗→∗∗∗** 71 75 76 77 78 79

Village famous for Germany's leading wine-school. Best v'yds. incl. Rothenberg, Kläuserweg. Grosslage: Burgweg.

Gemeinde

A commune or parish.

Gewürztraminer

Spicy grape of Alsace, used a little in s. Germany, esp. Rheinpfalz.

Gimmeldingen Rhpf. w. **∗→** 〔∗∗〕 75 76 77 78 79

Village just s. of MITTEL-HAARDT. Similar wines. Grosslage: Meerspinne.

Goldener Oktober

Popular Rhine-wine and Mosel blend from ST. URSULA.

Graach M-M w. **∗∗→** 〔∗∗∗〕 71 75 76 77 78 79

Small village between BERNKASTEL and WEHLEN. Top v'yds.: Himmelreich, Domprobst, Abstberg, Josephshöfer. Grosslage: Münzlay.

Grosslage

See Introduction, p. 59

Guntersblum Rhh. w. **∗→∗∗∗** 75 76 77 78 79

Big wine-town s. of OPPENHEIM. Grosslages: Krötenbrunnen, Vogelsgarten.

Guntrum, Louis

Fine 130-acre family estate in NIERSTEIN, OPPENHEIM, etc.

Gutedel

German for the Chasselas grape, used in s. BADEN.

Halbtrocken

"Half-dry". Containing less than 18 grams per litre unfermented sugar. A rather vague category of wine intended for meal-times.

Hallgarten   Rhg. w. ∗∗→∗∗∗ 71 75 76 77 78 79

Important little wine-town behind HATTENHEIM. Robust full-bodied wines. Top v'yds. incl. Schönhell, Jungfer. Grosslage: Mehrhölzchen.

Hallgarten, House of

Well-known London-based wine-merchant.

Hanns Christof

Top brand of LIEBFRAUMILCH from DEINHARD'S.

Hattenheim   Rhg. w. ∗∗→∗∗∗∗ 71 75 76 77 78 79

Superlative 500-acre wine-town. V'yds. incl. STEINBERG, MARCOBRUNN, Nüssbrunnen, Mannberg, etc. Grosslage: Deutelsberg.

Heilbronn   Württ. w. r. ∗→∗∗ 75 76 77 78 79

Wine-town with many small growers and a big co-op. Seat of DLG competition.

Hessische Bergstrasse   Rhh. w. ∗∗→∗∗∗ 75 76 77 78 79

Minor (700-acre) region s. of Frankfurt. Pleasant Riesling from State domain v'yds. in Heppenheim and Bensheim.

Hessische Forschungsanstalt für Wein- Obst- & Gartenbau

Germany's top wine-school and research establishment, at GEISENHEIM.

Heyl zu Herrnsheim

Fine 50-acre estate at NIERSTEIN.

Hochfeinste

"Very finest." Traditional label-term, now illegal.

Hochheim   Rhg. w. ∗∗→∗∗∗ 71 75 76 77 78 79

500-acre wine-town 15 miles e. of RHEINGAU. Similar fine wines. Top v'yds.: Domdechaney, Kirchenstück, Hölle, Königin Viktoria Berg. Grosslage: Daubhaus.

Hock

English term for Rhine-wine, derived from HOCHHEIM.

Huxelrebe

Modern very fruity grape variety.

Ihringen   Bad. (r.) w. ∗→∗∗∗ 75 76 77 78 79

One of the best villages of the KAISERSTUHL, BADEN. Heavy dryish wines.

Ilbesheim   Rhpf. w. ∗→ ∗∗ 75 76 77 78 79

Base of important growers co-operative of SÜDLICHE WEIN-STRASSE. See also Schweigen.

Ingelheim   Rhh. r. or w. ∗ 75 76 77 79

Village on Rhine known for red wine.

Iphofen   Franc. w. ∗∗→ ∗∗∗ 71 75 76 77 78 79

Village e. of WÜRZBURG. Top v'yd.: Julius-Echter-Berg. Grosslage: Burgweg.

Jesuitengarten

V'yd. in FORST. One of Germany's best.

Johannisberg   Rhg. w. ∗∗→∗∗∗ 71 75 76 77 78 79

260-acre village with superlative subtle wine. Top v'yds. incl. SCHLOSS JOHANNISBERG, Hölle, Klaus, etc. Grosslage: Erntebringer.

Johannisberg (Bereich)

District name of the entire RHEINGAU.

Josephshöfer

Fine v'yd. at GRAACH, the property of von KESSELSTATT.

Juliusspital

Ancient charity at WÜRZBURG with top FRANKEN v'yds.

Kabinett

The term for the driest and least expensive natural unsugared (QmP) wines.

Kaiserstuhl-Tuniberg (Bereich)

Best v'yd. area of BADEN. Villages incl. IHRINGEM, ACHKARREN.

Kallstadt Rhpf. w. (r.) ★★→★★★ 71 75 76 77 78 79

Village just n. of MITTEL-HAARDT. Fine rich wines. Top v'yd.: ANNABERG. Grosslages: Kobnert, Feuerberg.

Kanzem M-S-R (Saar) w. ★★→★★★ 71 75 76 77 78 79

Small but excellent neighbour of WILTINGEN. Top v'yds.: Sonnenberg, Altenberg. Grosslage: Scharzberg.

Kasel M-S-R (Ruwer) w. ★★ 71 75 76 77 78 79

Village with attractive light wines. Grosslage: Römerlay.

Keller

Wine-cellar or winery.

Kerner

Modern very flowery grape variety.

Kesselstatt, von

The biggest private Mosel Estate, 600 years old. 150 acres in GRAACH, PIESPORT, KASEL, MENNIG, WILTINGEN, etc.

Kesten M-W w. ★→★★★ 71 75 76 77 78 79

Neighbour of BRAUNEBERG. Best wines (from Paulinshofberg v'yd.) similar. Grosslage: Kurfürstlay.

Kiedrich Rhg. w. ★★→★★★★ 71 75 76 77 78 79

Neighbour of RAUENTHAL; almost as splendid and high flavoured. Top v'yds.: Gräfenberg, Wasseros, Sandgrub. Grosslage: Heiligenstock.

Klevner (or Clevner)

Term for the Traminer grape used in BADEN-WÜRTTEMBERG. Red Klevner is supposedly Italian Chiavenna, an early-ripening black Pinot.

Kloster Eberbach

Glorious 12th-century Abbey at HATTENHEIM, Rheingau, now State domain property and H.Q. of the German Wine Academy. See panel, p. 62.

Klüsserath M-M w. ★★→ [★★★] 71 75 76 78 79

Minor Mosel village worth trying in good vintages. Best v'yds.: Brüderschaft, Königsberg. Grosslage: St. Michael.

Kreuznach (Bereich)

District name for the entire northern NAHE. See also Bad Kreuznach.

Kröv M-M w. ★→★★★ 75 76 78 79

Popular tourist resort famous for its Grosslage name: Nacktarsch, meaning "bare bottom".

Landespreismünze

Prizes for quality at state, rather than national, level. Considered by some more discriminating than DLG medals.

Landgräflich Hessisches Weingut

75-acre estate in JOHANNISBERG, WINKEL, etc.

Langenbach & Co.

Well-known merchants of London and WORMS.

Lauerburg

One of the three owners of the famous Doktor v'yd. in BERNKASTEL, with THANISCH and DEINHARD.

Liebfrauenstift

26-acre v'yd. in the city of WORMS, said to be the origin of the name LIEBFRAUMILCH.

Liebfraumilch

Legally defined as a QbA "of pleasant character" from RHEINHESSEN, RHEINPFALZ, NAHE or RHEINGAU, blended from RIESLING, SYLVANER or MÜLLER-THURGAU. Most is mild semi-sweet wine from Rheinhessen and Rheinpfalz.

Lieser M-M w. *→ ⭐⭐ **71 75 76** 77 78 79
    Little-known neighbour of BERNKASTEL. Grosslages: Beerenlay, Kurfürstlay.

Lorch Rhg. w. (r.) *→** **71 76** 78 79
    At extreme w. end of Rheingau. Secondary quality. Best grower: von Kanitz.

Löwenstein, Fürst
    70-acre FRANKEN estate: classic dry wines.

Maikammer Rhpf. w. (r.) *→ ⭐⭐ **75 76** 77 78 79
    Village of n. SÜDLICHE WEINSTRASSE. Very pleasant wines incl. those from co-op at Rietburg. Grosslage Mandelhöhe.

Maindreieck (Bereich)
    District name for central part of FRANKEN, incl. WÜRZBURG.

Mainviereck (Bereich)
    District name for minor w. part of FRANKEN.

Marcobrunn
    See Erbach

Markgräflerland (Bereich)
    Minor district s. of Freiburg (BADEN). GUTEDEL wine. Drink very young.

Martinsthal Rhg. w. **→ ⭐⭐⭐ **71 75 76** 77 78 79
    Little-known neighbour of RAUENTHAL. Top v'yds.: Langenberg, Wildsau. Grosslage: Steinmacher.

Matuschka-Greiffenclau, Graf
    Owner of the ancient SCHLOSS VOLLRADS estate.

Maximin Grünhaus M-S-R (Ruwer) w. ⭐⭐⭐⭐ **71 75 76** 77 78 79
    Supreme RUWER estate of 52 acres at Mertesdorf.

Mennig M-S-R (Saar) w. ⭐⭐ **71 75 76** 77 78 79
    Village between TRIER and the SAAR. Its Falkensteiner v'yd. is famous.

Mertesdorf
    See Maximin Grünhaus

Mittelheim Rhg. w. **→ ⭐⭐⭐ **71 75 76** 77 78 79
    Minor village between WINKEL and OESTRICH. Top grower: WEGELER. Grosslage: Honigberg.

Mittel-Haardt
    The n., best part, of RHEINPFALZ, incl. FORST, DEIDESHEIM, etc.

Mittel-Mosel
    The central and best part of the Mosel, incl. BERNKASTEL, PIESPORT, etc.

Mittelrhein
    Northern Rhine area of secondary quality, incl. BACHARACH.

Morio Muskat
    Stridently aromatic grape variety.

Moselblümchen
    The "LIEBFRAUMILCH" of the Mosel, but on a lower quality level: TAFELWEIN not QbA.

Mosel-Saar-Ruwer
    Huge wine area, incl. MITTEL-MOSEL, SAAR, RUWER and lesser areas.

Müller-Thurgau
    Fruity, low-acid grape variety; the commonest in RHEINPFALZ and RHEINHESSEN, but increasingly planted in all areas.

Mumm, von
    111-acre estate in JOHANNISBERG, RUDESHEIM, etc.

Munster Nahe w. *→⭐⭐⭐ **71 75 76** 77 78 79
    Best village of n. NAHE, with fine delicate wines. Top grower: State Domain. Grosslage: Schlosskapelle.

Nackenheim Rhh. w. *→⭐⭐⭐ **71 75 76** 77 78 79
    Neighbour of NIERSTEIN; best wines (Engelsberg, Rothenberg) similar. Grosslages: Spiegelberg, Gutes Domtal.

Nahe

Tributary of the Rhine and quality wine region. Balanced, fresh and clean but full-flavoured wines. Two Bereiche: KREUZNACH and SCHLOSS BÖCKELHEIM.

Neef M-S-R w. ★→ ☐ ★★ 71 75 76 78 79

Village of lower Mosel with one fine v'yd.: Frauenberg.

Neipperg, Graf

62-acre top WÜRTTEMBERG estate at Schwaigern.

Nell, von

40-acre family estate at TRIER and AYL, etc.

Neumagen-Dhron M-M w. ★★→★★★ 71 75 76 77 78 79

Neighbour of PIESPORT. Top v'yd.: Hofberger. Grosslage: Michelsberg.

Neustadt

Central city of Rheinpfalz, with famous wine school.

Niederhausen Na. w. ★★→ ☐★★★★ 71 75 76 77 78 79

Neighbour of SCHLOSS BÖCKELHEIM and H.Q. of Nahe State Domain. Wines of grace and power. Top v'yds. incl. Hermannshöhle, Steinberg. Grosslage: Burgweg.

Niedermennig

See Mennig

Niederwalluf

See Walluf

Nierstein (Bereich)

Large e. RHEINHESSEN district of very mixed quality.

Nierstein Rhh. w. ★→★★★ 71 75 76 77 78 79

Famous but treacherous name. 1,300 acres incl. superb v'yds.: Hipping, Orbel, Pettenthal, etc., and their Grosslages Rehbach, Spiegelberg, Auflangen: ripe, racy wines. But beware Grosslage Gutes Domtal: no guarantee of anything.

Norheim Nahe w. ★→★★★ 71 75 76 77 78 79

Neighbour of NIEDERHAUSEN. Top v'yds.: Klosterberg, Kafels, Kirschheck. Grosslage: Burgweg.

Oberemmel M-S-R (Saar) w. ★★→★★★ 71 75 76 77 78 79

Next village to WILTINGEN. Very fine wines from Rosenberg, Hütte, etc. Grosslage: Scharzberg.

Obermosel (Bereich)

District name for the upper Mosel above TRIER. Generally poor wines from the Elbling grape.

Ockfen M-S-R (Saar) w. ★★→★★★ 71 75 76 77 78 79

200-acre hill with superb fragrant austere wines. Top v'yds.: Bockstein, Herrenberg. Grosslage: Scharzberg.

Oechsle

Scale for sugar-content of grape-juice (see page 155).

Oestrich Rhg. w. ★★→★★★ 71 75 76 77 78 79

Big village; good but rarely top grade. V'yds. incl. Doosberg, Lenchen. Grosslage: Gottesthal.

Oppenheim Rhh. w. ★→★★★ 71 75 76 77 78 79

Town just s. of NIERSTEIN, best wines (Kreuz, Sackträger, etc.) similar. Grosslages: Guldenmorgen (★★★) Krotenbrunnen (★★).

Originalabfüllung

Bottled by the grower. An obsolete term.

Ortenau (Bereich)

District just s. of Baden-Baden. Soft wines to drink young. Best village DURBACH.

Palatinate

English for RHEINPFALZ.

Pfalz

See Rheinpfalz

Perlwein

Semi-sparkling wine.

Piesport   M–M w. ****→****   71 75 76** 77 78 79
> Tiny village with famous amphitheatre of vines giving fine gentle fruity wine. Top v'yds.: Goldtröpfchen, Gunterslay, Falkenberg. Treppchen is on flatter land and inferior. Grosslage: Michelsberg.

Plettenberg, von
> Fine 100-acre Nahe estate at BAD KREUZNACH.

Pokalwein
> Café wine. A pokal is a big glass.

Portugieser
> Second-rate red-wine grape.

Prädikat
> Special attributes or qualities. See QmP.

Prüfungsnummer
> The official identifying test-number of a quality wine.

Prüm, J. J.
> Superlative 35-acre Mosel estate in WEHLEN, GRAACH, BERNKASTEL.

Qualitätswein bestimmter Anbaugebiete (QbA)
> The middle quality of German wine, with added sugar but strictly controlled as to grape areas, etc.

Qualitätswein mit Prädikat (QmP)
> Top category, incl. all wines ripe enough to be unsugared, from KABINETT to TROCKENBEERENAUSLESE.

Randersacker   Franc. w. ****→***   71 75 76** 77 78 79
> Leading village for distinctive dry wine. Top v'yds. incl. Teufelskeller. Grosslage: Ewig Leben.

Rauenthal   Rhg. w.   *****   →****   71 75 76** 77 78 79
> Supreme village for powerful spicy wine. Top v'yds. incl. Baiken, Gehrn, Wulfen. Grosslage: Steinmacher. The State Domain is an important grower.

Rautenstrauch Erben
> Owners of the splendid Karthäuserhof, EITELSBACH.

Rheinburgengau (Bereich)
> District name for the v'yds. of the MITTELRHEIN round the famous Rhine gorge. Moderate quality only.

Rheingau
> The best v'yd. region of the Rhine, near Wiesbaden. 5,000 acres. Classic, subtle but substantial RIESLING. Bereich name, JOHANNISBERG.

Rheinhessen
> Vast region (30,000 acres of v'yds.) between Mainz and the NAHE, mostly second-rate, but incl. NIERSTEIN, OPPENHEIM, etc.

Rheinpfalz
> Even vaster 35,000-acre v'yd. region s. of Rheinhessen. Wines inclined to sweetness. (See Mittel-Haardt and Südliche Weinstrasse.) This and the last are the chief sources of LIEBFRAUMILCH.

Rhodt
> Village of SÜDLICHE WEINSTRASSE with well-known co-operative. Agreeable fruity wines. Grosslage: Ordensgut.

Riesling
> The best German grape: fine, fragrant, fruity.

Ritter zu Groenesteyn, Baron
> Fine 37-acre estate in KIEDRICH and RÜDESHEIM.

Roseewein
> Rosé wine.

Rotenfelser Bastei
> See Traisen

Rotwein
> Red wine.

Rüdesheim Rhg. w. ★★→★★★ 71 75 76 79

Rhine resort with 650 acres of excellent v'yds.; the three best called Berg.... Full-bodied wines. Grosslage: Burgweg.

Rüdesheimer Rosengarten

Rüdesheim is also the name of a NAHE village near BAD KREUZNACH. Do not be misled by the ubiquitous blend going by this name. It has nothing to do with Rheingau RÜDESHEIM.

Ruländer

The PINOT GRIS: grape giving soft heavy wine. Best in BADEN.

Ruppertsberg Rhpf. w. ★★→ ★★★ 71 75 76 77 78 79

Southern village of MITTEL-HAARDT. Top v'yds. incl. Gaisbohl, Hoheburg. Grosslage: Hofstück.

Ruwer

Tributary of Mosel near TRIER. Very fine delicate wines. Villages incl. EITELSBACH, MERTESDORF, KASEL.

Saar

Tributary of Mosel s. of RUWER. Brilliant austere wines. Villages incl. WILTINGEN, AYL, OCKFEN, SERRIG.

Saar-Ruwer (Bereich)

District incl. the two above.

St. Ursula

Well-known merchants at BINGEN.

Scharzberger

Grosslage name of WILTINGEN and neighbours.

Scharzhofberger Saar w. ★★★★ 71 75 76 77 78 79

Superlative 30-acre SAAR v'yd.: austerely beautiful wines, the perfection of RIESLING. Do not confuse with the last.

Schaumwein

Sparkling wine.

Scheurebe

Fruity aromatic grape used in RHEINPFALZ.

Schillerwein

Light red or rosé QbA from WÜRTTEMBERG.

Schlossabzug

Bottled at the Schloss (castle).

Schloss Böckelheim Nahe w. ★★→★★★★ 71 75 76 77 78 79

Village with the best NAHE v'yds., incl. Kupfergrübe, Felsenberg. Firm yet delicate wine. Grosslage: Burgweg.

Schloss Böckelheim (Bereich)

District name for the whole s. NAHE.

Schloss Johannisberg

Famous RHEINGAU estate of 66 acres belonging to the Metternich family. Polished, elegant wine.

Schloss Reinhartshausen

Fine 99-acre estate in ERBACH, HATTENHEIM, etc.

Schloss Vollrads Rhg. w. ★★★→★★★★ 71 75 76 77 78 79

Great estate at WINKEL, since 1300. 81 acres producing classical RHEINGAU RIESLING. TROCKEN wines a speciality.

Schmitt, Gustav Adolf

Fine old 124-acre family estate at NIERSTEIN.

Schmitt, Franz Karl

Even older 74-acre ditto.

Schönborn, Graf von

One of the biggest and best Rheingau estates, based at HATTENHEIM. Full-blooded wines. Also SEKT.

Schoppenwein

Café wine: i.e. wine by the glass.

Schubert, von

Owner of MAXIMIN GRÜNHAUS.

Schweigen Rhpf. w. ★→ ★★ 75 76 77 78 79

Southernmost Rheinpfalz village with big co-operative, Deutsches WEINTOR. Grosslage: Guttenberg.

Sekt

German (QbA) sparkling wine.

Serrig M-S-R (Saar) w. ★★→★★★ 71 75 76 77 78 79

Village known for "steely" wine, excellent in hot years. Top growers: VEREINIGTE HOSPITIEN and State Domain. Grosslage: Scharzberg.

Sichel H., Söhne

Famous wine-merchants of London and Mainz.

Silvaner

Common German white grape, best in FRANKEN.

Simmern, von

94-acre family estate at HATTENHEIM since 1464 and in ELTVILLE, RAUENTHAL, etc.

Sonnenuhr

"Sun-dial." Name of several famous v'yds., esp. one at WEHLEN.

Every wine district has its own favourite pattern of glass for bringing out the character of the local product. For practical purposes at home, however, three shapes/sizes are enough. These three were designed by Professor Lord Queensberry of the Royal College of Art and the author for Ravenhead Glass as ideal glasses for, respectively, sherry/port, fine red wines, white wine/general purpose.

Spätburgunder

PINOT NOIR: the best red-wine grape in Germany.

Spätlese

"Late gathered." One better (stronger or sweeter) than KABINETT.

Spiess, Georg Fr.

50-acre family estate at Kleinkarlbach, MITTEL-HAARDT. Clean, typical Rieslings. Good SEKT.

Spindler

Fine 33-acre family estate at FORST, Rheinpfalz.

Staatsweingut (or Staatliche Weinbaudomäne)

The State wine estate or domain.

Steigerwald (Bereich)

District name for e. part of FRANKEN.

Steinberg Rhg. w. ★★★→★★★★ 71 75 76 77 78 79

Famous 62-acre v'yd. at HATTENHEIM walled by Cistercians 700 yrs. ago. Now property of the State.

Steinwein

Wine from WÜRZBURG's best v'yd., Stein. Loosely used for all Franconian wine.

Stuttgart

Chief city of WÜRTTEMBERG, producer of some pleasant wines, not exported.

Südliche Weinstrasse (Bereich)

District name for the s. RHEINPFALZ.

Tafelwein

"Table wine." The vin ordinaire of Germany. Can be blended with other EEC wines. But Deutscher Tafelwein must come from Germany alone.

Thanisch, Dr.

32-acre BERNKASTEL family estate, incl. part of Doktor v'yd.

Traben-Trarbach M-W w. $\boxed{\text{**}}$ 75 76 78 79

Secondary wine-town, some good light wines. Top v'yds. incl. Schlossberg, Ungsberg. Grosslage: Schwarzlay.

Traisen Na. w. $\boxed{\text{***}}$ 71 75 76 77 78 79

Small village incl. superlative Bastei v'yd., making wine of great concentration and class.

Traminer

See Gewürztraminer

Trier M-S-R w. ★★→★★★★

Important wine city of Roman origin, on the Mosel, adjacent to RUWER, now incl. AVELSBACH and EITELSBACH. Grosslage: Römerlay.

Trittenheim M-M w. $\boxed{\text{**}}$ →★★★ 71 75 76 77 78 79

Attractive light wines. Top v'yds.: Apotheke, Altärchen. Grosslage: Michelsberg.

Trocken

Dry. On labels Trocken *alone* means with a statutory maximum of unfermented sugar (9 grams per litre). But see next entry.

Trockenbeerenauslese

The sweetest and most expensive category of wine, made from selected withered grapes. See also Edelfäule.

Trollinger

Common red grape of WÜRTTEMBERG: poor quality.

Ungstein Rhpf. w. ★★→ $\boxed{\text{***}}$ 71 75 76 77 78 79

MITTEL-HAARDT village with fine harmonious wines. Top v'yd. Herrenberg. Top grower Führmann (weingut Pfeffingen). Grosslage Hönigsackel.

Ürzig M-M w. $\boxed{\text{***}}$ 71 75 76 77 78 79

Village famous for lively spicy wine. Top v'yd.: Würzgarten. Grosslage: Schwarzlay.

Vereinigte Hospitien

"United Hospitals." Ancient charity with large holdings in SERRIG, WILTINGEN, TRIER, PIESPORT, etc.

Verwaltung

Property.

Villa Sachsen

75-acre BINGEN estate belonging to ST. URSULA Weingut.

Wachenheim Rhpf. w. $\boxed{\text{***}}$ →★★★★ 71 75 76 77 78 79

840 acres, incl. exceptionally fine Rieslings. V'yds. incl. Gerümpel, Böhlig, Rechbächel, etc. Top grower: Bürklin-Wolf. Grosslages: Schenkenbohl, Schnepfenflug, Mariengarten.

Waldrach M-S-R (Ruwer) w. $\boxed{\text{**}}$ 75 76 77 78 79

Some charming light wines. Grosslage: (Trierer) Römerlay.

Walluf Rhg. w. $\boxed{\text{**}}$ 73 75 76 77 79

Neighbour of ELTVILLE; formerly Nieder- and Ober-Walluf. Good but not top wines. Grosslage: Steinmacher.

Walporzheim-Ahrtal (Bereich)

District name for the whole AHR valley.

Wawern M-S-R (Saar) w. ★★→★★★ 71 75 76 77 78 79

Small village with fine Rieslings. Grosslage: Scharzberg.

Wegeler Erben

138-acre Rheingau estate owned by DEINHARD'S. V'yds. in OESTRICH, MITTELHEIM, WINKEL, GEISENHEIM, RÜDESHEIM, etc.

Wehlen M-M w. $\boxed{\text{***}}$ →★★★★ 71 75 76 77 78 79

Neighbour of BERNKASTEL with equally fine, somewhat richer, wine. Best v'yd.: Sonnenuhr. Top growers: Prüm family. Grosslage: Münzlay.

Weil, Dr.

    45-acre private estate at KIEDRICH. Very fine wines.

Weingut

    Wine estate. Can only be used by estates that grow all their own grapes.

Weinkellerei

    Wine cellars or winery.

Weinstrasse

    "Wine road." Scenic route through v'yds. Germany has several, the most famous in RHEINPFALZ.

Weintor, Deutsches

    See Schweigen

Weissenheim-am-Sand Rhpf. w. (r.) ★→★★ 75 76 77 78 79

    Big northern Pfalz village on sandy soil. Light wines.

Weissherbst

    Rosé of QbA standard, speciality of BADEN and WÜRTTEMBERG.

Werner, Domdechant

    Fine 32-acre family estate at HOCHHEIM.

Wiltingen Saar w. ★★→★★★★ 71 75 76 77 78 79

    The centre of the Saar. 330 acres. Beautiful subtle austere wine. Top v'yds. incl. SCHARZHOFBERG, Braune Kupp, Braunfels, Klosterberg. Grosslage (for the whole Saar): Scharzberg.

Winkel Rhg. w. ★★★→★★★★ 71 75 76 77 78 79

    Village famous for fragrant, elegant wine, incl. SCHLOSS VOLLRADS. Other v'yds. incl. Hasensprung, Jesuitengarten. Grosslage: Hönigberg.

Wintrich M-M w. ★★→★★★ 71 75 76 77 78 79

    Neighbour of PIESPORT; similar wines. Top v'yds.: Grosser Herrgott, Ohligsberg, Sonnenseite. Grosslage: Kurfürstlay.

Winzergenossenschaft

    Wine-growers' co-operative, often making good and reasonably priced wine.

Winzerverein

    The same as the last.

Wonnegau (Bereich)

    District name for S. RHEINHESSEN.

Worms Rhh. w. ★★

    City with the famous LIEBFRAUENSTIFT v'yd.

Württemberg

    Vast S. area with scattered v'yds. of variable quality.

Würzburg Frank. ★★→★★★★ 71 75 76 77 78 79

    Great baroque city on the Main, centre of Franconian (FRANKEN) wine: fine, full-bodied and dry. Top v'yds.: Stein, Leiste, Schlossberg. No Grosslage. See also Maindreieck.

ZBW (Zentralkellerei Baden-Württemberg)

    Germany's biggest ultra-modern co-operative, at Breisach, BADEN.

Zell M-S-R w. ★→★★ 75 76 77 78 79

    Lower Mosel village famous for its Grosslage name Schwarze Katze ("Black Cat"). No fine wines.

Zell (Bereich)

    District name for the whole lower Mosel from Zell to Koblenz.

Zeltingen-Rachtig M-M w. ★★ →★★★★ 71 75 76 77 78 79

    Important Mosel village next to WEHLEN. Typically lively but full-bodied wine. Top v'yds.: Sonnenuhr, Schlossberg. Grosslage: Münzlay.

Switzerland

Switzerland has some of the world's most efficient and productive vineyards. Costs are high and nothing less is viable. All the most important are lined along the south-facing slopes of the upper Rhône valley and Lake Geneva, respectively the Valais and the Vaud. Wines are known both by place-names, grape-names, and legally controlled type-names. All three, with those of leading growers and merchants, appear in the following list. On the whole, D.Y.A.

Aigle Vaud w. dr. ★★
  Principal town of CHABLAIS, between La. Geneva and the VALAIS. Dry whites of appropriately transitional style: at best strong and well balanced.

Amigne
  Traditional white grape of the VALAIS. Heavy but tasty wine, usually made dry.

Arvine
  Another old VALAIS white grape, similar to the last; perhaps better. Makes good dessert wine.

Auvernier Neuchâtel r. p. w. dr. (sp.) ★★
  Village s. of NEUCHÂTEL known for PINOT NOIR, CHASSELAS and ŒIL DE PERDRIX.

Blauburgunder
  One of the names given to the form of PINOT NOIR grown in German Switzerland.

Bonvin
  Old-established growers and merchants at SION.

Chablais Vaud (r.) w. dr. ★★
  The district between Montreux on La. Geneva and Martigny where the Rhône leaves the VALAIS. Good DORIN wines. Best villages: AIGLE, YVORNE, Bex.

Chasselas
  The principal white grape of Switzerland, neutral in flavour but taking local character. Known as FENDANT in VALAIS, DORIN in VAUD and PERLAN round Geneva.

Clevner (or Klevner)
  Another name for BLAUBURGUNDER.

Cortaillod Neuchâtel r. (p. w.) ★★
  Village near NEUCHÂTEL specializing in light PINOT NOIR reds.

Côte, La
  The n. shore of La. Geneva between Geneva and Lausanne. Pleasant DORIN and SALVAGNIN. Best villages incl. Féchy and Rolle.

Dézaley   Vaud w. dr. ★★★

Best-known village of LAVAUX, between Lausanne and Montreux. Steep s. slopes to the lake make fine fruity DORIN. Dézaley-Marsens is equally good.

Dôle   Valais r. ★★

Term for red VALAIS wine of PINOT NOIR or GAMAY or both grapes, reaching a statutory level of strength and quality.

Domaine Château Lichten

Property making first-class VALAIS wines at Loèche Ville.

Dorin   Vaud w. dr. ★→★★

The name for CHASSELAS wine in the VAUD, the equivalent of FENDANT from the VALAIS.

Epesses   Vaud w. dr. ★★

Well-known lakeside village of LAVAUX. Good dry DORIN.

Ermitage

VALAIS name for white wine from MARSANNE grapes. Rich, concentrated and heavy; usually dry.

Fendant   Valais w. dr. ★→★★★

The name for CHASSELAS wine in the VALAIS, where it reaches its ripest and strongest. SION is the centre.

Flétri

Withered grapes for making sweet wine, often MALVOISIE.

Glacier, vin du

Almost legendary long-matured white stored at high altitudes. Virtually extinct today.

Goron   Valais r. ★

Red VALAIS wine that fails to reach the DÔLE standard.

Herrschaft   Grisons r. (w. sw.) ★→★★★

District near the border of Austria and Liechtenstein. Small amount of light PINOT NOIR reds and a few sweet whites.

Humagne

Rare old VALAIS grape. Some red Humagne is sold: decent country wine. Apparently there was formerly white as well.

Johannisberg

The Valais name for SYLVANER, which makes pleasant soft dry wine here.

Lavaux   Vaud r. w. dr. ★→★★★

The n. shore of La. Geneva between Lausanne and Montreux. The e. half of the VAUD. Best villages incl. DÉZALEY, EPESSES, Villette, Lutry, ST-SAPHORIN.

Légèrement doux

Most Swiss wines are dry. Any with measurable sugar must be labelled thus or as "avec sucre résiduel".

Malvoisie

VALAIS name for PINOT GRIS.

Mandement   Geneva r. (p.) w. dr. ★

Wine district just w. of Geneva, (see Vin-Union-Genève). Very light reds, chiefly GAMAY, and whites (PERLAN).

Marsanne

The white grape of Hermitage on the French Rhône, used in the VALAIS to make ERMITAGE.

Merlot

Bordeaux red grape (see Grapes for red wine) used to make the better wine of Italian Switzerland (TICINO). See also Viti.

Mont d'Or, Domaine du   Valais w. dr. sw. ★★★★

The best wine estate of Switzerland: 60 acres of steep hillside near SION. Good FENDANT, JOHANNISBERG, AMIGNE, etc., and real Riesling. Very rich concentrated wines.

Neuchâtel   Neuchâtel r. p. w. dr. sp. ★→★★★

City of n.w. Switzerland and the wine from the n. shore of its lake. Pleasant light PINOT NOIR and attractive sometimes sparkling CHASSELAS.

Nostrano

Word meaning "ours" applied to the lesser red wine of the TICINO, made from a mixture of native and Italian grapes, in contrast to MERLOT from Bordeaux.

Oeil de Perdrix

Pale rosé of PINOT NOIR.

Orsat

Important and reliable wine firm at Martigny, VALAIS.

Perlan Geneva w. dr. ★

The MANDEMENT name for the ubiquitous CHASSELAS, here at its palest, driest and least impressive.

Premier Cru

Any wine from the maker's own estate can call itself this.

Provins

One of the best-known producers of VALAIS wine.

Rèze

The grape, now rare, used for VIN DU GLACIER.

Rivaz Vaud r. w. dr. ★★

Well-known village of LAVAUX.

St-Saphorin Vaud w. dr. ★★

One of the principal villages of LAVAUX: wines drier and more austere than DÉZALEY OR EPESSES.

Salvagnin Vaud r. ★→★★

Red VAUD wine of tested quality: the equivalent of DÔLE.

Savagnin

Swiss name for the TRAMINER, called Païen in the VALAIS.

Schafiser Bern (r.) w. dr. ★→★★

The n. shore of La. Bienne (Bielersee) is well known for light CHASSELAS sold as either Schafiser or Twanner.

Sion Valais w. dr. ★→★★★

Centre of the VALAIS wine region, famous for its FENDANT.

Spätburgunder

PINOT NOIR: by far the commonest grape of German Switzerland, making very light wines.

Testuz

Well-known growers and merchants at Cully, LAVAUX.

Ticino

Italian-speaking s. Switzerland. See Merlot, Viti, Nostrano.

Twanner

See Schafiser

Valais

The Rhône valley between Brig and Martigny. Its n. side is an admirable dry sunny and sheltered v'yd., planted mainly, alas, to the second-rate CHASSELAS grape, which here makes its best wine.

Vaud

The region of La. Geneva. Its n. shore is Switzerland's biggest v'yd. and in places as good as any. DORIN and SALVAGNIN are the main wines.

Vétroz Valais (r.) w. dr. ★★

Village near SION in the best part of the VALAIS.

Vevey

Town near Montreux with a famous wine festival once every 30-odd years. The last was in 1977.

Vin-Union-Genève

Big growers' co-operative at Satigny in the MANDEMENT. Light reds and white PERLAN are Geneva's local wine.

Viti Ticino r. ★★

Legal designation of better-quality TICINO red, made of MERLOT and with at least 12% alcohol.

Yvorne

Village near AIGLE with some of the best CHABLAIS v'yds.

Italy

Valle d'Aosta **Vd'A**

•Turin

Milan•

Piemonte
Piem

Liguria **Lig**

Italy is the world's biggest wine producer with the biggest per capita consumption: 130 bottles a year. She is so at home with wine that she can seem alarmingly casual about it. A sense of humour is as important as a corkscrew to anyone who steps off the well-beaten track.

The chief clue to Italian wine is the DOC system, an approximate equivalent of France's Appellations Controlées, which has been taking shape since the 1960s. Most of Italy's worthwhile wines now have defined areas and standards under the new system. A few, like Chianti Classico, it must be said, had them long before. A few, however, have not—and DOCs have been granted to many areas of only local interest: so the mere existence of a DOC proves little. The entries in this book ignore a score of unimportant DOCs and include a score or so non-DOCs.

They also include a large number of grape-name entries. Italian wines are named in a variety of ways: some geographical like French wines, some historical, some folklorical, and many of the best from their grapes. These include old "native" grapes such as Barbera and Sangiovese and more and more imported "international" grapes from France and Germany. Many of the DOCs, particularly in the north-east, are area names applying to widely different wines from as many as a dozen different varieties. No overall comment on the quality of such a diversity is really possible, except to say that general standards are rising steadily and a small number of producers are emerging as outstanding by international standards.

Another rather disconcerting aspect of Italian wine is clear from the following pages: in many cases the same name applies to wine which can be red or white or in between, sweet or dry or in between, still or sparkling or in between. This must be taken into account when interpreting the necessarily cryptic grades of quality and vintage notes. Vintage notes are given when specific information has been available. Where there is no comment the best plan is to aim for the youngest available white wine and experiment with the oldest available red . . . within reason.

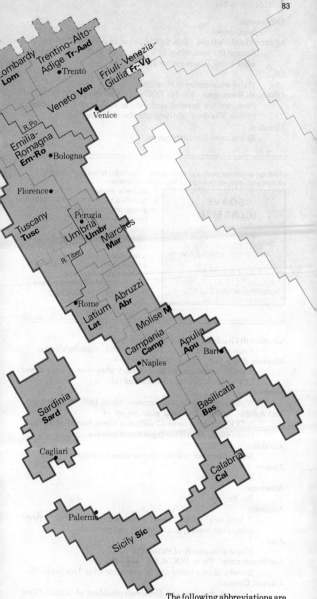

83

The map is the key to the province names used for locating each entry.

Abbreviations of province names shown in bold type are used in the text.

The following abbreviations are used in the Italian section

Pa. passito
Pr. Province
Com. commune
f. fortified

See also key to symbols opposite Contents

Abboccato
>   Semi-sweet.

Aglianico del Vulture   Bas. DOC r. (s/sw. sp.) ★★★ **75 77** 78
>   Among the best wines of s. Italy. Ages well. Called Vecchio
>   after 3 yrs., Riserva after 5 yrs.

Alba
>   Major wine-centre of PIEMONTE.

Albana di Romagna   Em-Ro. DOC w. dr. s/sw. (sp.) ★★ 76 77 78 79
>   Produced for several centuries in Romagna from Albana
>   grapes. The dry slightly tannic, the semi-sweet fruity.

Aleatico
>   Red muscat-flavoured grape.

Most Italian wines have a simple name, in contrast to the combination
village and vineyard names of France and Germany.

**SOAVE
CLASSICO**

VINO A DENOMINAZIONE DI
ORIGINE CONTROLLATA

IMBOTTIGLIATO DAL
PRODUTTORE ALL 'ORIGINE
CANTINA SOCIALE DI SOAVE

Soave is the name of this wine. It is
qualified only by the word Classico,
a legal term for the central
(normally the best) part of many
long-established wine regions.
"Denominazione di Origine
Controllata" is the official
guarantee of authenticity.
Imbottigliato . . . all origine means
bottled by the producer.
Cantina Sociale di Soave means
the growers' co-operative of
Soave.

Aleatico di Gradoli   Lat. DOC r. sw. or f. ★★
>   Aromatic, fresh, fruity, alcohol 12–15%, made in Viterbo.

Aleatico di Puglia   Apu. DOC r. sw. or f. ★★
>   Aleatico grapes make good dessert wine over a large area.
>   14% alcohol or more, aromatic and full.

Allegrini
>   Well-known producer of Veronese wines, incl. VALPOLICELLA.

Alto Adige   Tr-AAd. DOC r. p. w. dr. sw. sp. ★★
>   A DOC covering some 17 different wines named after their
>   grape varieties in 33 villages round Bolzano.

Amabile
>   Semi-sweet, but usually sweeter than ABBOCCATO.

Amaro
>   Bitter.

Amarone
>   See Recioto

Antinori
>   A long-established Tuscan house of repute producing first-
>   rate, if not truly typical, CHIANTI and ORVIETO.

Asti
>   Major wine-centre of PIEMONTE.

Asti Spumante   Piem. DOC w. sp. ★★★ NV
>   Sweet and very fruity muscat sparkling wine. Low in alcohol.

Attems, Count
>   Leading producer and Consorzio president of COLLIO. Good
>   PINOT GRIGIO, MERLOT, etc.

Badia a Coltibuono
>   Fine Chianti-maker at Gaiole with a restaurant and remark-
>   able collection of old vintages.

Barbacarlo (Oltrepo' Pavese)   Lomb. DOC r. dr. or sw. ★★ 76 77 78
>   Delicately flavoured with bitter after-taste, made in the Com.
>   of Broni in the Pr. of Pavia.

Barbaresco Piem. DOC r. dr. ★★★ **70 71 74** 78 79

Neighbour of BAROLO from the same grapes but lighter, ageing sooner. At best subtle and fine. At 3 yrs. becomes Riserva.

Barbera

Dark acidic red grape, a speciality of Piemonte also used in Lombardy, Veneto, Friuli and other n. provinces. Its best wines are:

Barbera d'Alba Piem. DOC r. dr. ★★ **73 74** 78 79

Round ALBA NEBBIOLO is sometimes added. Clean, tasty, fragrant red improves for 3–4 yrs.

Barbera d'Asti Piem. DOC r. dr. (s/sw.) ★★ **73 74** 78 79

Reputedly the best of the Barberas; all Barbera grapes; dark, grapy and appetizing. Ages up to 7–8 yrs.

Barbera del Monferrato Piem. DOC r. dr. (s/sw.) ★ **76 77** 78 79

From a large area in the Pr. of Alessandria and ASTI. Pleasant, slightly fizzy, sometimes sweetish.

Bardolino Ven. DOC r. dr. (p.) ★★ D.Y.A.

Pale, light, slightly bitter red from e. shore of La Garda. Bardolino Chiaretto is even paler and lighter.

Barolo Piem. DOC r. dr. ★★★ **67 68 70 71 74** 78 79

Small area s. of Turin with one of the best Italian red wines, dark, rich, alcoholic (minimum 12°), dry but deep in flavour. From NEBBIOLO grapes. Ages for up to 15 yrs.

Bertani

Well-known producers of quality Veronese wines (VALPOLICELLA, SOAVE, etc.).

Bertolli, Francesco

Among the best-known producers of CHIANTI CLASSICO. Cellars at Castellina in Chianti, n. of Siena.

Bianco

White.

Bianco di Pitigliano Tusc. DOC w. dr ★ D.Y.A.

A soft, fruity, lively wine made near Grosseto.

Bigi

Famous producers of ORVIETO and other wines of Umbria and Tuscany.

Biondi-Santi

One of the leading producers of BRUNELLO with cellars in Montalcino (Siena).

Boca Piem. DOC r. dr. ★★ **70 71 74 75** 76 78 79

From same grape as BAROLO in n. of PIEMONTE, Pr. of Novara.

Bolla

Famous Veronese firm producing VALPOLICELLA, SOAVE, etc.

Bonarda

Minor red grape widely grown in PIEMONTE and Lombardy.

Bonarda (Oltrepo' Pavese) Lomb. DOC r. dr. ★★ **73 74 75 76** 77

Soft, fresh, pleasant red from s. of Pavia.

Bosca

Wine-producers from PIEMONTE known for their ASTI SPUMANTE and Vermouths.

Botticino Lomb. DOC r. dr. ★ **73 74 76** 77 78 79

Strong, full-bodied red from Brescia.

Brachetto d'Acqui Piem. DOC r. sw. (sp.) ★ **76** 78 79

Sweet sparkling red with pleasant muscat aroma.

Brolio

The oldest (c. 1200) and most famous CHIANTI CLASSICO estate now owned by Seagrams.

Brunello di Montalcino Tusc. DOC r. dr. ★★★★ **66 67 70 73** 75 77 78

Italy's most expensive wine. Strong, full-bodied, high-flavoured and long-lived. After 5 yrs. is called Riserva. Produced for over a century 15 miles s. of Siena.

Cabernet

Bordeaux grape much used in n.e. Italy. See place names, e.g.:

Cabernet di Pramaggiore   Ven. DOC r. dr. ★★ **73 75 77** 78 79

Good, herb-scented, rather tannic, middle-weight red. Riserva after 3 yrs.

Calcinaia

First-class CHIANTI CLASSICO estate for centuries in the Caponi family.

Caldaro or Lago di Caldaro   Tr-AAd. DOC r. dr. ★★ **75 76 77** 78

Light, soft, slightly bitter-almond red. Classico from a smaller area is better. From s. of Bolzano.

Calissano

A long-established House of PIEMONTE producing ASTI SPUMANTE, Vermouths and red wines of that region.

Caluso Passito   Piem. DOC w. sw. (f.) ★★ **70 71 74 75** 78

Made from selected Erbaluce grapes left to partly dry; delicate scent, velvety taste. From a large area in the Pr. of Turin and Vercelli.

Cannonau di Sardegna   Sard. DOC r. dr. or s/sw. (f.) ★★ **74 76 77** 78

One of the good wines of the island capable of ageing.

Cantina

1. Cellar or winery. 2. Cantina Sociale = growers' co-op.

Capena   Lat. DOC w. dr. s/sw ★ D.Y.A.

A sound wine for daily drinking from n. of Rome.

Capri

Widely abused name of the famous island in the Bay of Naples. No guarantee of quality.

Carema   Piem. DOC r. dr. ★★ **71 73 74 75** 78 79

Old speciality of Val d'Aosta. NEBBIOLO grapes traditionally fermented Beaujolais-style before crushing. (See France: Macération carbonique.) More conventional today.

Carmignano   Tusc. DOC r. dr. ★★→ ★★★   **75** 78 79

Section of CHIANTI using CABERNET to make good wine.

Casa fondata nel . . .

Firm founded in . . .

Castel del Monte   Apu. DOC r. p. w. dr. ★★ **73 74 75 76 77** 78 79

Dry, fresh, well-balanced southern wines. The red becomes Riserva after 3 yrs.

Castel S. Michele

A good red made of Cabernet and Merlot grapes by the Trentino Agricultural College near Trento.

CAVIT

CAntina VITicultori, a co-operative of co-operatives near Trento, producing large quantities of table wine.

Cellatica   Lomb. DOC r. dr. ★★ **75 76 77** 78 79

Light red with slightly bitter after-taste, from Brescia.

Cerveteri   Lat. DOC w. dr. ★

Sound wines produced n.w. of Rome between Lake Bracciano and the Tyrrhenian Sea.

Chianti   Tusc. DOC r. dr. ★★   **71 75 77** 78 79

The lively local wine of Florence. Fresh but warmly fruity when young, usually sold in straw-covered flasks. Ages moderately. Montalbano, Rufina and Colli Fiorentini, Senesi, Aretini, Colline Pisane are sub-districts.

Chianti Classico   Tusc. DOC r. dr. ★★★   **70 71 75 77** 78 79

Senior Chianti from the central area. Many estates make fine powerful scented wine. Riservas (after 3 yrs.) often have the bouquet of age in oak.

Chianti Putto

Often high-quality Chianti from a league of producers outside the Classico zone. Designated by a neck-label of a pink and white cherub.

Cinque Terre   Lig. DOC w. dr. or sw. or pa. ★★★
Fragrant, fruity white made for centuries near La Spezia. The PASSITO is known as Sciacchetra.

Cinzano
A Vermouth company also known for its ASTI SPUMANTE from PIEMONTE.

Cirò   Cal. DOC r. (p. w.) dr. ★★ **73 74 75 77** 78 79
The wine of the ancient Olympic games. Very strong red, fruity white (to drink young).

Classico
Term for wines from a restricted, usually central, area within the limits of a DOC. By implication, and often in practice, the best of the region.

Clastidio   Lomb. r. (p.) w. dr. ★★ **73 74 75 76 77** 78 79
Pleasant, sour touch to the white. The red full, slightly tannic.

Collavini, Cantina
High-quality producers of GRAVE DEL FRIULI wines: PINOT GRIGIO, RIESLING, MERLOT, PINOT NERO, etc.

Colli   Means "hills" in many wine-names.

Colli Albani   Lat. DOC w. dr. or s/sw. (sp.) ★★ **77 78** 79
Soft fruity wine of the Roman hills.

Colli Bolognesi Em-Ro. DOC r.p. w. dr. ★ D.Y.A.
From the hills s.w. of Bologna.

Colli Euganei   Ven. DOC r. w. dr. or s/sw. (sp.) ★★ **75 76 77 78** 79
A DOC applicable to 3 wines produced s.w. of Padua. The red is scarcely memorable, the white soft and pleasant. The table wine of Venice.

Colli Orientali del Friuli   Fr-VG. DOC r. w. dr. or sw. ★ **75 77 78** 79
12 different wines are produced under this DOC on the hills e. of Udine and named after their grapes.

Collio (Goriziano)   Fr-VG. DOC r. w. dr.   ★★   76 77 78 79
Ten different wines named after their grapes from a small area w. of Gorizia nr. the Yugoslav border. Top grower: ATTEMS.

Contratto
Piemonte firm known for BAROLO, ASTI SPUMANTE, etc.

Cora
A leading House producing ASTI SPUMANTE and Vermouth from PIEMONTE.

Cori   Lat DOC w. r. dr./sw.   ★
Soft and well-balanced wines made 30 miles s. of Rome.

Cortese di Gavi   Piem. DOC w. dr. (sp.) ★★ D.Y.A.
Delicate fresh white from between Alessandria and Genoa.

Cortese (Oltrepo' Pavese)   Lomb. DOC w. dr. ★ D.Y.A.
The same from w. Lombardy.

Corvo   Sic. r. w. dr. ★★
Popular Sicilian wines. Sound dry red, pleasant soft white.

D'Ambra
Well-known producer of ELBA and other wines of that island.

Dolce   Sweet.

Dolceacqua
See Rossese di Dolceacqua

Dolcetto
Common low-acid red grape of PIEMONTE, giving its name to:

Dolcetto d'Acqui   Piem. DOC r. dr. ★ D.Y.A.
Good standard table wine from s. of ASTI.

Dolcetto d'Alba   Piem. DOC r. dr. ★★ **74 78** 79
Among the best Dolcetti, with a trace of bitter-almond.

Dolcetto d'Asti   Piem. DOC r. dr. ★ D.Y.A.

Donnaz   Vd'A. DOC dr. ★
A mountain NEBBIOLO, fragrant, pale and faintly bitter. Aged for a statutory 3 yrs.

Donnici   Cal. DOC r. (p.) dr. ★
    Middle-weight southern red from Cosenza.

Elba   Tusc. r. w. dr. (sp.)   ⬛ **77 78** 79
    The island's white is better: admirable with fish.

Enfer d'Arvier   Vd'A. DOC r. dr. ★★
    An Alpine speciality: pale, pleasantly bitter, light red.

Enoteca
    Italian for "wine library", of which there are many in the country, the most comprehensive being the Enoteca Italica Permanente of Siena. Chianti has one at Greve

Erbaluce di Caluso   Piem. DOC w. dr. ★ **76 78** 79
    Pleasant fresh hot-weather wine.

Est! Est!! Est!!!   Lat. DOC w. dr. or s/sw. ★★ D.Y.A.
    Famous soft fruity white from La. Bolsena, n. of Rome. The name is more remarkable than the wine.

Etna   Sic. DOC r. p. w. dr.   ⬛★★⬛ **70 73 74 75 77** 78 79
    Wine from the volcanic slopes. The red is warm, full, balanced and ages well; the white is distinctly grapy.

Falerio dei Colli Ascolani   Mar. DOC w. dr. ★ D.Y.A.
    Made in the Pr. of Ascoli Piceno. Pleasant, fresh, fruity; a wine for the summer.

Falerno   Camp. r. w. dr. ★
    One of the best-known wines of ancient times, but nothing special today. Strong red, fruity white.

Fara   Piem. DOC r. dr. ★★ **70 71 74 75 76** 77 79
    Good NEBBIOLO wine from Novara, n. PIEMONTE. Fragrant; worth ageing. Small production.

Faro   Sic. r. dr. ★★ **75 77** 78 79
    Sound strong Sicilian red, made in sight of the Straits of Messina.

Fazi-Battaglia
    Well-known producer of VERDICCHIO, etc.

Ferrari
    Firm making Italy's best dry sparkling wine by the champagne method nr. Trento, Trentino-Alto Adige.

Fiorano   Lat. r. ★★
    Interesting reds of Cabernet Sauvignon and Merlot.

Folonari
    Leading producers of quality Veronese wines as well as other table wines from various parts of Italy.

Fontana Candida
    One of the biggest producers of FRASCATI.

Fontanafredda
    Leading producer of Piemontese wines, incl. BAROLO.

Fracia   Lomb. DOC r. dr. ★★ **73 75 76** 78 79
    Good light but fragrant red from Valtellina.

Franciacorta Pinot   Lomb. DOC w. dr. (sp.) ★★
    Agreeable soft white made of PINOT BIANCO.

Franciacorta Rosso   Lomb. DOC r. dr. ★★ **75 76 77** 78 79
    Lightish red of mixed CABERNET and BARBERA from Brescia.

Frascati   Lat. DOC w. dr. s/sw. sw. (sp.)   ⬛★★⬛ **78** 79
    Best-known wine of the Roman hills: soft, ripe, golden, tasting of whole grapes. The sweet is known as Cannellino.

Frecciarossa   Lomb. r. w. dr. ★★ **71 73 76 77 78** 79
    Sound wines produced nr. Casteggio in the Oltrepo' Pavese; the white is better known.

Freisa d'Asti   Piem. DOC r. s/sw. or sw. (sp.) ★★ **73 74 78** 79
    Sweet, often sparkling red, said to taste of raspberries and roses.

Frescobaldi
    Leading pioneers of CHIANTI PUTTO at Nippozano, e. of Florence. Also elegant white POMINO.

Frizzante

Semi-sparkling or "pétillant", a word used to describe wines such as LAMBRUSCO.

Gambellara Ven. DOC w. dr. or s/sw. (sp.) ★ 76 77 78 79

Neighbour of SOAVE. Dry wine similar. Sweet (known as RECIOTO DI GAMBELLARA), agreeably fruity.

Gancia

Famous ASTI SPUMANTE house from Piemonte, also produces vermouth.

Gattinara Piem. DOC r. dr. ★★★ 69 70 74 75 76 78 79

Excellent big-scale BAROLO-type red from n. PIEMONTE. Made from NEBBIOLO, locally known as Spanna.

Gavi Piem. w. dr. ★★→★★★

At best almost burgundian dry white. Gavi dei Gavi from Rovereto di Gavi Ligure is best. Needs two or three years ageing.

Ghemme Piem. DOC r. dr. ★★ 70 71 73 74 78 79

Neighbour of GATTINARA, capable of Bordeaux-style finesse.

Giacobazzi

Well-known producers of Lambrusco wines with cellars in Nonantola and Sorbara, near Modena.

Giacosa, Bruno

Old family business making excellent Barolo and other Piemonte wines at Neive (Cuneo).

Gradi

Degrees (of alcohol) i.e. percent by volume.

Grave del Friuli Fr-VG. DOC r. w. dr. ★★ 75 76 77 78 79

A DOC covering 7 different wines named after their grapes, from near the Yugoslav border.

Greco di Tufo Camp. DOC w. dr. s/sw. ★★ 76 77 78 79

One of the best whites of the south, fruity and slightly bitter.

Grignolino d'Asti Piem. DOC r. dr. ★ 74 76 78 79

Pleasant lively standard wine of PIEMONTE.

Grumello Lomb. DOC r. dr. ★★ 71 73 75 76 78 79

NEBBIOLO wine from Valtellina, can be delicate and fine.

Gutturnio dei Colli Piacentini Em-Ro. DOC r. dr. (s/sw.) ★★ 70 71 74 77 78 79

Full-bodied wine of character from the hills of Piacenza. Named after a large Roman drinking cup.

Inferno Lomb. DOC r. dr. ★★ 70 73 75 76 78 79

Similar to GRUMELLO and like it classified as VALTELLINA Superiore.

Ischia Camp. DOC (r.) w. dr. ★ 75 77 78 79

The wine of the island off Naples. The slightly sharp white is best; ideal with fish.

Isonzo Fr-VG. DOC r. w. dr. ★

DOC covering 10 varietal wines in the extreme n.e.

Kalterersee

German name for LAGO DI CALDARO.

Kretzer

German term for rosé used in the Italian Tyrol.

Lacrima Cristi del Vesuvio Camp. r. p. w. (f.) dr. (sw.) ★

Famous but frankly ordinary wines in great variety from the slopes of Mount Vesuvius.

Lago di Caldaro

See Caldaro

Lagrein del Trentino Tr-AAd. DOC r. dr. ★★ 76 78 79

Lagrein is a Tyrolean grape with a bitter twist. Good fruity light wine.

Lamberti

Producers of SOAVE, VALPOLICELLA and BARDOLINO at Lazise on the e. shore of La. Garda.

Lambrusco di Sorbara   Em-Ro. DOC r. (w.) dr. or s/sw. sp. ✦✦✦ 76 77 78

Bizarre but popular fizzy red from near Modena.

Lambrusco Grasparossa di Castelvetro   Em-Ro. DOC r. dr. or s/sw. sp. ✦✦ 76 77 78

Similar to above. Highly scented, pleasantly acidic; often drunk with rich food.

Lambrusco Salamino di Santa Croce   Em-Ro. DOC r. dr. or s/sw. sp. ✦ 75 78

Similar to above. Fruity smell, high acidity and a thick "head".

Langhe

The hills of central PIEMONTE.

Latisana   Fr-VG. DOC r. w. dr. ✦✦

DOC for 7 varietal wines from some 50 miles n.e. of Venice.

Lessona   Piem. DOC r. d. ✦✦ 74 78 79

Soft, dry, claret-like wine produced in the province of Vercelli from Nebbiolo grapes.

Liquoroso

Strong and usually sweet, e.g. like Tuscan Vinsanto.

Locorotondo   Apu. DOC w. dr. ✦ D.Y.A.

A pleasantly fresh southern white.

Lugana   Lomb. DOC w. dr. ✦✦✦ 77 78 79

One of the best white wines of s. La Garda: fragrant and delicate.

Lungarotti

Leading producers of TORGIANO wine, with cellars and an outstanding Wine Museum near Perugia.

Malvasia

Important white or red grape for luscious wines, incl. Madeira's Malmsey. Used all over Italy.

Malvasia di Bosa   Sard. DOC w. dr. sw. or f. ✦✦

A wine of character. Strong and aromatic with a slightly bitter after-taste. A liquoroso (fortified) version is best.

Malvasia di Cagliari   Sard. DOC w. dr. s/sw. or sw. (f. dr. s.) ✦✦

Interesting strong Sardinian wine, fragrant and slightly bitter.

Malvasia di Casorzo d'Asti   Piem. DOC r. p. sw. sp. ✦✦ 74 76 78 79

Fragrant grapy sweet red, sometimes sparkling.

Malvasia di Castelnuovo Don Bosco   Piem. DOC r. sw. (sp.) ✦✦

Peculiar method of interrupted fermentation gives very sweet aromatic red.

Malvasia delle Lipari   Sic. DOC w. sw. (pa. f.) ✦✦✦ 73 76 77 78 79

Among the very best Malvasias, aromatic and rich, produced on the Lipari or Aeolian Islands n. of Sicily.

Malvasia di Nus   Vd'A. w. dr. ✦✦✦

Rare Alpine white, with a deep bouquet of honey. Small production and high reputation. Can age remarkably well.

Mamertino   Sic. w. s/sw. ✦✦ 74 75 76 77 78 79

Made near Messina since Roman times. Sweet-scented, rich in glycerine. Mentioned several times by Caesar in *De Bello Gallico*.

Manduria (Primitivo di)   Apu. DOC r. s/sw. (f. dr. or sw.) ✦✦

Heady red, naturally strong but often fortified. From nr. Taranto. Primitivo is a southern grape.

Mantonico   Cal. w. sw. f. ✦✦

Fruity deep amber dessert wine from Reggio Calabria. Can age remarkably well. Named from the Greek for "prophetic".

Marino   Lat. DOC w. dr. or s/sw. ✦ 77 78 79

A neighbour of FRASCATI with similar wine.

Marsala Sic. DOC br. dr. s/sw. or sw. f. ★★★ NV
Dark sherry-type wine invented by the Woodhouse Brothers from Liverpool in 1773; excellent apéritif or for dessert. The dry ("virgin") made by the solera system.

Marsala Speciali
These are Marsalas with added flavours of egg, almond, strawberry, etc.

Martinafranca Apu. DOC w. dr. ★ D.Y.A.
Agreeable but rather neutral southern white.

Martini & Rossi
Well-known vermouth House also famous for its fine wine museum in Pessione, PIEMONTE.

Marzemino (del Trentino) Tr-AAd. DOC r. dr. ★ 75 76 77 78 79
Pleasant local red of Trento. Fruity fragrance; slightly bitter taste.

Masi, Cantina
Well-known specialist producers of VALPOLICELLA, RECIOTO, SOAVE, etc., incl. fine red Campo Fiorin.

Mastroberardino
Leading wine-producer of Campania, incl. TAURASI and LACRIMA CRISTI DEL VESUVIO.

Melini
Long-established and important producers of CHIANTI CLASSICO at Pontassieve. Inventors of the standard *fiasco*, or litre flask.

Melissa Cal. r. dr. ★★ 74 75 77 78 79
Mostly made from Gaglioppo grapes in the Pr. of Catanzaro. Delicate, balanced, ages rather well.

Meranese di Collina Tr-AAd. DOC r. dr. ★ 76 77 78 79
Light red of Merano, known in German as Meraner.

Merlot
Adaptable red Bordeaux grape widely grown in n.e. Italy and elsewhere.

Merlot di Aprilia Lat. DOC r. dr. ★ 75 77 78 79
Harsh at first, softer after 2–3 yrs.

Merlot Colli Berici Ven. DOC r. dr. ★ D.Y.A.
Pleasantly light and soft.

Merlot Colli Orientali del Friuli Fr-VG. DOC r. dr. ★
Pleasant herby character, best at 2–3 yrs.

Merlot Collio Goriziano Fr-VG. DOC r. dr. ★
Grassy scent, slightly bitter taste. Best at 2–3 yrs.

Merlot Grave del Friuli Fr-VG. DOC r. dr. ★
Pleasant light wine, best at 1–2 yrs.

Merlot (Isonzo) Fr-VG. DOC r. dr. ★
A DOC in Gorizia. Dry, herby, agreeable wine.

Merlot del Piave Ven. DOC r. dr. ★★ 75 77 78 79
Sound tasty red, best at 2–3 yrs.

Merlot di Pramaggiore Ven. DOC r. dr. ★★ 74 75 76 77 78 79
A cut above other Merlots; improves in bottle. Riserva after 3 yrs.

Merlot (del Trentino) Tr-AAd. DOC r. dr. ⌐★⌐ 76 78 79
Full flavour, slightly grassy scent, improves for 2–3 yrs.

Monica di Cagliari Sard. DOC r. dr. or sw. (f. dr. or sw.) ★★ 73 77 78 79
Strong spicy red, often fortified and comparable with Spanish MALAGA. Monica is a Sardinian grape.

Monica di Sardegna Sard. DOC r. sw. ★ NV
Commoner form of above, not fortified.

Montecarlo Tusc. DOC w. dr. ★★
One of Tuscany's best whites, smooth and delicate, achieving a Graves-like style after 3–4 years. From near Lucca.

Montecompatri-Colonna   Lat. DOC w. dr. or s/sw. ★
A neighbour of FRASCATI. Similar wine.

Montepaldi
Well-known producers and merchants of CHIANTI CLASSICO at San Casciano Val di Pesa. Owned by the Corsini family.

Montepulciano d'Abruzzo (or Molise)   Abr&M. DOC r. p. dr.   **★★★**   **74 75 77** 78 79
One of Italy's best reds, from Adriatic coast round Pescara. Soft, slightly tannic, reminiscent of MARSALA when aged. Best from Francavilla al Mare, Sulmona, Pratola Peligna.

Monterosso (Val d'Arda)   Em-Ro. DOC w. dr. or sw. (sp.) ★ D.Y.A.
Agreeable and fresh minor white from Piacenza.

Moscato
Fruitily fragrant grape grown all over Italy.

Moscato d'Asti   Piem. DOC w. sw. sp. ★ NV
Low-strength sweet fruity sparkler made in bulk. ASTI SPUMANTE is the superior version.

Moscato dei Colli Euganei   Ven. DOC w. sw. (sp.) ★★ **77 78** 79
Golden wine, fruity and smooth, from nr. Padua.

Moscato Naturale d'Asti   Piem. DOC w. sw. ★ D.Y.A.
The light and fruity base wine for Moscato d'Asti.

Moscato di Noto   Sic. DOC w. s/sw. or sw. or sp. or f. ★ NV
Light sweet still and sparkling versions, or strong Liquoroso. Noto is near Siracusa.

Moscato (Oltrepo' Pavese)   Lomb. DOC w. sw. (sp.) ★★ 78 **79**
The Lombardy equivalent of Moscato d'Asti.

Moscato di Pantelleria   Sic. DOC w. sw. (sp.) (f. pa.) ★★★
Italy's best muscat, from the island of Pantelleria close to the Tunisian coast; rich, fruity and aromatic. Ages well.

Moscato di Siracusa   Sic. DOC w. sw.   **★★**   NV
Strong amber dessert wine from Siracuse. Can be superb.

Moscato di Sorso Sennori   Sard. DOC w. sw. (f.)   **★**
Strong golden dessert wine from Sassari, n. Sardinia.

Moscato di Trani   Apu. DOC w. sw. or f. ★ **74 76 77** 79
Another strong golden dessert wine, sometimes fortified, with "bouquet of faded roses".

Moscato (Trentino)   Tr-AAd. DOC w. sw. ★
Typical muscat: high strength for the north.

Nasco di Cagliari   Sard. DOC w. dr. or sw. (f. dr. or sw.) ★ **72 73 74**
Sardinian speciality, light bitter taste, high alcoholic content.

Nebbiolo
The best red grape of PIEMONTE and Lombardy.

Nebbiolo d'Alba   Piem. DOC r. dr. s/sw. (sp.)   **★★**   **74 76 77 78** 79
Like light-weight BAROLO; often good. Barolo that fails to reach the statutory 12° alcohol is sold under this name. Some prefer it so.

Negri, Nino
Famous house of VALTELLINA known for its excellent reds.

Nipozzano, Castello di
The most important CHIANTI producer outside the Classico zone, to the n. near Florence. Owned by FRESCOBALDI.

Nozzole
Famous estate in the heart of Chianti, n. of Greve.

Nuraghe Majore   Sard. w. dr. ★★ D.Y.A.
Sardinian white: delicate, fresh, among the island's best.

Nuragus di Cagliari   Sard. DOC w. dr. ★ **77 78 79**
Lively Sardinian white, not too strong.

Oliena   Sard. r. dr. ★
Interesting strong fragrant red; a touch bitter.

Oltrepo' Pavese   Lomb. DOC r. w. dr. sw. sp. ★→★★
DOC applicable to 7 wines produced in the Pr. of Pavia, named after their grapes.

Orvieto Umb. DOC w. dr. or s/sw. ⟦★★→★★★⟧ 77 78 79
   The classical Umbrian golden-white, smooth and substantial.
   O. Classico is superior.
Ostuni Apu. DOC w. dr. ★★
   Rather delicate, dry, balanced; produced in the Pr. of Brindisi.
Parrina Tusc. r. or w. dr. ★★ D.Y.A.
   Light red and fresh appetizing white from n. Tuscany.
Passito
   Strong sweet wine from grapes dried either in the sun or
   indoors.
Per' e' Palummo Camp. r. dr. ★★
   Excellent red produced on the island of Ischia; delicate,
   slightly grassy, a bit tannic, balanced.
Piave DOC r. or w. dr. ★★ 75 76 78 79
   DOC covering 4 wines, 2 red and 2 white, named after their
   grapes.
Picolit (Colli Orientali del Friuli) Fr-VG. DOC w. s/sw. or sw.
   ★★★★ 64 69 71 72 73 74 75 77 78 79
   Known as Italy's Château d'Yquem. Delicate bouquet, well
   balanced, high alcoholic content. Ages very well.
Piemonte
   The most important Italian region for quality wine. Turin
   is the capital, Asti the wine-centre. See Barolo, Barbera,
   Grignolino, Moscato, etc.
Pieropan
   Outstanding producers of SOAVE.
Pinot Bianco
   Rather neutral grape popular in n.e., good for sparkling wine.
Pinot Bianco (dei Colli Berici) Ven. DOC w. dr. ★★
   Straight satisfying dry white.
Pinot Bianco (Colli Orientali del Friuli) Fr-VG. DOC w. dr. ★★
   75 76 77 78 79
   Good white; smooth rather than showy.
Pinot Bianco (Collio Goriziano) Fr-VG. DOC w. dr. ★★ 77 78 79
   Similar to the above.
Pinot Bianco (Grave del Friuli) Fr-VG. DOC w. dr. ★★
   Same again.
Pinot Grigio
   Tasty, low-acid white grape popular in n.e.
Pinot Grigio (Collio Goriziano) Fr-VG. DOC w. dr. ★★ 76 77 78 79
   Fruity, soft, agreeable dry white. The best age well.
Pinot Grigio (Grave del Friuli) Fr-VG. DOC w. dr. ★★ 76 77 78 79
   Hardly distinguishable from the above.
Pinot Grigio (Oltrepo' Pavese) Lomb. DOC w. dr. (sp.) ⟦★★⟧ 74
   75 77 78 79
   Lombardy's P.G. is considered best.
Pinot Nero Trentino Tr-AAd. DOC r. dr. ⟦★★⟧ 75 76 77 78 79
   Pinot Nero (Noir) gives lively burgundy-scented light wine in
   much of n.e. Italy, incl. Trentino.
Pio Cesare
   A producer of quality red wines of PIEMONTE, incl. outstanding
   BAROLO.
Pomino
   Fine Tuscan white, partly Chardonnay, from FRESCOBALDI.
Primitivo di Apulia Apu. r. dr. ⟦★★⟧
   One of the best southern reds. Fruity when young, soft and
   full-flavoured with age. (See also Manduria.)
Prosecco di Conegliano Ven. DOC w. dr. or s/sw. (sp.) ★★★
   Popular sparkling wine of the n.e. Slight fruity bouquet, the
   dry pleasantly bitter, the sw. fruity; the best are known as
   Superiore di Cartizze. Best producer: Carpene-Malvolti.

Raboso del Piave Ven. r. dr. ★★ **71 73 74 75 76** 78 79
>   Powerful but sharp country red; needs age.

Ramandolo
>   See Verduzzo Colli Orientali del Friuli.

Ravello Camp. r. p. w. dr. ★★
>   Among the best wines of Campania: full dry red, fresh clean
>   white. Caruso is the best-known brand.

Recioto
>   Wine made of half-dried grapes. Speciality of Veneto.

Italian bottle shapes

1 Orvieto 2 Chianti 3 Verdicchio 4 Barolo

Recioto di Gambellara Ven. DOC w. s/sw. sp. ★
>   Sweetish golden wine, often half-sparkling.

Recioto di Soave Ven. DOC w. s/sw. (sp.) ★★
>   Soave made from selected half-dried grapes; sweet, fruity,
>   fresh, slightly almondy: high alcohol.

Recioto della Valpolicella Ven. DOC r.s/sw. sp. ★★ **74 77 78** 79
>   Strong rather sweet red, sometimes sparkling.

Recioto Amarone della Valpolicella Ven. DOC r. dr. ★★★★ **64 66
68 70 74 77** 78 79
>   Dry version of the above; strong concentrated flavour, rather
>   bitter. Impressive and expensive.

Refosco (Colli Orientali del Friuli) Fr-VG. DOC r. dr. ★★ **75 77** 78
>   Full-bodied dry red; Riserva after 2 yrs. Refosco is a grape of
>   little character.

Refosco (Grave del Friuli) Fr-VG. DOC r. dr. ★★
>   Similar to above but slightly lighter.

Regaleali Sic. w. r. p. ☐★
>   Among the better Sicilian table wines, produced between
>   Caltanissetta and Palermo.

Ribolla (Colli Orientali del Friuli) Fr-VG. DOC w. dr. ★ D.Y.A.
>   Clean and fruity n.e. white.

Ricasoli
>   Famous Tuscan family, "inventors" of CHIANTI, whose Chian-
>   ti is named after their BROLIO estate and castle.

Riesling
>   Normally refers to Italian (R. Italico). German Riesling,
>   uncommon, is R. Renano.

Riesling Italico (Collio Goriziano) Fr-VG. DOC w. dr. ★★ **77 78 79**
>   Pleasantly fruity, fairly full-bodied n.e. white.

Riesling (Oltrepo' Pavese) Lomb. DOC w. dr. (sp.) ★★
>   The Lombardy version, quite light and fresh. Occasionally
>   sparkling. Keeps well.

Riesling (Trentino) Tr-AAd. DOC w. dr. ★★ D.Y.A.
>   Delicate, slightly acid, very fruity.

Riserva
>   Wine aged for a statutory period in barrels.

Riunite
>   Cantine Sociali, a Co-operative cellar near Reggio Emilia
>   producing large quantities of LAMBRUSCO.

Rivera

Important and reliable wine-makers at Andria, near Bari, with good red and CASTEL DEL MONTE rosé.

Riviera Rosso Stravecchio Apu. r. dr. ★★ 67 70 73 74 75 76 78 79

Good dry full-bodied red from Castel del Monte. Ages well.

Riviera del Garda Chiaretto Ven. DOC p. dr. ★★ D.Y.A.

Charming cherry-pink, fresh and slightly bitter, from s.w. Garda esp. round Moniga del Garda.

Riviera del Garda Rosso Ven. DOC r. dr. ★★ 75 76 77 78 79

Red version of the above; ages surprisingly well.

Rosato

Rosé.

Rosato del Salento Apu. DOC p. dr. ★ D.Y.A.

Strong but refreshing southern rosé from round Brindisi.

Rossese di Dolceacqua Lig. DOC r. dr. ★★ 75 76 78 79

Well-known fragrant light red of the Riviera with typical touch of bitterness. Superiore is stronger.

Rosso

Red.

Rosso delle Colline Lucchesi Tusc. DOC r. dr. ★★ 75 77 78 79

Produced round Lucca but not greatly different from CHIANTI.

Rosso Conero Mar. DOC r. dr. ★★ 75 77 78 79

Substantial CHIANTI-style wine from the Adriatic coast.

Rosso Piceno Mar. DOC r. dr. ★ 75 77 78 79

Unremarkable Adriatic red.

Rubesco

See Torgiano

Rubino di Cantavenna Piem. DOC r. dr. ★★

Lively red, principally BARBERA, from a well-known co-operative s.e. of Turin.

Rufina

A sub-region of CHIANTI in the hills e. of Florence.

Ruffino

Well-known CHIANTI merchants.

Runchet (Valtellina) Lomb. DOC r. dr. ★★

Small production, soft bouquet, slightly tannic, drink relatively young.

Sangiovese

Principal red grape of CHIANTI, used alone for:

Sangiovese d'Aprilia Lat. DOC p. dr. ★ 77 78 79

Strong dry rosé from s. of Rome.

Sangiovese di Romagna Em-Ro. DOC r. dr. ★★ 75 78 79

Pleasant standard red; gains character with a little age.

Sangue di Giuda (Oltrepo' Pavese) Lomb. DOC r. dr. ★★

"Judas' blood". Strong rather tannic red of w. Lombardy.

San Severo Apu. DOC r. p. w. dr. ★ 75 77 78 79

Sound neutral southern wine; not particularly strong.

Santa Maddalena Tr-AAd. DOC r. dr. ★★ 71 73 75 78 79

Perhaps the best Tyrolean red. Round and warm, slightly almondy. From Bolzano.

Sassella

A CHIANTI CLASSICO estate of Melini producing an excellent single-vineyard wine.

Sassella (Valtellina) Lomb. DOC r. dr. ★★★ 71 73 75 78 79

Considerable NEBBIOLO wine, tough when young. Known since Roman times, mentioned by Leonardo da Vinci.

Sassicaia Tusc. D.O.C. r. dr. ★★★★ 75 76

Perhaps Italy's best red wine, produced in the Tenuta San Guido of the Incisa family, at Bolgheri near Livorno since 1968. In the manner of first-growth claret. Tiny production.

Sauvignon

The Sauvignon Blanc: excellent white grape used in n.e.

Sauvignon (Colli Berici)   Ven. DOC w. dr. ★★ D.Y.A.
Delicate, slightly aromatic, fresh white from near Vicenza.

Sauvignon (Colli Orientali del Friuli)   Fr-VG. DOC w. dr. ★★ 75 77 78 79
Full, smooth, freshly aromatic n.e. white.

Sauvignon (Collio Goriziano)   Fr-VG. DOC w. dr. ★★ 76 77 78 79
Very similar to the last; slightly higher alcohol.

Savuto   Cal. DOC r. p. dr. ★★
The ancient Savuto produced in the Pr. of Cosenza and Catanzaro. Big juicy wine.

Sciacchetra d'
See Cinque Terre

Secco
Dry.

Sella & Mosca
Major Sardinian growers and merchants at Alghero.

Sforzato (Valtellina)   Lomb. DOC r. dr. ★★★ 67 68 70 71 75 78 79
Valtellina equivalent of RECIOTO AMARONE made with partly dried grapes. Velvety, strong, ages remarkably well. Also called Sfursat.

Sizzano   Piem. DOC r. dr. ★★ 71 74 75 76 78 79
Attractive full-bodied red produced at Sizzano in the Pr. of Novara, mostly from NEBBIOLO.

Soave   Ven. DOC w. dr. ★★★ D.Y.A.
Famous, if not very characterful, Veronese white. Fresh with attractive texture. Classico is more restricted and better.

Solopaca   Camp. DOC r. w. dr. ★
Comes from nr. Benevento, rather sharp when young, the white soft and fruity.

Sorni   Tr-AAd. r. w. dr. ★★ 78 79
Made in the Pr. of Trento. Light, fresh and soft. Drink young.

Spanna
See Gattinara

Spumante
Sparkling.

Squinzano   Apu. r. p. dr. ★
Strong southern red from Lecce.

Stravecchio
Very old.

Sylvaner
German white grape successful in ALTO ADIGE and elsewhere.

Sylvaner (Alto Adige)   Tr-AAd. DOC w. dr. ★★ 77 78 79
Pleasant grapy well-balanced white.

Sylvaner (Terlano)   Tr-AAd. DOC w. dr. ★★ 78 79
Attractive lively and delicate wines.

Sylvaner (Valle Isarco)   Tr-AAd. DOC w. dr. ★★
Similar to the last.

Taurasi   Camp. DOC r. dr. ★★ 70 71 73 75 77 78 79
The best Campanian red, from Avellino. Bouquet of cherries. Harsh when young, improves with age. Riserva after 4 yrs.

Terlano   Tr-AAd. DOC w. dr. ★★ 76 77 78 79
A DOC applicable to 6 white wines from the Pr. of Bolzano, named after their grapes. Terlaner in German.

Termeno   Tr-AAd. r. w. dr. ★★
Village nr. Bolzano. Tramin in German, reputedly the origin of the TRAMINER. Its red is light and slightly bitter.

Teroldego Rotaliano   Tr-AAd. DOC r. dr. ★★ 75 76 77 78 79
The attractive local red of Trento. Blackberry-scented, slight bitter after-taste, ages moderately.

Tignanello   Tusc. r. dr. ★★★ 71 75 77 78
One of the new style of Bordeaux-inspired Tuscan reds, made by ANTINORI. Small production.

Tocai

North-east Italian white grape; no relation of Hungarian but possibly related to Alsace Tokay.

Tocai di Lison Ven. DOC w. dr. ** 76 77

From Treviso, delicate smoky/fruity scent, fruity taste. Classico is better.

Tocai (Colli Berici) Ven. DOC w. dr. *

Less character than the last.

Tocai (Grave del Friuli) Fr-VG. DOC w. dr. **

Similar to TOCAI DI LISON, generally rather milder.

Tocai di S. Martino della Battaglia Lomb. DOC w. dr. ** D.Y.A.

Small production s. of La. Garda. Light, slightly bitter.

Torbato Sard. w. dr. (pa.) **

Good n. Sardinian table wine, also PASSITO of high quality.

Torgiano, Rubesco di Umb. DOC r. w. dr. [***] 70 71 73 75 77 78

Excellent red from near Perugia comparable with CHIANTI CLASSICO. Small production. White Torre di Giano also good, but not as outstanding as the red.

Traminer Aromatico (Trentino) Tr-AAd. DOC w. dr. ** D.Y.A.

Delicate, aromatic, rather soft Traminer.

Trebbiano

The principal white grape of Tuscany and most of central Italy. Ugni Blanc in French.

A new top category, DOCG, Denominazione Controllata e Garantita, is to be added to the Italian wine classification in due course. It will be awarded only to certain wines from top-quality zones-within-zones which have been bottled and sealed with a government seal by the producer. So far no wine has been classified as DOCG. Barolo will probably be the first.

Trebbiano d'Abruzzo Abr&M. DOC w. dr. * D.Y.A.

Gentle, rather neutral, slightly tannic. From round Pescara.

Trebbiano d'Aprilia Lat. DOC w. dr. * D.Y.A.

Heady, mild-flavoured, rather yellow. From s. of Rome.

Trebbiano di Romagna Em-Ro. DOC w. dr. or s/sw. (sp.) * 75 77 78

Clean, pleasant white from near Bologna.

Trentino Tr-AAd. DOC r. w. dr. or sw. *→**

DOC applicable to 10 wines named after their grapes.

Uzzano

Fine old estate at Greve. First-class CHIANTI CLASSICO.

Valcalepio Lomb. DOC r. w. dr. * 74 77 78 79

From nr. Bergamo. Pleasant red; lightly scented, fresh white.

Valdadige Tr-AAd. DOC r. w. dr. or s/sw. *

Name for the ordinary table wines of the Adige valley—in German Etschtal.

Valgella (Valtellina) Lomb. DOC r. dr. [**] 73 74 75 76 78 79

One of the VALTELLINA NEBBIOLOS: good dry red growing nutty with age. Riserva at 4 yrs.

Valle Isarco Tr-AAd. DOC w. dr. *→**

A DOC applicable to 5 varietal wines made n.e. of Bolzano.

Valpolicella Ven. DOC r. dr. *** 78 79

Attractive light red from nr. Verona; most attractive when young. Delicate nutty scent, slightly bitter taste. Classico more restricted; Superiore has 12% alcohol and 1 yr. of age.

Valtellina Lomb. DOC r. dr. **→***

A DOC applicable to wines made principally from Chiavennasca (NEBBIOLO) grapes in the Pr. of Sondrio, n. Lombardy. V. Superiore is better.

Velletri Lat. DOC r. w. dr. or s/sw. **
> Agreeable Roman dry red and smooth white. Drink young.

Vendemmia
> Vintage.

Venegazzu' Fr-VG. r. dr. *** 72 74 78
> Little-known rustic Bordeaux-style red produced nr. Treviso.
> Rich bouquet, soft, warm taste, 13.5% alcohol, ages well.

Verdicchio dei Castelli di Jesi Mar. DOC w. dr. (sp.) *** D.Y.A.
> Ancient, famous and very pleasant fresh pale white from
> nr. Ancona. Goes back to the Etruscans. Classico is more
> restricted. Comes in amphora-shaped bottles.

Verdicchio di Matelica Mar. DOC w. dr. (sp.) **
> Similar to the last, though less well known.

Verdiso
> Native white grape of n.e., used for PROSECCO.

Verduzzo (Colli Orientali del Friuli) Fr-VG. DOC w. dr. s/sw.
or sw. **
> Full-bodied white from a native grape. The sweet is called
> Ramandolo.

Verduzzo (Del Piave) Ven. DOC w. dr. **
> Similar to the last but dry.

Vermentino Lig. w. dr. ** D.Y.A.
> The best dry white of the Riviera: good clean seafood wine
> made at Pietra Ligure and San Remo.

Vermentino di Gallura Sard. DOC w. dr. **
> Soft, dry, rather strong white from n. Sardinia.

Vernaccia di Oristano Sard. DOC w. dr. (f.) *** 74 75 76 77 78
> Sardinian speciality, like light sherry, a touch bitter, full-
> bodied and interesting. Superiore with 15.5% alcohol and 3
> yrs. of age.

Vernaccia di San Gimignano Tosc. DOC w. dr. (f.) ** 75 77 78 79
> Distinctive strong high-flavoured wine from nr. Siena.
> Michelangelo's favourite.

Vernaccia di Serrapetrona Mar. DOC r. dr. s/sw. sw. sp. **
> Comes from the Pr. of Macerata; aromatic bouquet,
> pleasantly bitter after-taste.

Vignamaggio
> Historic and beautiful CHIANTI CLASSICO estate controlled by
> ANTINORI.

Villa Terciona
> Important CHIANTI CLASSICO estate.

Vino da arrosto
> "Wine for roast meat", i.e. good dry red.

Vino da pasto
> Table wine: i.e. nothing special.

Vino Nobile di Montepulciano Tusc. DOC r. dr. *** 67 70 73 75 78
> Impressive traditional Tuscan red with bouquet and style.
> Aged for 3 yrs. Riserva; for 4 yrs. Riserva Speciale.

Vinsanto
> Term for certain strong sweet wines esp. in Tuscany: usually
> PASSITI.

Vinsanto di Gambellara Ven. DOC w. sw. **
> Powerful, velvety, golden: made near Vicenza and Verona.

Vinsanto Toscano Tusc. w. s/sw. **
> Made in the Pr. of Siena. Aromatic bouquet, rich and smooth.
> Aged in very small barrels known as Carratelli.

VQPRD
> Often found on the labels of DOC wines to signify "Vini di
> Qualita Prodotti in Regioni Delimitate", or quality wines
> from restricted areas in accordance with E.E.C. regulations.

Zagarolo Lat. DOC w. dr. or s/sw. **
> Neighbour of FRASCATI, similar wine.

Spain & Portugal

Abbreviations of regional names shown in bold type are used in the text.

The following additional abbreviations are used in the Spanish section (see p. 104):

R'a.A. Rioja Alta
R'a.Al. Rioja Alavesa
Res. Reserva
g. see Vino generoso

The very finest wines of Spain and Portugal are respectively sherry and port and madeira, which have a section to themselves on pages 150 to 154.

Spain's table wines divide naturally into those from the Mediterranean climate of the centre, south and east and those from the Atlantic climate of the north and west. The former are strong and with rare exceptions dull. The latter include the very good wines of Rioja, certainly, with the Penedès in Catalonia, the most important quality table-wine region of the peninsula.

Rainy north-west Spain and northern Portugal make their very similar "green" wines. Central Portugal has an excellent climate for wines like full-bodied Bordeaux.

The Portuguese system of controlled appellation is old and unrealistic today: it includes areas of dwindling interest and excludes several good new areas. The Spanish system is new (since 1971) and for the moment over-optimistic, delimiting some areas of purely local interest.

The listing here includes the best and most interesting types and regions of each country, whether legally delimited or not. Geographical references (see map) are to the traditional division of Spain into the old kingdoms, and the major provinces of Portugal.

Spain

Alavesas, Bodegas R'a. Al. r. (w. dr.) res. ★★→★★★ 68 70 73
The pale orange-red Solar de Samaniego is one of the most delicate of the soft, fast-maturing Alavesa wines.

Albariño del Palacio Gal. w. dr. ★★
Flowery "green wine" from FEFIÑANES near Cambados, made with the Albariño grape, the best of the region.

Alella Cat. r. (p.) w. dr. or sw. ★★
Small demarcated region just n. of Barcelona. Makes pleasantly fresh and fruity wines in limited amounts. (See Marfil.)

Alicante Lev. r. (w.) ★
Demarcated region. Its wines tend to be "earthy", high in alcohol and heavy.

Almansa Lev. r. ★
Demarcated region w. of ALICANTE, producing heavy wines high in alcohol.

Aloque N. Cas. r. ★
A light (though not in alcohol) variety of VALDEPEÑAS, made by fermenting together red and white grapes.

Almendralejo Ext. r. w. ★
Commercial wine centre of the Extremadura. Much of its produce is distilled to make the spirit for fortifying sherry.

Ampurdán
See Perelada.

Año
4° Año (or Años) means 4 years old when bottled.

Benicarló Lev. r. ★
Town on the Mediterranean. Its strong red wines were formerly used for adding colour and body to Bordeaux.

Berberana, Bodegas R'a.A. r. (w. dr.) res. ★→★★★ 66 70 72 74
Best are the fruity, full-bodied reds: the 3° año Carta de Plata, the 5° año Carta de Oro and the smooth velvety reservas.

Bilbainas, Bodegas R'a.A. r. (p.) w. dr. sw. or sp. res. ★★ →★★★ 66 69 70 71 72
Large bodega in HARO, making a wide range of reliable wines, including Viña Pomal, Viña Zaco, Vendimia Especial Reserves and "Royal Carlton" by the champagne method.

Blanco
White.

Bodega
1. a wineshop; 2. a concern occupied in the making, blending and/or shipping of wine.

Campanas, Las Nav. r. (w.) ★★
Small wine area near Pamplona. Clarete Campanas is a sturdy red. Mature 5° año Castillo de Tiebas is like a heavy RIOJA Reserva.

Campo Viejo, Bodegas R'a.A. r. (w. dr.) res. ★→★★★ 61 63 64 66 70 71 78
Branch of Savin s.a., one of Spain's largest wine companies. Makes the popular 2° año San Asensio and some big, fruity red reservas.

Cañamero Ext. w. ★
Remote village near Guadalupe whose wines grow FLOR and acquire a sherry-like taste.

Caralt, Cavas Conde de Cat. sp. ★★
Sparkling wines from SAN SADURNÍ DE NOYA, made by the champagne method.

Cariñena Ara. r. (p.w.) ★
Demarcated region and large-scale supplier of strong wine for everyday drinking.

Castillo Ygay
See Marques de Murrieta.

Cava

> 1. an establishment making sparkling wines by the champagne method; 2. a Spanish name for such wines.

Cenicero

> Wine township in the RIOJA ALTA.

Cepa

> Wine or grape variety.

Chacolí Gui. (r.) w. *

> Alarmingly sharp "GREEN WINE" from the Basque coast, containing only 8% to 9% alcohol.

Champaña

> "Champagne": i.e. Spanish sparkling wine.

Cheste Lev. r. w. *

> Demarcated region inland of VALENCIA. Blackstrap wines with 13% to 15% alcohol.

Clarete

> Light red wine (occasionally dark rosé).

Codorníu, S.A. Cat. sp. ★★★

> Best known of the firms in SAN SADURNI DE NOYA making good sparkling wines by the champagne method. Ask for the *bruto* (extra dry).

Compañía Vinícola del Norte de España (C.V.N.E.) R'a.A. r. (p.)
w. dr. or sw. res. ★★→★★★ 66 70 73 74 75

> The 3° año is among the best of young red Riojas and Monopol one of the best dry whites. Excellent red Imperial and Viña Real reservas.

Consejo Regulador

> Official organization for the defence, control and promotion of a DENOMINACIÓN DE ORIGEN.

Cosecha

> Crop or vintage.

Criado y embotellado por . . .

> Grown and bottled by . . .

Cumbrero

> See Montecillo, Bodegas.

Domecq Domain R'a.A. r. ★★ 73

> A reliable red Rioja made by Pedro Domecq in their new bodega near Laguardia.

Denominación de origen

> Officially regulated wine region. (See introduction p. 4.)

Dulce Sweet.

Elaborado y añejado por . . .

> Made and aged by . . .

Elciego

> Village in the Rioja Alavesa surrounded by vineyards.

Espumoso

> Sparkling.

Fefiñanes Palacio Gal. w. res. ★★★

> Best of all the ALBARIÑO wines, though hardly "green", since it is aged for 2–6 years.

Ferrer, José L. Mallorca r. res. *

> His wines, made in Binisalem, are the only ones of any distinction from Mallorca.

Flor

> A wine yeast peculiar to sherry and certain other wines that oxidize slowly and tastily under its influence.

Franco-Españolas, Bodegas R'a.A. r. w. dr. or sw. res. *→★★ 64 73

> Reliable wines from LOGROÑO. The sweet white Diamante is a favourite in Spain.

Freixenet, S.A., Cavas Cat. sp. ★★→★★★

> Cava, next in size to CODORNIU, making a range of good sparkling wines by the champagne method.

Fuenmayor

Wine township in the RIOJA ALTA.

Gaseoso

A cheap sparkler made by pumping carbon dioxide into wine.

Gonzalez y Dubosc, S.A. Cavas   Cat. sp. ★★→★★★

Cavas making pleasant sparkling wines by the champagne method.

Gran Vas

Pressurized tanks (*cuvés closes*) for making inexpensive sparkling wines; also used to describe this type of wine.

Green Wines

See under Portugal, p. 107.

Haro

The wine centre of the RIOJA ALTA.

Huelva   And. r. w. br. ★→★★

Demarcated region w. of Cadiz. The best of its wine is not on sale, since it goes to JEREZ for blending.

Jerez de la Frontera

The city of sherry. (See p. 152.)

Jumilla   Lev. r. ★

Demarcated region in the mountains north of MURCIA. Its full-bodied wines may approach 18% alcohol.

Laguardia

Picturesque walled town at the centre of the wine-growing district of LA RIOJA ALAVESA.

Lan, Bodegas   R'a.A. r. (p.w.) ★★→★★★ 70 73

A huge new bodega, lavishly equipped and making red Riojas of quality.

La Rioja Alta, Bodegas   R'a.A. r. (p.) w. dr. (or sw.) res. ★★→★★★ 64 70 73 76

Excellent wines, esp. the red 3° año Viña Alberdi, the velvety 5° año Ardanza, the lighter 6° año Arana, the fruity Reserva 904 and dry white Metropol Extra.

León   O.Cas. r. p. w. ★→★★

Its wines, particularly those from the unfortunately named V.I.L.E. (Planta de Elaboración y Embotellado de Vinos) are light, bone-dry and refreshing.

Logroño

Principal town of the RIOJA region.

López de Heredia, S.A.   R'a.A. r. (p.) w. dr. or sw. res. ★★→ ★★★ 68 70 73 76 78

Old established bodega in HARO with typical and good dry red Viña Tondonia of 6° año or more. Its wines are exceptionally long-lasting, and the Tondonia whites are also impressive, like old-fashioned Graves.

Malaga   And. br. sw. ★★→★★

Demarcated region around the city of Malaga. At their best, its dessert wines yield nothing to tawny port.

Mallorca

No wine of interest except from José FERRER.

Mancha/Manchuela   N.Cas. r. w. ★

Large demarcated region n. and n.e. of VALDEPEÑAS, but wines without the light and fresh flavour of the latter.

Marqués de Caceres, Bodegas   R'a.A. r. w. dr. ★★→★★★ 70 71 73 78

Good red Riojas of various ages made by French methods and also a surprisingly light and fragrant white.

Marqués de Monistrol, Bodegas   Cat. w. r. (dr. or sw.) sp. res. ★★→★★★

A family firm, just taken over by Martini and Rossi. Refreshing whites, esp. the Vin nature, a good red and an odd sweet red wine.

Marqués de Murrieta, S.A. R'a.A. r. w. dr. res. ★★→ ★★★ 64 68
70 74 78

> Highly reputed bodega near LOGROÑO. Makes 4° año Etiqueta
> Blanca, superb red Castillo Ygay and a dry fruity white.

Marqués de Riscal, S.A. R'a.Al. r. (p. and w. dr.) res. ★→★★★ 73 76
78

> The best-known bodega of the RIOJA ALAVESA. Its red wines
> are relatively light and dry. Recently disappointing.

Masía Bach · Cat. r. p. w. dr. or sw. ★★ →★★★ 70 74 78

> Extrísimo Bach from SAN SADURNÍ DE NOYA, luscious and
> oaky, is one of the best sweet white wines of Spain.

Marfíl Cat. r. (p.) w. ★★

> Brand name of Alella Vinicola (Bodegas Cooperativas), best
> known of the producers in ALELLA. Means "ivory".

Méntrida N.Cas. r. w. ★

> Demarcated region w. of Madrid, supplying everyday wine to
> the capital.

Monopole

> See Compania Vinicola del Norte de España.

Montánchez Ext. r. g. ★

> Village near Mérida, interesting because its red wines grow
> FLOR yeast like FINO sherry.

Montecillo, Bodegas R'a.A. r. w. (p.) ★★ 75 76

> Rioja bodega owned by Osborne (see Sherry), best known for
> its red and dry white Cumbrero, most reasonably priced and
> currently among the best of the 3° año wines.

Monterrey Gal. r. ★

> Demarcated region near the n. border of Portugal, making
> wines like those of VERIN.

Montilla-Moriles And. g. ★★★

> Demarcated region near Cordoba. Its crisp, sherry-like FINO
> and AMONTILLADO contain 14% to 17.5% natural alcohol and
> remain unfortified and singularly toothsome.

Muga, Bodegas R'a.A. r. (w.) res. ★★★ 70 73

> Small family firm in HARO, making some of the best red Rioja
> now available by strictly traditional methods in oak. Its wines
> are fruity, intensely aromatic, with long complex finish.

Navarra Nav. r. (w.) ★→★★

> Demarcated region, rather better than sturdy wine for everyday drinking.

Olarra, Bodegas R'a.A. r. (w. p.) ★★→★★★ 70 73 75

> A new and vast bodega near LOGROÑO, one of the show-pieces
> of the RIOJA, making good red and white wines and excellent
> Cerro Año reserves.

Paternina, S.A., Bodegas R'a.A. r. (p.) w. dr. or sw. res. ★→★★★★ 28
59 67 71 73 76 78

> Bodega at Ollauri and a household name. Its best wines are
> the red Viña Vial and the magnificent older reservas.

Pazo Gal. r. p. w. dr. ★

> Brand name of the co-operative at RIBEIRO, making "GREEN
> WINES". The rasping red is the local favourite. The pleasant
> fizzy white is safer.

Peñafiel O.Cas. r. and w. dr. ★★

> Sturdy red wine and well-made white, "Peñascal", from the
> village of the same name on the R. Duero near Valladolid.

Penedès Cat. r. w. dr. sp. ★→★★★

> Demarcated region including Vilafranca del Penedès, SAN
> SADURNÍ DE NOYA and SITGES. See also Torres.

Perelada Cat. (r. p.) w. sp. ★★

> In the demarcated region of AMPURDAN on the Costa Brava.
> Best known for sparkling wines made both by the champagne
> and tank or *cuve close* system.

Priorato Cat. br. dr. r. ★★

Demarcated region, an enclave in that of TARRAGONA, known for its alcoholic "rancio" wines and also for strong dark full-bodied reds, often used for blending. Lighter blended Priorato is a good carafe wine in Barcelona restaurants.

Reserva

Good-quality wine matured for long periods in cask.

Ribeiro Gal. r. (p.) w. dr. ★→★★

Demarcated region on the n. border of Portugal—the heart of the "GREEN WINE" country.

Rioja O.Cas. r. p. w. sp. esp. **64 66 68 70 73 75** 76 78

This upland region along the R. Ebro in the n. of Spain produces most of the country's best table wines in some 50 BODEGAS DE EXPORTACIÓN. It is sub-divided into:

Rioja Alavesa

North of the R. Ebro, the R'a.Al. produces fine red wines, mostly the lighter CLARETES.

Rioja Alta

South of the R. Ebro and w. of LOGROÑO, the R'a.A. grows fine red and white wines and also makes some rosé.

Rioja Baja

Stretching e. from LOGROÑO, the Rioja Baja makes coarser red wines, high in alcohol and often used for blending.

Riojanas, Bodegas R'a.A. r. (w. p.) res. ★★→★★★ **34 42 56 64 66 68 70 72**

One of the older bodegas, making a good traditional Viña Albina. Its Monte Real reservas are big, mellow wines above average.

Rioja Santiago, S.A. R'a.A. r. (w. dr. or sw. p.) res. ★→★★★

Bodega at HARO with well-known wines. The flavour sometimes suffers from pasteurization, and appropriately, as it now belongs to Pepsi-Cola, it makes the biggest-selling bottled SANGRÍA.

Rosado

Rosé.

Rueda O.Cas. w. ★→★★

Village-name given to the golden FLOR-growing wines with sherry-like taste and up to 17% alcohol, grown w. of Valladolid.

Rumasa

The great Spanish conglomerate, which has absorbed Williams and Humbert, Garvey, Paternina, Franco-Españolas and, in England, Augustus Barnett.

Sangre de Toro

Brand name for a rich-flavoured red wine from TORRES S.A.

Sangría

Cold red wine cup, best made fresh by adding ice, citrus fruit, fizzy lemonade and brandy to red wine.

Sanlúcar de Barrameda

Centre of the Manzanilla district. (See Sherry p. 153.)

San Sadurní de Noya Cat. sp. ★★→★★★

Town s. of Barcelona, hollow with cellars where dozens of firms produce sparkling wine by the champagne method. Standards are high, even if the ultimate finesse is lacking.

Sarría, Senorio de Nav. r. (p. w. dr.) res. ★★→★★★ **70 73** 75 78

The model winery of H. Beaumont y Cia. near Pamplona produces wines up to RIOJA standards.

Scholtz, Hermanos, S.A. And. br. ★→ ★★★

Makers of the best MALAGA, notably Solera Scholtz 1885.

Seco

Dry.

Sitges Cat. w. sw. ★★
> Coastal resort s. of Barcelona noted for sweet dessert wine made from Moscatel and Malvasia grapes.

Tarragona Cat. r. w. dr. or sw. br. ★
> 1. The demarcated region produces little wine of note. 2. The town makes vermouth and exports cheap wine.

Tierra del Vino O.Cas. w. ★→★★
> Area w. of Valladolid including the wine villages of La Nava and RUEDA.

Tinto
> Red.

Toro O.Cas. r. ★→★★
> Town, 150 m. n.w. of Madrid, and its powerful (to 16°) wine. Leading producer Bodegas Mateos. His 3 año is good.

Torres, Bodegas Cat. r. w. dr. or semi-sw. p. res. ★★→★★★★ 70 71 73 74 75
> Distinguished family firm making the best wines of Penedés, esp. the flowery white Viña Sol and Gran Viña Sol, the red Tres Torres and Gran Sangredetoro, the beautiful Gran Coronas reservas, and the red Santa Digna from the Pinot Noir grape.

Utiel-Requeña Lev. r. (w.) ★
> Demarcated region w. of Valencia. The CLARETES from the mountainous hinterland are best.

Valbuena O.Cas. r. ★★★
> Made with the same grapes as VEGA SICILIA but sold as 3° año or 5° año.

Valdeorras Gal. r. w. dr. ★→★★
> Demarcated region e. of Orense. Dry and refreshing wines.

Valdepeñas N.Cas. r. (w.) ★→★★
> Demarcated region near the border of Andalucia. The supplier of most of the carafe wine to Madrid. Its wines, though high in alcohol, are sometimes surprisingly light in flavour.

Valencia Lev. r. w. ★
> Demarcated region producing earthy high-strength wine.

Vega Sicilia O.Cas. r. res. ★★★★ 41 48 53 59 61 64 66 67
> One of the very best Spanish wines, full-bodied, fruity and almost impossible to find. Containing up to 16% alcohol.

Vendimia
> Vintage.

Verín Gal. r. ★
> Town near n. border of Portugal. Its wines are the strongest from Galicia, without a bubble, and up to 14% alcohol.

Vicente, Suso y Pérez, S.A. Ara. r. ★★
> A bodega s. of Sarragossa producing superior Cariñena.

Viña Vineyard.

Vino Blanco
> White wine.

Vino commun/corriente Ordinary wine.
> **clarete** Light red wine.
> **dulce** Sweet wine.
> **espumoso** Sparkling wine.
> **generoso** Apéritif or dessert wine rich in alcohol.
> **rancio** Maderized (brown) white wine.
> **rosado** Rosé wine.
> **seco** Dry wine.
> **tinto** Red wine.
> **verde** See Green wine under Portugal.

Yecla Lev. r. w. ★
> Demarcated region n. of Murcia. Its co-operative-made wines, once heavy-weight champions, have been lightened and improved for export.

Portugal

For Port and Madeira see pages 150 to 154.

Adega
> A cellar or winery.

Aguardente
> The Portuguese word for brandy, made by a multiplicity of firms. Safest to ask for Adega Velha from Aveleda or one from a port concern.

Algarve Alg. r. w. ★
> Lagoa is the wine centre of the holiday area. It is nothing to write home about.

Aliança Caves r. w. dr. sp. res. ★★→★★★
> Large Oporto-based firm, making sparkling wine by the champagne method and a variety of reds and whites, including mature DÃOS.

Amarante
> Sub-region in the VINHOS VERDES area. Rather heavier and stronger wines than those from farther n.

Aveleda Douro w. dr. ★★
> A first-class "GREEN WINE" made on the Aveleda estate of the Guedes family, proprietors of SOGRAPE. Sold dry in Portugal but sweetened for export.

Bagaceira
> A potent spirit made like the Spanish *aguardiente*. One of the best is CEPA VELHA from MONÇÃO.

Bairrada Bei. Lit. r. and sp. ★→★★
> Undemarcated region supplying much of Oporto's (often good) carafe wine. Also makes good-quality sparkling wines by the champagne method.

Barca Velha (Ferreirinha) Trás-os-M. r. res. ★★★★ 57 64 66
> One of Portugal's best wines, made in very limited quantity by the port firm of Ferreira. Fruity and fine with deep bouquet.

Basto
> A sub-region of the VINHOS VERDES area on the R. Tamega, producing more astringent red wine than white.

Borba Alen. r. ★
> Small enclave near Evora, making the only wine of any class from Alentejo (s. of the R. Tagus).

Braga
> Sub-region of the VINHOS VERDES area, good for both red and white.

Buçaco B'a.Al. r. (w.) res. ★★★ 40 45 47 51 53 59 62 63 70
> The speciality of the luxury Buçaco hotel near Coimbra, not seen elsewhere.

Bucelas Est'a. w. dr. ★★★
> Tiny demarcated region just n. of Lisbon. João Camilo Alves Lda. and Caves Velhas make delicate, perfumed wines with 11% to 12% alcohol.

Camarate Est'a. r. ★★
> Reliable CLARETE from FONSECA at Ageitão, s. of Lisbon.

Carcavelos Est'a. br. sw. ★★★
> Minute demarcated region w. of Lisbon. Its excellent sweet wines average 19% alcohol and are drunk cold as an apéritif or with dessert.

Cartaxo Rib. r. w. ★
> Brand name of adequate carafe wine from the Ribatejo n. of Lisbon, popular in the capital.

Casal García Douro w. dr. ★★
> One of the biggest-selling "GREEN WINES" in Portugal, made by SOGRAPE.

Casal Mendes M'o. w. dr. ★★
> The "GREEN WINE" from Caves Aliança.

Casaleiro

Trade mark of Caves Dom Teodosio—João T. Barbosa, who make a variety of reliable wines: DÃO, VINHOS VERDES, etc.

Cepa Velha M'o. (r.) w. dr. ★★★

Brand name of Vinhos de Monção, Lda. Their Alvarinho, from the grape of that name, is one of the best "GREEN WINES".

Clarete

Light red wine.

Colares Est'a. r. ★★★

Small demarcated region on the coast w. of Lisbon. Its classical dark red wines, rich in tannin, are from vines which survived the phylloxera epidemic. Drink the oldest available.

Conde de Santar B'a.A. r. (w. dr.) res. ★★→★★★

The only estate-grown DÃO, later matured and sold by Carvalho, Ribeiro & Ferreira. The reserves are fruity, full-bodied and exceptionally smooth.

Dão B'a.Al. r. w. res. ★→ ★★★

Demarcated region round Viseu on the R. Mondego. Produces some of Portugal's best table wines: solid reds of some subtlety with age; substantial dry whites. All are sold under brand names. 1970 was the best year of the decade.

Douro

The n. river whose valley produces port and more than adequate (though undemarcated) table wines.

Evel Trás-os-M. r. ★→★★

Reliable middle-weight red made near VILA REAL by Real Companhia Vinícola do Norte de Portugal. Ages well in bottle.

Faisca Est'a. p. ★

Big-selling sweet carbonated rosé from J. M. da Fonseca.

Fonseca, J. M. da

See Camarate and Moscatel de Setúbal.

Gaeiras Est'a. r. ★★

Dry, full-bodied and well-balanced red made in the neighbourhood of Óbidos.

Gatão M'o. w. dr. ★★

Reliable "GREEN WINE" from the firm of Borges & Irnão, fragrant but somewhat sweetened.

Grão Vasco B'a.A. r. w. res. ★★→★★★

One of the best brands of DÃO, blended and matured at Viseu by SOGRAPE. Fine red reservas; fresh young white (D.Y.A.).

Green Wine (Vinho verde)

Wine made from barely ripe grapes and undergoing a special secondary fermentation, which leaves it with a slight sparkle. Ready for drinking in the spring after the harvest. It may be white or red.

Lagoa See Algarve.

Lagosta M'o. w. dr. ★★

Well-known "GREEN WINE" from the Real Companhia Vinícola do Norte de Portugal.

Lancers Est'a. p. ★

Sweet carbonated rosé extensively shipped to the USA by J. M. da Fonseca.

Lima

Sub-region in the n. of the VINHOS VERDES area making mainly harsh red wines.

Madeira Island br. dr./sw. ★★→★★★★

Producer of the famous apéritif and dessert wines. See pages 150 to 154.

Mateus Rosé Trás-os-M. p. ★

World's biggest-selling medium-sweet carbonated rosé, made by SOGRAPE at VILA REAL.

Monção
> Sub-region of the VINHOS VERDES area on the R. Minho, producing the best of the "GREEN WINES" from the ALVARINHO grape.

Moscatel de Setúbal Est'a. br. ★★★
> Small demarcated region s. of the R. Tagus, where J. M. da Fonseca make an aromatic dessert muscat, 6 and 25 years old.

Palacio de Brejoeira M'o. (r.) w. dr. ★★★
> Outstanding estate-made "GREEN WINE" from Monção, with astonishing fragrant nose and full, fruity flavour.

Penafiel
> Sub-region in the s. of the VINHOS VERDES area.

Periquita Est'a. r. ★★
> One of Portugal's more robust reds, made by J. M. da Fonseca at Azeitão s. of Lisbon from a grape of that name.

Pinhel B'a.Al. r. ★
> Undemarcated region e. of the DÃO, making similar wine.

Quinta de S. Claudio M'o. w. dr. ★★★
> Estate at Esposende and maker of the best "GREEN WINE" outside MONÇÃO.

Quinta do Corval Trás-os-M. r. ★★
> Estate near Pinhão making good light CLARETES.

Raposeira B'a.Al. sp. ★★
> One of the best-known Portuguese sparkling wines, made by the champagne method at Lamego. Ask for the *bruto* (extra dry).

Serradayres Est'a. r. (w.) res. ★★→★★★
> Blended table wines from Carvalho, Ribeiro & Ferreira, Lda. Sound and very drinkable.

Setúbal
> See Moscatel.

Sogrape
> Sociedad Comercial dos Vinhos de Mesa de Portugal. Largest wine concern in the country, making VINHOS VERDES, DÃO, MATEUS ROSÉ, VILA REAL red, etc.

Terras Altas B'a.Al. r. w. res. ★★
> Good DÃO wines made by J. M. da Fonseca.

Vila Real Trás-os-M. r. ★→ ★★
> Town in the upper DOURO now making some good undemarcated red table wine.

Vinho branco White wine.
> **consumo** Ordinary wine.
> **doce** Sweet wine.
> **espumante** Sparkling wine.
> **garrafeira** A reserve with long bottle age.
> **generoso** Apéritif or dessert wine rich in alcohol.
> **maduro** A normal, mature table wine—as opposed to a VINHO VERDE.
> **rosado** Rosé wine.
> **seco** Dry wine.
> **tinto** Red wine.
> **verde** See under Green Wines.

Vinhos Verdes M'o. and D'o. r. ★ w. dr. ★→★★★
> Demarcated region between R. Douro and n. frontier with Spain, producing "GREEN WINES".

North Africa & Asia

Algeria

The massive v'yds. of Algeria have dwindled in the last ten years from 860,000 acres to under 600,000. Red wines of some quality are made in the coastal hills of Tlemcen, Mascara, Haut-Dahra, Zaccar and Ain-Bessem. Most goes for blending today. The Soviet Union is the biggest buyer.

Israel

Israeli wine, since the industry was re-established by a Rothschild in the 1880s, has been primarily of Kosher interest until recently, when CABERNET, SAUVIGNON BLANC, SEMILLON and GRENACHE of fair quality have been introduced. Carmel is the principal brand.

Lebanon

The small Lebanese wine industry, based on Ksara, has made red wine of real vigour and quality. Château Musar has the character of fine Burgundy.

Morocco

Morocco today makes North Africa's best wine from v'yds. along the Atlantic coast and round Meknes. In ten years the v'yds. have declined from 190,000 to 170,000 acres. Sidi Larbi and Dar Bel Amri are the best reds; Gris de Boulaouane a very dry pale rosé.

Tunisia

Tunisia now has 90,000 acres compared with 120,000 ten years ago. Her speciality is sweet muscat, but reasonable reds come from Carthage, Grombalia and Cap Bon.

Turkey

Most of Turkey's huge v'yds. produce table grapes. But her wines, from Thrace, Anatolia and the Aegean, are remarkably good. Trakya (Thrace) white and Buzbag red are the well-known standards of the State wineries. Doluca and Kavaklidere are private firms of good quality. Villa Doluca red is remarkable: dry, full-bodied, deep-flavoured and vigorous.

USSR

With over 3 million acres of v'yds. the USSR is the world's fourth-biggest wine-producer—but almost entirely for home consumption. The Ukraine (incl. the Crimea) is the biggest v'yd. republic, followed by Moldavia, the Russian Republic and Georgia. The Soviet consumer has a sweet tooth, for both table and dessert wines. Of the latter the best come from the Crimea (esp. Massandra). Moldavia and the Ukraine use the same grapes as Romania, plus Cabernet, Riesling, Pinot Gris, etc. The Russian Republic makes the best Rieslings (esp. Arbau, Beshtau, Anapa) and sweet sparkling Tsimlanskoye "Champanski". Georgia uses mainly traditional grapes (esp. white Tsinandali and red Mukuzani) for good table wines.

Soviet wines are classified as ordinary (unmatured), "named" (matured in cask or vat) or "kollektsionye" (which are matured both in cask and bottle).

Japan

Japan has a small wine industry in Yamanashi Prefecture, w. of Tokyo. Standard wines are mainly blended with imports from Argentina, E. Europe, etc. Premium wines of Semillon, Cabernet and the local white grape, Koshu, are light but can be good, though expensive. Remarkable sweet wines with noble rot have been made in an area with high humidity. The main producers are Suntory, Mercian, Mann's. '77 was a good vintage.

Central & South-east Europe

Langenlois
Wachau
Weinviertel
Vienna

AUSTRIA

Burgenland
Sopron
Somló
Mátraalya

Budapest •

Styria
Balaton
HUNGARY

Lutomer

Ljubljana •
Vilanyi-Pecs

Slovenia
Slavonia • Zagreb

Vojvodina

Croatia

Bosnia-
Herzegovina
JUGOSLAVIA

Dalmatia
Sarajevo •

Montenegro

ALBAN

Corfu

The huge range of wines from the countries covered by this map offers some of the best value for money in the world today. Quality is moderate to high, tending to improve, and reliability on the whole is excellent.

The references are arranged country by country, with all geographical references back to the map on this page.

Labelling in all the countries involved except Greece is based on the German, now international, pattern of place-name plus grape-variety. The main grape-varieties are therefore included alongside areas and other terms in the alphabetical listings. Quality ratings in this section are given where there is enough information to warrant it.

Austria

Austria is new to the international wine trade—her domestic market has hitherto absorbed her whole crop—and consequently is still undervalued. Most of her practices and terms are similar to the German; the basic difference is a higher alcoholic degree in almost all her wine. New legislation is in force to control names and qualities. The Austrian Wine Quality Seal (Weingutesiegel or WGS), in the form of a red, white and gold disc on the bottle, means the wine has met fixed standards, been officially tested and approved.

Recent vintages:
- **1979** Reduced crop; excellent quality.
- **1978** Average quantity and quality.
- **1977** Average quantity; very good quality.
- **1976** Big; good average quality.
- **1975** Big, high quality, alcoholic. Some wines lacked acid.

Apetlon Burgenland w. s./sw. or sw. ★→ **★★**
> Village of the SEEWINKEL making tasty whites on sandy soil, incl. very good sweet wines.

Ausbruch
> Means "syrupy"; specifically used for very sweet wines between Beerenauslese and Trockenbeerenauslese (see Germany) in richness.

Baden Vienna (r.) w. dr. or sw. ★→★★★★
> Town and area s. of VIENNA incl. GUMPOLDSKIRCHEN. Good lively high-flavoured wines, best from ROTGIPFLER and ZIERFÄNDLER grapes.

Blaufränkisch
> The GAMAY grape.

Bouvier
> Native Austrian grape giving soft but aromatic wine.

Burgenland Burgenland r. w. dr. sw. ★→ **★★★★**
> Region on the Hungarian border with ideal conditions for sweet wines. "Noble rot" occurs regularly and Ausleses are abundant. (See Rust, etc.)

Dürnstein w. dr. sw. ★★→★★★
> Wine centre of the WACHAU with a famous ruined castle and important Winzergenossenschaft (co-op.). Some of Austria's best whites, esp. Rheinriesling and GRÜNER VELTLINER.

Eisenstadt Burgenland (r.) w. dr. or sw. ★★→★★★★
> Town in BURGENLAND and historic seat of the ESTERHAZY family and their splendid cellars.

Esterhazy
> Quasi-royal family whose AUSBRUCH and other BURGENLAND wines are of superlative quality.

Grinzing Vienna w. ★★ D.Y.A.
> Suburb of VIENNA with delicious lively HEURIGE wines.

Grüner Veltliner
> Austria's most characteristic white grape (31% of her white v'yds.) making short-lived but marvellously spicy and flowery, racy and vital wine.

Gumpoldskirchen Vienna (r.) w. dr. or sw. ★★→★★★
> Pretty resort s. of VIENNA with wines of great character.

Heiligenkreuz, Stift
> Cistercian Monastery at THALLERN making some of Austria's best wine, particularly from a fine steep v'yd.: Wiege.

Heurige
> Means both new wine and the tavern where it is drunk.

Kahlenberg Vienna w. ★★ D.Y.A.
> Village and v'yd. hill n. of VIENNA, famous for HEURIGEN.

Kamp Langenlois (r.) w. dr. or sw. ★→★★

Tributary of the Danube (Donau) giving its name to wines from its valley, n. and e. of the WACHAU, incl. pleasant Veltliner (see Grüner Veltliner) and RIESLING.

Klöch Steiermark (r.) p. w. ★→★★

The chief wine town of Styria, the s.e. province. No famous wines, but agreeable ones, esp. Traminer.

Klosterneuburg

Famous monastery, now a wine college and research station with magnificent cellars, just n. of VIENNA.

Krems Danube. w. ★→★★★

Town and district just e. of the WACHAU with good GRÜNER VELTLINER and Rheinriesling (see Riesling).

Langenlois Langenlois r. w. ★→★★

Chief town of the KAMP valley with many modest and some good wines, esp. peppery GRÜNER VELTLINER and Rhein-riesling (see Riesling). Reds less interesting.

Lenz Moser

Austria's best known and most progressive grower, invented a high vine system and makes good to excellent wine at Röhrendorf near KREMS, APETLON, MAILBERG and elsewhere.

Mailberg Weinviertel w. ★★

Town of the WEINVIERTEL known for lively light wine, esp. LENZ MOSER's Malteser.

Morandell, Alois

Big-scale Viennese wine-merchant.

Mörbisch Burgenland r. w. dr. or sw. ★→★★★

Leading wine-village of BURGENLAND. Good sweet wines. Reds and dry whites not inspiring.

Müller-Thurgau

9% of all Austria's white grapes are Müller-Thurgau.

Muskat-Ottonel

The strain of muscat grape grown in e. Europe, incl. Austria.

Niederösterreich

Lower Austria: i.e. all the n.e. corner of the country.

Neuberger

Popular white grape: pleasant wine in KREMS/LANGENLOIS but soft and coarse in BURGENLAND.

Neusiedlersee

Shallow lake in sandy country on the Hungarian border, creating autumn mists and giving character to the sweet wines of BURGENLAND.

Nussdorf Vienna w. ★★

Suburb of VIENNA with well-known HEURIGEN.

Oggau Burgenland (r.) w. sw. ★★→★★★

One of the wine-centres of BURGENLAND, famous for Beerenausleses (see Germany) and AUSBRUCH.

Portugieser

With BLAUFRÄNKISCH, one of the two main red-wine grapes of Austria, giving dark but rather characterless wine.

Retz Weinviertel (r.) w. ★

Leading wine-centre of the WEINVIERTEL, known for pleasant GRÜNER VELTLINER, etc.

Ried

Vineyard: when named it is usually a good one.

Riesling

German Riesling is always called Rheinriesling. "Riesling" is Wälschriesling.

Rotgipfler

Good and high-flavoured grape peculiar to BADEN and GUMPOLDSKIRCHEN. Used with ZIERFÄNDLER to make lively whites. Very heavy/sweet on its own.

Ruländer
The PINOT GRIS grape.

Rust Burgenland (r.) w. dr. or sw. ★→★★★
Most famous wine centre of BURGENLAND, long and justly famous for its AUSBRUCH, often made of mixed grape varieties.

St. Laurent
Traditional Austrian red grape, faintly muscat-flavoured.

Schilcher
Pleasant sharp rosé, speciality of STYRIA.

Schloss Grafenegg
Famous property of the Metternich family near KREMS. Good standard white and excellent Ausleses.

Schluck
Name for the common white wine of the WACHAU, good when drunk very young.

Seewinkel
"Sea corner": the sandy district around the NEUSIEDLERSEE.

Sievering Vienna w. ★★
Suburb of VIENNA with notable HEURIGEN.

Spätrot
Another name for ZIERFÄNDLER.

Spitzenwein
Top wines—as opposed to TISCHWEIN: ordinary table wines.

Steiermark
Province in the s.e., not remarkable for wine but well-supplied with it.

Stift
The word for a monastery. Monasteries have been, and still are, very important in Austria's wine-making, combining tradition and high standards with modern resources.

Styria
English name for STEIERMARK.

Thallern Vienna (r.) w. dr. or sw. ★★ →★★★
Village near GUMPOLDSKIRCHEN and trade-name of wines from Stift HEILIGENKREUZ.

Tischwein
Everyday wine, as opposed to SPITZENWEIN.

Traiskirchen Vienna (r.) w. ★★
Village near GUMPOLDSKIRCHEN with similar wine.

Veltliner
See Grüner Veltliner

Vienna
See Wien

Vöslau Baden r. (w.) ★
Spa town s. of BADEN (and VIENNA) known for its reds made of PORTUGIESER and BLAUFRÄNKISCH: sound and refreshing but no more.

Wachau
District on the n. bank of the Danube round DÜRNSTEIN with cliff-like slopes giving some of Austria's best whites, esp. Rheinriesling (see Riesling) and GRÜNER VELTLINER.

Weinviertel
"The wine quarter": name given to the huge and productive district between VIENNA and the Czech border. Mainly light white wines.

Wien (Vienna)
The capital city, with 1,800 acres of v'yds. in its suburbs to supply its cafés and HEURIGEN.

Zierfändler
White grape of high flavour peculiar to the BADEN area. Used with ROTGIPFLER.

Hungary

Aszu
Word meaning "syrupy" applied to very sweet wines, esp. Tokay (TOKAJI), where the "aszu" is late-picked and "nobly rotten" as in Sauternes. (See p. 41.)

Badacsony Balaton w. dr. sw. `**→***`
1,400 ft. hill on the n. shore of La. BALATON whose basalt soil gives rich high-flavoured wines, among Hungary's best.

Balatonfüred Balaton (r.) w. dr. sw. `**`
Town on the n. shore of La. BALATON e. of BADACSONY. Good but softer, less fiery wines.

Balaton Balaton r. w. dr. sw. `*` `→***`
Hungary's inland sea and Europe's largest lake. Many wines take its name and most are good. The ending "i" (e.g. Balatoni, Egri) is the equivalent of -er in German names, or in Londoner.

Bársonyos-Császár
Wine-district of n. Hungary. MÓR is its best-known centre.

Bikavér
"Bull's Blood"—or words to that effect. The historic name of the best-selling red wine of EGER: full-bodied and well-balanced, improving considerably with age.

Csopak
Village next to BALATONFÜRED, with similar wines.

Debrö Mátraalya w. sw. `***`
Important centre of the MÁTRAALYA famous for its pale, aromatic and sweet HÁRSLEVELÜ.

Eger Mátraalya r. w. dr. sw. `*→` `**`
Best-known MÁTRAALYA wine-centre: fine baroque city of cellars full of BIKAVÉR. Also delicate white LEANYKA and dark sweetish MERLOT, known as MÉDOC NOIR.

Eszencia
The fabulous quintessence of Tokay (TOKAJI): intensely sweet grape-juice of very low, if any, alcoholic strength, reputed to have miraculous properties. Now almost unobtainable.

Ezerjó
The grape grown at MÓR to make one of Hungary's best dry white wines: distinguished, fragrant and fine.

Furmint
The classic grape of Tokay (TOKAJI), with great flavour and fire, also grown for table wine on La. BALATON with excellent results.

Hajós Mecsek r. `*`
Town in s. Hungary becoming known as a centre for good CABERNET SAUVIGNON reds.

Hárslevelü
The "lime-leaved" grape used at DEBRÖ to make good gently sweet wine.

Kadarka
The commonest red grape of Hungary, grown in vast quantities for everyday wine on the plains in the s.; also used at EGER; capable of ample flavour and interesting maturity.

Kékfrankos
Hungarian for GAMAY, literally "blue French". Makes good light red at SOPRON on the Austrian border.

Kéknelyü
High-flavoured white grape making the best and "stiffest" wine of Mt. BADACSONY: fiery and spicy stuff.

Leanyka
East-European white grape better known in Romania but making admirable pale soft wine at EGER.

Mátraalya
Wine-district in the foothills of the Matra range in n. Hungary, incl. DEBRŐ and EGER.

Mecsek
District in s. Hungary known for the good reds of VILÁNY and whites of PÉCS.

Médoc Noir
Hungarian name for MERLOT, used to make sweet red at EGER.

Monimpex
The Hungarian state export monopoly, with great cellars at Budafok, near Budapest.

Mór North Hungary w. dr. ★★★
Town in n. Hungary famous for its fresh dry EZERJÓ.

Muskotály
Hungarian muscat, used to add aroma to Tokay (TOKAJI) and occasionally alone at EGER, where its wine is long-lived and worth tasting.

Nágyburgundi
Literally "black burgundy"—the PINOT NOIR makes admirable wine in s. Hungary, esp. round VILÁNY.

Olasz Riesling
The Hungarian name for the Italian, or Wälschriesling.

Pécs Mecsek (r.) w. dr. ★★
Town in the Mecsek hills known in the West for its agreeable well-balanced (if rather sweet) Riesling.

Puttonyos
The measure of sweetness in Tokay (TOKAJI). A 7-gal. container from which ASZU is added to SZAMORODNI. One "putt" makes it sweetish; 5 (the maximum) very sweet indeed.

Siller
Pale red or rosé. Usually made from KADARKA grapes.

Somló North Hungary w. dr. ★★★
Isolated small v'yd. district n. of BALATON making intense white wines of high repute from FURMINT and RIESLING.

Sopron Burgenland r. ★★
Little Hungarian enclave in Burgenland s. of the Neusiedlersee (see Austria) specializing in KÉKFRANKOS (Gamay) red.

Szamorodni
Word meaning "as it comes": i.e. fully fermented (therefore dry) wine from all the grapes not specially selected. Used to describe the unsweetened form of Tokay (TOKAJI).

Szürkebarát
Literally means "grey friar": Hungarian for PINOT GRIS, which makes rich heavy wine in the BALATON v'yds.

Szekszárdi Vörös Mecsek r. ★★
The red (KADARKA) wine of Szekszárd in south-central Hungary. Dark strong wine which needs age.

Tokaji (Tokay) Tokaji w. dr. sw. ★★ →★★★★
Hungary's famous strong sweet wine, comparable to an oxidized Sauternes, from hills on the Russian border in the n.e. See Aszu, Eszencia, Furmint, Puttonyos, Szamorodni.

Tramini
The TRAMINER grape; little grown in Hungary.

Vilány Mecsek r. p. (w.) ★★
Southernmost city of Hungary and well-known centre of red wine production. Vilányi Burgundi is largely PINOT NOIR—and very good.

Wälschriesling
Austrian name sometimes used for Olasz (Italian) Riesling.

Zöldszilváni
"Green Sylvaner"—i.e. Sylvaner. Grown round La. BALATON.

Romania

Alba Iulia

Town in the TIRNAVE area in Transylvania, known for off-dry whites blended from Italian Riesling, FETEASCA and MUSKAT-OTTONEL.

Aligoté

The junior white burgundy grape makes pleasantly fresh white wine in Romania.

Babeasca

Traditional red grape of the FOCSANI area: agreeably sharp wine tasting slightly of cloves.

Banat

The plain on the border with Serbia. Workaday Riesling and light red CADARCA.

Cabernet

Increasingly grown in Romania, particularly at DEALUL MARE, to make dark intense wines often too sweet for French-trained palates.

Cadarca

Romanian spelling of the Hungarian Kadarka.

Chardonnay

The great white burgundy grape is used at MURFATLAR to make honey-sweet dessert wine.

Cotesti

Part of the FOCSANI area making reds of PINOT NOIR, MERLOT, etc., and dry whites said to resemble Alsace wines.

Cotnari

Romania's most famous historical wine: light dessert wine from MOLDAVIA. Like very delicate Tokay.

Dealul Mare

Important up-to-date v'yd. area in the s.e. Carpathian foot-hills. Red wines from CABERNET, MERLOT, PINOT NOIR, etc.

Dobruja

Black Sea region round the port of Constanta. MURFATLAR is the main v'yd. area.

Dragasani

Region on the R. Olt s. of the Carpathians, growing both traditional and "modern" grapes. Good MUSKAT-OTTONEL.

Feteasca

Romanian white grape of mild character, the same as Hungary's Leanyka (and some say Switzerland's Chasselas).

Focsani

Important eastern wine region including those of COTESTI, ODOBESTI and NICORESTI.

Grasa

A form of the Hungarian Furmint grape grown in Romania and used in, among other wines, COTNARI.

Moldavia

The n.e. province, now largely within the USSR.

Murfatlar

Big modern v'yds. near the Black Sea specializing in sweet wines, incl. very sweet CHARDONNAY.

Muskat-Ottonel

The e. European muscat, at its best in Romania.

Nicoresti

Eastern area of FOCSANI best known for its red BABEASCA.

Odobesti

The central part of FOCSANI; mainly white wines of FETEASCA, RIESLING, etc.

Perla

The speciality of TIRNAVE: a pleasant blended semi-sweet white of RIESLING, FETEASCA and MUSKAT-OTTONEL.

Pitesti

Principal town of the Arges region s. of the Carpathians. Traditionally whites from FETEASCA, TAMIIOASA, RIESLING.

Premiat

Reliable range of mid-quality wines for export.

Riesling

Italian Riesling. Very widely planted. No exceptional wines.

Sadova

Town in the SEGARCEA area exporting a rosé.

Segarcea

Southern wine area near the Danube. Exports rather sweet CABERNET.

Tamiioasa

A traditional white-wine grape variety of no very distinct character.

Tirnave

Important Transylvanian wine region, known for its PERLA and MUSKAT-OTTONEL.

Valea Calugareasca

"The Valley of the Monks", part of the DEALUL MARE v'yd. with a well-known research station. CABERNET, MERLOT and PINOT NOIR are made into heavy sweet wines.

Jugoslavia

Amselfelder

German marketing name for the Red Burgundac (Spätburgunder or PINOT NOIR) wine of KOSOVO.

Banat

North-eastern area, partly in Romania, with up-to-date wineries making adequate RIESLING.

Beli Pinot

The PINOT BLANC, a popular grape in SLOVENIA.

Bijelo

White.

Blatina

The red grape and wine of MOSTAR. Not in the same class as the white ZILAVKA.

Bogdanuşa

Local white grape of the Dalmatian islands, esp. Hvar and Brac. Pleasant fresh faintly fragrant wine.

Burgundac Bijeli

The CHARDONNAY, grown a little in SLAVONIA and VOJVODINA.

Cabernet

See grapes for red wine. Now introduced in many places, so far with pleasant, not outstanding, results.

Crno

Black—i.e. red wine.

Ćvićek

Traditional pale red or dark rosé of SLOVENIA.

Dalmacijavino

Important co-operative based at Split and selling a full range of coastal and island wines.

Dalmatia

The middle coast of Jugoslavia from Rijeka to Dubrovnik. Has a remarkable variety of wines of character.

Dingac

Heavy sweetish red from the local PLAVAC grape, speciality of the mid-Dalmatian coast.

Fruska Gora

Hills in VOJVODINA, on the Danube n.w. of Belgrade, with a growing modern v'yd. and a wide range of wines, incl. good Traminer and Sauvignon Blanc.

Graševina

Slovenian for Italian Riesling (also called Walschriesling, LASKI RIZLING, etc.). The normal Riesling of Jugoslavia.

Grk

Strong almost sherry-like white from the Grk grape. Speciality of the island of Korcula.

Istria

Peninsula in the n. Adriatic, Porec its centre, with a variety of pleasant wines, the MERLOT as good as any.

Jerusalem

Jugoslavia's most famous v'yd., at LJUTOMER.

Kadarka

The major red grape of Hungary, widely grown in SERBIA.

Kosovo

Region in the s., between SERBIA and Macedonia, with modern v'yds. The source of AMSELFELDER.

Laski Rizling

Yet another name for Italian Riesling.

Ljutomer (or Lutomer)-Ormoz

Jugoslavia's best known and probably best wine district, in n.e. SLOVENIA, famous for its RIESLING: full-flavoured, full-strength and at its best rich and satisfying wine.

Malvasia

White grape giving luscious heavy wine, used in w. SLOVENIA.

Marastina

Strong dry white of the Dalmatian islands.

Maribor

Important wine-centre of n. SLOVENIA. White wines incl. SIPON, Ruländer, etc., as well as RIESLING and Austrian BOUVIER (see Austria).

Merlot

The Bordeaux red grape, grown in SLOVENIA and ISTRIA with reasonable results.

Mostar

Islamic-looking little city inland from DALMATIA, making admirable dry white from the ZILAVKA grape. Also BLATINA.

Muskat-Ottonel

The East European muscat, grown in VOJVODINA.

Navip

The big growers' co-operative of SERBIA, with its headquarters at Belgrade.

Opol

Pleasantly light pale red made of PLAVAĆ grapes round Split and Sibenik in DALMATIA.

Plavać Mali

Native red grape of SLOVENIA and DALMATIA: makes DINGAC, POSTUP, OPOL, etc.

Plavina

Light red of the DALMATIAN coast round Zadar.

Plovdina

Native red grape of Macedonia in the s., giving mild wine. Grown and generally blended with PROKUPAC.

Portugizac

Austria's Portugieser: plain red wine.

Posip

Pleasant, not-too-heavy white wine of the Dalmatian islands, notably Korcula.

Postup
> Sweet and heavy DALMATIAN red from the Peljesac peninsula near Korcula. Highly esteemed locally.

Prokupac
> Principal native red grape of s. SERBIA and Macedonia: 85% of the production. Makes good dark rosé (RUZICA) and full-bodied red of character. Some of the best comes from ZUPA. PLOVDINA is often added for smoothness.

Prosek
> The dessert wine of DALMATIA, of stupefying natural strength and variable quality. The best is excellent, but hard to find.

Radgonska Ranina
> Ranina is Austria's BOUVIER grape (see Austria). Radgona is near MARIBOR. The wine is sweet and carries the trade name TIGROVO MLJEKO (Tiger's Milk).

Rajnski Rizling
> The Rhine Riesling, rare in Jugoslavia but grown a little in LJUTOMER-ORMOZ.

Refosco
> Italian grape grown in e. SLOVENIA and ISTRIA under the name TERAN.

Renski Rizling
> Alternative spelling for Rhine Riesling.

Riesling
> Without qualification means Italian Riesling.

Ruzica
> Rosé, usually from PROKUPAC. Darker than most; and better.

Serbia
> The e. state of Jugoslavia, with nearly half the country's v'yds., stretching from VOJVODINA to Macedonia.

Sipon
> Jugoslav name for the FURMINT grape of Hungary, also grown in SLOVENIA.

Slavonia
> Northern Croatia, on the Hungarian border between SLOVENIA and SERBIA. A big producer of standard wines, mainly white.

Slovenia
> The n.w. state, incl. Jugoslavia's most European-style v'yds. and wines: LJUTOMER, etc. Slovenija-vino, the sales organization, is Jugoslavia's biggest.

Teran
> Stout dark red of ISTRIA. See REFOSCO.

Tigrovo Mljeko
> See Radgonska Ranina

Tocai
> The PINOT GRIS, making rather heavy white wine in SLOVENIA.

Traminac
> The TRAMINER. Grown in SLOVENIA and VOJVODINA. Particularly successful in the latter.

Vojvodina
> An autonomous province of n. SERBIA with substantial, growing and improving v'yds. Wide range of grapes, both European and Balkan.

Zilavka
> The white wine of MOSTAR in Hercegovina. One of Jugoslavia's best: dry, pungent and memorably fruity, with a faint flavour of apricots.

Zupa
> Central SERBIAN district giving its name to above-average red and rosé (or dark and light red) of PROKUPAC and PLOVDINA: respectively Zupsko Crno and Zupsko Ruzica.

Bulgaria

Cabernet
> The Bordeaux grape is highly successful in n. Bulgaria. Excellent dark, vigorous, fruity and well-balanced wine.

Chardonnay
> The white burgundy grape is scarcely less successful . Very dry but full and deep-flavoured wine.

Dimiat
> The common native white grape, grown in the e. towards the coast. Agreeable dry white without memorable character.

Euxinograd
> Brand of blended white wine produced for export.

Fetiaska
> The same grape as Romania's Feteasca and Hungary's Leanyka. Rather neutral but pleasant pale wine, best a trifle sweet, sold as Donau Perle.

Gamza
> The common red grape, Hungary's Kadarka: gives fairly light but "stiff" and worthwhile wine.

Hemus
> A pale medium to sweet muscat from KARLOVO.

Iskra
> The national brand of sparkling wine, normally sweet but of fair quality.

Karlovo
> Town in central Bulgaria famous for the "Valley of Roses" and its very pleasant white MISKET.

Mavrud
> Darkly plummy red from s. Bulgaria. Improves with age.

Melnik
> City of the extreme s.e. Such concentrated MAVRUD that the locals say it can be carried in a handkerchief.

Misket
> Bulgaria's muscat: locally popular flavour in sweet whites.

Pamid
> The light, quite soft, everyday red of s. and central Bulgaria.

Rcatzitelli
> One of Russia's favourite white grapes for strong sweet wine. Grown in n.e. Bulgaria.

Riesling
> Normally refers to Italian Riesling, though some Rhine Riesling is grown. In the brand known as Rosenthaler Riesling (for export to Germany) the two are blended.

Saperavi
> Russian red grape, presumably used for export to Russia: the biggest export market.

Sonnenküste
> Brand of medium-sweet white sold in Germany.

Sungurlare
> Eastern town giving its name to a sweet MISKET, similar to that of KARLOVO.

Sylvaner
> Some pleasant dry SYLVANER is exported as "Klosterkeller".

Tamianka
> Sweet white; sweeter than HEMUS.

Tirnovo
> Strong sweet red wine.

Trakia
> "Thrace". Brand name of a good export range.

Vinimpex
> The "State Commercial Enterprise for Export and Import of Wines and Spirits".

Greece

Achaia-Clauss
>The best-known Greek wine-merchant, with cellars at Patras, n. PELOPONNESE.

Attica
>Region round Athens, the chief source of RETSINA.

Cambas, Andrew
>Important Athenian wine-growers and merchants.

Castel Danielis
>One of the best brands of dry red wine, from ACHAIA-CLAUSS.

Corfu
>Adriatic island with wines scarcely worthy of it. Ropa is the traditional red.

Crete
>Island with the name for some of Greece's better wine, esp. MAVRO ROMEIKO.

Demestica
>A reliable standard brand of dry red and white from ACHAIA-CLAUSS.

Hymettus
>Standard brand of red and dry white without resin.

Kokkineli
>The rosé version of RETSINA: like the white. Drink very cold.

Lindos
>Name for the higher quality of RHODES wine, whether from Lindos itself or not. Acceptable; no more.

Malvasia
>The famous grape is said to originate from Monemvasia in the s. PELOPONNESE.

Mavro
>"Black"—the word for dark red wine.

Mavrodaphne
>Literally "black laurel": dark sweet concentrated red; a speciality of the Patras region, n. PELOPONNESE.

Mavro Romeiko
>The best red wine of Crete, reputedly among the best of Greece: dry and full-bodied.

Mavroudi
>The red wine of Delphi and the n. shore of the Gulf of Corinth: dark and plummy.

Naoussa
>Above-average strong dry red from Macedonia in the n.

Nemea
>Town in the e. PELOPONNESE famous for its lion (a victim of Hercules) and its fittingly forceful MAVRO.

Peloponnese
>The s. landmass of mainland Greece, with a third of the whole country's v'yds.

Pendeli
>Reliable brand of dry red from ATTICA, grown and bottled by Andrew CAMBAS.

Retsina
>White wine with pine resin added, tasting of turpentine and oddly appropriate with Greek food. The speciality of ATTICA. Drink it very cold.

Rhodes
>Easternmost Greek island. Its sweet MALVASIAS are its best wines. LINDOS is the brand name for tolerable table wines.

Rombola
>The dry white of Cephalonia; island off the Gulf of Corinth.

Ropa
>See Corfu

Samos

Island off the Turkish coast with a reputation for its sweet pale-golden muscat. The normal commercial quality is nothing much.

Santorin

Island north of Crete, making sweet Vinsanto from sun-dried grapes, and dry white Thira.

Verdea

The dry white of Zakinthos, the island just w. of the PELOPONNESE.

Cyprus

Afames

Village at the foot of Mt. Olympus, giving its name to one of the better red (MAVRON) wines.

Aphrodite

Full-bodied medium-dry white, named after the Greek goddess of love.

Arsinöe

Dry white wine, named after an unfortunate female whom Aphrodite turned to stone.

Bellapais

Rather fizzy medium-sweet white named after the famous abbey near Kyrenia.

Christoforou

Family-directed wine firm at LIMASSOL.

Commandaria

Good-quality brown dessert wine made since ancient times and named after a crusading order of knights. The best is superb, of incredible sweetness. Normal qualities are much used as Communion wine.

Haggipavlu

Well-known wine-merchant at LIMASSOL.

Keo

One of the biggest firms in the wine trade at LIMASSOL.

Kokkineli

Rosé: the name is related to "cochineal".

Limassol

"The Bordeaux of Cyprus". The wine-port in the s.

Mavron

The black grape of Cyprus (and Greece) and its dark wine.

Mosaic

The brand-name of KEO's Cyprus sherries.

Othello

Perhaps the best dry red: solid, satisfying wine.

Pitsilia

Region s. of Mt. Olympus producing the best white and COMMANDARIA wines.

Rosella

Brand of strong medium-sweet rosé.

St Panteleimon

Brand of strong sweet white.

Sherry

Cyprus makes a full range of sherry-style wines, the best (particularly the dry) of very good quality.

SODAP

Major wine firm at LIMASSOL.

Xynisteri

The native white grape of Cyprus.

California

California has been making wine for 150 years, but her modern wine industry has grown from scratch in scarcely more than 25. Today it leads the world in good-quality cheap wines and startles it with a handful of luxury wines of brilliant quality. In the last six years the industry has expanded and altered at a frenzied pace, which is reflected in the entries that follow: nearly 40 of them start "new winery...". Quality ratings must therefore be tentative.

Grape-varieties (combined with brand-names) are the key to California wine. Since grapes in California play many new roles they are separately listed on the next two pages. For recent vintages see p. 125.

The areas referred to in the winery entries (and shown on the map) are listed below.

Vineyard areas

Amador
County in the Sierra foothills e. of Sacramento. Grows fine Zinfandel.

Central Coast
A long sweep of coast with scattered wine activity, from San Francisco Bay s. to Santa Barbara.

Central Coast/Santa Barbara
Some of the newest planting in the state is round the Santa Maria river n. of Santa Barbara, where coastal fog gives particularly cool conditions.

Central Coast/Santa Cruz Mts.
Wineries are scattered round the Santa Cruz Mts. s. of San Francisco Bay, from Saratoga down to the HECKER PASS.

Central Coast/Hecker Pass
Pass through the Santa Cruz Mts. s. of San Francisco Bay with a cluster of small old-style wineries.

Central Coast/Salinas Valley
The main concentration of new planting in the Central Coast: the Salinas Valley runs inland s.e. from Monterey.

Livermore
Valley e. of San Francisco Bay long famous for white wines but now largely built over.

Lodi Town and district at the n. end of the San Joaquin Valley, its hot climate modified by a westerly air-stream.

Mendocino
Northernmost coastal wine country; a varied climate, much of it hotter than Sonoma and Napa farther s.

Napa The Napa Valley, n. of San Francisco Bay, well established as the top-quality wine area.

San Joaquin Valley
The great central valley of California, fertile and hot, the source of most of the jug wines and dessert wines in the State.

Sonoma and Sonoma/Russian River (R-R.)
County n. of San Francisco Bay, between Napa and the sea. Most v'yds. are in the n. round the Russian River. A few, historically important, are in the Valley of the Moon in the s.

Sonoma/Alexander Valley
New quality area in Sonoma county, along the Russian River n. of the Napa Valley.

Temecula (Rancho California)
Very new small area in s. California, 25 miles inland halfway between San Diego and Riverside.

Recent Vintages

The Californian climate is far from being as consistent as its reputation. Although on the whole the grapes ripen regularly, they are subject to severe spring frosts in many areas, sometimes a wet harvest-time, and such occasional calamities as the two-year drought of 1975–7.

Wines from the San Joaquin Valley tend to be most consistent year by year. The vintage date on these, where there is one, is more important for telling the age of the wine than its character.

Vineyards in the Central Coast are mainly so new that no pattern of vintage qualities has yet emerged.

The Napa Valley is the one area where comment can be made on the last ten vintages of the top varietal wines: Cabernet Sauvignon and Chardonnay.

	Chardonnay	Cabernet Sauvignon
1979	Promising.	Early rain. V. difficult
1978	Promising	Promising
1977	Generally excellent.	Scarcely ripe. Few good.
1976	Difficult: variable.	Small crop but splendid.
1975	Good.	Good. Underrated.
1974	Good.	Difficult: but many superb.
1973	Very good.	Big and good.
1972	The best wines of a cool year.	Uneven: rain: many poor wines.
1971	Good balance: long lived.	Average.
1970	Good all round: not great: mature.	Best ever.
1969	Weak.	Good, not great.
1968	Well-balanced: now ageing.	Fine, well balanced, now ageing.
1967	Weak.	Weak.

California: grape varieties

Barbera
Darkly plummy variety from Piemonte (see Italy). Gives full-blooded and astringent wine in cool areas, good but softer wine in hot ones.

Cabernet Sauvignon
The best red-wine grape in California with a wide range of styles from delicately woody to overpoweringly fruity. The classic Napa grape.

Carignane
Common bulk-producing red grape rarely used as a "varietal", but occasionally with some success.

Charbono
Rare red grape of Italian origin and no distinction.

Chardonnay
The best white-wine grape—indeed the best wine-grape—in California. Styles of making vary from merely clean and grapy to rich and complex like the best white burgundies.

Chenin Blanc
A work-horse white grape with a surprising turn of speed when made dry and in limited, concentrated quantities. But usually made soft and sweet.

Emerald Riesling
A Californian original in the German manner. Clean, flowery/fruity and a touch tart.

Flora
California-bred white. Mildly flowery; best made sweet.

French Colombard
High-acid white coming into favour for clean semi-dry wines made more German-style than French.

Fumé Blanc
See Sauvignon Blanc.

Gamay (or Napa Gamay)
The red grape of Beaujolais. Never remarkable in California.

Gamay Beaujolais
Not the red grape of Beaujolais, but a selection of Pinot Noir good for light summer wines.

Gewürztraminer
Generally softer and less aromatically thrilling in California than in France, but at best one of the real successes.

Green Hungarian
A minority interest: rather tasteless white. Can be lively.

Grenache
The most successful grape for rosé in California; generally, alas, made sweet.

Grey Riesling
Not a Riesling. Full-bodied but scarcely notable white.

Grignolino
Highly seasoned grape good for young reds and rosés.

Johannisberg Riesling
Real Rhine Riesling (also known as White Riesling). Often rather strong and bland in California, but at its best (esp. in Auslese-style wines) gloriously complex and satisfying.

Merlot
The St-Emilion grape has a growing acreage in California. Very good heavy reds have been made.

Muscat
Light sweet pale gold muscat is one of California's treats.

Petite Syrah or **Syrah**
The name of the Rhône's and Australia's great red grape has been wrongly applied to a poor one. Generally used in Burgundy blends. But the real one is present in small quantities, and has great promise.

Pinot Blanc

Much in the shade of the better Chardonnay.

Pinot Noir

Has yet to reach consummation in California. Most wine with the name is disappointing; a minute proportion thrilling.

Pinot St George

Only used by one winery—The Christian Brothers—to make a thoroughly agreeable sturdy red.

Riesling

See Johannisberg Riesling. Also Sylvaner.

Ruby Cabernet

A California-bred cross between Carignan and Cabernet Sauvignon with enough of the character of the latter to be interesting. Good in hot conditions.

Sauvignon Blanc

Excellent white grape used either Sancerre style (fresh, aromatic, effervescent) or Graves style (fat, chewable). The former usually called Fumé Blanc.

Semillon

High-flavoured whites from the cooler areas; bland ones from hotter places. The most memorable are sweet.

Zinfandel

California's own red grape, open to many interpretations from light-weight fruity to galumphing. Capable of ageing to great quality.

California wineries

Alexander Valley Vineyards Alexander Valley. Table ★★→★★★

New small winery. CHARDONNAY, JOH. RIESLING esp. good.

Almaden Central Coast. Full range ★→ ★★

Big winery famous for pioneer varietal labelling and pioneer planting in the Central Coast. Now owned by National Distillers. Best regular wines incl. SAUV BL., CABERNET. New Charles le Franc label for top vintage wines.

Ambassador

Brand name of PERELLI-MINETTI.

Assumption Abbey

Brand name of BROOKSIDE.

Barengo Lodi. Table and dessert ★→★

Small firm making wines of character, especially ZINFANDEL and RUBY CABERNET.

Beaulieu Napa. Table and sp. ★★→★★★★

Rightly famous medium-size growers and makers of esp. CABERNET. CHARDONNAY now less good. Top wine: De Latour Private Reserve Cabernet. Now owned by Heublein Corp.

Beringer Napa. Table and dessert ★★ →★★★

Century-old winery recently modernized by Nestlé Co. Increasingly interesting wines incl. Auslese types.

Boeger Amador. Table ★→★★

Small winery in Sierra foothills. Good ZIN.

Brookside S. California. Table and dessert ★→★★

Traditional dessert wine firm also making table varietals from TEMECULA under the Assumption Abbey label.

Bruce, David Central Coast. Table ★★★

Small luxury winery with heavy-weight old-style wines.

Buena Vista Sonoma. Table ★★

Historic pioneer winery with inproving recent record esp. in whites (RIESLING, FUMÉ BLANC). Reds include old-style ZINFANDEL from its reputed original v'yd.

Burgess Cellars Napa. Table ★★★
>   Small hillside winery, originally called Souverain, making good CHARDONNAY, late harvest RIESLING, CABERNET.

B.V. Abbreviation of BEAULIEU VINEYARDS used on their labels.

Cakebread Napa. Table ★★
>   Started 1974. Increasing reputation, esp. for SAUVIGNON BLANC; also CHARDONNAY, CABERNET, ZIN.

Calera Monterey-San Benito. Table ★★
>   New winery with good ZIN and ambitious with PINOT NOIR.

California Growers San Joaquin. Table and dessert ★
>   Known for sherry and brandy, now also varietal table wines, some labelled Setrakian (now the owner).

Callaway S. California. Table ★★
>   Small new winery in new territory at TEMECULA. Early reds are strong, dark, conservative.

Caymus Napa. Table ★★★
>   New small winery at Rutherford with Spätlese-style RIESLING and notable CABERNET.

Carneros Creek Napa. Table ★★★
>   The first winery in the cool Carneros area between Napa and San Francisco Bay. First PINOT NOIR ('77) was sensational. Fine CHARDONNAY (Giles v'yd.) and AMADOR ZIN.

Chalone Central Coast/Salinas. Table ★★★★
>   Unique small hilltop v'yd. Good CABERNET SAUVIGNON and RIESLING.

Chappellet Napa. Table ★★★★
>   Small modern luxury winery and hillside v'yd. Good CABERNET SAUVIGNON and RIESLING, very good dry CHENIN BLANC.

Château Montelena Napa. Table ★★→★★★
>   New small winery making good distinctive RIESLING, CHARDONNAY, ZINFANDEL and CABERNET SAUVIGNON.

Château St Jean Sonoma. Table and sp. ★★★★
>   New small winery specializing in richly flavoured whites from individual v'yds., incl. CHARDONNAY, PINOT BLANC and esp. late harvest RIESLING.

Christian Brothers Napa and San Joaquin. Full range ★★→★★★
>   The biggest Napa winery, run by a religious order, specializing in consistent blends, incl. excellent CABERNET, useful PINOT ST GEORGE, sweet white Ch. La Salle and very good brandy. Also vintage-dated special lots.

Clos du Val Napa. Table ★★★
>   New small French-owned winery making strong rustic ZINFANDEL and fine delicate CABERNET.

Concannon Livermore. Table ★★
>   Substantial winery famous for SAUVIGNON BLANC and SEMILLON, but with reds of similar quality. In new ownership.

Congress Springs Santa Clara/Santa Cruz. Table ★★
>   Tiny new winery above Saratoga. Well-made whites, esp. SAUVIGNON BLANC, SEMILLON.

Conn Creek Napa. Table ★★→★★★
>   Still formative. New winery building on Silverado Trail. 1974 CABERNET was a critical success.

Cresta Blanca Mendocino and San Joaquin. Table and dessert ★★
>   Old name from Livermore revived on the n. coast by new owners, GUILD co-op. Husky ZIN and SYRAH. Mild whites.

Cuvaison Napa. Table ★★→★★★
>   Small winery with expert new direction. Shows promise. Austere CABERNET and CHARDONNAY for long ageing.

Davis Bynum Sonoma. Table ★→★★
>   Established maker of standard varieties, w. of Healdsburg.

Dehlinger Sonoma. Table ★★→★★★
> Small winery and v'yd. w. of Santa Rosa. Promising CHARDON-NAY, CABERNET and ZIN since 1976.

Diamond Creek Napa. Table ★★★
> Small winery since the 60s with CABERNET from hills w. of Calistoga. Growing in reputation.

Domaine Chandon Napa. sp. ★★★
> Californian outpost of Moët & Chandon Champagne. Launched 1976. Early promise is being fulfilled.

Dry Creek Sonoma. Table ★★★
> New small winery with high ideals, making old-fashioned dry wines, esp. whites, incl. CHARDONNAY, CHENIN BLANC and FUMÉ BLANC.

Durney Vineyard Central Coast/Monterey. Table?
> Good CABERNET from Carmel Valley, riper than most in Monterey. Also CHENIN BLANC. Since '76.

East-Side San Joaquin. Table and dessert ★
> Progressive growers' co-operative best known for its Royal Host label. Good RUBY CABERNET, EMERALD RIESLING, ZIN.

Edmeades Mendocino. Table ★★
> Tiny winery in Anderson Valley near Pacific. Known for CABERNET and a French Colombard Ice Wine.

Eleven Cellars
> Brand name of PERELLI-MINETTI.

Estrella River San Luis Obispo/Santa Barbara. Table ★★
> Impressive new winery with 600 acres. CHARDONNAY, RIES-LING, MUSCAT, SYRAH are promising.

Felton-Empire Vineyards Cent. Coast/Santa Cruz Mts. Table ★★.
> The old Hallcrest property recently revived by new owners. Excellent first RIESLING. A label to watch.

Fetzer Mendocino. Table ★★
> Rapidly expanding 12-year-old winery with interesting but inconsistent wines, incl. CABERNET, SAUVIGNON BLANC, ZIN, RIESLING.

Ficklin San Joaquin. Dessert (and table) ★★★
> Family firm making California's best "port" and minute quantities of table wine.

Field Stone Sonoma (Alexander Valley). Table ★★
> Newcomer owned by mechanical harvester manufacturer, pressing grapes in the v'yd. for whites and CABERNET rosé.

Firestone Central Coast/Santa Barbara. Table ★★★
> Ambitious new (1975) winery in a new area n. of Santa Barbara. Cool conditions are producing interesting wines, incl. PINOT NOIR and RIESLING.

Foppiano Sonoma. Table ★★
> Old winery at Healdsburg refurbished with vintage varieties incl. CHENIN BLANC, FUMÉ BLANC, CAB, ZIN, PETITE SYRAH.

Franciscan Vineyard Napa. Table ★★→★★★
> Small-to-medium winery run by an ex-Christian Brother. Good ZINFANDEL, CABERNET, CHARDONNAY and RIESLING.

Franzia San Joaquin. Full range ★
> Large old family winery now owned by Coca Cola Bottling Co. of N.Y. Various labels, but all say "made and bottled in Ripon". Noteworthy Burgundy and ZINFANDEL.

Freemark Abbey Napa. Table ★★★
> Small connoisseur's winery with high reputation for CABER-NET, CHARDONNAY, PINOT NOIR and RIESLING.

Gallo, E. & J. San Joaquin. Full range ★→★★
> The world's biggest winery, pioneer in both quantity and quality. Family owned. Hearty Burgundy and Chablis Blanc set national standards. Varietals incl. GEWÜRZ, RIESLING, CHARDONNAY, CABERNET.

Gemello Santa Clara/Santa Cruz. Full range ★★
Old winery with reputation for reds, esp. PETITE SYRAH, ZIN.

Geyser Peak Sonoma. Table ★★
Old winery recently revived and expanded by Schlitz
Brewery. More steady than inspired.

Giumarra San Joaquin. Table ★
Recent installation. Sound RUBY CABERNET and PETITE SYRAH
from family v'yds. in hottest part of valley.

Grand Cru Sonoma. Table ★★→★★★
New small winery making good GEWÜRZ and increasingly
CABERNET and SAUVIGNON BLANC.

Grgich-Hills Cellars Napa. Table ★★★
New winery. Grgich (formerly of CH. MONTELENA) is wine-
maker, Hills grows the grapes—esp. CHARDONNAY and
RIESLING.

Guild San Joaquin. Table and dessert ★
Big growers' co-operative famous for Vino da Tavola semi-
sweet red and B. Cribari label. New line of varietals with
Winemasters label incl. good ZINFANDEL.

Gundlach-Bundschu Sonoma. Table ★★★
Very old small family winery revived by the new generation.
Excellent CABERNET, MERLOT, ZIN and good whites: CHARDON-
NAY, GEWÜRZ, RIESLING.

Hacienda Sonoma. Table ★★→★★★
New small winery specializing in high-quality CHARDONNAY.

Hanzell Sonoma. Table ★★★
Small winery which revolutionized Californian
CHARDONNAYS in the '50s under its founder, now in
new hands. PINOT NOIR now also good.

Harbor Winery San Joaquin. Table ★★★
Tiny winery using AMADOR and NAPA grapes to make first-
rate ZINFANDEL and CHARDONNAY.

Heitz Napa. Table (and dessert) ★★★★
In many eyes the first name in California. An inspired
individual wine-maker who has set standards for the whole
industry. His CABERNETS (esp. "Martha's Vineyard") are
dark, deep and emphatic, his best CHARDONNAYS peers of
Montrachet.

Hoffmann Mtn. Ranch Cen. Coast San Luis Obispo. Table ★★★
New small winery in new area near Paso Robles.
CHARDONNAY and PINOT NOIR are promising.

Inglenook Napa and San Joaquin. Table and dessert ★ →★★★
One of the great old Napa wineries recently much changed
by new owners: Heublein Corp. Special Cask CABERNET
SAUVIGNON remains best wine. Other varieties sound.
Inglenook Vintage is a second label, Inglenook Navalle a
third and the best value: good cheap RUBY, ZINFANDEL and
FRENCH COLOMBARD.

(Italian Swiss) Colony San Joaquin and Sonoma. Full range ★→★★
Honourable old name from Sonoma transferred to
San Joaquin by new owners: Heublein Corp. Adequate
standards. Lejon is a second label.

Jekel Vineyards Central Coast/Monterey. Table?
Well-made RIESLING and CHARDONNAY. Perhaps technique
better than grapes.

Johnsons of Alexander Valley Sonoma. Table (Probable ★★)
New small winery with good v'yd. land.

Jordan Sonoma. Table ★★★
Extravagant winery specializing in CABERNET. First vintage,
'76, released in 1980, exceptionally elegant at a fair price.

Kenwood Vineyards Sonoma. Table ★★→★★★
Steady small producer of increasingly stylish reds, esp.
CABERNET and ZIN. Also good CHARDONNAY and CHENIN BLANC.

Korbel Sonoma. Sp. and table ★★★

Long-established sparkling wine specialists. "Natural" and "Brut" are among California's best standard "champagnes".

Kornell Napa. Sp. ★★★

Fine sparkling wine house making excellent full-flavoured dry wines: Brut and Sehr Trocken.

Krug, Charles Napa. Table and dessert ★★→★★★

Important old winery with reliable range, incl. good CABERNET SAUVIGNON, CHARDONNAY, sweet CHENIN BLANC and very sweet Moscato di Canelli. C.K. is the jug-wine brand.

Lambert Bridge Sonoma. Table ★★

New small winery nr. Healdsburg has made promising CHARDONNAY; also CABERNET.

Lamont, M. San Joaquin. Table and dessert ★

New name for old Bear Mountain co-op, now owned by Labatt brewery. Well-made varietals, incl. FRENCH COLOMBARD.

Landmark Sonoma. Table ★★

New winery nr. Windsor with sound CHARDONNAY and CABERNET tending to improve.

Lawrence Winery Central Coast/San Luis Obispo. Table?

Ambitious new mid-size winery.

Lejon Brand name of ITALIAN SWISS COLONY.

Long Vineyards Napa. Table?

New small winery in eastern hills nr. CHAPPELLET. Long is husband of SIMI wine-maker Zelma. So far good CHARDONNAY and late-harvest RIESLING.

Los Hermanos

Second label of BERINGER.

Mark West Sonoma Table ★★

New winery in cool sub-region starting well with whites: GEWÜRZ, RIESLING.

Markham Napa. Table ★★?

New winery with 200 acres. Early releases show promise.

Martin Ray Central Coast/S. Cruz Mts. Table ★★★

Eccentric small winery famous for high prices and unpredictable wines, occasionally very good.

Martini, Louis Napa. Table and dessert ★★→ ★★★

Large but individual winery with very high standards, from jug wines (called "Mountain") up. CABERNET SAUVIGNON one of California's best. BARBERA, PINOT NOIR, ZINFANDEL, GEWÜRZ, FOLLE BLANCHE and Moscato Amabile are all fine.

Martini & Prati Sonoma. Table ★★

Important winery selling mainly in bulk to others. Uses the name Fountaingrove for a small quantity of good CABERNET.

Masson, Paul Central Coast. Full range ★→ ★★

Big, lively and reliable middle-quality winery with good-value varietals, incl. Emerald Dry (EM. RIES.) Rubion (RUBY), CHARDONNAY, ZINFANDEL, good cheap sparkling and very good Souzão port-type.

Matanzas Creek Sonoma. Table?

First wines ('79) are GEWÜRZ and very good PINOT BLANC. CHARDONNAY and CABERNET to come.

Mayacamas Napa. Table ★★★★

First-rate very small v'yd. and winery offering CABERNET SAUVIGNON, CHARDONNAY, ZINFANDEL (sometimes).

Mill Creek Sonoma. Table ★★

New winery near Healdsburg with ex-SIMI winemaker Mary Ann Graf. First wines are CHARDONNAY, MERLOT, CABERNET.

Mirassou Central Coast. Full range ★★→★★★

Dynamic mid-sized growers and makers, the fifth generation of the family. Pioneers in SALINAS v'yds. Notable ZINFANDEL, GAMAY BEAUJOLAIS, PETITE SYRAH, GEWÜRZ and sparkling.

Mondavi, Robert Napa. Table ★★★
Ten-year-old winery with a brilliant record of innovation in styles, equipment and technique. Wines of grace and character incl. CABERNET SAUVIGNON, SAUVIGNON BLANC (sold as Fumé Blanc), CHARDONNAY, PINOT NOIR.

Monterey Peninsula Central Coast/Salinas. Table ★★★
Very small new winery near Carmel making chunky chewable ZINFANDEL and CABERNET from SALINAS grapes.

Monterey Vineyard Central Coast/Salinas. Table ★★→★★★
The first big modern winery of SALINAS, opened 1974. Now owned by Coca Cola. Good ZINFANDEL, GEWÜRZ and SYLVANER and fruity feather-weight GAMAY BEAUJOLAIS.

Monteviña Amador. Table ★★
Pioneer small winery in new area: the Shenandoah Valley, Amador County, in the Sierra foothills. ZINFANDEL, BARBERA and SAUVIGNON BLANC.

J. W. Morris North Coast (Oakland). Table and dessert ★★★
Small specialist in high-quality port-types, both vintage and wood-aged. Mainly SONOMA grapes. Good CHARD., CAB. S., ZIN.

Mount Eden Central Coast. Table ★★
New company owning a major share of what were MARTIN RAY Vineyards. Excellent (and expensive) first wines.

Mount Veeder Napa. Table ★★
Ambitious little new winery. High prices but early signs of quality.

Nichelini Napa. Table ★★
Small old-style family winery selling sound varietals at the cellar door.

Novitiate of Los Gatos Central Coast. Dessert and Table ★★
Jesuit-run altar-wine-orientated unrevolutionary winery with some adequate varietals, inadequately distributed.

Papagni, Angelo San Joaquin. Table and sp. ★★→★★★
Grower of an old family with a technically outstanding modern winery at Madera. Dry coastal-style varietals include excellent ZINFANDEL, good Alicante Bouschet, light "Moscato d'Angelo".

Parducci Mendocino. Table ★★
Well-established mid-sized winery with v'yds. in several locations. Good sturdy reds: CABERNET SAUVIGNON, PETITE SYRAH, ZINFANDEL, Burgundy. Also pleasant slightly sweet CHENIN BLANC and FRENCH COLOMBARD.

Pedroncelli Sonoma R-R. Table ★★
Second-generation family business with recent reputation for well-above-average ZINFANDEL, PINOT NOIR and CHARDONNAY in a ripe rural style.

Perelli-Minetti San Joaquin. Table and dessert ★
Big firm with chequered history as California Wine Association, now in family hands. Two principal labels: Ambassador and Guasti.

Phelps, Joseph Napa. Table ★★★→★★★★
New very de luxe small winery and v'yd. Late harvest RIESLING exceptional. Very good CHARDONNAY, CABERNET and ZIN.

Preston Sonoma. Table (Possible ★★★)
Tiny new winery with very high standards in Dry Creek Valley, Healdsburg. So far SAUVIGNON BLANC and CABERNET.

Rafanelli, J. Sonoma. Table ★★
Tiny local cellar specializing in outstanding ZIN; also GAMAY BEAUJOLAIS.

Raymond Vineyards Napa. Table ★★★
New small winery near St. Helena with experienced owners. Early ZIN, CHARDONNAY, CHENIN BLANC and CABERNET all excellent.

Ridge Central Coast S. CRUZ. Table ★★★★
Small winery of high repute among connoisseurs for powerful concentrated reds needing long maturing in bottle. Notable CABERNET and very strong ZINFANDEL.

Robert Keenan Napa. Table (Possible ★★★)
Newcomer with very good first CHARDONNAY and CABERNET. V'yds. on Spring Mountain; wine-maker ex-CHAPPELLET.

Robert Pecota Napa. Table (Probable ★★)
New small cellar of ex-Beringer man with high standards. Wines are FLORA, PETITE SIRAH, SAUVIGNON BLANC.

Roudon-Smith Santa Clara/Santa Cruz. ★★→ ★★★
New small winery. Really stylish CHARDONNAY.

Royal Host
Brand name for EAST-SIDE winery.

Rutherford Hill Napa. Table ★★
Recent larger stable-mate of FREEMARK ABBEY. Good early GEWÜRZ, MERLOT, ZIN. Promising CHARDONNAY and CABERNET.

Rutherford Vintners Napa. Table ★★★
New small winery started in 1977 by Bernard Skoda, former LOUIS MARTINI manager. CABERNET and RIESLING will be specialities; also PINOT NOIR, MERLOT, CHARDONNAY.

St. Clement Napa. Table ★★★
Small production of very good CABERNET and CHARDONNAY. Both need age.

Sandford and Benedict Santa Barbara Table ★★★
New winery whose first CHARDONNAY and PINOT NOIR (1976) caused a stir.

San Martin Central Coast. Table and dessert ★★→ ★★★
Newly restructured old company using SALINAS and SAN LUIS OBISPO grapes to make clean, correct varietals of increasing quality, esp. soft (low-alcohol) RIESLING and ZIN from AMADOR.

San Pascal S. California. Table ★→★★★
New winery near San Diego with pleasant whites, esp. CHENIN BLANC, SAUVIGNON BLANC.

Santa Ynez San Luis Obispo/Santa Barbara. Table ★★
Promising whites, esp. SAUVIGNON BLANC, from new winery.

Schramsberg Napa. Sp. ★★★★
A dedicated specialist using historic old cellars to make California's best "champagne".

Sebastiani Sonoma. Table and dessert ★★
Substantial and distinguished old family firm with robust appetizing wines, esp. BARBERA, GAMAY BEAUJOLAIS, PINOT NOIR. Top wines have SONOMA appellation.

Setrakian
See California Growers.

Simi Alexander Valley. Table ★★★
Restored old winery with expert direction. Several notable wines, incl. racy GEWÜRZ, gentle ZINFANDEL, delicate CABERNET.

Smith-Madrone Napa. Table ★★→★★★
New v'yd. high on Spring Mountain made good RIESLING in '77. '78 CHARDONNAY excellent.

Smothers Santa Clara/Santa Cruz. Table
Tiny winery owned by T.V. comic made remarkable first wines, esp. late-harvest GEWÜRZ. First reds due 1980.

Sonoma Vineyards Sonoma R-R. Table and sp. ★★ →★★★
Quick-growing business, well-regarded for varietals, esp. RIESLING and CHARDONNAY. Range includes single-v'yd. wines, esp. Alexander's Crown CABERNET.

Souverain Alexander Valley. Table ★★
Luxurious new mid-sized winery with highly competent wines, both red and white, if no great ones.

Spring Mountain Napa. Table ★★★
> Recently renovated small 19th-century property with new winery already noted for good CHARDONNAY, SAUVIGNON BLANC and CABERNET.

Stag's Leap Wine Cellars Napa. Table ★★★→★★★★
> New small v'yd. and cellar with high standards. Excellent CABERNET, fresh GAMAY, soft RIESLING, fine CHARDONNAY.

Sterling Napa. Table ★★★
> Spectacular new mid-sized winery, now owned by Coca-Cola, with already startling achievements. Strong, tart SAUVIGNON BLANC and CHARDONNAY; fruity CABERNET and MERLOT.

Stonegate Napa. Table ★★→★★★
> Small privately-owned winery and v'yd. making CHENIN BLANC, SAUVIGNON BLANC, CHARDONNAY, PINOT NOIR.

Stony Hill Napa. Table ★★★★
> Many of California's very best whites have come from this minute winery over 25 years. Alas owner Fred McCrea died in 1977, but his wife Eleanor carries on. Stony Hill CHARDONNAY, GEWÜRZ and RIESLING are all delicate and fine.

Story Vineyard Amador County. Table ★★
> Old vineyard produces very good ZIN grapes, but wine-making is erratic.

Sutter Home Napa. Table ★★
> Small winery revived, specializing in ZINFANDEL from Amador County grapes: excellent heavy-weight.

Swan, J. Sonoma. Table ★★
> New one-man winery with a name for rich ZINFANDEL.

Trefethen Napa. Table ★★★→★★★★
> Small family-owned winery in Napa's finest old wooden building. Good RIESLING, and CABERNET. Brilliant CHARDONNAY.

Trentadue Sonoma R-R. Table ★★
> Small v'yd. and smaller winery making sound big-flavoured wines, incl. some from unorthodox varieties.

Tulocay Napa. Table?
> Tiny new winery at Napa City. First wines are good PINOT NOIR and CABERNET.

Turgeon & Lohr Central Coast. Table ★★
> Small winery in San Jose with its own v'yds. in SALINAS. Reliable PINOT BLANC and CABERNET.

Veedercrest Napa. Table ★★
> Still nascent small winery with promise of talent.

Ventana Central Coast/Monterey. Table?
> New in '78 with flavoury PINOT BLANC and CHARDONNAY.

Villa Armando Livermore/San Joaquin. Table ★
> Specialist in the American-Italian market for coarse sweet table wines.

Villa Mount Eden Napa. ★★★
> Small Oakville estate with excellent dry CHENIN BLANC, good CHARDONNAY, and CABERNET outstanding.

Weibel Central Coast. Table and sp. ★
> Veteran mid-sized winery without high ambitions.

Wente Livermore and Central Coast. Table ★★→★★★
> Important and historic specialists in Bordeaux-style whites. Fourth-generation Wentes are as dynamic as ever. CHARDONNAY, SAUVIGNON BLANC and RIESLING are all standards. PINOT NOIR is also good.

Winemasters
> Brand name of GUILD.

Z-D Wines Napa. Table ★★★
> Very small winery (moved from Sonoma to Rutherford) with a name for powerful PINOT NOIR and CHARDONNAY.

New York

New York State and its neighbours Ohio and Ontario make their own style of wine from grapes of native American ancestry, rather than the European vines of California. American grapes have a flavour known as "foxy"; a taste acquired by many easterners. Fashion is slowly moving in favour of hybrids between these and European grapes with less, or no, foxiness. The entries below include both wineries and grape varieties.

Aurora
One of the best white French-American hybrid grapes, the most widely planted in New York. Formerly known as Seibel 5279. Good for sparkling wine.

Baco Noir
One of the better red French-American hybrid grapes. High acidity but good clean dark wine.

Benmarl
Highly regarded and expanding v'yd. and winery at Marlboro on the Hudson River. Wines are mainly from French-American hybrids, but European vines also make good wine.

Boordy Vineyards
The winery which pioneered French-American hybrid grapes in the USA. Started by Philip Wagner in Maryland in the '50s.

Brights
Canada's biggest winery, in Ontario, now tending towards French-American hybrids and experiments with European vines. Their CHELOIS and BACO NOIR are pleasant reds, respectively lighter and more full-bodied.

Bully Hill
New (since 1970) FINGER LAKES winery using both American and hybrid grapes to make varietal wines.

Château Gai
Canadian (Ontario) winery making European and hybrid wines, incl. successful GAMAY and PINOT NOIR.

Catawba
One of the first American wine-grapes, still the second most widely grown. Pale red and foxy flavoured.

Chautauqua
The biggest grape-growing district in the e., along the s. shore of La. Erie from New York to Ohio.

Chelois
Popular red French-American hybrid grape, formerly called Seibel 10878. Makes dry red wine with some richness, slightly foxy.

Concord
The archetypal American grape, dark red, strongly foxy, making good grape jelly but dreadful wine. By far the most widely planted in New York (23,000 acres).

Delaware
Old American white-wine grape making pleasant, slightly foxy dry wines. Used in "Champagne" and for still wine.

De Chaunac
A good red French-American hybrid grape, popular in Canada as well as New York. Full-bodied dark wine.

Finger Lakes
Century-old wine district in upper New York State, best-known for its "Champagne". The centre is Hammondsport.

Fournier, Charles
The top quality of "Champagne" made by the GOLD SEAL company, named for a former distinguished and pioneering wine-maker.

Frank, Dr. Konstantin
> A controversial figure in the FINGER LAKES: the protagonist of European vinifera vines. See Vinifera Wines.

Gold Seal
> One of New York's biggest wineries, makers of Charles FOURNIER "Champagne" and the HENRI MARCHANT range. Known for high quality and readiness to experiment.

Great Western
> The brand name of the PLEASANT VALLEY WINE CO's "Champagne", one of New York's best wines.

Henri Marchant
> Brand name of GOLD SEAL's standard range of mainly traditional American-grape wines.

Inniskillin
> Small new Canadian winery at Niagara making European and hybrid wines, incl. good MARÉCHAL FOCH.

Isabella
> Old CONCORD-style red grape making strongly foxy wine.

Phylloxera is an insect that lives on the roots of the vine. Its arrival in Europe from North America in the 1860s was an international catastrophe. It destroyed almost every vineyard on the continent before it was discovered that the native American vine is immune to its attacks. The remedy was (and still is) to graft European vines on to American rootstocks. Virtually all Europe's vineyards are so grafted today. Whether their produce is just as good as the wine of pre-phylloxera days is a favourite debate among old-school wine-lovers.

Maréchal Foch
> Promising red French hybrid between PINOT NOIR and GAMAY. Makes good burgundy-style wine in Ontario.

Morre's Diamond
> Old American white grape still grown in New York.

Niagara
> Old American white grape used for sweet wine. Very foxy.

Pleasant Valley Wine Co.
> Winery at Hammondsport, FINGER LAKES, owned by TAYLOR'S, producing GREAT WESTERN wines.

Seibel
> One of the most famous French grape hybridists, responsible for many successful French-American crosses originally known by numbers, since christened with such names as AURORA, DE CHAUNAC, CHELOIS.

Seyve-Villard
> Another well-known French hybridist. His best-known cross, no. 5276, is known as Seyval Blanc.

Taylor's
> The biggest wine-company of the Eastern States, based at Hammondsport in the FINGER LAKES. Brands incl. GREAT WESTERN and LAKE COUNTRY. Most vines are American.

Vinifera Wines
> Small but influential winery of Dr Frank, pioneer in growing European vines, incl. RIESLING, CHARDONNAY and PINOT NOIR, in the FINGER LAKES area. Some excellent wines.

Widmers
> Major FINGER LAKES winery selling native American varietal wines: DELAWARE, NIAGARA, etc.

South America

The flourishing vineyards of Argentina (the world's fifth largest) and Chile are known to the world chiefly as a source of cheap wine of sometimes remarkable quality. Most of it is drunk within South America.

ARGENTINA

The quality vineyards are concentrated in Mendoza province in the Andean foothills at about 2,000 feet. They are all irrigated. San Raphael, 140 miles s. of Mendoza city, is centre of a slightly cooler area. San Juan, to the north, is hotter and specializes in sherry and brandy.

Bianchi, Bodegas

Well-known premium wine producer at San Raphael. "Don Valentin" is a best-seller. "1887" and "particular" are top Cabernets.

Cooperation San Raphael

Enormous cooperative for bulk wines and concentrated grape juice.

Crillon, Bodegas

Brand-new (1972) winery owned by Seagram's, principally for tank-method sparkling wines.

Furlotti, Angel

Big bodega at Maipu, Mendoza. 2,500 acres making its best red wine from a blend of CABERNET, MERLOT and Lambrusco, white from PINOT BLANC and RIESLING.

Giol

The State winery of Maipu province. Mainly bulk wines. Premium range is called "Canciller".

Gonzales Videla, Bodegas

Old-established family firm re-equipped for modern methods. Brands include "Tromel" and "Panquehua".

Goyenechea, Bodegas

Basque family firm making old-style wines.

Greco Hermanos

1,750-acre v'yds. at St. Martin, Mendoza, with Malbec, Lambrusco, BARBERA, SEMILLON, PALOMINO, etc. Range incl. El Greco "selection" and Oro del Rhin (PINOT BLANC).

La Rural, Bodegas

Family-run winery at Coquimbito specializing in Riesling and Traminer whites.

Lopez, Bodegas

Family firm best known for their 10-year-old "Château Montchenot" Cabernet/Malbec red.

Norton, Bodegas

Old firm, originally English, at Perdriol. "Perdriel" is brand-name of 10-year-old premium Cabernet in flask-bottle.

Orfila, José

Long-established bodega at St. Martin, Mendoza. Top export wines are CABERNET and white Extra Dry (PINOT BLANC).

Penaflor

Four bodegas and 3,000 acres in San Juan and Mendoza. Specialities: sherry and dessert wine, also red in cans. Tio Quinto is their popular medium sherry.

Proviar, Bodega

Producers of "champana" (sparkling wine) under contract with MOET ET CHANDON! Premium brand is "Baron B".

Santa Ana, Bodegas

Old-established family firm at Guaymallen. Wide range of wines.

Suter, Bodegas

Swiss-founded firm best-known for "Etiquetta Marron" white and "Juan Suter" reds.

Toso, Pascual
> Old Mendoza winery at San José, making one of Argentina's best reds, Cabernet Toso. Also RIESLING and sparkling wines.

CHILE
> The principal bodegas exporting wine from Chile are:

Canepa, José
> A modern establishment at Valparaiso handling wine from several areas. Very good French-style CABERNET from Lontüé, Talca, 100 miles south; dry SEMILLON, sweet Moscatel. Exports to Switzerland, Mexico, U.K., etc.

Concha y Toro
> The biggest wine firm, with several bodegas and 2,500 acres in the Maipo valley. Remarkable dark and deep CABERNET, MERLOT, Verdot. Good SAUVIGNON BLANC. Wines go to Venezuela, Brazil, etc., Canada and Germany.

Cousiño Macul
> Distinguished estate near Santiago. Very dry "green" SEMILLON and CHARDONNAY. Don Luis light red, Don Matias dark and tannic, tastes of oak and cheese. Colombia is a big market, also Benelux.

Santa Carolina
> A bodega with pleasant widely available dry wines.

San Pedro
> Brand name for Wagner Stein & Co., long established at Lontüé, Talca. Range of good wines sold all over S. America, esp. Bordeaux-like CABERNET.

Santa Rita
> Bodega in the Maipo valley s. of Santiago. Pleasant soft wines including the "120" brand.

Tocornal, José
> Considerable exporter to Venezuela and Canada.

Undurraga
> Famous family business; one of the first to export to the U.S.A. Wines in both old and modern styles: good clean SAUVIGNON BLANC and oaky yellow "Viejo Roble". "Gran Vino Tinto" is one of the best buys in Chile.

England

The English wine industry started again in earnest in the late 1960s after a pause of some 400 years. More than a million bottles a year are now being made; almost all white and generally Germanic in style, many from new German and French grape varieties designed to ripen well in cool weather. In such a young industry results of prize competitions are studied with interest. The annual Gore-Brown Trophy is awarded for the best English wine.

Adgestone nr. Sandown, Isle of Wight. K. C. Barlow
> Prize-winning 9-acre v'yd on chalky hill site. Vines are MÜLLER-THURGAU, Reichensteiner, SEYVAL BLANC. First vintage was 1970. Light, fragrant, dryish wines.

Beaulieu Abbey nr. Lymington, Hampshire. The Hon. Ralph Douglas Scott-Montagu
> 6-acre v'yd, principally of MÜLLER-THURGAU, established in 1960 by the Gore-Brown family on an old monastic site.

Biddenden nr. Tenterden, Kent. R. A. Barnes
> 16-acre mixed v'yd since 1973 making crisp med-dry white of Huxelrebe and MÜLLER-THURGAU; also a rosé with PINOT NOIR. First vintage 1973. Also makes wine for other growers.

Cavendish Manor nr. Sudbury, Suffolk. B. T. Ambrose
10-acre v'yd of MÜLLER-THURGAU planted on a farm. Fruity dry wine has won several awards at home and abroad since 1974.

Chilford Hundred Linton, nr. Cambridge. S. Alper
16 acres of MÜLLER-THURGAU, Schönburger, Huxelrebe, Siegerrebe and Ortega making fairly dry wines since 1974.

Chilsdown nr. Chichester, Sussex. I. R. Paget
10½ acres of MÜLLER-THURGAU, Reichensteiner and SEYVAL BLANC making full dry French-style white since 1974.

Elmham Park nr. East Dereham, Norfolk. R. Don
7½-acre v'yd of a wine-merchant/fruit farmer, planted with MÜLLER-THURGAU, Madeleine-Angevine, etc. "Mosel-style" light dry flowery wines. First vintage 1974. "Jubilee Cask" is '76/'77 blend.

Felstar Felsted, nr. Dunmow, Essex J. G. Barrett
Well-established 10½-acre v'yd of many varieties, selling Madeleine Sylvaner, MÜLLER-THURGAU, SEYVAL BLANC/ CHARDONNAY, MUSCAT, a PINOT NOIR red and an occasional Auslese.

Hambledon nr. Petersfield, Hampshire. Maj. Gen. Sir Guy Salisbury Jones
The first modern English v'yd., planted in 1954 on a chalk slope with advice from Champagne. Grapes are SEYVAL BLANC and Pinot Meunier. Now 5½ acres. Fairly dry wines.

Hascombe Godalming, Surrey. Lt. Cdr. T. P. Baillie-Grohman
5¾-acre v'yd., principally MÜLLER-THURGAU, making dry delicate wines since 1971.

Kelsale nr. Saxmundham, Suffolk. S. T. Edgerley
2¼-acre v'yd. owned by a retired barrister, making stylish wines. Winner of 1977 Gore-Brown Trophy with a Madeleine Angevine.

Lamberhurst Priory nr. Tunbridge Wells, Kent. K. McAlpine
England's biggest v'yd. with 35 acres, planted 1972. Largely MÜLLER-THURGAU, SEYVAL BLANC, also Reichensteiner, Schönburger, Gutedel, RIESLING and PINOT NOIR. Production capacity up to half a million bottles a year including wine-making for other small v'yds.

Merrydown Wine Co. Heathfield, E. Sussex. J. L. Ward
A major influence on English wine-making, having started in 1946 with cider and since 1969 acted as a co-operative for the young wine industry. Now making an estate MÜLLER-THURGAU, "Horam Manor" (2 acres).

New Hall nr. Maldon, Essex. S. W. Greenwood
22 acres of a mixed farm making award-winning whites, chiefly of the fragrant Huxelrebe. Experimental reds.

Pilton Manor nr. Shepton Mallet, Somerset. N. de m. Godden
4½-acre hillside v'yd., chiefly of MÜLLER-THURGAU and SEYVAL BLANC, planted 1966. Twice winner of Gore-Brown Trophy. Also a méthode champenoise sparkling wine.

Pulham nr. Norwich, Norfolk. P. W. Cook
New 6-acre v'yd. (since 1976); principally MÜLLER-THURGAU and experimental Bacchus.

Rock Lodge nr. Haywards Heath, Sussex. N. C. Cowderoy
2½-acre v'yd. of MÜLLER-THURGAU and Reichensteiner making very dry white since 1970.

St. Etheldreda nr. Ely, Cambridge. N. Sneesby
2½-acre mixed v'yd. making a MÜLLER-THURGAU and a CHARDONNAY since 1974.

Wootton nr. Wells, Somerset. Major C. L. B. Gillespie
6-acre v'yd. of Schönburger, MÜLLER-THURGAU, SEYVAL BLANC, etc., making award-winning fresh and fruity wines since 1973.

Australia

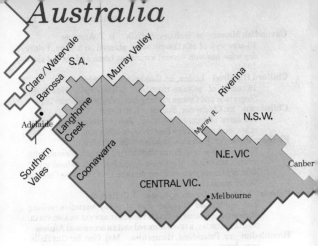

It is only 20 years since modern wine technology revolutionized Australia's 150-year-old wine industry, ending the dominance of fortified wines and making table wines of top quality possible. Already the results are as impressive as California's. The Australians know it: little is left for export.

Traditional-style Australian wines were thick-set and burly Shiraz reds or Semillon or Riesling whites. The modern taste is for lighter wines, especially Rhine Rieslings, and for Cabernet reds, but the best still have great character and the ability to age splendidly.

Australia's wine labels are among the world's most communicative. Since Australians started to take their own wine seriously they have become longer and longer winded, with information about grapes, soil, sunshine, fermenting periods and temperatures, wine-makers' biographies and serving hints. Little of this is pure salesmanship. It is intended to be, and really is, helpful. Bin-numbers mean something. They need to be noted and remembered. Prizes in shows (which are highly competitive) mean a great deal. In a country without any sort of established grades of quality the buyer needs all the help he can get.

Wine areas

The vintages mentioned here are those rated as good or excellent for the reds of the areas in question in an authoritative chart published by the Rothbury Estate Society.

Adelaide 66 67 70 71 72 73 75 76 77 79
> The capital of South Australia had the state's first v'yds. A few are still making wine.

Barossa 66 68 72 73 75 76 77 79
> Australia's biggest quality area, of German origin, specializing in white (esp. Riesling; best from the Eden Valley at 1,500 feet), good-quality reds and good dessert wines.

Clare-Watervale 66 68 70 71 72 75 76 77 78 79
> Small cool-climate area 90 miles n. of Adelaide best known for Riesling; also planted with Shiraz and Cabernet.

Central Victoria 66 68 71 73 74 76 79

Scattered v'yds. remaining from vast pre-phylloxera plantings include GT. WESTERN, CH. TAHBILK, AVOCA and BENDEGO.

Coonawarra 66 68 70 71 72 73 74 75 76 77 79

Southernmost v'yd. of South Australia, long famous for well-balanced reds, recently successful with Riesling.

Hunter Valley 66 67 70 72 73 74 75 76 77 79

The great name in N.S.W. Broad deep Shiraz reds and Semillon whites with a style of their own. Now also Cabernet and Chardonnay. Recent expansion at Wybong, etc., to the w.

Keppoch/Padthaway

Large new area in southern S. Australia being developed by big companies as an overspill of Coonawarra. Cool climate and good potential for commercial reds and whites.

Langhorne Creek

See Southern Vales.

Lilydale/Yarra Valley

Historic wine area near Melbourne destroyed by phylloxera, now being redeveloped by enthusiasts with small wineries. A bewildering range of varieties and styles.

N.E. Victoria 66 70 71 72 73 75 76

Historic area incl. Rutherglen, Corowa, Wangaratta. Heavy reds and magnificent sweet dessert wines.

Margaret River/Busselton

New area of great promise for fine wines, s. of Perth in W. Australia.

McLaren Vale and S. Adelaide

See Southern Vales

Mudgee

Small traditional wine area in a N.S.W. fruit-growing district. Big reds of great colour and flavour and full coarse whites.

Murray Valley N.V.

Important scattered v'yds. irrigated from the Murray river, incl. Swan Hill, Mildura, Renmark, Berri, Loxton, Waikerie. Largely sherry, brandy, "jug" and dessert wines.

Riverina N.V.

Fruit- and vine-growing district irrigated from the Murrumbidgee river. Mainly jug wines, but good light "varietals".

Southern Vales 66 67 70 71 72 73 75 76 77 79

General name for several small pockets of wine-growing s. of Adelaide of which McLaren Vale is the most important. Big full-blooded reds and rather coarse whites.

Swan Valley

The main v'yd. of Western Australia, on the n. outskirts of Perth. Hot climate makes strong low-acid wines.

Upper Hunter

New region 60 miles N.W. of Hunter Valley, N.S.W. with more extreme climate, specializing in white wines, lighter and quicker-developing than Hunter whites.

Wineries

All Saints N.E. Vic. Full range ★→★★

Big old family-run winery in dessert-wine country. Sturdy reds. Sweet brown MUSCAT is sometimes exceptional.

Angove's S.A. Table and dessert ★→★★

Family business in Adelaide and Renmark in the Murray Valley. Sound traditional wines.

Arrowfield N.S.W. Table ★

The largest Upper Hunter vineyard, on irrigated land. Some pleasant dry whites, including RH. RIESLING.

Bailey's N.E. Vic. Table and dessert ******
Small family concern making rich old-fashioned reds of great character, esp. Bundarra Hermitage and dessert MUSCAT.

Balgownie Vic. Table ***
Specialist in fine reds, particularly straight CABERNET.

Berri Coop. S. Aus. full range ***→****
Aus's largest winery, selling mostly to other companies. Now developing own name with success; esp. robust oaky reds.

Best's Central Vic. Full range *→**
Conservative old family winery at Great Western with good strong old-style claret, hock, etc.

Bilyara N. Barossa. S. Aus. Table and Sp. **→***
Wolf Blass is the ebullient German wine-maker with dazzling products and propaganda. His oak wines are not for keeping.

Bleasdale Langhorne Creek, S.A. Full range *→**
Small family business making above-average reds of CABERNET and SHIRAZ.

Brand Coonawarra, S.A. Table *******
Small privately owned winery. Outstandingly fine and stylish CABERNET and SHIRAZ under the Laira label.

Brokenwood N.S.W. Dry red. ***
New small winery owned by lawyers. Exciting quality of CABERNET SAUVIGNON since 1973.

Brown Brothers Milawa, N.E. Victoria. Full range ***→*****
Old family firm with new ideas, wide range of rather delicate wines, including several well-made varietals, a refreshing change from the blood-and-guts style of the area.

Buring, Leo Barossa, S.A. Full range *→***
"Château Leonay", old white-wine specialists, now owned by LINDEMAN. Very good "Reserve Bin" RHINE RIESLING.

Château Tahbilk Central Vic. Table *→***
Family-owned wine-estate making CABERNET, SHIRAZ, RHINE RIESLING and Marsanne. "Special Bins" are outstanding.

Château Yaldara Barossa, S.A. Full range *
A showpiece of Barossa, popular with tourists. Sparkling wines are a speciality.

Craigmoor N.S.W. Table and Port *→**
The oldest Mudgee winery. Robust reds and whites, and port matured in rum barrels.

d'Arenberg McLaren Vale, S.A. Table and dessert *→**
Small-scale old-style family outfit s. of Adelaide. Strapping rustic reds; CABERNET, SHIRAZ and Burgundy.

Drayton Hunter Valley, N.S.W. Table ******
Traditional Hunter wines, Hermitage red and SEMILLON white, from the old Bellevue estate.

Elliott Hunter Valley, N.S.W. Table **
Long-established grower. "Tallawanta" reds and "Belford" whites are in the bosomy, deep-flavoured Hunter style.

Emu S.A. Table and dessert *
Bulk shippers of high-strength wine to Britain and Canada.

Gramp Barossa, S.A. Full range *→***
Great pioneering family company, now owned by Reckitt & Colman. Range includes sweet fizzy "Barossa Pearl", good standard CABERNET, etc., and some of Australia's best RHINE RIESLING: Steingarten. Typed labels on special wines.

Hamilton's S. Adelaide and Barossa, S.A. Full range *
Big family business making popular rather light and "modern" wines, e.g. Ewell Moselle and Springton Riesling.

Hardy's Southern Vales, S.A., Barossa, etc. Full range *→**
Famous wide-spread family-run company using and blending wines from several areas, incl. a CABERNET, reliable light St. Thomas Burgundy and good Old Castle Riesling.

Henschke Barossa, S.A. Table ★

> Family business known for white wines, esp. RHINE RIESLING.

Houghton Swan Valley, W.A. Table and dessert ★→★★

> The one famous winery of W. Australia. Soft, ripe "White Burgundy" is the top wine. Now also excellent CABERNET.

Hungerford Hill Hunter Valley, N.S.W. Table ★→★★

> Big new winery with over 1,000 acres and modern ideas.

Huntingdon Estate N.S.W. Table ★→★★

> New small winery; the best in Mudgee. Fine award-winning reds and clean SEMILLON and CHARDONNAY.

Kaiser Stuhl Barossa, S.A. Full range ★→★★★

> The Barossa growers' co-operative. A fine modern winery with high standards. "Individual v'yd." Rieslings are excellent. So is "Special Reserve" CABERNET.

Lake's Folly Hunter Valley, N.S.W. Table ★★★

> The work of an inspired surgeon from Sydney. A new style for the Hunter Valley: CABERNET and new barrels to make rich complex California-style reds. Also excellent CHARDONNAY.

Lindeman Orig. Hunter, now everywhere. Full range ★→★★★

> One of the oldest firms, now a giant owned by Phillip Morris Corp. Its Ben Ean "Moselle" is Australia's best-selling wine. Owns BURINGS in Barossa and Rouge Homme in Coonawarra. Dessert-wine v'yds. at Corowa, N. Victoria. Many inter-state blends. Pioneers in modernizing wine styles.

McWilliams Hunter Valley and Riverina, N.S.W. Full range ★→★★★

> Famous and first-rate Hunter wine-makers at Mount Pleasant and Lovedale (HERMITAGE and SEMILLON). Pioneers in RIVERINA with lighter wines, incl. sweet white "Lexia" and fine varieties.

Mildara Murray Valley, S.A. Full range ★→★★★

> Sherry and brandy specialists at Mildura on the Murray river also making fine CABERNET and RIESLING at COONAWARRA.

Morris N.E. Vic. Table and dessert ★★→★★★★

> Old winery at Rutherglen making Australia's best brown "liqueur" muscat. Now owned by Reckitt & Colman.

Orlando See GRAMPS.

Penfold's Orig. Adelaide, now everywhere. Full range ★→★★★★

> Ubiquitous and excellent company: in BAROSSA, HUNTER VALLEY, RIVERINA, COONAWARRA, etc. Grange Hermitage is ★★★★, St. Henri Claret not far behind. Bin-numbered wines are usually outstanding. "Grandfather Port" is remarkable.

Petaluma S.A. ★★★

> Very promising newcomer, a recent rocket-like success with CHARDONNAY and RIESLING, now centred around new winery in ADELAIDE HILLS.

Quelltaler Clare-Watervale, S.A. Full range ★→★★

> Old winery n. of Adelaide known for good "Granfiesta" sherry and full dry "hock". Recently good Rhine Riesling.

Redman Coonawarra, S.A. Table ★★★

> Small new winery making only COONAWARRA claret of SHIRAZ and CABERNET of top quality.

Reynella Southern Vales, S.A. Full range ★→★★★

> Red-wine specialists s. of ADELAIDE. Highly esteemed rich CABERNET and "Vintage Reserve" claret.

Rosemount N.S.W. Table ★→★★

> Bustling newcomer in Upper HUNTER. Agreeable RH. RIESLING and Traminer/Riesling blend.

Rothbury Estate Hunter Valley, N.S.W. Table ★★★

> Important syndicate-owned wine estate concentrating on traditional HUNTER wines: "Hermitage" and long-lived SEMILLON. Also new plantings of CABERNET, CHARDONNAY, PINOT NOIR.

Ryecroft McLaren Vale, S.A. Table ★→★★
Specialists in typical sturdy CABERNET and SHIRAZ.

Saltram Barossa, S.A. Full range ★→★★★
One of the smaller wineries making a notable CABERNET, "Mamre Brook" and good "Selected Vintage" claret and RHINE RIESLING.

Sandalford W. Aus. Table ★→★★
New small winery with contrasting styles of red and white varietals from Swan and Margaret River.

Saxonvale N.S.W. Table ★★
Large newcomer at Fordwich, N.W. of Hunter. After early difficulties now making very good SEMILLON and CHARDONNAY.

Seaview Southern Vales, S.A. Table and dessert ★★
Old-established winery now owned by Toohey's Brewery. Well-known CABERNET, SAUVIGNON and RHINE RIESLING.

Seppelt Barossa, S.A. Central Vic. and elsewhere. Full range ★→★★★
Far-flung producers of Australia's best "champagne" (Gt. Western Brut), good dessert wines (from Rutherglen, the Murray Valley, Barossa), the reliable Moyston claret and some good private bin wines from Gt. Western in Victoria.

Smith's Yalumba Barossa, S.A. Full range ★→★★★
Big old family firm. Best wines incl. Rhine Riesling from Pewsey Vale above Barossa, good "Galway Vintage" claret, "Galway Pipe" port and Chiquita sherry.

Southern Vales Wine Co. S. Aus. Full range ★→★★
Co-op in McLaren Vale developing fine table wines, esp. dry white varietals.

Stanley Clare, S. Aus. Full range ★→★★
Important medium-size quality winery owned by Heinz. Among Aus.'s best RH. RIESLING and CABERNET SAUVIGNON and complex Cabernet-Shiraz-Malbec blends under Leasingham label.

Stonyfell Adelaide, S.A. Full range ★→★★
Long-established company best known for "Metala" CABERNET SHIRAZ from Langhorne Creek.

Tollana Barossa, S.A. Full range ★→★★
Old company famous for brandy, has latterly made some remarkable CABERNET and RHINE RIESLING.

Tulloch Hunter Valley, N.S.W. Table ★★
An old name at Pokolbin, with good dry reds and "Riesling".

Tyrrell Hunter Valley, N.S.W. Table ★★→ ★★★
Up-to-date old family business at "Ashman's". Some of the best traditional Hunter wines, Hermitage and RIESLING, are distinguished by Vat Numbers. Also big rich CHARDONNAY and delicate PINOT NOIR becoming known in Europe.

Valencia W. Aus. Full range ★→★★
W. Aus.'s largest company owned by Thos. Hardy, located in Swan Valley. Interesting white varietals of CHENIN BLANC from Gin Gin w. of Perth.

Woodleys Adel, S. Aus. Table ★★
Melbourne-owned; well-known for Queen Adelaide label claret and Riesling.

Wyndham Estate Branxton, N.S.W. Full range ★→★★
Frantic marketers of full range, but some fine Hunter varietals occasionally emerge. Geo. Wyndham's original estate is now a tourist attraction.

Wynns S. Aus. and N.S.W. Table ★→★★★
Large inter-state company, originators of flagon wines, with winery in RIVERINA and vineyards at Coonawarra, making good CABERNET. Owned by Toohey's Brewery.

South Africa

South Africa has made excellent sherry and port for many years, but has taken table wine seriously only in the last decade. Since 1972 a new system of Wines of Origin and registered "estates" has started a new era of competitive modern wine-making. The following list includes areas of origin, wineries, grape varieties and other label terms. Star-ratings have been omitted for the present until more information is available.

Allesverloren
Estate in MALMESBURY with over 325 acres of v'yds., formerly well known for "port", now specializing in red wines made with modern technology. Distributed by BERGKELDER.

Alphen
Estate originally at Constantia, owned by the famous Cloete family (see GROOT CONSTANTIA), now at Somerset West with a new winery. Expert direction should make good wines.

Alto
STELLENBOSCH estate of about 200 acres best known for massive-bodied CABERNET and a good blend: Alto Rouge. Distributed by BERGKELDER.

Audacia
Estate in STELLENBOSCH district producing CABERNET, PINOTAGE and CINSAUT.

Backsberg
Name formerly associated with commercial blends, now a prize-winning 400-acre estate at PAARL with notably good varietal reds.

Benede-Oranje
Newly demarcated wine region in the Orange River irrigation area. The northernmost region.

Bergkelder
Big wine concern at STELLENBOSCH, member of the OUDE MEESTER group, making and distributing many brands and estate wines, incl. FLEUR DU CAP, ALTO, HAZENDAL, etc. Now combined with STELLENBOSCH FARMERS' WINERY. See Cape Wine and Distillers Ltd.

Bertrams
Major wine company owned by Gilbeys with a wide range of well-made varietals.

Blaauwklippen
Estate s. of STELLENBOSCH.

Boberg
Controlled region of origin consisting of the districts of PAARL and TULBAGH.

Bonfoi Estate in STELLENBOSCH district. White wines marketed through the BERGKELDER.

Boschendal
Estate in PAARL area being developed on old fruit farm. Anglo-American owned.

Breede River Valley
Demarcated wine region.

Bukettraube
New German white-wine grapes with acidity and aroma, popular in S. Africa for blending.

Cabernet
The great Bordeaux grape particularly successful in the STELLENBOSCH area. Sturdy, long-ageing wines.

Cape Wine and Distillers Ltd.
The holding company for the reconstructed liquor interests of Oudemeester, STELLENBOSCH FARMERS' WINERIES, etc.

Cavendish Cape
Range of remarkably good sherries from the K.W.V..

Château Libertas

Also Oude Libertas. Two standard good-quality blended reds from the STELLENBOSCH FARMERS' WINERY.

Cinsaut

Bulk-producing French red grape formerly known as Hermitage in S. Africa. Chiefly blended with CABERNET, but can make good wine on its own.

Coastal Region

Demarcated wine region.

Colombard

The "FRENCH COLOMBARD" of California. Prized in S. Africa for its high acidity and fruity flavour.

Constantia

Once the world's most famous muscat wine, from the Cape. Now the southernmost district of origin ("Constantia and Durbanville"). See also GROOT CONSTANTIA.

Delheim

Winery at Driesprong in the best and highest area of STELLENBOSCH, known for delicate STEEN whites and also light reds, PINOTAGE, SHIRAZ and CABERNET.

De Wetshof

Estate in ROBERTSON district. Prize-winning Riesling marketed by BERGKELDER.

Drostdy

Well-known growers' co-operative in TULBAGH.

Estate wine

A strictly controlled term applying only to some 40 registered estates making wines made of grapes grown on the same property.

Fleur du Cap

Popular and well-made range of wines from the BERGKELDER, Stellenbosch. Particularly good SHIRAZ.

Gewürztraminer

The famous spicy grape of Alsace, successfully grown in the TULBAGH area.

La Gratitude

Well-known brand of dry white from the STELLENBOSCH FARMERS' WINERY.

Goede Hoop

Estate in STELLENBOSCH district. Red wines bottled and sold by BERGKELDER.

Groot Constantia

Historic estate, now government-owned, near Cape Town. Source of superlative muscat wine in the early 19th century. Now making CABERNET, PINOT NOIR, PINOTAGE and SHIRAZ reds, the Shiraz is apparently best. Also a blend Heerenrood.

Grünberger

A good brand of dry STEEN white from the BERGKELDER, though flagrantly dressed up as a German Franconian "Steinwein".

Hazendal

Family estate in w. STELLENBOSCH making STEEN, CINSAUT and PINOTAGE, all marketed by the BERGKELDER.

Jacobsdal

Estate in STELLENBOSCH district, overlooking False Bay. PINOTAGE and CINSAUT bottled and sold by BERGKELDER.

Kanonkop

Estate in n. STELLENBOSCH, specializing in high-quality and particularly full-bodied CABERNET and PINOTAGE.

Klein Karoo

The easternmost S. African wine district, warm and dry, specializing in dessert and distilling wine.

Kerner Flowery grape variety recently introduced from Germany.

K.W.V. The Kooperatieve Wijnbouwers Vereniging, S. Africa's national wine co-operative (now independent) originally organized by the State to absorb embarrassing surpluses, now at vast and splendidly equipped premises in PAARL making a range of good wines, particularly sherries.

Laborie
New K.W.V.-owned estate on Paarl Mtn. Showpiece cellars, restaurant and guesthouse.

Landgoed
South African for Estate; a word which appears on all estate-wine labels and official seals.

Landskroon
Family estate owned by Paul and Hugo de Villiers. Mainly port-type wines for K.W.V. but recently some exc. dry reds – PINOTAGE and Tintas das Baroccas.

Malmesbury
Centre of the SWARTLAND wine district, on the w. coast n. of Cape Town, specializing in dry whites and distilling wine.

Meerendal
Estate near Durbanville producing robust reds marketed by the BERGKELDER.

Meerlust
Estate s. of STELLENBOSCH making CABERNET marketed by the BERGKELDER.

Monis Well-known wine concern of PAARL now merged with the STELLENBOSCH FARMERS' WINERY.

Montagne
Relatively new but successful estate of 300+ acres near STELLENBOSCH. Wines incl. CABERNET, STEEN (sold as "Chenin Blanc"), RIESLING, and a dry rosé now owned by Gilbeys.

Montpellier
Famous pioneering TULBAGH estate with 350 acres of v'yds. specializing in white wine. Produced the first two whites to be officially designated SUPERIOR (RIESLING and GEWÜRZTRAMINER), also French CHENIN BLANC and a small quantity of excellent méthode champenoise sparkling wine.

Muratie
Ancient estate in STELLENBOSCH, best known for its Pinot Noir. 160 acres of v'yds. also grow CABERNET, RIESLING, STEEN and CINSAUT.

Nederburg
The most famous wine farm in modern S. Africa, now operated by the STELLENBOSCH FARMERS' WINERY. Pioneer in modern cellar practice, popularized both CABERNET and the idea of estate wines, although no longer technically an estate itself. Recent innovations have included an outstanding Auslese-type STEEN: Nederburg Edelkeur.

Olifantsrivier
Northerly demarcated wine region with a warm dry climate. Mainly distilling wine.

Overberg
Demarcated wine district in the Caledon area, Coastal Region.

Overgaauw
Estate w. of STELLENBOSCH making good whites and reds.

Paarl South Africa's wine capital, 50 miles n.e. of Cape Town, and the surrounding demarcated district, among the best in the country, particularly for white wine and sherry. Most of its wine is made by co-operatives.

Paarlsack
Well-known range of sherries made at PAARL by the K.W.V.

Pinotage
South African red grape, a cross between PINOT NOIR and CINSAUT, useful for high yields, hardiness and good quality.

Piquetberg
Small demarcated district on the w. coast round Porterville. A warm dry climate gives mainly dessert and distilling wine.

Riesling
South African Riesling makes some of the country's better white wines, but is not the same as Rhine Riesling, which has only recently been planted in any quantity in S. Africa.

Robertson
Small demarcated district e. of the Cape and inland. Mainly dessert wines (notably MUSCAT), but red and white table wines are on the increase.

Roodeberg
High-quality brand of blended red wine from the K.W.V. Has good colour, body and flavour and ages well in bottle.

Rustenberg
Effectively, if not officially, an estate red wine from just n.e. of STELLENBOSCH. Rustenberg and SCHOONGEZICHT are managed together and the name Rustenberg used for the red of CABERNET and CINSAUT, one of S. Africa's best.

Schoongezicht
Partner of RUSTENBERG, one of S. Africa's most beautiful old farms and producer of agreeable white wine from STEEN, RIESLING and Clairette Blanche. Now registered as an estate.

Shiraz The red Rhône grape, recently gaining in popularity in S. Africa for rich deep-coloured wine.

Simonsig
Estate owned by F.J. Malan, Chairman of the Cape Estate Wine Producers' Association. Produces a successful "Méthode Champenoise" wine among others.

Simonsvlei
One of S. Africa's best-known co-operative cellars, just outside PAARL. A prize-winner with both whites and reds.

Spier Estate of five farms w. of STELLENBOSCH producing reds and whites.

Steen South Africa's commonest white grape, said to be a clone of the CHENIN BLANC. It gives strong, tasty and lively wine, sweet or dry, normally better than S. African RIESLING.

Stein Name used for any medium dry white wine.

Stellenbosch
Town and demarcated district 30 miles e. of Cape Town, extending to the Ocean at False Bay. Most of the best estates, esp. for red wine, are in the mountain foothills of the region.

Stellenbosch Farmers' Winery
South Africa's biggest winery (after the K.W.V.) with several ranges of wines, incl. NEDERBURG, ZONNEBLOEM, Lanzerac, Oude Libertas and the popular TASSENBERG. Also new low-alcohol white and rosé "Vinotas Light". See Cape Wine and Distillers Ltd.

Superior
An official designation of quality for WINES OF ORIGIN. The wine must meet standards set by the Wine & Spirit Board.

Swartland
Demarcated district around MALMESBURY.

Swellendam
Demarcated district of the s.e., with Bonnievale as its centre. Dessert, distilling and light table wines.

Sylvaner
Recently introduced variety. OVERGAAUW makes a pleasant version.

Taskelder

Range of good value wines from the STELLENBOSCH FARMERS' WINERY, including CH. LIBERTAS, Lanzerac Rosé, LA GRATITUDE and Tasheimer.

Tassenberg

Popular and good-value red table wine known to thousands as Tassie. "Oom Tas" is a low-price white.

Tawny In Portugal means port-style wines aged in wood.

Theuniskraal

Well-known TULBAGH estate specializing in white wines, esp. RIESLING. Also STEEN, Semillon and GEWÜRZTRAMINER. Distributed by the BERGKELDER.

Tulbagh

Demarcated district n. of PAARL best known for the white wines of its three famous estates, MONTPELLIER, THEUNISKRAAL and TWEE JONGEGEZELLEN, and the dessert wines of its co-operative at Drostdy. See also BOBERG.

Twee Jongegezellen

Estate at TULBAGH. One of the great pioneers which revolutionized S. African wine in the 1950s, still in the family of its 18th-century founder. Mainly white wine, incl. RIESLING, STEEN and SEMILLON. Best wine: "T.J.39". The name means "two young friends". Now also producing a CABERNET grown by a large dam (reservoir) to get the "Médoc" effect.

Uiterwyk

Estate w. of STELLENBOSCH making a very good CABERNET SAUVIGNON.

Uitkyk

Old estate at STELLENBOSCH formerly famous for Cabernet red and Carlsheim white, recently recovering from a bad patch with good CABERNET, STEEN, etc. Now over 350 acres. Distribution by BERGKELDER.

Union Wine

Company with HQ in Wellington, Boberg area. Brand names Culemborg, Bellingham and Val du Charron.

Van Riebeck

Co-operative at Riebeck Kasteel, MALMESBURY, known for pioneering work in white wine technology.

Verdun

Estate w. of STELLENBOSCH, best known for its Gamay red, but also producing an excellent SAUVIGNON BLANC.

Vergenoegd

Old family estate in s. STELLENBOSCH supplying high-quality sherry to the K.W.V. but recently offering prize-winning reds under an estate label.

Weisser Riesling

A fairly recent introduction from Germany. Rather different from the S.A. Riesling, which it is replacing.

Wine of Origin

The S. African equivalent of Appellation Controlée. The demarcated regions involved are all described on these pages.

Worcester

Demarcated wine district round the Breede and Hex river valleys, e. of PAARL. Many co-operative cellars make mainly dessert wines, brandy and dry whites.

Zandvliet

Estate in the Robertson area marketing a SHIRAZ red through the BERGKELDER. Later will add a Cabernet-Merlot blend.

Zonnebloem

Popular brand of CABERNET, RIESLING, PINOTAGE, SHIRAZ and STEEN from the STELLENBOSCH FARMERS' WINERY. The Cabernet is vintage-dated and ages well in bottle.

Sherry, Port & Madeira

The original, classical sherries of Spain, ports of Portugal and madeiras of Madeira are listed in the A–Z below. Their many imitators in South Africa, California, Australia, Cyprus, Argentina are not. References to them will be found under their respective countries.

The map on page 99 locates the port and sherry districts. Madeira is an island 400 miles out in the Atlantic from the coast of Morocco, a port of call for west-bound ships: hence its traditional market in North America.

In this section most of the entries are shippers' names followed by a brief account of their wines. The names of wine-types are included in the alphabetical listing.

Amontillado
> In general use means medium sherry; technically means a wine which has been aged to become more powerful and pungent. A FINO can be amontillado.

Amoroso
> A style of sweet sherry, not noticeably different from a sweet OLOROSO.

Barbeito
> Shippers of good-quality Madeira, including the driest and best apéritif Madeira, "Island Dry".

Bertola
> Sherry shippers, owned by the giant Rumasa group, best known for their Bertola Cream Sherry.

Blandy
> Old family firm of Madeira shippers at Funchal. Duke of Clarence Malmsey is their most famous wine.

Blazquez
> Sherry bodega at JEREZ with outstanding FINO, "Carta Blanca", and "Carta Oro" amontillado "al natural" (unsweetened).

Brown sherry
> British term for a style of dark sweet sherry, not normally of the best quality.

Bual
> One of the grapes of Madeira, making a soft smoky sweet wine, not as sweet as Malmsey.

Caballero
> Sherry shippers best known for Gran Señor Choice Old Cream. Their best FINO is Don Guisa.

Cockburn
> British-owned port shippers with a range of good wines. Fine vintage port from very high v'yds. can look deceptively light when young, but has great lasting power. Vintages: 55 60 63 67 70 75.

Cossart Gordon
> Leading firm of Madeira shippers founded 1745, best known for their "Good Company" range of wines but also producing old vintages and soleras.

Cream sherry
> A style of fairly pale sweet sherry made by sweetening a blend of well-aged OLOROSOS.

Crofts
> One of the oldest firms shipping vintage port: 300 years old in 1978. Bought early this century by Gilbey's. Well-balanced

vintage wines last as long as any. Vintages: **55 60** 63 66 70 75 77, and lighter vintage wines under the name of their Quinta da Roeda in several other years. Also now in the sherry business with Croft Original (pale cream), Delicado (fino).

Crusted

Term for a vintage-style port, but blended from several vintages not one, bottled young and aged in bottle, so forming a "crust" in the bottle. Needs decanting.

Cuvillo

Sherry bodega at Puerto de Santa Maria best known for their Cream, dry Oloroso Sangre y Trabajadero and Fino "C" and a fine Palo Cortado.

Delaforce

Port shippers particularly well known in Germany. "His Eminence" is an excellent tawny. "Vintage character" is also good. Vintage wines are very fine, among the lighter kind: **55 58 60** 63 **66** 70 75 77.

Domecq

Giant family-owned sherry bodega at JEREZ. Double Century Oloroso is their biggest brand, La Ina their excellent FINO. Other famous wines incl. Celebration Cream, Botaina (old amontillado) and Rio Viejo (dry oloroso). Now also in Rioja (p. 104).

Dow

Old name used on the British market by the port shippers Silva & Cosens, well known for their relatively early maturing vintage wines, said to have a faint "cedarwood" character. Vintages: **55 57 58 60** 63 66 70 75 77.

Duff Gordon

Sherry shippers best known for their El Cid AMONTILLADO. Owned by the big Spanish firm Bodegas Osborne.

Ferreira

Portuguese-owned port growers and shippers (since 1751) well-known for old tawnies and good, relatively light, vintages: **60 63 66** 70 75 77. Also Special Reserve (vintage character) Donna Antonia.

Findlater's

Old established London wine merchant shipping his own very successful brand of medium sherry: Dry Fly amontillado.

Fino

Term for the lightest and finest of sherries, completely dry, very pale and with great delicacy. Fino should always be drunk cool and fresh: it deteriorates rapidly once opened. TIO PEPE is the classic example.

Flor

The characteristic natural yeast which gives FINO sherry its unique flavour.

Fonseca

British-owned port shipper of high reputation. Vintage character "Bin 27" makes robust, deeply coloured vintage wine, sometimes said to have a slight "burnt" flavour. Vintages: **55 60 63** 66 70 75 77.

Garvey's

Famous old sherry shippers at JEREZ. Their finest wines are Fino San Patricio, Tio Guillermo Dry Amontillado and Ochavico Dry Oloroso. San Angelo Medium Amontillado is their most popular.

Gonzalez Byass

Enormous concern shipping the world's most famous and one of the best sherries: Tio Pepe. Other brands incl. La Concha Medium Amontillado, Elegante Dry Fino, San Domingo Pale Cream, Romano Cream.

Graham
　　Port shippers famous for one of the richest and sweetest of vintage ports, largely from their own Quinta Malvedos, also excellent brands, incl. Ruby and Tawny and 'Late Bottled Vintage'. Vintages: **55 58 60 63** 66 70 75 77.

Harvey's
　　World-famous Bristol shippers of Bristol Cream and Bristol Milk sweet sherries, Club Amontillado and Bristol Dry, which are medium. Luncheon Dry and Bristol Fino, which are dry.

Henriques & Henriques
　　Well-known Madeira shippers of Funchal. Their wide range includes a good dry apéritif wine: Ribeiro Seco.

Jerez de la Frontera
　　Centre of the sherry industry, between Cadiz and Seville in s. Spain. The word sherry is a corruption of the name, pronounced in Spanish "Hereth". In French, Xérés.

Late-bottled vintage
　　Port of a single good vintage kept in wood for twice as long as vintage port (about 5 years). Therefore lighter when bottled and ageing quicker.

Leacock
　　One of the oldest firms of Madeira shippers. Most famous wine is "Penny Black" Malmsey.

Lustau
　　The largest independent family-owned sherry bodega in JEREZ, making many wines for other shippers, but with a very good "Dry Lustau" range and "Emilio" Palo Cortado.

Macharnudo
　　One of the best parts of the sherry v'yds., n. of Jerez, famous for wines of the highest quality, both FINO and OLOROSO.

Malmsey
　　The sweetest form of Madeira; dark amber, rich and honeyed yet with Madeira's unique sharp tang.

Manzanilla
　　Sherry, normally FINO, which has acquired a peculiar bracing salty character from being kept in bodegas at Sanlucar de Barrameda, on the Guadalquivir estuary near JEREZ.

Offley Forester
　　Port shippers and owners of the famous Quinta Boa Vista. Their vintage wines tend to be round, "fat" and sweet, good for relatively early drinking. Vintages: **55 60 62 63 66 67** 70 72 75 77 (an exception to the "early-drinking" rule).

Oloroso
　　Style of sherry, heavier and less brilliant than FINO when young, but maturing to greater richness and roundness. Naturally dry, but generally sweetened for sale, as CREAM.

Palo Cortado
　　A style of sherry close to OLOROSO but with some of the character of a FINO. Dry but rich and soft. Not often seen.

Palomino & Vergara
　　Sherry shippers of JEREZ, best known for Palomino Cream, Medium and Dry. Best FINO: Tio Mateo. Rumasa group.

Puerto de Santa Maria
　　The port and second city of the sherry area with a number of important bodegas.

P.X.
　　Short for Pedro Ximenez, the grape used in JEREZ for sweetening blends. P.X. wine alone is almost like treacle.

Quinta　Portuguese for "estate".

Quinta do Noval

Great Portuguese port house making splendidly dark, rich and full-bodied vintage port; a few pre-phylloxera vines still at the Quinta make a small quantity of "Nacional"—very dark, full and slow-maturing wine. Vintages: 55 58 60 63 66 67 70 75.

Rainwater

A fairly light, not very sweet blend of Madeira—in fact of VERDELHO wine—popular in the USA and Canada.

Real Tesoro, Marques de

Sherry shippers of SANLUCAR, specializing in MANZANILLA, esp. "La Capitala".

Rebello Valente

Name used for the vintage port of ROBERTSON. Their vintage wines are light but elegant and well-balanced, maturing rather early. Vintages: 55 60 63 66 67 70 75.

La Riva

Distinguished firm of sherry shippers making one of the best FINOS, Tres Palmas, among many good wines.

Rivero

Considerable sherry concern best known for CZ range of wines.

Robertson

Subsidiary of SANDEMAN'S, shipping REBELLO VALENTE vintage port and Gamebird Tawny and Ruby.

Ruby

The youngest (and cheapest) style of port: very sweet and red. The best are vigorous and full of flavour. Others can be merely strong and rather thin.

Ruiz Mateos

The sherry bodega which gave its name to the mammoth Rumasa group of bodegas, banks, etc. Its Don Zoilo sherries are some of the most expensive and best. Ruiz Hermanos is a cheaper range.

Rutherford & Miles

Madeira shippers with one of the best known of all Bual wines: Old Trinity House.

Saccone & Speed

British sherry shippers owned by Courage's the Brewers, make the popular Troubador and Lysonder ranges and a good Fino.

Sandeman

Giant of the port trade and a major figure in the sherry one. Still family controlled. "Partners" is their best-known tawny port; their vintage wines are robust—some of the old vintages were superlative [55 58 60 63 66 67 70 75]. Of the sherries, Medium Dry Amontillado is the best-seller, their Fino "Apitiv" is particularly good and Armada Cream and Dry Don Amontillado are both well known.

Sanlucar

Seaside sherry-town (see Manzanilla) 15 miles from JEREZ.

Sercial

Grape (reputedly a RIESLING) grown in Madeira to make the driest of the island's wines—a good apéritif.

Solera

System used in making both sherry and Madeira, also some port. It consists of topping up progressively more mature barrels with slightly younger wine of the same sort: the object to attain continuity in the final wine. Most commercial sherries are blends of several solera wines.

Tarquinio Lomelino

Madeira shippers famous for their collection of antique wines. Their standard range is called Dom Henriques.

Tawny

A style of port aged for many years in wood (in contrast to vintage port, which is aged in bottle) until it becomes tawny in colour.

Taylor

One of the best port shippers, particularly for their full, rich, long-lived vintage wine and tawnies of stated age (40-year-old, 30-year-old, etc.). Their Quinta de Vargellas is said to give Taylor's its distinctive scent of violets. Vintages: **55 60** 63 66 70 75 77. Some lesser vintages are shipped with the Quinta name.

De Terry, Carlos y Javier

Family-owned bodega at PUERTO DE SANTA MARIA with a good range of sherries.

Tio Pepe

The most famous of FINO sherries (see Gonzalez Byass).

Valdespino

Famous bodega at JEREZ, owner of the Inocente v'yd., making the excellent FINO of the same name. Tio Diego is their splendid dry AMONTILLADO, Solera 1842 a ditto oloroso, Matador the name of their popular range.

Varela Sherry shippers, members of the Rumasa group, best-known for their Varela Medium and Cream.

Verdelho

Madeira grape making fairly dry wine without the distinction of SERCIAL. A pleasant apéritif.

Vintage Port

The best port of exceptional vintages is bottled after only 2 years in wood and matures very slowly, for up to 20 years or even more, in its bottle. It always leaves a heavy deposit and therefore needs decanting.

Vintage port is almost as much a ritual as a drink. It always needs to be decanted with great care (since the method of making it leaves a heavy deposit in the bottle). The simplest and surest way of doing this is by filtering it through clean muslin or a coffee filter-paper into either a decanter or a well-rinsed bottle. All except very old ports can safely be decanted the day before drinking. At table the decanter is traditionally passed from guest to guest clockwise.

Vintage port can be immensely long-lived. Particularly good vintages older than those mentioned in the text include 1950, 48, 45, 35, 34, 27, 20, 11, 08, 04.

Vintage Character

Somewhat misleading term used for a good-quality full and meaty port like a first-class RUBY made by the solera system. Lacks the splendid "nose" of vintage port.

Warre

Probably the oldest of all port shippers (since 1670). Fine long-maturing vintage wines, a good TAWNY, Nimrod and Vintage Character Warrior. Vintages: **55 60** 63 66 70 75 77.

White Port

Port made of white grapes and therefore golden in colour. Formerly made sweet, now more often dry: a good apéritif but a heavy one.

Williams & Humbert

Famous and first-class sherry bodega now owned by the giant Rumasa group. Dry Sack (medium AMONTILLADO) is their best-selling wine. Pando is an excellent FINO. Canasta Cream and Walnut Brown are good in their class.

Wine newspeak

The last ten years has seen a revolution in wine technology. They have also heard a matching revolution in wine-talk. Attempts to express the characters of wines used to get little further than terms as vague as "fruity" and "full-bodied". Your modern wine-lover is made of sterner stuff. He is satisfied with nothing less than the jargon of laboratory analysis. Rather than expound the old imagery (which should after all be self-explanatory) I therefore give below a summary of the new hard-edge wine-talk.

The most frequent references are to the ripeness of grapes at picking; the resultant alcohol and sugar content of the wine; various measures of its acidity; the amount of sulphur dioxide used as a preservative, and the amount of "dry extract"—the sum of all the things that give wine its characteristic flavours.

The **sugar** in wine is mainly glucose and fructose, with traces of arabinose, xylose and other sugars that are not fermentable by yeast, but can be attacked by bacteria. Each country has its own system for measuring the sugar content or ripeness of grapes, known as the **"must-weight"**. The chart below relates the three principal ones (German, French and American) to each other, to specific gravity, and to the potential alcohol of the resulting wine if all the sugar is fermented out.

Specific Gravity	°O °Oechsle	Baumé	Brix	% Potential Alcohol v/v
1.065	65	8.8	15.8	8.1
1.070	70	9.4	17.0	8.8
1.075	75	10.1	18.1	9.4
1.080	80	10.7	19.3	10.0
1.085	85	11.3	20.4	10.6
1.090	90	11.9	21.5	11.3
1.095	95	12.5	22.5	11.9
1.100	100	13.1	23.7	12.5
1.105	105	13.7	24.8	13.1
1.110	110	14.3	25.8	13.8
1.115	115	14.9	26.9	14.4
1.120	120	15.5	28.0	15.0

Residual sugar is the sugar left after fermentation has finished or been artificially stopped, measured in grammes per litre.

Alcohol content (mainly ethyl alcohol) is expressed as a percentage by volume of the total liquid.

Acidity is both fixed and volatile. **Fixed acidity** consists principally of tartaric, malic and citric acids which are all found in the grape, and lactic and succinic acids, which are produced during fermentation. **Volatile acidity** consists mainly of acetic acid, which is rapidly formed by bacteria in the presence of oxygen. A small amount of volatile acidity is inevitable and attractive. With a larger amount the wine becomes "pricked"—i.e. starts to turn to vinegar.

Total acidity is fixed and volatile acidity combined. As a rule of thumb for a well-balanced wine it should be in the region of 1 gramme/thousand for each 10°Oechsle (see above).

pH is a measure of the strength of the acidity, rather than its volume. A pH above 7 is alkaline; below is acid; the lower the figure the more acid. Wine normally ranges in pH from 2.8 to 3.8. Cold northerly climates with less ripe grapes tend to lower pHs; winemakers in hot climates can have problems getting the pH low enough. Lower pH gives better colour, helps prevent bacterial spoilage, allows more of the SO_2 to be free and active as a preservative.

Sulphur dioxide (SO_2) is added to prevent oxidation and other accidents in wine-making. Some of it combines with sugars, etc., and is known as "bound". Only the **"free SO_2"** that remains in the wine is effective as a preservative. **Total SO_2** is controlled by law according to the level of residual sugar: the more sugar the more SO_2 is needed.

QUICK REFERENCE VINTAGE CHARTS FOR FRANCE AND GERMANY

These charts give a picture of the range of qualities made in the principal areas (every year has its relative successes and failures) and a guide to whether the wine is ready to drink or should be kept.

0   no good   10   the best

⌇   drink now   ➥   needs keeping

✓   can be drunk with pleasure now, but the better wines will continue to improve

Combinations of these symbols mean that there are wines in more than one of the categories.

FRANCE

| | Red Bordeaux | | White Bordeaux | |
	Médoc/Graves	Pom/St-Em.	Sauternes & sw.	Graves & dr.
79	5–8	5–9	6–9	6–9
78	6–9	6–8	4–6	7–9
77	3–5	2–5	2–4	6–9
76	6–8	7–8	7–8	4–8
75	9–10	8–10	9–10	8–10
74	4–6	3–5	0	6–7
73	5–6	5–7	0–4	7–8
72	2–5	2–4	2–4	4–7
71	5–8	6–8	8–9	8–10
70	9–10	9–10	9–10	9–10
69	1–4	0–3	6–7	8–9
68	0–2	0	0	0
67	5–7	6–8	7–10	8–10
66	7–9	8–9	4–7	7–8
64	2–7	5–9		
62	4–8	3–6		
61	10	10		

| | Red Burgundy | White Burgundy | | |
	Côte d'Or	Côte d'Or	Chablis	Alsace
79	4–8	6–8	6–8	7–8
78	8–10	7–9	7–9	6–8
77	2–4	4–7	5–7	6–7
76	9–10	7–9	8–9	10
75	0–5	4–8	8–10	9
74	2–5	6–8	6–8	6–7
73	4–7	8	7–8	7–8
72	4–9	5–8	1–4	3
71	8–10	8–10	7–9	10
70	6–8	7–8	6–8	7–8
69	9–10	8–10	7–9	

Beaujolais: 79 and 78 are the vintages to buy. Mâcon-Villages (white): 79 and 78 are good now.
Loire: Sweet wines of Anjou and Touraine. Best recent vintages: 79, 78, 76, 73, 71, 70, 69, 64.
Upper Loire: Sancerre and Pouilly-Fumé 79, 78, 76 are all good now.
Muscadet: Drink the new vintage.

GERMANY

	Rhône			Rhine	Moselle
79	6–8	79		6–8	6–8
78	8–10	78		5–7	4–7
77	5–7	77		5–7	4–6
76	6–9	76		9–10	9–10
75	0–5	75		8–10	9–10
74	4–7	74		3–6	2–4
73	5–8	73		6–7	6–8
72	6–9	72		2–5	1–4
71	7–9	71		9–10	10

N.B. Fully detailed charts will be found on pages 20, 21 (France), 65 (Germany).